SO-CFX-525

Human Behavior in the Social Environment

Human Behavior in the Social Environment

JOHN F. LONGRES

UNIVERSITY OF WISCONSIN, MADISON

F. E. PEACOCK PUBLISHERS, INC.
ITASCA, ILLINOIS

THIS BOOK IS DEDICATED TO

MY MOTHER

AND TO THE MEMORY OF

MY FATHER

Copyright © 1990
F. E. Peacock Publishers, Inc.
All rights reserved.
Library of Congress Catalog
Card Number: 89-063451
ISBN: 0-87581-336-4
Printed in the U.S.A.

93 Year
5 6 7 8 9 10 Printing

Brief Contents

PART I

A CRITICAL PERSPECTIVE ON SOCIAL SYSTEMS   1

 1. A CRITICAL PERSPECTIVE   2
 2. A SYSTEMS APPROACH TO HUMAN BEHAVIOR   18

PART II

COMMUNITIES IN SOCIETY 55

 3. DIVERSITY IN COMMUNITY LIFE   ✗   8·65   56
 4. A SOCIAL HISTORY OF ETHNIC COMMUNITIES
   IN THE UNITED STATES   92
 5. THE NEW ARRIVALS   131
 6. ETHNIC-COMMUNITY RELATIONS IN
   CONTEMPORARY AMERICAN SOCIETY   146

PART III

FAMILY LIFE 181

 7. THE FAMILY AS A SOCIAL INSTITUTION   182
 8. DIVERSITY IN FAMILY LIFESTYLES   226
 9. THE FAMILY AS A SOCIAL ORGANIZATION:
   IDENTIFYING WELL-BEING   265
 10. THE FAMILY AS A SOCIAL ORGANIZATION:
   ANALYZING WELL-BEING   300

PART IV

THE INDIVIDUAL AS A SYSTEM   343

11. PSYCHOLOGICAL WELL-BEING   344
12. INTERPERSONAL WELL-BEING:
     BEHAVIORAL AND MARXIAN THEORIES   367
13. INTERPERSONAL WELL-BEING: STRUCTURAL FUNCTIONAL
     AND SYMBOLIC INTERACTION THEORIES   407
14. INTRAPERSONAL WELL-BEING: EGO PSYCHOLOGY
     AND COGNITIVE DEVELOPMENT THEORIES   447
15. EGO PSYCHOLOGY AND DEVELOPMENT
     ACROSS THE LIFE COURSE   488

PART V

EPILOGUE   537

16. TOWARD A REFORM-ORIENTED THEORY FOR PRACTICE   538

SUBJECT INDEX   549

AUTHOR INDEX   561

Contents

PREFACE   *xvii*

PART I

A CRITICAL PERSPECTIVE ON SOCIAL SYSTEMS   **1**

CHAPTER 1. A CRITICAL PERSPECTIVE   2

A Theory for Practice   3
    Thinking about Social Service Work   4
    Control and Change in Social Service Work   4
The Critical Perspective   5
    Prescription Rather Than Description   6
    Critical Analysis in Contemporary Social Service   6
Questioning the Critical Perspective   7
    Unintended Consequences of Social Change   7
    The Possibility of Human Progress   8
Working with the Interaction between Individual and Society   9
    Blame the Victim or Blame Society?   9
    The Multicentered and Transactional Points of View   11
    Private Troubles and Public Issues   11
    The Dual Nature of Social Service Practice   14
Critical Theory and Social Change   14

CHAPTER 2. A SYSTEMS APPROACH TO HUMAN BEHAVIOR   18

A Systems Approach   19
Human Systems   20

Human Nature: Biological and Cultural Determinants   20

A Theory of Human Nature   21

Male and Female Differences   21

The Individual as a System   22

The Biophysical Domain   22

The Psychological Domain   24

Levels of Systems within Individuals   25

Dynamics of the Individual as a System   26

Change and Development   27

Homeostasis and Feedback   29

System Boundaries   30

Social Systems and the Social Environment   31

Social Systems   32

Social Norms   35

Social Institutions   35

Institutionalized Social Arrangements   38

Stability and Conflict in Social Systems   39

Roles: Person in Environment   41

The Concept of Role   41

Transactions between Individuals and Social Systems   43

The Person-in-Environment Relationship   45

Implications for Practice   45

The Problem-Solving Process   47

Practice Principles for Social Work Assessment   47

Demonstrating the Practice Principles   48

A Look Ahead   51

PART II

COMMUNITIES IN SOCIETY   55

CHAPTER 3. DIVERSITY IN COMMUNITY LIFE   56

Communities as Social Systems   57

Types of Communities   58

Attributes of Identificational Communities   60

Some Variations in Community Life   61

Social Classes as Communities   61

Religious Denominations as Communities   68

Emergence of a Gay and Lesbian Community   69

Racial and Ethnic Communities   73

    The Meaning of Race   73

    Ethnic Communities and Ethnicity   76

    Community Relations   80

Minority and Majority Groups   80

    Ethnic Minorities and Minority Individuals   81

    Types of Minorities   82

    Women as a Minority   83

    Minority-Majority Relations   85

Implications for Practice   86

    Building a Helping Relationship   87

CHAPTER 4. A SOCIAL HISTORY OF ETHNIC COMMUNITIES
IN THE UNITED STATES   92

Socioeconomic Achievement and Ethnic Communities   93

    Socioeconomic Well-Being, 1960–1976   94

    Socioeconomic Well-Being Since 1976   95

    Inequalities among Ethnic Communities   97

Understanding Racial and Ethnic Relations   98

    Theories of Minority-Majority Relations   98

    Immigrant and Colonialist Analogies   101

    The Minority Response to Subordination   103

U.S. Immigration Policies   103

    The Setting of Quotas   104

Socioeconomic Success of European Immigrants   106

    Northern and Western European Immigrants   106

    Southern and Eastern European Immigrants   109

Socioeconomic Success and Third World People of Color   113

    Native Americans and Alaskan Natives   113

    American Blacks and Afro-Americans   117

    Mexican Americans (Chicanos)   120

    Puerto Ricans   122

    Asian Americans   124

Implications for Practice   126

    Human Needs   126

    Intergroup Conflict and Competition   127

CHAPTER 5. THE NEW ARRIVALS   131

   The New Americans   132
   The New Immigrants   134
      East Indian Immigrants   134
   Refugees and Displaced Persons   136
      Indochinese Refugees   138
   Undocumented Aliens   139
      Mexicans   139
      Haitians   140
   Implications for Practice   142

CHAPTER 6. ETHNIC-COMMUNITY RELATIONS IN
CONTEMPORARY AMERICAN SOCIETY   146

   The Social Context of Minority-Majority Relations   147
      Racism and Ethnocentrism   148
      Prejudice and Discrimination   149
      The Principle of Nondiscrimination   151
   Institutional Racism   156
      Social Institutions and Institutional Arrangements   156
      Racism as an Institutional Arrangement   156
      Institutional Racism in Contemporary American Society   158
      The Continuing Influence of Informal Intentional Racism   162
   Biological Attributes of Minority Communities   162
      Differences in Intelligence-Test Scores   163
   Cultural Attributes of Minority Communities   165
      The Culture of Poverty   165
      Cultural Values and Traditions   167
      Cultural Traits Needed for Success   169
      The Dual Perspective on Acculturation   170
   Prospects for Progress in Minority-Majority Relations   174
      Happy Endings: Assimilation and Cultural Pluralism   174
      Unhappy Endings: From Extermination to Secession   175
   Implications for Practice   176

PART III

FAMILY LIFE   181

CHAPTER 7. THE FAMILY AS A SOCIAL INSTITUTION   182

The Family as an Institution: An Antisexist Approach   184

   Recent Trends in Family Life   185

   Defining Family Life   187

   Types of Institutionalized Families   189

Functions of the Family   191

   Manifest Functions: Procreation and Socialization   191

   Latent Functions: Maintaining Differences   192

   Other Manifest Functions: Production, Consumption,

   and Emotional Support   193

   A Social History of Family Emotional Climate   195

Variations in the Structure of Family Life   199

   Two-Parent and Married-Couple Families   200

   The One-Parent Family   201

   Stepfamilies or Reconstituted Families   202

   Cohabiting Couples   203

   Gay and Lesbian Couples   203

   Single Persons   205

Changes in Role Expectations among Family Members   205

   Family Politics in American Society: Women, Children, the Elderly   206

   Changing Gender Roles in Family Life   211

   Psychogenetic Factors in Parent-Child Relationships   217

   Family Relationships with the Elderly   219

Implications for Practice   220

CHAPTER 8. DIVERSITY IN FAMILY LIFESTYLES   226

Social Class and Family Life   227

   Middle-Class Families   227

   Working-Class Families   228

   Poverty-Class Families   230

   The Families of the Rich   232

Family Life in Racial and Ethnic Communities   234

   Generalizations on Family Ideals and Norms   236

   An Overview of Racial- and Ethnic-Minority Families   244

Family Life Outside Marriage: Gay and Lesbian Couples   252

   Homosexual Couples in a Heterogeneous World   252

   Crafting a Contemporary Lifestyle   254

   Lesbians and Gay Men as Heterosexual Family Members   257

Implications for Practice   259

CHAPTER 9. THE FAMILY AS A SOCIAL ORGANIZATION:
IDENTIFYING WELL-BEING   265

Identifying Family Well-Being: Healthy Families and Happy Marriages   266
   Characteristics of Healthy Families   268
   Variations in Happy Marriages   268
Family Functioning   272
   Needs Satisfaction   272
   Family Boundaries   274
   Structural Patterns and Family Well-Being   275
   Interactional Patterns and Family Well-Being   276
Family Problems: Domestic Violence   278
   Spouse Abuse   280
   Elder Abuse   281
   Child Abuse and Neglect   282
Family Problems: Marriage, Divorce, Remarriage   286
   Marriage and Divorce Rates   287
   The Never-Married and the Remarried   287
   Interpreting the Data   289
Stressful Family Patterns   289
   The Stress of Divorce   290
   The Stress of Single Parenthood after Divorce   291
   Families of Unwed Mothers   292
   The Stress of Remarriage   294
   Stresses in Cohabitation   295
Implications for Practice   295
   Primary Prevention, Early Intervention, and Rehabilitation   296

CHAPTER 10. THE FAMILY AS A SOCIAL ORGANIZATION:
ANALYZING WELL-BEING   300

Perspectives on Family Functioning   301
The Ecological Perspective   301
   Macrosystems and Ecosystems   302
   The Family and Economic Stress   302
   The Eco-Map: Studying the Social Context of the Family   307
   The Genogram: Studying the Individual in the Family System   311
The Psychodynamic Perspective   316
The Developmental or Life-Cycle Perspective   318
   The Normal Troubles of Family Life   318

Diversity in the Family Life Cycle   320

Usefulness of the Family Life-Cycle Model   322

Role Theory and the Family   322

Dynamics of Role Relationships   324

Role Conflict or Strain   325

Family Responses to Role Conflict or Strain   330

Conflict Theory and the Family   332

The Family as an Oasis in Capitalism   333

Inequalities in the Family Institution   333

Conflict between Husbands and Wives   334

Conflict between Parents and Children   336

Implications for Practice   337

PART IV

THE INDIVIDUAL

AS A SYSTEM   343

CHAPTER 11. PSYCHOLOGICAL WELL-BEING   344

Domains of Psychological Well-Being   345

The Study of Abnormality: Mental Disorders   346

Evaluation of the *DSM-III*   348

The Study of Normality   349

Normality as Average   349

Normality as Health   350

Normality as Utopia   354

Normality as Transactional Systems   357

Toward an Integrated Approach to Normality   358

The Transactional Context of Psychological Normality   359

Normality and the Disabled   361

Implications for Practice   362

CHAPTER 12. INTERPERSONAL WELL-BEING: BEHAVIORAL

AND MARXIAN THEORIES   367

Behavioral Theories: Social Exchange and Learning   370

Learning Theories and Principles of Learning   370

Classical Conditioning   371

Operant Conditioning   371

Social-Learning Theory   374

Social Exchange Theory: Equity   376

    The Marketplace Analogy and the Systems Approach   377

    Intimate Relations and Exchange Relationships   378

    The Calculation of Rewards in Exchange Transactions   379

    Cooperation, Reciprocity, and Fairness in Social Exchange   380

    Implications of Social Exchange for Social Service Practice   384

Marxian Theory: Exploitation and Alienation   386

    Marx's Theory of Social Behavior   386

    Capitalism as a Social Relationship   387

    Marx's Solution for Exploitation and Alienation   392

    Alienation in Contemporary Society   393

    Contemporary Views on Resolving Exploitation and Alienation   398

    Implications of Marxian Theory for Social Service Practice   402

CHAPTER 13. INTERPERSONAL WELL-BEING: STRUCTURAL
FUNCTIONAL AND SYMBOLIC INTERACTION THEORIES   407

Structural Functionalism and Anomie   408

    The Utopian Vision   408

    Anomie Theory: Breakdowns in the Social System   409

    Comparing Merton, Marx, and Social Exchange   414

    Anomie and Juvenile Delinquency   415

Stress as a Form of Anomie   418

    The General Adaptation Syndrome   419

    Stressors in the Environment   420

    The Psychological Response to Stress   423

    Stress Theory and Management in Social Service Practice   423

Implications of Structural Functionalism for Practice   424

Symbolic Interactionism   425

    Mind and Self in the Context of Society   426

    The Development of the Self   427

    Social Interaction   429

    The Effects of Social Interaction on the Self   432

Symbolic Interactionism and Labeling   432

    Labeling in Everyday Life   433

    Achieved Labels: Blemishes to Individual Character   433

    Ascribed Labels: Tribal Stigmas   438

    Responding to Labels   441

Social Service Work and Labeling   441

Implications of Symbolic Interactionism for Practice   442

CHAPTER 14. INTRAPERSONAL WELL-BEING: EGO PSYCHOLOGY
AND COGNITIVE DEVELOPMENT THEORIES   447

The Study of Ego Psychology and Psychosocial Development   449

Development and Change   450

The Freudian Base of Ego Psychology   451

A Theory of Psychosexual Development   451

Freud's Developmental Stages   454

Freud on Female Development   457

The Complex Process of Sex-Role Development   458

Freud's Contributions to the Study of Human Behavior   464

Ego Psychology   465

The Ego in Conflict: Ego-Defense Mechanisms   465

The Ego in Harmony: Autonomous Functions   466

The Study of Object Relations   469

Cognitive Development   471

Piaget's Stages of Cognitive Development   471

Kohlberg's Stages of Moral Development   474

Women's Moral Development   478

The Roots of Moral Behavior   480

Implications for Practice   481

Points of View on Human Development   482

Application in Assessment and Intervention   483

CHAPTER 15. EGO PSYCHOLOGY AND DEVELOPMENT ACROSS
THE LIFE COURSE   488

Stages of Development   489

Biological, Social, and Psychological Clocks   490

Prenatal Development and Birth   491

The Parents' Influence   491

Genetic Inheritance   493

The Embryonic and Fetal Periods   494

Birth   495

The Newborn Baby   496

Developmental Tasks across the Life Course   496

Havighurst's Classification of Tasks   497

Erikson's Psychosocial Crises   501

    Eight Stages of Psychosocial Development   501

    Early-Life Stages of Development   504

    School Age and Adolescence   508

    Young Adults and Adulthood   512

    Old Age   516

Developmental Crises in Maturity   519

    Levinson and the Seasons of Life   520

    Peck on Development in Old Age   524

The Role of Crises in Development   525

    The Adolescent Crisis Debate   525

    Is There a Crisis in Mid-Life?   527

    Reconsidering Crises across the Life Course   527

Implications for Practice   528

    Dealing with Developmental Difficulties   529

PART V

EPILOGUE   537

CHAPTER 16. TOWARD A REFORM-ORIENTED
THEORY FOR PRACTICE   538

Communities in Society   539

    The Critical Themes: Majority-Minority Relations   540

    The Systems Approach to the Issues   541

Family Life   541

    The Critical Themes: Changing Roles and Expectations   542

    The Systems Approach to the Issues   543

The Individual as a System   544

    The Critical Themes: Achieving Psychological Well-Being   544

    The Systems Approach to the Issues   545

SUBJECT INDEX   549

AUTHOR INDEX   561

ABOUT THE AUTHOR   563

Preface

W HY SHOULD you use this text? That's a good question, and it deserves an answer. Until recently, it was also a moot question, because there were no, or at least few, texts on human behavior in the social environment from which to choose. Instructors designed their own courses and developed a set of reading assignments to accompany them. Instructors may still choose this option, but a number of texts now are available, and instructors are more likely to take the time to evaluate these and choose one for their courses. There are a number of reasons why the choice of this text is a good one.

All these texts aspire to satisfy the broad guidelines of the Council on Social Work Education. According to its Curriculum Policy for the Master's Degree and Baccalaureate Degree Programs in Social Work Education, educators are to keep within a "person in environment" perspective and to bring to students a focus on individuals as members of families, groups, organizations, and communities. They are enjoined to present human behavior as a function of biological, social, psychological, and cultural systems and to underscore the consequences of ethnicity, race, class, and sexual orientation. Furthermore, the council requires the material to be organized in a coherent approach and to consider implications for social service practice.

This text meets these guidelines. It utilizes a coherent perspective incorporating critical analysis and a systems approach. In addition, it considers a number of other important social and psychological theories and perspectives, including structural functionalism, the ecological approach, anomie, stress, Marxian theory, social exchange, learning, symbolic interactionism, labeling, role theory, ego psychology, self psychology, cognitive development, and psychosocial development. Information from the biological sciences is included in discussions on human nature, gender differences, IQ differences and race, disabilities, prenatal development, and physical changes across the life course. Social and political knowledge frequently is incorporated to illuminate the content.

The consequences of differences in ethnicity, race, class, and sexual orientation, as well as gender, age, and disability status, are highlighted. There is considerable material on individuals throughout the life course, as members of communities and families, and in transaction with others in the society, as well as in groups and organizations. The chapters have sections on implications for social service practice, especially in the assessment process, that is, the identification and analysis of client problems and the plans for intervention that follow.

The principal reason for choosing this text, however, is not so much that it meets the guidelines as that it is a reliable presentation of the material which has been uniquely developed from my professional background in social service work and education. My undergraduate training was in psychology; my masters in social welfare stressed practice with individuals and families; and my doctorate was in social work and social psychology at the University of Michigan. My first faculty position was a joint appointment in a school of social work and a department of sociology. I have been teaching courses on human behavior and on social psychology throughout my academic career. This book therefore is the result of years of thinking about the place of human behavior courses in the education of social work practitioners. It is influenced by the human behavior courses I took as a social work graduate student, as well as by my field work and subsequent paid and volunteer experience as a social worker in public welfare, mental health, hospital social services, services for juveniles, and services with minority populations, especially Hispanics. And, of course, it is influenced by my own developing professional interests and commitments.

The Systems Approach

There are two different ways in which courses on human behavior and the social environment are usually organized. One stresses the psychosocial development of the individual, often referred to as "growth and development." The other includes material on groups, families, communities, organizations, and society and stresses the "social environment." In my own courses I have always preferred to emphasize that the individual is only one system among a number of systems with which social workers must deal. While they must know about individual growth and development, they must also know about the society in which their clients live, especially where community and family life are concerned.

In this regard the organization of the book — although not its content — is indebted to the successful editions of *Human Behavior and the Social Environment: A Systems Approach*, by Ralph Anderson and Irl Carter (3rd edition, 1984, Aldine Publishing Company, New York). Their text first presents a general theoretical framework applicable to all human systems and then elucidates it with respect to particular human systems: community, organization, small group, family, and individual. This type of organization has always appealed to me

because it recognizes that social service workers take on diverse roles. Most social workers work directly with individuals and families. Some work with communities as organizers and planners. Others promote social policy, develop
and administer programs, or supervise those programs. And some become
generalists, moving from one level of practice to another, depending on the
needs of clients and services. Human behavior and social environment courses
must lay the foundation for all forms of social service practice.

In organizing this text I, too, start by presenting a general theoretical framework (Part I), followed by four chapters on community life (Part II), four chapters on family life (Part III), and five chapters on the individual (Part IV).
While there are no separate chapters on groups and organizations, material
relevant to these systems is incorporated, particularly in the chapters on the
interpersonal well-being of individuals in Part IV. Part V is a final chapter
which serves as a summary and helps provide a synthesis of the content.

This text thus takes a "systems approach" akin to Anderson and Carter's, but
it does not follow their structural functional or "systems theory" perspective.
For years I denied that I was a systems theorist, but every time I gave a presentation on my approach to the study of human behavior I was told that is what
I was. As you will see, I still tend to reject systems theory, but I support a systems approach. A systems approach aspires to be a content-free model for examining human behavior. At its core, it guides the social worker to look simultaneously at the environment of a system and at the system itself. My definition
of a systems approach acknowledges that the behavior of any particular
system — be it an individual, family, or community — is always a function of the
transactions between it and its environment. This systems approach is apparent in all four parts of this text. It allows for the introduction of a number of
structural functional as well as non-structural functional approaches to the
study of systems, including such "conflict perspectives" as social exchange and
Marxian theories. It also allows for the incorporation of psychological theory,
which cannot easily be integrated into the terminology associated with structural functional approaches to systems.

The Critical Approach

The critical approach of this text is also of special note. Critical theory has long
been a tradition within both psychology and sociology. A critical approach emphasizes the search for social progress through evaluation of the effects of existing social structural arrangements on society and on individual well-being.
This perspective is useful to the social work profession for two reasons. First,
it recognizes that the study of human behavior cannot stop at mere description
but must proceed to prescription. When social service workers make policy,
design and administer programs, and assess, analyze, and intervene in the
lives of individuals and families, they cannot avoid taking positions on what
is likely to improve social functioning. In this respect social workers are
prescribers. The second reason follows from the first. A critical approach ac-

knowledges the importance of values in human behavior. It supports the belief that social workers operate not just on knowledge but on certain humanist principles as embodied in their code of ethics.

Because of its critical approach, this text is unusual in its depth of coverage of issues related to race and ethnicity, social class, gender, and sexual orientation. It rarely strays far from these issues, although in some chapters discussion of one or another of them may predominate. The chapters on community life focus largely on ethnic and racial minority communities. Considerable attention is given to their social history, to groups that have recently entered the United States, and to the study of prejudice, discrimination, racism, and culture. There is also ample discussion of social class and poverty in the chapters on community and family life. Gender, women's issues, and issues related to sexual orientation are particularly important in the chapters on family life but are also highlighted in the chapters on individuals and addressed in some of the chapters on community life.

Theoretical Orientation and Style

In spite of my own theoretical preferences and critical inclinations, I try hard to present a number of theories as impartially as possible. I sincerely believe that the use of a systems and critical approach is enhanced by recognizing the contributions of a number of theories. Since so many of the theories of social scientists have not been completely tested, it is premature for social workers to be committed to any particular viewpoint. Rather, they should continually test and evaluate the utility of various theories in their practice. Thus rather than promoting one particular perspective, I identify the contributions of many of them. It is up to students to integrate them into their own practice in ways that make sense to them.

Throughout the text I have attempted to create a readable and lively style. I present theory and findings from studies and tackle controversial issues in ways that I hope will keep students interested. Each chapter begins with an introduction of the major themes to be discussed. Although no glossary is included, key concepts are highlighted and defined within context. All the chapters end with study questions which should be useful in organizing class discussion and designing examinations. An instructor's manual to facilitate the development of tests is also available.

In using drafts of the chapters with my own students and getting feedback from other faculty who have graciously used my drafts, I feel relatively secure in saying that students will be able to understand the content and will enjoy reading it. I have been helped enormously in this task by Gloria Reardon, the editor assigned to me by F. E. Peacock Publishers. Although I have generally had great respect for editors, she is without doubt the best I have ever worked with. If you enjoy using the book, she will have had a lot to do with it.

Acknowledgments

In closing, I want to acknowledge that I have been helped along by many people. My parents and my three sisters have always been emotionally supportive and have made me feel special. My good friend, James Nattinger, was always kind and considerate. Some of the professors and professional associates who inspired my thinking are Harry Kitano, Jerome Cohen, Eugene Litwak, Eileen McCloud, Gordon Hearn, Peter Leonard, Norman Wyers, Jefry Galper, Herbert Kelman, Albert Reiss, Jr., and Guy Swanson. I have received encouragement from a number of friends and associates, past and present, including Gary Lloyd, Anne Minahan, Arecelis Frances, Julio Morales, J. Julian Rivera, Sheldon Rose, Carmen Fidelina de Rodriguez, June Hopps, Diane Kravetz, Betsy DeBeer Smith, Bernard Ross, Mona Wasow, and Berit Ingersoll Dayton. A number of associates read drafts of this manuscript, and I would like to give special thanks to them: Grant Farr, Allen Pincus, Naomi Farber, Aaron Brower, Eileen Brennan, and Gary Seltzer. Jodi Schmitz helped me research the material on adolescent employment which appears in Chapter 13. Mary Kasparek was the most diligent and competent work-study student I have ever worked with; thanks to her, all the footnotes should be correct. I would be remiss not to mention that Ted Peacock, my publisher, is a fine person, and I am proud to publish under his banner.

January 1990   JOHN F. LONGRES

PART I

A Critical Perspective on Social Systems

CHAPTER 1

A Critical Perspective

M AJOR THEMES DISCUSSED IN THIS CHAPTER:

1. *A theory for practice*. The groundwork for a reform-oriented social service practice is laid by distinguishing among three kinds of theory: a theory for practice, a theory of practice, and a theory of caring.

2. *The critical perspective*. A theory for practice and a theory of caring merge to form a critical perspective. In this perspective, social service workers participate in debates about social problems and take sides in building a better society.

3. *Questioning the critical perspective*. A critical perspective is not without detractors. As students begin social service practice, they must develop their own ideas about the strengths and limitations of a particular perspective.

4. *Working with the interaction between individual and society*. Those who accept a critical perspective must recognize that social conditions, good or bad, are not the product of either individuals or society alone. Individuals influence society just as they are influenced by society, and the troubles individuals face in their own lives are inseparable from the problems society experiences as a whole. The goal of critical social service practice, therefore, is to understand and resolve difficulties in the interaction between individual and society.

T HE IDEA that real social progress is possible underlies social welfare institutions and social work practice. Social service policymakers and practitioners truly believe that if the right programs are developed and delivered effectively, clients, be they individuals or communities or whole societies, can progress from a relatively negative to a relatively positive condition.

A critical theory for social service practice is in keeping with such a social change philosophy. It is less concerned with what social service is than with what it might be and might accomplish. Unlike a theory *of* practice, which is derived from observations of social service workers' norms and roles, a theory *for* practice provides explanations to guide practice.

A THEORY FOR PRACTICE

One way to formulate a **theory of practice** would be to observe social service workers as they go about their work, and then codify what they are doing. From observations it should be possible to specify what social workers do and what results they get: How they run groups and handle conflict; how they assess problems in a particular client or in a family; how they identify harmony and conflict in organizational decision making, and so on. Theory building in this way is encumbered by the norms of the profession and the work organization, as well as by the policy-derived roles of social service workers. A theory constructed from observations may describe present practices, but it has a limited ability to improve it or to bring about social change.

A **theory for practice**, in contrast, is a system of ideas or statements which explain social service practice. It provides for the development of practice models and principles out of which actual social service practice might evolve. Rather than being based in the norms and roles of social service, it is more likely to be indebted to the social and biological sciences. The proposed theory for practice which could be developed from the ideas and content in this book would incorporate knowledge from other disciplines, sociology and psychology in particular, and history, anthropology, economics, political science, and biology more generally.

A theory for practice is a prerequisite for the development of a **practice theory**, which is undoubtedly the ultimate goal of those who try to formulate social service theory. Robert Vinter describes a practice theory as consisting of "a body of principles, more or less systematically developed and anchored in scientific knowledge, that seeks to guide and direct practitioner action." These principles are "directed not at understanding reality, but at achieving control over it."[1]

Since a theory for practice precedes practice theory, it can be understood as a system of statements intended to explain human behavior and make it comprehensible, toward the ultimate purpose of learning how to control human behavior. While we may use such a theory to explain *all* human behavior, this book primarily focuses on explaining the problems and needs, strengths, and weaknesses of *clients*. It contributes to practice theory by developing a *meta-theory* for practice, that is, "a synthesis of several theories of knowledge from a social systems perspective."[2]

THINKING ABOUT SOCIAL SERVICE WORK

A theory for practice would guide social service workers at all levels in thinking about the problems they encounter in their work. Consider the following case example:

> Maria Santos came to the area from Texas some five years ago. She left high school when she became pregnant, and she is now the mother of a three-year old asthmatic son. Though she is separated from the father, she still sees him on and off. He contributes very sporadically to their economic support. They recently quarreled about his jealous temper, and Maria says she isn't counting on seeing him again.
>
> Maria Santos has never applied for public assistance, although her mother has received Aid to Families with Dependent Children (AFDC) payments since they have been in the city. For a while she managed by working at odd jobs, but during the past year she has not worked steadily because of a series of minor illnesses. She says she doesn't want to end up as "another Mexican failure."
>
> She lives in a two-room apartment, is three months behind in her rent, and has received a notice of eviction. Her mother and younger sister live nearby. They babysit for her now and then, but she says they have their own problems to worry about and can't be worried about her.
>
> During the interview she did not express a great deal of emotion, although she did say she was unhappy about her predicament. She stated a number of times that she didn't know what to do or where to turn and hoped that the services offered by the center could help her.[3]

The case of Maria Santos is a hypothetical case study, but the problems presented in the case are not unlike those social services workers confront in everyday practice. Social workers, counselors, and other line workers work directly with people like Maria Santos, and they must determine ways to relieve or ameliorate the problems these people present. Supervisors must assist the line workers who bring them their questions about possibilities for helping people in situations like the ones in which Maria finds herself. Administrators, program developers, and social policy planners would work indirectly with these people. They must see how the range of problems Maria presents is typical of a class of clients and develop and organize services accordingly.

How should social services workers think about the problems presented in a case like that of Maria Santos? Why does she find herself in her present predicament? What are her problems and needs? What are her strengths and limitations? What kinds of things can be done to help her out of her predicament? Thinking about the problems presented by clients and how to intervene in them is the subject of this book.

CONTROL AND CHANGE IN SOCIAL SERVICE WORK

Social scientists generally agree that the purpose or function served by the social services is to help people like Maria Santos out of their predicaments. In the process of doing this, it is hoped, a better society will be built.

Behind such vague, general statements there lie many contradictions and complexities, however. Does social service help Maria and society by helping her adjust and cope with the realities and demands of the larger society? Or does it help her and society by championing her cause and insisting that society accommodate to her needs? Those who would help her by asking that she learn to adjust and cope are acting in keeping with a **social control** philosophy. Those who support her rights and ask that society accommodate to them and try to improve her situation are following a **social change** philosophy.

It is not always easy to distinguish between the social control and social change philosophies. Most social service practice seems to be oriented somewhere in between. What might be called a liberal philosophy, accepting a certain degree of conformity while working for a certain degree of within-system change, is followed.[4]

By tradition, most social service workers operate on the basis of a **theory of caring**. While theories of practice and for practice strive to be empirical and therefore free of values, a theory of caring is value-dominated.[5] Social service workers adopt the value that it is good to show care, and they support their practice with political and ideological values concerning the best ways to show care. This is both necessary and good (a value statement), but practice cannot be based solely on values. **Values**, which are statements of good or bad which people reject or accept and place their faith in, may inform practice and should infuse it. They cannot substitute for practice theory, however. The issue of conformity versus change is a value issue which is debated among professionals. Ultimately, it is an individual choice.

This book aspires to develop a theory for social service practice which is in keeping with a social change philosophy. As we outline the systems approach and present theories of human behavior, therefore, we will evaluate them from a perspective that emphasizes the need to be concerned about social issues and social change.

THE CRITICAL PERSPECTIVE

The theory for social service practice being proposed in this book adopts a critical perspective on society. From this perspective, it is not enough to merely observe and describe social conditions and interactions. Rather, they must be looked at critically and analytically, with a view to identifying problems and solving them. Some social scientists relate the critical perspective to the idea of social justice and the elimination or reduction of inequalities. Charles Anderson and Jeffry Gibson define a critical perspective as "the dual task of developing a critique of all forms of social oppression [and] . . . assist[ing] in the development of alternative social forms that uphold human dignity and provide the conditions for the positive cultivation of human mental and physical ability."[6]

Critical perspectives have a long history in the social sciences and social service. Ernest Becker notes that in the nineteenth century the social sciences were not as divided as they are today.[7] Those who took up the profession did not think of themselves as psychologists or sociologists or economists or social workers, for instance, but as social scientists. They also seem to have been guided by a more clear-cut understanding of what questions needed to be answered. Unlike contemporary times, when there appear to be no identifiable central issues in social science, in the nineteenth century social scientists were collectively concerned with "the problem of the soul." They asked themselves: What is the happy life? What is the good society? And they didn't stop there. They also asked: How can the happy life and the good society be achieved? The central function of the social sciences, as they perceived it, was to provide ideas and prescriptions for building the best society possible.

PRESCRIPTION RATHER THAN DESCRIPTION

AD → PD
EC → PP
Becker identifies two kinds of social science research with different methods and outcomes. In his terms, research that is **analytic descriptive** makes for **placid descriptions**. It merely reports observations and describes what is going on in human interactions. The other type of research, which is **evaluative critical** in nature, provides **passionate prescriptions** for the conditions it identifies. Rather than just describing a situation, it seeks to prescribe the means to improve it.[8]

Becker prefers research that provides such passionate prescriptions. By implication, he would say that a theory for social service practice cannot be merely analytic descriptive. It ought also to be evaluative critical, acknowledging that scientists need to make judgments about society and the circumstances people find themselves in. We might say that a theory of caring ought to be infused into a theory for practice.

Thus, in thinking about social service work such as the problems of Maria Santos, the worker's aim is not merely to make a "placid description" of her life and experiences or of her present relationships and psychological functioning. The worker's goal is to make a "passionate prescription" for Maria; to help her, and thus to help society, meet the highest possible standards.

CRITICAL ANALYSIS IN CONTEMPORARY SOCIAL SERVICE

In the twentieth century, many social scientists have renewed the emphasis on critical evaluation or analysis of the human condition. Change is considered possible because the social sciences are not natural sciences. For example, as Anthony Giddens points out, the social processes studied in sociology are not governed by unalterable laws of nature:

> As human beings, we are not condemned to be swept along by forces that have the inevitability of laws of nature. But this means we must be conscious of the alternative futures that are potentially open to us. . . . the task of sociology is contributing to *the critique of existing forms of society*.[9]

Social service work is inherently critical because it is oriented to social concern and social change. Edwin Thomas notes three ways in which practice theory differs from what he refers to as scientific theory: practice theory is "oriented to the objective of control rather than that of understanding alone, it tends to be value laden rather than value free, and it is prescriptive as well as descriptive."[10] The very process of assessing the case of Maria Santos, or of any other individual, group, family, or community, requires a value judgment about the well-being of the individuals and the functioning of society. The very process of planning an intervention requires a prescriptive judgment on what alternatives are most likely to reduce personal happiness and the good society. In social service work, values go hand in hand with skills.

QUESTIONING THE CRITICAL PERSPECTIVE

All social scientists do not believe the human condition can be improved through planned social change. One of these is Peter Berger, who describes himself as a "conservative humanist." Berger's **conservative humanism** opposes values and ideologies that assume the human condition can be changed in any significant way. His preliminary definition of a conservative outlook is "fundamental hesitation regarding social change." Berger concludes, "The prototypical conservative maxim can be put as follows. 'Other things being equal, let society remain the way it is.' The prototypical maxim of the 'left,' be it liberal or radical in its particular coloration, can then be formulated: 'Other things being equal, let society change.' " He goes on to add, "A conservative accepts the messiness of history and is suspicious of the idea of progress."[11]

UNINTENDED CONSEQUENCES OF SOCIAL CHANGE

Berger makes another point which should not be overlooked: Changing society is no easy matter, and in the process people are likely to be hurt. The American War of Independence and the French Revolution had noble aspirations to secure the blessings of liberty, equality, brotherhood, and the free pursuit of happiness for all the people, but the fact is that in the process of trying to achieve these goals, many lives were lost or socially and economically shattered. Social change always has costs as well as benefits. If Congress tries to create a just and fair system of taxation, for example, citizens who have become accustomed to loopholes, tax shelters, and the like will be outraged if they are asked to start paying their share of the costs of government.

Similarly, if a social agency tries to get the father of Maria Santos's child to provide consistent child support, the father's personal liberties would be curtailed, and he would not be happy at the social progress being made to assure that parents accept responsibility for their children. A liberal or radical humanist (as opposed to Berger's conservative humanist) may advocate change but must also be concerned with the difficulty of bringing it about and the possibility of creating harm as well as happiness.

Social reforms, however noble in their aspirations, do not always work perfectly. They may have a number of unintended negative consequences. A recent example is the effort to deinstitutionalize the care of individuals with mental health troubles or "problems in living."[12] In the 1960s, mental hospitals and institutions were judged to be harming patients more than curing them, and civil rights of the institutionalized were being routinely violated. Social workers and others in the helping professions led the way in developing a national community-based mental health program that would have eventually closed down the institutions for the "mentally ill." Legislation was passed authorizing the construction and staffing of community mental health facilities, but many of them were never built and sufficient funds were not allotted to develop effective community-based programs. The movement toward deinstitutionalization therefore has had some adverse results.[13] Without community health centers to provide clinical services and counseling, and without adequate means of support, many formerly institutionalized patients have been forced to cope with daily living on their own. Not only is their own situation often desperate, but they have congregated in cities and neighborhoods which do not welcome them and consider them a burden.

The Possibility of Human Progress

The belief in progress and human perfectibility through planned change which is inherent in the critical perspective expresses values that are essentially Western. People raised outside the Judeo-Christian rationalist tradition are likely to be skeptical of the critical perspective.

Russel Means, cofounder of the American Indian movement, is one of those who question European **rationalism** and its assumption that progress is possible through the use of technological inventions — including the technology of social welfare — to overcome human suffering. He finds "Christians, capitalists, Marxists" to be all the same in that they represent European intellectual development: "They do what they do in order that European culture can continue to exist and develop according to its needs." Means endorses instead a Native American spiritual position which is concerned with what he calls the natural order: "Rational[ism] is a curse since it can cause humans to forget the natural order of things. A wolf never forgets his or her place in the natural order. Europeans do."[14]

Whether human progress is possible is something that only continual monitoring through history will demonstrate. In the meantime, social service workers ought to realize that progress through the use of rational planned change, an idea which reflects European intellectual tradition, is what the social services stand for. The history of the social welfare movement in the United States and other Western countries has been a history of putting the concept of planned, rational social progress in motion.

Ralf Dahrendorf has reflected on the relationship between history and human progress. His point of view is one with which many in the social services are likely to agree:

> There may thus be a progress of liberty. There may be societies which give more space than others to the desire of men to reduce constraints; there may be more open and more developed societies in which life chances are enhanced and extended further. And since this is so, we must never rest in our quest for advancing the frontiers of freedom.[15]

WORKING WITH THE INTERACTION BETWEEN INDIVIDUAL AND SOCIETY

The critical theory for social service practice we are proposing is based on the idea that social conditions, good or bad, are not the product of either individuals or society alone. Rather, they are derived from the interactions between the two. Thus the problems individuals face in their own lives and the problems society recognizes and tries to solve in order to achieve human progress are interrelated.

BLAME THE VICTIM OR BLAME SOCIETY? *Ryan* *soc. reactions to people with problems*

The term **blaming the victim** was coined by William Ryan as a way of expressing society's reaction to people with problems and advancing the cause for social change.[16] In Maria Santos, Ryan would see a victim of American society, a woman exploited by an economic system that cannot function to achieve its goals of producing profits without the presence of unemployment and social inequalities. In this view, Maria is discriminated against in a culture where Hispanic values, traditions, and physical appearance are looked down upon, and she is abused by a sexist society which keeps women vulnerable and dependent. Such victims should not be blamed for the predicaments they find themselves in, Ryan says.

Nevertheless, Ryan claimed that in the 1970s, when he was presenting this idea, social service systems were in fact blaming people like Maria Santos. He did not suggest that social service organizations and workers were being mean or nasty, or that they were deliberately setting out to blame clients. Most people who enter the social service professions undoubtedly mean well and intend to demonstrate care and concern. Since Ryan's book came out, in fact, many social workers have taken pains to inform certain clients that they are not to blame for their situations. But they are missing the point; even as they tell clients of their blamelessness, they may participate in victim blaming.

Blaming the victim entails more than suggesting a client is at fault in a particular circumstance. Social service workers also blame the victim when they acknowledge the societal causes of problems but intervene only at the level of the individual. From line workers to administrators and policy formulators, social service practitioners often participate in this very contradiction. Ryan explains how:

> The old-fashioned conservative could hold firmly to the belief that the oppressed and the victimized were born that way — "that way" being defective or inadequate in character or ability. The new ideology attributes defect and inadequacy to the malignant nature of poverty, injustice, slum life, and racial difficulties. The stigma that marks the victim and accounts for his victimization is an acquired stigma, a stigma of social, rather than genetic origin. But the stigma, the defect, the fatal difference — though derived in the past from environmental forces — is still located within the victim, inside his skin. With such an elegant formulation, the humanitarian can have it both ways. He can, all at the same time, concentrate his charitable interests on the defects of the victim, condemn the vague social and environmental stresses that produced the defect (some time ago), and ignore the continuing effect of victimizing social forces (right now), ...[17]

Ryan perceives a "terrifying sameness" in the programs that arise from this kind of analysis:

> All of this happens so smoothly that it seems downright rational. First, identify the social problem. Second, study those affected by the problem and discover in what ways they are different from the rest of us as a consequence of deprivation and injustice. Third, define the differences as the cause of the social problem itself. Finally, of course, assign a . . . bureaucrat to invent a humanitarian action program to correct the differences.[18]

In blaming Maria Santos for her predicament, a social service worker might focus on her psychological condition, her emotional and cognitive state (perhaps depression), or her personality makeup. The worker might explore Maria's inability to get along with her mother or try to determine what she had done (or not done) so that the father of her child was no longer around. Her need to learn work skills so she could be employed and parenting skills so she would not end up as she had would also be addressed. In short, the social service worker would focus on the things about Maria — her attitudes, beliefs, and behaviors — that are unique to her or, presumably, to others in her circumstances. These are the things that can be assumed to have produced her present crisis and that now require assistance.

Rather than blaming the victim in this way, Ryan would say, an assessment of Maria Santos should focus instead on the environmental stresses and the continuing effects of the social forces that are victimizing her. He would, in short, blame the society in order to change the society.

This might very well be a trap, however. Blaming the victim would fit a theory of human behavior which suggests that people make their own destinies, for better or worse, and they are completely responsible for what happens to them. Blaming the society, on the other hand, would fit a theory of human behavior which suggests that people are completely shaped by environmental forces and are passive victims of societal circumstances that cannot be controlled. It suggests that somehow society, "the system," is out there somewhere, some kind of vague, dark monster, working people over in ways that they are powerless to influence.

The Multicentered and Transactional Points of View

If we are to avoid victim blaming and society blaming, Jill Kagle and Charles Cowger suggest that we must begin to think of social work in both multicentered and transaction-centered terms.[19] The difficulties experienced by clients are described in **multicentered** terms when attention is called to the ways in which the environment and the individual both contribute to the problem. For example, a social worker might describe a child's school problems as "The child is misbehaving in the classroom, and the teacher does not know how to handle it." In a multicentered approach, the social worker needs to work independently with the child (and the child's family) to change the misbehavior and must also work independently with the teacher (and the school) to assure that teachers are trained to handle misbehavior in the classroom. The difficulties experienced by clients are defined in **transaction-centered** terms when the focus is on the simultaneous interaction between the individual and the environment. For example, the social worker might describe the child's school problems as "a breakdown in communication between child and teacher." In a transaction-centered approach, the social worker must bring the child and the teacher together to work on how they can communicate with each other better.

Following the lead of Kagle and Cowger, the point of view taken in this book will be to acknowledge that both society and individuals contribute to problems. People are not completely responsible for what happens to them, but neither are they completely shaped by environmental forces. The individual and society are equally basic and primary; each influences and is influenced by the other, and they are inseparable. In taking this position, we will point out the multicentered factors and transactional processes that lead to the difficulties experienced by clients.

Private Troubles and Public Issues

The transactions between a society and the individuals who comprise it are diverse and varied in their scope and impact. The problems that arise in these transactions are likely to involve the **micro environment** of individual beliefs, attitudes, and behaviors, as well as the **macro environment** of social institutions and processes. In the terms coined by C. Wright Mills, they may be either private troubles or public issues — or both.[20]

The term **private troubles** refers to the ways individuals experience problems. According to Mills, "*Troubles* occur within the character of the individual and within the range of his immediate relations with others; they have to do with his self and with those limited areas of social life of which he is directly and personally aware."[21]

Maria Santos feels miserable; she doesn't want to be a failure in life, she is worried about getting a job and paying the rent, she is concerned for her health and the health of her child, she is quarreling with her boyfriend and with her mother. These are her troubles, and she experiences them in a very personal or private way. They are her private troubles, not the troubles of other people.

The term **public issues** refers to the ways society experiences problems. According to Mills, "*Issues* have to do with matters that transcend these local environments of the individual and the range of his inner life." They have to do with the institutions of society as a whole, "the larger structure of social and historical life." Public issues also reflect contradictions and conflict in the ways society is organized:

> An issue is a public matter, some value cherished by publics is felt to be threatened. Often there is a debate about what the value really is and about what it is that really threatens it. This debate is often without focus if only because it is the very nature of an issue, unlike even widespread trouble, that it can not very well be defined in terms of the immediate and everyday environments of ordinary men.[22]

Public issues are not directly observable in the case of Maria Santos, but they can be sensed in the background. For one thing, there are many Maria Santos's who pass through social service caseloads. Their shared troubles give evidence of the public issues, the debates about social problems that make up the political, social, and economic concerns of the nation. Why are divorce rates so high, and what should be done about them? Why is there persistent unemployment, and how can it be prevented? Should there be a national policy of health insurance so everyone has the right to medical services, not just those who can afford them?

Mills gives several examples of how to tell them when a private trouble reflects a public issue. One is unemployment:

> When, in a city of 100,000, only one man is unemployed, that is his personal trouble, and for its relief we properly look to the character of the man, his skills, and his immediate opportunities. But when in a nation of 50 million employees, 15 million men are unemployed, that is an issue, and we may not hope to find its solution with the range of opportunities open to any one individual.[23]

Another is marriage:

> Inside a marriage a man and a woman may experience personal troubles, but when the divorce rate during the first four years of marriage is 250 out of every 1,000 attempts, this is an indication of a structural issue having to do with the institutions of marriage and the family and other institutions that bear upon them.[24]

Thus, while private troubles can be independent of public issues, often they are not. When there is a private trouble that is clearly unrelated to public issues, it would be reasonable to blame the person or persons experiencing the difficulty. The services provided might try to overcome the personal limitations that apparently have caused the problem. When private troubles clearly reflect public issues, then it is unreasonable to blame the individuals for them or to

The rights of citizens is a public issue about which there is constant debate. Social activists join together to push the cause of social justice. *AP/Wide World Photos*.

see the troubles they are experiencing as a sign of their personal limitations. In such circumstances, there is a dual obligation to try to resolve both the trouble and the issue.

The Dual Nature of Social Service Practice

Sociologists have used different terms for the need for social services to attend to both the individual and the society: micro and macro, direct and indirect services, social work and social welfare. William Schwartz points out that the need to deal with both private troubles and public issues is responsible for the dual nature of social work practice, or intervention.[25] Neil Gilbert and Harry Specht make a distinction between the direct-service worker, who provides assistance to those in need, and the social welfare specialist, who focuses on the institutional structure through which those in need are served.[26]

This book maintains that social service workers must all take into account the dual nature of social service practice. Social service line workers deal with individuals experiencing troubles, but they also need to have a vision of the issues that lie behind these troubles. They must find ways in which they can contribute, in however restrained a fashion, to the resolution of such issues. Social service administrators and planners deal with public issues and cannot translate them solely into the private troubles of individuals, but they must acknowledge these troubles. The goal of the social services, taken as a whole, is to try to resolve both private troubles and public issues simultaneously.

CRITICAL THEORY AND SOCIAL CHANGE

The relation of public issues in society to private troubles in the individual's inner life and everyday experiences points up the need for social service workers to take a broad, comprehensive viewpoint in their efforts to understand and alleviate human suffering. The micro-environmental troubles of an individual in need of help must be understood in terms of the larger environmental problems affecting that individual. The opposite is also true.

The idea that individual problems are usually social problems is a basic assumption of critical theory, according to Peter Findlay:

> Critical theory assumes that most individual problems are in fact social problems, caused by an inequitable social structure; that this social structure is fundamentally determined by the economic organization of society . . . ; that social institutions . . . maintain this social structure even while trying to ameliorate its harmful social consequences; that many of the dominant cultural forms sustain this structure . . . .[27]

The way to deal with this situation, Findlay says, is through analysis of socioeconomic structures and their configuration in society. In making this statement, Findlay expresses to a large extent the value position taken in this book. He also points out an important limitation in the usefulness of critical theory, however. According to Findlay, "The problem critical theory poses for social work" is "the lack of middle-range guidelines for analysis and action."[28] Such guidelines would support change on neither the micro nor the macro level, in neither the individual nor the society. Rather, they would call for action on the basis of study of the transactions between the two.

The tendency for critical theory to channel attention to the need for large-scale, society-wide, even revolutionary social transformations reduces the effectiveness of its application to social service. Social workers caught up in searching for the big change often become impotent when face to face with clients like Maria Santos. The troubles she is experiencing might indeed reflect important public issues. These issues might be (probably are) related to inequitable and exploitative economic structures. However, the obligation of the direct-service worker face to face with Maria Santos, or the role of the program developer setting up services for her, is to help her deal with inequality and exploitation as she experiences and defines them in her everyday life. It does her little good for a worker to declare that she is a victim of social injustice, when only a major revolution could change that. Critical theory can only be of use by trying to develop strategies in the here and now which link individual and social change.

This is not a book about how to work with social service clients, though attention is given to practice methods and techniques. It is, rather, a book which is concerned with learning how to *think about* the problems presented by clients and determining how to intervene in them effectively. In it we examine the explanations offered in various theories of human behavior and consider how they might be applied to communities, families, and individuals in American society. In doing this, we begin to build a theory for social service practice which provides a specific rationale or way of thinking about such work—a critical theory which incorporates a social systems approach to human behavior. Our aim is to provide the background for a theory for practice in which the everyday services social workers provide for troubled clients could, by extension, bring about the changes necessary to improve the ability of social institutions to secure the common good.

DISCUSSION QUESTIONS AND CLASS PROJECTS

1. Identify and describe the following concepts:
   - theory for practice
   - theory of practice
   - theory of caring
   - placid description
   - passionate prescription
   - conservative humanism
   - rationalism
   - the natural order of things
   - blaming the victim
   - blaming society
   - public issues
   - private troubles

2. A critical perspective requires that social workers evaluate the strengths and weaknesses of society and, through their practice, enter into the process of social

change and reform. What does this task mean to you? In what ways do you feel comfortable with this task?

3. Describe two criticisms which have been leveled at the critical perspective. What do you think of these criticisms?

4. Do you believe that human progress is possible through social work practice?

5. In the case of Maria Santos, how would you explain the troubles she is experiencing without either blaming the victim or blaming the society? How would you describe them in multicentered terms? How would you describe them in transactional terms?

6. Identify the public issues that are evident in the case of Maria Santos.

NOTES

1. Robert D. Vinter, "Problems and Processes in Developing Social Work Practice Principles," in E. J. Thomas (editor), *Behavioral Science for Social Workers* (New York: Free Press, 1967), pp. 425–32.

2. Joseph Vigilante et al. "Searching for Theory: Following Hearn," paper presented at the 1981 Annual Program Meeting, Council on Social Work Education, Louisville, Kentucky.

3. John F. Longres, "Social Work Practice with Racial Minorities: A Study of Contemporary Norms and Their Ideological Implications," *California Sociologist*, vol. 4, (Winter 1981), pp. 55–56.

4. Ibid., pp. 54–71.

5. Vigilante et al., "Searching for Theory," p. 25.

6. Charles H. Anderson and Jeffry Royle Gibson, *Toward a New Sociology*, 3rd ed. (Homewood, IL: Dorsey Press, 1978), p. 17.

7. Ernest Becker, "The Rediscovery of the Science of Man," in J. M. Romanshyn (editor), *Social Science and Social Welfare* (New York: Council on Social Work Education, 1974), pp. 7–32.

8. Ibid., pp. 17–23.

9. Anthony Giddens, *Sociology: A Brief But Critical Introduction* (New York: Harcourt, Brace, Jovanovich, 1982), p. 26; italics in original.

10. Edwin J. Thomas, "Types of Contributions Behavioral Science Makes to Social Work," in E. J. Thomas (editor), *Behavioral Science for Social Workers* (New York: Free Press, 1967), p. 6.

11. Peter Berger, "On Conservative Humanism," in P. L. Berger and R. J. Neuhaus (editors), *Movement and Revolution* (New York: Doubleday, 1970), pp. 20–30.

12. Thomas Szasz, *The Myth of Mental Illness* (New York: Harper and Row, 1961).

13. Mona Wasow, "Deinstitutionalization," *Practice Digest*, vol. 6 (Spring 1984), pp. 10–12.

14. Russell Means, "Fighting Words: On the Future of the Earth," *Mother Jones*, December 1980, pp. 24–28, 30, 31, 38.

15. Ralf Dahrendorf, *Life Chances* (Chicago: University of Chicago Press, 1979), p. 20.

16. William Ryan, *Blaming the Victim* (New York: Vintage Books, 1971).

17. Ibid., p. 7.

18. Ibid., p. 8.

19. Jill Doner Kagle and Charles D. Cowger, "Blaming the Client: Implicit Agenda in Practice Research?" *Social Work*, vol. 29 (July-August 1984), pp. 347–52.

20. C. Wright Mills, *The Sociological Imagination* (New York: Penguin Books, 1971).

21. Ibid., pp. 14–15; italics in original.

22. Ibid., p. 15; italics in original.

23. Ibid., p. 15.

24. Ibid., p. 16.

25. William Schwartz, "Private Troubles and Public Issues: One Social Work Job or Two?" *The Social Welfare Forum* (New

York: Columbia University Press, 1969), pp. 22–43.

26. Neil Gilbert and Harry Specht, "The Incomplete Profession," *Social Work*, vol. 19 (November 1974), pp. 655–74.

27. Peter C. Findlay, "Critical Theory and Social Work Practice," *Catalyst*, No. 3 (1978), p. 55.

28. Ibid., p. 59.

CHAPTER 2

A Systems Approach to Human Behavior

M AJOR THEMES DISCUSSED IN THIS CHAPTER:

1. *A systems approach*. A systems approach to social service practice which follows from the critical perspective is described. Human behavior is seen as the result of a multiplicity of factors, both internal and external, operating in transaction. A systems approach is an orienting framework rather than a specific theory of human behavior.

2. *Human systems*. A system is a dynamic order of parts and processes standing in mutual interaction. There are many kinds of systems, animate and inanimate, but social service workers are interested in those systems that are composed of interacting human beings.

3. *The individual as a system*. Individuals, like all other systems, are comprised of dynamic parts and processes, each making up a subsystem or domain. Within the individual, the biophysical and the psychological are the principal domains. In the psychological domain are cognitive, affective, and behavioral subsystems.

4. *Social systems and the social environment*. People live out their lives within the context of social systems and the norms and institutions which are generated through social interaction within these systems. The ever-changing social environment serves both as a source of stress and a source of support.

5. *Roles: Person in environment*. Individuals are connected to social systems through the roles they occupy in them. Definitions of role are considered, and role dynamics and role-related transactions are discussed.

6. *Implications for practice*. The systems approach can be useful in a number of phases of social service practice. Its application to the assessment phase of direct-service social work practice is demonstrated.

T HE CONCEPT of system has been a mainstay in the social service literature for over two decades, and a number of leading practice theory and human behavior texts have been organized around it.[1] As used by social workers, this concept originated in what sociologists refer to as structural functional theory.[2] (See Chapter 13.) At least two variants are presently popular in social work: the general systems model, introduced by Gordon Hearn, and the ecological model, introduced by Carol Germain and Alex Gitterman.[3] These models not only have produced important social work contributions, they also have reinforced the need to see clients "not as isolated, self-contained entities, but rather as interdependent systems interacting in complex larger systems, as persons-in-situation, persons-in-environment."[4]

A SYSTEMS APPROACH

Despite their origin in structural functional theory, the notion of system and the emphasis on person in environment are implicit in any number of social and psychological theories. For this reason, we will conceive of systems in the broadest way, one which acknowledges the contribution of structural functional thinking but is not limited to it. We will take what is referred to as a **systems approach**, "a loose cluster of several theories and hypotheses emerging from various disciplines."[5] In other words, in the systems approach used here, we will attempt to be as free of concrete substantive knowledge and point of view as possible.

Nevertheless, in the systems approach to human behavior, we will make two general substantive assumptions:

1. The state or condition of a system, at any one point in time, is a function of the interaction between it and the environment in which it operates.
2. Change and conflict are always evident in a system.

These assumptions follow from the discussion of critical theory presented in Chapter 1. Human behavior must be understood as the result of a multiplicity of factors, both internal and external, operating in transaction with one another. Individuals are not robots completely determined by their environment, nor are they independent actors operating solely on free will. Individuals both influence their environments and are influenced by them. Processes of mutual influence generate change and development.

A systems approach serves best as an orienting model or framework through which an analysis of human behavior can be made. It tells us everything and yet it tells us nothing at all. For the systems approach to come to life in social service practice, a whole range of concepts and perspectives must be incorporated into it. In this chapter we will lay out the approach, highlighting its major concepts. In the remainder of the book we will use these concepts selectively to examine communities, families, and individuals as examples of systems.

HUMAN SYSTEMS

A system is a "dynamic order of parts and processes standing in mutual interaction."[6] There are many kinds of systems in nature. A machine can be thought of as an inanimate system, for example, and a plant can be thought of as an organic system. These examples of systems usually do not interest social service workers, however. What is of interest to them are systems composed of human beings, or human systems. A **human system** is one in which one or more individuals are found. The **individual**, as a system, is the basic human system. A **social system**, stripped to its essential characteristics, is simply a collection of interacting individuals.

Human Nature: Biological and Cultural Determinants

Not only are individuals basic human systems in their own right, but they constitute the basic element in all social systems. Individuals also are the driving force or energy of all social systems. Some discussion of the innate nature of human motives, needs, and drives therefore is inevitable in the systems approach. There is considerable debate, however, about human nature, even as to whether there is such a thing.

One debate centers on the relative importance of biological or cultural determinants of human behavior. At one extreme are those who argue that humans are born in a blank state or **tabula rasa**, with no human nature beyond obvious biological features such as a large brain, erect posture, opposable thumbs, and vocal abilities. These theorists maintain that human motives, needs, and drives are completely learned through social conditioning or cultural transmission.[7] At the other extreme are those who argue in favor of biological determinism and who see individual and societal behavior as solely a function of genetic programming. This position is taken less often, but there has been a recent surge in interest in the biological origins of human behavior.[8]

A second debate has to do with the extent to which human behavior differs from animal behavior qualitatively or quantitatively. Many researchers maintain that humans are so unique that propositions based on the study of other animals do not hold for them, and humans can only be understood on their own terms. Ronald Fernandez, for instance, argues that "people are unique, different in kind from every other animal on Earth."[9] Others insist that the social sciences have not progressed to the status of a full science largely because they have ignored the comparative study of animals, including humans. On the basis of comparative study of mammals and other animal species, Pierre van den Berghe concluded that "the uniqueness of human behavior has been misunderstood." Human behavior, like the behavior of every other species, is unique in some respects, but it is not radically different from the behavior of other species.[10]

We will take the position that biological and cultural determinants of human behavior are equally important, and while Homo sapiens have unique qualities they are also similar to other animals in many ways. Human evolution is a function of the interaction between biology and environment, so much so that it is impossible to separate the two. While human drives and motives may seem to be biological in nature, they are never free of the influence of learning and culture. For instance, sex is often believed to be a purely biological drive. Yet studies indicate that environmental factors not only can block the development of sexual maturity but also can shape sexual expression in very profound ways. Harvey Gochros suggests, therefore, that "sexual behavior must be viewed . . . within the social context in which it exists."[11]

A THEORY OF HUMAN NATURE

Human Nature
Biological   Cultural factors

Although it is clear that human nature is guided by the continually evolving interplay between biological and cultural factors, it is difficult to pin down its exact properties. Milton Gordon advances a theory of human nature which cogently summarizes the generally accepted view.[12]

Gordon
1. physiological needs
2. emotional expressions
3. cognitive capacities
4. Drive motivations
5. Derived behavioral patterns — cooperation Agression

Gordon suggests that at least five elements make up human nature. First, there are physiological needs, such as hunger, thirst, and sexual desire. Second, there is the capacity for basic emotional or affective expressions, such as feeling anger, fear, anxiety, attachment, and dependence. Somewhat after birth, and only partly as a result of learning, the capacities to feel shame and pride also become apparent. Third, there are cognitive capacities — the ability to conceptualize, to apprehend, to evaluate, and to rationalize ourselves and others. Fourth, there are overarching drive motivations which represent the implacable tendencies of the total organism and are not traceable to any specific neurological mechanisms or sources. Presumably these drives are products of evolutionary development which can be attributed to self-preservative tendencies in the lower animals but which must be conceptualized and described in much more complex terms for humans. These include the search for pleasure and avoidance of pain, the need to defend the self from disapproval and denigration, and the desire for immortality. The fifth element in human nature is derived behavioral patterns, the most important of which, Gordon believes, are cooperation and aggression. Both are presumed to be elicited by environmental and cultural factors acting on the biological organism.

MALE AND FEMALE DIFFERENCES

One question about human nature is whether there is only one or there are in fact two, a male human nature and a female human nature. The anatomical, biological differences between physiologically normal men and women are obvious. Generally, men are larger and stronger than women, and while only men can impregnate, only women can menstruate, gestate, and lactate.[13] The question is whether these biological differences generate clear-cut cognitive, emotional, and behavioral differences between the sexes.

Some say the answer to this question is decidedly yes. Men, they argue, are by nature active, aggressive, rational, mathematical, and concerned with autonomy. Women, they say, are by nature passive, nurturant, emotional, verbal, and concerned with relationships. Others say the answer is just as decidedly no. Human nature, they assert, is not sexbound. The differences that may exist between the sexes are generated by cultural norms and instilled through socialization processes. This biology versus culture controversy is an important issue in the study of changing gender roles (see Chapter 7).

The research literature demonstrates the existence of any number of statistically significant male-female differences. In one of the most exhaustive literature reviews undertaken, Eleanor Maccoby and Carol Jacklin report a number of consistent findings, some of which support the contentions of those who believe that there are differences in the nature of males and females, but most of which do not.[14] For instance, a good deal of the research concurs that, especially after age 11, girls surpass boys in verbal ability and that, after age 13, boys outperform girls on mathematical tests. Boys also seem to be better able to manipulate three-dimensional objects and to perceive differences between a figure and its surroundings. Males seem to be more active as infants and more aggressive throughout life. More recent research by Carol Gilligan suggests that cognitive, moral development is distinguished by separate female and male "voices." Men are concerned with personal autonomy and independence, while women have been more concerned with welfare and relationships (see Chapter 14).[15]

Close inspection of the literature on the research which has uncovered these male-female differences has failed to indicate whether the results reflect biological or cultural differences, however. Many of the samples in these studies are small, much of the methodology is flawed, and few of the differences seem to hold up across the board. When statistically significant differences are consistently found, they often are so small as to be virtually meaningless.[16] Thus science has yet to determine if the anatomical and biological differences between men and women lead to innate cognitive, emotional, and behavioral differences.

THE INDIVIDUAL AS A SYSTEM

Individuals, like all other systems, are comprised of dynamic parts and processes, each making up a subsystem or domain (see box, The Individual as a System). Two such domains are usually described in the literature, the biophysical and the psychological.

THE BIOPHYSICAL DOMAIN

The **biophysical domain** is the basic building block or infrastructure of the individual as a system. Biological capacities most directly determine human nature. In addition to inborn capacities, the biophysical domain includes all those elements necessary for the functioning of the organism. Examples include the skeletal, sensorimotor, respiratory, endocrine, circulatory, waste elimination, sexual-reproductive, digestive, and nervous systems. This domain is affected by genetic endowments as well as by disease, illness, and accident. Because the biophysical system is associated with the processes of maturation and aging, its normal functioning differs across the life span.

Biophysical processes are extremely important to human behavior. Social workers looking for explanations of human behavior tend to emphasize social and psychological processes and to underestimate the importance of biology. But biology is fundamentally important to individual functioning in at least four ways.

First, biophysical states and processes unique to the species provide the outer

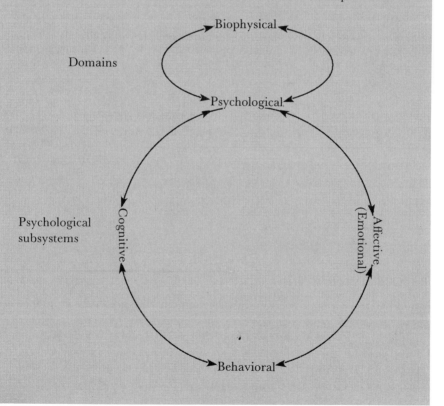

THE INDIVIDUAL AS A SYSTEM

Individuals are comprised of dynamically related biophysical and psychological domains. In the psychological domain are subsystems made up of cognitive, behavioral, and affective or emotional states and processes.

Domains

Biophysical

Psychological

Psychological subsystems

Cognitive

Affective (Emotional)

Behavioral

limit of human behavior and development. This limit is related to the issue of the basis of human nature. Not only are cognitive, affective, and behavioral capacities firmly rooted in biology, but so are aging and the length of life attainable by humans. Although medical advances have increased the likelihood that more and more people will live to a ripe old age, there is little indication that humans are able to live for much more than 110 to 120 years. This seems to be an outer biological or species-related limit.

Second, individual genetic inheritance has an important function in individual psychological development. Although there is considerable debate surrounding the relative importance of genetics to human behavior and development, no one really doubts that it is of some importance. Individual intelligence, personality, abilities, health, and disease all have genetic components. Mental health experts, for instance, are becoming increasingly aware of the importance of genetic background in such illnesses as schizophrenia and severe depression.

Third, alterations in a person's physical condition through illness, injury, or disability may lead to alterations in cognitive, affective, or behavioral performance. People who are ill experience changes in mood, in perceptions, and in their ability to perform everyday tasks. Often, especially if the condition can be reversed, the alterations prove to be temporary.

Fourth, physical growth — from sperm and ovum, to embryo, to fetus, to newborn, to infant, to toddler, to child, to pubescent youth, to mature adult — provokes personal change and development. Similarly, physical decline, including decline in the capacity to procreate, also produces cognitive, affective, and behavioral changes. However, this is a very slow process during which a good deal of compensatory development may occur.

The Psychological Domain

Building on the infrastructure of the biophysical domain is the **psychological domain**. This domain may be thought of as a series of interrelated subsystems made up of cognitive, affective, and behavioral states and processes. It is of central importance in social service work because many of the assessment and intervention tasks performed by workers have to do with promoting healthy psychological functioning.

The Cognitive Subsystem

Cognitive states and processes include perception, sensation, memory, imagination, judgment, and language, as well as intelligence and other aspects of intellectual functioning such as knowledge, beliefs, and opinions. Through these processes, the individual assigns and attributes meaning and understanding to the world. The meanings attached to places, objects, and situations, to society and other human beings, and, above all, to the self are involved.

The study of cognitive states and processes is especially important to direct-service social workers, since much of what transpires between them and the individuals and families they serve is the exchange of meanings about human experience. As a preliminary step in assessing the needs of clients and formulating plans for intervention, social service workers attempt to understand how they see and interpret their experiences. Often the intervention process itself has to do with supporting or altering the ways in which clients understand their lives.

The Affective Subsystem   *emotional life* *crises & adaptation to them*

Affective states and processes usually are concerned with the emotional life of individuals — their motivations, needs, drives, feelings, and interests. This subsystem also involves the crises individuals may be experiencing and their adaptations to these crises.   *directly assoc. with well-being or ill-being*

The affective subsystem is most directly associated with the client's sense of well-being or ill-being. As such, it is often understood as the underlying reason why many clients need or seek services. This domain is of particular interest to social service workers in mental health and related settings.

The Behavioral Subsystem   *How man. express themselves in action. — actual things people say and do.*

Behavioral states and processes are concerned with the ways individuals express themselves in action. Behaviors differ from cognitive and affective processes in that they always involve the actual things people say and do. Mannerisms, habits, and interpersonal and communications skills are all behaviors.

Social service workers frequently are involved with individuals whose delinquent or other antisocial behaviors get them in trouble. Workers also are involved with individuals who are troubled by their own behavior, people who do not like the things they do or say and would like to change. Thus undesirable behaviors often are the "presenting problem" of clients in service, and workers are most concerned with understanding and analyzing such behaviors.

LEVELS OF SYSTEMS WITHIN INDIVIDUALS

The domains and subsystems described so far exist at the micro or most elementary level of states and processes comprising the individual. Within these, more complex states or processes may be differentiated. Thus it is possible to visualize the individual as an intricate pattern of increasingly larger and more complex levels of systems (see box, Levels of Systems within Individuals).

The biophysical domain, as we have noted, is the infrastructure for the existence of the psychological domain. The psychological subsystems arise from the interaction of the biological (nature) and environmental (nurture) transac-

Biophysical infrastructure to psych. domain   psychological ↑ ↑ Biological (nature) environmental (nurture)

tions. The psychological domain exists independently of its origins, however, and is not completely reducible to either the biological or the environmental. The cognitive, affective, and behavioral components which make up the psychological domain themselves combine to form increasingly larger and more complex systems within the individual. For instance, an attitude is a combination of beliefs (cognition), feelings (emotions), and behaviors. Single attitudes combine to form the individual's attitude system, value system, and belief system, and these in turn combine to form the individual's character, personality, self, and identity. These last four concepts, taken together, summarize the entire cognitive, affective, and behavioral makeup of the individual. Those who study personality and self are concerned with how these structures emerge and change and are reflected in private and social behavior.

DYNAMICS OF THE INDIVIDUAL AS A SYSTEM

All systems are marked by dynamic interaction among their component parts. Not only are the parts often inseparable from one another, but they are in a state of continual interaction and interdependence.

The subsystems comprising the individual are therefore dynamically interrelated, as are the various levels of systems. The differences among the cognitive, affective, and behavioral subsystems often blur, as do the differences

LEVELS OF SYSTEMS WITHIN INDIVIDUALS

It is possible to abstract many levels of systems and subsystems within the individual. They range from micro biophysical elements, through cognitive, affective, and behavioral states and processes in the psychological domain, through mezzo-level attitudes and belief and value systems, and finally to the macro structures of character, personality, the self, and personal identity.

Micro level	Biophysical domain

	Psychological domain
	    Cognitive, affective and
	    behavioral states and processes

Mezzo level	Attitudes, values, and beliefs Attitude, value, and belief systems
Macro level	Character, personality, self, and identity

among the micro, mezzo, and macro structures. By the same token, the processes taking place in each of the subsystems and between the various levels influence all the others. The biological and psychological mutually influence each other. We feel differently about ourselves, depending on our age and our physical health and abilities. A man might be 50 years old, for instance, but if he is in good health and has kept his body in condition, he could have a sense of being young. Similarly, cognition, emotion, and behavior mutually influence one another. If we believe something is not good, we are likely to act (or not to act) in accordance with our belief, and then we feel that we have done something good. For instance, regardless of how important an exam may be and how little prepared a woman is for it, if cheating goes against her moral principles she may choose to fail rather than cheat.

Although these subsystems mutually influence one another, it should not be assumed that one follows directly from the other. Those who have studied attitudes are quick to point out that our beliefs are often in contradiction with our actual behaviors. We may think and feel in one way and yet do something quite different.

CHANGE AND DEVELOPMENT

Individuals, like other systems, are never static but change and develop, grow and decline. The two types of dynamic processes which occur in the individual vary along a time dimension. Psychological processes have to do with the more immediate changes going on at any one moment, and developmental processes have to do with changes going on across the life span.

Psychological processes define how knowledge, beliefs, emotions, attitudes, and behaviors are acquired, maintained, and changed. These changes occur as a function of biological, psychological, and social factors. The study of psychological processes includes the various theories of learning, such as classical and operant conditioning and social learning theory, as well as theories of social interaction, such as social exchange theory and symbolic interactionism (see Chapters 12 and 13).

Developmental processes define how changes in personality functioning occur throughout the entire life span. Human development rests on the biological facts of birth and death and takes place through biological development, or the growth and decline in biogenetic capacities. This includes all the changes that take place in a person's body throughout the course of life; changes in height and weight, for instance, as well as in glands, muscles, the brain, and sensory and reproductive organs. It also includes the development of motor skills, such as the ability to walk, to balance one's self, and to manipulate and use tools.

Unless accident or injury produces irreversible physical damage, the early years of life are marked by sharp growth, the middle years by a good deal of stability, and the later years by gradual decline. But under normal circumstances, physical decline is a very slow process which does not affect all parts of the organism in the same way. Just as different individuals age differently, so do different parts of the body. Similarly, physical decline does not necessarily mean intellectual and psychosocial decline.

For social service workers, the interest in biological development lies largely in its effects on cognitive, affective, and behavioral processes. The developmental processes that they are concerned with have as their outcome normal or abnormal psychological functioning. Models of personality development which trace individual emotional and inner-life experiences across the life cycle have been constructed by Sigmund Freud and his followers, such as Erik Erikson. Jean Piaget and other cognitive theorists have also devised developmental models which trace changes in individual intellectual development from childhood to adulthood. While these models have been modified across the years and are not always accepted in their entirety, they continue to have a profound influence on our understanding of individual behavior (see Chapters 14 and 15).

Progressive Growth, Stability, or Decline

Darwinian evolutionary theory is the forerunner of most thinking about human development. The influence of this theory is evident in a number of ways. For instance, developmental processes are often believed to be time-ordered changes in the condition of a system which are generated by biologically based survival needs. Developmental processes are also believed to propel human systems in an orderly progression, from less developed stages to increasingly more advanced stages. As individuals advance into adulthood it is assumed that they go from cognitive, behavioral, and emotional immaturity to increasingly higher levels of maturity. One text on individual development across the life span, for instance, builds on the assumption that "growth occurs at every period of life, from conception through old age."[17]

Developmental perspectives are not limited to the study of individuals. Models of group development and of family development also have been proposed.[18] Similarly, many theorists adopt developmental perspectives on whole societies and world systems. Nineteenth-century thinkers, including such ideologically diverse scientists as Karl Marx and Herbert Spencer, described inevitable evolutionary or developmental processes.[19]

The notion of inevitable progress, therefore, is built into many developmental perspectives. Yet it is not altogether clear that, over the short or long run, the continual changes taking place in systems somehow automatically lead to progress. Gerhard and Jean Lenski, in discussing societal development, acknowledge that progressive growth and development have not been typical of all societies. "Societal stasis" (the condition of standing still) and even "societal regression" are as likely to occur as societal progress.[20]

Recent evidence suggests that development in individuals also is not necessarily linear and progressive. Change always occurs, but the change need not be toward growth. According to Paul Baltes, individual development across the life span is nonsequential, multidirectional, and at times even reversible.

He notes that developmental changes in individuals may be thought of in three ways:[21]

1. Changes may show growth and improvement at one point in time, stability at another, and decline at still another.
2. The rate at which change occurs may vary across the life cycle; change may be rapid and steep at one point and slow, slight, or nonexistent at another.
3. While some changes may follow similar patterns among various individuals, developmental change often varies considerably from one person to the next.

Thus progressive growth in individuals, as in societies, is not automatic. The task of the social service worker in this respect is to help generate psychological development and prevent psychological decay. Growth is one of the major goals of a critical perspective on social service practice and an important social work value, rather than an inevitable fact of life.

Homeostasis and Feedback

In early systems theory, it was suggested that systems are self-regulating entities which exist in a state of balance or equilibrium known as **homeostasis**.[22] In this view, balance is achieved as each element in a system successively serves as input, throughput, and output, generating the **feedback** which enables elements to adapt to one another constantly. Survival of the system is thus assured.

More recent thinking on systems has pointed out limitations to the concepts of homeostasis and feedback. Ludwig von Bertalanffy argues that homeostasis makes sense when referring to inanimate, mechanical systems but not when referring to complex, developing, dynamic systems like living organisms. He posits instead the concept of steady state.[23]

Living systems are in the process of continuous generation, decay, and regeneration. This process takes place for one of two reasons: because tensions existing inside a system demand readjustment, or because disturbances in the environment force readjustment. **Steady state** is the self-regulation and readjustment which take place to enable the organism to be "maintained approximately constant."[24] The steady state ensures that organisms do change, but slowly, and, as has been pointed out, in no particular direction. From one point to the next organisms are not the same, but they are similar.

The steady state also ensures that there is no one way by which an organism goes from one state to the next. Although feedback helps to regulate systems, it should not be regarded as the only way by which systems maintain themselves. The **principle of equifinality** refers to "achieving similar results from different initial conditions."[25] How a system achieves steady state is largely indeterminate and involves a great deal of flexibility and creativity.

A system in a steady state, according to Ralph Anderson and Irl Carter, "is maintaining a viable relationship with its environment and its components, and its functions are being performed in such fashion as to ensure continued existence."[26] Yet it would be misleading to say that all systems always achieve steady state. They may aim to and they may hope to, but they do not always succeed. Very often when clients seek social services it is because the tensions within them and the disturbances coming from their environment have destroyed any semblance of balance; their very survival may be in jeopardy. The worker must help them figure out the flexible and creative solutions that could restore a steady state.

System Boundaries

All systems have boundaries, in the sense that the elements making them up are distinguishable from the elements making up their environment. The boundaries of a system are not easily determined, however, and they do not exist as a legal demarcation, as the boundaries of a nation do. The boundaries of a system are always dynamic, changing, and developing, and they are more or less evident from time to time. To some extent, therefore, they are one and the same with their environment.

Take, for instance, the boundary of an ethnic community. We might say that the Asian community is made up of all Asians living in the United States. Well and good, but just who is and isn't included in this community? Are we referring only to those who have American citizenship, those whose parents are both Asian, those who live in a particular neighborhood or geographic area, or those who identify with being Asian?

The boundary of an individual is also dynamic and not clearly demarcated. It is clearest at the physical level; the skin, hair, and other visible features certainly form a boundary. But what of the psychological boundary of the individual? Much of the personality is learned and much of the information about the self comes from the various groups and individuals with whom the individual interacts in everyday life. The "I" and the "me" are intimately connected to the "they" and the "them." As we develop we gain a sense of our own uniqueness, our own separate ways of feeling, thinking, and behaving. We become self-conscious and take on an identity, and this subjective understanding of ourselves becomes our boundary.

The tightness of the boundary of a system is important because it affects the degree to which a system (the "I" and "me") will be influenced by its environment (the "they" and "them"). Because human systems are interdependent, they are **open systems**. To the extent that individuals close themselves off from others, they are **closed systems**, and they have no means of surviving. Humans are innately social animals dependent on others for the fulfillment of basic and higher-level needs like hunger, shelter, protection, love, belonging, and personal fulfillment. Human systems therefore must respond to their environment and can never be completely self-sufficient.

Nevertheless, individuals differ in the degree to which they open themselves up to others, and this can have important implications for their development. Some mental health theorists believe that too much openness or too little openness can create difficulties. Family practitioners, for instance, postulate that the individuals composing a family need to maintain some degree of openness to other family members if they are to contribute to the family and meet their own needs. In "enmeshed" families, the members have opened themselves up so much that their own individuality has been lost. In "disengaged" families, the members are closed off to one another, and there is no give and take in their interaction (see Chapter 9). Both extremes are considered indications of poor interpersonal relations.[27]

Working at the boundary between systems is often seen as a primary task in social work. Among the intervention tasks derived from boundary considerations that have been identified, the foremost is to bring about mutual adjustments: coping and adaptation on the part of the client system, and alteration and change on the part of environmental systems.[28]

SOCIAL SYSTEMS AND THE SOCIAL ENVIRONMENT

Perhaps the most important fact about systems is that they are **holons**; they are a whole — units unto themselves — and a part of a whole, both at the same time (see Chapter 9). Human systems do not exist in isolation. The idea that an individual comes to have a self-conscious identity clearly acknowledges the presence of an environment. There can be no "I" without an "it," "you," "he," "she," and "they."

Individuals exist, therefore, only within social and physical environments. The **physical environment** of a system encompasses the geographically or spatially structured context in which it exists. The physical environment includes such things as climate, land and its resources, and buildings and neighborhoods and their physical organization. The **social environment** of a system includes its location within a socially and historically determined context. Social service workers are usually, although certainly not always, concerned with social environments — the interactions among individuals and groups of individuals. The emphasis in this book will be on the social context of system behavior.

The social context or environment of individuals is important for at least two reasons. First, private troubles often arise from larger, societally based social problems or public issues. Thus the self-confidence and sense of well-being of children is influenced by how much they are loved and how well they are treated by parents, which in turn is influenced by the availability of economic and social resources. Similarly, the troubles of a minority-group member may be connected to the prejudice and discrimination operating in a society.

Second, environments often supply the strengths and resources by which troubles may be overcome or at least ameliorated. Environments can cause trouble, but they also can give strength. A family suffering from economic troubles might find strength in the financial support of relatives and the help of friends and neighbors in finding work. Or an ethnic community faced with prejudice and discrimination can impart courage and a sense of worth to its otherwise demoralized members. This function of environments is well documented in the literature on natural helping networks.[29]

SOCIAL SYSTEMS

The primary element in the social environment is the social system. The smallest social system is the **dyad**, a system composed of only two individuals. Successively larger and more complex systems are the **triad**, the small group, the family, the community, the bureaucracy or organization, the nation, and the international community. Regardless of size, social systems, like individuals, are dynamic orders of parts and processes standing in mutual interaction.

At their core, social systems are simply collections of individuals, but they are much more than this. The individuals in a social system share a common identity, a "we" and "us" which separates them from outsiders; that is, they have a boundary which is larger than the boundary of any individual in the system. The individuals also are organized in terms of roles and statuses and, especially in complex systems, divided into units or departments, each of which has separate functions. The roles and units are often organized vertically and horizontally to show authority and power, as in an organizational chart (see box). The roles and units making up the system are also held together by working agreements, norms, and traditions, which give the system its unique culture or way of operating. Finally, all the parts of a system are in dynamic interaction with one another, so change and development are constantly taking place.

With respect to the everyday lives of individuals, a number of dimensions of social systems are relevant. Transactions between the individual and society can take place at the interactional level and at the sociocultural level.[30]

At the interactional level, transactions involve face-to-face contact, and relatively deep personal commitments and attachments are often apparent. Social systems which generate such transactions are usually referred to as **primary groups** because they are believed to be basic to an individual's identity and personality. Examples of primary groups are friends and peers; family, kin, and other intimate relations; and community, especially communities based on common identities such as nationality, religion, or race and ethnicity.

Transactions at the sociocultural level are more impersonal and usually take place within the larger, more complex social systems and institutions making up the environment. Social systems typified by impersonal transactions are referred to as **secondary groups**. The assumption is that, because these groups are less immediately personal, they are less central to the personality of an individual. The needs met by secondary systems are more utilitarian, such as the needs for income and physical comfort. Secondary groups include work organizations, schools, political parties, religions, and other associations in

The Holon, a sculpture by Don Wilson, was
dedicated to Gordon Hearn, the founding dean of the
School of Social Work at Portland State University
and the person largely responsible for introducing the
systems perspective into social work.

EXAMPLE OF AN ORGANIZATIONAL CHART

The familiar organizational chart demonstrates the composition of systems as dynamic units and parts in vertical and horizontal relationship to one another.

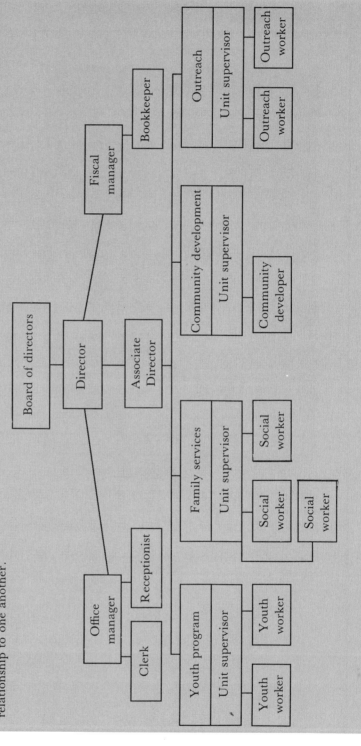

which individuals assume such roles as citizen, producer, consumer, and client.

Social Norms

The most important attribute of a social system is the social norms which hold it together. **Norms** consist of all the agreements, formal or informal, explicit or implicit, which regulate and give order and purpose to a system, be it a primary or secondary group. Examples include goals and objectives; values and ideologies; traditions, lifestyles, and folkways or mores; dogmas, laws, policies, and procedures; and rules, regulations, obligations, and duties. Social norms are experienced by individuals as **expectations**, the expectations of other people as well as the expectations that emerge from the self as a function of participation with other people. A person entering the social work profession, for instance, is expected to abide by a set of professional ethics which have been collectively agreed to (see box).

An example of social norms on a larger organizational scale is the Bill of Rights, the first ten amendments to the United States Constitution, passed by Congress in September 1789 and ratified in December 1791. For about 200 years, these amendments, setting forth the rules by which the power of government is to be limited and the rights of citizens are to be protected, have guided the political organization of the United States. The first amendment, for instance, is:

> Congress shall make no law respecting an establishment of religion, or prohibiting the free exercise thereof; or abridging the freedom of speech, or of the press; or the right of the people peaceably to assemble, and to petition the Government for a redress of grievances.

Norms evolve through democratic as well as nondemocratic processes; sometimes people earnestly believe in the agreements that regulate their transactions, but other times they are experienced as coercive. Norms give stability and a sense of unity to social systems, but they are also a major source of conflict in social systems. For this reason, all norms are best thought of as working agreements which are continually being invented, worked out, debated, and negotiated.

Social Institutions

In large industrial societies such as the United States, there are certain kinds of norms known as **social institutions** which include clusters or orders of social systems sharing similar functions. The Lenskis note that institutions develop in the following way: "Because human societies have so many needs, and because these needs persist over long periods of time, every society develops more or less standardized and traditional ways of dealing with them. These 'continuing answers' to 'continuing problems' are known as institutions and institutional systems."[31]

But social institutions are not just standardized and traditional ways of dealing with problems. As Hans Gerth and C. Wright Mills point out, social institutions are the organization of roles and systems that are "guaranteed by authority."[32] Institutions are considered the *correct* way to deal with problems, and those who choose not to follow them or who wish to alter them can expect

SOCIAL WORK PROFESSIONAL ETHICS:
An Example of Social Norms

Adopted by the 1979 Delegate Assembly of the National Association of Social Workers.

Preamble

This code is intended to serve as a guide to the everyday conduct of members of the social work profession and as a basis for the adjudication of issues in ethics when the conduct of social workers is alleged to deviate from the standards expressed or implied in this code . . .

SUMMARY OF MAJOR PRINCIPLES

I. The Social Worker's Conduct and Comportment as a Social Worker
  A. Propriety. The social worker should maintain high standards of personal conduct in the capacity or identity as social worker.
  B. Competence and Professional Development. The social worker should strive to become and remain proficient in professional practice and the performance of professional functions.
  C. Service. The social worker should regard as primary the service obligation of the social work profession.
  D. Integrity. The social worker should act in accordance with the highest standards of professional integrity.
  E. Scholarship and Research. The social worker engaged in study and research should be guided by the conventions of scholarly inquiry.
II. The Social Worker's Ethical Responsibility to Clients
  F. Primacy of Clients' Interests. The social worker's primary responsibility is to clients.
  G. Rights and Prerogatives of Clients. The social worker should make every effort to foster maximum self-determination on the part of clients.
  H. Confidentiality and Privacy. The social worker should respect the

that social control will be applied to ensure that the organization remains intact.

Social institutions are usually discussed in terms of the common, manifest functions they serve for society as a whole. Gerth and Mills describe five major institutional orders in industrial societies:[33]

I. The **political order**, which regulates the distribution of power and authority.

privacy of clients and hold in confidence all information obtained in the course of professional service.

I. Fees. When setting fees, the social worker should ensure that they are fair, reasonable, considerate, and commensurate with the service performed and with due regard for the clients' ability to pay.

III. The Social Worker's Ethical Responsibility to Colleagues

J. Respect, Fairness, and Courtesy. The social worker should treat colleagues with respect, courtesy, fairness, and good faith.

K. Dealing with Colleagues' Clients. The social worker has the responsibility to relate to the clients of colleagues with full professional consideration.

IV. The Social Worker's Ethical Responsibility to Employers and Employing Organizations

L. Commitments to Employing Organizations. The social worker should adhere to commitments made to the employing organizations.

V. The Social Worker's Ethical Responsibility to the Social Work Profession

M. Maintaining the Integrity of the Profession. The social worker should uphold and advance the values, ethics, knowledge, and mission of the profession.

N. Community Service. The social worker should assist the profession in making social services available to the general public.

O. Development of Knowledge. The social worker should take responsibility for identifying, developing, and fully utilizing knowledge for professional practice.

VI. The Social Worker's Ethical Responsibility to Society

P. Promoting the General Welfare. The social worker should promote the general welfare of society.

Source: Adapted from Appendix I, "Code of Ethics of the National Association of Social Workers," in *Encyclopedia of Social Work*, 18th ed. (Silver Spring, MD: National Association of Social Workers, 1987), pp. 951–56.

2. The economy or **economic order**, which regulates the production and distribution of goods and resources.
3. The **military order**, which regulates the legitimate use of violence.
4. The **kinship order**, or marriage and the family, which regulates sexual behavior, procreation, and the rearing of children.
5. The **religious order**, which regulates the worship of God or other dieties.

Other institutional orders could be added to this list. The **welfare order**, for instance, expresses the traditional and authoritative ways developed by the society to deal with problems of individual well-being.[34]

Because social institutions are experienced by individuals through participation in specific primary and secondary groups, they influence individuals profoundly. Being norms, they come into individuals' cognitive and emotional systems as expectations for proper behavior. The United States is a representative democracy, with a profit-making, achievement-oriented, free-market or capitalist economy and a Judeo-Christian religious tradition. It is a society with a kinship order which is oriented to the nuclear family and heterosexual coupling and which is somewhat patriarchal in its authority structure (see Part III). Young people are instructed in the "correct ways" of participating in American society and are expected to conform to them. Those who do not or cannot succeed in meeting the expectations generated by social institutions are likely to experience difficulties in their personal lives. Social service workers often are involved in helping people cope with the expectations of social institutions.

Institutionalized Social Arrangements

There are other kinds of social norms which pervade society but which do not necessarily reflect an ordering of functions. Rather, they reflect agreements that crosscut and therefore characterize all social institutions. Like institutions, however, they are guaranteed by authority and represent continuing solutions to continuing problems. These norms will be referred to as institutionalized social arrangements, or **institutional arrangements**.

Symbols and cultural backgrounds are major examples of such arrangements. In the United States, for instance, American English, derived from a northern European cultural heritage, is the valued and officially sanctioned way for people to express themselves verbally and in writing. Similarly, there are status divisions in society which represent working agreements about the distribution of wealth, power, and prestige. In many societies, hierarchies are institutionalized around socioeconomic opportunities and the prestige and privilege associated with race, ethnicity, gender, age, or sexual orientation.

Institutional arrangements, like social norms more generally, create stability in a society, but they also generate a good deal of conflict and change. Newcomers such as immigrants and refugees coming into a society often have problems because they are unfamiliar with the symbols and culture that are taken for granted by those already there. Certain institutionalized inequities are particularly important to social service workers because of the troubles they create for clients. The United States has a class society based on differential access to education, employment, and, ultimately, wealth. It is a society in which racial and ethnic groups have limited prestige and power, gender roles hinder the full development of men and women, and age, sexual orientation, or physical ability can provoke discrimination. Terms such as *classism, racism, sexism*, and *ageism* are used to describe these inequities and to underscore both how they harm people and how they need to be changed. The question of whether the United States can be said to have a racist society is examined in Chapter 6.

Stability and Conflict in Social Systems

Social theorists continually debate questions about how much stability or consensus and how much conflict or change can be expected in social systems and what their normal state is. Should social relations be expected to be orderly and harmonious or to be conflict-ridden and chaotic? Different answers are offered by two different sociological theories on social systems, structural functionalism and conflict theory (see box, Conflict or Consensus).

In **structural functional theory**, social systems are said to exist in a relatively continuous state of harmony (see Chapter 13). Each element making up the system serves a function which assures the maintenance (that is, the survival) of the system, and the functions are coordinated so that the system emerges as a well-integrated whole. Social systems are held together through a consensus of shared norms and values; everyone agrees on the goals and purposes of the system and works hard to achieve them. As a result, conflict and change are looked upon as dysfunctional, a threat to the survival of the system, and conformity is championed as necessary.[35]

Conflict theory promotes an alternative picture of social systems (see Chapter 12). Instead of a shared consensus, the elements of a system are said to operate from competitive, self-interested motives. Systems are poorly integrated and riddled with dissension. Interest-group politics predominate, so that change and conflict are the normal state of a system. People in a system are always trying to get others to do what they want so they can shape the system in their own image. Every element contributes to the disintegration rather than the maintenance of the system. Conflict theorists look upon stability and harmony as suspect, a sign of coercion and forced compliance, and an indication of underlying tensions.[36]

In fact, social systems are at the same time riddled with conflict and bathed in the harmony that comes from a consensus on values. The two theories are two sides of the same coin. Depending on which side you look at, social systems can seem to be harmonious and stable or conflict-ridden and chaotic. If you ask yourselves why you are reading this book, for example, you might say, "Because I'm interested in the subject matter and think it will help me become a good social worker." Or you might say, "Because if I don't, I won't pass the exam, and then where will I be?" The first response reflects the structural functional vision of the world: People do things because they want to do them; they believe in the norms and values of the system (in this example, education), and therefore they willingly do what is expected of them. The second response reflects the conflict vision of the world: People do things because they have to do them; they don't particularly believe in the system and the way it is organized, but they comply because they don't really see any alternative. If they could have their way, they would completely alter the system.

The Functions of Conflict

The two sociological theories on social systems are in need of a synthesis. In fact, there has been a merging of the conflict and structural functional viewpoints. Structural functional thinking, in particular, has evolved so that conflict, change, and nonconformity are not always seen as dysfunctional. Lewis Coser has proposed that conflict serves positive functions. It may draw

CONFLICT OR CONSENSUS:
A Comparison of Structural Functional and Conflict Theories

Assumptions of Structural Functionalism:

1. The working agreements in a system derive from a consensus of shared values among the members and units.
2. Every system has a well-integrated social organization; each of its elements serves a function by contributing to its maintenance.
3. Harmony and stability are the natural state or condition of a system.
4. Conflict and change are normal, but only when they contribute to the ultimate survival of the system and they occur within a range of acceptable behaviors.

Assumptions of Conflict Theory:

1. The working agreements in a system derive from the ability of some elements to make other elements agree with them.
2. Every system is a poorly integrated social organization; each element serves a function by contributing to its disintegration.
3. Conflict and change are the natural state or condition of a system.
4. Harmony and stability are good only when they reflect equity and equality in opportunities and outcomes among the elements.

Source: Adapted from Ralf Dahrendorf, *Class and Class Conflict in Industrial Society* (Palo Alto, CA: Stanford University Press, 1959), pp. 161–62.

a group together against a common enemy and thereby promote solidarity, or it may promote innovation and creativity. Conflict also may help the system confront realistic sources of tension; it may help release tensions; or it may encourage those in positions of power to acknowledge that problems must be confronted.[37]

In spite of such attempts at synthesis, the structural functional and conflict theories continue to have different implications for social service practice. Workers following structural functional theory are forced to make an assessment whether conflict is functional or dysfunctional. They must always be concerned about the survival of the system they are working with. Conflict theory puts no such constraints on workers, since it asserts that all conflict, regardless of whether it leads to the survival or the disintegration of a social system, is positive.

This difference is especially important in a critical approach to practice. Certainly social service workers ought to be concerned about the survival of social systems and their norms, institutions, and institutional arrangements. Conflict and change create a great deal of havoc for people, and numerous unintended negative consequences are possible. Yet every social system, and the institutions and institutional arrangements it represents, is not worth maintaining. Many workers are committed to ending racism and sexism and the classism that supports a free-market economy. They believe these systems are not worthy of saving in some steady state but should be totally transformed.

Recognizing the importance of system-disintegrating as well as system-maintaining functions goes right to the heart of a critical approach to social service practice. To the extent that workers concern themselves only with the survival needs of social systems, they inadvertently limit change and reinforce the status quo. Jeffry Galper's definition of social work as "conservative politics" focuses on precisely this issue. He argues that too much of the attention of social workers is directed to assuring the maintenance and survival of existing systems and too little is directed to system change and disintegration.[38]

ROLES: PERSON IN ENVIRONMENT

Individuals are connected to social systems through the roles they occupy in them. Roles are at the same time an element of the individual and an element of a social system. They represent the joint boundary between the two, the point at which person meets environment.

THE CONCEPT OF ROLE

The concept of role has been borrowed from the theater. Most of what it conveys in the theatrical sense it also conveys in the social scientific sense. For instance, the role of Hamlet was written by Shakespeare in the seventeenth century. Over the years numerous actors have taken the part, each giving their own interpretations, but the role of Hamlet continues, regardless of who is playing it. In the same way, the roles we play in life or the positions we occupy are a part of the social systems to which we belong, and they somehow exist separate from ourselves. Husbands and sons, wives and daughters, students and teachers, social workers and clients exist as parts in the theater of everyday life. People enter the roles and leave them, but the system and the roles that comprise them usually continue.

Status differs from role in that it locates individuals in terms of their social position. It is a description of where they fit within a chain of command or in an authority or power structure. A direct-service social worker, for instance, can be located between the client, to whom service is given, and the supervisor, who assures that agency policies and professional principles are followed. **Role** refers to the more dynamic aspects of a status or position. It is concerned with specifying the attitudes and behaviors expected of people in particular positions.

Role is not an easy concept to define, partly because of the tension which usually exists between roles and the individuals who take them. In the theatrical imagery, the role of Hamlet exists as a series of lines to be spoken by an actor. The actor has to speak them if he is to play the role, and so the role constrains the actor. In real life, roles also constrain individuals. Mothers, students, and clients are expected to behave in certain ways. But roles in real life rarely constrain us in the same way roles in the theater do. There are no exact lines that must be declaimed. Life is a living drama in which the individual actors often become authors who rewrite the drama.

The rewriting of roles in everyday life creates tensions. On the one hand, all the other members of the system have their ideas of how the role should be performed. On the other hand, the person in the role has his or her own idea about the role. How the role is eventually performed is a function of the negotiations taking place among the actors.

It is not surprising, then, that a person's role is usually defined in not one but three ways, as Morton Deutsch and Robert Krauss have done (see box, Definitions of Role). In one way, often identified with sociology, role is defined from the point of view of the other actors, that is, in terms of "the expectations which exist in the social world surrounding the status." This has been defined as the expected or **prescribed role**. In another way, more identified with psychology, role is defined from the point of view of the actor in the role, that is, "those specific expectations the occupant of a position perceives as applicable to his own behavior when he interacts with the occupants of some other position." This has been defined as the subjective or **perceived role**. And role is also defined in terms of the actual outcome of the interaction between the actor and the other actors, that is, "the specific overt behaviors of the occupant of a position when he interacts with the occupants of some other position." This has been referred to as the **enacted role**.[39]

In the role of social worker, all three of these definitions of role apply. The role of the social worker is at once defined by the expectations of the administrator, the supervisor, and the client about what the worker is to do, the expectations of the worker about what is to be done, and the actual behaviors of the worker.

TRANSACTIONS BETWEEN INDIVIDUALS AND SOCIAL SYSTEMS

Roles are acquired, maintained, and changed through a series of **transactions** between individuals and social systems. George McCall and J. L. Simmons describe five overlapping "basic social processes" which are transactional in nature. These processes are related to the tasks through which systems attempt to maintain and alter themselves: recruitment, socialization, interaction, innovation, and control.[40]

Recruitment refers to the processes by which the individual's participation in a social system is determined. Through recruitment processes, criteria for membership in statuses and roles are decided and selections are made for these statuses and roles. The basis for selection may be **ascriptive**, that is, deter-

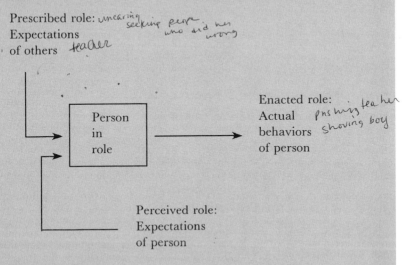

DEFINITIONS OF ROLE

A person's role in any situation is defined in three ways: from the perspective of the expectations of others for people in that role (the prescribed role), the expectations of the person taking the role (the perceived role), and that person's actual behaviors (the enacted role).

Prescribed role: *uncaring* *seeking peope who did hers wrong*
Expectations
of others *teacher*

Person
in
role

Enacted role: *teacher*
Actual *pnshing*
behaviors *shoving boy*
of person

Perceived role:
Expectations
of person

Source: Based on Morton Deutsch and Robert M. Krauss, *Social Psychology* (New York: Basic Books, 1965), pp. 175–77.

mined by birth; **conscriptive**, that is, determined by law; or **achieved**, that is, determined by merit. Recruitment through ascription is found in many social systems; certain roles and statuses may be set aside on the basis of such characteristics as sex, race and ethnicity, social class, or age. Conscriptive processes are seen in military drafts and other laws which require participation by certain types of people. Achievement processes involve the setting of cognitive, behavioral, or affective standards which allow membership only to those who are capable of meeting the standards.

Socialization refers to the processes through which individual participation is defined and refined as individuals learn to function as system members. Included are the processes by which people become aware of the expectations of others and learn the attitudes, knowledge, and abilities necessary to comply with those expectations. While socialization is often thought of in terms of infants and children, it is a broader phenomenon which takes place throughout the life cycle whenever an individual participates in social life. By the same token, socialization is not a one-way process whereby established members simply pass on expectations which new recruits are compelled to accept. The process of socialization in most systems is a negotiation between old and new in which new expectations evolve.

Interaction refers to the processes through which participation in the system is implemented. Through the continual, overarching process of interaction, members influence one another and social systems are shaped and reshaped. Interaction takes place through formal and informal channels, through face-to-face contact, or through more impersonal means such as letters and phone calls. The size of the social system has a lot to do with the means through which interactional processes take place. In general, the smaller the social system, the more likely is interaction to be informal and face to face. However, even in large, complex systems, informal, face-to-face processes exist along with formal, impersonal processes.

Innovation refers to the processes through which a person's participation in a system is altered or changed. Innovations may be externally imposed, as when changes in the physical environment force system members to rethink the ways they relate to their environment, or internally planned, as when conditions within a society force new laws into being. Much of the time, however, innovation comes about through improvisation. This is especially evident at the level of statuses and roles. Individuals' personalities or particular abilities may lead them to begin to change the expectations connected with a role or status.

Social control refers to the processes through which a person's participation in a system is limited or constrained. Social control may be implemented through positive or negative means. Often systems of reward are devised to assure compliance with group expectations. If you go to school, get an education, and apply yourself, you are more likely to be rewarded with a good job and less likely to confront the inequities in the society's economic opportunities. But social control also includes various punishments or sanctions. Rewards may be taken away, restrictions may be forcefully placed on behavior, a person may be ignored or ostracized or even physically punished.

The Person-in-Environment Relationship

The relationship between person and environment can be depicted in such a way as to bring together most of the concepts discussed in this chapter (see box, Person in Environment). The individual, a dynamic ordering of biophysical and psychological processes, is in transaction with the environment, a dynamic ordering of primary and secondary social systems, norms, institutions, and institutional arrangements. Individuals and environment are joined together by roles. The transactions taking place, be they recruitment, socialization, interaction, innovation, or control, always juxtapose the expectations of the person against the expectations of the social environment. Through the **negotiation of roles**, specific behaviors are enacted which have the effect of maintaining or altering the individual and the society.

Social service workers must take into account the roles and statuses that make up the client systems with which they work. Humans are never just individuals trying to meet their own needs. They are social in nature and live out their lives in the context of social systems and their constituent roles. The meeting of individual needs is intimately caught up in the dynamics of the system as a whole. Clients, like workers, exist in a world where the expectations of others are always impinging on the expectations of self. The task of the worker often is to clarify the various expectations and negotiate the working agreements that lead to rewriting the drama and the roles. In this way, workers contribute to individual and social change and renewal.

IMPLICATIONS FOR PRACTICE

Work in the social services requires that theory be put into practice. Since service workers occupy many different positions, working with or on behalf of many different client populations and around many different problem areas, formulating the implications for practice of a systems approach is no simple task. An administrator trying to put together a program suitable for an inner-city community, for instance, will have needs different from those of a rural, mid-America, child welfare worker handling cases of abuse and neglect. Similarly, an employment opportunities policy planner must deal with constituencies and interest groups that a social worker in practice with suburban, middle-class families might never have to consider. In short, because of complex practice situations, roles, agencies, and services, there is no one specific way to apply the systems approach to practice.

To illustrate the use of the systems approach, we will describe its application to the assessment phase of direct-service practice. Most social workers are in direct practice with individuals, groups, and families. The principles described, however, are not limited to assessment by these workers. All social ser-

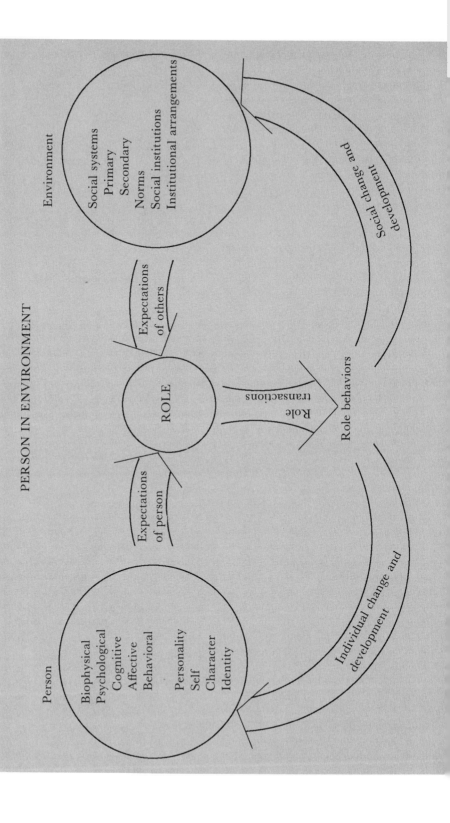

PERSON IN ENVIRONMENT

Environment

Social systems
Primary
Secondary
Norms
Social institutions
Institutional arrangements

Expectations
of others

ROLE

Role
transactions

Expectations
of person

Social change and
development

Role behaviors

Individual change and
development

Person

Biophysical
Psychological
Cognitive
Affective
Behavioral

Personality
Self
Character
Identity

vice practice begins with assessment, and workers in all social service areas should find this application useful.

The Problem-Solving Process

Practice theory is aimed at prevention or amelioration and generally is concerned with giving help to clients through a logical, problem-solving process. This process has been described in diverse terms such as "the basic helping approach" or "practice skill areas," but the underlying process is the same.[41] The first step in problem-solving is assessment, that is, making an accurate determination of the problems and needs of clients. The second step is determining the objectives of the intervention and formulating a plan for reaching them. The third step is putting into practice intervention strategies designed to resolve the problem and meet the need. And the last step is evaluating the intervention to determine if its objectives have been met.

The use of terms such as *steps* to describe the problem-solving process is itself a heuristic or problem-solving mechanism. In actual practice the steps blend, merge, and overlap, and problem-solving is more a circular process than a linear one. It is not unusual to reach one step and find that it is necessary to go back over the whole process again. For example, determining the exact needs of clients and constituencies sometimes requires three and four reviews. A social worker, for instance, may think she understands a presenting problem, but as she tries to put a plan for resolving it into operation she comes to see that her understanding is off target.

Practice Principles for Social Work Assessment

The process of accurately assessing the needs of clients involves three subprocesses: identifying problems and needs, analyzing the causes or factors contributing to problems and needs, and identifying strengths and resources. The systems approach offers six general assessment principles which are applicable to these three subprocesses.

In **problem and need identification**, the assessment principles are:

1. Identify the system to be assessed.
2. Identify the condition in that system to be understood.

In **problem analysis**, the principles stem from the basic assumption on which the systems approach has been constructed: *the state or condition of a system, at any one point in time, is a function of the interaction between it and the environment in which it operates.* Put another way, the needs and problems of clients and constituents are always a product of the transactions between them and the individuals and groups that make up their environment. These assessment principles are:

3. Identify the factors about the system itself that contribute to the condition.
4. Identify the factors in the social context of the system that contribute to the condition.

In **resource identification**, an understanding is developed of the resources available to clients and constituents which may be useful in resolving problems and fulfilling needs. Social work intervention is based on the recognition and use of existing resources, both strengths existing within the client and supports existing in the environment. These assessment principles are:

5. Identify the resources that exist within the system itself.
6. Identify the resources that exist within the environment of the system.

Demonstrating the Practice Principles

To demonstrate the application of these six principles, we will review the concepts discussed in this chapter in the context of social work assessment. As an example, we will consider the case of Mary, a 20-year-old university student. She has come in voluntarily for counseling, saying she feels discouraged and unable to control how she completes her courses and participates in peer-group activities.

The Focal System

Before a systems analysis can be undertaken, the social worker must be able to clearly distinguish the system to be assessed. This is referred to as the **focal system**. Usually the system to be assessed is the **client system** or the person actually receiving the service. In the example, Mary is the focal system when she comes in for counseling. But it is also possible to assess what has been referred to as the **target system**, the system to be influenced, changed, or altered. In many social work situations the client system and the target system are one and the same, that is, the person receiving the service is likely to be the target for change. But it is also possible that the target system will be some other person or group or condition.

The focal system chosen for assessment depends on a number of things, including the nature of the agency and how far along the service delivery process might be. In the beginning phases of service, it is likely that the client system will be the focal system. Later, especially if it is determined that environmental change is necessary, other systems may be targeted. These systems would then become the focal system.

The target system may be an individual or a social system. Social workers most often work with individuals as clients and as targets, and this chapter has focused on the individual as a system. But this is not always the case. Many social workers work with groups, with families, and with communities, and assessment of the individual is only of secondary concern to them.

The Focal Condition

From a person-in-environment perspective, the assessment of individuals focuses on the roles they occupy and the role transactions in which they are involved. This is not to say that social workers are unconcerned about such levels of individual systems as biophysical functioning, cognitive and affective processes, behavioral skills, or personality development. They certainly are concerned with all of these. But individuals' roles and role transactions become essential considerations in analyzing the problems and needs of individuals in relation to the role transactions in which they are involved.

The **focal condition** to be assessed has to do with role transactions and behaviors. In the example, the social worker, by empathic responses to Mary's feelings and concerns, leads her to the conclusion that her troubles at school are related to what appears to be an unsuccessful, tension-provoking relationship with her parents. From our perspective, the worker sees the problem as one of failed transactions over role innovation and control. Mary wants her parents to treat her as an adult and allow her autonomy to develop her own plans in such areas as career, marriage, and friends. Her parents appear to have their own expectations of how a young adult daughter ought to behave, and this does not allow for a great deal of independence from family traditions and norms. The focal condition is the struggle going on between Mary's attempt to change her parents' understanding of the daughter role and the parents' attempt to control the daughter.

The values of social workers are frequently being tested. In this example, the worker's own values about parent-young adult daughter relations and, more generally, about the role and status of women in society are being tested. Inevitably, the worker must make a decision to take the point of view of the parents and social tradition, or to take the point of view of the daughter and social innovation.

Social workers are among those interest groups in society today that are promoting more equitable gender-role expectations. Thus it is likely that a social worker who shares this goal, and whose service supports it, will be inclined to foster the young woman's desire for greater autonomy over her life. Yet this does not mean that the social worker will ignore the expectations of the parents or simply attempt to turn Mary against her parents. The social worker will work at the *boundary* between the person and her social environment in order to help bring about the best fit. It may be possible that the situation can be worked out among them so that the relationship can be renewed and rebuilt along different lines.

Factors and Resources in the Focal System

Individuals clearly contribute to their own problems. Acknowledging this does not mean that Mary is being blamed, however, if the worker also acknowledges Mary's strengths and resources and is prepared to identify factors in the environment that contribute to her troubles. Having stated Mary's problem in transactional terms, as a problem in the relationship between her and her parents, the worker now is ready to inquire how Mary functions as an individual occupying the role of daughter. In doing this, it is possible to take account of Mary's strengths as well as her deficiencies.

First, interviews and other diagnostic tools might be used to explore Mary's health and physical state to see if these are contributing to the problem. Since this cannot be done completely by the worker alone, Mary might be referred for a medical examination. If she is found to be healthy and fit, this is acknowledged as a strength. Then attention can be turned to such things as Mary's intelligence and her ability to reason, judge, and accurately perceive the expectations being held by her parents and herself. The worker might also try to determine Mary's emotional maturity and to explore any internal emotional crises taking place in her life. Since Mary is a young adult, the degree to which she has a clear identity, a clear sense of present and future goals, and a strong sense of self-esteem, and the extent to which she is ready to make deep interpersonal commitments, might be examined. The aim is to determine if she is ready to assume the autonomy and independence she so desires. Then the worker might examine Mary's behavioral skills and abilities. Does she know how to express herself clearly when speaking to her parents? Does she know how to be assertive and let her wishes be known?

After such inquiries, Mary, facilitated by the social worker, might determine that although she is healthy and intelligent and has a clear sense of her own identity and goals, she really does not know how to express her own ideas about her life in face-to-face encounters with her parents. Her skills in communicating her needs, especially when people she loves are involved, need to be improved.

Factors and Resources in the Social Environment

There are two ways to assess the environment when working with an individual. The environment can be understood subjectively, through the perceptions and attitudes of the client, or it can be understood objectively, through independent study by the social worker. A good assessment requires that both the subjective and objective environments be analyzed.

The **subjective environment** is important because individuals' attributions and meanings, or their definitions of the situation, are central to understanding the problems they are experiencing. It is essential for the worker to inquire about how Mary perceives the expectations being directed to her by her parents and the society more generally; that is, the expectations supported by social institutions and institutional arrangements. For instance, it will be important to understand if she believes that the troubles she is experiencing have anything to do with the inequitable gender-role norms of society as interpreted by her parents, her friends, or the organizations in which she may work, study, or otherwise participate. Similarly, it will be important to inquire into the supports which she perceives to exist in the environment. Social norms are in a state of continual change. This means there are likely to be people and groups who have very different opinions about how young women ought to lead their lives. It will be necessary, therefore, to determine the supports the young woman feels she has among her kin and among her friends and peers.

After inquiring into Mary's subjective environment, the worker may lead her to realize that many of her relatives and all of her friends are quite supportive of her, but she really does not understand her parents' expectations. They do not talk to her comfortably, and they often give her mixed messages, at one moment seeming to encourage her independence and at the next seeming to squash her attempts to be independent. The difficulty, from her point of view, is that she and her parents never seem able to talk about it without quarrelling.

Since Mary's problem seems to focus on the inadequate communication patterns between her and her parents, the social worker may decide to directly assess the **objective environment**. The parents may be visited or asked to come in for a talk so the worker can check out their actual expectations and abilities to communicate clearly and consistently. If, after such an examination, the social worker corroborates that the problem does have to do with inadequate communication skills, she or he may recommend that the intervention involve both Mary and her parents. In this way all of them can work out and clarify their own needs and expectations and, if the intervention proves successful, come to a new understanding of them and of one another.

The example of Mary is at best a sketch of how the systems approach can be used in the assessment phase of direct-service practice. The aim of this simplified description is to illustrate the uses of the concepts rather than to teach social work assessment. Further knowledge can be gained through courses in practice theory, through actual field experiences with clients, and through further study of issues in human behavior.

A LOOK AHEAD

The next three sections of this book focus on three systems which are integral to the study of human behavior in the social environment. Part II turns attention to the community as a system. Advanced industrial societies such as the United States are made up of diverse ethnic and racial and other subcultures, and the relations among subcultures have a lot to do with the behaviors of individuals. Part III considers the family both as a social institution and as an organization or system within which most people live out most of their lives. The family is perhaps the most important system in terms of individual change and development, and many social service workers see it as central to good practice. Part IV, which is concerned with the individual as a system, discusses perspectives on interpersonal transactions and examines the contributions of ego psychology and developmental theory to the study of human behavior. Part V consists of a final chapter which summarizes and synthesizes the content and reviews how the critical and systems approaches might contribute to a reform-oriented theory for practice.

DISCUSSION QUESTIONS AND CLASS PROJECTS

1. In reviewing Gordon's theory of human nature, notice that he says nothing about a "spiritual nature." To what extent do you believe that humans are spiritual by nature? To what extent do you believe that humans are spiritual because of learning?

2. What does the research literature say about innate differences between men and women?

3. Define what is meant by a system. Give at least four examples of human systems.

4. Systems are made up of parts or elements. List and describe the parts of the individual as a social system discussed in this chapter.

5. Do change and development in human systems always follow a progressive path?

6. Describe and give examples of the following concepts: homeostasis, feedback, steady state, equifinality, holon.

7. Why is the study of biophysical processes important to human behavior?

8. Why is the study of the social environment important to human behavior?

9. Describe and discuss the differences between the interactional and the sociocultural levels of social systems.

10. Compare social norms, social institutions, and institutional arrangements.

11. Compare the visions of social systems found in structural functional and conflict theories. In what ways do their views about conflict differ? Do you think the structural functional approach or the conflict approach to the study of systems is better for social work?

12. The concept of role has been defined in three ways. Describe and give examples of each.

13. Describe five major forms of transactions that take place between individuals and social systems and give examples of each.

14. The box titled "Person in Environment" pulls together the concepts discussed in this chapter. Can you use it to describe an individual client you have or are working with?

NOTES

1. See such popular texts as Allen Pincus and Anne Minahan, *Social Work Practice: Model and Method* (Itasca, IL: F. E. Peacock Publishers, 1973); Carol Germain and Alex Gitterman, *The Life Model of Social Work Practice* (New York: Columbia University Press, 1980); and Ralph E. Anderson and Irl Carter, *Human Behavior in the Social Environment: A Social Systems Approach*, 3rd ed. (Hawthorne, NY: Aldine, 1984).

2. Jonathan Turner, *The Structure of Sociological Theory*, rev. ed. (Homewood, IL: Dorsey Press, 1978).

3. Gordon Hearn, *Theory Building in So-*

cial Work (Toronto, Ontario: University of Toronto Press, 1958), pp. 38–51; Germain and Gitterman, *Life Model of Social Work Practice*.

4. Genevieve De Hoyos and Claigh Jensen, "The Systems Approach in American Social Work," *Social Casework*, vol. 66 (October 1985), pp. 490–96.

5. Anderson and Carter, *Human Behavior in the Social Environment*, p. 1. Note, however, that while Anderson and Carter claim to present a systems approach, they declare that theirs is a "functionalist one," that is, systems theory (p. 7).

6. Ludwig von Bertalanffy, *General Systems Theory*, rev. ed. (New York: George Braziller, 1968), p. 208.

7. Burrhus F. Skinner, *Beyond Freedom and Dignity* (New York: Alfred A. Knopf, 1971); Ruth Benedict, *Patterns of Culture*, 2nd ed. (Boston: Houghton Mifflin, 1959).

8. For readings in sociobiology, see Edward O. Wilson, *On Human Nature* (Cambridge, MA: Harvard University Press, 1978); and T. H. Clutton-Brock and Paul H. Harvey (editors), *Readings in Sociobiology* (San Francisco: W. H. Freeman, 1978).

9. Ronald Fernandez, *The I, The Me, and You: An Introduction to Social Psychology* (New York: Frederick A. Praeger, 1977), p. 20.

10. Pierre L. van den Berghe, *Man in Society: A Biosocial View*, 2nd ed. (New York: Elsevier, 1978), p. 34.

11. Harvey L. Gochros, "Sexuality," in *Encyclopedia of Social Work*, 18th ed. (Silver Springs, MD: National Association of Social Workers, 1987), p. 581.

12. Milton M. Gordon, *Human Nature, Class, and Ethnicity* (New York: Oxford University Press, 1978), pp. 48–64.

13. John Money and Patricia Tucker, *Sexual Signatures: On Being a Man or a Woman* (Boston: Little Brown, 1975), p. 38.

14. Eleanor Maccoby and Carol Jacklin, *The Psychology of Sex Differences* (Stanford, CA: Stanford University Press, 1974).

15. Carol Gilligan, *In a Different Voice: Psychological Theory and Women's Development* (Cambridge, MA: Harvard University Press, 1982).

16. Marie Richmond-Abbott, *Masculine and Feminine: Sex Roles Over the Life Cycle* (New York: Newberry Award Records, 1983), pp. 41–81.

17. Barbara M. Newman and Philip R. Newman, *Development through Life: A Psychosocial Approach*, 4th ed. (Chicago: Dorsey Press, 1987), p. 4.

18. Rodney W. Napier and Matti K. Gershenfeld, *Groups: Theory and Experience*, 2nd ed. (Boston: Houghton Mifflin, 1981); Elizabeth A. Carter and Monica McGoldrick (editors), *The Family Life Cycle: A Framework for Family Therapy* (New York: Gardner, 1980).

19. David Macarov, *The Design of Social Welfare* (New York: Holt, Rinehart & Winston, 1978), pp. 191–200.

20. Gerhard Lenski and Jean Lenski, *Human Societies*, 4th ed. (New York: McGraw-Hill, 1982), p. 73.

21. Paul B. Baltes, "Life-Span Developmental Psychology: Some Converging Observations on History and Theory," in P. B. Baltes and O. G. Brim, Jr. (editors), *Life Span Development and Behavior*, vol 2. (New York: Academic Press, 1979), p. 263.

22. See the discussion of the work of W. B. Cannon in Ludwig von Bertalanffy, *General System Theory*, rev. ed. (New York: George Braziller, 1968), pp. 160–63.

23. von Bertalanffy, *General Systems Theory*, pp. 156–60.

24. Ibid., p. 158.

25. Hearn, *Theory Building in Social Work*, p. 44.

26. Anderson and Carter, *Human Behavior in Social Environment*, p. 21.

27. Salvador Minuchin et al., *Families of the Slums: An Exploration of Their Structure and Treatment* (New York: Basic Books), 1967).

28. Gordon Hearn, "General Systems Theory and Social Work," in F. J. Turner (editor), *Social Work Treatment: Interlocking Theoretical Approaches*, 2nd ed. (New York: Free Press, 1979), pp. 333–59.

29. See Diane L. Pancoast and Alice Collins, "Natural Helping Networks," in *Encyclopedia of Social Work*, 18th ed., vol. 2 (Silver Spring, MD: National Association of Social Workers, 1987), pp. 171–81.

30. See the discussion by Genevieve De Hoyos, Arturo De Hoyos, and Christian B. Anderson, "Sociocultural Dislocation: Beyond the Dual Perspective," *Social Work*, vol. 21 (January–February 1986), pp. 61–67.

31. Lenski and Lenski, *Human Societies*, p. 54.

32. Hans Gerth and C. Wright Mills, *Character and Social Structure: The Psychology of Social Institutions* (New York: Harbinger Books, 1964), p. 23.

33. Ibid., p. 26.

34. Neil Gilbert and Harry Specht, *The Emergence of Social Welfare and Social Work*, 2nd ed. (Itasca, IL: F. E. Peacock, 1981).

35. Ralph Lehninger, "Systems Theory," *Journal of Sociology and Social Welfare*, vol. 5 (July 1978), pp. 481–98.

36. Ralf Dahrendorf, *Class and Class Conflict in Industrial Society* (Palo Alto, CA: Stanford University Press, 1959).

37. Lewis A. Coser, *The Functions of Social Conflict* (New York: Free Press, 1956).

38. Jeffry H. Galper, *The Politics of Social Services* (Englewood Cliffs, NJ: Prentice-Hall, 1975), pp. 88–110.

39. Morton Deutsch and Robert M. Krauss, *Social Psychology* (New York: Basic Books, 1965), pp. 175–77.

40. George J. McCall and J. L. Simmons, *Social Psychology: A Sociological Approach* (New York: Free Press, 1982).

41. Max Siporin, *Introduction to Social Work Practice* (New York: Macmillan, 1975), pp. 17–36; Pincus and Minahan, *Social Work Practice*.

PART II

Communities in Society

CHAPTER 3

Diversity in Community Life

M AJOR THEMES DISCUSSED IN THIS CHAPTER:

1. *Communities.* Three types of communities are identified: locational, based on common residence; identificational, based on common identity; and interest, based on common goals and objectives. The focus is on identificational communities.

2. *Variations in community life.* Some contemporary forms of identificational communities are based on a shared social class, religious belief, or sexual orientation. More pervasive influences on the formation and maintenance of communities in American society are racial and ethnic heritage and minority or majority status.

3. *Implications for practice.* Communities form a major social context in which people live out their everyday lives. Individuals' attitudes and values, needs and problems, strengths and resources are all associated with community life. The cultural uniqueness of communities and their status in a society must be taken into account when working with clients, especially clients in communities which diverge from majority communities.

T HE STUDY of community life is important for good social service practice. Some of the major roles people hold in a society derive from their membership in various communities within the society. Most of these are citizen roles. Americans may have such roles as urban dweller or rural dweller; white, black, Hispanic, or Asian; lower-class, middle-class, or affluent; Protestant, Catholic, Jewish, or Islamic; and heterosexual or homosexual, among others. Connected to these roles are statuses: majority or minority; upper-class or lower-class; deviant or "normal." Moreover, the communities in which people live and with which they identify form a major social context for human behavior and development. Many of our attitudes and values derive directly from the continual transactions—recruitment, socialization, interaction, innovation, and control—which take place in and through community life. Communities also supply many of the resources and social supports essential for individual social and psychological well-being. The organizations, associations, families, kin, and friendship groups which comprise communities all can contribute to healthy human behavior and development.

There is also a darker side to community life. Because many of the needs and problems of people originate in a community context, the everyday transactions among individuals in communities can create problems. Perhaps even more important, from a critical perspective, community life acts as a link between individuals and the society as a whole. A complex industrial society such as the contemporary American society of the United States is composed of many communities, often in competition or conflict with one another. The relationships among communities, as well as the status of each community within a society, have important implications for the social and psychological well-being of community members. To the extent that individuals are connected to communities which are powerful and valued and which have a wealth of resources, they will experience advantages over those who are connected to communities which are less powerful, less valued, and have more limited resources. This does not mean that there is a one-to-one relationship between community and individual well-being. The influence of other social systems, in particular the family, and the adaptive capacities of individuals have a lot to do with how they experience and resolve their needs and problems. Nevertheless, it is clear that communities do help shape individuals' chances for well-being.

If social service workers are to serve individuals and families, or if they are to plan and develop policy and programs for communities as a whole, they must recognize the important links between individuals and communities. They must respect and understand the attitudes and values that permeate communities, recognize their strengths and resources, and learn how to use them in problem resolution. They need to acknowledge that they affect the chances for well-being of the individuals and families that comprise the communities in which they are working.

COMMUNITIES AS SOCIAL SYSTEMS

Communities are types of social systems which are distinguished by the personal or affective nature of the ties that hold their members together. They are groups of people who sense a common identity and bond with one another and who are attached to one another through regular interaction. Sociologists often describe these types of communities as a **gemeinshaft**, that is, a societal group characterized by "a high degree of personal intimacy, emotional depth, moral commitment, social cohesion, and continuity in time."[1]

Communities are very similar to other groups such as the family and the society. These, too, are based on common identity and interpersonal bonding. If we go back far enough in history, there probably were no differences among these three types of groups. The national society, in which large, centrally regulated states supersede regional communal ties, is a relatively new phenomenon. Similarly, in many cultures and historical eras, communities have incorporated numerous attributes which are associated with families today.

Probably the greatest differences among the community, the family, and the society have to do with size and the degree to which intimacy is possible. At least in contemporary industrial societies, families are typically quite small, and membership is expressed in intimate personal attachments. National societies are usually quite large, and personal attachments most often are expressed through patriotic rituals mediated through impersonal bureaucracies such as government and business. Many national societies are **pluralist**, that is, composed of many subcultures or community groups. Communities lie somewhere between family and society in these respects. They are relatively **homogeneous**, or uniform in composition, neither very small nor very large, and not very intimate but not very bureaucratic, either.

TYPES OF COMMUNITIES

Sociologists have identified three principal types of communities.[2] Some communities are **locational**, based on a common residence or territory. Such communities are believed to have developed with the evolution of agriculture, as nomadic hunters and gatherers began to settle in one place. Thus, in part, the bonding and attachment in a community are to the place as much as to the people. Perhaps the most pertinent example of communities based on location is the neighborhood. Neighborhoods vary a great deal; some offer evidence of the strong interpersonal attachments and closeness of the gemeinshaft, but others do not. Many observers today believe that neighborhoods in American society are losing the sense of community which typified them in the past. Inner-city neighborhoods, for instance, have been described as disorganized, conflict-ridden, impersonal, and with little sense of attachment among the residents, since sociologists first turned their attention to urban living.[3] Even contemporary suburban neighborhoods may lack a sense of community. Philip Slater describes American suburban communities as being in "pursuit of loneliness": families living in individual houses, glorying in their privacy, fencing or hedging themselves in, and limiting their contacts with neighbors.[4]

Another type of community is **identificational**, based on a common identity. Jessie Bernard uses the term *the community* to refer to locational communities and the term *community* to refer to identificational communities.[5] In identificational communities residence is of less consequence than ties based on

Community cohesion, spirit, and identity are
celebrated in neighborhood block parties throughout
the United States. *Elizabeth Hamlin/Stock, Boston.*

affection and common identity. Examples include social class, racial and ethnic, and religious communities, and, more recently, communities based on sexual orientation. Blacks, Italians, and Catholics are good examples. Their sense of commonality and affection derives from the historical experiences which they have in common and which they carry around within themselves, regardless of where they may live.

The third type of community is based on a shared **interest**, with common goals and objectives. Although locational and identificational communities also are held together by common interests, their interests are likely to be more general and inclusive. In interest communities, the affection and attachment derive from a much more narrowly focused interest. Interest communities include professional or occupational associations; science, for instance, has been described by Thomas Kuhn as the work of communities of scientists. It is also common for social workers and other groups within the helping professions to think of themselves as a community.[6]

ATTRIBUTES OF IDENTIFICATIONAL COMMUNITIES

The focus of this chapter is on identificational communities. However, there is a considerable overlap between locational and indentificational communities. In many societies, identificational communities occupy particular territories. Great Britain is composed of Scottish, Welsh, Irish, and English populations, each primarily occupying a particular region. Czechoslovakia is composed of Czechs and Slovaks occupying different geographic sectors.

The United States is composed of a number of communities existing in relative physical segregation. The most obvious basis for such segregation is race and ethnicity. Blacks, Puerto Ricans on the continent, and Mexican Americans are likely to live in segregated communities, often in decaying inner-city areas. Because of social policies dating back to the nineteenth century, many Native Americans (Indians) still live on segregated reservations. Segregation also is evident on the basis of social class; American neighborhoods are shaped by the residents' income or wealth. Some religious communities are more-or-less segregated, though often, as in the case of Catholics and Jewish people, the basis for separation may be more a matter of ethnicity than of religion. Recently, neighborhoods composed of lesbians and gay men have become apparent in some cities.

Because of such patterns of segregation in American society, identificational communities are also likely to be locational communities. Indeed, when social service workers become involved with community work they are likely to do so through the neighborhoods served by their agencies. But identificational communities go beyond locational communities in two respects; they incorporate the issues of the larger group, rather than being limited to the needs and problems of a particular area or neighborhood, and they include communities which are important to individuals and families but which may not exist as clearly demarcated neighborhoods. The focus on identificational communities makes it possible to incorporate the study of neighborhoods with the study of larger groupings of people who consider themselves communities.

There are two other attributes which distinguish identificational communities: Each community develops a unique culture, and each is accorded a certain status. The concept of group culture is usually associated with ethnic groups, but it is equally relevant to other communities. **Culture** is not an easy concept to define, but it generally means all the beliefs, values, norms, and traditions that are shared in a community and govern social interactions among community members or between members and outsiders. The values and norms of the various social classes, of religious denominations, of gays and lesbians, of ethnic and racial groups constitute their cultures. Such communities also vary in terms of their status in the society. Ethnic minorities and minority individuals, who are devalued and experience hostility as a result of their group membership, have low social status; ethnic majorities and majority individuals enjoy a higher status. Differences in status are explicit in the notion of social classes, and religious denominations, which often are linked to social class and ethnicity, also differ in terms of status.

SOME VARIATIONS IN COMMUNITY LIFE

In examining community life, we will consider the different kinds of identificational communities which have already been introduced. Social class communities, religious denominations, and the gay and lesbian community are discussed in this section. A more pervasive type of identificational community in American society is based on race and ethnicity or on minority or majority status. These topics, which are considered in the next two sections, are the focus of discussion in Part II. The remaining chapters in this part describe the history and present conditions of racial and ethnic groups and minority-majority relations in the United States.

SOCIAL CLASSES AS COMMUNITIES

Social classes are not communities in the sense of being based on a shared location, identification, or interest. Nevertheless, they can give rise to communal action, that is, to the development of common neighborhoods, a common identity, and common interests.[7] The term **social class** has a distinctly economic meaning. It is used to describe people in terms of the economic opportunities available to them, the economic goods and resources they command, and the occupations or positions they hold in the economy.

Two Approaches to the Study of Social Class

Sociologists approach the study of social class in two basic ways, regarding it as a descriptive tool or an analytic tool (see box, Social Stratification and Social Classes). Most approach it as a descriptive tool, in terms of **social stratifica-**

tion; that is, society is described as a ladder composed of a series of rungs or **prestige rankings**, each a step higher than the preceding one. Individuals in the society are located on this vertical ladder according to such standards as the amount of money they earn, the level of education they have completed, the prestige of their occupation, or the prestige conferred on them by others in the community. Then the ladder is divided in some logical but nevertheless arbitrary way. For instance, those whose education, income, and job status only get them up the first two or three rungs are said to be lower-class. Those whose education, salary, and job status get them all the way to the top are said to be upper-class. Those located at the middle rungs are the middle class.[8] In this way, sociologists have designated various social classes. W. Lloyd Warner, for instance, proposed a schema with six classes: upper-upper, lower-upper, upper-middle, lower-middle, upper-lower, and lower-lower.[9]

Marxian-influenced sociologists use classes as an analytic tool. Social classes are defined in a structure of associations or **social roles** in the workplace. The work organization in a free-market or capitalist economy is divided into a number of roles, each with a set of responsibilities, privileges, duties, and obligations. **Owners** put up the capital for the business or service, define what the product or service will be, and decide how the work will be done. They are the ultimate authority on who will be hired, how much will be paid in wages, and who will be fired. **Managers** follow the direction of the owners and put the

SOCIAL STRATIFICATION AND SOCIAL CLASSES

Some sociologists define social classes descriptively, as a series of prestige rankings, while others define them analytically, in terms of the role a person occupies in the economy.

DESCRIPTIVE APPROACH	ANALYTIC APPROACH
Classes as Prestige Rankings	Classes as Social Roles in Production and Service
Upper-upper class	Owner
Upper class	
Lower-upper class	Manager
Upper-middle class	
Middle class	White-collar worker
Lower-middle class	
Upper-lower class	Blue-collar worker
Lower class	
Lower-lower class	

Because of social class segregation, lower-class neighborhoods marked by dilapidated housing are found in all cities, suburbs, and towns. *Brent Jones*.

plans for service and production into operation; they are likely to do the actual hiring and firing. Thus owners and managers often are regarded as two different strata within the same social class. **Workers** offer their mental and physical skills to the managers and owners in return for wages. Workers also may be considered as different strata in the same class, such as white-collar workers, skilled workers, and semiskilled workers.[10]

According to this definition, class is a position a person occupies within a hierarchy or authority structure. The essential element has to do with domination and subordination. In this sense social class is more than a description of prestige rankings and can be used as a tool for analyzing social relationships. With the concept of social class, we can look at the potential for role conflict, or, in the Marxian terminology, **class conflict**. We can understand the circumstances that will make a worker content and can evaluate if workers are being underpaid or overworked. We can examine whether workers are allowed to be autonomous or creative and whether owners and managers are being authoritarian or exploitive.

In contemporary industrial societies, social class distinctions are very complex. The simple designations of owner, manager, and worker are replaced with far more complicated patterns. Traditionally the two principal categories of workers have been blue-collar or white-collar, ordinarily determined on the basis of whether they work more with their hands (construction workers) or with their minds (bookkeepers). There are also the categories of unskilled workers (janitors, waiters), skilled workers (computer technicians and programmers), and professional workers (lawyers, urban developers). Managers may include supervisors, department heads, and executives. Owners are those who own small and medium-size businesses, as well as those who have controlling interests in large companies and corporations. The American class structure, based on roles and statuses within roles, is an example of such a complex hierarchy.[11]

Social Class Position

Although the two ways of approaching the study of social class are quite different, there are overlapping areas between them. Owners of businesses, especially large businesses, are likely to be educated and to have a great deal of income and a fair amount of occupational prestige. Managers and professionals similarly are likely to have high educational, prestige, and income rankings. Both groups, therefore, are likely to be found among the upper classes. White-collar workers are likely to have middle-level incomes, education, and occupational prestige, and blue-collar workers, especially nonunionized, unskilled workers, are most likely to be in the lower-middle to lower classes. In poverty-class families (see Chapter 8), the head of the household is chronically unemployed, underemployed, or dependent on welfare, or at best working for a subsistence wage.

Regardless of how social class position is defined, it is highly correlated with

many variables of human behavior. Compared to people in lower socioeconomic positions, those in higher positions gain more wealth and income, experience greater social prestige, and command greater power. Thus they have
greater **life chances** and better **life conditions** (see box, Life Chances and Life
Conditions in Social Classes).

LIFE CHANCES AND LIFE CONDITIONS IN SOCIAL CLASSES

Vincent Jeffries has described five social classes and the conditions or circumstances that can be expected for members of each class.

Upper class. The upper classes will have very high income and a great
deal of wealth. The wealth often goes back a number of generations. They
are very highly respected in their communities. They are in positions
where they can make fundamental decisions and exert considerable control over the economy and over civic affairs. They are likely to be members
of boards of directors of large organizations. Their own education and that
of their children is likely to be at elite schools.

Upper-middle class. They will have high incomes but not necessarily a lot
of family wealth. They often own property and have a good deal of savings.
They are likely to be professionals, administrators, or executives who are
just below the very top in the organizational hierarchy. They approach
their occupations as a lifelong career. Generally, they are college-
educated.

Lower-middle class. They will have more modest incomes and savings.
Often they will work in less-prestigious professions or as small businesspeople. More likely they will be in clerical or sales occupations. Many will
not have college educations. They are likely to put a great deal of emphasis
on respectability.

Working class. They will likely have low incomes, minimal savings, and
work in skilled and semiskilled jobs. Many will have completed high
school, but many will not have. They will live adequately but on a narrow
margin. Their principal concern is getting by day by day.

Lower class. Their income is likely to be at poverty level, even when they
work. It is likely that they will be unskilled laborers in the lowest-paying
jobs. It is also likely that they will experience a good deal of unemployment. Few of them will have completed high school, and some might not
have completed elementary school. They are often looked down upon by
others in society.

Source: Adapted from Vincent Jeffries, "Basic Concepts and Theories of Class Stratification," in V. Jeffries and H. E. Ransford, *Social Stratification* (Boston: Allyn and Bacon, 1980),
p. 121.

Social class position has a lot to do with neighborhood formation. American neighborhoods are segregated by class, that is, they tend to be inhabited by people holding similar economic positions in the society, with similar incomes and occupational and educational backgrounds. A walk through most American cities readily indicates where the rich, the middle classes, and the poor live. This was not always the case, however; there used to be much more social class mixing in neighborhoods. For instance, middle- and lower-class blacks formerly tended to be grouped in "black neighborhoods." Today, black, inner-city neighborhoods are described as being inhabited by an **underclass**, which essentially consists of unemployed or marginally employed unskilled workers (see Chapter 6). Upper- and middle-class blacks are not identified with black neighborhoods.[12]

Class Consciousness

Class position forms a basis for the development of community spirit. In the United States, this type of spirit has emerged periodically in various communities, but it has never persisted. For instance, no labor party has taken hold in the United States in the same way such political organizations have developed in European nations.

Researchers have found that although most Americans believe there are social classes in the society, the great majority think of themselves as being middle-class and do not identify strongly with a particular social class.[13] Very few of those who are members of the upper class according to financial standards acknowledge that status, for instance. Thus Americans do not have a great deal of class consciousness.

In some situations, however, communities of interest based on class position do emerge. In the United States, the labor movement, that is, the development of trade unions and other workers' organizations, grew out of the common interests of skilled and unskilled blue-collar workers. Most of the welfare programs developed during the Great Depression of the 1930s and the War on Poverty of the 1960s were instituted because lower- and middle-income workers joined together and pushed for them.[14] These workers saw the need for a strong "safety net" as protection from economic troubles over which they had no control, in the form of such government programs as social security, unemployment insurance, Aid to Families with Dependent Children, community mental health, and support for education. Indeed, the inability of the Reagan administration to completely dismantle the welfare state, as such programs are collectively referred to, is testimony that at least some basic level of class consciousness among lower- and middle-income groups still exists in the United States.

Irving Krauss suggests that if community is to emerge from class, five conditions must be met:[15]

1. There must be a common associational context; that is, people must see that their roles in the workplace and the things that are happening to them as a result of those roles are pretty much the same.

2. There must be a high degree of similarity in background and in life chances. People's incomes and educations have to be similar.
3. There must be a shared awareness of undesirable conditions.
4. People must agree that others in the association (owners, managers, or other categories of workers) are the cause of the undesirable conditions.
5. Some kind of organized attempts to bring about change must take place. In this process, leaders must emerge to direct the energies of the class.

Social Classes and Racial and Ethnic Stratification

The differences in class status and in racial and ethnic status in the United States overlap considerably. Large percentages of people of color—Afro-Americans, Puerto Ricans, Mexican Americans, and Native Americans, in particular—are found in the lower social class. Researchers have coined the term **ethclass** to describe the relation between social class and minority status.[16] Especially where minorities of color are involved, social class as well as subcultural factors must be taken into account. As Wynetta Devore and Elfriede Schlesinger note, "this intersect of ethnicity and social class generates identifiable dispositions and behaviors."[17]

It would be inaccurate, however, to maintain that only ethnic and racial minorities have lower-class status in the United States. Many white ethnics— part of the majority white group—find themselves with lower-class status, fearful of unemployment and living on low incomes, even in poverty. The problems of the "white poor" in the South and in Appalachia have been the subject of many studies,[18] as have the white, working-class ethnic neighborhoods in such sections of the country as the Northeast and the Midwest. The delivery of effective social services to these groups depends on recognition and understanding of their unique characteristics.

Michael Novak describes white southern and eastern European ethnic groups affectionately as "PIGS" (Polish, Italians, Greeks, and Slavs), because they tended to be identified with factions opposing the civil rights movement in the 1960s and 1970s. He insists, however, that their attitudes were not racist (in the sense that they believed that blacks are inherently inferior) but rather were rooted in their own ethnic and class-based interests. Novak eloquently described the history of these largely Catholic and Jewish groups in the United States and the kinds of struggles they encountered and the adaptations they had to make in a society dominated by whites, Anglo-Saxons, and Protestants. They had to become more individualistic and competitive and less oriented to family and community. They also had to redefine the way they understood their sexuality. Protestantism, Catholicism, and Judaism all constrain sexual activity and preach that sex outside of marriage is sinful. But in Protestantism, sex is not only sinful, it is also dirty. For Catholics and Jews from southern and eastern Europe, sex may have been sinful, but it also was "delicious."[19]

In a like manner, Richard Sennett and Jonathan Cobb have described the life of white ethnics and the "hidden injuries of class" they suffer. Not having "made it" economically, they come to believe that their relatively low status is their own fault, and they live for the possibility that their children will not repeat what they believe were their own mistakes.[20]

RELIGIOUS DENOMINATIONS AS COMMUNITIES

Religion is another factor around which community life is organized. In the United States, unlike other nations, there is no official religion. Nevertheless, a strong Protestant Christian tradition has shaped this nation's heritage.

Today the United States is a mosaic of religions, Protestant, Catholic, Jewish, and others. According to the National Opinion Research Center (NORC), 64 percent of all Americans define themselves as Protestant, 25 percent as Catholic, 2 percent as Jews, and 1 percent as "other." Some 7 percent of Americans do not identify with any religion.[21] Within religions, especially among Protestants, Jews, and "others" there is considerable variation. Protestants, for instance, may be Episcopalian, Baptist, Lutheran, or any number of other denominations. Jews may be Sephardic, Orthodox, Conservative, and so on. Other religions practiced by Americans include Muslim, Buddhist, and Hindu. Each religion or denomination unites people not only in terms of religious doctrine but also in terms of social and cultural values.

Religion is difficult to define in community terms because, like social class and, to some extent, ethnicity, the degree to which an individual or family identifies with a religion can vary a great deal. To say that a person is a Protestant does not describe the degree to which that person believes in the principles of the Protestant faith, nor does it describe the person's level of participation in a church and its activities. Religious attachment seems to differ among denominations. For instance, in the past 15 years or so, Protestant fundamentalist denominations appear to have created the greatest sense of attachment: 51 percent attend weekly services, and 58 percent rate their faith strong. Catholicism also seems to be promoting a strong identity: just over 40 percent of Catholics rate their participation and their faith strong. Episcopalianism commands less affiliation, with 18 percent saying they attend weekly services and 31 percent rating their faith strong.[22]

Religious Affiliation and Social Attitudes

The NORC has been documenting the relation between religious affiliation and social attitudes since 1972.[23] One of their findings is that certain Protestant denominations can be grouped together along a liberal-conservative continuum. Protestant liberal religions include Episcopalians, Unitarians, Presbyterians, and Congregationalists. Protestant moderates include Methodists and Lutherans. Protestant conservatives include a number of fundamentalist groups, as well as Baptists and Southern Baptists. Sectarian differences among Jews (Reformed, Orthodox, Conservative, etc.) are not documented in these studies, but Jews in general are seen as quite liberal. Such distinctions are useful in analyzing social and cultural attitudes.

Protestant fundamentalists and Baptists evidence the most conservative attitudes. According to the NORC criteria, they are "often unwilling to allow an atheist the basic civil liberties — to make a speech, teach in a college, or have a book in a public library." Only about 20 percent in this group support all three of these rights. The percentage of support is much higher in other religious groups: 40 percent among Catholics, 54 percent in liberal Protestant denominations, and 61 percent among Jews.

Similar differences are apparent with regard to attitudes about sex, marriage, and child rearing. Fundamentalists and Baptists express the most conservative attitudes. They condemn homosexual behavior, premarital sex, abortion, birth control information for teens, divorce, and new roles for women. Catholics resemble fundamentalists, especially with regard to attitudes on abortion, divorce, birth control information for teens, and new roles for women. Protestant liberal denominations and Jews are the most progressive on all of these issues, with moderate Protestant denominations somewhere in the middle.

Fundamentalists and Baptists also put great emphasis on the obedience of children to parents; 45 percent see it as among the top three most important child-rearing values. Lutherans, Methodists, and Catholics see obedience as less important; around 30 percent of these groups rate it among the top three child-rearing values. Only around 18 percent of Jews and Episcopalians include it among the top three values.

Despite these differences on sex, marriage, and child rearing, religious groups hardly differ with respect to their level of marital satisfaction reported in the NORC studies. About 45 percent of the people in each religion and denomination report "a very great deal of satisfaction" with their family life.

EMERGENCE OF A GAY AND LESBIAN COMMUNITY

The recent emergence of a community of gay men and lesbians provides an excellent example of how communities develop in a society. There is a question, however, as to whether gays and lesbians represent one "homosexual" community or two distinct communities. Although gay men and lesbians share a number of common experiences, they also have had different kinds of experiences. For instance, Philip Blumstein and Pepper Schwartz find that gay men share a common male socialization experience with "straight" men which makes them more similar in thought and action to other men than to lesbian women. The same is true the other way around; lesbians generally have more commonalities with heterosexual women than they do with gay men.[24] Frances Fitzgerald observes that gay men and lesbians also differ in their relationships to one another and in the way they have developed community life. While acknowledging the many healthy strengths in the gay and lesbian communities, she points out that gay men tend to form atomistic and impersonal communities and to be very business-oriented, rationalistic, and hierarchical. Lesbians tend to be far more communal; even their business groups are likely to include encounter groups and other structures which encourage open communication and cooperation. She also notes that lesbians tend to become involved in close and emotionally intense friendships, "private and intimate to the point of suffocation."[25]

Two characteristics distinguish the lesbian and gay community or communities from heterosexual communities. First, gays and lesbians are not socialized into the homosexual community as children; that is, they do not learn the roles, values, and expectations of the society in the normal process of growing up. They learn the ways of the homosexual community after they have "come out," that is, after they have made a more-or-less conscious choice to become a part of that community. Second, because of the severe stigmatization they experience, gays and lesbians tend to be enveloped in a certain amount of protective secrecy, and relations with heterosexual outgroup members are often guarded.[26]

Deviant Group or Minority Group?

Everyone would not agree that gays and lesbians ought to be seen as a community or communities. In the past, they have been defined as deviants and therefore distinguishable from minorities. Homosexual conduct has been studied in courses on abnormal psychology and social deviance, rather than in courses on normal growth and development. William Newman sees a good deal of commonality in deviant groups and minority groups, in that both are devalued, experience hostility, and have little social power. But deviants, he believes, "explicitly reject and violate legal norms" and would not be recognized as having a legitimate *claim* to power.[27] Newman correctly notes the need to distinguish between minority groups and deviant groups, but doing so raises other questions. When blacks rejected and violated Jim Crow laws which forced them to sit in the back of the bus or to drink from a segregated water fountain, were they acting as deviants rather than as minorities who were calling attention to unjust laws? Similarly, are homosexuals who reject and violate legal norms about homosexual behavior being deviant, or are they clamoring against injustice?

Deviant and minority groups represent opposite ends of a continuum of group status. From a labeling perspective, social movements can change perceptions about the status of groups in a society.[28] When enough members of a society recognize a just cause and struggle to achieve it, deviant status may be overcome. The gay and lesbian rights movement of the past two decades or so appears to be just such a social movement. Lesbians and gay men have claimed the right to be seen as minority communities, not as deviants. As Donald Webster Cory, one of the earliest defenders of homosexual rights, observes:

. . . our minority status is similar, in a variety of respects, to that of national, religious, and other ethnic groups: in the denial of civil liberties; in the legal, extra-legal, and quasi-legal discrimination; in the assignment of an inferior social position; in the exclusion from the mainstreams of life and culture; in the development of the protection and security of intragroup association; in the development of a special language and literature and a set of moral tenets within our group.[29]

In many countries, including the United States, it is legal to discriminate against lesbians and gays. Meredith Gould maintains that statutory (legal) oppression and **homophobia**, or irrational fear of homosexuals, characterize all American social institutions.[30] "Good citizens" are instructed by governments and many religions to treat homosexuals as immoral criminals or mentally ill individuals. Sexual behavior not intended for procreation was condemned as unnatural after Constantine proclaimed Christianity the official religion of the Roman Empire, early in the fourth century AD. For centuries, under church law, men and women suspected of homosexual behavior were tortured, mutilated, or burned at the stake. After a return to secular law in the twelfth century, antihomosexual attitudes became a cultural value supported by the developing science of medicine. Beginning in the nineteenth century, psychiatry also gave credence to antihomosexual values.[31]

Such discrimination recently has been challenged by a strong civil rights movement among gays and lesbians, supported by sympathetic heterosexuals. This has led to increased, although certainly not total, acceptance of gays and lesbians by the general public. The American Psychiatric Association no longer considers homosexual behavior as a mental disorder. Laws forbidding discrimination on the basis of sexual orientation have been passed in some cities and one state, Wisconsin. A "gay rights" ordinance was vigorously resisted in the Chicago City Council, but it was passed by a vote of 28–17 in December 1988 after it had been renamed a "human rights" ordinance and protection against discrimination in housing, employment, and public accommodations was extended not only to homosexuals but to anyone whose marital or parental status, military discharge status, or source of income might be a source of discrimination. The traditional race, color, sex, age, and religious groupings were also included.

Emergence of the Community

The emergence of a gay and lesbian community appears to be a unique historical phenomenon. While homosexuality has been practiced in almost every society and in every historical period, a common homosexual identity, with an emphasis on coupling and the development of community, appears to be related to advanced industrial, free-market societies. Barry Adam hypothesizes that the same forces which shaped changes in heterosexual family life with the development of capitalism also promoted the modern homosexual community. He asserts that as a feudal, agricultural society changed to a modern, industrial, free-market society, homosexual relations were released from a dominant heterosexual kinship system. Exclusive homosexuality became possible, and autonomous, self-aware homosexual communities came into being.[32]

Gay and lesbian voluntary associations have existed in the United States throughout most of the twentieth century.[33] Vigorous organizing activities in the community followed the "Stonewall riots" in 1969, when New York City police who were hassling the clients of bars frequented by "counterculture" gays and some lesbians met with resistance as they tried to shut down the Stonewall Inn. A "gay liberation front" emerged, accompanied by a number of gay and lesbian civil rights organizations, social clubs, business organizations, newspapers and magazines, and social service associations. As a result, a strong community spirit developed both within neighborhoods and across the country.

The gay and lesbian community is largely identificational, made up of people who share a common identity and who have developed unique subcultural lifestyles. In certain large cities, however, it also has become a locational community based in certain neighborhoods. This is particularly true for gay men. Such areas as West Los Angeles, the Castro in San Francisco, and Christopher Street in New York are largely gay neighborhoods. In smaller cities, the tendency is for gays to live near one another. The lesbian neighborhood is not so common, and lesbian communities are regarded not as geographical locations but as being comprised of individuals loosely joined by history, jargon, and significant activities. Deborah Goleman Wolf uses this definition in noting that the term *lesbian community* is "used by the women themselves to refer to the continuing social networks of lesbians who are committed to the lesbian-feminist lifestyle, who participate in various community activities and projects, and who congregate socially."[34] She concludes that there is a "sociopsychological unity" which holds lesbians together. In a similar vein, Fitzgerald observes that in San Francisco there are some small, loose enclaves of lesbians, but they are not nearly as clearly defined as those in which gay men live.[35]

Out of the community experience, a gay and lesbian culture has been emerging. The richness and diversity of the community has been described in a number of works, and it is no longer commonly believed that gays and lesbians are homogeneous groups which can be easily identified by the behaviors and lifestyles of their members. This is the major point made by Alan Bell and Martin Weinberg in their book *Homosexualities*.[36]

Lesbians and gay men are found in all racial and ethnic groups, in all social classes, and undoubtedly in all religions. The experience of being homosexual and being part of another community or class may add to the difficulties they face. Some religions are extremely intolerant of homosexuals. Ethnic and racial communities also vary in terms of their acceptance of homosexual conduct and identity.[37] Hispanics are often assumed to be particularly repressive of homosexual behavior. Native Americans, who often accorded social approval and dignity to homosexual behavior before they were conquered and displaced by Europeans, now appear to have adopted more hostile attitudes toward it.

Recognition of the gay and lesbian community has improv·
vices provided to members. Until recently, according to B
only 'help' that homosexuals could expect from the human
was in the direction of being made over to become 'norma·
Now the gay and lesbian community has become a focus of socia·
vention, including support services for parents of gays and lesbians, wo·
teenagers, counseling for couples, senior citizen services, and help for peop·
with sexually transmitted diseases, such as acquired immune deficiency syndrome (AIDS).[39]

RACIAL AND ETHNIC COMMUNITIES

The United States, like many other national societies, is composed of many racially and ethnically diverse communities. To examine this diversity, the concepts of race and ethnicity must first be understood. Along with the concept
of minority and majority status, to be discussed in the next section, these concepts focus on different ways to develop an understanding of the strengths and
problems that may become evident in the diverse groups in a society. Together
they are extremely important in planning and providing social services.

THE MEANING OF RACE

Race refers to biological differences among groups of people. Although we use
the term frequently in everyday language, it is relatively new, originating in
the Enlightenment period of eighteenth-century Europe.[40] Naturalists, who
used scientific methods to study human variation, began to classify people according to their visible differences. The use of classification systems, or **taxonomies**, is one of the oldest and most respected methods in science.

Attempts at Racial Classification

In a work on the unity of man and nature which was published in 1735, Carolus
Linnaeus, a Swedish botanist, identified the human species and classified humans into four color groups. He saw these as fixed subgroups within the species
but acknowledged that the division was arbitrary. He did not, however, refer
to these four groups as races.

George Louis LeClerc was the first to use the term *race*. He distinguished six
races but saw them not as fixed subgroups but as existing in a continual, flexible, ever-changing process. Johann Blumenbach, the father of physical anthropology, later proposed a typology of five races based on differences in human
skull measurements. He created the "science" of phrenology but, like Linnaeus, he maintained that his division into five races was arbitrary and that
human differences are so complex they defy the creation of a reliable classification system.

It was nineteenth-century scholars and political officials who developed the

.deas of race and racism. Whereas eighteenth-century naturalists studied differences, nineteenth-century thinkers looked for **individious differences** of an objectionable nature which could cause envy, discontent, or resentment. Arthur de Gobineau, a French aristocrat, argued in 1854 that the French nobility had descended directly from a noble Aryan race and thus was superior to the peasants and city dwellers who had promoted the French Revolution. Some 50 years later, in Britain, Henry Stewart Chamberlain argued for a connection between race and culture, maintaining that because Aryans were of a superior race their culture also was superior, and they were deserving of the empires they had built. Francis Galton, a British anthropologist who developed the science of eugenics, went even further with his dictum that only superior people should populate the world. Influenced by these ideas, Adolf Hitler would argue in the twentieth century for the superiority of Aryans and would attempt to eliminate the "inferior" Jewish race.[41]

The ideas of thinkers such as these came to be regarded as "common knowledge" and "common sense" about race. According to these early ideas, a small, fixed number of pure races or racial types exists. These races consist of a series of highly interrelated physical attributes (skin color, blood, hair type, etc.) which are passed down in their entirety from one generation to another. Thus races are immutable differences which can be traced back to the dawn of creation. External physical attributes are passed on as a package, and the mixing of people from two different races leads to a fairly predictable blending of the races. These externally visible racial characteristics determine culture and individual behavior. And, when races are placed on an evolutionary scale, certain races can be shown to be superior, as evidenced by their culture and behavior.

At the same time this kind of thinking was pervading everyday life — and to some extent it still may be — evidence was being gathered to disprove it. Though his work was virtually ignored for years, Gregor Mendel, a nineteenth-century Austrian botanist, patiently studied the genetics of inheritance and mapped out the **law of segregation**, which maintains that inheritance rests "not on blends of parental qualities, but on combinations of parental genes, units that preserve their own particular nature unchanged through the generations. Every individual is a new combination of existing genes." [42] In short, Mendel taught that **phenotype**, or external physical characteristics, could not indicate anything about **genotype**, or internal characteristics. Knowing what a group of people look like today is no indication of what they might have looked like in some distant past.

While Mendel's work was being ignored, scientists were continually trying to classify humans into discrete or separate races. No two scientists, it would appear, were ever able to agree on the number of races. While some said there were 4, others said there were 34.[43] In popular culture in the United States, the idea of three pure races — Caucasoid, Mongoloid, and Negroid — was adopted.

All attempts to classify humans into discrete races are inevitably doomed to failure, since most differences which exist among peoples are continuous, not qualitative. Classification systems based on continuous differences, such as height, skin color, or skull shape, are necessarily arbitrary. Height, for instance, is measured in inches (or centimeters), and each person can be rated as relatively tall or short. But one person may be 5'10" and another 5'11" or 5'9". Where can the lines possibly be drawn to divide the world's populations into short, tall, and medium height? Another example is skin tone, which is determined by the relative mix of three hormones possessed by all humans: melanin, hemoglobin, and carotene. From the north pole to the equator, the residents show less hemoglobin and more melanin, but there is no clear dividing line between those who are dark and those who are light. There are some differences among people which are qualitative, however. Blood is the best example; blood types may be A, B, AB, or O. But blood types cannot be used successfully to divide the races. There is no such thing as "black blood" or "white blood." All groups have all blood types, to a lesser or greater extent.

Contemporary Ideas on Race

Today, theorists generally either reject the concept of race altogether or define it in terms of gene pools or breeding populations.[44] The idea of race as **breeding populations** starts from the Mendelian law of segregation and accepts that races come about essentially through groups of people living in geographical or social isolation.[45] Peoples who live and procreate among themselves inevitably develop a pool of genes out of which similarities in physical appearance emerge. The most physically and socially distant are the most likely to be noticeably different in appearance. This view acknowledges, however, that races are not discrete, distinct groups but simply "local limitations in the total variation in man." [46] Those who reject the idea of race altogether argue that since any designation of race is essentially arbitrary in nature, and since the concept has caused so much harm, it should be dismissed from scientific discourse.

Regardless of whether or not the concept of race should be rejected, its political and social nature cannot be ignored. Race may or may not be a biological fact, but it is certainly a social fact. In the political sense, race can be understood as "a social construction of reality," something created by peoples and used for political purposes as a way of justifying enslavement, colonial conquest, or genocide. To understand the politics of this social construction we need only compare how race is defined in the United States with how it is defined in other societies.

In American society, traditional definitions of the "Negro" race, for instance, stipulate that a person is black to the extent that he or she has any identifiable features which indicate African ancestry. In some states, court decisions have produced legal definitions. In Louisiana, "colored persons" were defined as a result of *Lee* v. *New Orleans Great Northern RR Co.* (1910). "Colored persons," the decision read, were "all persons with any appreciable mixture of Negro blood."

ne states, such as Arkansas, have statutes which define race: "Persons of Negro race" are "any person who has in his or her veins any Negro blood
whatever." [47]

If it were possible to stand back from the "common sense" of American culture, we could ask why members of the white race are not defined as people
"with any appreciable mixture of white blood" or "any person who has in his
or her veins any Caucasian blood whatsoever." In the United States, to be
white is to be "pure," and to be black is to be tainted. A child born of a white
father and a black mother might just as easily be considered white as black.
Puerto Rico is a society which traditionally has taken this approach. Until very
recently, Puerto Ricans measured their whiteness; to be considered black
(*prieto*), a person had to be virtually of pure African ancestry. Puerto Ricans
used a host of terms, such as *mulatto*, *trigueño*, and *moreno*, to describe people
who are white but might have some African ancestry. The word *negro* (black)
was not used to designate a race but simply to designate the color black, or it
was used as a term of endearment between spouses, lovers, and friends; it carried absolutely no connotation of skin color. Only recently did the word begin
to be used to designate skin color, an unfortunate consequence of colonializa-
tion in Puerto Rico.

Defining a person as nonwhite proves just as difficult. Native Americans
(Indians) and Asians are designated as nonwhite in the U.S. Census. Native
Americans are defined by law; to be on the roll of most tribes, a person must
be at least 25 percent American Indian. Definitions of Asian are more difficult;
there is no standard for how many generations of Asian ancestry are required
for this designation. Hispanics are designated as white unless a particular
Hispanic person says she or he is not white. This is the case even though most
Mexican Americans are *mestizo*, that is, of mixed Spanish and Indian
heritage.[48]

ETHNIC COMMUNITIES AND ETHNICITY

The difficulties of defining race are one reason we have referred to racial *and*
ethnic communities rather than racial *or* ethnic communities. We consider the
concepts of ethnicity and race to be equally inclusive. Races can include peoples of many ethnic groups. Ethnic groups can include people of any color.

An **ethnic group** has been defined by Richard Burkey as "a community
group based upon the ascribed status of a diffuse ancestry that is maintained
by similarities of culture, language, and/or phenotype" [49] and by Richard
Shermerhorn as "a collectivity within a larger society having a real or putative
common ancestry."[50] These definitions take into account four important features of ethnic groups.

First, ethnic groups generally are subcommunities within a larger national
state. Thus, where everyone might be American, individuals might also be
Anglo-Americans, Afro-Americans, Jewish Americans, or Irish Americans.

Jews are a heterogeneous religious and ethnic
community. Here a conservative Rabbi celebrates a
wedding. The men wear yarmulkes. The bride and
groom stand under a chupah, which is inscribed with
the words "Voice of the bride." *Barbara Alper/Stock,
Boston.*

Or, where everyone might be a citizen of the Soviet Union, individuals might also be Russians, Ukrainians, Uzbeks, Byelorussians, Lithuanians, Estonians, Jews, Georgians, White Russians, Armenians, Latvians, or members of other ethnic groups.[51]

Second, ethnic groups are based on a sense of common ancestry. That is, the subjective reality, the perception of members that they are as one and are perceived by others in the same way, is more important than the objective reality, actually being of a common ancestry. Many peoples who became part of the ethnic mix of the United States did not arrive with a sense of common ancestry but only developed such a sense once they were here. The people we think of as Italian Americans in actuality came to the United States as Sicilians, Calabrians, and a myriad of other identities. While often these identities still are important in individual families, they tend to get lost in the identity of Italian American. When blacks were forced to come to the United States, they were brought from different parts of Africa and from different tribes within Africa. Their identity as a group in the United States emerged only as a result of their being forced together by whites.

The sense of common ancestry emerges in the course of history as new experiences with other nations and communities are encountered. It comes about because other communities define a people as of similar ancestry, and they come to accept that definition and start to act as a separate, distinct community. It follows, of course, that ethnic groups also decompose. In this respect there are two opposing views of American social development. The idea of the society as a melting pot implies that ethnic identities should eventually disappear and only a single American identity should remain (see Chapter 4). The idea of a multicultural society implies that ethnic identities should not be amalgamated, and American society should remain a mosaic of separate, diverse, and equally proud identities.

Third, ethnic groups are, at their root, collections of families with a common ancestry. Ancestry implies marriage, procreation, birth, and socialization of the young. Ethnic groups thus are pools of possible partners for mating, and new members enter primarily through birth or adoption. Selection for membership is on an ascriptive basis, determined by characteristics present at birth (see Chapter 2), and members of ethnic groups hold an **ascribed status**. An **achieved status**, in contrast, results when selection is on an achievement basis. Members join these groups more or less because they want to. In sum, ethnic groups are those that people are born into and are reared to cherish.

Fourth, the sense of shared ancestry is reflected in the development of an ethnic identity, or ethnicity. Ethnic groups are held together for a number of reasons, including coercive experiences from outside or within the particular group. However, the most important ingredient holding an ethnic group together usually is its ethnicity. **Ethnicity** can be thought of as the psychological or attitudinal core of the group. It reflects all those things the members believe they share in common.[52]

Factors Associated with Ethnicity

Three factors commonly associated with ethnicity are language, culture, and physical type.[53]

Language. The boundaries between ethnic groups are most often structured around language and styles of speech. Ethnic-group members maintain and, in many cases, develop their own language and socialize each other to speak it properly. Outgroup members become "foreigners." This phenomenon is apparent even when ethnic groups share the same language as the host society. Members develop subtle styles and inflections and unique words and phrases, and in this way they set themselves apart. Black Americans are believed to have developed a special way of speaking English which is based in part on African influences and in part on their own need to celebrate their uniqueness.[54]

Culture. The term *culture*, as we have noted, generally means "shared symbolic meanings,"[55] that is, all the beliefs, values, norms, and traditions that govern social interaction among members of a society or between members and outsiders. But, although shared symbolic meanings form the attitudinal core out of which actual behaviors emerge, behaviors are not always a good indication of beliefs, values, and norms. It is not uncommon for situations, especially those that are cross-cultural in nature, to demand a behavior which is not in keeping with the culture. Similarly, as James Green aptly points out, culture and ethnicity should not be thought of as some fixed set of traits which define a group and make for easy categorization of it.[56] Social workers who presume that members of particular ethnic groups can be pigeonholed into categories will unwisely stereotype their clients. Ethnic culture is dynamic and constantly emerging and changing.

Physical Type. The practice of continual intermarriage in ethnic communities leads to the development of certain kinds of physical features which distinguish members from other groups. There is considerable debate about the reality of race, as we have seen, and there is no such thing as a pure race. Races are formed essentially through the social, environmental, and biological processes surrounding birth and mate selection. Thus, ethnic communities (Italians, Afro-Americans, Swedes, etc.) acquire certain physically distinguishing characteristics, not because they originated from some pure race which existed in antiquity but simply because, as they have come to see themselves as one, they have increasingly intermarried and procreated. Of course, there is considerable variation in physical appearance within these groups. Many members do not look at all as they might be expected to look. Moreover, sometimes what appears different about people's appearance is not so much what they look like but how they act. Two first cousins, both of Polish ancestry, looked like they could have been twins. But one was born in Argentina and the other in the United States, and one had an obviously Hispanic demeanor while the other was just as obviously American. Anyone seeing them separately would not mistake their ethnic origin, but seeing them together was startling.

COMMUNITY RELATIONS

As ethnic communities emerge, they celebrate their sense of common ancestry by developing organizations or associations which serve to hold the group together as well as to help the group meet its goals and obtain needed resources. Ethnic associations include churches, lodges, clubs, businesses, political parties, banks, and interest groups or lobbies. It is not uncommon for social services to be provided by ethnic groups. These associations often represent the "natural helping systems" within the community.

Those who understand multigroup societies in terms of ethnic groups and ethnicity generally emphasize that the source of problems between groups has to do with cultural differences and the difficulty of bridging the cultural gap between groups. Problems between Hispanics and Anglos (whites), for instance, are believed to relate to the fact that Hispanics have developed language and cultural values and norms which are very different from those developed by Anglos. When members of these groups get together, communication often breaks down and expectations get confused. Similarly, when the problems that are assumed to exist between whites and blacks are seen in terms of ethnicity, the focus is on differences in communication styles.[57] When a social worker of one ethnic group meets a client of another ethnic group, for instance, the worker must become aware of the ethnically distinct origins of her own behavior, while respecting and trying to tune into the ethnically distinct origins of her client.

MINORITY AND MAJORITY GROUPS

Another way multiethnic societies can be understood is through the concepts of minority group and majority group. Some racial and ethnic groups come to be minority groups in a society, while others become majority groups. For instance, in contemporary American society, Anglo-Americans, including all those with origins in northern and western Europe, are ethnic groups, but they are not minority groups. Afro-Americans, Puerto Ricans, Mexican Americans, and Native Americans are ethnic groups which are also minority groups.

In everyday usage, *minority* and *majority* are terms which refer to the size of a group; minorities are groups that are believed to be relatively small in size, whereas majorities are believed to be relatively large. But this everyday usage somehow falls short in the case of specific examples. For instance, the white community of apartheid South Africa would seldom be referred to as a minority group, even though whites represent less than 10 percent of the population of South Africa. Similarly, in the United States, it is not unusual for women to be referred to as a minority group, although they constitute slightly more than half of the population. Size may be a consideration in determining minority status, but size per se is not the distinguishing characteristic of minority and majority groups.

When sociologists use the term **minority groups** they usually mean groups that are negatively valued and treated with hostility within a society. Perhaps the most frequently quoted definition was written by Louis Wirth. He describes a minority group as "a group of people who, because of their physical or cultural characteristics, are singled out from others in the society in which they live for differential and unequal treatment and who therefore regard themselves as objects of collective discrimination."[58]

Other definitions generally focus on the same issues. According to John R. Howard, "the fundamental fact of ethnic stratification is domination of one group by another. Members of minority groups experience stigma on categorical grounds."[59] Edward Sagarin notes that "it is when the social differentiation takes place followed by the social inequality, . . . resulting in collective and irrelevant discrimination, that the minority emerges."[60]

While definitions of minorities abound, definitions of majorities are seldom found. As a result, the concept of majority group is less well understood, and this in turn produces a less-then-full understanding of minority groups.

Newman uses the criteria of relative group size, social differences, and power to distinguish minority from majority:

> Minority groups may be defined as groups that vary from the social norms or archetypes in some manner, are subordinate with regard to the distribution of social power, and rarely constitute more than one-half of the population of the society in which they are found. . . . In contrast to minority groups, majority groups may be defined as those groups that create or enforce the social norms or exemplify the social archetypes (trait characteristics of groups that are the most highly desired or rewarded), are superordinate with regard to the distribution of power, and are neither extremely large nor extremely small.[61]

Aside from the issue of group size, the two key features of Newman's definition are that majorities "create or enforce the social norms" and are "superordinate with regard to the distribution of power." If words like *stigmatized, victimized, discriminated against, oppressed*, and *disadvantaged* are associated with ethnic minorities and minority individuals, then words like *advantaged* and *powerful* are associated with ethnic majorities and majority individuals. **Majority groups** create the stigmas attached to minorities and are powerful enough to victimize, discriminate against, and take advantage of them.

ETHNIC MINORITIES AND MINORITY INDIVIDUALS

Minority status is generally an ascribed status in that the people making up the minority group have been born into the status or at least are believed to have had little choice in the matter. Therefore, minority groups often are ethnic groups, that is, collections of families, and they constitute **ethnic minorities**. Examples include Afro-Americans, Mexican Americans, Puerto Ricans, and Filipinos. Their stigmas and disadvantages are suffered collectively in family life, and their children must learn to deal with a hostile environment.[62] The whole family confronts hostility and devaluation by the larger society.

n contemporary usage, however, minority groups are not always collections of families. Women, the aged, sexual minorities, and the disabled are groups which often are referred to as minorities and are believed to suffer common devaluation and hostility, but they are not collections of families. Membership in such groups is ascribed on the basis of people's characteristics as individuals, not as family members. To distinguish members of these groups from ethnic minorities, we refer to them as **minority individuals**. The position of women, children, and the elderly in society is examined in Chapter 7 in the section on family politics. The position of the disabled as a minority group capable of being mainstreamed in society is discussed in Chapter 11 in the section on normality and the disabled.

TYPES OF MINORITIES

Minority groups are singled out on the basis of particular traits members are believed to have in common. Not only is the group perceived to be different from the majority in the particular trait, but the difference is considered undesirable. Groups differ in different ways. Some differences are accorded high value and assure people of supportive experiences, while others are accorded low value and result in hostile experiences. Having a British accent or eating French food are differences that often are considered good in American society. Having a Mexican accent or eating soul food have not been so valued, at least until recently.

Newman postulates that minority status — both ethnic-minority and minority-individual status — evolves around physical, cognitive, or behavioral characteristics.[63] While these categories are not mutually exclusive, they are useful in thinking about the various kinds of minority groups that are possible.

Physical minorities are those that look different from the majority. Perhaps the most important example is race. Afro-Americans have been singled out for differential treatment largely on the basis of their skin color. To be dark-skinned and have tightly curled hair in a society which equates beauty with fair skin and blondness is to suffer minority status. Other physical differences can be used as a basis for singling out minorities, however. According to Newman, to the extent that people with disabilities and the aged are considered minority groups or minority individuals, they would also be physical minorities.

Cognitive minorities are those whose low status has evolved around the beliefs and values they hold. Ethnic and religious groups are the most obvious examples; they believe and follow different cultural and religious traditions. Minority status also can evolve around political beliefs. The Communist party in the United States might be considered a minority, distinguishable from the Democratic and Republican majority. Newman asserts that women who are part of the women's movement are a cognitive minority because they hold beliefs that are at variance with the gender-role norms of society.

Behavioral minorities are those that do not so much look or think differently from the majority but that behave in ways the majority believes are undesirable. Perhaps the most obvious example, according to Newman, is gays and lesbians. They do not necessarily think differently from the heterosexual majority, and they do not necessarily look different. Many "unliberated" and "in the closet" homosexuals may actually yearn to be heterosexual and may believe that heterosexuals are correct in exhibiting hostility toward them. It is their behavior, their attempt to sexually fulfill themselves, which is not valued in society and produces their minority status.

WOMEN AS A MINORITY

Women constitute a very slight majority in the population of the United States; in 1986, there were 94.8 males for every 100 females.[64] Nevertheless, women usually are included in discussions of minority groups. Certainly, as the chapters on family life in Part III will discuss more fully, women are the object of economic and other forms of discrimination. Women's wages still were just 70 percent of men's in 1987; median weekly earnings for men were $445, while for women they were $309. Single mothers heading families are the most disadvantaged; in 1985, when the median money income for all families was $27,735, it was just $13,660 for households headed by women (see Chapter 7). Women also continue to have a subordinate social status. While the religious and secular laws that gave men authority over women in the family and in society have largely been discarded, women's position continues to be subordinated. Women still may be regarded as somehow deviant, treated as sexual objects, spoken to rather than listened to, excluded from occupational and political leadership, segregated into female-oriented occupations, or expected to function largely within the realm of family life.[65]

Nevertheless, despite such evidence of discriminatory treatment, it is not clear that the term *minority group* pertains to women. As we have noted, minority groups have traditionally been understood as collections of ethnic or racial families. By themselves, heterosexual women do not form families or communities, though homosexual women may do so. The status of all women, therefore, cannot be adequately understood by defining them as a separate community or as a group independent of the communities of which they are a part. The ways in which women are tied to various social class, religious, and ethnic and racial communities to a large extent determines the nature and extent of subordination they experience. Their status also differs across time and space; all women are not discriminated against in the same ways.[66]

Newman does not consider women in general to be a minority group. While the fact that women represent more than half the population in itself does not preclude minority status, he points out that the norms of heterosexual women do not differ from the norms of society. Societal expectations are that women will be heterosexual and function within family and social life. He does consider women involved in the women's movement to be a cognitive minority group, however, as we have noted.[67]

But categorizing women as those who are a minority and those who are not is unwarranted. The position we take is that all women in contemporary society are subordinated, but their status is best understood in terms of the class, religious, and racial and ethnic communities of which they are a part. The question is not whether women are subordinate to men but why it is that some women perceive themselves to be subordinate members of their communities and other women do not. The issues are very similar to those about social class consciousness raised earlier in this chapter. For feminist consciousness to emerge, a number of social and psychological preconditions are necessary: There must be a common associational context, a high degree of similarity in background, a shared awareness of undesirable status, an agreement as to the cause of this status, and some kind of organized attempt at change. There must also be opportunities within the communities for a feminist view to take hold. Obviously, these conditions are not met in all communities today, and women of different communities have very different understandings of their status.

Three Forms of Feminism

Although feminist consciousness is evident among some racial- and ethnic-minority women, it is most apparent among affluent white women of European background and with mainstream Jewish or Christian beliefs. Yet feminist consciousness itself takes different forms. Janet A. Nes and Peter Iadicola identify three strains within feminism: liberal, radical, and socialist. The three differ on a number of dimensions, including their understanding of human nature, inequality and the factors perpetuating it, and the good society and how it is to be achieved.[68]

According to Nes and Iadicola, **liberal feminists** believe that men and women do not differ in their human nature; inequality becomes a problem only when there is too much of it or it results from discrimination. They also maintain that gender-role socialization teaches women to deny discrimination exists and that a better society can be achieved by working within the system to bring about equal opportunity. **Radical feminists** believe that women are different from men; women are more caring, loving, and spiritual and less competitive and individualistic. Inequality is not natural to humans but stems from patriarchy, that is, from the sex-gender oppression of men. Sex inequality is perpetuated largely because men benefit from it and work in their own self-interest. The good radical society is one in which women's values become dominant, and it can only come about through self-help, separatism, consciousness raising, and the promotion of **androgyny** (attitudes, beliefs, and behaviors that are not specific to one gender). **Socialist feminists** believe that women and men have different values due to the structure of sex and gender roles in society. Inequality is rooted in social class as well as in patriarchy, and it is maintained not only because men benefit but also because capitalist interests benefit; a sex-segregated labor force and unpaid labor in the home (housework) assure greater profit. The good socialist society is one in which all forms of oppression are eradicated, including those based on social class and sex or gender. This society can only be achieved by organizing all oppressed groups and building coalitions among them.

MINORITY-MAJORITY RELATIONS

Because minority groups and individuals exist in a social relationship with majority groups and individuals, they must be understood in terms of that relationship. Newman's differentiation between minority and majority groups on the basis of the social power of the majority to stigmatize and discriminate against the minority (discussed above) is useful in developing such an understanding.

Competition and Conflict

The relationship between minority and majority essentially is one of hostility; competition and conflict are inherent in the distinctions between the two groups. This hostility is generated not only because the groups may have developed different languages and cultures, so their communication is hampered, but because they have very different interests. Majorities are interested in maintaining their advantage; they want to continue to create and enforce the social norms and to hold their superordinate position. Minorities are interested in reducing or overcoming their stigma and disadvantage. They want a hand in creating and enforcing the norms, and they want to be able to experience some degree of autonomy and power.

Just what is it that minorities and majorities are fighting over? The nature of the hostility obviously will vary, depending on the type of minority group involved. In the broadest sense the struggle is about dominance and control, and since the struggle of minority and majority takes place within a national society, the prize they are seeking is dominance and control of the state. Burkey makes the point abundantly clear: "A dominant ethnic group or race exists when the majority of the major positions of the state are occupied by the members of one ethnic group or race."[69] The struggle, however, often is played out around more specific issues. With respect to ethnic and racial minority groups, at least two areas of competition and conflict can be identified. One is economic, and the other involves national character or cultural ascendancy.

In part the hostility between minority and majority groups is economic and is demonstrated in social class relationships. As workers, minorities and majorities often are part of the same class, and the conflict is about which group will get the good jobs, the seniority, the security, and the good paycheck. Economic issues such as jobs and housing are believed to be at the root of much of the conflict between minorities of color and dominant whites in the United States today.[70]

Minorities and majorities also are engaged in conflict over the national character. This struggle can be defined in two ways. In the first, the struggle is over whose cultural characteristics are to typify the nation; whose language will be official, whose heroes will be honored, whose traditions and holidays will be observed. This struggle is most often associated with ethnic and religious differences, but it is also in the background of other differences. In the second, the struggle is over whose physical and behavioral characteristics are to typify the national *image*. In the United States, this involves decisions about what physical features are to be taken as the standard in identifying beauty and personifying the typical American. What does Uncle Sam look like? Who will be chosen as Miss America, the typical all-American boy, or the girl next door?

Limitations to Hostility

Although the relationship between majority and minority is by definition hostile, the hostility need not always be open, nor must it necessarily be intense. It is not unusual for a semblance of harmony to appear in the relations between minorities and majorities. At one time there may be civil strife, while at another the relationship may actually appear amicable. During the latter periods, majority-group members may assume there is no problem, and minority-group members may be happy. It is also quite possible for the stigma and disadvantage to operate in subtle ways rather than being evident. In some periods hostility may take the form of warfare or genocide, while in others it takes the form of social snobbery or failure to extend friendship.

Moreover, even though hostility typifies minority-majority relations, minority and majority persons are not always aware of it. Hostility is often obscured by "the way things are." Where we live and whom we make friends with are often shaped by the hostility that pervades minority-majority relationships, but few in the majority group would assume that they are acting in a hostile manner when they make friends and choose a place to live. They perceive their behavior as normal and natural, merely a matter of finding a good place to live and making compatible friendships. Nevertheless, minority-group members are likely to feel the hostility which is perhaps inadvertently generated by the majority-group members in making such decisions.

IMPLICATIONS FOR PRACTICE

This chapter has explored the nature of community life in the United States, giving special attention to communities based on identification: those communities that are held together by affection, historical circumstances, and a sense of common destiny.

Identificational communities are important to social service workers for at least three reasons. First, many of the attitudes and values of individuals derive from their everyday experiences in communities. Second, many of the social and psychological troubles experienced by individuals and families have their origin in the public issues connected to the communities in which they live.

Third, communities support their members, and thus they build strengths and resources to help individuals and families cope and adapt. Social service workers, therefore, need to orient themselves to the community context of client behavior.

BUILDING A HELPING RELATIONSHIP

There are many ways to incorporate the notion of identificational community into social service practice with individuals and families. In these concluding comments, we will synthesize the discussion of community life by focusing on how direct-service social workers build helping relationships with clients whose communities differ from their own. To build a helping relationship, the worker must generate accurate empathy and rapport and thus come to understand the client's needs and problems from the point of view of the client. A good helping relationship is a vital first step in effective practice.

Throughout this chapter two attributes of identificational communities have been stressed. Each community develops a unique culture, and each carries with it a certain status. In order to empathize and build rapport accurately, social workers must become sensitive to both of these attributes of communities.

When things go wrong in the relationship between a client and a social worker, the source of the difficulty may very well be in the cultural gap which exists between them. A black social worker, raised in her own culture, may make assumptions about the society which are foreign to her white, Hispanic, or Hmong clients. A social worker with an affluent, Episcopalian background is likely to hold very different values and norms than a poverty-class client who is a Southern Baptist would. Experiences in different communities can generate breakdowns in communication and lack of clarity in expectations on the part of workers and clients. When they come from different communities, they usually have been socialized to think and feel in particular ways and may fail to understand one another. Client "resistance" may then be evidenced in lower service utilization rates, higher rates of dropping out of service or missing appointments, and difficulties in reaching agreement as to the nature of a presenting problem and an appropriate intervention plan.

In establishing a helping relationship, social workers also must take into account how communities vary in terms of their status in a society. The important point for social work practice is that differences in *interest* are inherent in status differences. This has been brought out in the discussions in this chapter of majorities and minorities, social classes, and the lesbian and gay community. Lower-status groups are interested in improving their status, while higher-status groups are interested in maintaining theirs. The two goals may very well conflict, especially in a society of limited opportunities and resources. As a result, a special kind of dynamic may be present in relationships between clients from lower-status communities and social workers from higher-status communities.

Lower-status clients are not likely to accept the notion that higher-status social workers have their best interests in mind. They are more likely to perceive workers as members of "the system" who are not really interested in helping them. Gay men and lesbians are likely to distrust heterosexual social workers; ethnic-minority and lower-class clients are likely to distrust ethnic-majority and affluent, more educated social workers. Much of the resistance of lower-status clients, therefore, may originate in the status differences they perceive between themselves and social workers. If social workers are to establish a good helping relationship, they usually must attempt to see the problem from the perspective of clients who are of lower status than they themselves are. They must appreciate their clients' struggle to get ahead in spite of the devaluation and hostility they experience in the larger society. And they must demonstrate, through their attitudes and behaviors, that they are working in the best interests of their clients.

In summary, the study of community life helps social workers to anticipate potential difficulties in helping clients. Building a helping relationship requires getting beyond differences in culture and status and avoiding a breakdown in communication between social workers and clients. They may fail to communicate because they hold different attitudes, values, norms, and traditions or because clients do not trust workers to have their best interests at heart.

DISCUSSION QUESTIONS AND CLASS PROJECTS

1. Three reasons for studying community life are discussed in this chapter. Describe each of these. Give some other reasons why it is important for social workers to study communities.

2. Define what is meant by locational, identificational, and interest communities. Using these concepts, identify the communities to which you belong.

3. Describe the two ways in which sociologists have studied social classes.

4. Do you think the United States is a class society? How do you define classes, and how many classes do you think there are in American society? To what class do you belong? Do you think it is important for people to have a strong identification with or consciousness of their social class?

5. Are you a member of a religious denomination? How active are you in this denomination? Can you identify the values and attitudes you hold which are associated with this denomination? Do you think it is important for people to have a strong identification or consciousness of their religion?

6. Do you consider gay men and lesbians a "deviant group" or a minority group? What do you know about the gay and lesbian community in your area?

7. What is a race? How many races are there? Are American blacks a race?

8. Define and distinguish among the following:

ethnic group
ethnicity
ethnic minority
ethnic majority
minority group
majority group
minority individuals
genotype
phenotype
racial group

9. Select a community from your area (a social class community, a religious denomination community, gays and lesbians, an ethnic or racial community, a majority or minority community). With respect to this community gather information on the following: its culture (attitudes, values, norms, and traditions), its status, its strengths and resources, and its problems and needs.

NOTES

1. Robert B. Nisbett, *The Sociological Tradition* (New York: Basic Books, 1967), p. 47. The term *gemeinschaft* was coined by Ferdinand Tönnies in the nineteenth century to define a primary or folk community as one of two types of society. The other type, a *gesellschaft*, is an association with a common purpose which members join voluntarily.

2. Jessie Bernard, *The Sociology of Community* (Glenview, IL: Scott, Foresman, 1973), pp. 3–5.

3. An example of such descriptions of urban life is given in Robert E. Park, Ernest W. Burgess, and Roderick D. McKenzie, *The City* (Chicago: University of Chicago Press, 1967).

4. Philip E. Slater, *The Pursuit of Loneliness* (Boston: Beacon Press, 1970).

5. Bernard, *Sociology of Community*, pp. 3–4.

6. Ibid., p. 5. The idea of social work as a community underlies Gary A. Lloyd's *The Culture and Politics of Social Work* (San Jose, CA: San Jose State University, School of Social Work, 1978).

7. Max Weber, "Class, Status, Party," in V. Jeffries and H. E. Ransford (editors), *Social Stratification: A Multiple Hierarchy Approach* (Boston: Allyn and Bacon, 1980), pp. 89–98.

8. See Irving Krauss, *Stratification, Class, and Conflict* (New York: Free Press, 1976), pp. 12–17.

9. W. Lloyd Warner and Paul S. Lunt, *The Social Life of a Modern Community* (New Haven, CT: Yale University Press, 1941).

10. For a Marxist description of social classes, see K. Charles Loren, *Classes in the United States* (Davis, CA: Cardinal, 1977).

11. Erik Olin Wright, Cynthia Costello, David Hachen, and Joey Sprague, "The American Class Structure," *American Sociological Review*, vol. 47 (December 1982), pp. 709–26.

12. William Julius Wilson, *The Declining Significance of Race* (Chicago: University of Chicago Press, 1980).

13. Roger Brown, *Social Psychology* (New York: Free Press, 1966), pp. 113–35.

14. The writings of Frances Fox Piven and Richard A. Cloward stress this point. See especially their *Poor People's Movements: Why They Succeed, How They Fail* (New York: Pantheon, 1977).

15. Krauss, *Stratification, Class, and Conflict*, pp. 23–27.

16. Wynetta Devore and Elfriede G. Schlesinger, *Ethnic-Sensitive Social Work*, 2nd ed. (St. Louis, MO: C. V. Mosby, 1981), pp. 4–6.

17. Ibid., p. 5.

18. Mark Pilisuk and Phyllis Pilisuk (editors), *Poor Americans: How the White Poor Live* (New Brunswick, NJ: Transaction Books, 1970).

19. Michael Novak, *The Rise of the Unmeltable Ethnics* (New York: Macmillan, 1973).

20. Richard Sennett and Jonathan Cobb, *The Hidden Injuries of Class* (New York: Vintage Books, 1972).

21. Tom W. Smith, "America's Religious Mosaic," *American Demographics*, vol. 6 (June 1984), pp. 19–23.

22. Ibid.

23. Ibid.

24. Philip Blumstein and Pepper Schwartz, *American Couples: Money, Work, Sex* (New York: William Morrow, 1983), pp. 324–30.

25. Frances Fitzgerald, "A Reporter at

Large (The Castro—I)," *The New Yorker* July 21, 1986, pp. 59–60.

26. Carol A. B. Warren, *Identity and Community in the Gay World* (New York: John Wiley and Sons, 1974), p. 4.

27. William M. Newman, *American Pluralism: A Study of Minority Groups and Social Theory* (New York: Harper and Row, 1973), p. 21.

28. Edwin M. Schur, *Labeling Deviant Behavior* (New York: Harper and Row, 1971), pp. 100–114.

29. Donald Webster Cory, *The Homosexual in America* (New York, Paperback Library, 1963), p. 24.

30. Meredith Gould, "Statutory Oppression: An Overview of Legalized Homophobia," in M. P. Levine (editor), *Gay Men: The Sociology of Male Homosexuality* (New York: Harper Colophon, 1979), pp. 51–67. Also see Jeannine Gramick, "Homophobia: A New Challenge," *Social Work*, vol. 28 (March–April 1983), pp. 137–41.

31. Gould, "Statutory Oppression," pp. 51–52.

32. Barry D. Adam, "Structural Foundations of the Gay World," *Comparative Studies in Society and History*, vol. 27 (October 1985), pp. 658–70.

33. Toby Marotta, *The Politics of Homosexuality* (Boston: Houghton Mifflin, 1981), pp. 3–21.

34. Deborah Goleman Wolf, *The Lesbian Community* (Berkeley: University of California Press, 1979), p. 73.

35. Fitzgerald, "A Reporter at Large."

36. Alan P. Bell and Martin S. Weinberg, *Homosexualities: A Study of Diversity among Men and Women* (New York: Simon and Schuster, 1978).

37. For an interesting set of readings on black gays, see Joseph Beam, *In the Life: A Black Gay Anthology* (Boston: Alyson, 1986).

38. Betty Sancier, "A Challenge to the Profession," *Practice Digest*, vol. 7 (Summer 1984), p. 3.

39. See the issue of *Practice Digest* titled "Working with Gay and Lesbian Clients," vol. 7 (Summer 1984).

40. Michael Banton and Jonathan Harwood, *The Race Concept* (New York: Frederick A. Praeger, 1975).

41. Newman, *American Pluralism*, pp. 252–61. Also see Banton and Harwood, *Race Concept*, pp. 35–42, 61–90.

42. William W. Howells, "The Meaning of Race," in R. H. Osborne (editor), *The Biological and Social Meaning of Race* (San Francisco: W. H. Freeman, 1971), p. 3.

43. James W. Vander Zanden, *American Minority Relations*, 4th ed. (New York: Alfred A. Knopf, 1983), pp. 32–60.

44. Ibid., pp. 36–37. Also see Banton and Harwood, *Race Concept*, pp. 47–60.

45. Howells, "Meaning of Race," pp. 3–10.

46. Ibid., p. 8.

47. Pauli Murray (editor), *States' Laws on Race and Color* (Cincinnati, OH: Women's Division of Christian Service, Board of Missions and Church Extension, Methodist Church, 1951), pp. 173–74; 39.

48. Carlos E. Cortes, "Mexicans," in S. Thernstrom (ed.), *Harvard Encyclopedia of American Ethnic Groups* (Cambridge, MA: Belknap Press, 1980), p. 699.

49. Richard M. Burkey, *Ethnic and Racial Groups* (Menlo Park, CA: Cummings, 1978), p. 12.

50. Quoted in ibid., p. 5.

51. Theresa Rakowska-Harmstone, "Ethnic Autonomy in the Soviet Union, *Society*, vol. 12 (January–February 1975), pp. 44–50.

52. James W. Green, *Cultural Awareness in the Human Services* (Englewood Cliffs, NJ: Prentice-Hall, 1982), pp. 9–13.

53. Burkey, *Ethnic and Racial Groups*, pp. 9–17.

54. David Dalby, "Black through White: Patterns of Communication in Africa and the New World," in W. Wolfram and N. Clarke (editors), *Black-White Speech Relationships* (Washington, DC: Center for Applied Linguistics, 1971), pp. 99–138.

55. Burkey, *Ethnic and Racial Groups*, p. 7.

56. Green, *Cultural Awareness in the Human Services*, p. 9.

57. R. L. McNeely and Mary Kenny Badami, "Interracial Communication in School Social Work," *Social Work*, vol. 29 (January–February 1984), pp. 17–28.

58. Louis Wirth, "The Problem of Minority Groups," in R. Linton (editor),

The Science of Man in the World Crisis (New York: Columbia University Press, 1945), p. 347.

59. John R. Howard (editor), *Awakening Minorities* (New Brunswick, NJ: Transaction Books, 1970), p. 3.

60. Edward Sagarin (editor), *The Other Minorities* (Watham, MA: Xerox College Publishing, 1971), p. 17.

61. Newman, *American Pluralism*, pp. 33–41.

62. See Leon W. Chestang, "The Black Family and Black Culture: A Study in Coping," in M. Sotomayor (editor), *Cross Cultural Perspectives in Social Work Practice and Education* (Houston, TX: Graduate School of Social Work, University of Houston, 1976). Also see Harriette Pipes McAdoo (editor), *Black Families* (Beverly Hills, CA: Sage, 1981).

63. Newman, *American Pluralism*, pp. 20–21.

64. U.S. Bureau of the Census, *Statistical Abstract of the United States* 1988 (Washington, DC, 1987), Table 16.

65. Virginia Sapiro, *Women in American Society* (Palo Alto, CA: Mayfield Publishing, 1986), pp. 169–91, 221–336. Also see Edwin M. Schur, *Labeling Women Deviant* (New York: Random House, 1984).

66. Johnnetta B. Cole, "Commonalities and Differences," in J. B. Cole (editor), *All American Women: Lines That Divide, Ties That Bind* (New York: Free Press, 1986), pp. 1–30.

67. Newman, *American Pluralism*, pp. 135–37.

68. Janet A. Nes and Peter Iadicola, "Toward a Definition of Feminist Social Work: A Comparison of Liberal, Radical and Socialist Models," *Social Work*, vol. 34 (January 1989), pp. 12–22.

69. Burkey, *Ethnic and Racial Groups*, pp. 20–21.

70. Ronald F. Walters, "Race, Resources, Conflict," *Social Work*, vol. 27 (January 1982). pp. 24–30.

CHAPTER 4

A Social History of Ethnic Communities in the United States

M AJOR THEMES DISCUSSED IN THIS CHAPTER:

1. *Socioeconomic achievement.* Socioeconomic achievement is related to ethnic and racial status. In the United States, four ethnic minorities continue to lag well behind the white majority. These are Afro-Americans, Mexican Americans, Puerto Ricans, and Native Americans (American Indians) and Alaskan Natives. In addition, Chinese, Filipino, and Japanese minorities may find their success blocked at the top of the achievement ladder.

2. *Understanding racial and ethnic relations.* When racial and ethnic communities come together, a stratification system is likely to develop in which some groups become dominant and others become subordinate. Certain processes lead to the development and maintenance of ethnic stratification systems.

3. *U.S. immigration policies.* Over the years, the immigration policies of the United States have determined the extent to which people of various nationalities, races, and ethnic backgrounds have been welcomed and, once here, have been able to participate in the American dream. The open-door policy of the young Republic, by which virtually everyone who wanted to could enter, was replaced by regulations. The entry of Asians was severely restricted, and quotas were set to limit the immigration of eastern and southern Europeans.

4. *Historical factors in socioeconomic success.* The histories of how northern

and western Europeans, southern and eastern Europeans, and Third World people of color became part of American society is related to their socioeconomic achievement. The achievement of each group has had to do with the manner in which it was recruited into the United States, the economic opportunities it was offered, and the amount of hostility it received from dominant ethnics. The values held by a group, its willingness to be cohesive and help its members, and its preparation for entering the United States also are important in understanding its achievements.

5. *Implications for practice.* Two points are made for social workers: The socioeconomic well-being of individuals is related to the status of the ethnic and racial groups to which they belong, and attempts to help ethnic minorities must acknowledge historical processes of group conflict and competition.

T HE COMMUNITIES to which people belong have a good deal to do with the problems and needs they experience. Nowhere is this more true than in the connection between socioeconomic achievement and racial and ethnic communities. The data on socioeconomic well-being — that is, the data on education, occupation, and income — reveal vast disparities based on racial and ethnic differences.

Five racial and ethnic communities in the United States have been officially designated as minorities: Afro-Americans, Native Americans (American Indians) and Alaskan Natives, Asian Americans, Mexican Americans, and Puerto Ricans. They have been identified as **ethnic minorities** because of the prejudice and discrimination they have faced in American society, as a result of which they are likely to live in poverty or to be denied full participation in the economic resources generated by the society. The other ethnic groups making up American society, mostly white and of European origin, are considered **ethnic majorities**.

As an outcome of the civil rights legislation in the 1960s and 1970s, a policy of **affirmative action** has been developed to improve access to educational and occupational opportunities for ethnic-minority communities. This policy was challenged in the 1980s by administrative actions and legal rulings, but it has been upheld in principle, and progress has been made by some sectors of some ethnic minorities in achieving socioeconomic success.

SOCIOECONOMIC ACHIEVEMENT AND ETHNIC COMMUNITIES

Socioeconomic achievement is studied through **social indicators**, quantitative measures which have been mapped out over extended periods of time so trends can be traced. Social indicators attempt to measure well-being, that is, whether attainment by a particular group in a particular socioeconomic factor can be considered to have been good or not so good. By looking at trends it is possible to evaluate whether a situation is not only good or bad but whether it is getting better or worse or staying the same.[1] This section will consider a number of social indicators: income, occupation, education, and satisfaction with one's economic condition.

Some social indicators are based on **subjective measures** such as people's perceptions of how satisfied they are with their economic condition. This is what researchers call the "sense of well-being" or "direct perceptions of well-being."[2] Angus Campbell and his associates at the University of Michigan have done an important series of studies on the sense of well-being of Americans in a number of "domains" or areas of life. These include areas associated with economic well-being, such as satisfaction with income, jobs, and place of residence.[3] While it would be helpful to have good comparisons between ethnic majorities and minorities on such indicators, most studies do not systematically make such comparisons. Usually the comparison is between whites and blacks. Campbell summarizes a number of findings comparing these two groups between 1970 and 1978:

> The situation of low-income black people is unique; they suffer both from being poor and from being black. Poor white people also have relatively low feelings of well-being, but they are clearly more positive than those of black people in the same low-income category. Black people of all income levels describe their lives less positively than white people do.
>
> A high income raises a black person's sense of well-being, but not to the level of a white person of that income. Black people lack what income alone will not give them, equal social and political status. Their sense of inequity is sharply expressed in the large proportion of black people who feel they have had less than their share of the happiness a person can reasonably expect in life — over twice the proportion found among white people.[4]

Other social indicators are based on **objective measures** rooted in inferences about well-being which are externally based. Usually, these measures are derived from statistics provided by government agencies and departments such as the U.S. Census Bureau. Although objective measures and subjective measures are significantly correlated, the correlation is less strong than might be imagined. Campbell demonstrates that while the objective economic well-being of Americans rose dramatically in the 1950s and 1960s, their psychological well-being did not change and actually seemed to decrease.

SOCIOECONOMIC WELL-BEING, 1960–1976

Trends in the period 1960–1976 were examined in a publication of the U.S. Civil Rights Commission, *Social Indicators of Equality for Minorities and Women.*[5] This report, based on objective measures, is of great importance because it is the only one to compare systematically the five designated minority groups with one another and with the majority white population. The report gave equal attention to minorities and women, and a major conclusion was that sexual inequality is at least as important as racial and ethnic inequality, if not more important.

During the period 1960–1976, the educational, economic, and occupational achievement of most Americans was improving dramatically. Yet the achievement of four minority groups—Afro-Americans, Native Americans and Alaskan Natives, Mexican Americans, and Puerto Ricans—continued to lag behind, and there was no indication that they were catching up. These groups were likely to have lower rates of college completion, jobs in lower-prestige occupations, higher rates of unemployment for both teenagers and adults, lower per capita household incomes, and higher rates of poverty. In addition, the commission found that differences in income between these four minority groups and the white majority continued to be evident even when age, occupational prestige, number of weeks worked, hours worked during the previous week, and average income in the state of residence were taken into account.

The fifth minority group examined by the commission, Asian Americans, included Japanese, Chinese, and Filipinos. These three groups did much better than the other four minorities and sometimes did even better than the white majority. For instance, the rates of college completion and the prestige ranking of occupations were comparable for the three Asian groups and whites. Japanese families, on average, earned significantly more income than white families. But Asians did not always do as well as the white majority. In particular, they had significantly higher rates of college overqualification than whites. This means that Filipino, Japanese, and Chinese people tended to be employed in occupations for which they were overqualified and in which they could not use the education and skills they had acquired. Overqualification also showed up in income levels. College-educated male Asians tended to earn less income than college-educated male whites. No differences were apparent between college-educated women, however.

Socioeconomic Well-Being Since 1976

The report of the commission on Civil Rights for 1960–1976 represents a standard of excellence that has not been equaled since. More recent data systematically comparing groups are not readily available. Information is more likely to come from separate reports and studies comparing whites and blacks and, occasionally, Hispanics. **Hispanic** refers to all Spanish-heritage groups in the United States, not just Mexican Americans and Puerto Ricans.

The evidence that is available suggests that the disadvantages apparent in 1976 have been maintained. Economists have shown that 1977 was a high-water mark for equality in the United States. Between the depression years of the 1930s and 1977, economic inequality in the United States generally shrank. The 1980s, however, has been a period of growing inequality. Even among whites, the rich have gotten richer and the poor have gotten poorer, and middle-class incomes have failed to grow.[6] Other data show that the share of total money income earned by families in the bottom fifth of the population (by income level) declined steadily between 1968 and 1986, while the share earned by families in the top fifth just as steadily increased (see box, Changing Shares of Money Income of Families).

It is not surprising, therefore, that the economic situations of blacks and Hispanics have not shown significant improvement in recent years. For instance, mean incomes for families with children, when adjusted for inflation, show a steady decline between 1973 and 1984 for white, black, and Hispanic families alike. The effect of this overall decline, however, is that the relative difference in family income among all these groups has barely changed. Compared to whites, black and Hispanic families are generally in no better position than they were in 1973.[7]

There have been some changes, of course. Conservative blacks, particularly, have pointed to certain improvements: a growing black middle class,

CHANGING SHARES OF MONEY INCOME OF FAMILIES, 1968–1986

This table presents data on money income of families, a concept used by the Bureau of the Census which considers family income received without taking into account taxes or certain government benefits. Money income does not reflect the facts that some families have greater tax liabilities and some receive part of their income in noncash benefits such as food stamps, health benefits, and subsidized housing; goods produced and consumed by farmers; or job benefits such as company cars and retirement programs.

| | Percentage of Total Family Income Earned by: | |
Year	Bottom Fifth (20%) of Population	Top Fifth (20%) of Population
1968	5.6%	40.5%
1973	5.5	41.1
1977	5.2	41.5
1980	5.1	41.6
1982	4.7	42.7
1984	4.7	42.9
1986	4.6	43.7

Sources: Data from U.S. Bureau of the Census, *Current Population Reports*, Series P-60, and *Statistical Abstract of the United States*, various issues. Definition of money income from *Statistical Abstract of the United States 1988* (Washington, DC, 1987), p. 405.

more black-owned industrial enterprises, and increases in the number of blacks who have moved from deteriorated inner-city neighborhoods to the suburbs.[8] Looked at another way, however, these changes may not actually mean improvement for the society as a whole. Sheldon Danziger and Peter Gottschalk demonstrate how the level of inequality between rich and poor has increased for families with children. Among these families, the top fifth (20 percent) by income level earned 38.5 percent of all income earned in 1967 and 42 percent of all income earned in 1984. The growth of this inequality is even more evident among black and Hispanic families. The top fifth of black families with children earned 42 percent of all income earned by such families in 1967 and 48 percent of their earnings in 1984. Likewise, the top fifth of Hispanic families with children earned 40 percent of all income earned by these families in 1973 and 44 percent of their earnings in 1984.[9]

INEQUALITIES AMONG ETHNIC COMMUNITIES

Based on the available reports, we can conclude that two groupings of ethnic minorities have developed in the United States. One, composed of blacks, Native Americans, Mexican Americans, and Puerto Ricans, includes a large number of people who are seriously disadvantaged in meeting the basic human needs of everyday life. The other, composed of Chinese, Japanese, and Filipinos, includes large numbers who are largely able to meet their basic human needs but find themselves blocked at the upper levels of American society. Edna Bonacich calls these **middlemen minorities**.[10] They have the skills and education required to reach the top but tend to be overqualified for the jobs they hold, and their earnings seldom are comparable to those of their white counterparts. In the competition for socioeconomic success in American society, both of these ethnic-minority groupings must vie with the predominant white, European-based ethnic majority.

What accounts for the socioeconomic differences among racial and ethnic groups? Following a systems approach, we can conclude that socioeconomic success or failure is a function of the historical and contemporary transactions taking place between minority and majority ethnic groups. It results from the things minorities do to propel themselves forward and the things majorities do to facilitate or hinder the advance of minorities. Although well-being is a function of such transactions, this does not necessarily mean that minorities and majorities contribute equally. Sometimes minorities achieve success in spite of all obstacles thrown at them. Sometimes failure comes about in spite of superhuman efforts to avoid it. Sometimes majorities help minorities along, and sometimes they make every effort to keep them down. In this chapter we will look at one facet of the transactions between minorities and majorities, those that took place as ethnic groups were being recruited and socialized into the United States, primarily in the nineteenth and early twentieth centuries.

UNDERSTANDING RACIAL AND ETHNIC RELATIONS

When ethnic groups come in contact with one another, the transactions between them are likely to result in the formation of a stratification system in which one becomes dominant and the other remains subordinate. According to Donald Noel, three conditions are necessary for stratification to occur: ethnocentrism, competition, and differential power.[11]

Ethnocentrism has been described as the view whereby one's own group is seen as the best, and all others are evaluated in reference to it. **Ethnocentrism**, in other words, is the glorification of one's own group over all others. **Competition** has to do with the interaction between two or more groups striving to achieve or acquire the same scarce goal or resource, such as wealth, land, or prestige. **Power** is usually described as the ability to get one's way. A group is powerful to the extent that it has the technical, military, or legal capacity to exploit other groups. Power may be exercised through force but also through the control of rewards.

Noel demonstrates that these three conditions were evident in the relationships between early American colonists and blacks, and they led to the enslavement of blacks. It would not be difficult to prove that in early American society, ethnocentrism, the emphasis on competition, and differences in power and ability to exploit led to minority-group status for a number of groups entering the society.

Nevertheless, many groups have evolved from minority status to inclusion in the majority in American society. The major examples are the European immigrants who came to the United States during the nineteenth and twentieth centuries. Many of them arrived in poverty and were greeted with hostility, but they eventually became participants in the American dream. Thus conditions also exist in American society which encourage advancement and allow the elimination of minority status.

THEORIES OF MINORITY-MAJORITY RELATIONS

With the experience of southern and eastern Europeans in mind, Robert Park developed a theory of group relations based on a **cycle of race relations**.[12] Park assumes that racial and ethnic relations proceed in a specific, inevitable manner. He postulates that as groups come into **contact** through exploration, migration, or some other process, **competition** among them naturally emerges for land, natural resources, and various scarce goods and services. This competition may erupt into violent **conflict** or remain relatively peaceful, but as an outcome of the competition one group establishes dominance. The period of competition and the establishment of dominance is followed by a process of **accommodation** through which there is a "progressive merging" of the subordinated group into the dominant group. Eventually, **assimilation** takes place, and all distinguishing signs of group differences disappear.

In rethinking Park's cycle of race relations, Milton Gordon makes the point that assimilation is better conceived of as a collection of subprocesses rather than a single process.[13] He distinguishes among a number of forms of assimilation: cultural, structural, marital, identificational, and civic. These subprocesses of assimilation are not stages of development in the usual sense, since one does not lead automatically to the others and each may occur to a greater or lesser extent. **Cultural assimilation**, referred to as **acculturation**, is often the first to take place. It involves changing one's cultural patterns and language to those of the dominant or "host" society. **Structural assimilation** involves large-scale entrance and participation in cliques, clubs, and institutions of the dominant society, and the development of primary-group friendship ties. **Marital assimilation** is apparent when large-scale intermarriage occurs. **Identificational assimilation** occurs when the subordinate group develops a sense of peoplehood based exclusively on the dominant society. **Civic assimilation** is present when there is an absence of value and power conflict.

According to Gordon, in the United States the process of assimilation has produced not a single melting pot, in which the various racial and ethnic groups lose their separate identities and are melded into a uniquely American culture, but various melting pots[14] (see box, Where "The Melting Pot" Came From). Three of these involve religious groups; Protestants, Catholics, and Jews generally have erased their ethnic subdivisions. Another has to do with race. An example of how racial assimilation occurs can be seen in the example of contemporary Haitian immigrants.[15] The United States uses a definition of race which, by rule of thumb, labels as black any person with an African ancestry. This is a uniquely American definition of race. New groups coming into the country often are confronted with the necessity to "assimilate" into one of

---

WHERE "THE MELTING POT" CAME FROM

The term *the melting pot* is accredited to an author, Israel Zangwill, who used it in a play which opened in this country in 1908. With this term, he dramatically described the assimilationist doctrine of the times:

> America is God's crucible, the great Melting Pot where all the races of Europe are melting and re-forming! Here you stand, good folk, think I, when I see them at Ellis Esland, here you stand in your fifty groups, with your fifty languages and histories, and your fifty blood hatreds and rivalries. But you won't be long like that, brothers, for these are the fires of God you've come to—these are the fires of God. A fig for your feuds and vendettas! Germans and Frenchmen, Irishmen and Englishmen, Jews and Russians—into the crucible with you all! God is making the American.

Source: Quoted in Milton M. Gordon, *Assimilation in American Life: The Role of Race, Religion, and National Origin* (New York: Oxford University Press, 1964), p. 120.

the existing American racial categories. Thus within two generations after coming to the United States from Haiti, the Haitian identity begins to fade and the black identity emerges. Regardless of the "pot" into which new arrivals "melt," Gordon, as well as Park, acknowledges that the change is always toward accepting the ways of the dominant group.

The theory of a cycle of race relations, with its emphasis on assimilation into the ways of the dominant group, has been criticized for assuming that the experiences of European immigrants represent a natural law of assimilation. A second way of looking at minority-majority group relations is **conflict theory**, which does not hold that these relations ultimately lead to accommodation and assimilation. William Newman believes that minority and majority group status and conflict are inevitable, unalterable features of society. He does suggest, however, that, through conflict, majorities may become minorities, minorities may become majorities, and minorities and majorities may coalesce and create

TWO APPROACHES TO MINORITY-MAJORITY RELATIONS

Some sociologists believe that relations between minority and majority groups and individuals inevitably will take the form of harmonious assimilation. Others believe that, although new alignments may take place, conflict will always mark group relations. Two prominent theories of minority-majority group relations are graphically presented here.

Park's and Gordon's Cycle of Race Relations

Contact → Competition/Conflict → Accommodation → Assimilation
a. Cultural
b. Structural
c. Marital
d. Identificational
e. Civic

Newman's Conflict Theory of Majority-Minority Relations

Contact → Competition/Conflict → Majority/Minority Status → Competition/Conflict → Realignment of status → Competition/Conflict → Realignment

Sources: Robert E. Park, *Race and Culture* (New York: Free Press 1964); Milton M. Gordon, *Assimilation in American Life* (New York: Oxford University Press, 1964); William Newman, *American Pluralism: A Study of Minority Groups and Social Theory* (New York: Harper and Row, 1973).

new minorities. Thus he sees society as a continual conflict among groups which leads to constant realignment and redefinition of status.[16]

Together, these two approaches to minority-majority group relations, the cycle of race relations proposed by Park and Gordon and the conflict theory suggested by Newman, are essential to an understanding of racial and ethnic relations (see box, Two Approaches to Minority-Majority Group Relations). As we shall see, the thinking of Park and Gordon captures a certain reality in American race relations: Most groups have assimilated in some basic ways to the dominant Anglo culture. We think of ourselves as black-Americans, Irish-Americans, Mexican-Americans, Italian-Americans, and so on. At the same time, however, minority-majority status has not disappeared, and realignments have taken place. In the course of the twentieth century, southern and eastern Europeans have blended into the northern and western European majority in American society. Blacks, Hispanics, and other people of color remain as a new minority aligned against this changed majority. What realignments the future might bring are unclear, but it is important to understand how people of color have come to be the minority groups in the latter half of the twentieth century.

IMMIGRANT AND COLONIALIST ANALOGIES

It is generally believed that the United States is a land of immigrants. In fact, this is not the case. **Immigrants** take up stakes, more or less voluntarily, in one national society and migrate to another land, where they become part of a new national society. Many groups in the United States were indeed immigrants, but some were not. In terms of minority-majority group relations, whether or not a person is an immigrant has a lot to do with that person's likelihood of success. Southern and eastern European immigrant groups chose to come to the United States and in making that choice assumed they would have to accommodate to American society. The dominant white Anglo-Saxon Protestant community, while not completely receptive to these largely Catholic and Jewish immigrants, nevertheless offered them basic opportunities for accommodation and ultimate socioeconomic success. Because of this dynamic, it was fairly easy for these immigrant groups to attain success in the United States. But for significant numbers of Americans who unwillingly became immersed in the American melting pot, such an **immigrant analogy** did not apply.

Robert Blauner uses the **colonialist analogy** to describe the experiences of those who were forced to become part of American society and who, as a result of this forced inclusion, never were given the opportunities for success and assimilation that European immigrants enjoyed.[17] Blauner refers to these as **colonized groups**, principally Afro-Americans and Native Americans (Indians) and Alaskan Natives. There is evidence, however, that other groups might also be thought of as colonized groups.

In using a colonialist analogy, Blauner distinguishes between classical colonialism and internal colonialism. In **classical colonialism**, as in the British

Empire at the turn of the twentieth century, the colonized natives usually constitute the majority of the population. Accordingly their culture pervades the land and continues to develop, although they are accorded less prestige than the colonizers. The colonized do not have the rights of citizens of the empire, but they generally are free to continue their cultural traditions. The colonizers are more interested in taking out and using up the wealth and resources of the colony than it shaping its culture. In **internal colonialism,** many aspects of classical colonialism prevail. The wealth and resources of internally colonized groups are removed from their communities, to the benefit of the dominant group. However, the "natives" are less dominant; the colonized groups are generally smaller, and their culture is not as evident. The colonizers have come to live in and take over the colony.

The differences between the experiences of immigrants and internally colonized Americans are best described by reference to three differing circumstances: the manner in which they became part of American society, the opportunities they were given for participation in American economic institutions, and the degree of cultural oppression they experienced at the hands of the American majority (see box, Differences between Immigrant and Colonized Groups).

DIFFERENCES BETWEEN IMMIGRANT AND COLONIZED GROUPS

Ethnic and racial groups have entered American society in different ways, some as immigrants and some as colonized peoples. As a result they have had different experiences in the economy and in social relationships with the majority.

This table lists the differences between immigrant and colonized groups in American society as ideal types. Ideal types are not intended to portray specific categories but rather to describe characteristics along particular dimensions, thus making it possible to compare types.

Circumstance	Immigrant Groups	Colonized Groups
Entry into society	Voluntary	Forced
Participation in labor market	Mainstreamed	Secondary labor market
Cultural oppression	Minimal	Total

Source: Adapted from Robert Blauner, *Racial Oppression in America* (New York: Harper and Row, 1972).

The immigrant and colonialist analogies describe relationships between social systems. In terms of the focal system, they call attention to the motives of the people coming into a country. Immigrants are basically motivated to participate in the economy and to strive for achievement, while colonized groups are basically motivated to escape their confinement and to seek autonomy. In terms of the social context, these analogies call attention to the motivations and behaviors of the dominant groups. Essentially, dominant groups lend a helping hand to immigrants, while they put obstacles in the way of colonized groups.

The Minority Response to Subordination

Some theorists argue that all groups coming into the United States have experienced hostility from the dominant groups. To a great extent this is true, although the degree of hostility experienced varies considerably. In any event, these theorists have focused on the ways new groups respond to the obstacles that have been put in their way.

Thomas Sowell describes at least three dimensions of the response of new groups to obstacles to socioeconomic success: the preparedness, cohesiveness, and value system of the group. Whether immigrant groups do well in competition with other groups depends to some extent on whether their occupational experiences in the home country prepare them for similar experiences in the adopted country. Thus immigrants from rural, agricultural communities in the homeland who are offered only urban, industrial jobs in the new country will not adapt readily to the new environment. Success in the new country also depends on how well immigrants pull together to help each other out. A cohesive immigrant group has a better chance of overcoming the obstacles imposed by the dominant group. Since many immigrant groups come in waves, the cohesion between the various waves is as important as the cohesion within any one wave. Perhaps of greatest importance is the value system of the group. Certain kinds of values are more important than others; values of thrift, hard work, and orientation to future rather than immediate fulfillment facilitate socioeconomic success, regardless of the obstacles confronted.[18]

U.S. IMMIGRATION POLICIES

The success of ethnic communities in the United States is closely related to the governmental policies connected with their immigration. Official views on whether a racial or ethnic group was to be welcomed or their immigration was to be limited varied as social and economic conditions dictated. Immigration policies both reflected and helped shape the environment confronted by various immigrant groups as they attempted to enter and to achieve success in a new land.

William Bernard traces four periods of immigration to the United States. The first period, 1776–1881, was the **open door period**; virtually anyone who wanted to immigrate to the United States could do so. The second period, 1882-1916, was the **era of regulation**; for the first time, immigration was controlled. The first laws excluded categories of people such as convicts, lunatics, idiots, illiterates, incapacitated persons who might become public charges, mental defectives and persons involved in crimes of moral turpitude, anarchists, paupers and beggars, and the like. In this period, also, laws were passed to exclude Chinese immigrants, and steps were taken to control immigration from Japan. In the period 1917-1964, the **era of restriction**, laws were passed setting up quotas based on national origin and race. This is the period that will most concern us in this chapter. In the present period, the **era of liberalization**, quotas based on national origin and race have been eliminated.[19] Instead, preference is given to refugees and immigrants with certain personal qualifications.

The "open door" began to close in 1882, when passage of the Chinese Exclusion Act barred all foreign-born Chinese from acquiring U.S. citizenship. The legal precedent was the Naturalization Act of 1790, under which citizenship was limited to "free white persons." The Chinese Exclusion Act was to be in effect for ten years but was renewed. It became unnecessary with passage of the immigration acts of 1921 and 1924, which allowed no quotas for Orientals.

Beginning in 1882, also, patterns of European immigration into the United States began to change. Until then, approximately 87 percent of Europeans who immigrated were from northern and western European nations such as Great Britain, Germany, Holland, France, and the Scandinavian countries. After 1882, the bulk of the immigrants were from southern and eastern European nations such as Italy, Greece, and Russia, and Slavic and Polish-speaking peoples. Several million immigrants arrived between 1890 and 1914 alone. The flood was abated only by periodic economic problems in the United States.

In the eyes of many "native Americans," the term used in that era to refer to Europeans born in the United States, the peoples from southern and eastern Europe were decidedly undesirable. It was believed that something should be done to keep them from entering the country. From the point of view of economic elites, they represented a class of people who would adopt socialist ideas and were willing to participate in labor organizations. From the point of view of working people, they represented cheap labor which could be used as "scabs" to undercut wages and break strikes. To Americans in general, they represented inferior "races" who would mongrelize the nation and dilute the prized Aryan stock.[20]

THE SETTING OF QUOTAS

As a result of this kind of sentiment, the U.S. Congress passed an act in 1921 setting immigration quotas. The unabashed purpose of this legislation was to limit the influx of immigrants from southern and eastern Europe. In addition to putting a ceiling on the number of immigrants who could enter, the act set annual quotas for immigrants from each nation, based on 3 percent of the number from that nation who had entered the United States, according to the 1910 census. This law was considered ineffective and was amended by the Immigration Act of 1924, which set national quotas based on 2 percent of the number from each nation residing in the United States in 1890. The law then gave 84 percent of the quotas to northern and western European nations and 14 percent to southern and eastern European nations. It also reaffirmed the Chinese Exclusion Act and barred many groups from the so-called Asian-Pacific triangle, who had been declared racially ineligible for citizenship by a 1922 Supreme Court decision. For groups like the Japanese, no quotas were set.

As a consequence of this legislation, immigration was considerably reshaped to realize the racist and ethnocentric goals of its framers. The law drastically changed the "complexion" of those who immigrated (see box, Effects of Quotas on European Immigration). In effect, it provided affirmative action in favor of white, Anglo-Saxon Protestants.

The immigration laws were changed from time to time. The "permanent" quotas for each country, which went into effect in 1929, were based on the national origins of the population of the United States in 1920. The quota system based on national origin was abolished by the Immigration Act of 1965. Instead, the eastern hemisphere (Europe, Africa, and Asia) was given a quota of 170,000 a year, with a maximum of 20,000 from any one country, and the western hemisphere (Canada and Latin America) was given a quota of 120,000 a year. No national quotas were imposed, but preference was given to people

EFFECTS OF QUOTAS ON EUROPEAN IMMIGRATION

Patterns in the volume and sources of immigration to the United States drastically changed as an effect of the immigration laws passed early in the 1920s. Quotas based on national origin were set which severely limited immigration from southern and eastern Europe. The decline in number of immigrants from northern and western Europe was much less spectacular.

| | No. of Immigrants from: | |
Period	Northern and Western Europe (yearly average)	Southern and Eastern Europe (yearly average)
1907–1914	176,683	685,531
After 1921 act	198,082	158,367
After 1924 act	140,999	20,847

Source: Stephen Thernstrom (editor), *Harvard Encyclopedia of Ethnic and Racial Groups* (Cambridge, MA: Belknap Press, 1980), p. 493.

with family members in the United States and those who have skills or professional occupations that are needed here. The inscription on the Statue of Liberty, "Give me your tired, your poor, your huddled masses yearning to breathe free" no longer reflects government policy, nor does it describe who now immigrates to the United States (see Chapter 5).

SOCIOECONOMIC SUCCESS OF EUROPEAN IMMIGRANTS

The following sections will present a historical sketch of the conditions confronted by various groups as they became a part of American society. The principal purpose is to explain why some groups have been able to "make it" socially and economically, while other groups have not. In this analysis we will argue that immigrant groups — those that more or less chose to come to the United States and were more or less positively received by Americans — had an easier time than groups that were forced into the country. The underlying motivations for entry and the receptivity of the dominant group weigh heavily in determining the eventual success of an incoming group, but they do not explain everything about it. In Sowell's terms (discussed earlier), the preparedness of the group, its cohesiveness, and its value system also must be taken into account, especially when the social context of the new society is particularly hostile.

This section considers factors affecting the ability of two groups of European immigrants — from northern and western Europe and from southern and eastern Europe — to achieve socioeconomic success. The next section describes how Third World people of color in the United States have struggled to achieve similar socioeconomic success, despite their position as ethnic minorities.

Northern and Western European Immigrants

Peoples from northern and western Europe, in general, found it easiest to realize the American dream. The hard part was getting here. Many aspiring immigrants met death or disease while crossing the ocean in steerage, crowded into the hulls of small, unsanitary cargo vessels. It was estimated, for instance, that 2,000 Germans died at sea on voyages to Philadelphia in 1749.[21] Once in this country, it was common for northern and western European immigrants to put in a period of indentured servitude before they were free to hold jobs. Most of them, however, arrived during the colonial era or in the early days of the Republic, when there were few immigration laws and land was readily available for settlement.

The early American economy was based on agriculture, and the new arrivals became landowners and farmers, participating in the mainstream of that economic system. Colonial governments eagerly sought immigrants from northern and western Europe and not only provided information about the colonies and transportation to them but also subsidized the purchase of lands and tools for new settlers.[22] The early national government of the United States, however, did little to promote immigration, leaving it up to market conditions to set the demand and to state and territorial governments to see to it that workers were supplied. Some states had publicity agents who sent out brochures written in the European languages, extolling the virtues of settling in their states. As an inducement, public lands could be purchased for as little as $1.25 an acre. Northern and western Europeans were certainly welcomed.

As these immigrants settled in the new country, regional and communal segregation patterns developed. Germans settled in Pennsylvania, the Ohio Valley, and the Midwest; the Scotch-Irish in Appalachia; Scandinavians in the upper Mississippi area; the Dutch in upstate New York. This allowed the new arrivals to maintain their languages and traditions for some time. The Germans even toyed with the idea of creating a separate state. A public school system was barely evident, so there was no incentive to learn to read and speak English. Many groups maintained their own newspapers and schools. Although there are recorded incidents of violence and hostility toward these ethnic groups, it is difficult to say that they were ever considered minorities in the United States. The history of such groups as Germans and Norwegians makes this clear.[23]

The Irish Catholics in the United States

One exception among the northern and western European immigrant groups was the Irish, who have been described as the first major immigrant minority group in the United States.[24] Irish immigration took place throughout the colonial era but began to increase significantly around 1820 and represented the first major wave of immigration to the United States. The hostile experiences the Irish faced were as difficult as those encountered by any immigrant group before or since. Not until the beginning of the twentieth century did the Irish begin to show evidence of "making it" in American society.[25] In comparison, most European immigrants could do so in about two generations.[26]

Why was entry into American society so difficult for the Irish? They had a number of advantages that ought to have made it easier for them.[27] They spoke English, regarded by many immigrant peoples as necessary to success. They had a respected literature, which helped Americans to understand and appreciate the Irish cultural heritage. They were also familiar with the Anglo-Saxon legal system, which was not shared with most other European groups. Furthermore, although Ireland was a devastatingly poor country and Irish immigrants were poor by American standards, they seldom came from among the very poorest of the Irish.[28] But in spite of these apparent advantages, other conditions were operating which indeed put them at a disadvantage.

In many ways the Irish did not really immigrate at all. Immigration always involves a certain amount of push and pull—people who feel they have to leave and who at the same time want to leave. For the Irish, the push away from Ireland was far stronger than the pull to the United States. Potato harvest failures in the nineteenth century deprived the Irish poor of their principal food source and made the choice either to immigrate or to die. According to Oscar Handlin, "Irishmen fled with no hope in their hearts—degraded, humiliated, mourning reluctantly-abandoned and dearly-loved homes."[29]

The decision to come to the United States was not that much of a choice, in any case. Ireland was not a free country but a colony of the British. The Irish were a classically colonized group, making their way from one sector of the British Empire to a recently liberated but nevertheless culturally enmeshed ex-colony. While Irish immigrated to many parts of the world, by far the greatest number came to the United States. This had a lot to do with the limitations imposed by the available means of travel; a person traveled by trading ship and went where the ships went. Since Irish immigrants left from British ports, they mostly ended up in Boston and other ports on the northeastern coast. Relatively few went to the South or to the frontier, although by the nineteenth century, significant numbers had made their way to San Francisco and other parts of the West.

Once in the United States, the Irish were forced to live in squalor. The men could find work only as manual laborers in the dirtiest, hardest, and most unstable jobs, and the women became servants to fashionable New Englanders. The worst slum areas of the cities became home for the Irish. They were crowded into "shanty towns" where indoor plumbing was unheard of and disease and death were everyday occurrences. Crime rates were high; alcoholism and family dissolution were common. Prejudice and discrimination hounded them; they were seen as dirty, thriftless, boisterous, and worthless, and "Irish need not apply" signs rebuffed them when they searched for work. They were a prime target of the American political party, whose members were called Know-Nothings because they refused to discuss their program: a pledge to vote only for native Americans, demands for a 21-year naturalization period, and vigorous opposition to Catholicism.

Thus the Irish found themselves a despised minority in the United States not only because they were a colonized people but because they were Catholic. At one time, religious hostilities were a dominant factor in ethnic relations. Europeans fought wars over religion; England endured a civil war when the state separated from the Catholic Church, and Anglo-Saxon Protestants were alienated from Anglo-Saxon Catholics. The intense, violent conflict in Northern Ireland today should give a sense of the extreme hostility faced by the Catholic Irish in coming to the United States, an English-speaking country.

The Irish-Catholic immigrants were despised even by Protestants of their own nationality. In the colonial era the term *Irish* referred to any people from Ireland, but much of the early immigration was from the Protestant North. The immigration that took place during the third and fourth decades of the nineteenth century was from the Catholic South. The Protestant Irish established in the new country rejected the Catholic Irish and coined the term *Scotch-Irish* to distinguish themselves from the later arrivals. No helping hands were extended, and the Catholics and Protestants certainly did not become a cohesive Irish group and pull together.[30]

The Irish response to obstacles to their socioeconomic success also was lacking in the other two dimensions identified by Sowell (discussed above).[31] In these respects, they were less well equipped to succeed than other northern and western European groups who arrived at about the same time. The Irish became urban dwellers, though they had been agricultural and small-town people back home. Unable to reproduce their lifestyle in the United States, they did not join the economic mainstream but became day laborers and servants. Sowell points out that efforts were made to encourage the Irish to disperse from the cities to the farmlands, but they resisted. One reason was that the kind of land on which they had grown potatoes in Ireland was very different from the kind of land available in the United States. Another was that, due to their cultural nature, they did not enjoy living on isolated farms; they were too gregarious for American rural living, with its vast open spaces.

This gregariousness and similar values also hindered their progress. They were an expressive people, given to enjoying the moment, convivial and loquacious. These qualities made the Irish very creative and likeable, and they became excellent political organizers. Eventually they exerted considerable control over politics in the cities they inhabited. With such a value system, however, they failed to acknowledge the need to delay immediate gratification or to put their energies into building an economic base in their communities.

Southern and Eastern European Immigrants

The immigrant experiences of southern and eastern Europeans — peoples from such nations as Italy, Greece, Poland, and Russia — were quite a bit different from those of most peoples from northern and western Europe. In the struggle for socioeconomic success, they were more like the Irish.

Southern and eastern Europeans began to immigrate to the United States after the Civil War, and their immigration reached a peak during the latter part of the nineteenth and early part of the twentieth century. All of them did not plan to stay permanently in this country, however. With transatlantic passenger ships now running regular routes, new arrivals knew they could return if they chose. Many Italians came as sojourners, intending to stay only until they had amassed enough money so they could go home and live more comfortably. It was not unusual for sojourners to go back and forth several times before deciding to stay in the United States.[32] Others came with the hope of starting a new life away from the hardships they were experiencing in their native lands. Russian Jews, for instance, were being subjected to pogroms, or government-sanctioned violence against them, and to discriminatory laws which controlled where they could live, where they could go, and the occupations to which they could aspire.[33] The pull of the United States was also strong for these groups. The Statue of Liberty being placed in New York harbor symbolized the promise of a better life and greater opportunities.

The economy found by these newcomers to the United States was different from the agricultural system that had been encountered by earlier immigrants from northern and western Europe. As the United States underwent industri-alization, southern and eastern Europeans were actually recruited and en-couraged to immigrate. They became industrial workers in the factories and mines and helped to build the bridges, railroads, and cities. They came as free laborers, able to move about the country in search of the best industrial em-ployment or other opportunities they could find. For many who had been serfs and urban dwellers in Europe, in a society which was still quite medieval and controlled by landed aristocrats, this was an enormously liberating experience. While the best jobs were not available to them, their work could lead to self-improvement and advancement, if not for themselves, at least for their chil-dren. Moreover, opportunities as free laborers in a free-market economy al-lowed them to aspire to majority status in the United States. Fundamentally, these immigrants were programmed for success; the opportunities were there.

Nevertheless, for many southern and eastern European immigrants, the way was not easy. They did hold minority status in the United States and were con-fronted with ethnocentrism, prejudice, and even racism, as we have noted. Racist fears led to the development of the first federal immigration laws, aimed specifically at controlling the flow of immigrants from southern and eastern Eu-rope and preserving the dominance of Aryan peoples from northern and west-ern Europe. Peoples who were not Aryan or Anglo-Saxon were seen as being not only of different nationalities but of different races.

It probably is incorrect to state that peoples from southern and eastern Eu-rope are still minorities in the United States. Yet their status as ethnic-majority groups is not entirely secure, either. In general, Italians, Poles, and other such groups have done well economically, but there are pockets of poverty among them. Moreover, groups such as Jewish Americans, who have been very suc-cessful, seldom have been accepted at the top of the socioeconomic status hier-archy. No Jewish person has become president of the United States or been appointed to a directorate in certain major business sectors, such as banking. Jewish success has generally come in such areas as radio, television, and pub-lishing.[34] And prejudice against southern and eastern Europeans lingers in American public opinion. "Polish jokes" swept the nation in the late 1970s, for instance; Italian criminal stereotypes are still apparent; and anti-Semitism is not unusual. Thus, while southern and eastern Europeans generally have achieved socioeconomic success, they still are not free of minority status.

Italian Americans

The experience of Italians was fairly typical for southern and eastern European immigrants. Early immigration tended to be from the richer northern states of Italy, but by the turn of the century it came primarily from the rural, im-poverished South. Immigrating Italians were generally peasants from rural and small-town backgrounds. In the United States, they crowded into "little Italy" sectors in the slums of eastern cities. The men worked at the manual-labor jobs that were being vacated by the Irish. Often they were at the mercy

The Statue of Liberty offered hope to the homeless, huddled masses from southern and eastern European countries. *Historical Pictures Service, Chicago.*

of unscrupulous *padrinos* who helped them find jobs but milked them of their earnings in return.[35]

The Italian immigrants became alienated from the Catholic Church, which was largely controlled in the United States by the Irish. The Italians brought no tradition of education, and problems with the public school systems, dominated by Anglo-Saxons, were common. Protestant social workers attempting to Americanize the Italians often made them feel inferior in the process. It was not unusual for violence to be directed at them, especially in the South; in some areas, Italian children were required to attend segregated schools.[36] Despite these problems, the Italians accepted the economic opportunities available to them and coalesced to gain community strength. Together, they began to achieve socioeconomic success by the third generation.

Russian Jews in the United States

An atypical experience among southern and eastern European immigrants was that of the Russian Jews. They were one of the most impoverished groups to come to the United States, and they faced severe religious prejudice and discrimination. Nevertheless, within one generation members of this ethnic group were already showing signs of significant success.[37]

The three factors affecting the struggle of immigrant groups to overcome the obstacles facing them in American society cited by Sowell — cohesiveness, preparedness, and values — help explain the rapid success of Russian Jews.[38] Considerable credit has to be given to the ability of Russian Jews and German Jews to coalesce in an ethnic community. The differences between the religious orientations of Russian Jews and German Jews, who had come to the United States earlier in the nineteenth century, were at least as pronounced as the differences between Catholic and Protestant Irish. The two Jewish groups did not necessarily like each other, but the Germans did not turn their backs on the Russians when they arrived. Instead, they helped set up social services which laid the groundwork for the success of the Russian Jews in the United States.

Another factor in their success was preparedness to enter the American economy. Though they were impoverished, they brought with them industrial and urban skills which proved as good as, if not better than, money. In Russia (indeed, in many parts of Europe), Jews could not own land and were forced into urban occupations. By some twist of fate, this form of oppression turned out to have beneficial effects in the United States. Rather than taking manual-labor jobs, as the Italians were forced to do, they became factory workers, tailors, or merchants, creating an ethnic economy which often served to provide jobs for newcomers. It is estimated that 64 percent of the gainfully employed Russian Jews were skilled workers.

The values Russian Jews brought with them also facilitated their success. They had a profound respect for education and eagerly took advantage of the opportunities available through the public school systems. They also had a strong commitment to economic success and pursued it by using their ethnic economy as a springboard to the mainstream economy. They were willing to delay immediate gratification for long-term economic goals.

SOCIOECONOMIC SUCCESS
AND THIRD WORLD PEOPLE OF COLOR

The term **Third World** first was used to describe peoples from nations that formerly were included in European colonial empires. Thus it includes racial and ethnic groups from Africa, Asia, and South America. In the United States, Third World also has been used to refer to the indigenous Native American or American Indian and Alaskan Native populations. All these peoples also have been described in the social science literature as **people of color**.[39]

According to Blauner, these groups are best seen not through the immigrant analogy but through the colonialist analogy.[40] It seems especially appropriate to describe the experiences of blacks and Native Americans in these terms. Puerto Ricans also fit the analogy fairly well, but the evidence for including Mexican Americans and Chinese and Japanese immigrants to the United States is not so clear-cut. In each case, the hostilities experienced by the "colonized" groups and the opportunities they were offered severely constrained their ability to achieve socioeconomic success in American society.

NATIVE AMERICANS AND ALASKAN NATIVES

The designation *Indian* is a fiction imposed on the indigenous or native peoples who inhabited the western hemisphere at the time European explorers and settlers first arrived. Upward of 200 different tribes, or nations, as the Europeans called them, existed at that time, and there still are some 173 different groups, each with its own culture and language.[41] The appropriate term to use with respect to this extremely heterogeneous group is still debated. Generally, we prefer the designation *Native American* to the term *American Indian*. Indigenous people from Alaska — Eskimos and Aleuts — are usually referred to as *Alaskan Natives*.

With some exceptions, noticeably the Quakers and some German immigrants, the new settlers treated the Native Americans harshly. The hostility probably had relatively little to do with the race of the original population and quite a bit to do with their religion; they were considered barbarians and heathens because they did not acknowledge Christianity.[42] But race did play a part, especially under government policies with regard to the native populations.

Native Americans did not choose to become part of the United States; they are a conquered people. In Alaska, Indians as well as Alaskan Natives were not so much conquered as "purchased." Neither the United States nor Russia, from which Alaska was purchased in 1867, asked the native population whether it wanted to be purchased. Aleuts, who were fairly well acculturated into Russian civilization, and Eskimos were not considered part of the "uncivilized tribes" living outside the Russian settlements.[43] Native Americans, during much of U.S. history, did not have rights to land, to jobs, or even to citizenship. They were not incorporated into the economy as free workers, as European immigrants were. The initial policy of the federal government was to remove the native populations from the land coveted by the settlers. Starting in the 1820s, "voluntary removal" was undertaken at government expense all along the frontier, from Canada to the Gulf of Mexico, and one by one Indian tribes were escorted to lands west of the Mississippi.

Forced Resettlement

At first neither the Native American population nor the invading colonists wanted accommodation to one another. Some Indians did accommodate to the American culture in the Southeast. The "five civilized tribes" — Cherokee, Choctaw, Chickasaw, Seminole, and Creek — settled into a relatively American way of life, owning their homes, living as farmers, developing a written script and becoming literate, and joining in a loosely federated republic with a bicameral legislature and an appellate judiciary. But they were not to be given a place in American society. In 1828 and 1829, the state of Georgia annexed their lands, and the native populations sued. The Supreme Court, in *Cherokee Nation* v. *Georgia* (1831), set what has become national policy ever since. Chief Justice John Marshall argued that the Cherokees were not a foreign nation; in his written opinion he noted that "tribes which reside within the acknowledged boundaries of the United States . . . may more correctly, perhaps, be denominated domestic dependent nations." In *Worcester* v. *Georgia* (1832), however, Marshall did assert that "the Cherokee Nation is a distinct community, occupying its own territory . . . in which the laws of Georgia can have no force." [44]

Regardless of these rulings, President Andrew Jackson adopted a policy of forced resettlement. Under the Indian Removal Act of 1830, the tribes were coerced to abandon their lands. The 900-mile march from Georgia to what is now Oklahoma is often referred to as the **Trail of Tears**. The U.S. Army forcibly removed some 100,000 Indians from the southern states, costing the lives of thousands and shattering any trust they might have placed in their European dominators.

As the white settlers moved on to the lands west of the Mississippi and began to covet Indian lands there, a new government policy was adopted. Indian wars were declared, and the adage "The only good Indian is a dead Indian" expressed the attitude of the government and the white settlers. The effect was near genocide. Indians who were not killed by bullets were starved to death as soldiers and settlers slaughtered the buffalo, the principal food for many Native Americans on the central plains.

Native Americans did not immigrate to the United States. The "Trail of Tears" painting by Robert Lindneux commemorates the suffering the Five Civilized Tribes endured as they were pushed off their land. *Reproduced with permission of the Woolaroc Museum, Bartlesville, Oklahoma.*

Reservations and Cultural Repression

Under the system of reservations, the natives were required to live on lands that usually were unsuited to either agriculture or industry. Edward Spicer refers to this system as operating on a policy of **coercive assimilation**, whereby whites aimed to "replace Indian ways with their own ways and to help [Indians] become self-sufficient farmers and artisans, under conditions dictated by whites." [45] This policy was embodied in the Dawes Act of 1887, which was promoted by Christian religious and political leaders as a solution to the Indian wars. Thus, as the United States was being industrialized, Native Americans were being trained to the ways of Christian family life on farms that could not support it. Furthermore, the policy was instituted at a time when the rural American society was in decline and being drained to feed the growing urban and industrial populations of the Northeast and the West. [46]

Moreover, efforts were made to destroy the cultures of American Indian tribes. In many instances, their religious traditions and ceremonies were outlawed. Christian missionaries were in fact extremely successful, so that by 1930 the majority of Native Americans professed a Christian affiliation. Systematic attempts also were made to extinguish the various Native American languages and dialects. Children often were required to leave the reservations and attend boarding schools hundreds of miles away, where they could be Americanized. The Dawes Act called for breaking up the tribal lands, with 160 acres to be allotted to each family. Titles were to be held in trust by the government for 25 years, and "surplus" land was to be sold to the United States. Tribes that would not agree to these provisions had their tribal governments dissolved under an act of Congress.

The first federal statute granting citizenship to an entire tribe (the Brothertons) was passed in 1839, but the effect of the law was to dissolve the tribe. The Winnebagos were offered the option of becoming citizens in 1870, provided they could prove that they were sufficiently intelligent and prudent, that they had adopted habits of "civilized life," and that they had supported themselves and their families for the preceding five years. It was not until 1924 that citizenship was granted unconditionally to all Native Americans. Because of confusion over their wardship status in Arizona and New Mexico, however, the right to vote was not extended in these states until 1948. [47]

Reorganization and Termination

The Indian Reorganization Act, which reversed much of the previous policy, was passed in 1934. This act recognized the cultural distinctiveness of the tribes and stipulated that no efforts were to be made to alter them further. Nevertheless, the tribes were encouraged to adopt governing structures modeled after state and federal governments. Under these more humane policies, intertribal organizations emerged, the educational level of Native Americans rose, and the Native American population began to increase.

In 1953, the federal government instituted a **policy of termination**, whereby protection and assistance for Native American tribal communities was to be withdrawn. A number of small tribes and two large ones, the Menominee of Wisconsin and the Klamath of Oregon, lost their tribal status, though the Menominee regained theirs in 1973. In some ways this policy made sense, since American Indians had been made prisoners on reservations where only limited economic development was possible. Yet the policy of termination proved to be disastrous for the Indians, who were deprived of their land and whatever economic potential it had. Some tribes began to fight back, filing suit to reclaim the lands that had been taken from them almost 200 years ago. In 1970, the Oneida Nation of Wisconsin challenged the legality of a 1795 purchase by New York State because it had been made without the authority of the federal government, which had exclusive jurisdiction to deal with the Indians under the Constitution and the Indian Trade and Intercourse Act of 1793. A Supreme Court ruling on this suit in 1985 established that an Indian tribe holds a common-law right to recover land wrongfully taken after the effective date of the Constitution. This principle is being used by the Oneida and other Indian nations to press claims to additional land.

AMERICAN BLACKS AND AFRO-AMERICANS

The ancestry of many ethnic groups in the United States can be traced to Africa. Included are American blacks, whose forefathers were largely slaves in the United States, as well as other African groups such as those from the West Indies — Jamaicans and Haitians, Virgin Islanders, and some Puerto Ricans, Cubans, and Dominicans. Also included are recent immigrants directly from African nations. As a group, these peoples often are referred to as **Afro-Americans**. In the following discussion, however, we will focus largely on American blacks. Use of the term *African Americans* has recently been proposed as a means for American blacks to acknowledge their heritage to their mother-land, in the same way terms such as *Mexican Americans* and *Asian Americans* have been adopted. With popular use, the term *African American* could replace *black*, in the same way that proud use of the term *black* in the 1960s made it preferable to *Negro*, which earlier had replaced *colored*.

Slavery in American Society

American blacks were forced to migrate to the United States. They came not as people with rights to land and participation in a free-market economy but as indentured servants. Many European whites also were indentured, but after a brief, fixed period they became free workers. Blacks were relegated to slave status, which was perpetual and cross-generational, handed down from parent to child. To be a slave meant being owned by slaveholders or masters and having no right to seek opportunities to improve one's own lot or that of one's family. In fact, family life was deliberately undermined to make it easier for slave owners to buy and sell humans according to their need for labor and profit. American whites have never been subjected to such degradation (see box, An Abolitionist's View of American Slavery).

The place of blacks in the United States has always presented a problem for whites. The framers of the Constitution did not know what to do about slaves. They "conceived the nation in liberty," as Abraham Lincoln would later declare, and stated that all men were created equal, but still they allowed slavery. This contradiction continues to this day; American values hold that all men are created equal, yet American blacks and the dominant white ethnic groups are not treated equally. Gunner Myrdal refers to this contradiction as "an American dilemma."[48]

In no other society did slavery exist quite the way it did in the United States.[49] It was situated within a decentralized democracy, in which the doctrine of "states rights" worked to put slavery under local control, out of the jurisdiction of the federal government. It was largely a southern rural phenomenon, flourishing in a mild climate where slaves could work the fields year round so they would not be a drain on the financial resources of the slaveholders. Some northern "free states," such as Oregon, prohibited slavery not because of moral outrage but simply because their climate was too harsh and would not allow for year-round work.[50] The rural plantation setting also allowed slaveholders to retain considerable control over their slaves and made

AN ABOLITIONIST'S VIEW OF AMERICAN SLAVERY

In *American Slavery as It Is: Testimony of a Thousand Witnesses*, published by the American Anti-Slavery Society in May 1839, Theodore Weld exposed the inhumanity of the American slave system. He reproduced observations on the cruelties being inflicted on slaves and answered the arguments of the slaveholders one by one. In his Introduction, Weld compared the conditions of free workers and slaves:

Two millions seven hundred thousand persons in these States are in this condition [slavery]. They were made slaves and are held such by force, and by being put in fear, and this for no crime! Reader, what have you to say of such treatment? Is it right, just, benevolent? Suppose I should seize you, rob you of your liberty, drive you into the field, and make you work without pay as long as you live, would that be justice and kindness, or monstrous injustice and cruelty? Now, everybody knows that the slaveholders do these things to the slaves every day, and yet it is stoutly affirmed that they treat them well and kindly, and that their tender regard for their slaves restrains the masters from inflicting cruelties upon them. We shall go into no metaphysics to show the absurdity of this pretence. The man who *robs* you every day, is forsooth, quite too tenderhearted ever to cuff or kick you! True, he can snatch your money, but he does it gently lest he should hurt you. He can empty your pockets with qualms, but if your *stomach*

escape difficult. Plantation slaves had nothing they could call their own and were completely dependent on the owner. In the cities, it was easier for slaves to learn to read and write and to escape or seek their freedom. Throughout the slavery period there were some free blacks in the United States, but severe restrictions were placed on their ability to participate in government or many economic enterprises.[51]

Freedom and Segregation

The United States is the only nation in which a civil war was necessary to free the slaves. This conflict occurred just about the time industrialization was beginning to redefine the American economy. After the war, blacks could have been used as free workers in the burgeoning industries that European peasant immigrants were being invited to enter. Instead, after a postwar period of considerable freedom, blacks were subjected to **Jim Crow laws**, which restricted their physical movement and social position. These laws regulated racial relations in such aspects of daily living as travel and transportation, eating and sleeping, friendship and sexual fulfillment, and ability to vote in elections. The laws were incorporated into a **separate but equal** federal policy which sanctioned discrimination. As a result, many blacks were reduced to the status of sharecroppers, working the land for a landowner in return for a share of the

is empty, it cuts him to the quick. He can make you work a life time without pay, but loves you too well to let you go hungry. He fleeces you of your *rights* with a relish, but is shocked if you work bareheaded in summer, or in winter without warm stockings. He can make you go without your *liberty*, but never without a shirt. He can crush, in you, all hope of bettering your condition, by vowing that you shall die his slave, but though he can coolly torture your feelings, he is too compassionate to lacerate your back — he can break your heart, but he is very tender of your skin. He can strip you of all protection and thus expose you to all outrages, but if you are exposed to the *weather*, half clad and half sheltered, how yearn his tender bowels! What! Slaveholders talk of treating men well, and yet not only rob them of all they get, and as fast as they get it, but rob them of *themselves*, also; their very hands and feet, all their muscles, and limbs, and senses, their bodies and minds, their time and liberty and earnings, their free speech and rights of conscience, and their right to acquire knowledge, and property, and reputation; — and yet they, who plunder them of all these, would fain make us believe that their soft hearts ooze out so lovingly toward their slaves that they always keep them well housed and well clad, never push them too hard in the field, never make their dear backs smart, nor let their dear stomachs get empty.

Source: Richard O. Curry and Joanna Dunlap Cowden, *Slavery in America: Theodore Weld's American Slavery as It Is* (Itasca, Il: F.E. Peacock Publishers, 1973), pp. 4–5.

crop, minus expenses. This was little better than slave status, since it was tied to the land and the authority and economic domination of the landowners. Thomas Holt describes this post-Civil War period as "the failure of freedom."[52]

Cultural oppression against blacks was as total as it was against the Native American populations. In the slave trade, peoples of different tribes and languages were mixed together. Since blacks were not able to talk to one another freely, they developed a dialect which still retains many traces of African languages. They were unable to practice their religions, and the slave owners' total control made family life extremely difficult for blacks. That they survived centuries of misery is testimony to their strength. Their contributions to the political and cultural dimensions of American society have been enormous.[53]

Not until the twentieth century did blacks begin to migrate from the rural South to the industrial North and West. They were recruited as cheap labor by industrialists to break strikes and the organizing efforts of labor unions. Not incidentally, they were greeted by hostile white workers who were fearful of losing their jobs and favored continued oppression of blacks. The competition for jobs between two newcomers, European immigrants and southern blacks, helped provoke "race riots" in which bodily harm was inflicted on blacks by whites, even the police. The situation for blacks did not improve appreciably until after World War II and the civil rights legislation of the 1960s (see Chapter 6).

MEXICAN AMERICANS (CHICANOS)

The term *Mexican American* refers to all groups in the United States with an ancestral origin in Mexico or what was once Mexican territory. But there is no satisfactory term to describe this large and diverse group of people. They may refer to themselves as Mexican Americans or, especially in New Mexico, as Hispanics or Latinos. During the 1960s the term **Chicano** became popular, especially among those committed to the civil rights movement. The roots and meaning of this word are unclear, however, and because of its political connotations, there are Americans of Mexican descent who do not feel comfortable with it. Social service workers therefore should be cautious about applying the term to clients.

Almost all of the southwestern part of the United States was obtained as a result of territorial conflict with Mexico. Northern Mexico had four major provinces: Texas, New Mexico, Arizona, and California. The boundaries of these settlements stretched as far north as the present states of Nevada, Colorado, and Wyoming. New Mexico had the largest population and an extensively developed cultural life centered in Santa Fe. California was also fairly well developed, with missions, towns, and ranches up and down the coast. Texas, with its center in San Antonio, and Arizona, with its center in Tucson, were less densely settled.

In Texas, American settlers, invited to immigrate into the territory, quickly outnumbered the Mexican population and rebelled against the Mexican government. In spite of their loss at the Alamo, they were eventually victorious and created the Lone Star Republic. Texas became a state in 1845, and the following year the United States became engaged in war with Mexico over disputed boundaries. The United States offered to purchase areas in the Southwest, and when the Mexican government refused to part with them, the U.S. Army attacked, marching through New Mexico and toward California, which already was in the process of separating from Mexico. Though little blood was shed, eventually there was armed retaliation by Mexican citizens. Mexico City was captured in 1848, and the war ended with the signing of the Treaty of Guadalupe Hidalgo. Article VIII gave Mexicans the right to remain where they were or to withdraw to Mexico within two years. Those who stayed in the United States were given the option of becoming American citizens or retaining Mexican citizenship. All rights to property belonging to Mexicans in the territory were to be guaranteed and protected by law.

Little by little, however, the Mexicans who stayed behind lost their lands to Americans who laid claim to them. Instead of automatically accepting all land titles, in the spirit in which the treaty had been written, American officials put the burden of proof of ownership on the Mexican landholders. Americans were allowed to take over the land, and Mexicans soon found themselves with the status of second-class citizens. Often they resisted, and, as late as 1915, they periodically resorted to arms in attempts to right such injustices. By the end of the nineteenth century, Mexicans were the numerical minority in all states which had previously been part of Mexican provinces, with the exception of New Mexico. This area was a special case because of its cultural center and leadership by an economic and social elite. New Mexico entered the Union as an officially bilingual state. As elsewhere in the Southwest, Mexicans lost land and Anglo governors were appointed, but only in the recent past have Anglos begun to outnumber Mexicans and take political control in New Mexico.

It is clear that conquest played an important role in the history of the Southwest, but whether Mexican Americans can be considered a conquered group is open to debate. Joan Moore points out that at the time of conquest, relatively few Mexicans were living in that vast area. She estimates that the largest population of Mexicans, some 60,000, were in New Mexico, and there were about 7,500 in California, 5,000 in Texas, and 1,000 in Arizona.[54] Most Mexican Americans do not trace their background to the period of conquest and annexation. Mexicans began to immigrate to the United States in large numbers about 1912, pushed by civil strife and poverty in Mexico. The extent to which these Mexicans regarded themselves as immigrating to the United States is questionable, however. Blauner points out that until the 1940s, Mexican schoolchildren were taught that the Southwest was Mexican territory under the control of the American government. He argues that many early immigrants believed they were going from one part of Mexico to another, and thus they were not immigrating so much as going to their rightful place.[55]

Mexicans continue to cross the U.S. border today in large numbers, both as documented immigrants or visitors and as undocumented aliens (see Chapter 5). In March 1986 the Current Population Survey of the U.S. Census Bureau counted 11,200,000 Americans of Mexican descent in the United States, by far the largest population of Spanish origin.[56] The number of such residents who are not counted is impossible to estimate.

It has been suggested that the slow assimilation of Mexicans in American society is related to the proximity of the United States to Mexico, which encourages them to retain their national identity and loyalty. The hostility encountered by many Mexicans in the United States undoubtedly contributes to this loyalty. The experiences of Mexicans in the American labor market provide evidence of their subordinate status. While Mexicans were neither enslaved nor forced onto reservations, their opportunities for work have been as constrained as those of blacks and Native Americans. Historically, Mexican Americans were used as farm labor, which formerly was not subject to minimum-wage restrictions or social security contributions. They also were employed in unskilled jobs on ranches and in mining, food processing, construction, and the railroads, even though many of them had the skills and experience necessary for supervisory positions.

Mexican Americans also have experienced harsh cultural oppression. Although their language and religion were not outlawed, they were subjected to segregation laws. In Texas, where southern whites made up the bulk of the Anglo migration, and in California, the law effectively segregated Mexicans from the mainstream populations, restricting them to certain schools, recreational facilities, restaurants, and theaters. During the 1930s the U.S. government adopted a repatriation program through which 500,000 Mexicans were forced to leave the country, though many of them were American citizens. It is estimated that the Mexican-American population of Texas declined by 40 percent as a result. Even in New Mexico, some 9,000 Hispanics lost their small farms and ranches because of inability to pay taxes. Again in the period 1953–1955, 2.2 million Mexicans in the United States were rounded up and sent back over the border; some were deported more than once.[57]

PUERTO RICANS

In many ways Puerto Ricans who have come to the U.S. mainland from the island appear to have immigrated. If only this movement is considered, this is probably the case. However, to ignore the social relationship between the island of Puerto Rico and the government of the United States is a serious error. Moreover, among Puerto Ricans there has been a continual social movement favoring independence from the United States.

Puerto Rico was annexed by the United States as a result of the Treaty of Paris (1898), which settled the Spanish American War. American armed forces had invaded Puerto Rico and marched across the island, proclaiming it American territory. Although there was no insurrection by Puerto Ricans against the American soldiers and even a certain amount of support for them, there also was no referendum to allow Puerto Ricans to choose their destiny. Many who supported the U.S. invasion believed that Puerto Rican independence would follow. This was not to be the case.[58]

Since prior to the conquest the United States had never owned overseas territories, it was necessary to clarify the use of the term *territory* with respect to Puerto Rico. Previously, a territory within the continental United States had rights to statehood; when the territory had been incorporated and a provisional government had been set up, it could acquire the status of a state. However, in a 1905 Supreme Court case, *Downes* v. *Bidwell*, Puerto Rico and similar territories were declared unincorporated and therefore not eligible for statehood. The rationale for this decision was in keeping with the racism prevalent at the turn of the century. Puerto Rico could not become a state because it was a racially mixed society.[59]

After the conquest Puerto Ricans were removed from power, English became the language of public school instruction, and Protestant missionaries came in large numbers. In the Foraker Act of 1900, political power was taken away from Puerto Ricans and placed in the hands of Americans. U.S. officials appointed the governor and the eleven-member Executive Council, only five of whom had to be Puerto Rican. Puerto Ricans were allowed only to elect representatives to the lower house, though there was an elected "resident commissioner" who could speak in the House of Representatives but could not vote. Puerto Ricans could not set their tariffs or participate in the negotiation of commercial treaties with foreign countries. Not until Louis Múnoz Marín took office as the first freely elected governor in 1948 and instituted a program for industrial development called **Operation Bootstrap** was Puerto Rican culture allowed to reassert itself. English, for instance, is no longer the language of public school instruction.

Puerto Ricans were granted U.S. citizenship in 1917. Presently, Puerto Rico is a commonwealth of the United States. Its citizens do not go through any naturalization procedure and may travel freely in the states in search of employment. While the status of **commonwealth** is believed to be equal to statehood, the meaning of the term is quite unclear.[60] Sizable numbers of Puerto Ricans of all political persuasions believe that *commonwealth* in reality means little more than *territory*. The population of the island is presently divided on the issue. While most Puerto Ricans seem to be content to leave well enough alone and not challenge the commonwealth status, there is a strong movement in favor of statehood and another in favor of independence.

Puerto Ricans coming to live in the United States do so more-or-less willingly, as the southern and eastern Europeans did, and, within the limitations of their skills, they can seek employment in a free-market economy. Discrimination has been cited as a reason for their continued poverty, unemployment, and underemployment. Yet the hostility the Puerto Ricans have experienced from Americans on the continent is probably not very different from that experienced by southern and eastern European immigrants. Their religion has not been challenged, and there has been no overt attempt to break up family life. However, since the Puerto Rican ethnic mix is essentially a blend of European (Spanish) and African, with traces of Native American, many Puerto Rican immigrants have endured the same kinds of racial prejudice in the United States as blacks have.

ASIAN AMERICANS

Historically, the two largest Asian groups in the United States have been the Japanese and the Chinese. Only recently has a wider range of Asian groups begun to enter in large numbers. The Chinese replaced the Japanese as the largest Asian group in 1980, but demographers predicted that Filipinos would have this distinction by 1990.[61]

The Chinese and Japanese are considered immigrant groups by most scholars. No conquest or forced entry marked their arrival in the United States. The decision to immigrate was largely voluntary, with push-and-pull factors that were not too different from those for European immigrants: economic and political difficulties at home, coupled with perceived opportunities in the United States. Like the Italians, many Chinese and Japanese came as sojourners expecting to return to the homeland after making their fortune in the United States. As a consequence, most of the early immigrants were men, and family life was relatively slowly established. Yet there are elements of the Japanese and Chinese experience which suggest that their entry and their quest for well-being in the United States also resembled those of groups that were forced in. For instance, their immigration has to be seen as part of the social upheavals caused by the forced opening of China and Japan to American and European markets. Similarly, belief in the racial undesirability of Asians provoked intense hostility and severely strained Asian opportunities in the U.S. labor market, to a degree not experienced by most Europeans.[62]

The Chinese Immigrant Experience

The immigration of the Chinese was closely monitored. As a result of the Opium Wars, England opened isolationist China to European exploitation. The Chinese economy, already in decline, worsened, thus setting the stage for emigration. Between 1850 and 1882, an estimated 322,000 Chinese entered the United States. Large numbers also went to the independent kingdom of Hawaii, where they constituted the main labor force on the sugar plantations.[63] In both Hawaii and the United States they met with considerable hostility. The Chinese worked the railroads, mines, and canneries and did farm labor. Soon they began to gravitate to small industries such as shoe and garment factories and to develop farms of their own. As the Chinese became successful, anti-Chinese sentiment flourished, spearheaded by labor unions but also supported by small entrepreneurs and farmers. Violent riots of whites against Chinese were not uncommon in the mining towns of California and in Oregon. In some towns in the West, Chinese were evicted. In San Francisco, a city ordinance restricted their use of the streets. The Chinese were also subjected to segregated schools and theaters. In Hawaii, attempts were made to limit inter-marriage with Chinese. Anti-Chinese sentiment culminated in the passage of the Chinese Exclusion Act of 1882, which barred all foreign-born Chinese from acquiring U.S. citizenship.

The Japanese Immigrant Experience

As the number of Chinese immigrants declined, business interests needing a cheap labor supply began to encourage Japanese immigration. Between 1891 and 1924 the records show that 295,820 Japanese entered legally.[64] Previously, equally large numbers had entered the kingdom of Hawaii. The kinds of im-migrants leaving Japan were quite different from the kinds leaving China or most of those leaving Europe. When Japanese immigration first started, vagrants were recruited off the streets of Tokyo. Trouble in Hawaii over these "first-year men" soon led Japanese officials to be more selective about whom they allowed to immigrate. In order to avoid the difficulties confronted earlier by the Chinese, the Japanese sent workers who were suited to contract labor.[65] The result was a more capable, more middle-class type of Japanese immigrant.

The Japanese worked in many of the same areas as the Chinese, but soon they found that the most advancement was possible in agriculture. A Japanese immigrant might begin as an ordinary laborer, progress to contract farming, share tenancy, and cash leasing, and finally achieve truck-farm ownership. Their success in this labor market soon inspired anti-Japanese sentiment. Le-gal support for discrimination against them was found in laws which stipulated that Asians were aliens who were ineligible for citizenship. Not only were first-generation Japanese (*Issei*) refused citizenship, but they could be blocked from owning or leasing agricultural lands. Attempts were also made to block them from passing on previously owned lands to their second-generation American-born children (*Nisei*), but these were not successful.

The Japanese government took an important role in the relations between Japanese immigrants and the U.S. government. In 1907, the Japanese and American governments signed a **gentlemen's agreement**, whereby Japan set up self-imposed quotas to limit immigration. Chinese immigrants had fought the Exclusion Act of 1882, but they could not count on a strong government to force concessions by the United States. Regardless, when the U.S. immigra-tion quotas were being devised in the 1920s, the Japanese, like other Asian groups, were denied a quota. The Japanese government experienced this as a complete rebuff of the "gentlemen's agreement," and there is no doubt that the new immigration laws played a part in provoking Japanese hostilities in World War II.

When strong governments become enemies, enemy nationals can expect to suffer. German Americans, for instance, endured a great deal of hostility dur-ing World War I. The Japanese, an "undesirable race" from an undesirable country, were subjected to even more. After the bombing of Pearl Harbor, a move to "relocate" Japanese Americans took hold in California. Curfews and other restrictions were imposed on Japanese neighborhoods. In 1942, President Franklin D. Roosevelt signed an executive order which forced the evacuation of Japanese Americans to internment camps. In the process, Japanese community and family life was seriously disrupted, and many of them were economically ruined. Although the Japanese in Hawaii also were faced with some restrictions, the size of the Japanese population there, coupled with more liberal racial attitudes, precluded evacuation and internment.

In 1944, the U.S. Supreme Court determined that the relocation of the Japanese, whose loyalty to the United States was not at issue, had been unconstitutional. After the war many Japanese relocated to states other than California. The situation for them, as for all Asian groups, improved enormously. While many had lost their livelihood and their land, some compensation was given, and the Japanese community was able to draw together again.

Since the war the Japanese have done well, both economically and politically, especially in Hawaii but also on the mainland. Yet there is danger that the Japanese, like the Chinese and Filipinos, may have become trapped in the middleman status described earlier in this chapter, blocked from reaching the upper levels of socioeconomic success. As Harry Kitano notes, "[Japanese] progress, if measured by their movement upward, is impressive, but if progress is measured by their distribution at the top, it is less so. Few are in the highest leadership positions and many are overqualified for the jobs they hold."[66]

IMPLICATIONS FOR PRACTICE

This chapter emphasizes two points for social service workers. It demonstrates that the socioeconomic well-being of Americans is very much related to the status of their ethnic or racial groups. It also demonstrates that as workers attempt to help members of racial or ethnic minorities, they are getting involved in a larger historical process of group conflict and competition.

HUMAN NEEDS

Abraham Maslow has developed the idea that human needs exist in hierarchical form (see Chapter 11). At the bottom of his hierarchy are the basic human needs, such as food and shelter, which are essential to survival. At the top are higher-level needs such as belongingness, self-esteem, and self-actualization. Maslow makes the point that higher-level needs cannot be satisfied until lower level, more basic needs have been met.[67]

Taking Maslow's lead, we should expect to find that black, Native American, Puerto Rican, and Mexican-American clients are caught up in the struggle to meet basic human needs. This does not imply that all clients in these groups have the same basic needs or that white clients never have these needs. In general, however, these ethnic minorities are more likely than other ethnics to be struggling to survive. Asian Americans, at least the Chinese, Japanese, and Filipinos discussed in this chapter, are likely to evidence a different set of needs which are more akin to those of white Americans. Their self-actualization, however, is likely to be blocked at the top. Their high education levels and hard work do not always pay off for them as much as they do for whites.

One of the dilemmas of social work as a profession is that it is increasingly divorcing itself from the struggles of poor people.[68] Professional social workers today are less likely to be working with the poor and the unemployed in the income maintenance programs of public agencies and more likely to be working for private, not-for-profit or profit-making organizations or in private practice, offering services geared to meet the more-advanced human needs. Social workers who do encounter ethnic minorities and the poor may have become insensitive to the importance of meeting basic human needs. They may have good intentions and sincerely wish to serve such people, but the nature of the organizations for which they work and the services they have been trained to provide may in fact not be the kinds required by individuals and families in these groups. To be of help to them, social workers must become as adept at assessing and intervening in basic human needs as they are in meeting advanced needs.

Intergroup Conflict and Competition

Helping minorities and the poor involves historical processes of competition and conflict. Thus a social worker dealing with the private troubles of a minority individual or family also must try to resolve larger public issues of group competition and conflict.

The social histories of racial and ethnic groups presented in this chapter supply a background for understanding the larger issues. In the same way social workers take a case history of an individual or family, this chapter has taken case histories of ethnic and racial groups. These histories demonstrate that the needs and problems of individuals and families are very much related to events and conditions which occurred in their ethnic and racial communities in the past and over which they had no control. By accident of birth, the chances for meeting basic human needs are diminished for people of color and enhanced for white ethnics.

Knowing the social history of these groups makes it possible for social workers to go a step further in establishing accurate empathy and rapport with ethnic minority clients. Rather than blaming a client as an individual for the troubles being experienced, a worker may be able to see the connection between the individual's problems and the problems of the community as a whole. This makes it easier for the worker to recognize that the distrust the client may express has its basis in the reality of past group conflict. The worker also may appreciate the strengths of clients who continue to prevail despite a history of abuse. Finally, the worker may recognize that helping to solve the problems of ethnic minority clients requires her or his own personal and professional involvement in the eradication of group conflict and competition in the society.

Knowing the social history of racial and ethnic groups also gives social workers a sense of hope. European and Asian ethnics have done fairly well as communities in the United States, and there is every reason to believe that the system is open enough to allow for the eventual advance of many American blacks, Native Americans and Alaskan Natives, Mexican Americans, and Puerto Ricans. Social workers who are willing to work with and on behalf of ethnic minorities can help to speed up the process by which these communities become part of the majority.

DISCUSSION QUESTIONS AND CLASS PROJECTS

1. Search in your library for data on the social and economic achievements of a racial or ethnic group of your choice. Determine for yourself the educational, income, and occupational needs of the group and compare it with at least one other such group.

2. Describe and compare the approaches of the cycle of race relations and conflict theory to the study of ethnic and racial stratification. Which approach do you think describes more accurately what has happened and can take place in the United States?

3. Describe what is meant by the following concepts:
social indicators
ethnocentrism
cultural assimilation
structural assimilation
marital assimilation
identificational assimilation
civic assimilation
immigrant and colonialist analogies

4. Is the United States a land of immigrants?

5. Compare and contrast the history of one or more European ethnic groups and one or more Third World people of color in the United States.

6. Identify your ethnic community or communities of origin. Read up on the history of your community and talk to your parents, grandparents, or other relatives to see how the history of your family fits the history of the community.

7. Identify the significance of:
the Trail of Tears
coercive assimilation
policy of termination
an American dilemma
the Naturalization Act of 1790
the Treaty of Guadalupe Hidalgo
Operation Bootstrap
the Foraker Act
the Chinese Exclusion Act of 1882
the gentlemen's agreement
middlemen minorities

NOTES

1. Howard E. Freeman and Eleanor Bernert Sheldon, "Social Indicators," *Encyclopedia of Social Work*, 17th ed, vol. 2 (New York: National Association of Social Workers, 1977), pp. 1350–55.

2. Arthur G. Neal, *Social Psychology: A Social Perspective* (Reading, MA: Addison-Wesley, 1983), pp. 477–94; Frank M. Andrews and Stephen B. Withey, *Social Indicators of Well-Being: Americans' Perceptions of*

Life Quality (New York: Plenum Press, 1976), p. 23.

3. Angus Campbell, *The Sense of Well-Being In America: Recent Patterns and Trends* (New York: McGraw-Hill, 1981).

4. Ibid., pp. 232-33.

5. U.S. Commission on Civil Rights, *Social Indicators of Equality for Minorities and Women* (Washington, DC: United States Government Printing Office, August 1978).

6. Barbara Ehrenreich, "Is the Middle Class Doomed?" *The New York Times Magazine*, September 7, 1986, pp. 44, 50, 54, 62, 64.

7. Sheldon Danziger and Peter Gottschalk, "How Have Families with Children Been Faring?" paper prepared for the Joint Economic Committee of the Congress (Madison, WI: Institute for Research on Poverty, November 1985).

8. Reverend E. V. Hill, Glenn Loury, G. A. Parker, Joseph Perkins, Clarence Thomas, and Robert Woodson, "Black America under the Reagan Administration: A Symposium of Black Conservatives," *Policy Review*, No. 34. (Fall 1985), pp. 27-41.

9. Danziger and Gottschalk, "Families with Children," p. 17.

10. Edna Bonacich, "A Theory of Middlemen Minorities," *American Sociological Review*, vol. 38 (October 1973), pp. 583-94.

11. Donald L. Noel, "A Theory of the Origin of Ethnic Stratification," in N. R. Yetman and C. H. Steele (editors), *Minority and Majority* (Boston, MA: Allyn and Bacon, 1971), pp. 109-20.

12. Robert E. Park, *Race and Culture* (New York: Free Press, 1964).

13. Milton M. Gordon, *Assimilation in American Life* (New York: Oxford University Press, 1964).

14. Ibid., pp. 60-83, 115-31.

15. Tekle Wodemikael, "Becoming Black Americans: The Case of Haitian Immigrants," paper presented at the 78th Annual Meeting of the American Sociological Association, August–September 1983, Detroit, Michigan.

16. William Newman, *American Pluralism: A Study of Minority Groups and Social Theory* (New York: Harper and Row, 1973), pp. 97-190.

17. Robert Blauner, *Racial Oppression in America* (New York: Harper and Row, 1972), pp. 51-75.

18. Thomas Sowell, *Race and Economics* (New York: David McKay, 1975).

19. William S. Bernard, "Immigration: History of U.S. Policy," in S. Thernstrom (editor), *Harvard Encyclopedia of American Ethnic Groups* (Cambridge, MA: Belknap Press, 1980), pp. 486-95.

20. Richard M. Burkey, *Ethnic and Racial Groups (Menlo Park, CA: Cummings,* 1978), pp. 246-51.

21. Thomas Sowell, *Ethnic America* (New York: Basic Books, 1981), p. 48.

22. Bernard, "Immigration," p. 487.

23. See Kathleen Neils Conzen, "Germans," and Peter A. Munch, "Norwegians," in *Harvard Encyclopedia of American Ethnic Groups*, pp. 406, 750-61; also see Dietmar Rothermund, "The German Problem of Colonial Pennsylvania," and Carl Wittke, "Ohio's Germans, 1840-75," in L. Dinnerstein and F. C. Jaher (editors), *Uncertain Americans: Readings in Ethnic History* (New York: Oxford University Press, 1977), pp. 48-57, 114-23.

24. Sowell, *Ethnic America*, pp. 17-42.

25. Patrick J. Blessing, "Irish," in *Harvard Encyclopedia of American Ethnic Groups*, pp. 539-40.

26. Sowell, *Race and Economics*, pp. 71-80.

27. Michael Novak, *The Rise of the Unmeltable Ethnics* (New York: Macmillan, 1971), pp. 85-136.

28. Sowell, *Ethnic America*, pp. 17-42.

29. Oscar Handlin, *Boston's Immigrants, 1790-1865: A Study in Acculturation*, rev. ed. (Cambridge, MA: Harvard University Press, 1941), p. 129.

30. Sowell, *Race and Economics*, pp. 76-78.

31. Ibid., pp. 142-48.

32. Humbert S. Nelli, "Italians," in *Harvard Encyclopedia of American Ethnic Groups*, pp. 547-49.

33. Arthur A. Goren, "Jews," in *Harvard Encyclopedia of American Ethnic Groups*, p. 579.

34. Joe R. Feagin, *Racial and Ethnic Relations* (Englewood Cliffs, NJ: Prentice-Hall, 1984), pp. 153-58.

35. See Sowell, *Race and Economics*, pp. 80-90. Also see Nelli, "Italians," pp. 545-60.

36. Feagin, *Racial and Ethnic Relations*, pp. 129, 116.

37. See Goren, "Jews," pp. 579-88.

38. Sowell, *Race and Economics*, pp. 665-71, 115-57.

39. Doman Lum, *Social Work Practice and People of Color* (Monterey, CA: Brooks/Cole, 1986).

40. Blauner, *Racial Oppression in America*, pp. 10-14, 51-75.

41. Edward H. Spicer, "American Indians," in *Harvard Encyclopedia of American Ethnic Groups*, p. 58.

42. Newman, *American Pluralism* (New York: Harper and Row, 1973), pp. 35-36.

43. Dorothy M. Jones, "Aleuts," and Arthur E. Hippler, "Eskimos," in *Harvard Encyclopedia of American Ethnic Groups*, pp. 28-29, 336-39.

44. C. Dale McLemore, *Racial and Ethnic Relations in America*, 2nd ed. (Boston, MA: Allyn and Bacon, 1983), p. 334.

45. Edward H. Spicer, "American Indians: Federal Policy Toward," in *Harvard Encyclopedia of American Ethnic Groups*, p. 114.

46. Joseph G. Jorgensen, "Indians and the Metropolis," in J. O. Waddel and O. M. Watson (editors), *The American Indian in Urban Society* (Boston, MA: Little, Brown, 1971), pp. 67-113.

47. James E. Officer, "The American Indian and Federal Policy," in *American Indian in Urban Society*, pp. 9-65.

48. Gunnar Myrdal, *An American Dilemma: The Negro Problem and Modern Democracy* (New York: Harper and Brothers, 1944).

49. Sowell, *Race and Economics*, pp. 3-33.

50. Daniel G. Hill, Jr., *The Negro in Oregon: A Survey*, unpublished masters thesis, University of Oregon, Eugene, June 1932.

51. Sowell, *Race and Economics*, pp. 11-18.

52. Thomas C. Holt, "Afro-Americans, in *Harvard Encyclopedia of American Ethnic Groups*, p. 13.

53. See, for instance, Holt's description of their contributions to literature, ibid., pp. 16-17.

54. Joan Moore, "Colonialism: The Case of the Mexican Americans," *Social Problems*, vol. 17 (Spring 1970), pp. 463-72.

55. Blauner, *Racial Oppression in America*, pp. 53-70.

56. U.S. Bureau of the Census, *Statistical Abstract of the United States 1988* (Washington, DC, 1987), Table 43.

57. Carlos E. Cortes, "Mexicans," in *Harvard Encyclopedia of American Ethnic Groups*, pp. 707, 711; Otto Friedrich, "The Changing Face of America," *Time*, July 8, 1985, p. 28.

58. Manuel Maldonado-Denis, *Puerto Rico: A Socio-Historic Interpretation* (New York: Vintage Books, 1972), pp. 52-62, 65-129. Also see Juan Angel Selin, *We the Puerto Rican People: A Story of Oppression and Resistance* (New York: Monthly Review Press, 1971), pp. 60-66.

59. Diana Christopulos, "Puerto Rico in the Twentieth Century," in A. Lopez and J. Petras (editors), *Puerto Rico and Puerto Ricans* (New York: John Wiley, 1974), pp. 126-27. Also see Maldonado-Denis, *Puerto Rico*, pp. 83-129.

60. See, for instance, Henry Wells, "Puerto Rico's Commonwealth Status and Its Relevance to the U.S. Virgin Islands: An Outline," in J. A. Bough and R. C. Macridis (editors), *Virgin Islands: America's Caribbean Outpost* (Wakefield, MA: W. F. Williams, 1970), pp. 174-80.

61. Leon F. Bouvier and Anthony J. Agresta, "The Fastest Growing Minority," *American Demographics*, vol. 7 (May 1985), pp. 31-33.

62. See Harry H. L. Kitano, "Japanese," and H. M. Lai, "Chinese," in *Harvard Encyclopedia of American Ethnic Groups*, pp. 560-71 and 217-34.

63. Lai, "Chinese," pp. 218, 231.

64. Kitano, "Japanese," pp. 560-71.

65. Ibid., pp. 561-62. Also see McLemore, *Racial and Ethnic Relations in America*, pp. 163-65.

66. Kitano, "Japanese," pp. 570-71.

67. Abraham H. Maslow, *Motivation and Personality* (New York: Harper and Row, 1954).

68. See Norman L. Wyers, "Income Maintenance and Social Work: A Broken Tie," *Social Work*, vol. 28 (July-August 1983), pp. 261-68, and "Whatever Happened to the Income Maintenance Line Worker?" *Social Work*, vol. 25 (July 1980), pp. 259-63. Also see Linda Cherrey Reeser and Irwin Epstein, "Social Workers' Attitudes toward Poverty and Social Action: 1968-84," *Social Service Review*, vol. 61 (December 1987), pp. 610-11.

CHAPTER 5

The New Arrivals

Major themes discussed in this chapter:

1. *The new Americans.* New ethnic and racial groups continue to enter the United States, adding to the cultural mosaic and becoming incorporated into the status hierarchies. Some of the new groups are immigrants, others are refugees, and still others enter as undocumented aliens. None have been colonized by the United States.

2. *The new immigrants.* Immigrants now entering the United States are less likely to come from Europe. Because of new immigration laws, most immigrants have occupational skills which make it possible for them to succeed more quickly than immigrants of the past.

3. *Refugees and displaced persons.* Many new arrivals have come to the United States as refugees or displaced persons. Usually they have been forced out of countries that have been overtaken by socialist revolutions or regimes.

4. *Undocumented aliens.* This population, being largely unskilled, uneducated, and often rural in character, is more like the "teeming masses" which came from Europe at the turn of this century.

5. *Implications for practice.* Social service workers must try to assure that new arrivals to the United States do not take on the status of minority groups. They also have the responsibility of respecting and helping to sustain the cultural values and traditions of these groups while assuring that their socialization into American society takes place.

In the social history of racial and ethnic minority communities in the United States outlined in Chapter 4, it was pointed out that groups entering the country commonly experienced socioeconomic difficulties and low status. Some of these groups overcame the difficulties with relative ease, while others did not.

In general, European groups and certain racial groups, in particular the Chinese and Japanese, have greatly improved their socioeconomic status. The European groups immigrated to the United States more-or-less willingly and were offered opportunities as free workers in a market economy. Some others, such as the Japanese, had unique skills and sets of values which enabled them to overcome extremely hostile early experiences. The ethnic and racial minority groups that have not done well in the United States did not immigrate, or their immigration was severely restricted. They were systematically excluded from the competitive labor market and experienced severe prejudice and discrimination and cultural oppression in American society.

This chapter turns from the social history of immigrant and colonized groups to consider arrivals in the contemporary era. New ethnic and racial groups entering the United States are adding their own distinctive traditions, norms, and values to the cultural mosaic.[1] Of the 601,700 legal immigrants who entered the United Staes in 1986, 101,600 were from the Caribbean, over 39,000 more than came from all of Europe. The largest number from a single nation came from Mexico (66,500), followed by the Philippines (52,600) and Korea (35,800).[2]

Immigration law now sets an annual ceiling of 270,000 on immigrants, with a maximum of 20,000 from any single country. But husbands, wives, parents, and children of U.S. citizens are not included in the limits, and under the Refugee Act of 1980 the president can determine an additional number of people to be admitted because they have a "well-founded fear of persecution" on account of race, religion, nationality, membership in a social group, or political opinion. The proportions of immigrants or refugees from various nations or parts of the world admitted into the United States in a specific year thus are related to national political policy. In 1985, two-thirds of all the immigration in the world consisted of people entering the United States.[3]

THE NEW AMERICANS

The study of ethnic and racial minority communities in contemporary society is complex. Since the mid-1960s, several waves of new arrivals have washed up on the shores of the United States.[4] Most of them are neither white nor European, and many represent ethnic and cultural differences that have been relatively unknown in the United States (see box, New Arrivals by Continent of Birth). The reasons for their entry vary widely. None was conquered or forced to enter by the U.S. government. Some have immigrated, but under immigration laws that are quite a bit different from those of the late nineteenth and early twentieth centuries. Others have come as refugees, having been driven out of or fleeing from regimes in their native countries which threatened to oppress them. Still others have come as undocumented or illegal immigrants, willing to enter but not willingly accepted socially or politically. The new immigrants and refugees have entered the country as free workers; that is, they can enter the labor market directly or try to obtain the education necessary to advance themselves. But undocumented aliens face severe restrictions in the labor market. Often they are forced to work for below-minimum wage, without social security and other fringe benefits, and under constant threat of being discovered and deported.

The new arrivals are clearly ethnic groups, but it is not clear that they are all minority groups. Minority groups, as described in Chapter 3, are oppressed groups *within* society, and the oppression must be widespread both in time and place. The new immigrant and refugee groups are too new to be automatically considered minority groups in the United States. They enter during periods when the values of cultural pluralism and a multicultural society are being championed (see Chapter 6). Therefore, while the new arrivals have met with hostility in some instances, it is much less detrimental than that experienced by enslaved Afro-Americans, conquered Native Americans, or immigrating Catholic Irish; it is probably even less than the hostility directed to many southern and eastern Europeans at the turn of the twentieth century. Many of the new arrivals probably never will be relegated to minority status in the United

NEW ARRIVALS BY CONTINENT OF BIRTH, 1961–1985

Patterns of immigration to the United States have changed dramatically since the 1960s. In the two decades between 1961 and 1980, the number of legal entrants from Europe declined by one-third while the number from Asia increased almost four-fold. The numbers from North and South America continued to increase; the data for North America include Mexico, Central America, and the Caribbean as well as Canada. These data from the U.S. Immigration and Naturalization Service show the number of immigrants in thousands but do not include estimates of undocumented aliens.

	Period Covered		
	1961–70 (000)	1971–80 (000)	1981–85 (000)
Europe	1,238.6	801.3	321.8
Asia	445.3	1,633.8	1,376.3
North America	1,351.1	1,645.0	885.7
South America	228.3	284.4	184.0
Africa	39.3	91.5	77.0

Source: U.S. Bureau of the Census, *Statistical Abstract of the United States 1988* (Washington, DC, 1987), Table 8.

States. The provision of social services to immigrants and refugees can help avoid this outcome.

Undocumented aliens are another matter. Since they are largely either African (e.g., Haitian) or Hispanic (e.g., Mexican or Central American) in origin, they have a very strong likelihood of either being incorporated into existing black or Hispanic minorities or becoming new minority groups. The following sections consider the experiences of new immigrants, refugees, and undocumented aliens entering the United States today.

THE NEW IMMIGRANTS

Immigrants, as we noted in Chapter 4, are natives or residents of one nation who move more-or-less voluntarily to another nation. They become part of the new national society, and many of them take up citizenship in the new nation. To some extent, the immigrants arriving today differ from those who came to the United States from the early days of the Republic to the mid-twentieth century. The Hart-Cellar Act passed in 1965 significantly altered immigration patterns. The law, which went into effect in 1968, abolished quotas based on national origin and abandoned use of the designation *Asian-Pacific Triangle* as an area from which the immigration of Asians had been severely restricted. A limit on total immigration was set which allowed 290,000 immigrants to enter annually, with no more than 20,000 from any one nation. While the law did not assign preferences by national origin, in practice people from the eastern hemisphere with family members in the United States and with occupational training and skills which were in demand were more likely to be admitted. The western hemisphere act passed in 1976 gave similar preferences to people from the Americas with family ties and occupational training.[5]

The new immigration laws thus changed the types of persons likely to be admitted into the United States. Immigrants still come from Europe; in the late 1980s, for instance, provisions were made to admit a number of Russians, including Jews, who finally were allowed to leave the Soviet Union under that nation's new policy of *glasnost*, or openness. The largest numbers are arriving from Latin America and Asia, however. Today's immigrants are likely to be relatively well educated and prepared for life in the United States. They still face problems—leaving one's homeland and giving up one's culture is never easy. But immigrants arriving today are very unlike those impoverished and illiterate southern and eastern Europeans who flocked to the United States at the turn of the twentieth century.

EAST INDIAN IMMIGRANTS

An example of a new immigrant group is the East Indians, sometimes called Asian Indians. Between 1820 and 1965, fewer than 17,000 East Indians had entered the United States, in large part because they were included in the Asian groups that were barred from immigration. Since 1965, over 100,000 have come to the United States; over 30,000 have settled in the New York City area, and there are sizable settlements in California and Illinois.[6]

East Indians are a heterogeneous group. India is a large country divided into 30 territories and states, with a wide range of diverse racial, religious, and linguistic groups. The Indian government recognizes 15 national languages, among them English, which most immigrants speak fluently. Hinduism is the dominant religion in India, and Hindus make up the largest group of East Indian immigrants to the United States.

It might have been predicted that East Indian immigrants would have a difficult time adjusting to life in American society, considering the attitudes that Americans had demonstrated toward them in the past. In 1926, when Emory Borgardus first reported **social distance** scores, East Indians were ranked lowest on the list of 30 groups studied; this was lower than all the racial minorities we have been discussing. As recently as 1966, East Indians were still seen as the least desirable group for neighborhoods, for friendship, and for marriage.[7] East Indians also experience considerable prejudice and discrimination in Great Britain and South Africa, where they are considered "colored." Yet in spite of these disadvantages, the transition to American life appears to be relatively easy for recent East Indian immigrants.

One likely explanation is that, like most contemporary immigrants, many East Indians are highly trained professionals. Although there are exceptions, most of them are well educated and immigrate with their families. It has been estimated that about 46,000 East Indian engineers, physicians, scientists, professors, teachers, and businesspeople entered the United States between 1965 and 1975, along with almost 47,000 of their wives and children.[8] According to the 1980 census, 50 percent of Asian Indians in the United States were in management or professional positions. This percentage was higher than that for any other Asian group and considerably higher than that for white Americans, only 25 percent of whom held such positions. Similarly, 52 percent of Asian Indians 25 years of age and older in the United States were college graduates in 1980, compared to 17 percent of whites.[9]

Undoubtedly their relatively high level of training and their ability to speak English have made the transition into American society relatively smooth for East Indians. Upon arrival, many of these immigrants live in residential hotels until they find permanent employment or professional positions. Adults often enroll in colleges and universities for additional training, and children generally adjust well to the public schools.

Becoming an American is not free of difficulty for all East Indians, however. Some have experienced discrimination, especially as they have attempted to move into administrative and top-level management positions. Traditional family life has been disrupted as the women join the labor force and the role of wife and mother undergoes change. The respect traditionally shown by East Indian children for their elders has also been eroded by contact with American culture. Nevertheless, most East Indians have tried to maintain their heritage and resist assimilation. New immigrants have joined together to develop voluntary associations and promote cultural programs, and community schools have been formed where children can learn regional languages, music, and dance.

REFUGEES AND DISPLACED PERSONS

The number of new arrivals coming to the United States who enter as refugees is sizable. **Refugees** differ from immigrants in that they do not voluntarily leave their native country to come to another; they are forced out. Refugees also differ from colonized groups; they have not been forced into another society by a colonizing or conquering state.

Laws covering the entrance of displaced persons are relatively new in the United States. Their history is tied to international politics and the relations between communist and capitalist nations. After World War II, displaced persons from war-torn eastern European Baltic nations, which were then coming under Russian domination, were allowed to enter the United States. The first Displaced Persons Act, passed in 1948, allowed 220,000 Baltic-nation refugees to enter the United States under "mortgaged" immigration quotas; that is, they could borrow against future quota allowances. Because the legislation was written to favor Protestants and discriminated against Catholics and Jews, President Harry Truman signed the bill reluctantly and asked for its speedy amendment. The discriminatory aspects of the law were changed in 1950, and by 1953 displaced persons could enter as "nonquota immigrants." Three years later, annual quotas on displaced persons were ended. Special provisions were made under the Refugee Act of 1980 to allow entry of a limited number who fear persecution or oppression in their native land, but the definition of who qualifies under these rules is controversial.

Although humanitarian motives were involved in the displaced-persons acts, their principal use has been as a weapon in Cold War politics. On the whole, they have favored opponents of communist regimes, including Hungary in 1956, Dutch Indonesia in 1957, and Cuba and China in 1960. More recently, refugees from communist-controlled Southeast Asia have been allowed to enter under these acts.

Refugees now entering the United States tend to be more like the new immigrants than the immigrants of the late nineteenth and early twentieth centuries. While there is wide variation among them, they generally are educated and skilled, and they have benefited from government programs aimed at helping them make a smooth transition to life in the United States. In no way should the suffering these refugees endured in leaving their homelands and building a new life for themselves be minimized. But, simply put, on the whole refugee groups have not been oppressed in the United States and probably should not be thought of as subordinated minority groups.

With the fall of capitalism, many upper- and middle-class Vietnamese were forced to flee their country. In the United States, they are taking the opportunities provided and working hard to achieve the American Dream, as exemplified by this Vietnamese immigrant family in front of their Chicago restaurant. *Mike Tappin.*

INDOCHINESE REFUGEES

The term **Indochinese** includes the many Southeast Asian peoples under French colonial rule in the nineteenth century. Of these, the Vietnamese, the Cambodians, and the Laotians are the three major groups that have come to the United States. Each is a linguistically and culturally distinct group.

During World War II, Indochina was occupied and controlled by the Japanese forces. Toward the end of the war France proposed a plan of reunification and sought to regain control, but a coalition of Vietnamese nationalists and communists refused to accept, and war broke out between the French and both factions. After the French were defeated at Dienbienphu in 1954, Vietnam was partitioned into the Democratic Republic of Vietnam (the communists) in the North and the Republic of Vietnam (the nationalists) in the South. Proposed elections to reunify Vietnam under a single government were canceled by the South, with the backing of the United States, and war broke out between the North and South Vietnamese. U.S. military forces became heavily involved in the civil war, which lasted for almost 20 years, seriously disrupting the economy and the culture of the Vietnamese. Thousands of Americans in military service lost their lives, and there was turmoil in the United States as young people, led by university students and others, protested U.S. involvement. In April 1975 the South Vietnamese government collapsed, and the communists took control.[10]

Relatively few Indochinese were living in the United States prior to 1975, and there are no data on the Cambodians and Laotians in this country. The Vietnamese who had immigrated generally were wives or children of American servicemen. But within five months of the collapse of the South Vietnamese government, almost 190,000 Vietnamese, Laotians, and Cambodians arrived, and this first wave of refugees did not represent a cross section of the Indochinese people. By and large they were from the urban, affluent, better-educated sectors. Most were young (82 percent were under 35) and male. Forty percent were Catholic, though only 10 percent of the Vietnamese population was Catholic. Almost 75 percent of the refugees were North Vietnamese who had resettled in South Vietnam at the time of the 1954 partition.[11]

Four temporary refugee camps were set up, and funds for services to help settle and integrate the refugees were allotted under the Indochinese Migration and Refugee Assistance Act of 1975. In the camps, the refugees received educational and medical services: schooling for children, language and vocational training for adults, and lessons in such skills as shopping, applying for jobs, and renting apartments. The services also attempted to locate sponsors for the refugees, American citizens who would assume responsibility for helping refugee individuals and families enter American society. But life in the camps was difficult. The programs were criticized for attempting to assimilate refugees without sufficient attention to their cultural history and preferences. Some parents refused to let their children attend school. Many of the refugees arrived with extended families, and since sponsors were reluctant to assume responsibility for an entire family, family networks were often broken up. While many sponsors proved extremely helpful, others exploited the new refugees.[12]

Between 1980 and 1985, more than 250,000 Vietnamese entered the United States—more than half the total previously in the country. There were still some 100,000 Vietnamese in refugee camps in Asia in 1985, many of whom had expressed a preference for entering the United States. The recent Indochinese refugees are not so educated or skilled as the first wave. According to the 1980 census, only 13 percent of the Vietnamese in the United States held managerial or professional positions, and their median family income was $13,000. On both these indexes they were below not only white Americans but all other Asian-American groups.[13] More recent refugees also have not had the government benefits or the access to sponsors that were available to the first wave. They have been described as being more willing to start at the bottom and to accept hardship.[14]

UNDOCUMENTED ALIENS

Changes in immigration laws over the years which have attempted to control access to the United States have resulted in a patchwork of regulations which often have unintended consequences. As a result of the changes favoring immigrants with work skills and professional expertise in demand in the United States, the "illegal" immigration of unskilled workers has increased considerably. The latest legislative effort to deal with the "immigration problem," the Immigration Reform and Control Act of 1986, targets residents who have entered the country illegally (see box, Immigration Reform and the Undocumented Alien).

The actual number of such **undocumented aliens** in the United States is not known, but the estimate has been put as high as 8 million. The U.S. Immigration and Naturalization Service reports that up to 500,000 undocumented aliens are arrested and deported each year.[15] This population, being largely unskilled, uneducated, and rural, is more like the "teeming masses" that came from southern and eastern Europe at the turn of the twentieth century.

Alejandro Portes notes that illegal immigration is caused not only by push factors in the country of origin but by pull factors in the country of destination, since U.S. businesses encourage the illegal immigration of low-wage workers to maximize profit. The flow of illegal aliens, Portes says, is a movement of people who are not searching for a welfare handout but looking for honest work to fulfill basic human needs. Moreover, illegal immigration is not always permanent but often is a cyclical process in which people move back and forth between nations according to the opportunities available to them.[16]

MEXICANS

The majority of illegal immigrants come from Mexico, but by no means are all undocumented aliens in the United States Mexican. Others have come from

Haiti, the Dominican Republic, Guatemala, Honduras, El Salvador, and even Canada. Most Mexican Americans are legal citizens of the United States. They either have been in this country since before the American takeover of the Southwest or have immigrated legally.

Mexicans who enter illegally come largely from the rural, northern parts of Mexico. Their movement is pushed by poverty and unemployment in Mexico and pulled by agricultural and other business interests in the United States which welcome them as a source of cheap labor willing to do work that most Americans will not do. Undocumented Mexicans also contribute to the American economy in other ways; for instance, they pay taxes. The Department of Labor estimated that in 1976 almost 75 percent of undocumented Mexicans were paying federal income and social security taxes. They also are not a burden on public welfare; in 1976, less than 4 percent had children in school, and only 0.5 percent received welfare benefits.[17]

HAITIANS

Haitians have recently been identified as another ethnic group with large numbers of undocumented aliens in the United States, though Haitians have been

IMMIGRATION REFORM AND THE UNDOCUMENTED ALIEN

The three major sections of the Immigration Reform and Control Act of 1986 are concerned with legalization of residency, provisions for temporary agricultural workers, and sanctions against employers who hire undocumented workers.

The legalization section provided a method for legalizing the status of many aliens who could prove they had entered the United States before January 1, 1982. Applicants were to be granted temporary-resident status for 18 months and then would earn permanent-resident status if they had a minimal knowledge of spoken English and civics. After five more years, during which they are not to be entitled to welfare benefits, they are to become U.S. citizens. The Immigration and Naturalization Service opened special offices to process applications, and private groups encouraged aliens to overcome their fear and distrust of the government and register. But when this yearlong program expired on May 4, 1988, only 1.7 million amnesty applications had been filed, far short of the 3 million expected.

The temporary agricultural workers provision of the law stipulated that growers wishing to hire alien migrant farm workers must file a petition with the U.S. Department of Labor. The petition will be granted if there are not already enough workers who are able, willing, qualified, and availin this country since colonial times. A troop of 800 "men of color" from Haiti fought on behalf of American independence, and the first permanent settler and founder of the city of Chicago was Haitian.[18] Recent Haitian immigration began in 1957 with the totalitarian regime of Francois "Papa Doc" Duvalier, who was elected president and subsequently named himself President for Life. It intensified in the turmoil which followed the exile of Duvalier's successor, his son "Baby Doc," and the appointment of a military-civilian council.

Most Haitians have come to the United States as immigrants, generally representing the middle class of this impoverished island. In the early 1960s, about 50 percent of gainfully employed Haitian immigrants were professionals or white-collar workers.[19] Since 1970, however, the occupational and educational profile of Haitian immigrants has changed. Included in recent waves have been "boat people" who leave the island on their own, using small boats to make the dangerous crossing to Florida. They are mostly rural peasants fleeing poverty and political repression, but instead of being accepted into this country as refugees they have been considered illegal immigrants. Many were apprehended and held for deportation, even though return to Haiti meant certain death. Under a special provision of the Immigration Reform and Control Act of 1986, however, qualified aliens who are in the category of

able to do the work, and if there will be no adverse effects on wages and working conditions. Temporary agricultural workers were also to be allowed to seek U.S. residency status under a special amnesty program which had a later deadline than the legalization program. To qualify, workers had to show they had done such work for 90 days between May 1, 1985, and May 1, 1986. Normally, about 600,000 aliens come to the United States each year to work on farms or pick crops, but when this program ended in December 1988, some 1.2 million applications had been received. It was speculated that many who could not qualify under the stricter residency requirements of the legalization program sought to stay by representing themselves as farm workers.

Under the employer sanctions section of the legislation, civil penalties were to be imposed on employers who knowingly hire, recruit, or refer aliens who are not authorized to work in the United States; criminal penalties were possible for habitual offenders. Employer sanctions were to start in May 1987 but were delayed by Congress until after a 12-month education period ending in September 1988.

Sources: "U.S. Immigration Law," *World Almanac and Book of Facts, 1988* (New York: World Almanac, 1987), p. 747; "A Stampede Story," *Time*, May 9, 1988, p. 45; "A Million Late Arrivals," *Time*, December 12, 1988, p. 33.

Cuban/Haitian Entrant (Status Pending) are eligible to adjust to permanent residence status.[20]

IMPLICATIONS FOR PRACTICE

Social service workers have at least two goals in working with new arrivals. One is to assure that none of the new groups becomes a minority group. The other is to assure that socialization into American society takes place, while respecting and helping to sustain the cultural values and traditions of the new arrivals.

The new arrivals today are not colonized groups, forced into the United States and therefore subjected to minority status. Both the immigrants and some of the refugees are more likely to succeed than either immigrants or colonized peoples in the past. Because of their educational background and occupational skills, they are better prepared to achieve socioeconomic success. Moreover, social services often are available to help them move quickly into the American mainstream. Undocumented aliens present another problem. Although they come to the United States voluntarily, looking for work, they live under threat of being expelled. Often they are associated with ethnic groups such as Mexican Americans and blacks who already hold minority status in the United States.

The task of the social service worker in working with new arrivals is the same as it was with earlier arrivals, however. Leaving one country and taking up residence in another always involves social and economic hardships. The crucial objective of workers is to help new arrivals make their transitions into American society without experiencing the severe hostility that produces minority status for a group. The social service worker can do this through advocacy, as well as by developing social and economic opportunities, providing appropriate services, and making referrals to other needed services.

In working with new arrivals, social service workers become involved in their clients' socialization into the attitudes and values, norms and traditions of American society. In the past, the task of socialization was often accomplished at the expense of the new arrivals' own cultures. Workers advocated assimilation into the society and often acted as if the old ways were of no value. Today, they are more likely to espouse **cultural pluralism**, the value that the United States should be culturally diverse and everyone should not be forced into a single mold (see Chapter 6). Tied to this value is the idea that new arrivals should become **bicultural**, that is, able to function competently within the norms, traditions, and values of their own culture, as well as in the culture of the United States.

A theory of **bicultural socialization** proposed by Diane de Anda is relevant to social service work with new arrivals.[21] She maintains that social and personal well-being requires being adequately socialized within both one's own culture and the dominant culture. While new arrivals may understand what is expected in order to be successful within their own communities, they lack

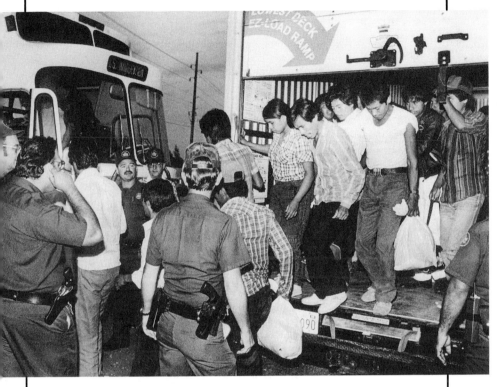

The roundup of suspected illegal immigrants is common in the border areas of the southwest. With changes in immigration laws, today's illegal immigrants are like the "huddled masses" from southern and eastern Europe who came to the United States seeking to escape poverty. *AP/Wide World Photos*.

knowledge of what is expected in order to be successful in the majority community.

The factors facilitating successful bicultural socialization are described in Chapter 6, but two of them offer ideas about how social workers can help new arrivals become bicultural. One is the use of translators and models from the same ethnic group as their clients, to help the clients develop an understanding of the values of the majority community and learn the behavior patterns expected in it, while maintaining their own values and behavior patterns. Workers also can use mediators from the dominant group to serve as guides for ethnic minorities.[22] The second factor is the provision of corrective feedback. Social service workers themselves can serve as translators, models, and mediators and can offer corrective feedback. A worker who is of the same ethnic group as the client can serve as a translator or model. A worker who is not can serve as a mediator and give feedback.

DISCUSSION QUESTIONS AND CLASS PROJECTS

1. Distinguish among the following: immigrants, refugees, and undocumented aliens. Give examples of each and describe their experiences in coming to the United States.

2. Select an immigrant or refugee group that is settling in your area and collect information on them by searching your library or conducting interviews with people knowledgeable about them. See what you can learn about their cultural values and traditions, their strengths and resources, and their needs and problems.

3. From your experience, would you say that any new immigrant or refugee group is in danger of becoming a minority group in the United States? Why or why not?

4. In what ways can social workers be helpful to new arrivals?

NOTES

1. For an interesting, well-illustrated account of the diverse new racial and ethnic groups which are "rapidly and permanently changing the face of America," see the special issue of *Time*, "Immigrants," July 8, 1985.

2. U.S. Bureau of the Census, *Statistical Abstract 1988* (Washington, DC, 1987), Table 8.

3. "U.S. Immigration Law," *World Almanac and Book of Facts 1988* (New York, World Almanac, 1987), p. 747; Otto Friedrich, "The Changing Face of America," *Time*, July 8, 1985, p. 29.

4. See the issue of *Practice Digest* titled "The New Arrivals," vol. 5 (March 1983).

5. William S. Bernard, "Immigration: History of U.S. Policy," in S. Thernstrom

(editor), *Harvard Encyclopedia of American Ethnic Groups* (Cambridge, MA: Belknap Press, 1980), pp. 486–96.

6. Joan M. Jensen, "East Indians," in *Harvard Encyclopedia of American Ethnic Groups*, pp. 296–301.

7. Emory S. Bogardus, "Comparing Racial Distance in Ethiopia, South Africa, and the United States," *Sociology and Social Research*, vol. 52 (January 1968), p. 162.

8. Jensen, "East Indians," p. 299.

9. Leon F. Bouvier and Anthony J. Agresta, "The Fastest Growing Minority," *American Demographics*, vol. 7 (May 1985), pp. 31–33.

10. Mary Bowen Wright, "Indochinese," in *Harvard Encyclopedia of American Ethnic Groups*, pp. 508–13.

11. Ibid., pp. 509–11.

12. Ibid., pp. 511–12.

13. Bouvier and Agresta, "Fastest Growing Minority."

14. Bowen Wright, "Indochinese," pp. 512–13.

15. Bernard, "Immigration: History of U.S. Policy," p. 495.

16. Alejandro Portes, "Illegal Immigration and the International System, Lessons from Recent Legal Mexican Immigrants to the United States," *Social Problems*, vol. 26 (April 1979), pp. 425–27.

17. Carlos E. Cortes, "Mexicans," in *Harvard Encyclopedia of American Ethnic Groups*, p. 704.

18. Michel S. Laguerre, "Haitians," in *Harvard Encyclopedia of American Ethnic Groups*, p. 446.

19. Ibid., p. 447.

20. "U.S. Immigration Law," p. 747.

21. Diane de Anda, "Bicultural Socialization: Factors Affecting the Minority Experience," *Social Work*, vol. 29 (March–April 1984), pp. 101–107.

22. Ibid., p. 104.

CHAPTER 6

Ethnic-Community Relations in Contemporary American Society

M AJOR THEMES DISCUSSED IN THIS CHAPTER:

1. *The social context of minority-majority relations.* In contemporary American society, blacks, Native Americans, Mexican Americans, and Puerto Ricans continue to encounter poverty, unemployment, and other social problems in numbers disproportionate to their representation in the population as a whole. To what extent is their situation a product of racism and ethnocentrism? Do prejudice and discrimination still operate to make American society racist?

2. *Institutional racism.* Racism can exist independent of the attitudes and beliefs of individuals. When it is built into the norms, traditions, laws, and policies of a society, so that even those who have nonracist beliefs are compelled to act otherwise, racism is said to be institutionalized.

3. *Biological and cultural attributes of ethnic-minority communities.* A systems approach not only examines the social context of ethnic-minority communities but assesses factors in focal systems which may contribute to their needs and problems. Two of these factors, biological or genetic and cultural attributes, are highly controversial areas of study.

4. *Prospects for progress in minority-majority relations.* Successful outcomes

for ethnic relations, in the form of assimilation or cultural pluralism, are possible but not guaranteed. As a result of ethnic and racial conflict and competition, some minority groups have been exterminated or expelled, and some have seceded or violently rebelled against the majority.

5. *Implications for practice.* Social workers must strive to alter the conditions that limit success in the larger society and in minority groups. The problems of individuals and families in minority groups can never be divorced from the problems of their communities. Social workers must be able to assess the continuing effects of prejudice and discrimination on the progress of their clients.

THIS CHAPTER looks at the "here and now" of racial-and ethnic-minority communities, in particular the "old," established minorities: Afro-Americans, Native Americans, Mexican Americans, and Puerto Ricans. As noted in Chapter 4, many members of these groups continue to be mired in adverse socioeconomic conditions such as unemployment, underemployment, and poverty. Although historical circumstances have shaped their situations, contemporary socioeconomic conditions are of even greater consequence. It is in the present that minorities must struggle to achieve social, economic, and political success and social service workers must address the disadvantages to which minorities have been subjected. And it is in the present that the social changes necessary to a better future for these groups must be initiated. In order to understand the contemporary situation, we will consider both what factors in the social environment of ethnic-minority communities and what factors within the communities themselves are currently acting to hinder or facilitate their achievement of socioeconomic well-being.

THE SOCIAL CONTEXT OF
MINORITY- MAJORITY RELATIONS

Minority-majority relations in American society are carried out within the context of social systems which include both ethnic-minority and ethnic-majority communities and the individuals who comprise them. Underlying these relations are the norms and other institutions and institutional arrangements which are generated through social interactions within these systems (see Chapter 2). The question to be considered in this section is whether the social context currently confronted by ethnic-minority communities is a hostile one which acts to block their progress to secure socioeconomic well-being. If the answer is yes, we can go a long way toward understanding the disadvantages still being experienced by minorities.

RACISM AND ETHNOCENTRISM

Does the United States have a racist society? **Racism** is most often defined as a set of beliefs which attributes inferiority to others because of their presumed physical characteristics: their skin color, "blood," or some other aspect of their physical or genetic makeup. A society that is racist would be one that promotes such beliefs.

Contemporary scholars are quick to point out that this traditional definition of racism needs to be updated in the light of present circumstances. Social scientists have documented that relatively few Americans now believe in the doctrine of innate inferiority of racial groups. With respect to Afro-Americans, John McConahay and Joseph Hough argue that symbolic racism now is more characteristic of the thinking of whites, especially affluent suburban whites.[1] **Symbolic racism** rejects doctrines of racial inferiority and even segregation and focuses on three affective elements:

1. Feelings that minorities are pushing too much and demanding too much in an attempt to get more than they merit.
2. Beliefs that minorities are not playing by "the rules of the game" and want success but do not want to work hard or to delay gratification in order to get it.
3. Negative feelings about welfare, urban riots, crime in the streets, affirmative action, and quota systems, all of which are associated with minority groups.

The question might equally well be: Does the United States have an ethnocentric society? William Graham Sumner defines **ethnocentrism** as "this view of things in which one's own group is the center of everything, and all others are scaled and rated with reference to it."[2] James Vander Zanden describes it as:

> . . . the tendency of group members to appraise peoples of other cultures by the standards of judgement prevailing in their own culture. Individuals assume that in *the nature of things* other people should be organized according to the same assumptions as prevail within their own group. Ethnocentrism entails strong positive feelings toward an ingroup, even ingroup glorification.[3]

In the past it was clear that American society was both racist and ethnocentric. There is evidence that residents of the United States used to be more open about their prejudices, more flagrant in their discrimination, and more demanding that new arrivals assimilate to American ways. Moreover, laws and government policies which formerly gave official sanction to discrimination no longer exist. Whereas 30 states had laws prohibiting interracial marriage in 1950, for instance, there are no such laws presently.[4]

The evidence for the existence of significant ethnocentrism and racism in American society has been increasingly harder to find. Scholars—even those from minority communities themselves—are divided about the relative importance of racism in holding back minorities today. Some, such as William J. Wilson, believe that while racism still is evident, it is no longer of consequence for economic success.[5] Others, such as Ronald Walters, see the struggle for economic resources as a continuing factor in prejudice and discrimination.[6] Before considering this debate, we must clarify the concepts of prejudice and discrimination.

PREJUDICE AND DISCRIMINATION

Racism and ethnocentrism are forms of prejudice in that they have to do with people's beliefs and attitudes. Sociologically, the term **prejudice** is used in a specific way. William Newman defines prejudice as "any set of ideas and beliefs that negatively prejudge groups or individuals as members of groups on the basis of real or alleged group traits or characteristics."[7] Four components make up this definition.

First, prejudice is a state of mind in that it refers to thoughts, feelings, and intentions but does not refer to actions or behaviors. It is studied by asking people what they think, feel, or intend to do.

Second, prejudice is group-based and thus a social phenomenon. For social scientists, prejudice is not the study of individual biases or personal likes and dislikes but the study of how the attitudes of individuals reflect their group membership. It is the study of how "I" as a member of one group dislike "you" as a member of another group.

Third, prejudice is a prejudgment and exists regardless of the experiences an individual might have with members of another group. People who never have had contacts with outgroup members still can form stereotypes and expectations about what such people are like.

Fourth, prejudice represents negative beliefs and attitudes about others. While favorable prejudices certainly might be held, social scientists have been more concerned with documenting negative, group-based prejudices.

Newman defines **discrimination** as "any act of differential treatment toward a group or an individual perceived as a member of a group." Moreover, he notes, "the intent and/or effect of differential treatment is to create a disadvantage of some sort."[8] Thus discrimination differs from prejudice primarily in that one defines an attitude and the other defines a behavior. Both reflect group processes whereby in-group members express negative attitudes or behaviors toward outgroup members. To study discrimination we would have to observe the actual behaviors of people and organizations.

Discrimination is extremely difficult to measure. In studying prejudice people can be asked what they feel, think, and intend to do, but studying discrimination requires observation in some fairly direct ways of what people actually do. Because of the difficulty of studying discrimination, social scientists have largely focused on prejudices, on the assumption that there is at least a reasonable link between what people believe, feel, and think they will do and what they actually do. As we shall see, however, this may not be altogether a good assumption.

In an early investigation of whether prejudice and discrimination go hand in hand, Melvin DeFleur and Frank Westie wrote to motel owners asking them if they would accept Chinese patrons (the study was published in 1958).[9] The majority who wrote back indicated that they would not, but when the researchers actually brought Chinese patrons to these motels, their business was rarely turned away. Depending on personality and situational factors, prejudicial attitudes may not lead to discriminatory behavior, and discrimination may come about even when prejudice is not apparent.

Robert Merton distinguishes between prejudice and discrimination by referring to four possible types of adaptation (see box, Prejudice and Discrimination Typology).[10] The term **bigot** usually refers to someone who is both filled with prejudice and consistently discriminates. Old-style southern political leaders come readily to mind. The term **liberal**, in this sense, applies to a person who is consistent in attitude and behavior in that he or she neither is prejudiced nor discriminates. Most people who aspire to work in the social services would like to think of themselves in these terms.

There are, however, prejudiced people who, because of particular constraints, do not act on their prejudices. An example is the university bureaucrat or the agency administrator who would rather not follow affirmative action guidelines in recruiting students and workers but nevertheless does obey the letter of the law. Merton refers to such people as **timid bigots**. There also are

PREJUDICE AND DISCRIMINATION TYPOLOGY

Prejudice and discrimination do not always go hand in hand. The situations people find themselves in can alter such attitudes and behaviors.

Person is Person	Discriminates	Does not discriminate
Prejudiced	Bigot	Timid bigot
Not prejudiced	Fair-weather liberal	Liberal

Source: Based on Robert Merton, "Discrimination and the American Creed," in R. MacIver (editor), *Discrimination and National Welfare* (New York: Harper and Row, 1949).

many people who sincerely do not believe they are prejudiced but who nevertheless might discriminate in particular situations. This is the **fair-weather liberal**. One example is the worker or manager who sees discrimination going on in the workplace but does nothing about it. Another is the unprejudiced person who would not move into an integrated neighborhood or might even block neighborhood integration efforts, not because of personal opinions deriding racial and ethnic minorities but because of a desire to avoid creating problems in the neighborhood.

The Principle of Nondiscrimination

If American society is to be defined as racist, then there would have to be, at a minimum, fairly widespread prejudice and fairly open discrimination by individuals. On the whole, Americans would have to believe in principle that discrimination is a good thing. The attitudes and actions of a handful of bigots are not sufficient evidence that the United States has a racist society. It is necessary to consider what kinds of attitudes about ethnic-minority group members are expressed by the white ethnic-majority community.

On the surface there is less evidence of bigotry in the United States now than in the past. Researchers have noted that during the most active period of the civil rights movement, whites' attitudes toward blacks (the focus of the bulk of these studies) and toward most other minority groups changed appreciably in a positive direction. Examining public opinion and other surveys of racial attitudes dating back to 1942, Howard Schuman, Charlotte Steeh, and Lawrence Bobo showed that prior to World War II, the population of the United States generally supported the principle of segregation of minorities and discrimination against them. After the civil rights movement of the 1960s, however, this principle lost popular support. By and large, white Americans now believe that there should be equal job opportunities, that everyone should be able to live where they wish, that all students should attend the same schools, that means of transportation should not be segregated, and that interracial marriages should not be prohibited. In other words, they believe in the **principle of nondiscrimination**.[11]

In 1942, for instance, 42 percent of Americans believed that "Negroes have the same intelligence as white people, given the same education and training." By 1963 the proportion who agreed with this statement had jumped to 78 percent. Similarly, support for "Jim Crow" segregational laws seems to have declined a great deal. In 1942, 44 percent believed "there should not be separate sections for Negroes in streetcars and buses." By 1963, this proportion had jumped to 79 percent and by 1970 to 88 percent. Even in terms of neighborhood integration, there seems to have been a decline in prejudicial attitudes. In 1942, 35 percent of American whites believed that "if a Negro with just as much income and education as you had moved into your block, it would not make any difference." By 1963, 64 percent of white Americans said they believed this; by 1972, 81 percent agreed.[12] There is also evidence that Americans are increasingly uncomfortable with **stereotypes** of the group characteristics of racial and ethnic minorities (see box, Stereotypes: Negative and Positive).

There are also indications that white Americans are more willing to intermingle with members of ethnic and racial minority groups. In his studies on social distance, Emory Bogardus attempted to measure **racial distance** by asking whites how willing they were to welcome members of such groups to "employment in my occupation," "my street as neighbors," "my club as personal chums," and "close kinship by marriage." These studies were completed in 1926, 1946, 1956, and 1966, and throughout this period the rankings of the groups remained relatively constant. In general, ethnic groups from northern and western Europe were seen as more desirable than groups from eastern and southern Europe, who were in turn seen as more desirable than Third World groups. Nevertheless, significant changes were apparent over the years. The distance white Americans felt obligated to maintain in 1926 had shrunk a good deal by 1966. Whereas white Americans were drawing the line against Third World groups at neighborhood integration in 1926, by 1966 they were drawing it at the level of friendships.[13]

The degree to which there has been a broad change toward less racism and

STEREOTYPES: NEGATIVE AND POSITIVE

Stereotypes are rigid opinions about people in which characteristics are uncritically attributed to all members of a particular group. Stereotypes may be negative or positive. Negative stereotypes are applied to members of outgroups by members of in-groups, who may view the same characteristics in others as positive stereotypes. Robert Merton cites as an example Abraham Lincoln's habit of working far into the night, which is regarded as evidence that he was "industrious, resolute, perseverant, and eager to realize his capacities to the full." But if outgroups such as Jews or Japanese work equally hard, this is likely to be considered evidence of "their sweatshop mentality, their ruthless undercutting of American standards, their unfair competitive practices."

The concept of stereotyping was explored in a series of studies in which Princeton University students were asked in 1933, 1951, and 1967 to characterize various ethnic and racial groups. A large percentage of the students in 1933 easily agreed that Negroes were superstitious, lazy, happy-go-lucky, and ignorant; that the Chinese were superstitious, sly, and conservative; that Italians were artistic, impulsive, and passionate; and that the English were sportsmanlike, intelligent, and conventional. By 1951, student willingness to make such stereotypical generalizations had declined significantly, and many expressed irritation at being asked to do

ethnocentrism, as expressed in attitudes, depends on the particular issue or sphere of life being examined. By 1972 virtually all Americans said they believed that discrimination in employment was wrong and that equal economic opportunity should exist for all Americans. Nevertheless, 25 percent of them also said they would not vote for a black president.[14] Intermarriage is another area in which the principle of nondiscrimination seems to fall short. By 1983 only about 35 percent of white Americans approved of interracial marriages — about the same level of approval that integrated transportation had achieved in the 1940s.[15]

Taking data such as these into account, Schuman, Steeh, and Bobo concluded that "this overall picture of change points to a broad cultural shift in the norms that influence white attitudes toward the treatment of blacks in America."[16] White Americans, they argue, are by and large not bigots but believe, in principle, in equal treatment and opportunity for all. While these authors focused on attitudes toward blacks, it can be generalized that their findings are applicable to other ethnic and racial communities as well. In support of their findings, they reject the possibility that there are many "timid bigots" among Americans who say things they do not really mean when they

so. As a result, a "fading effect" was predicted for such stereotypes. Princeton students in 1967 also expressed indignation at being asked to come up with stereotypes and regarded the task as an insult to their intelligence.

The 1967 students who undertook the task of stereotyping nevertheless produced several important results. Their stereotypes were more uniform; that is, the students could agree on what the stereotypical traits of each group were. There was also a fair amount of consistency between the stereotypes noted in 1933 and those noted in 1967. However, the content of the stereotypes did change. In general, the negative stereotypes declined and were replaced by more positive stereotypes. For instance, only 14 percent of the students in 1967 stereotyped blacks as superstitious, down from 84 percent in 1933, and 47 percent described blacks as musical, up from 26 percent in 1933. Similarly, 6 percent of the students in 1967 described the Chinese as sly, down from 29 percent in 1933, and 50 percent described them as "loyal to family ties," up from 22 percent in 1933.

Sources: Robert Merton, *Social Theory and Social Structure*, 2nd ed. (New York: Free Press, 1968); Daniel Katz and Kenneth W. Braly, "Racial Stereotypes of One Hundred College Students," *Journal of Abnormal and Social Psychology*, vol. 28 (October-December 1933), pp. 280–90; Richard Centers, "An Effective Classroom Demonstration of Stereotypes," *Journal of Social Psychology*, vol. 34, 1st half (August 1951), pp. 41–46; Marvin Karlins, Thomas L. Coffman, and Gary Walters, "On the Fading of Social Stereotypes: Studies in Three Generations of College Students," *Journal of Personality and Social Psychology*, vol. 13 (September 1969), pp. 1–16.

are confronted by interviewers: "Outright lying is probably rare in these data; there is compelling evidence that most people assume that others — in this case white interviewers — agree with their own views."[17]

Yet it is possible that considerable bigotry does exist in American society, since there is evidence that progress in rejecting racism and ethnocentrism has slowed in the recent past. The early 1970s, in fact, seem to have been a high point in more tolerant racial attitudes among white Americans, and since that time the growth of such progressive attitudes has leveled off. Little change in attitudes about intermarriage, for instance, has been documented since the early 1970s. According to Schuman, Steeh, and Bobo, "In fact, on a broad question about the desirability of desegregation in general, there was even a partial reversal of trend."[18] If we realize that the late 1960s and 1970s were a period of liberalism in the United States and that the 1980s have been a period of conservatism, we should expect that the "timid bigots" would now feel freer to express their views. But research does support the possibility that, with changing cultural sanctions, social constraints against expressing prejudice or following through on discriminatory behavior may appear even among seemingly prejudiced persons.[19]

Implementing the Principle of Nondiscrimination

While Schuman, Steeh, and Bobo document a cultural shift to the principle of nondiscrimination, they also note that there is considerable disagreement among white and black Americans on the ways in which that principle should be implemented. It is one thing to accept the belief that nondiscrimination is good and another to agree on specific ways to implement it. For instance, should there be busing to achieve racial integration of schools? Should there be affirmative action programs to ensure the hiring of racial minorities? Should there be bilingual programs to help non-native speakers learn standard American English? Should neighborhoods actively attempt integration? These are not easy questions, and Americans are much more divided on them than they are on the principle of nondiscrimination. White Americans, for example, show much lower support for government intervention on behalf of nondiscrimination than for the principle of nondiscrimination itself. In only rare instances does support for particular policies to implement equal treatment surpass 50 percent. For instance, very few whites say they would resist the presence of one or a few blacks in a neighborhood or school, but such resistance is more likely as the hypothesized number of blacks increases.[20]

Afro-Americans themselves are not in total agreement on how to implement the principle of nondiscrimination. In some cases attitudes among blacks are no different from attitudes among whites. Attitudes toward busing is a case in point. Both groups show less support for busing than for any other implementation issue, although blacks are generally more supportive of busing than whites are.[21]

Is it racist to oppose a particular approach to achieving the principle of non-

TO BE SOLD *by* William

Yeomans, *(in Charles Town Merchant,)* a
parcel of good  Time Cre-
Plantation ... dit, Securi-
Slaves. En- ... ty to be gi-
couragement ... ven if requi-
will be gi- ... red There's
ven by taling ... likewise to
Rice in Pay- ... be sold, very
ment, or any ... good Troop-
ing saddles and Furniture, choice Barbados
and Boston Rum, also Cordial Waters
and Limejuice, as well as a parcel of extraordinary Indian trading Goods, and many of o-
ther sorts suitable for the Season.

American blacks were forced to immigrate as unfree
workers. This 1744 advertisement proudly announces
the sale of plantation slaves in South Carolina. *North
Wind Picture Archives*.

discrimination? Are people prejudiced if they are against busing or want to dismantle affirmative action programs? As long as the principle of nondiscrimination is valued, we can accept honest disagreements over the best ways to achieve nondiscrimination as being constructive debate and conflict. However, when such attitudes mask underlying disrespect for the principle, we can brand them as unfair.

INSTITUTIONAL RACISM

The study of attitudes and behaviors of individuals goes only part of the way in developing an understanding of what is meant by a racist society. To determine whether or not American society still should be considered racist, we must also study what has been called institutional racism and its corollary, institutional discrimination. It may very well be that while most Americans sincerely believe in the principle of nondiscrimination, they nevertheless support racism because in their everyday lives they live up to norms and traditions that are racist.

SOCIAL INSTITUTIONS AND INSTITUTIONAL ARRANGEMENTS

Social institutions and institutional arrangements were introduced in Chapter 2. Both may be seen as systems of norms which instruct people as to what constitutes "good behavior," thereby contributing to social stability. They provide continuing answers to continuing problems,[22] and they are guaranteed by authority, since failure to act according to social norms elicits punishment.[23] Social institutions are sets of norms which reflect an ordering of the major functions of a society. In an industrial society, the principal institutions are the political system, the economy, the military, kinship, and religion. Institutional arrangements, in contrast, are systems of norms which reflect agreements that crosscut these institutions and characterize all of them. Status hierarchies and cultural backgrounds are examples.

People experience social institutions and institutional arrangements through the norms expressed as laws, policies, and standard operating procedures by secondary groups or formal organizations such as social service agencies and schools. They also experience them through the norms adopted in primary groups or in informal social relationships such as neighborhoods, friendship cliques, and deep interpersonal relations. Some examples of these norms are family traditions, interpersonal expectations and behaviors, and neighborhood and social club membership values and expectations. At the informal level, the system of norms is often not written down or explicitly stated but exists on an implicit, between-the-lines, nonverbal basis.

RACISM AS AN INSTITUTIONAL ARRANGEMENT

In order to answer the question of whether the United States has a racist society, it is necessary to examine the institutional arrangements that regulate everyday social interaction. To what extent do the norms that govern economic, political, religious, and family life reward prejudice and discrimination on the basis of race or ethnicity? To what extent do the norms of formal and informal groups lead respected members of a society to adopt racism?

Like other institutional arrangements, racism takes a variety of forms which represent different combinations of formal or informal and intentional or inadvertent characteristics (see box, Institutional Racism Typology). There is disagreement as to whether deliberation and intent must be present before institutional racism and institutional discrimination can be said to exist in a society. Some norms intend to discriminate; there are rules and regulations that specifically aim to punish one group in favor of another. The apartheid system of South Africa is an excellent example. Other rules and regulations do not intend to discriminate but nevertheless do so, as in the use of intelligence tests and some forms of merit testing. Although such tests aim to distinguish on the basis of intellectual, attitudinal, or behavioral merit, due to unintentional biases in the test instruments they often distinguish on the basis of race and ethnicity. Louis Knowles and Kenneth Prewitt argue that regardless of intent, rules and regulations that discriminate on this basis are racist:

> A university admissions policy which provides for entrance only to students who score high on tests designed primarily for white suburban high schools necessarily excludes black ghetto-educated students. Unlike the legal policies of Mississippi [in the past], the university admission criteria are not intended to be racist, but

INSTITUTIONAL RACISM TYPOLOGY

One reason racism can pervade a society is that it takes many forms, ranging from formal policy and written legislation to individual attitudes. The results may be intentional outcomes or inadvertent consequences.

Results \ Form	Formal	Informal
Intentional	Written laws, such as quota act of 1921 and "Jim Crow" laws	Unwritten laws, such as friendship norms and norms of mate selection
Inadvertent	Merit and other procedures with non-racist criteria which nevertheless place members of certain groups at a disadvantage	Being willing to help friends get jobs, but having no friends who are members of other groups, so effect is discrimination

the university is pursuing a course which perpetuates institutional racism . . . Both the individual act of racism and the racist institutional policy may
occur without the presence of conscious bigotry, and both may be masked intentionally or innocently.[24]

Richard Burkey disagrees, arguing that the term *institutional discrimination*
should only be used to mean *intentional* discrimination: "Discrimination is a
form of conflict and therefore is intentional. It is to be distinguished from other
social conditions and policies that may perpetuate inequality but that are not
intentional."[25]

Whether or not discrimination is intentional, it is harmful. In social service
work, one question is the proper terminology to be used in trying to deal with
discrimination. An organization should be labeled as racist if its policies and
procedures deliberately discriminate. But when this is not the case, workers
schooled in interpersonal skills might do better to refer to "inadvertent racism"
or the "discriminatory effects" of particular procedures. Implying intention
when none is present can only cause confusion and offense and may work
against the achievement of common goals.

INSTITUTIONAL RACISM IN CONTEMPORARY AMERICAN SOCIETY

Important social changes have altered the nature of racism in the United States
today. Formal intentional racism, which formerly limited access to educational
and occupational opportunities, has given way to informal intentional racism,
which effectively excludes racial minorities from the self-help, support networks which people often use to locate opportunities, promote achievement,
and secure economic advancement.

Informal Intentional Racism: Interpersonal Relationships

At the informal intentional level, it is easy to document the racist character of
the society of the United States. Neighborhood segregation, which is apparent
in almost every American city, stands as a bastion of racism in spite of laws
that prohibit discrimination in selling or leasing property. Similarly, people's
usual interpersonal friendships and marital partners confirm that intimate
relationships are bounded by racism. While laws prohibiting interracial marriage or association no longer exist, most intimate relationships rarely cross
ethnic and racial boundaries. From an early age, Americans know who they
are supposed to live next to, become friends with, and make love to. These patterns exist over and above the attitudes of individuals, because social life is organized in such a way that they become inevitable. Individuals have to go out
of their way to avoid maintaining racism, and when they do, society often
reacts with negative sanctions. Americans therefore maintain racism simply by
where they buy or rent housing and whom they choose as friends and marriage
partners. Thus informal racist norms govern ordinary, everyday behavior.

In his studies of social distance, Bogardus demonstrates the existence of normative racist patterns controlling neighborhood, friendship, and marital patterns.[26] Such studies have shown that these informal laws operate not only in the white community but in minority communities as well.[27] People learn racist expectations in a number of ways. Sometimes they are reminded of them intentionally by parents and friends. Harry Kitano has demonstrated that the roots of prejudice and discrimination can be found in family life; children learn them as they are taught by their parents to be good family members.[28] They are also learned casually through the media, in motion pictures, on television, and in advertising and periodicals. Sometimes such learning occurs in ways that are not very obvious. Since community life is structured so that groups are separated, the absence of contact socializes individuals into believing that such attitudes and behaviors are of no concern. Informal racism is so normal and natural that often people do not even recognize its presence. At this level, the pervasiveness of racism is astonishing. We maintain a racist system through the ordinary activities of our everyday lives.

Informal racism is related to some forms of personal success and well-being: being part of the "in crowd," living in the right neighborhood, marrying the most "socially valued" person. But the question we have been addressing in Part II is more concerned with whether racism is important to socioeconomic well-being: educational, occupational, and financial success. To answer this question we need to look at more formal forms of institutional racism.

Formal Intentional Racism: Government Laws and Policies

The racist character of the society of the United States formerly was clear. As we saw in Chapter 4, federal laws and policies worked to promote the well-being of immigrants from northern and western Europe at the expense of those from southern and eastern Europe, and they worked even more stringently to the disadvantage of non-Europeans. This disparity was evident in immigration laws, voting regulations, and legal access to employment opportunities, housing, transportation, public accommodations, and education, among other areas of daily living. Native Americans, Afro-Americans, and Asians were excluded from citizenship at various times, and a "separate but equal" philosophy justified discrimination against minorities.

In the past three decades, however, American society has changed a good deal. Some scholars contend that it has entered a new era in which the effects of racism on the lives of people of color have been much diminished. With regard to blacks, William J. Wilson maintains that

> race relations in the United States have undergone fundamental changes in recent years, so much so that now the life chances of individual blacks have more to do with their economic class position than with their day-to-day encounters with whites. . . .
> In the pre-Civil War period, and in the latter half of the nineteenth through the

first half of the twentieth century, the continuous and explicit efforts of whites to construct racial barriers profoundly affected the lives of black Americans.[29]

Wilson traces three periods of race relations with respect to blacks in the United States. The first two follow the social history of the Afro-American community discussed in Chapter 4. After the American Revolution, race relations in the preindustrial South were institutionalized in the form of slavery or a caste system of oppression, with a small landed aristocracy in control of the plantation economy. After the Civil War, blacks became citizens, protected under the Constitution, but a series of Jim Crow laws restricted them to a life of sharecropping and little mobility. Legally, blacks were "separate but equal," but the laws were worked out to assure the separate rather than the equal aspects of this relationship. These laws no longer reflected the power and needs of the landed aristocracy. Rather, they developed out of the potential competition between white and nonwhite workers.

With the end of World War II, first federal and then state and local laws began to change. The civil rights movement forced governments to make a major shift — from supporting whites against nonwhites to supporting the equal rights of all groups. Civil rights laws replaced the Jim Crow laws. Affirmative action laws were developed to allow minorities to "catch up" after the systematic discrimination of the past. All government agencies and firms doing business with the federal government were required to safeguard the rights of racial and ethnic minorities. Discrimination on the basis of race, religion, or national origin was no longer permitted.

Because of these important changes, Wilson believes that racism no longer is a deterrent to the socioeconomic success of blacks and other racial minorities in the United States. Affirmative action policies helped to make upward mobility possible for a relatively small number of upper-class blacks, whose daily lives are comparable to those of upper-class whites. But government policy did not help the bulk of the blacks, who emerged as an urban underclass, living in poverty with little hope for advancement. This underclass is held back, not by individual or institutional discrimination, but by the operation of an advanced industrial, capitalist economy. As Wilson observes, "class is clearly more important than race in predetermining job placement and occupational mobility."[30]

Class conflict, however, has little role in Wilson's thinking. He believes poverty for blacks results not because management needs cheap labor or because workers compete for a limited number of jobs, but because the inner cities have decayed and economic opportunities have moved to the suburbs. Blacks are poor because they are isolated from the mainstream economy. The theme of black isolation rather than racism has been promoted by other leading black scholars as well.[31]

Yet Wilson does not maintain that racism is of no contemporary consequence whatever. He cites the racial division of labor which has been created by centuries of discrimination and prejudice. This division is reinforced, he

Current posters like this show that racism is yet to be eradicated in the United States. *AP/Wide World Photos.*

says, "because those in the low-wage sector of the economy are more adversely affected by impersonal economic shifts in advanced industrial society."[32]

THE CONTINUING INFLUENCE OF INFORMAL INTENTIONAL RACISM

Though intentional racism and discrimination have been prohibited by government laws and policies, they still operate in contemporary American society to limit the socioeconomic success of blacks and, by extension, other minority groups. Charles Willie contends that economic well-being must be seen as a complex structure which includes social and personal conditions as well as government laws and policies. Thus he argues that patterns of neighborhood, social, and friendship segregation which are still very evident today are intimately connected with economic well-being. Put another way, informal institutional racism still impedes the progress of blacks. Willie cites evidence from other studies which demonstrates an association between economic opportunity, educational opportunity, and residential location. Furthermore, he argues that Wilson's class perspective "tends to mask the presence of opportunities that are institutionally based such as attending the 'right' school, seeking employment in the 'right' company or firm, and being of the 'right' race."[33]

Willie also believes that the black upper class is not free of racism, as Wilson would have us imagine. Blacks and other minorities who have achieved success with the help of affirmative action policies are often treated as if they could not have made it any other way, as if they were really unqualified and merely symbols or tokens. Self-doubt and the constant need to establish their worth have created major socially induced stress for blacks. On the basis of his case studies of black families who have moved into racially integrated neighborhoods and work situations, he concludes that "race for some of these pioneers is a consuming experience. They seldom can get away from it. When special opportunities are created . . . the minorities who take advantage of them must constantly prove themselves."[34]

Willie suggests that the struggle against racism should be shifted to neighborhood integration and friendship development. His thesis supports the view that informal residential, friendship, and kinship patterns mediate social achievement. It might be suggested that acquaintance processes, or social affiliations a step below friendship, also are influenced by racism and mediate achievement. Acquaintances made in clubs, civic service groups, and other voluntary associations often can provide information about economic and educational opportunities. Minorities who are routinely denied these opportunities cannot profit from what Mark Granovetter calls "the strength of weak ties."[35]

BIOLOGICAL ATTRIBUTES OF MINORITY COMMUNITIES

In addition to the obstacles to the socioeconomic well-being of racial and ethnic minorities which are inherent in the social context of minority-majority rela-

tions, there are factors *within* these racial and ethnic min⟨
their quest for the American dream. Researchers have
in the relative importance of the biological and cultᵣ
minorities. Both of these types of attributes are be'
cioeconomic achievement, though these beliefs hav
troversy and debate. Intelligence is a biological attribuᵤ
this section. The following section considers such cultural deᵤ
culture of poverty and cultural values and traditions.

The biological foundations for the concept of race were discussed in Chᵤ₎
3. Attempts to classify humans into discrete races on a biological basis have
generally been unsuccessful, but currently some credence is given to the definition of race in terms of gene pools or breeding populations. Considerable research also has examined belief that differences in socioeconomic well-being
can be attributed to genetically based deficiencies in the intellectual capacities
of minorities. The hypothesis is that significant differences in intelligence exist
between races, in particular between whites and blacks, and that these differences have an effect on socioeconomic well-being.

Differences in Intelligence-Test Scores

Intelligence tests have been used by educational psychologists to measure intelligence for almost a century, and the results have documented significant
differences among ethnic groups, as well as differences between rural and urban groups. Early tests found evidence to support the superiority of people
from northern and western Europe over those from southern and eastern Europe.[36] In Great Britain, significant differences favoring the English over the
Irish continue to be reported.[37] Such findings have provoked controversy in the
past and continue to be controversial.

The current controversy centers on the differences in intelligence-test scores
of American blacks and whites in general. The studies have focused on these
two groups, so whites have not been compared with a "pure" black race. In
reviewing research on intelligence tests, Arthur Jensen found that, on average,
they show a 15-point difference in IQ scores favoring whites over blacks.[38]
There is no dispute over this finding; the dispute lies in how to interpret it.
Hereditarians attribute the difference to biological or genetic variables, and
environmentalists attribute it to the effects of social class and racism. Neither
side in the debate has been able to prove its point conclusively, but the environmentalists seem to have the upper hand.

The Hereditarian Position

Along with Hans Eysenck, another outspoken hereditarian,[39] Jensen attributes
the black-white difference in IQ scores to inborn genetic traits. Hereditarians
note that in studies which take into account differences in family environment,
including socioeconomic status, these IQ differences are reduced, but they

in significant. Even in studies which use culture-fair tests, the differences present, and in some cases they are more pronounced. This is taken as evidence that cognitive ability is largely determined genetically.

Jensen estimates that genetic inheritance, or heritability, accounts for some 60 percent of the scores on intelligence tests. Genetic inheritance is measured through **heritability estimates**, which express "the proportion of variation in intelligence in a population which is attributable to genetic variation within the population." [40] Heritability does not measure individual genetic endowment; it is a group estimate. It also is a within-group, not between-group estimate, so the intelligence of blacks and whites is considered separately. To measure heritability, Jensen used studies of twins reared apart in which the subjects were mostly white twins of American, British, and Danish nationality. The proportion of variation in his heritability estimate for whites then was used as the basis for a heritability estimate for blacks.

In evaluating arguments for genetic inheritance, it is important to consider some of the things Jensen is *not* saying. He is not saying that all whites are superior in intelligence to all blacks. Rather, he is making a generalization, while noting that there are many instances in which blacks score as well as or higher than whites. Indeed, in a recent study, Jensen found that on certain dimensions of intelligence, blacks in general do better than whites in general.[41] He does not regard his findings as definitive but acknowledges the need for further confirmation. While recognizing the possibility of an environmental explanation of the differences, he maintains that, so far, none has been satisfactory.

The Environmentalist Position

Environmentalists reject the hereditarian position on the genetic determination of intelligence. Some question the value of IQ tests, arguing that only in a racist society would there be attempts to measure differences in IQ across racial and ethnic groups. They also question the relevance of IQ tests as a measure of intelligence. Intelligence is multidimensional, and forms of intelligence other than knowledge of vocabulary and mathematics would have to be measured. Thus they maintain that test scores predict not success in life but success in school.[42] People whose IQ scores were not high can become very successful, both socially and financially. Other environmentalists accept testing but point out the need for more sophisticated studies of family background. Without analysis of differences in such things as parenting styles and parental values, gross measures of occupation and education are insufficient explanations of family background.

Environmentalists also have taken a hard look at biases in the testing situation. Irwin Katz, for instance, has done a series of studies demonstrating that the anxiety provoked by testing is so great among blacks that their performance is inhibited. When black students are told they are being compared to students at predominantly white colleges, their performance is significantly lower than when they are told they are being compared to other black students.[43] In a somewhat different approach, Carl Milofsky compared testing procedures in schools with high and low percentages of black students. He found that though such testing or "child study" requires a good deal of time and care, much less time is spent on it in schools with a high percentage of blacks. In such schools child studies on average took 3.9 hours, compared to 6.3 hours in schools with a low percentage of blacks.[44]

Perhaps the most devastating critique of the hereditarian position has been done by Leon Kamin. By closely examining the studies used to develop heritability estimates, he was able to show that the results had been flagrantly falsified. Most of the studies done on heritability were conducted by Cyril Burt, a prominent English psychologist. Kamin noticed consistent errors in the reporting of correlation coefficients in these studies. The proof of falsification, however, came in an independent biography of Burt by an admirer and supporter who was forced to conclude that the figures had been falsified.[45]

More recent studies of twins reared apart have been able to eliminate some of the methodological problems of earlier studies and have demonstrated that the influence of the parent rearing the child is more important than the natural parent or the genetic background of the child. In correlating intelligence scores in adoptive parents who also had biological children, studies in Texas and Minnesota found that adopted and biological children reared by the same parents had pretty much the same IQ scores.[46]

CULTURAL ATTRIBUTES OF MINORITY COMMUNITIES

The term *culture*, as we noted in Chapter 3, usually refers to the beliefs, attitudes, values, norms, and traditions that are shared in a society or community and govern interactions among the members. The study of culture develops an understanding of the plasticity of human nature: Different groupings of individuals produce different shared meanings and behavior patterns. A number of social scientists have found a relationship between the culture of a group and its social and economic achievement.

This does not mean that the culture of a community is necessarily at fault when its members do not do as well as those of other communities. There are many strengths in ethnic-minority communities, but there also may be limitations and weaknesses. From a systems perspective, social service workers look at the attributes of the focal system in the context of the social environment. To avoid blaming the victim (see Chapter 1), they must not lose sight of the social context as they examine a particular focal system. With this caution in mind, we will consider some theories which attempt to explain how group culture affects the socioeconomic status of ethnic-minority communities.

The Culture of Poverty

Oscar Lewis, who coined the term **culture of poverty**, believed that the cultural adaptations poor people make to poverty make it extremely difficult for them to escape from that condition.[47] Lewis primarily studied Mexicans and Puerto Ricans,[48] but he concluded that the culture of poverty transcends regional, rural-urban, and national differences. Thus the term is not a description of a particular ethnic community but concerns many kinds of communities living in poverty.

A culture of poverty is both a cause and an effect of socioeconomic ill-being. It first comes about as an adaptation to poverty; that is, it is an effect of living under poverty conditions. Yet everyone who experiences poverty does not develop a culture of poverty. Many college students experience economic hardship as they struggle to get through school, but college students as a community do not develop a culture of poverty. Similarly, a culture of poverty would not be expected to emerge in a community of highly educated or skilled refugees or immigrants, who ordinarily experience enormous but temporary economic hardship in coming to the United States.

Development of the Poverty Culture

Lewis contends that a culture of poverty develops in communities with certain living conditions which are prevalent in Western, industrial or industrializing nations. The societies in which the culture can be seen have the following characteristics:[49]

1. A cash economy, labor for wages, and production for profit.
2. Persistently high rates of unemployment and underemployment.
3. Low wage scales.
4. Failure to provide social, political, and economic organization, on either a voluntary or government-sponsored basis.
5. A bilateral kinship system in which descent is determined by both the paternal and maternal lines and the nuclear family is the ideal.
6. Values in the dominant class which stress the accumulation of wealth and property.

A group's development of a culture of poverty, Lewis says, should not be seen as just a negative or dysfunctional reaction to economic deprivation. The culture of poverty develops as a positive or functional adaptation; it demonstrates the ability of people to cope and survive under the most debilitating circumstances. But it is both a reaction and an adaptation of the poor to their marginal position in society — an effort to cope with hopelessness and despair which develop from the realization of the improbability of achieving success. However, once this way of life comes into existence, it tends to perpetuate itself from generation to generation, through child-socialization processes. By the time children in a culture of poverty are 6 or 7 years old, they have usually absorbed the basic values and attitudes of their subculture and are not psychologically geared to take full advantage of changing conditions or increased opportunities which may be presented in their lifetime. Thus they may not be able to take advantage of the social services that are provided on their behalf. In this respect, the culture of poverty becomes a cause of further poverty.

Lewis defines the culture of poverty itself in terms of the following traits, which are said to be characteristic of members:[50]

1. A lack of effective participation and integration into the major institutions and the economic, political, and religious systems of the larger society.
2. Severely thwarted family life, typified by such factors as an absence of childhood; early initiation into sex, free unions, and consensual marriages; a tendency toward female-headed households; much greater knowledge of maternal relatives; a strong predisposition to authoritarianism; a lack of privacy; and a verbal emphasis on family solidarity, which is only rarely achieved in actuality.
3. A minimum of social organization beyond the level of family, so that while there may be a certain sense of commonality, there is very little ability to organize around community interests.
4. Individual attitudes of marginality, helplessness, dependence, and inferiority.

Evaluation of the Theory

Lewis's theory was criticized harshly, and in some respects the criticism was unfair. Lewis did attribute the development of the culture of poverty to the oppressive economic conditions the poor were forced to endure. However, this part of his theory tends to get lost in his description of the traits that become internalized by individuals and families and maintain them in poverty. Furthermore, the programs and policies derived by social service professionals from the work of Lewis emphasized the need to alter the culture, rather than the need to alter the harsh economic conditions that had created it.

While the theory of the culture of poverty is no longer widely cited, many of its "victim-blaming" particulars have resurfaced in descriptions of the predominantly minority urban underclass (see box, Explaining the Underclass).[51] The lifestyle characteristics of blacks and Hispanics living in poverty-stricken inner-city neighborhoods have been described in ways that emphasize lack of integration into the major social institutions, disorganized family life, inability to provide effective self-help, and feelings of marginality and helplessness. By the same token, conservative ideas, taken out of the context of the culture of poverty and the literature on the underclass, have been used to describe white, lower-class behavior. Charles Murray, in assessing teenage pregnancy rates, for instance, describes poor whites as "white trash," in line with what he believes is an internalized culture of poverty.[52]

CULTURAL VALUES AND TRADITIONS

Thomas Sowell's perspective on socioeconomic success differs somewhat from Lewis's. Sowell is primarily interested in comparing the socioeconomic advances made by the various racial and ethnic groups in American society. He contends that new groups achieve success — that is, economic parity with

Anglo-Saxon Protestants — in about two generations. Some groups suc-
nore quickly — the Japanese, Russian Jews, and East Indians, for
:e — and others succeed more slowly — the Irish in the nineteenth century, American blacks, Puerto Ricans, Mexican Americans. Sowell believes
that cultural differences explain these varying rates of success.[53]

Sowell maintains that racism and "other causes of poverty" do not greatly
affect such community progress. He argues that "low income origins, over-
crowded and substandard housing, prejudice and discrimination, inadequate
educational opportunities, and a general failure of public services — such as the
police, schools, and garbage collection" are not unique to contemporary
minority groups; rather, "all those things impeded the progress of all American
minorities."[54] He also argues that color or race, per se, does not preclude suc-

EXPLAINING THE UNDERCLASS

The culture of poverty is one of two explanations for the continued presence of an economic underclass in an otherwise prosperous society. In this
view, the underclass is attributed to the dominance of norms and values
which do not prepare members to take advantage of economic opportunities as they present themselves. Ill health, unemployment, and crime are
perpetuated, and the underclass is sustained by the existence of a welfare
state.

The other explanation sees the underclass as the effect of discrimination
against racial and ethnic groups as well as against the poor. In this view
the underclass, primarily composed of minorities, is a product of institutional racism operating in education, the job market, housing, and the
criminal justice system.

Joan Moore believes that both the culture-of-poverty and racism approaches are oversimplified. Both also focus on categories of individuals
rather than communities. The explanation for the existence of the underclass, she maintains, must be found in the dynamics at work within the
minority community. The focus should be on differentiation within such
communities, as in her study of Chicano youth gangs in East Los Angeles.
Within that community, she found social processes at work which both
were creating and could be used to eliminate the treatment of families as
members of the underclass.

Sources: Vincent N. Parrillo, "Minorities," in J. Stimson and A. Stimson (editors), *Sociology: Contemporary Readings* (Itasca, IL: F.E. Peacock, 1987), p.218; Joan W. Moore, "Isolation
and Stigmatization in the Development of an Underclass: The Case of Chicano Gangs in East
Los Angeles," *Social Problems,* vol. 23 (1985), pp. 1-12; reprinted in Stimson and Stimson, *Sociology,* pp. 224-32.

cess. While the record is "not unequivocal," it "provides at least some basis for believing that color acceptance is not impossible in the United States."[55]

Similarly, Sowell cites evidence that political power is of little importance in facilitating socioeconomic success. Groups such as the Jews and Japanese, on entering the United States, had little power to influence local, state, and federal elections and policies but nevertheless succeeded. The Irish and later the blacks have excelled at political organizing, but this has not necessarily helped them do well economically.

Thus Sowell takes a far more conservative stance than Lewis does. Where Lewis argues that a debilitating social environment can create a culture of poverty, Sowell maintains that all ethnic and racial groups in American society have confronted a similarly harsh environment, but some have been able to deal with it better than others. He does acknowledge, however, that the functioning of the economic system in the late twentieth century makes success somewhat more difficult now than in the past. Labor unions have not been responsive to the needs of minorities. The standardization of jobs, wages, and promotions through objective criteria like tests and formal credentials which minorities must deal with in the labor market today did not confront immigrants in the past. Whereas the problems of European immigrants were low wages and difficult working conditions, contemporary minorities can become mired in the underclass, where unemployment, underemployment, and public assistance prevail.

Cultural Traits Needed for Success

In order for groups to overcome their harsh environments, Sowell believes they must possess certain cultural traits such as group cohesiveness and family stability. **Group cohesiveness** (a sense of common identity) is important because communities that stick together, encourage mutual aid, and overcome inevitable internal conflicts are likely to do well. Moreover, the style in which the group identity is expressed is important. He suggests that Jews and Japanese were quiet about their identity, while blacks and Irish loudly proclaimed theirs. Since Jews and Japanese have been singularly successful, he proposes that blacks should be quieter in their expressions of solidarity.

While groups that have done well in American society have all evidenced stable family life, Sowell contends that family stability alone is insufficient to produce success. Some immigrant groups, such as Italians, that did have high family stability nevertheless did not succeed quickly. Family stability must be coupled with the teaching of particular values to children. When these values are taught within stable environments, success is more likely.

Sowell maintains that the cultural trait that seems to predict economic success best is a **future orientation**, that is, "a belief in a pattern of behavior that sacrifices present comforts and enjoyments while preparing for future success."[56] The cultural traits which appear to predict slow economic progress and which characterize the less successful minorities are "a high value on immediate 'fun,' 'excitement' and emotionalism." Thus, Sowell says, if an ethnic-minority community is to advance, parents should be encouraged to stabilize their family life and teach their children to delay gratification.

In proposing his point of view, Sowell says he does not want to cast blame: "There is no place for praise or blame . . . here." Nor does he suggest that cultural traits reflect "superior insight by one's ancestors." He maintains that culture develops as a response to historically specific demands, and developments at one point in time may or may not be helpful at other times. As we noted in Chapter 4, because Jews were not allowed to own land and were forced into urban occupations in Russia, they valued education and developed skills which turned out to be useful in the emerging industrial economy of the United States. The Irish and Italians, who were largely peasants from rural areas, developed cultural traditions which were appropriate in their native lands but which proved to be a hindrance to their success in this country.

While Sowell's ideas are interesting, some of his analysis is questionable. For instance, although it is true that the Japanese did not have the numbers to become a politically potent force within the United States, they did have the strong backing of the Japanese government. As an example, when the Japanese were being forced to attend segregated schools in the United States and laws were being considered which would exclude them from immigration, Japanese government officials protested.[57] Similarly, Sowell tends to overplay the importance of cultural traits while underplaying some of the important differences in the environmental conditions confronted by minorities. Thus he does not acknowledge the difference between colonized and immigrant groups or the role of formal intentional discrimination in preventing the success of blacks and Native Americans.

THE DUAL PERSPECTIVE ON ACCULTURATION

The dual or bicultural perspective on the acculturation of minorities which has been developed by social workers acknowledges the strengths of ethnic-minority communities. According to Dolores Norton, the concept of the **dual perspective** "grew out of the idea that every individual is a part of two systems: the larger system of the dominant society, and the smaller system of the client's immediate physical and social environment."[58]

The dual perspective proceeds from a particular philosophy about culture and cultural diversity. Social workers are asked to recognize the cultural roots of both their own and their clients' attitudes and behaviors. This perspective teaches an "empathic appreciation of both the majority societal system and the minority client system."[59] It rejects the idea that minority members must fully assimilate into the mainstream culture if they are to achieve well-being. Rather, it espouses **cultural pluralism**, the view that the society should allow for and appreciate cultural diversity. Biculturalism is presented as a social good.

Those who work within the dual perspective acknowledge the strengths of

Native Americans celebrate a proud and vibrant cultural heritage. *John Running/Stock, Boston.*

ethnic-minority communities. Leon Chestang, for instance, describes the ways in which the black community nurtures its members but sees no such strengths in the majority community which would help minorities. Rather, he shows that the majority community is not supportive of blacks and makes the development of healthy personalities difficult for them.[60]

Strengths have also been located in Hispanic communities. It is often believed that these communities lack cohesiveness and cannot organize in their own behalf. Salvador Alvarez disproves this by describing a wide range of formal voluntary associations, including labor unions, which have been developed by Mexican Americans.[61] Others have described the natural **support systems** often found in Puerto Rican communities. Melvin Delgado and Denise Humm-Delgado see such systems as "an inherent source of strength for individuals that can be explored as resources in the development of culture-specific counseling or in the development of service plans, programs, and policies."[62]

Bicultural Socialization

While the concept of the dual perspective has been the basis for a literature on the strengths of ethnic-minority communities, it also provides an explanation for why members of such groups may not succeed. Diane de Anda's construction of a theory of success or failure in American society based on the concept of bicultural socialization was introduced in Chapter 5. She believes social and personal well-being for ethnic minorities requires them to be adequately socialized within both the minority and the majority cultures. Minority-group members must know both what is expected of them if they are to be successful within their own community and what is expected of them if they are to be successful in the majority community. Success in the larger society is jeopardized when minority individuals do not understand how it operates.[63]

DeAnda hypothesizes that six factors are necessary for successful bicultural socialization. First, it is facilitated when there is a great deal of cultural overlap between ethnic groups. Failure is more likely when there are large differences between the minority and majority cultures. The values and attitudes of a minority group and the way members think about the world may be so different that they cannot operate successfully in both systems. De Anda claims that the bicultural socialization of Afro-Americans, Hispanics, and Asians is more difficult in American society because of the vast dissimilarities between their cultural background and that of Anglo-Americans.

Second, bicultural socialization is facilitated when people are available to act as translators, mediators, and models. **Translators** are successful bicultural minority-group members who are "able to share [their] own experiences, provide information that facilitates understanding of the values and perceptions of the majority culture, and convey ways to meet the behavioral demands made on minority members of the society without compromising ethnic values and norms." **Mediators** are majority-group members "who serve as providers of information and guides for ethnic minority persons." **Models** are minority-group members "whose behavior serves as a pattern to emulate in order to develop a behavioral repertoire consistent with the norms of the majority and minority culture."[64]

Third, bicultural socialization can be achieved through **corrective feedback**, or positive reinforcements by minority and majority socializing agents. With patience, these agents can point out the positive aspects in a minority person's behavior, be specific in pointing out errors, and give concrete suggestions about how to correct errors.

Fourth, bicultural socialization is more likely when the individual being socialized has problem-solving skills; that is, a cognitive style or "a repertoire of modes of perceiving and interpreting one's interpersonal and material environment." If minorities are to operate within the dominant system, according to deAnda, they must have a cognitive analytic style. To the extent that they are embedded in their own cultures and unable to develop such a style, they will not achieve adequate socialization.

Fifth, the degree of bilingual ability in a minority group also plays a part in successful bicultural socialization. Ethnic and racial groups with competence in both languages are most able to learn the norms of the majority culture.

Sixth, to the extent that the physical appearances of minority- and majority-group members are similar, bicultural socialization is more likely. De Anda notes that minority individuals with the ability "to pass," that is to go undetected among the majority, are better able to learn the majority culture. Not only are they directly exposed to that culture, but they also become aware of negative opinions about members of their own community. Thus they learn not only what to do but also, and perhaps more important, what not to do.

De Anda's perspective on dual socialization has the merit of fostering a culturally plural society. It also gives social workers some concrete ideas about how they can help minorities achieve success within the dominant society. But her perspective does have shortcomings. For one thing, new arrivals may have values and attitudes which are vastly different from those of the majority culture, but it is unlikely that the values and attitudes of the "old minorities"— blacks, Native Americans, Japanese, Chinese, Mexican Americans, and Puerto Ricans, whose families go back generations, are also vastly different. De Anda does not specify what these vast differences in values are. For the old minorities it seems, therefore, that more has to be taken into consideration than a lack of knowledge of expectations. Her perspective ignores an understanding of the process of conflict and competition and the ideologies of racism and ethnocentrism which are in operation among communities. The role of the majority community in preventing success for minorities is not considered in depth, although she does ask majority-group members to serve as mediators and calls on social workers to help majorities understand the values of minorities. Success also seems to mean conformity to the ways of the larger society. Thus, according to de Anda, minorities must learn to work within the dominant culture, adding a second level to their abilities, and should not aim to change the dominant culture.

PROSPECTS FOR PROGRESS
IN MINORITY-MAJORITY RELATIONS

As the chapters on community life in Part II have demonstrated, socioeconomic success is possible in the United States, although it is rarely achieved without great effort. Immigration minorities from Europe have done well for the most part, especially in socioeconomic terms. There is evidence that minorities of color are also "making it" in the United States. Many Asian Americans, in particular, have achieved social and economic success. Affluent and middle-class blacks, Hispanics, and Native Americans are increasingly evident. They are achieving success through their own efforts and because the legal obstacles that prevented it in the past have been for the most part eliminated. The principle of equal opportunity, in the form of affirmative action and civil rights legislation, has brought hope to racial and ethnic minorities in the United States.

But American society is still involved in a debate concerning ethnic community relations. Some champion the traditional desire for assimilation, and others champion the cause of cultural pluralism. These philosophies are quite different, and in some cases they conflict. For instance, in the cultural pluralist view, English is regarded as a second language for native speakers of another tongue. Advocates of the assimilation view see English as the only official language of the United States, and by 1988 this position had been adopted in 17 states. Assimilationists also are challenging multilingual provisions of the federal Voting Rights Act, seeking to limit bilingual education programs, and recommending the tightening of English-language proficiency standards for citizenship.[65]

HAPPY ENDINGS: ASSIMILATION AND CULTURAL PLURALISM

Assimilation has historically been championed by members of the dominant group as the eventual outcome of intercommunity relations. According to assimilation philosophy (see Chapter 4), all groups were expected to become "American," that is, white, Anglo-Saxon, and Protestant, leaving behind their own cultural traditions and values. When the philosophy was first espoused, nonwhite groups were seen as unassimilable and were excluded from the United States through immigration laws. Nonwhite groups already in the country were to be kept in a "separate but equal" status.

Cultural pluralism was envisioned as the outcome of immigration by minorities from southern and eastern Europe, and it continues to be the dream of many contemporary minority groups.[66] According to the philosophy of cultural pluralism, each group is to retain allegiance to its own traditions and values, and all groups in the society are to learn to respect these differences and allow them to flourish. Cultural pluralism always involves a bicultural perspective. The implicit assumption is that, rather than everyone becoming American, there will be Irish-Americans, Japanese-Americans, Afro-Americans, and so on. Each group is to retain its own traditions while also accepting a certain degree of Americanization.

Assimilation and cultural pluralism have one thing in common: They are happy endings. Assimilation is the ending envisioned by many in the dominant group: "They will all become like us." Cultural pluralism is the ending envisioned by minorities: "We will retain our own ways but adopt their ways as well." Both are happy endings in the sense that they see some ultimate good conclusion to cultural and ethnic conflict. These philosophies provide positive goals to shoot for. They keep attention focused on the need for solutions that advance the common good.

Unhappy Endings: From Extermination to Secession

Minority-majority relations do not always have happy endings, however. Neither assimilation nor cultural pluralism takes into account some harsh realities. Progress in intercommunity relations is neither linear nor automatic. There are no natural laws of social relationships to assure that societies will grow and develop in positive ways.

Historical evidence affirms the rise and fall of groups within a society. For instance, the history of Jews has been marked by success as well as oppression. Who would have predicted at the turn of the twentieth century that Jews in Germany, a group that was socioeconomically successful and even admired and respected, would within a few short years be systematically stripped of their possessions and subjected to the incredible humiliation and devastation of the World War II death camps. In the United States, negative turnarounds in the destiny of groups are also evident. With the end of the Civil War, a great liberal era was ushered in with the promise that the recently freed slaves would soon join the mainstream society. Yet by the end of the nineteenth century, Jim Crow laws were in place to assure their segregation.[67]

Burkey describes a number of possible unhappy endings to minority-majority relations. Extermination and expulsion are two ways that majority groups try to deal with the real or imagined threat of minority groups. **Extermination** occurs when the dominant group in a society attempts to annihilate a particular minority group. The Germans under Hitler attempted to annihilate Jews, and American military policy in the mid-nineteenth century was to exterminate Native Americans on the western plains. **Expulsion** of a minority group by a majority group is another adverse outcome. Jews were expelled from Spain when the Catholic monarchs Ferdinand and Isabella ascended to the throne, and in the Great Depression Mexican Americans were rounded up and deported from the United States.

There are also ways by which minorities can attempt to overcome their oppressors. **Revolution** is the use of armed force by subordinated groups to throw off the shackles of domination. Thus Native Americans rebelled against the onslaught of white settlers attempting to appropriate their lands on the frontier, and today armed rebellion is pitting blacks against whites in South Africa and Catholics against Protestants in Northern Ireland. **Secession** is an attempt by subordinated groups to leave the territory controlled by their dominators and relocate elsewhere. It can also be seen in attempts by minorities to carve out an independent territory within the area controlled by the dominant group and claim it as their own. Both types of secession movements have been seen in American history. Marcus Garvey led a back to Africa movement at the turn of the twentieth century, and Reies Lopez Tijerina tried to reclaim Mexican lands in New Mexico during the 1960s.[68] More recently, Puerto Rican islanders have debated the issue of secession to secure independence from the United States.[69]

Conflict between minorities and majorities is serious business. It should not be minimized as simply a misunderstanding or a breakdown in communication in an otherwise harmonious world. The stakes are often high — control over a government as well as control of the lion's share of a nation's wealth. With the stakes so high, anything can happen.

IMPLICATIONS FOR PRACTICE

In the past, social service work often was identified with the goal of assimilation for racial and ethnic minorities. Social workers, representing the dominant society, worked to control the aspirations of blacks, Native Americans, Asians, and Hispanics in the United States. But social service work has changed. Today social workers, whether they are members of the majority group or of a minority group, generally support the goal of cultural pluralism. While this is undoubtedly a worthy goal, the meaning of the term in social service work is not clear. In actual practice, the concept often resembles assimilation more than cultural pluralism. Nevertheless, at the attitudinal level, at least, and in their conscious intentions, most social workers accept the ideal of cultural pluralism and the happy endings it promises for minority-majority relations.

Social service workers often get caught up in the unhappy endings, however. When Mexican Americans were deported during the Great Depression, for instance, it was often social workers who identified those to be returned to Mexico. In the late 1970s, social workers in the state of Oregon were instructed to tell their Southeast Asian clients to leave the state, because no welfare funds were available to support them. The questions for social workers are difficult: How do they respond to such injunctions? Do they do what agency and department administrators tell them to do, or do they take a professional stance and advocate against such injustices? Social service workers need to work hard to secure a happy ending for minorities, while they steel themselves against the possibility of not being able to achieve this.

The problems of minority individuals and families should never be divorced from the problems of their communities. Prejudice and discrimination have declined since the early 1960s, both in individual attitudes and in informal social norms. But they are still evident in the United States; in fact, there has been evidence of a reversal of the trend to support the principle of nondiscrimination. At the informal institutional level, the persistence of racism is clearly evident in segregated neighborhoods and friendship patterns. At the formal institutional level, the civil rights legislation of the 1960s and early 1970s mandated equal opportunities for all racial and ethnic groups and prohibited discrimination in many areas of social life. But the mechanisms for enforcing provisions of the legislation were weakened in the 1980s by the policies, personnel appointments, and regulatory decisions of the Ronald Reagan administration.

Social service workers, therefore, must continue to be concerned with prejudice and discrimination. Direct-service social workers must become adept at assessing the ways that prejudice and discrimination continue to hinder the progress of their clients. To avoid blaming the victim, they must understand that the context of the social environment can have a negative influence on individuals and families. They must also, through advocacy and the development of social policies and programs, work to change the social context in which their clients are involved.

Change in the social context is likely to go hand in hand with change in individuals and families. To the extent that ethnic minorities have internalized values and attitudes which make social and economic success less likely for them, social workers must strive to alter these values and attitudes. In these efforts the use of models, mediators, and translators can be of value. So can the use of corrective feedback and the teaching of problem-solving skills. But in the process of helping minorities achieve, social service workers must continue to evaluate the goals of the larger society from a critical perspective.

DISCUSSION QUESTIONS AND CLASS PROJECTS

1. Define prejudice and discrimination. Do the two always go together?

2. How would you define racism? Does the United States still have a racist society?

3. Interview representative individuals from an ethnic-minority group in your area. Determine if they believe that prejudice and discrimination limit the achievement of group members. Ask them if they have ever been discriminated against.

4. What do you see as the problems of implementing the principle of non-discrimination? Is someone who doesn't believe in such things as busing to achieve integrated schools, affirmative action, or bilingual education programs racist?

5. Do you think social workers, when working face to face with individuals and families, should concern themselves about the possibility of discrimination? How should they try to determine if discrimination affects the lives of their clients?

6. Interview professional social workers to determine how they attempt to assess discrimination and intervene to resolve it when working with ethnic and racial minority individuals and families.

7. Describe the debate regarding intelligence testing. Would you say you are a hereditarian or an environmentalist on this issue? Do you favor testing, or are you against it?

8. Do you think the attitudes and values of a community have anything to do with the social and economic success of their members? What kinds of values, attitudes, and community norms are believed to favor success or to limit achievement?

9. Make a list of the attitudes and values you believe are important for social and economic success. Try to determine the extent to which they are present in an ethnic-minority population in your area by interviewing representative individuals from that community.

10. Define the following concepts:
symbolic racism
institutional racism
principle of nondiscrimination
culture of poverty
underclass
the dual perspective
bicultural socialization

NOTES

1. John B. McConahay and Joseph C. Hough, Jr., "Symbolic Racism," *Journal of Social Issues*, vol. 32 (Spring 1976), pp. 23-45.

2. Quoted in James W. Vander Zanden, *American Minority Relations*, 4th ed. (New York: Alfred A. Knopf, 1983), p. 68.

3. Ibid., p. 68; italics in original.

4. David M. Heer, "Intermarriage," in S. Thernstrom (editor), *Harvard Encyclopedia of American Ethnic Groups* (Cambridge, MA: Belknap Press, 1980), p. 514.

5. William Julius Wilson, *The Declining Significance of Race (Chicago: University of Chicago Press,* 1980).

6. Ronald Walters, "Race, Resources, Conflict," *Social Work*, vol. 27 *(January* 1982), pp. 24-31.

7. William M. Newman, *American Pluralism: A Study of Minority Groups and Social Theory* (New York: Harper and Row, 1973), pp. 196-99.

8. Ibid., pp. 199-201.

9. Melvin L. DeFleur and Frank R. Westie, "Verbal Attitudes and Overt Acts: An Experiment on the Salience of Attitudes," *American Sociological Review*, vol. 23 (December 1958), pp. 667-73.

10. Robert K. Merton, "Discrimination and the American Creed," in R. MacIver (editor), *Discrimination and National Welfare* (New York: Harper and Row, 1949), pp. 99-126.

11. Howard Schuman, Charlotte Steeh, and Lawrence Bobo, *Racial Attitudes in America: Trends and Interpretations* (Cambridge, MA: Harvard University Press, 1986).

12. Survey cited in Richard T. Schaefer, *Racial and Ethnic Groups* (Boston, MA: Little, Brown, 1979), p. 67.

13. Emory S. Bogardus, "Comparing Racial Distance in Ethiopia, South Africa, and the United States," *Sociology and Social Research*, vol. 52 (January 1968), pp. 149-56, and *A Forty-Year Racial Distance Study* (Los Angeles: University of Southern California, 1967).

14. Schuman, Steeh, and Bobo, *Racial Attitudes in America*, p. 195.

15. Ibid.

16. Ibid., p. 194.

17. Ibid., p. 203.

18. Ibid., p. 195.

19. Lyle G. Warner and Melvin L. DeFleur, "Attitude as an Interactional Concept: Social Constraint and Social Distance as Intervening Variables between Attitudes and Action," *American Sociological Review*, vol. 34 (April 1969), pp. 153-69.

20. Schuman, Steeh, and Bobo, *Racial Attitudes in America*, pp. 86-138.

21. Ibid., pp. 139-62.

22. Gerhard Lenski and Jean Lenski, *Human Societies* 4th ed. (New York: McGraw-Hill, 1982), p. 54.

23. Hans H. Gerth and C. Wright Mills, *Character and Social Structure: The Psychology of Social Institutions* (New York: Harbinger Books, 1964), p. 23.

24. Louis Knowles and Kenneth Prewitt, *Institutional Racism in America* (Englewood Cliffs, NJ: Prentice-Hall, 1969), p. 5.

25. Richard M. Burkey, *Ethnic and Racial Groups: The Dynamics of Dominance* (Menlo Park, CA: Cummings, 1978), p. 81.

26. Emory S. Bogardus, *Social Distance* (Yellow Springs, OH: Antioch Press, 1959).

27. Vander Zanden, *American Minority Relations*, pp. 96-97.

28. Harry H. L. Kitano, "Passive Discrimination: The Normal Person," *Journal of Social Psychology*, vol. 70 (October 1966), pp. 23-31.

29. William Julius Wilson, "The Declining Significance of Race," in N. R. Yetman with C. H. Steele, *Minority and Majority*, 3rd ed. (Boston, MA: Allyn and Bacon, 1982), p. 385.

30. Ibid., p. 390.

31. See Kenneth B. Clark and John Hope Franklin, *A Policy Framework for Racial Justice* (Washington, DC: Joint Center for Political Studies, 1983), pp. 9-13.

32. W. Julius Wilson, "Cycles of Deprivation and the Underclass Debate," *Social Service Review*, vol. 59 (December 1985), p. 550.

33. Charles V. Willie, "The Inclining Significance of Race," in Yetman and Steele, *Minority and Majority*, pp. 393-94.

34. Ibid., p. 398.

35. Mark S. Granovetter, "The Strength of Weak Ties," *American Journal of Sociology*, vol. 78 (May 1973), pp. 1360-80.

36. Hans J. Eysenck vs. Leon Kamin, *The Intelligence Controversy* (New York: John Wiley and Sons, 1981), pp. 90-95.

37. Ibid., pp. 77-79. Also see Michael Banton and Jonathan Harwood, *The Race Concept* (New York: Frederick A. Praeger, 1975), pp. 91-115.

38. Arthur R. Jensen, "How Much Can We Boost IQ and Scholastic Achievement?" *Harvard Educational Review*, vol. 39 (Winter 1969), pp. 1-123.

39. Eysenck vs. Kamin, *Intelligence Controversy*, pp. 1-90, 157-72.

40. Banton and Harwood, *Race Concept*, p. 96.

41. Cecil R. Reynolds and Arthur R. Jensen, "Wisc-R Subscale Patterns of Abilities of Black and Whites Matched on Full Scale IQ," *Journal of Educational Psychology*, vol. 75 (April, 1983), pp. 207-14.

42. Banton and Harwood, *Race Concept*, pp. 105-15.

43. Irwin Katz, "The Socialization of Academic Motivation in Minority Group Children," in D. Levine (editor), *Nebraska Symposium on Motivation* (Lincoln: University of Nebraska, 1967), pp. 133-91.

44. Carl Milofsky, "Intelligence Testing and Race in the Public Schools," paper presented at the American Sociological Association meeting, Detroit, Michigan, August-September 1983.

45. Eysenck vs. Kamin, *Intelligence Controversy*, pp. 98-105.

46. Ibid., pp. 114-25.

47. Oscar Lewis, "The Culture of Poverty," in M. Pilisuk and P. Pilisuk, *Poor Americans: How the White Poor Live* (New Brunswick, NJ: Transaction Books, 1971), pp. 20-26.

48. See Oscar Lewis, *The Children of Sanchez* (New York: Random House, 1961); *Five Families* (New York: Science Editions, 1962); *La Vida* (New York: Vintage Division of Random House, 1968).

49. Oscar Lewis, "The Culture of Poverty," in *La Vida*, pp. xlii-lii.

50. Ibid., pp. xlv-xlviii.

51. Ken Auletta, *The Underclass* (New York: Random House, 1982). For an excellent critique of the concept of the underclass, see Michael W. Sherraden, "Working over the 'Underclass,' " *Social Work*, vol. 29 (July-August 1984), pp. 391-92.

52. Charles Murray, "White Welfare, White Families, White Trash," *National Review*, vol. 38 (March 25, 1986), pp. 30-34.

53. Thomas Sowell, *Race and Economics* (New York: David McKay, 1975).

54. Ibid., p. 143.

55. Ibid., p. 142.

56. Ibid., p. 144.

57. Harry H. L. Kitano, "Japanese," in *Harvard Encyclopedia of American Ethnic Groups*, pp. 561-71.

58. Dolores Norton, with Eddie Frank Brown, Edwin Garth Brown, E. Arecelis Francis, Kenji Murase, and Ramon

Valle, *The Dual Perspective: Inclusion of Ethnic Minority Content in the Social Work Curriculum* (New York: Council on Social Work Education, 1978), p. 3.

59. Ibid.

60. Leon Chestang, "Environmental Influences on Social Functioning: The Black Experience," in P. Cafferty and L. Chestang (editors), *The Diverse Society: Implications for Social Policy* (Washington, DC: National Association of Social Workers, 1976), pp. 59–74.

61. Salvador Alvarez, "Mexican American Community Organizations," in O. Romano, V. (editor), *Voices: Readings from El Grito* (Berkeley, CA: Quinto Sol, 1971), pp. 91–100.

62. Melvin Delgado and Denise Humm-Delgado, "Natural Support Systems: Source of Strength in Hispanic Communities," *Social Work*, vol. 27 (January 1982), p. 83.

63. Diane de Anda, "Bicultural Socialization: Factors Affecting the Minority Experience," *Social Work*, vol. 29 (March–April 1984), pp. 101–07.

64. Ibid., p. 104.

65. Margaret Carlson, "Only English Spoken Here," *Time*, December 5, 1988, p. 29.

66. Newman, *American Pluralism*, pp. 67–68.

67. For an interesting book on the transition from post-Civil War reconstruction to segregation, see C. Vann Woodward, *The Strange Career of Jim Crow*, 2nd ed. (New York: Oxford University Press, 1966).

68. See discussion on Garvey in Burkey, *Ethnic and Racial Groups*, pp. 270–71. For a discussion on Tijernia, see F. Christ Garcia and Rudolp O. de la Garza, *The Chicano Political Experience: Three Perspectives* (North Scituate, MA: Duxbury, 1977), pp. 128, 155, 158.

69. For insights into the various positions on Puerto Rican independence see Manuel Maldonado-Denis, *Puerto Rico: A Socio-Historical Interpretation* (New York: Vintage Books, 1972); Adalberto Lopez and James Petras (editors), *Puerto Rico and Puerto Ricans* (New York: John Wiley and Sons, 1974).

PART III

Family Life

CHAPTER 7

The Family as a Social Institution

Major themes discussed in this chapter:

1. *The family as an institution: An antisexist approach.* Study of the family as a social institution involves examining what society believes is the good and correct way to create and maintain family life. In looking at the family in a cross-cultural light, we reflect on the traditions behind the organization of American families and describe the changing societal expectations which guide men and women as they form families and take family roles. Our value stance in studying the family is antisexist and feminist.

2. *The functions of family life.* The family serves a number of functions. It is the primary institution for the procreation and socialization of children, a means for providing affection and emotional stability, and a vehicle for economic production and consumption. It also has latent functions, such as sustaining racism and sexism.

3. *Variations in the structure of family life.* Family life is taking on a number of forms in contemporary society. Serial monogamy is increasing, as the married-couple, two-parent family is matched by single-parent families and stepfamilies. Cohabitation among unmarried heterosexual and gay and lesbian couples is increasingly evident, as are single people living alone or sharing households in nonsexual relationships.

4. *Changes in role expectations.* Expectations for the various roles in the family are related to male dominance and the position of women, children, and the elderly in the society. With the industrialization of Western societies, gender-role and parent-child relations began to change, and the family is becoming increasingly egalitarian and democratic. The extended-kin family is now rare, but relationships with the elderly are being maintained by adult children.

5. *Implications for practice.* The image of the family breaking down, which suggests that the institution is a fixed, closed system, forces social workers to try to maintain the past. Problems in the traditional family have generated a need for change. When social service workers intervene in the lives of families, they can help reshape the family as an institution.

THE STATE of the American family, which has become a social and political issue, is also a major factor in the critical perspective. As we noted in Chapter 2, most people live out their lives within the family, which is perhaps the most important system in terms of individual change and development. There is ample evidence that family forms and functions are changing, but whether these changes are contributing to the breakdown of the institution of the American family or are merely evidence of ongoing modifications in family life is open to question.

At the heart of this controversy are the competing goals of preserving the institution of the family or enhancing the well-being of family members. In discussing the changing roles and forms of the American family, Ronald Pavalko contrasts the **traditional family**, "a family form in which the roles of husband and wife are clearly separate and the husband monopolizes power and makes the major family decisions," with the **equal-partner marriage**, "a more democratic family form in which both husband and wife contribute to the family's economic resources, share authority and decision making, and work together in child rearing." He concludes that "the desire for independence and equality by each member of the family, including the children, is challenging the dominant position of the husband and father in the traditional form of the family."[1]

The effects of such challenges can be considered by viewing the family as a social institution or as a social system or organization (see box, The Family as Institution and Organization). As an institution, the family is concerned with societal ideals and contradictions and involves public issues. As a social organization it is concerned with how these ideals and contradictions are handled and involves private troubles. Together, however, the family as an institution and an organization form a single entity. Institutional norms—especially the contradictions in them, debates over them, and obstacles to changing or achieving them—create the problems that lead family members, voluntarily or involuntarily, to seek out social services. Moreover, the family's perceptions of the ways their lives are organized may not seem to fit their image of what family life ought to be. Work with clients on the organization of their everyday lives in families, therefore, is intrinsically involved with social control and innovation, and the way the helping situation is handled affects the maintenance or change of existing institutions. In this way, the private troubles of family life are related to the public issues of family life.

This chapter looks at the family as an institution, and the remaining chapters in Part III consider it more as a system. Chapter 8 discusses variations in the characteristics of family life in communities differentiated by social class or race and ethnicity and the family lifestyles being developed by gay and lesbian couples. Chapters 9 and 10 identify and analyze well-being in the family as a social organization.

THE FAMILY AS AN INSTITUTION:
AN ANTISEXIST APPROACH

The study of social institutions focuses on the ways people endow collective behavior with value and authority: value in the sense that certain behaviors are seen as preferred, and authority in the sense that failure to conform provokes sanctions and other forms of social control. Social institutions are often formalized in laws and regulations, but just as often they are distilled into the unwritten but binding traditions of a society. Study of the family as a social institu-

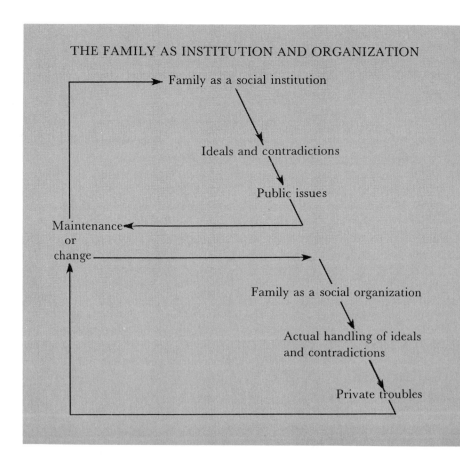

THE FAMILY AS INSTITUTION AND ORGANIZATION

Family as a social institution

Ideals and contradictions

Public issues

Maintenance
or
change

Family as a social organization

Actual handling of ideals
and contradictions

Private troubles

tion, therefore, examines what members of a society believe to be good and correct ways of creating and maintaining family life. It looks at the traditions underlying family life and the societal expectations that guide the formation of families and the assumption of family roles, and it examines how these preferred ways change over time.

It is difficult to maintain objectivity in studying the family. Family roles and relationships are very intense and shape our emotions and thoughts in basic ways. Our individual and collective positions in the public debate on the family also make it difficult to be objective. Is a family ideally a mother and father and two little children living in a private house in the suburbs? Can a family be an unmarried heterosexual couple with no desire to have children, or a lesbian couple rearing a child? Is the only proper goal of sexual relations to procreate, or is giving and receiving sensual pleasure an acceptable goal in itself? Is abortion the murder of innocent babies or the right of women to control their own bodies? Should mothers of young children work outside the home, and should fathers willingly do housework and care for the children? Should divorce be avoided at all costs?

These are examples of the intense public debates surrounding family life in contemporary society. At the heart of these debates are concerns about the role of women and the function of sexuality in society. A whole range of opinions on these matters can be found, but for simplification, people either favor supporting past traditions on women and sexuality, or they favor change. This and the following chapters on the family are not written from a value-neutral position. The theory of caring on which they are based stems from feminist and antisexist values.

Looking at the family from an antisexist point of view does not mean that objectivity must be abandoned, however. As noted in Chapter 3, feminism is not a single phenomenon but includes differing liberal, radical, and socialist ideas. Furthermore, no easy prescriptions for good family life can be found. There are only difficult questions and limited, complex answers. The family in Western society is a sexist institution because it subordinates the interests of women to those of men. It is also sexist in that social mores, or moral attitudes, restrain sexuality to the procreative function, thus condemning both heterosexual and homosexual sex for pleasure. As issues are raised about definitions of the family, family functions, family lifestyles, family problems, and theories about the family, we will strive for objectivity. Nevertheless, we will be concerned with encouraging social service workers to think critically about family life, to think from an antisexist viewpoint.

RECENT TRENDS IN FAMILY LIFE

In considering how the American family is changing, the starting point is the traditional family, a form which has developed over time on the basis of a number of assumptions. It is assumed that the family is a heterosexual institution, with prescriptions about how a man and a woman ought to be joined together and live together. The proper family form is assumed to be the nuclear family, that is, a family composed of a married man and woman and their children. It is assumed that the husband is the head of the family, with ultimate authority over wife and children, and that in their clearly separated roles the husband is the income-earner and the wife is the homemaker and provider of child care. It is also assumed that the family lives by itself in its own house or residence.

Observers of family life have suggested that numerous changes are taking place in this traditional American family form. Included are the following general observations about trends:[2]

1. More men and women seem to be living together before getting married.
2. Women and men seem to be marrying at a later age.
3. Married couples are having fewer children.
4. Unmarried women appear to be having more children.
5. Wives, even mothers with small children, are increasingly likely to be employed outside the home.
6. Marriages are more likely to end with divorce.
7. Single-parent families are more prevalent.
8. Remarriage is likely to follow divorce rather than widowhood.
9. Remarriage rates are declining, especially for women.

Some of these trends are clearer than others. Data on family life in the United States have been kept for about a century. "Good" data have been kept for a much shorter time, and much of the data that are available is very primitive. For instance, there can be no reliable data on the incidence of cohabitation, that is, the numbers of unmarried men and women living together in a sexual liaison. Similarly, there is insufficient data on out-of-wedlock births and the work experiences of mothers. For the most part, it can only be said that in general and in the recent past (say since the 1950s), the prevalence of cohabitation, out-of-wedlock births, and working mothers has increased.

Some trends, viewed in a long-range historical context, appear not to be trends at all. The age at which men and women normally marry is the same now as it was 100 years ago, though it has fluctuated; a short-range increase in the 1940s and 1950s due to widespread postponement of marriage in wartime made it appear that a change had occurred. Other trends appear to be following established patterns rather than representing a sharp break with tradition. Divorce rates have been increasing and families have been having fewer children for well over a century. Single-parent families and stepfamilies were very common in the past, although the reason for them was different. Many marriages formerly were dissolved and followed by remarriage because of the death of a parent or partner. Today single parenthood and remarriage are more likely to be a response to divorce.

Some social scientists see in these changes the breakdown of the family, to the detriment of the society. We take the position that family institutions and systems, like all human systems, are open, take many forms, and are constantly changing. In considering the family as an institution, therefore, we will describe the forms the family has taken and the ways it appears to be changing in contemporary society.

Defining Family Life

The concept of the family is difficult to define. Part of the difficulty is that in everyday language, the term *family* is used to describe a number of relationships. These range from the biological, nuclear family of mother, father, and child and siblings; to the more extended family which includes several generations of blood relatives or relatives through marriage; to close and intimate friends; even to humankind, or the "family of man." As popularly used, *family* has connotations about the quality or nature of the relationship: meaningful sexual relationships, loving parent-child relationships, permanent or long-lasting relationships, intimate relationships, faithful and loyal relationships. The term is also used to apply to the activities, tasks, or functions of the family: procreation activities, socializing activities, nursing and protective activities, materially helpful activities, or consumptive activities.

The wide variation in everyday usage is less apparent in formal definitions, but even here there is a lack of consensus. Formal definitions do not always fit informal definitions. The U.S. Bureau of the Census, which collects information used by social scientists, defines **family** as "a group of two or more persons related by blood, marriage, or adoption and residing together in a household." A **household** is comprised of "all persons who occupy a 'housing unit,' that is a house, an apartment, or other group of rooms, or a single room that constitutes 'separate living quarters.' "[3] This definition considers the family in terms of only its structure and legal status, not the qualities of the relationship or its functions or activities. The Census Bureau thus would accept as a family two legally related people who hated each other and were just living together for their mutual economic advantage. Their definition also includes sexual and nonsexual relations; married women and men living together in sexual unions are families, but so are brothers and sisters living together in nonsexual unions. In terms of family structure, the Census Bureau definition is quite inclusive. Nevertheless it considers unmarried couples as households, not families, though a parent-child dyad in such a household would be considered a family. Any others in the household are referred to as **unrelated individuals**.

Anthropologists and sociologists have offered different definitions. George Murdock's is perhaps the most commonly quoted. After examining descriptions of 250 representative societies, he concludes that "the family is a social group characterized by common residence, economic cooperation, and reproduction. It includes adults of both sexes, at least two of whom maintain a socially approved sexual relationship, and one or more children, own or adopted, of the sexually cohabiting adults." [4] This definition excludes all nonsexual relationships and all sexual relationships without the intention of procreation and child rearing. It would also appear to exclude those that allow for the rearing of children but not reproduction, such as a grandmother taking responsibility for care of a daughter's child born out of wedlock.

In Murdock's definition, study of the family would be limited to procreative, heterosexual marriages. But family life persists throughout the entire life cycle, not just the period in which husbands and wives are having and caring for children. Recognizing this, social scientists often distinguish between the family of origin and the family of procreation. Most of us are simultaneously members of two families: the **family of origin**, into which we are born and of which we are always considered a member, even if we leave it, and the **family of procreation**, which we join as adults for the purposes of procreation and rearing children.[5] Some social scientists also distinguish marriage from family and see the two as independent of one another. They argue that the family can exist regardless of whether the couple are married. Christopher Harris sees **marriage** as a public ceremony which joins together two kinship groups and in so doing lays out some important rights over children, domestic authority, and sexual matters.[6] Marriage is also the ritual through which children are made legitimate in the eyes of the parents and the society. Marriage therefore is a social ceremony, whereas family need not be.

In terms of family functions, most social scientists, like Murdock, consider the family as a means of procreation and socialization of children, as well as the development of interpersonal ties in carrying out these functions. Some definitions, however, would extend the use of the term **family** to social groups and activities that involve neither procreation nor socialization. In this direction, Ann Hartman and Joan Laird say that a family is created "when two or more people construct an intimate environment that they define as a family, an environment in which they generally will share a living space, commitment, and a variety of the roles and functions usually considered part of family life." Their definition implies that any two or more people can call themselves family as long as they are acting like family members. It is interesting because it measures the quality rather than the structure of the relationship, and it has deliberate, progressive social policy implications. Hartman and Laird believe family practice should be based on an "inclusive, self-determining, or phenomenological definition of the family."[7]

Karen Lindsey also explicitly includes other relationships in the family. In *Friends and Family*, she argues that ultimate choice should prevail in family development and processes. The concept of family should apply to "people who have shared history, who have loved each other and lived through major parts of each other's lives together." She notes that "friends, neighbors, co-workers have often lived through as many experiences together as husbands and wives — have created, perhaps unconsciously, equally strong bonds."[8] To Lindsey, the idea of family embodies not sexual relationships or even kin relationships, but strong emotional attachments.

Mark Poster defines the term *family* in still another way. His definition is more psychological and focuses on the kinds of interactions, role relationships, authority patterns, and typical conflicts that take place in families across time and place. While his definition implicitly accepts Murdock's emphasis on heterosexual coupling, procreation, and socialization, he considers family as "the place where psychic structure is formed and where experience is characterized in the first instance by emotional patterns." The family is also seen as "a distinct social space to the extent that it generates and embodies hierarchies of age and sex." This is "the social space where generations confront each other directly and where the two sexes define their differences and power relations."[9]

Rayna Rapp follows the U.S. Census Bureau definitions in making a distinction between family and household. Family implies only a procreation and socialization function and suggests a separation of family from the rest of society, in particular from economic institutions. Household, in addition to often being a procreative unit, is also an economic unit, since it is through households—the people we live with—that money and other goods and resources are transferred into and out of the economy through consumption. Family and household are connected in social norms which stress that the proper way for households to be set up is through nuclear families; other kinds of households are considered deviant. Rapp suggests abandoning the concept of family and substituting the concept of household. From the perspective that the social welfare of all members of a society, regardless of whether or not they live together in families, is a central concern, this suggestion has merit.[10]

In summary, many social scientists believe that a family is a socially approved, heterosexually oriented grouping of a male, a female, and their children through which the biologically based activities of procreation and socialization take place (in the family of procreation) and the lifelong bonds or kin relations initiated by these activities are nurtured (in the family of origin). While a significant number of social scientists do not see family solely in terms of hetereosexuality, marriage, procreation, socialization, and kinship activities, they are in the minority.

TYPES OF INSTITUTIONALIZED FAMILIES

Some sort of family life exists in all societies. Anthropologists have uncovered three major types of families which have been institutionalized in societies: the nuclear family, the extended-kin family, and the plural marriage or family. The **nuclear family** has been defined as "a family form composed of two adults of opposite sex living together in a socially approved sex relationship, together with their children."[11] In this form and the extended-kin family, marriage is **monogamous**; that is, to only one person at a time. In the **extended-kin family**, the parent-child relationship is broadened to include several generations. The key characteristic of the extended family, according to Harris, is that "adult children continue to be members of, and subject to the authority of, the group in which they were born."[12] The head of the family is always the oldest parent figure. In **plural marriages**, the husband-wife relationship is extended to include multiple spouses living together. Plural marriages may be both **po-**

lygamous, one husband with multiple wives, or **polyandrous**, one wife with multiple husbands. The polygamous form is far more common.

Although the nuclear family has been institutionalized in Western, industrial societies, it is not the most common type of family. In examining 192 societies for which there was documentation, Murdock found that the extended-kin and plural-marriage family types were more common than the nuclear family, especially among pre-industrial societies.[13] Nevertheless, he maintains that he could identify a nuclear unit in all societies. He regards extended-kin families and plural marriages as mere offshoots of the nuclear family. In his words, nuclear families are often combined "like atoms in a molecule" to form the other two types.

The Question of Universality

The idea that the nuclear family form is a universal one has been subjected to analysis by social scientists. It has been pointed out, for instance, that the term *nuclear family*, or a term which translates that way, is not found in every society. Indeed, as Clyde Kluckholm notes, the vocabularies of some nonliterate peoples do not include words that correspond with a procreative or biological unit.[14] In pre-industrial societies, *family* denoted only household, lineage, and kinship.[15] Harris concludes that the usage of the term *nuclear family* and the patterns of behavior to which it refers are distinctive aspects of Western, industrialized cultures. The term cannot be applied to other cultures without further definition.[16]

The most substantial evidence for the universality of the nuclear family comes from Western anthropologists who have identified it in other societies, even though the term, or its equivalent, is never used by their people. Murdock, for instance, argues that *he* could identify a nuclear unit in all societies regardless of how the people in those societies thought about themselves. Following the same line, Norman Bell and Ezra Vogel, the editors of a social work education text, conclude that

> if the nuclear family is a unit found in all societies, it is a stable point of reference for systematic analysis. Despite arguments to the contrary we maintain [it] is such a universal unit. The nuclear family may not be the normal household unit . . . *but we contend that it is always identifiable as a unit.*[17]

Murdock's assertion that the nuclear unit of mother, father, and child is the atom around which family life is formed has also been reevaluated. In considering the question, "Is the family universal?" Kathleen Gough studied the history of the Nayars, a primitive tribe in southern India. There was no concept of biological fatherhood in this culture. A Nayar woman might have as many as eight husbands, none of whom lived with her. The husband visited a wife after supper and left before breakfast the next morning, and he had no responsibility for maintaining the wife or their children. This responsibility fell to the mother's male kin or relatives. Nayar children used the terms *lord* or *leader* to refer to all their mother's lovers, without any connotation of paternity. In this culture, family was defined as "a relationship established between a woman and one or more other persons, which provides that a child born to the woman under circumstances not prohibited by the rules of the relationship, is accorded full birth status rights common to normal members of his society or social stratum."[18]

Harris concludes from such findings that the nuclear family unit is not the basis of family life. He emphasizes that the nuclear family unit is mother and children, not mother, father, and child, as Murdock proposes.[19] Indeed, the atoms around which family life is organized may very well be mother and child.

FUNCTIONS OF THE FAMILY

The family, like other evolving social institutions, is undergoing increased specialization. It has been relieved of the need to fulfill many arduous, basic functions, those that were "calculated to ensure the survival of members of the group, to secure their existence and to counter the threats of nature."[20] Families in the past were responsible for religion, government, raising armies and fighting wars, and providing basic medical care. They had to produce their own food, shelter, and materials for earning a living. Families today do not perform these functions in the same way or to the same degree that they did in the past. By the early twentieth century, at least six of the functions served by the American family in pre-industrial times had been lost or had undergone significant change: the economic, protective, religious, recreational, educational, and status-conferring functions.[21] The contemporary American family serves a narrower range of functions, some that are manifest and some that are latent.

MANIFEST FUNCTIONS: PROCREATION AND SOCIALIZATION

As we have shown, most definitions of the family explicitly include two **manifest functions**, or readily perceived activities: procreation and the socialization of children. The family is still the major institution through which procreative sexual behavior is organized and children are reared, especially in their early years. In contemporary society, day care and schools are agents of socialization, but the family continues to have the major responsibility for child rearing. In addition, the family has manifest productive, consumptive, and affective functions.

Most discussions of family emphasize those manifest functions that are believed to foster system maintenance and adaptation to the environment. In this regard, discussions of socialization usually center on the ways that societal values such as individuality, achievement and hard work, and the ability to delay gratification are passed on from one generation to the next. But socialization also can perform certain latent **functions**, which are unintended, often unrecognized, and can have negative consequences.[22]

LATENT FUNCTIONS: MAINTAINING DIFFERENCES

Through the socialization of children and the ways in which the cognitions, emotions, and behaviors of family members, both adults and children, are controlled, the family contributes to institutional arrangements (see Chapter 2). Thus the latent functions of the contemporary family can act to promote and sustain ethnocentrism, racism, and sexism in a society.

The Family and Ethnocentrism and Racism

Children are not born with prejudicial attitudes, and they do not automatically discriminate among racial and ethnic groups. Racism becomes institutionalized within a society when the social mores support status, power, and privilege differences along racial and ethnic lines. The antagonisms thus created can be supported only to the extent that they exert influence over how families are formed and children are socialized.

A number of authors have studied the ways by which the young are socialized into taking on the prejudicial attitudes of their families and communities. Mary Ellen Goodman describes a three-step process. First there is simple awareness; children learn that people differ according to color. Then an incipient racial orientation develops, and negative feelings are attached to color differences. The final stage is the development of full-fledged negative attitudes.[23] Phyllis Katz has developed an eight-stage model which, like Goodman's, begins with learning to distinguish racial cues and culminates with the crystallization of prejudicial attitudes. In between these two end points, she postulates a series of cognitive and perceptual elaborations aimed at showing how the attitudes are learned.[24]

Harry Kitano has shown that in the course of socialization, children normally learn the prejudices and discriminatory tendencies of their parents. This study is particularly interesting because it focuses on the Japanese community, which has itself been subjected to harsh prejudice and discrimination in the United States. Thus it demonstrates that regardless of a family's ethnic status, its children may be taught prejudice against other groups.[25]

The Family and Sexism

Socialization techniques have a lot to do with the ways in which gender-role status, privilege, and power are distributed in a society. Adults bring with them into the parent role societal expectations about appropriate behaviors for girls and boys. From the birth of their children, parents attribute to them the stereotypes associated with traditional masculine and feminine roles.[26] John Scanzoni points out that many studies have demonstrated how, from their earliest years, "males' in our society are socialized to adopt aggressive, active, forceful behaviors. Females, conversely, are socialized to accept passivity, conformity, and 'goodness of conduct.' "[27]

Parents treat girls and boys differently throughout childhood. Adults engage in roughhouse play with boys and provide them with toys, sports equipment, and clothing considered appropriate to the masculine role. Boys are repeatedly given the injunction "Big boys don't cry" and discouraged from showing their emotions. Girls imitate their mothers in play and usually are given toys and clothing appropriate to the feminine role. Teaching the feminine role may not be apparent to either the parent or the child, however. In a study of children and mothers, Robert Sears found that mothers reacted very differently to acts of aggression by girls than to such acts by boys. Girls were much more restricted in showing aggressive behavior toward neighborhood children or parents. They were not encouraged to fight back, though boys were expected to do so. Mothers usually disciplined the girls, using withdrawal of love, a psychological punishment. Boys were more likely to receive physical punishments, administered by their fathers.[28]

By the age of five boys and girls have become acquainted with the gender roles expected of them, and they project the same expectations on infants. In one study, kindergarten children were allowed to play with a four-month-old baby. Some saw the baby dressed as a boy and were told the baby's name was John. Others saw the same baby dressed as a girl and were told the name was Laura. When the children were asked to describe the baby after playing with it, those who had played with John described the baby as big and tough, while those had had played with Laura described the same baby as little and gentle.[29]

OTHER MANIFEST FUNCTIONS:
PRODUCTION, CONSUMPTION, AND EMOTIONAL SUPPORT

The manifest functions of the family, in addition to procreation and socialization, are production, consumption, and emotional support. The family's consumptive function is to purchase a good deal of the goods and services produced by the economy, and the family's productive function is to provide many of the services individuals need for interaction with the environment. The family's affective function is of special importance for the social service worker, for it is in the family setting that "the individual can freely express personality needs and expect to receive understanding, consideration, and love."[30]

Productive Functions

Families today no longer are required to produce the goods necessary to sustain their members. Generally, they do not grow their food, build their houses, make their furniture, sew their clothes, or fashion their means of transportation. But it would be a mistake to believe that the family is no longer a unit of economic production. It may not be a goods-producing unit, but it is certainly a service-producing unit. Ruth Schwartz Cowan demonstrates that the family, particularly the woman in the family, has in fact been assuming productive functions related to transportation and water, gas, electricity, and other utilities.[31] She makes the point that instead of making household production chores easier, advanced technology has made many of them more difficult. Merchants used to bring products to the home. Milk was delivered to the doorstep each morning; the Fuller brush man and other peddlers made their rounds; Sears Roebuck and Montgomery Ward made household products available through catalogs and mail orders; and purchases made at local stores were delivered. Public transportation proliferated with bus, train, and trolley systems. Today, the wife is both the shopper and provider of transportation. She is engaged in the production of services which are time-consuming and provided free of charge.

Consumptive Functions

The contemporary family is also a unit of consumption for the goods and services created in the economy. The family or the household is the organization through which the food, housing, furniture, clothes, and automobiles necessary for participation in society are purchased. Members must seek employment outside the home to earn wages so they can purchase the necessities of life. Thus the economy depends on the family to consume, and the family depends on the economy to produce.

As part of its consumptive functions, the family also has **cultural functions**. It has assumed responsibility for a multitude of activities which assure the participation of members in the community. Parents determine the cultural activities, such as concerts, sports, camping, movies, and gardening, which fill the leisure time of the family.[32]

Affective Functions

Along with changing productive and consumptive activities, the family has been taking on more affective functions. The contemporary family has become a private world in which members are expected to give the emotional support necessary to help members endure the harsh realities of an increasingly impersonal, industrial society. In Christopher Lasch's terms, the family is a "haven in a heartless world."[33]

The affective function of the family is sometimes seen as its most distinguishing feature. Indeed, most social service practice with families takes the affective function as the point of departure. The focus is on ways to maintain and improve emotional support, nurturance, and bonding among family members. The idea that family life is the seat of emotional support and deep personal commitment has been firmly established. In distinguishing family life from economic life, for instance, Talcott Parsons maintains that family life is personal and members are accepted for what they are, whereas economic life is impersonal and people are accepted for their talents and abilities.[34] Social historians point out, however, that this division between a public, impersonal economic world and a private, personal family world is a relatively recent phenomenon. The family of today may be largely concerned with subjectivity and emotional support, but this was not always the case.[35]

A SOCIAL HISTORY OF FAMILY EMOTIONAL CLIMATE

One way to trace the evolution of family functions is by noting how the affective function has changed. Poster synthesized the work of historians to demonstrate how the emotional climate of families has been mediated by social class conditions. Arguing that the emotional climate changed a good deal with the rise of capitalism and industrialization, he compares the artistocratic and peasant families of feudal Europe with the upper-middle-class and lower-class families of the turn of this century.[36]

Feudal Aristocratic Families

The aristocratic family of feudal times "placed little value on privacy, domesticity, maternal care, romantic love, and intimate relations with children."[37] These families were extremely large, often up to 200 members, including children, kin, servants, retainers, and clients. The great castles and chateaux in which they lived were public and political places with no privacy. Marriage was a political act, usually to join two relatively autonomous territories. The ideal marriage was not based on romantic love, and sexual respectability was not a particular concern. Extramarital sexual affairs were common. Women were considered to be as sexual as men.

The family was preoccupied with the status of the household within the social order. Land was the basis of wealth, not in order to exploit it but to maintain it and pass it on to heirs. Women and men participated in this effort. Men defended it and organized its economy; women bore sons and arranged for the social life of the household.

Women were little concerned with the management of the house or child rearing. Children were important because they were potential heirs. Mothers did not nurse infants but gave that function to servants, so the first attachments of children were not to the parents. Older children often did not live at home but were sent to live away from the family.

Child rearing was physically brutal; whipping was common, and obedience was a paramount goal. Obedience did not demonstrate attachment to a father or mother so much as respect for the family line and the hierarchy of the society.

Feudal Peasant Families

Most peasant families of feudal times lived in villages, the all-important social unit around which family life was structured. Kin and friends lived close by and households intruded on one another. Village norms and traditions were to be upheld, and the village held authority over families. Marriage took place through collective forms of courtship, with a strong role for the village in mate selection.

Men and women had separate functions, with women generally subordinate. However, social authority was not vested in men, and women's work was vital to the survival of the family and the village. The attachments of married couples came less from love than from trying to sustain the household in a difficult agricultural economy.

Children were needed for economic survival; a basic indifference to them was in part due to their high mortality rate. Infants were swaddled and fed by the mother but were often undernourished. Older children often were sent away from home to be apprenticed in a trade. The responsibility for rearing children was vested in the village, and failure to heed its will could lead to severe punishments and sanctions. As in the aristocratic family, children had a low sense of personal identity and an extremely high sense of social hierarchy and social order. Poster concludes:

> The child was not trained to defer its gratifications, to accustom itself to a clocklike schedule of rewards, to face the world alone and be prepared to make autonomous decisions, to regulate emotional energy for a competitive struggle against others. Life for peasants had a fixed pattern, governed by innumerable traditions which were not even to be questioned by individuals.[38]

Turn-of-the-Century Bourgeois Families

By the end of the nineteenth century there was a very different emotional climate in upper-middle-class, bourgeois families. Husbands owned businesses and factories or were professionals, and the families lived in private homes in urban areas, independent of kin. Romantic love was the predominant motive for marriage, but love and sex, like business, had a symbolic meaning. Business was considered rational and was assumed to express the essence of civilization and civility. Sex was considered irrational and assumed to express base, animal instincts; it had to be civilized. In the same way that a successful business career required the ability to delay gratification in the hope of long-term success, sexual gratification was to be delayed until true love was found in marriage, and it could only be realized through procreation. Having children would continue the economic success of the family.

Romantic love of husband for wife was expected to last only a short time; then they were supposed to live together in restrained respectability. The bourgeois woman was seen as basically asexual, giving in to sexual urges only because her husband demanded it. The bourgeois man was expected to be restrained in sexual relations with his wife but to turn to prostitutes to fulfill his "irrational" needs. Sexual repression thus characterized family life and marked the personality of male and female.

The roles of women and men in society and in the family were clearly differentiated. The ideal woman was homebound; she cared for the children, maintained a clean and comfortable home, and catered to the needs of her hus-

Madonna and Child (detail),
Segna di Buonaventura. *All
rights reserved. The Metropolitan
Museum of Art, New York.*

Virgin and Child, Master of
the Mansi Magdalen. *All rights
reserved. The Metropolitan
Museum of Art, New York.*

Painted two hundred years apart, these pictures show
cultural changes in the meaning of childhood and
motherhood. In the fourteenth century children were seen
as small adults and mothers were not expected to show
special affection for them. By the sixteenth century this
had changed.

band. The husband was autonomous in making the important economic and political decisions. The father also had almost complete authority over the children.

Children were to be loved deeply and thus trained for a successful, respectable place in society. They were asked to give up personal gratifications in return for the love of their parents. The wife was responsible for the everyday rearing of the children, and whatever might befall them always was seen as her fault. Child rearing became an extremely intimate, stressful experience.

The threat of withdrawal of love was the dominant means of disciplining children. In early infancy, breast feeding was organized according to rigid schedules. Toilet training was forced on children before they were physiologically capable, and masturbation was an anathema. In this context certain personality patterns emerged. Ambivalence was the principal emotion of children, who had to trade off satisfaction of their own needs for the affection of their parents. The anger children experienced could not be vented on their loving parents but instead was directed inward. Shame, doubt, and guilt marked the personality. Children learned to regard their bodies as disgusting, and they became desexualized. Identification with the sex roles of the parents was pronouced, as children unconsciously incorporated parental norms. A need for submission to authority and the belief that authority was inherently worthy of trust and devotion became embedded in the personality.

Twentieth-Century Working-Class Families

The origin of the lower-middle-class or working-class family was in the peasant family of feudal times. As peasants were recruited into the industrial working class, they tended to hold on to the patterns that had been instilled through village authority. While children in urban neighborhoods often worked, they were reared by the community in the street and by other workers in the factory. But wives and husbands both had to work outside the home to provide the family income. And, since working-class urban communities were not the self-contained islands of the rural villages, the norms regulating marriage and sexual relations failed to apply. There was considerable sexual promiscuity.

Concern for the perceived immorality of the working class was an impetus for the growth of social welfare policy and services. Middle-class women took on the role of "friendly visitors," who sought to protect and provide for working-class women and children. The charity organization societies helped secure child-labor and compulsory-education laws and family welfare legislation and services, and working-class people came to accept the family and sexual values of the middle class. Changes in the composition of the labor force, the development of skilled labor, and the family wage for the male head of the household also helped change the ideals of working-class family life. When urban neighborhoods were replaced by the suburbs in the 1950s, the identification of the working-class family with middle-class norms was complete. Wives and children left the labor force, and the mother presided in her private house, devoting her life to her children and to the emotional or sensual needs of her husband.

VARIATIONS IN THE STRUCTURE OF FAMILY LIFE

Along with changing functions, American family life is taking different forms. **Serial monogamy**, or repeated marriages to one person at a time after divorce or widowhood, is increasingly evident. A married-couple, two-parent family may be followed by a single-parent family or stepfamily. Cohabitation among unmarried couples and single people living alone are also more prevalent (see box, American Households in the 1980s).

AMERICAN HOUSEHOLDS IN THE 1980s

Married-couple households with children were declining in this decade, while less traditional household types were increasing. For instance, households headed by women living alone were expected to increase by one-fourth, and households headed by men living alone were expected to increase by just over one-third. The increase expected for all households was just 15 percent.

	1981	Projection 1990	Projected change 1981–90
All households (number)	82,368,000	95,076,000	15.4%
Married-couple households	59.8%	55.1%	6.2%
With children under 18	30.2	25.8	−1.9
No children under 18	29.6	29.3	14.2
Other, woman as householder	26.5%	29.0%	26.0%
With children under 18	6.8	7.9	33.0
No children under 18	19.7	21.1	23.6
Living alone	14.2	15.4	25.0
Other	5.5	5.7	19.6
Other, man as householder	13.6%	15.9%	35.4%
With children under 18	0.8	0.8	32.7
No children under 18	12.8	15.0	35.5
Living alone	8.8	10.3	34.4
Other	4.0	4.7	35.6

Source: Paul C. Glick, "How American Families Are Changing," *American Demographics*, vol. 6 (January 1984), p. 23.

TWO-PARENT AND MARRIED-COUPLE FAMILIES

The traditional nuclear family form is declining among households in the United States. In 1986, 71.9 percent of all households could be described as families, according to the U.S. Census definition, down from 73.7 percent in 1980. The number of families with children under age 18 also declined, from 52.6 percent of all families in 1980 to 49.8 percent in 1986. Married-couple families with children under age 18 represented 80.5 percent of all families in 1980 and 77.8 percent in 1986. The family with two children, a father in the labor force, and an at-home mother — the hallmark of the nuclear family — constituted only 9 percent of families with children in 1983.[39]

Perhaps the biggest change among two-parent families is the growing number of mothers in the labor force. Especially among families of limited means, the working mother has been a reality for some time. In certain periods, as during World War II, large numbers of women from all social classes, married and unmarried and with and without children, necessarily participated in the labor force. In the recent past, however, there has been an extraordinary increase in the participation rate of married women in the labor force, going from 30.5 percent in 1960 to 55.8 percent in 1987. The increase is notable among women with children under age six, going from 18.6 percent in 1960 to 56.8 percent in 1987.[40] The most dramatic increase in labor force participation has been among middle-class, well-educated women who formerly would have dropped out of the labor force during their child-rearing years.[41]

Racial and ethnic differences in the percentage of married mothers who participate in the labor force are narrowing somewhat. In 1970, 44 percent of white married mothers with children under age 18 were working, compared to 59 percent of black married mothers. In 1987, this proportion was 63 percent of whites and 76 percent of blacks. The rate of married mothers who work outside the home is lower for Hispanics than for either whites or blacks. In 1984, the rate was 47 percent for Hispanics, 56 percent for whites, and 69 percent for blacks.[42]

Changes in the labor force participation rates of married women have necessarily brought changes in the roles taken by men and women in the family. It has been estimated, for instance, that employed men with working wives spend about 2.7 hours more per week on household duties than men with wives at home. This is a small concession, however. According to Philip Blumstein and Pepper Schwartz, who studied thousands of American couples:

> Working wives do less housework than homemakers, but they still do the vast bulk of what needs to be done. Husbands of women who work help out more than husbands of homemakers, but their contribution is not impressive. Even if a husband is unemployed, he does much less housework than a wife who puts in a forty-hour week.[43]

A 1977 study of American families found that children, even those with working mothers, still see mothers as "good cooks and housekeepers" and fathers as these who "earn money for the family."[44] Nevertheless, the roles of women and men also are undergoing change in families with children, particularly when the mother works outside the home. Devising new ways of sharing the responsibility for child care is a challenge.

Working husbands and wives need to redefine their expectations for each other, and this process can be quite painful. People raised in traditional ways do not easily change. Lillian Rubin makes it clear that as women change they may experience enormous guilt, and as men change they may be frustrated and come to think of themselves as less of a man.[45] Even men and women who are sincere about their desire for change are likely to have these feelings. The theoretical and historical background for changing gender roles in the family is discussed in the next section.

The One-Parent Family

The number of one-parent families in the United States went from 3.8 million in 1970 to 8.9 million in 1986 and is expected to continue to rise through 1990 (see box, Changes in Families with Children). These families constituted 26.3 percent of all families with children under 18 in 1986, and by far the majority (23.1 percent) were headed by the mother. Only 3.2 percent of single-parent families were headed by the father alone.[46]

Although single-parent families are found in all social classes and in all ethnic groups, the likelihood of living in a single-parent family is greater among blacks and persons of Spanish origin than among whites. In March 1984, 56.4 percent of black children and 27.6 percent of children of Spanish origin under age 18 were living with just one parent, compared to 17.5 percent of white children.[47]

There have always been single-parent families, but now they are being formed in a different way. In the past, these families usually resulted from the death of a parent; now the are likely to be produced by divorce or unwed pregnancy (see Chapter 9).

While a number of special problems confront single-parent families headed by females, the major problem is economic survival.[48] Households in which women live alone with their children constitute a major poverty group in the United States; in 1986, 27.1 percent of households headed by married women with the husband absent and 17.4 percent of those headed by single (never-married) women had incomes of under $5,000, one-fifth the median money income of households that year ($24,897).[49] Not only are the incomes women can earn considerably lower than those obtainable by men, but the need to support the family while providing adequate child care presents a dilemma to many single-parent families. A large share of single mothers are employed. In 1984, for 69 percent of children between the ages of 6 and 17 and 50 percent of younger children with single mothers, the mothers worked outside the home.[50]

STEPFAMILIES OR RECONSTITUTED FAMILIES

Despite the decline in the number of two-parent families and the rise in the number of single-parent families, by far the majority of children in American society are reared by two parents. Increasingly often, however, one of the parents is not a biological or adoptive parent but has married into the family.[51] Estimates of the number of reconstituted, blended, or stepfamilies are difficult to find. It has been estimated that in 1980, 9.2 million U.S. households included a married couple in which at least one of the spouses had remarried after a di-

CHANGES IN FAMILIES WITH CHILDREN IN THE 1980s

The number of families in which children under 18 live with both parents was declining in this decade, while the number in which children live with one parent or in stepfamilies was increasing. The number of divorced mothers living with children was projected to increase by 36 percent, while the number of widowed mothers declined by 14 percent. The change was even greater for fathers; the number who had been divorced was expected to rise by 48 percent, while the number widowed declined by 27 percent.

	1981	Projection 1990	Projected change 1981-90
All families with children under 18 (number)	62,918,000	58,735,000	– 6.6%
Living with two parents	76.4%	69.4%	– 17.9%
Living with one parent	20.0	26.5	23.5
All other children	3.6	4.1	7.0
Living with mother	18.1%	24.0%	23.3
Divorced	7.8	11.3	35.7
Married	5.6	6.3	5.8
Separated	4.9	6.1	16.8
Widowed	1.8	1.7	– 13.7
Never married	2.9	4.5	47.5
Living with father	1.9%	2.5%	25.4%
Divorced	1.0	1.5	47.7
Married	0.5	0.5	2.0
Separated	0.4	0.5	28.0
Widowed	0.3	0.2	– 27.1
Never married	0.2	0.3	49.1

Source: Paul C. Glick, "How American Families are Changing," *American Demographics*, vol. 6 (January 1984), p. 25.

vorce.[52] Parent-child and sibling relationships within such families can be especially difficult, and some children are simultaneously members of two families. Andrew Cherlin, who has studied remarriages, notes that the emerging norms governing such relationships

> . . . seem to be moving in the direction of expanding the concept of the family to include step-relationships and other quasi-kin ties. Indeed, family ties after remarriage often extend across two or three households. The result is that our commonsense equation of "family" with "household" often breaks down. The basic question of what constitutes a family and what its boundaries are becomes less clear.[53]

Cohabiting Couples

Cohabitation, or two unrelated adults of the opposite sex living together outside of marriage, seems to be increasing, though the number of such couples is unknown. Cherlin notes that this change is recent; prior to about 1970, the practice was uncommon. The U.S. Census Bureau counted 523,000 households with two unrelated adults of the opposite sex in 1970 and 1,988,000 such households in 1984. The 1982 National Survey of Family Growth indicated that about 6 percent of all unmarried women aged 15 to 44 were cohabiting.[54]

Couples give various reasons for entering into and maintaining such households (see box, Reasons for Cohabitation). Cherlin differentiates between the kinds of couples who regard cohabitation as an alternative and those who see it as a prelude to married life. Young, college-educated, middle-class couples who cohabitate for a period and then either break up or are married generally consider it a test of compatibility prior to marriage. Other cohabiting couples, which usually involve at least one divorced or separated member, regard the practice as an alternative to marriage.[55]

Gay and Lesbian Couples

Most traditional definitions of the family specifically exclude the use of the terms *marriage* and *family* for cohabiting homosexual couples. Scanzoni points out, however, that some definitions of marriage allow for a much wider range of relationships than a heterosexual couple living together in a socially approved manner for purposes of procreation and child rearing. To make the point that marriages must provide for both economic and expressive relations, he cites the following statement by Murdock, whom we have recognized as the author of the conventional definition of family: "Sexual unions without economic cooperation are common, and there are relationships between men and women involving a division of labor without sexual gratification . . . but marriage exists only when the economic and the sexual are united into one relationship, and this combination occurs only in marriage."[56] Scanzoni adopts this definition in his work on the politics of power in the American marriage because, he says:

It is exceedingly parsimonious and flexible in that the form or structure of the economic and sexual (or expressive) relations could theoretically take any conceivable shape whatsoever, including polygynous or group marriage. It is also broad enough to subsume communal arrangements, as well as homosexual or lesbian relationships. All that is required is that the persons (whatever their number) in the marriage maintain both types of interdependencies.[57]

The desire of gay men and lesbians to form long-term relationships has not been well explored, as Blumstein and Schwartz point out in their study of American couples, a significant part of which concerns lesbian and gay male couples. They cite a study done at the Kinsey Institute in the late 1960s which found that 71 percent of the sample of gay men between the ages of 36 and 45 were living with a partner.[58] In a study of lesbians, Alan Bell and Martin Weinberg found that 82 percent of the women they talked to were living with someone, and for one-fourth of the women, being in a permanent arrangement was "the most important thing in life."[59]

Research on gay and lesbian couples is now being stimulated, however. Moreover, social service agencies and social workers in private practice have been using marital counseling and family therapy techniques with such cou-

REASONS FOR COHABITATION

Eleanor Macklin's typology of cohabiting arrangements indicates the wide range of differences in reasons why heterosexual couples decide to live together outside of marriage. Couples may see cohabitation as a matter of:

1. Temporary, casual convenience. These are couples who share living quarters because it is convenient and cost-effective.
2. Affectionate dating or going together. These are couples who stay together as long as the partners enjoy being with one another.
3. Trial marriage. These are couples who are "engaged to be engaged" or are consciously testing the relationship before making a permanent commitment.
4. Temporary alternative to marriage. In these couples the partners are committed to staying together but are waiting for the right time to marry.
5. Permanent alternative to marriage. In these couples the partners live together in a long-term, committed relationship similar to marriage, but without the traditional religious or legal ties.

Source: Eleanor Macklin, "Nonmarital Heterosexual Cohabitation," in A. Skolnick and J. Skolnick (editors), *Family in Transition* (Boston: Little, Brown, 1983).

ples.[60] We will not apply the terms *family* and *marriage* to gays and lesbians, even though many such couples do think of themselves as married or as families, because this would imply that they ought to be judged by heterosexual norms.[61] In Chapter 8, however, we refer to gay and lesbian couples as having a family lifestyle.

SINGLE PERSONS

Over 90 percent of the U.S. population marries at least once in a lifetime. While it appears that the number of people not marrying has increased recently, a closer examination of the data reveals that the number of marriages in the 1950s and 1960s, following World War II, was unusually high. By comparison with what it has been in the past, the proportion of never-married persons now in the population is not out of line.[62]

Nevertheless, according to the U.S. Census Bureau, the proportion of single (never married) persons age 18 and over in the population increased from 18.9 percent of males and 13.7 percent of females in 1970 to 25.3 percent of males and 18.3 percent of females in 1986. Both men and women are staying single longer; the median age at first marriage increased from 22.5 years for males and 20.6 years for females in 1970 to 24.6 years for males and 22.8 years for females in 1984.[63]

Single persons are a diverse group, since individuals live alone for a number of reasons. In addition to never-married men and women, there are sizable numbers of single persons who have been divorced or widowed (see box, Reasons for Staying Single). The ways in which bachelors and single women build their own households and connect with friends and family have not been studied. One finding in studies of single, heterosexual individuals is that they are often treated with suspicion and considered deviant.[64] Particularly for women, staying single is often attributed to lack of sex appeal, psychological problems, unwillingness to commit to a relationship, or homosexuality. Economic independence, social support from likeminded people, and increased autonomy would help solve the problems of single women.[65] Though the lives of single persons are commonly believed to be troubled by loneliness and insecurity, this is not always the case. Many singles, women as well as men, choose this way of life.

CHANGES IN ROLE
EXPECTATIONS AMONG FAMILY MEMBERS

Along with changes in the structure and function of family life, changes in the roles of family members are also evident in contemporary society. Within the family of procreation, relationships between spouses and between minor children and parents have both changed. In the extended-kin family, relationships between elderly parents and their adult children are also undergoing change.

Underlying all these changes in roles and societal expectations is the position of women, children, and the elderly in contemporary society.

FAMILY POLITICS IN AMERICAN SOCIETY: WOMEN, CHILDREN, THE ELDERLY

Study of the relationships among members of the family and societal expectations for the roles each is to perform has been described as **family politics**. The traditional American family is a **patriarchy**, a system in which power and authority are arbitrarily vested in the male head of the household. This position is being challenged by other members of the family, particularly the female partner but also the children and the elderly. In order to understand their roles in the family, it is necessary to consider their position as minority or subordinate individuals in the society (see Chapter 3).

Women in Society

The success of the women's movement of the second half of the twentieth century can be measured in terms of expanding the choices for women in the society and the family. The beginning of the movement has been associated with the founding of the National Organization for Women (NOW) in 1966. This group adopted a statement of purpose calling for attacks on discrimination in

REASONS FOR STAYING SINGLE

Peter Stein's typology of single persons distinguishes among four types, varying according to personal circumstances or preferences:

1. Voluntary singlehood. These individuals have never married or were formerly married but now choose to be single. They may not like the idea of marriage, or their religious convictions may prevent it.
2. Voluntary but temporary singlehood. These individuals have postponed marriage but are not opposed to it.
3. Involuntary but temporary singlehood. These individuals would like to marry but have not yet found an appropriate partner.
4. Involuntary singlehood. These individuals have never married or were previously married. They would like to marry but have not found a partner and are more-or-less resigned to living as a single person.

Source: Peter Stein, "The Lifestyles and Life Chances of the Never-Married," *Marriage and Family Review*, vol. 1 (July-August 1978), pp. 1–11.

the legal system, employment, and education, which had limited their ability to control their own lives. In regard to women's role in the family, the statement broke new ground with the declaration: "We believe that a true partnership between the sexes demands a different concept of marriage, an equitable sharing of the responsibilities of home and children and of the economic burdens of their support."[66]

While the condition of women in contemporary society has improved, a status in society and in the family which is fully equal to men's has yet to be achieved.[67] Despite the successes of women in securing legislation forbidding discrimination, **institutionalized sexism**, both formal and informal and both intentional and inadvertent, persists, and women continue to have unequal power and status in American society. As evidence, Thomas Kando has identified four kinds of oppression which have kept women in a disadvantaged position. Because of **structural discrimination**, women are less likely than men to be emotionally fulfilled and to achieve sexual satisfaction. Their ability to control conception and birth is threatened or restricted, and real equality of opportunity in education and access to meaningful jobs and careers is yet to be achieved. Because of **cultural discrimination**, the inferiority of women is embedded into the norms and beliefs of the society by means of language, socialization processes, and cultural stereotyping. Because of the **role strain** created by marriage and motherhood in the procreative family, women have suffered legal, economic, social, and psychological harm. And because of **sexual exploitation**, both inside and outside the family, women are still threatened by the double standard in sex favoring men, sexual harassment and intimidation, and violence in the form of abuse and rape.[68]

Women continue to be most disadvantaged by their lack of money, however. As Cynthia Harrison notes, "The women's movement has been able to do little to change the fact that by a large women who are not attached to men are poorer than single men and also poorer than married women."[69] In 1985, the median money income for all families was $27,735. For married-couple families it was $31,100; for families with male householders and no wife present, $22,622; and for those with women householders and no husband present, the median money income was just $13,660. For unrelated individuals, the median money income in 1985 was $14,921 for males and $9,865 for females.[70]

Even the fact that growing numbers of women are participating in the labor force has done little to improve their financial situation. In 1987, women's wages, on average, still were just 70 percent of men's. Median weekly earnings for men were $445; for women, $309.[71] As a group, women continue to be locked into low-paying, little-future, service-oriented jobs (see the box on comparable worth in Chapter 12). Despite some gains in accessibility to traditionally male work roles, in many occupations sex segregation is continuing or even increasing (see box, Women's Occupations and Men's Occupations).

The growing numbers of single women supporting children is a principal reason that poverty affects women and children more than men. The number of persons in families with a female householder and no husband present who were living below the poverty level increased from 13.5 million in 1979 to 16.9 million in 1986. When the poverty rate for the population as a whole was 13.6 percent in 1986, it was 19.8 percent for children under 18 in all families and 54.4 percent for children in families headed by the mother alone.[72]

In both married-couple and single-parent families with children, the principal drawback for women in their attempts to achieve equality in society is the

WOMEN'S OCCUPATIONS AND MEN'S OCCUPATIONS

Women are achieving parity with men in some occupations, such as bartender, bus driver, and editor or reporter. In the period 1975–1986, women's representation in a number of occupations substantially improved, going from 7 to 18 percent of all lawyers and judges, 9 to 21 percent of all mail carriers, and 13 to 39 percent of all economists. But they still represented 99 percent of dental assistants and only 4 percent of dentists; 85 percent of elementary school teachers and only 36 percent of college teachers, and 34 percent of computer systems analysts but 91 percent of data entry keyers.

Occupation	Women as Percent of Total Employed	
	1975	1986
Airline pilot	—	1.5
Architect	4.3	9.7
Bartender	35.2	48.8
Bus driver	37.7	50.4
Child care worker	98.4	97.4
Computer programmer	25.6	34.0
Computer systems analyst	14.8	34.4
Data entry keyer	92.8	91.1
Dentist	1.8	4.4
Dental assistant	100.0	99.0
Economist	13.1	39.3
Editor, reporter	44.6	50.5
Elementary school teacher	85.4	85.2
College/university teacher	31.1	36.0
Lawyer, judge	7.1	18.1
Librarian	81.1	85.9
Mail carrier	8.7	20.6
Physician	13.0	17.6
Registered nurse	97.0	94.3
Social worker	60.8	65.0

Source: Sara E. Rix (editor), *The American Woman 1988–89: A Status Report* (New York: W. W. Norton, 1988), Table 18, p. 382. Data from Bureau of Labor Statistics, *Employment and Earnings*, January 1976, Table 2, and January 1987, Table 22.

fact that their primary responsibility continues to be the care of the children. While many men as well as women have accepted the idea of sharing this responsibility, it still is vested in the mother, and she cannot match the father's dedication to work or public life. Nevertheless, the women's movement has brought gains in education, employment, law, and government. Legal discrimination has ended, and educational and occupational opportunities have been enlarged. There are as many women voters as men, and slightly more women in presidential elections. More women are holding public office, particularly in local and state governments. In many areas of daily living, women now have more choices in shaping their lives than they have ever had before.

Children in Society

There is disagreement about the extent to which the position of children in the United States continues to be dependent and subordinate, in the family as well as the society. Some believe childhood has never been better. According to Lloyd DeMause, for instance, as parent-child relations have evolved, children have been granted total care and appreciation by their parents.[73] Others argue that children are the individuals with the least power in American society, with no vote and no voice even in matters which directly concern them, such as school referendums. In socializing children, parents have the right as well as the duty to maintain discipline by setting rules and seeing to it that they are obeyed. Child advocates and child advocacy groups continue to argue for more attention to the needs of children in the society, as well as a more equitable position for them in the family.

Letty Cottin Pogrebin maintains that "America is a nation fundamentally ambivalent about its children, often afraid of its children, and frequently punitive toward its children."[74] This attitude underlies the failure in American society to adequately fund public education at all levels, child health programs, or child-care facilities, and the reluctance to prosecute parents as child abusers or to enforce child-support payment orders. The attitude also can be detected in public opinions and policies which keep one-fifth of all children under 18 in families living in poverty; in 1986, 15 percent of white children, 43 percent of black children, and 37 percent of Hispanic children were in families with incomes below poverty level.[75] Some do not have a roof over their heads; Jonathan Kozol estimates that there are about 500,000 homeless children in the United States, easily unseen because they are scattered in a thousand cities. In his study of the homeless, which focuses on the desperate condition of women and children in "welfare hotels" in New York City, he notes that Americans throughout the country seem to be afraid of homeless children:

> It is hard to know exactly what it is we fear (the children themselves, the sickness they may carry, the adolescents they will soon become if they survive, or the goad to our own conscience that they represent when they are visible, nearby); but the fear is very real. Our treatment of these children reaffirms the distancing that now has taken place. They are not of us. They are "the Other."[76]

The Elderly in Society

In the past, relatively few people lived to old age; most deaths, in fact, occurred at birth or in early childhood. In the twentieth century, however, the life expectancy of Americans has been increasing steadily. In 1920, both females and males at birth could expect to live 54 years. By 1950, life expectancy was 66 years for males and 71 years for females, and by 1986, it was 71 for males and 78 for females. About 12 percent of the total population was 65 years old and over in 1986. Because of their longer life expectancy, women represent a larger share of the elderly population; there were just 68.1 males to each 100 females in that age category in 1986.[77] Better nutrition, medical advances, and less strenuous lifestyles are among the reasons more people are reaching old age.

The social history of old age is still to be written. There is evidence to support the belief that the elderly experience many disadvantages in industrial societies. American society values youth, and prejudiced attitudes and discriminatory acts against old people have been documented. Even after the age of 50, job discrimination makes work hard to find, and the prevalence of corporate mergers, buyouts, and takeovers is multiplying the numbers of workers who are forced to retire even though they have the health, energy, and motivation to continue to produce. The elderly make up a significant portion of the poor, particularly among women and ethnic minorities. Some of the elderly must not only try to live on a subsistence income but also must cope with isolation, loneliness, ill health, abuse, or abandonment.

Such disadvantages suffered by the elderly have led some observers to conclude that **ageism** permeates American society; that is, there is an institutionalized age stratification system which generates inequality and conflict between younger adults and older persons. They contend that the elderly are systematically deprived of opportunities for participation in society and so should be thought of as a minority group or minority individuals. One of the first to advance this argument was Robert Butler, whose book *Why Survive? Being Old in America* described a "deep and profound prejudice against the elderly." Though the work of the elderly helped produce the affluent society, they are considered economic burdens, Butler says:

> In America, childhood is romanticized, youth is idolized, middle age does the work, wields the power and pays the bills, and old age, its days empty of purpose, gets little or nothing for what it has already done. The old are in the way, an ironic example of public-health progress and medical technology creating a huge group of people for whom survival is possible but satisfaction in living elusive.[78]

Whether or not the elderly should be seen as disadvantaged, however, depends on the particular roles or activities of the elderly that are being considered. P. K. Ragan and J. B. Wales point out that in terms of the differential distribution of the resources of a society according to age, it is apparent that "in certain respects (work roles, income, and prestige) the aged are systematically disadvantaged, while in other respects (political power, discretionary time, categorical benefits, and obligations) the aged are not disadvantaged."[79]

It also is not clear that the position of the elderly in urban, industrial societies is worse than it is in rural, undeveloped societies. According to Vern Bengtson, it is unwarranted to conclude that modernization causes a decline in favorable evaluations of aging or that relationships between young and old are marked by a severe generational gap. While there are differences in values depending on generation, there are also many similarities. Members of three-generational families — child, parent, and grandparent — showed similar rankings on the relative importance of respect, "loyalty to your own," and friendship as well as on the relative lack of importance of possessions and appearance.[80] Recent evidence that adult children in industrial societies show a great deal of care and affection for their elderly parents also has challenged the idea that the elderly can expect to be abandoned or alienated from their children.[81]

Social security and other benefits have greatly improved the economic position of the elderly. The percentage of all persons 65 years old and over living below poverty level fell from 24.6 percent in 1970 to 12.4 percent in 1986, somewhat less than the poverty rate for the population as a whole. For blacks 65 and over, however, the rate in 1986 was 31 percent, and for Hispanics, 22.5 percent. For females, there was a large difference between women 65 and over living in families and those living as unrelated individuals. For the former, the poverty rate was 11.8 percent; for the latter, it was 26.8 percent.[82] The elderly also have an advantage in the ratio of taxes paid to benefits received. Elderly households paid $60.7 billion in taxes in 1986, representing 10.4 percent of all income and payroll taxes. Social security recipients with higher incomes from pensions, investments, or employment now must pay taxes on a portion of their benefits, and beginning in 1989 a surcharge of up to $800 was to be collected for catastrophic health insurance. (As of this writing, however, it looks as if the surcharge will be repealed.) But those over 65 received $204 billion in government benefits in 1986, including Medicare and social security payments from the retirement insurance trust fund; this was 68.4 percent of all benefits paid to individuals that year.[83] In addition, numerous social services for the elderly, including meals programs, senior centers, transportation services, and activity programs, have been developed to help assure that the elderly live out their lives actively and with dignity.

CHANGING GENDER ROLES IN FAMILY LIFE

In the traditional family of Western societies, the division of rights and duties in the family was strictly separated along biological, male and female lines. The "man of the house" was expected to fulfill the duties and obligations of the head of the family and to receive in return certain rights and privileges. His duties included taking on the role of breadwinner, being committed to the world of work for pay, and providing for the material comfort of wife and children. The privileges he received for fulfilling his duties as **socioeconomic task leader** included the respect and obedience of the wife and children. The "woman of the house" was accorded the status of **socio-emotional leader**, the homemaker who maintained the livability of the hearth, nurtured the children, and comforted the husband. To her was given the responsibility for reducing tensions and assuring the equilibrium of family life. In return, her ways of rearing the children were to be supported by the husband, and her husband and children were to show her love, respect, and devotion. Certain other qualities were expected to infuse the roles of husband and wife. Husbands were to be assertive, competitive, rational, and achievement oriented; wives were to be passive, emotional, sensitive, and nurturing. The sexual relationship between husband and wife was to be monogamous, but it was recognized that the male had greater sexual urges and required more frequent satisfaction. Sons and daughters were expected to follow in the gender roles of fathers and mothers, respectively.

Biology versus Culture in Gender Roles

Those who support these traditional sex or gender roles argue that they are tied to the biological or "natural" order. Those who challenge the traditional roles argue that they are social and cultural inventions, learned through socializing.

From the family viewpoint the most important anatomical and biological differences between men and women are that only men can impregnate and only women can menstruate, gestate, and lactate. Other such differences, such as size and strength, are quantitative and distinguish women and men on the average, rather than absolutely. It is not clear, however, that these physiological differences lead to innate cognitive, emotional, and behavioral differences, as we noted in Chapter 2, or to psychological differences and in turn to social structural or gender-role differences.

John Money and Patricia Tucker have taken the position that humans are born tabula rasa, in a blank or empty state in which no gender-role predispositions are associated with a person's sex. They argue that gender differences are imposed through the medium of language; as languages developed, gender was applied to inanimate objects and subsequently to humans. The application of gender in language is absolutely arbitrary. In French, *sun* is male, while in German it is female. *Land* and *cloud* are masculine in French but neuter in German. In the same arbitrary manner, society has imposed certain psychological and social attributes of sex on women and men.[84]

Others maintain that there is a direct correlation between physiological sex differences and gender-role differences. They argue that male dominance is natural, since it is characteristic of most animal species and most human societies. Moreover, they argue that male dominance has come about largely through brute force and the generally superior size and strength of males, and it is facilitated by bonding among adult males. Men thus are naturally assertive and dominant. Female gender roles are tied directly to gestation and lactation, and there is bonding between mother and child. Women thus are naturally nurturant and submissive.[85]

Most social scientists find themselves somewhere in the middle on these two

Although it is still not common for men to take over
the chore of feeding a family, in many middle-class
families today men are changing. *Billy E. Barnes*.

positions. They believe that while there may be physiological differences which create psychological and social tendencies, gender roles are heavily overlaid by cultural and historical expectations. Further, most of them agree that biology and society interact to such an extent that trying to separate their effects is not warranted.[86]

Anthropologists have found certain cross-cultural patterns in gender roles which suggest biological origins. George Murdock and Caterina Provost, for instance, examined 224 societies at all levels of historical development and found that men were more likely to be involved in chores which require strength, such as hunting, mining, and land clearance, while women's tasks were related to the maintenance of the household, including cooking and making clothing.[87] Nevertheless, there is overwhelming evidence that the assignment of gender roles has a strong sociocultural overlay. In the study by Murdock and Provost, for instance, gender-role variation was found in such chores as house building, crop planting and tending, milking, and making leather products and weaving. Other anthropologists have found that psychological traits such as aggressiveness and passivity do not always conform to sex. Margaret Mead studied three primitive tribes in New Guinea. She found that among the Arapesh, passivity, cooperation, and peacefulness characterized both sexes; in the neighboring Mundugumor tribe, both were highly competitive and aggressive, and among the Tchambuli, women were dominant and impersonal and managed the affairs, while men were less responsible and emotionally dependent.[88] These kinds of studies make it clear that there is great malleability in the gender roles men and women assume.

The Historical Background of Changing Gender Roles

Changes in the roles of women and men in the family have been engendered by recent social movements, but they have a much longer social history. The dominant role of the male — the patriarchy — began to be challenged with the advent of industrialization and capitalism and the growth of the nuclear family form.[89] While Western societies are still governed in general by patriarchal norms, the absolute authority of the husband over the wife and children has been considerably diminished.

In hunting and gathering societies, the most primitive form of economy, male and female gender roles were relatively egalitarian. Male dominance became the norm with the development of agricultural economies. Since greater strength was needed for plowing and irrigation, men did the heavy agricultural labor. From control over the economy it was an easy step to control over the polity, the military, and religion. Patriarchy infused the social structure, and institutionalized sexism, based on formal and informal laws, norms, and policies, prevailed.

Early in the move to industrialization, male dominance was reinforced by religious teachings and men's continued hold on politics and the economy. Social structural arrangements favored men, and the socialization of children reinforced the institutionalized discrimination. But it soon became apparent that success in an industrial society is less dependent on physical strength than on personality and intelligence, in which the abilities of men are not superior to those of women. Men became less powerful in the society and lost authority in the family as they became less vital to the family's survival. Increasing industrialization reduced the husband's control of the family's productive function, and the availability of labor for wages reduced the importance of inheritance. By the twentieth century, the husband's role of patriarch had become more that of a companionate provider.[90]

Throughout the industrial era, conflict regarding gender roles and gender expectations has been growing. As a result of these conflicts between females and males, opportunities have opened up for relations between spouses to become more egalitarian. Thus, as we have noted, the traditional American family is being challenged by the equal-partner marriage (see box, From Wife as Property to Wife as Equal Partner).

The Men's Movement

The changes in the roles of men in the family brought on by industrialization have not been as fundamental as the changes in the roles of women. For men, the principal role still is related to earning a living in the world of work. Nevertheless, the dialogue calling for a more equal sharing of the instrumental, or socioeconomic, and expressive, or emotional, roles in marriage has opened up the range of choices for men as well as women. Men, too, have been questioning their traditional gender roles, and some observers have identified a men's movement which is comparable to the ongoing women's movement.[91]

More husbands are sharing household chores, and more fathers are providing child care than at any time in the past.[92] The principal change, however, has been in men's gender-role expectations. While it is clear that the traditional male role gives men an advantage in power, prestige, and privilege, in both the society and the family, that role is also a source of great strain.[93] It limits and constrains men, especially with regard to intimacy. Men typically reveal less personal information about themselves, have a tendency to have secrets, do not like being known by others, show a good deal of tension, often view others as threatening, and fear a sense of vulnerability and dependence. Because they tend to ignore their feelings, men also are less sensitive to signs of trouble in interpersonal relations. Difficulty with intimacy constrains not only male-female relations but friendships with other men, and accusations of homosexuality may be a threat.

Barbara Ehrenreich maintains that, from the emphasis on organizational norms in the "gray flannel suit" period of the 1950s through the beginnings of the men's movement in the late 1960s, men have been rebelling against the traditional male role which puts economic success and responsibility ahead of interpersonal success and responsibility. Men, like women, now are more likely to value an androgynous gender identity, with both masculine and feminine characteristics.[94] As Philip Lichtenberg notes, "Men will strive to be masculine based on unique traits and abilities: . . . some men will have preferences that were once identified as feminine and others will have traditional masculine tendencies; but all will be able to utilize various characteristics that are relevant to many new circumstances."[95]

The Feminization of Sexuality

One aspect of spouse relations in which significant change has taken place is the rights and obligations of consenting partners in the sexual act. Traditional norms surrounding sexual behavior allowed only one function, procreation. Yet there was a double standard; sexual satisfaction was considered to be the exclusive right of men. In addition to participating in procreation, men could take pleasure, both in marriage and outside it, in sexual intercourse. Women supposedly did not desire such satisfaction. They were expected to be monogamous and submissive, to satisfy the sexual needs of their husbands, and to bear children.

In popular opinion, recent changes in these norms are so far-reaching that a sexual revolution is said to have taken place. The revolution, however, is most apparent in the behaviors of women who have claimed equal rights with

FROM WIFE AS PROPERTY TO WIFE AS EQUAL PARTNER

John Scanzoni coined the term *equal-partner marriage*, using it in the 1972 first edition of *Sexual Bargaining: Power Politics in the American Marriage* to describe the ultimate goal of a process of ongoing change in relations between husbands and wives. He traces these changes to the beginning of the feminist movement in the early nineteenth century and places the wife's position on a continuum which ranges from property, to complement, to junior partner, to equal partner.

Scanzoni would place most married women in 1972 at or near the complement position, where the needs and interests of the husband and his work, as well as those of the children, are more important than the wife's, although she does have more authority than in the property position. A minority of wives, including most who work outside the home, would be placed around the junior-partner position. Only a "minute percentage" would be found at or near the equal-partner position. He concludes that "the actual social position possessed by women, both out of the family, and in it, remains subordinate to that of men."

Scanzoni does not change his evaluation of the position of women in the

men to sexual satisfaction.[96] Increasingly, women are likely to insist that sexual relations need not be limited to procreation, and a man has an obligation to satisfy the woman's sexual needs as well as his own. Women are learning to participate more fully in the "joy of sex" and are exploring diverse forms of sexual activity. Even in marital sex manuals published by conservatives, new freedom for women and new obligations for men in the sex act are being endorsed.[97] The nature of intimate relations between men and women has changed a great deal.

PSYCHOGENETIC FACTORS IN PARENT-CHILD RELATIONSHIPS

Parent-child relations have also changed appreciably since industrialization. DeMause has documented a series of changes in the authority relations between parents and children in Western cultures which parallels the changes in the emotional climate of the family identified by Poster, discussed earlier in this chapter. He asserts, however, that cultural and historical factors are not as important as psychogenetic factors, and he relates these changes to the biological evolution of the species. Thus in the history of parent-child relations, the power of parents over children has evolved from brutality to a commitment to the welfare of the child.[98]

second edition, published ten years later. He notes in the Preface to this edition that changes in family patterns have been occurring for almost 200 years and will continue in evolutionary fashion for the foreseeable future. The catalyst for these changes continues to be women's desire for equity — "for greater rewards and fewer costs relative to men's" — both in the family and in the world of work.

While women have a way to go before approaching parity with men, there has been a good deal of discussion about a greater *preference* among both men and women for equal rights and duties in marriage. Scanzoni points out that there is a difference between what people say they prefer and how they actually behave. Nevertheless, he perceives a trend in favor of the equal-partner marriage, in which there would be reciprocity between husband and wife in the essential instrumental (or socioeconomic) and expressive roles of marriage, and the provider role would be interchangeable.

Source: John Scanzoni, *Sexual Bargaining: Power Politics in the American Marriage*, first edition (Englewood Cliffs, NJ: Prentice-Hall, 1972), and second edition (Chicago: University of Chicago Press, 1982).

During antiquity and up to the fourth century of the Christian era, the **infanticide mode** of parent-child relations predominated. Social norms gave complete and absolute authority to parents to do with children as they wished. Their anxieties about the desirability or worth of children justified routine killing. In the feudal era, from the fourth to the thirteenth centuries, the **abandonment mode** prevailed. The idea that the child has a soul made killing unacceptable, so parental anxieties about children were relieved by abandonment or severe control. With the beginning of the Renaissance and up to the seventeenth century, parent-child relations were in an **ambivalent mode**. Parents of this era had more concern for their children, who were seen as soft wax to be molded by a caring but forceful hand. Parents attributed original sin to children, and anxieties about molding them correctly led to whipping or beating as a way to maintain control. The eighteenth century brought the **intrusive mode**, in which parents no longer visited their anxieties on their children but sought to conquer them and win them over. Parents prayed with children but did not play with them, and hitting was permissible but whipping was not. From the nineteenth to the mid-twentieth century, in the **socialization mode**, the object of parents was to train children and guide them into proper pursuits. Child labor was prohibited, and it became proper for children to spend their days at play.

DeMause refers to contemporary parent-child relations as the **helping mode**, the high point in their history. In this mode, children know better than their parents what their own needs are. Parents are not expected to discipline children or to encourage the formation of good habits, and striking children is no longer proper. Parents see themselves as the servants of children, tolerating their regressions, responding to their needs, and most of all helping them discover their own needs and ways of meeting them.

This view of the current state of childhood is controversial, however, as we have noted. Phillipe Aries describes the contemporary family as a "prison of love" in which the emotions are so intense that the relationship is destructive.[99] Valerie Suransky, in a more reasoned analysis, suggests that as adults have come to love and protect children, they have also attempted to structure, contain, and reduce their autonomy. Childhood, she says, has been eroded:

> We now separate children from the world of work; we dichotomize play from work; we deny the significance of the child's contribution to the cultural forms of everyday life. We infantilize children's perceptions and "school" their minds through the domestication of their critical curiosity and consciousness.[100]

We can conclude that for most children in American society, family experiences include a great deal of love and nurturance which at times may be stifling and constraining. It is clear, however, that parental treatment of children is moving away from authoritarian to more democratic patterns, with the primary goal of assisting children to determine and help satisfy their own needs and desires.

Family Relationships with the Elderly

Regardless of the structure of the family—married couple, single parent, reconstituted, cohabiting, or single person—most families in contemporary American society live apart from their kin. There are few **matrilocal** or **patrilocal families**, that is, kinfolk living in the household or under the authority of the eldest female or male. The usual form is **neolocal families**, in which a married couple or partners set up their own household apart from either set of parents. The existence of neolocal patterns, however, does not detract from ties to kin and elderly parents.[101] Although the classical extended-kin family form is rare, there are complexes of viable, supportive kin relationships which M. B. Susman refers to as the **modified-kin family**.[102]

Kin relationships continue to be very important to contemporary families. Grandparents often take on nurturant and affective roles in the neolocal family, as well as contributing financial support in various ways, from providing housing and paying tuition to buying shoes for the children. Grandchildren often give grandparents valued love, companionship, and physical assistance. But no kin relationship is more important than that between parents and their adult children.

The attachments that form between parents and children continue to develop as both mature. Even with the rise in social services for the elderly, their major source of emotional support often comes from their own families, particularly their adult children. It has been estimated that 78 to 90 percent of older people with living children visit with their children and are in contact with them by telephone at least once a week.[103] Although in part this contact derives from a sense of duty or obligation, affection seems to be the basic reason for it. One study found that about 90 percent of adult children felt "close" or "very close" to their elderly parents, and only 2 percent or less said their relationship was "not close at all." Most of the relationships are quite smooth, with only about 5 percent of adult children saying they were in frequent conflict with their parents.[104]

Considerable mutual help is exchanged between adult children and the elderly, both instrumental, as with transportation and housekeeping, and affective, such as companionship and sympathy. Early in life parents overwhelmingly give more help to children than children give to parents. Help from parents may continue for young adults whose education, early work experience, or troubles with jobs or in marriage keep them in a dependent position. This situation evens out when both generations are active and healthy adults, and eventually it is the adult child who gives most help.

Adult children appear to monitor the needs of their aging parents and are disposed to give help as required. Stress and conflict are clearly evident in the relationship when parents become very dependent on their adult children. Some 34 percent of adult children reported substantial strain as a result of helping their elderly parents, while an additional 52 percent reported some strain.[105] Adult children may feel physically and emotionally exhausted, frustrated by a seeming lack of appreciation, helpless, guilty, financially strapped, tied down, or caught between the needs of their parents, their own family members, and their personal lives. Since it is often the adult daughter who assumes most responsibility for care of elderly family members, women are particularly affected by the stress of providing such care. With people 80 years old and over the fastest growing segment of the 65-and-over population, Ken Dychtwald observes that "the average American woman can expect to spend more years caring for the parents than she did caring for her children."[106]

IMPLICATIONS FOR PRACTICE

The study of the family is particularly important for social service workers. The history of social services is very much concerned with family life and well-being; indeed, no other profession may be so involved with family issues. Many of these services are explicitly dedicated to family well-being, and even where the individual is the principal client, the family represents the major social context for assessing needs and problems and for providing support.

This chapter has reviewed the family as a changing social institution. No agreement exists among social scientists as to the meaning of the term *family*, but most use it to mean a socially approved, heterosexually oriented grouping of a male, a female, and their children through which the biologically based activities of procreation and socialization take place (in the family of procreation) and the lifelong bonds or kin relations initiated by these activities are nurtured (in the family of origin).

Although all societies devise ways to raise and care for children, there is no clear evidence of a universal nuclear family resembling the traditional family in American society. Family relations have taken any number of forms across time and place, and such values as heterosexuality, a male head, sexual fidelity, monogamy, nurturance, and emotionally laden interpersonal relationships have not always been found to be part of family life. The family in American society is best seen as a social invention, constructed out of a history of competing interests, which is continually provoking conflict and, through it, change.

While the family is a changing social institution, it is not breaking down. That is a conservative image in which the family is seen as a closed, fixed, and unchanging system. Rather, like all human systems, the family is an open system in which change is the natural state. The idea of the demise of the family would force social service workers into the role of guardians of tradition. There are many good things about the traditional nuclear family, but there were many problems in it as well. It is these problems that have generated the need for change.

Social service workers cannot help but participate in the changes in the family that are taking place. Through the social policies and programs they help to develop, they make statements about how family life ought to be. Through their everyday practice with families in need they reinforce or help dissolve the norms and traditions of society. To intervene in the lives of families is to help reshape the family as an institution. Social service workers can work to sustain clients in traditional nuclear family relations when the clients so desire it, but they also can help clients generate new and better interpersonal relationships.

Certain functions that exist in contemporary families have to be maintained. Workers can help clients form families in which procreation and child rearing can be carried out without producing the emotional problems they generated in nuclear families of the past. They can help clients find better ways to meet their needs for affection, productivity, and consumption. They can help rid the family of the latent functions of maintaining sexism and racism.

As social service workers help clients they must also take into account family ideals which seem to be worth striving for. For many people, the ideal family would be egalitarian and less constrained by rigid gender roles. Parent-child relations would be more democratic, and parents would serve as expediters, allowing children to develop according to their own needs and desires. This kind of family would attempt to maintain strong kin ties across generations. Social service workers can help today's families work toward these kinds of ideals and thereby influence how the institution of the family functions in American society.

DISCUSSION QUESTIONS AND CLASS PROJECTS

1. Identify at least three different definitions of the family used in the literature and evaluate their merits and limitations. How would you define *family*?

2. Define the following terms:
traditional family
nuclear family
extended-kin family
feminization of sexuality
household
family of origin
family of procreation
plural family
institutionalized sexism
equal-partner marriage

3. Describe the three major forms of families described by anthropologists.

4. Would you agree that the nuclear family unit — mother, father, child — is universal?

5. List and describe at least five manifest functions often associated with family life. Would you agree that the family also serves latent functions? If so, describe various latent functions served by family life.

6. Do you believe the family is a racist and sexist institution? Why or why not?

7. A lot of different forms of families can be seen in contemporary society. Describe the following types: single-parent families, stepparent families, cohabitating couples, single people, and married-couple, two-parent families. Working with others in the class, identify people who can be interviewed about these types of families and interview them to determine what needs and problems, as well as strengths and resources, are available in them.

8. Describe the four ways in which Kando says women are oppressed in contemporary society. Would you agree?

9. Do you agree that men are changing?

Make a list of traditional male activities and chores in the family. Make a list of the ways you believe the new male should be behaving. Conduct a survey of husbands and young sons to determine if these changes are coming about.

10. Describe the changes that DeMause believes have taken place in parent-child relations. Do you believe that parents today are more likely to want to help children discover their own needs and desires?

11. What is meant by the term *ageism*? Do you believe that ageism permeates American society, including family life? In what ways are the aged advantaged and disadvantaged in our society?

NOTES

1. Ronald M. Pavalko, *Social Problems* (Itasca, IL: F. E. Peacock Publishers, 1986), pp. 321–22, 286.

2. Andrew J. Cherlin, *Marriage, Divorce, Remarriage* (Cambridge, MA: Harvard University Press, 1981).

3. U.S. Bureau of the Census, *Statistical Abstract of the United States 1988* (Washington, DC, 1987), p. 5.

4. George Peter Murdock, "The Universality of the Nuclear Family," in N. W. Bell and E. F. Vogel (editors), *The Family* (Glencoe, IL: Free Press, 1960), p. 37.

5. Christopher C. Harris, *The Family and Industrial Society* (London, England: George Allen and Unwin, 1983), pp. 34–39.

6. Ibid., pp. 16–30.

7. Ann Hartman and Joan Laird, "Family Practice," in *Encyclopedia of Social Work*, 18th ed., vol. 1 (Silver Spring, MD: National Association of Social Workers, 1987), p. 576.

8. Karen Lindsey, *Friends as Family* (Boston, MA: Beacon Press, 1981), p. 13.

9. Mark Poster, *Critical Theory of the Family* (New York: Seabury Press, 1978), p. 143.

10. Rayna Rapp, "Family and Class in Contemporary America: Notes toward an Understanding of Ideology," in B. Thorne (editor) with M. Yalom, *Rethinking the Family: Some Feminist Questions* (New York: Longman, 1982).

11. Pavalko, *Social Problems*, p. 321.

12. Harris, *Family and Industrial Society*, p. 93.

13. Murdock, "Universality of the Nuclear Family," pp. 37–51.

14. Clyde Kluckholm, "Variations in the Human Family," in Bell and Vogel (editors), *The Family*, p. 48.

15. Poster, *Critical Theory of the Family*, p. 141.

16. Harris, *Family and Industrial Society*, pp. 30–31.

17. Norman W. Bell and Ezra F. Vogel, *The Family* (Glencoe, IL: Free Press, 1960), p. 32, italics added.

18. E. Kathleen Gough, "Is the Family Universal? The Nayar Case," in Bell and Vogel (editors), *The Family*, p. 90.

19. Harris, *Family and Industrial Society*, p. 40.

20. Michael Mitterauer and Reinhard Sieder, *The European Family* (Chicago: University of Chicago Press, 1982), p. 83.

21. See Lucille Duberman, *Marriage and Other Alternatives*, 2nd ed. (New York: Praeger, 1977), pp. 18–22.

22. Robert K. Merton, *Social Theory and Social Structure*, 3rd ed. (New York: Free Press, 1968).

23. Mary Ellen Goodman, *Race Awareness in Young Children* (New York: Collier, 1964).

24. Phyllis A. Katz, *Toward the Elimination of Racism* (New York: Pergamon Press, 1976).

25. Harry H. L. Kitano, "Passive Discrimination: The Normal Person," *Journal of Social Psychology*, vol. 70 (October 1966), pp. 23–31.

26. Mary Richmond Abbott, *Masculine and Feminine: Sex Roles over the Life Cycle*

(New York: Random House, 1983), pp. 89–98.

27. John Scanzoni, *Sexual Bargaining: Power Politics in the American Marriage*, 2nd ed. (Chicago: University of Chicago Press, 1982), p. 48.

28. Robert R. Sears, "Development of Gender Role," in F. A. Beach (editor), *Sex and Behavior* (New York: John Wiley and Sons, 1965), pp. 133–63.

29. Caroline Smith and Barbara Lloyd, "Material Behavior and Perceived Sex of Infant: Revisited," *Child Development*, vol. 49 (December 1978), pp. 1263–65.

30. Duberman, *Marriage and Other Alternatives*, p. 21.

31. Ruth Schwartz Cowan, *More Work for Mother* (New York: Basic Books, 1983).

32. Mitterauer and Sieder, *European Family*, pp. 83–84; Kenneth Kenniston, *All Our Children* (New York: Harcourt Brace Jovanovich, 1977), pp. 13–17.

33. Christopher Lasch, *Haven in a Heartless World: The Family Besieged* (New York: Basic Books, 1977).

34. Talcott Parsons, *The Social System* (New York: Free Press, 1964), pp. 58–67, 151–57. Also see Parsons, "The Normal American Family," in S. M. Farber, P. Mustacchi, and R. H. L. Wilson (editors), *Man and Civilization: The Family's Search for Survival* (New York: McGraw-Hill, 1965), pp. 31–50.

35. Eli Zaretsky, *Capitalism, The Family, and Personal Life* (New York: Harper Colophon, 1973), pp. 56–77.

36. Poster, *Critical Theory of the Family*, pp. 166–205.

37. Ibid., p. 183.

38. Ibid., p. 188.

39. U.S. Bureau of the Census, *Statistical Abstract 1988*, Tables 62, 66, 68; Sheila Kammerman, "Families, Nuclear," in *Encyclopedia of Social Work*, vol. 1, pp. 542–43.

40. U.S. Bureau of the Census, *Statistical Abstract 1988*, Table 624.

41. Nancy Barrett, "Women and the Economy," in S. E. Rix (editor), *The American Woman 1987–88: A Report in Depth* (New York: W. W. Norton, 1987), p. 100.

42. U.S. Bureau of the Census, *Statistical Abstract 1988*, Table 625; Kammerman, "Families, Nuclear."

43. Philip Blumstein and Pepper Schwartz, *American Couples: Money, Work, Sex* (New York: William Morrow, 1983), p. 144.

44. Yankelovich, Skelly, and White, *Raising Children in a Changing Society*, General Mills American Family Report, 1976–77 (Minneapolis, MN, 1977).

45. Lillian Rubin, *Intimate Strangers* (New York: Harper Colophon Books, 1984).

46. U.S. Bureau of the Census, *Statistical Abstract 1988*, Table 65.

47. Sara E. Rix (editor), *The American Woman 1987–88*, Figure 7, p. 298.

48. See U.S. Commission on Civil Rights, *A Growing Crisis: Disadvantaged Women and Their Children*, Clearinghouse Publication 78 (Washington, DC: U.S. Government Printing Office, 1983), and Ruth A. Brandwein, C. A. Brown, and E. M. Fox, "Women and Children Last: The Social Situation of Divorced Mothers and Their Families," *Journal of Marriage and the Family*, vol. 36 (August 1974), pp. 498–514.

49. U.S. Bureau of the Census, *Statistical Abstract 1988*, Table 692.

50. Rix (editor), *American Woman 1987–88*, Figure 11, p. 306.

51. Paul Glick, "How American Families Are Changing," *American Demographics*, vol. 6 (January 1984), pp. 23–24.

52. Andrew Cherlin, "Women and the Family," in Rix (editor), *American Woman 1987–88*, p. 67.

53. Ibid., p. 94.

54. Cherlin, "Women and the Family," pp. 74–75.

55. Cherlin, *Marriage, Divorce, Remarriage*, pp. 13–14.

56. George P. Murdock, *Social Structure* (New York: Macmillan, 1949), p. 8.

57. Scanzoni, *Sexual Bargaining*, p. 22.

58. Blumstein and Schwartz, *American Couples*, pp. 44–45.

59. Alan P. Bell and Martin S. Weinberg, *Homosexualities: A Study of Diversity among Men and Women* (New York: Simon and Schuster, 1978).

60. "Counseling for Gay and Lesbian Couples," *Practice Digest*, vol. 7 (Summer 1984), pp. 13–16.

61. Bell and Weinberg, *Homosexualities*, p. 219.

62. Cherlin, *Marriage, Divorce, Remarri-*

age, pp. 6–19. Also see Edward L. Kain, "Surprising Singles," *American Demographics*, vol. 6 (August 1984), pp. 16–19, 39.

63. U.S. Bureau of the Census, *Statistical Abstract 1988*, Tables 49, 126.

64. Margaret Adams, "The Single Woman in Today's Society: A Reappraisal," in H. Wortis and C. Rabinowitz (editors), *The Women's Movement* (New York: John Wiley and Sons, 1972), pp. 89–101.

65. Ibid. Also see Peter J. Stein, *Single* (Englewood Cliffs, NJ: Prentice-Hall, 1976).

66. Cynthia Harrison, "A Richer Life: A Reflection on the Women's Movement," in Rix (editor), *The American Woman 1988–89* (New York: W. W. Norton, 1988), p. 56.

67. Naomi Gottlieb, "Sex Discrimination and Inequality," in *Encyclopedia of Social Work*, vol. 2, pp. 561–69.

68. Thomas M. Kando, *Sexual Behavior and Family Life in Transition* (New York: Elsevier, 1978), pp. 345–54.

69. Harrison, "Richer Life," p. 73.

70. U.S. Bureau of the Census, *Statistical Abstract 1988*, Tables 703, 705.

71. News item, *Chicago Tribune*, February 2, 1988, Sect. 3, p. 1.

72. U.S. Bureau of the Census, *Statistical Abstract 1988*, Table 714.

73. Lloyd DeMause, "The Nightmare of Childhood," in B. Gross and E. Gross, *The Children's Rights Movement* (New York: Anchor Books, 1977), pp. 17–36.

74. Letty Cottin Pogrebin, *Family Politics: Love and Power on an Intimate Frontier* (New York: McGraw-Hill, 1983), p. 42.

75. U.S. Bureau of the Census, *Statistical Abstract 1988*, Table 717.

76. Jonathan Kozol, *Rachel and Her Children: Homeless Families in America* (New York: Fawcett Columbine, 1989), p. 181.

77. U.S. Bureau of the Census, *Statistical Abstract 1988*, Tables 106, 20, 18.

78. Robert N. Butler, *Why Survive? Being Old in America* (New York: Harper and Row, 1975), pp. xi–xiii.

79. P. K. Ragan and J. B. Wales, "Age Stratification and the Life Course," in J. Birren and R. Sloane (editors), *Handbook of Mental Health and Aging* (Englewood Cliffs, NJ: Prentice-Hall, 1980), p. 396.

80. Vern L. Bengtson, "Comparative Perspectives on the Microsociology of Aging: Methodological Problems and Theoretical Issues," in V. Marshall (editor), *Later Life: The Social Psychology of Aging* (Beverly Hills, CA: Sage, 1986), pp. 304–36.

81. Victor G. Cicirelli, "Adult Children and Their Elderly Parents," in T. H. Brubaker (editor), *Family Relationships in Later Life* (Beverly Hills, CA: Sage, 1983), p. 39.

82. U.S. Bureau of the Census, *Statistical Abstract 1988*, Tables 715, 716.

83. News item, *Chicago Tribune*, December 28, 1988, Sect. 1, p. 4.

84. John Money and Patricia Tucker, *Sexual Signatures: On Being a Man or a Woman* (Boston, MA: Little, Brown, 1975), p. 38.

85. See Pierre van den Berghe, *Man in Society: A Biosocial View*, 2nd ed. (New York: Elsevier, 1978).

86. See Marie Richmond-Abbott, *Masculine and Feminine: Sex Role over the Life Cycle* (New York: Random House, 1983), pp. 1–87.

87. George P. Murdock and Caterina Provost, "Factors in the Division of Labor by Sex: A Cross Cultural Analysis," *Ethnology*, vol. 12 (April 1973), pp. 203–25.

88. Margaret Mead, *Sex and Temperament in Three Primitive Societies* (New York: Dell, 1963).

89. Mitterauer and Sieder, *European Family*, pp. 86–90.

90. See Philip Lichtenberg, "Men," in *Encyclopedia of Social Work*, p. 97.

91. Ibid., pp. 95–102.

92. For a brief discussion of this point see Kammerman, "Family, Nuclear," pp. 544–45. Also see Joseph L. Pleck, "Men's Family Work: Three Perspectives and Some New Data," *The Family Coordinator*, vol. 28 (October 1979), pp. 481–88.

93. Joseph H. Pleck, *The Myth of Masculinity* (Cambridge, MA: MIT Press, 1981).

94. Barbara Ehrenreich, *The Hearts of Men* (New York: Anchor Books, 1983).

95. Lichtenberg, "Men," p. 100.

96. Barbara Ehrenreich, Elizabeth Hess, and Gloria Jacobs, *Remaking Love: The Feminization of Sexuality* (New York: Anchor Doubleday, 1986).

97. Ibid., pp. 74–102, 134–60.

98. DeMause, "Nightmare of Childhood."

99. Phillipe Aries, *Centuries of Childhood*, translated by Robert Baldick (New York: Vintage Books, 1962), pp. 411–15.

100. Valerie Polakow Suransky, *The Erosion of Childhood* (Chicago: University of Chicago Press, 1982), p. 8.

101. Eugene Litwak, "Extended Kin Relations in an Industrial Democratic Society," in E. Shanas and G. Strieb (editors), *Social Structure and the Family: Generational Relations* (Englewood Cliffs, NJ: Prentice-Hall, 1965), pp. 290–323.

102. M. B. Sussman, "Relationship of Adult Children with Their Parents in the United States," in Shanas and Strieb (editors), *Social Structure and the Family*, pp. 62–92.

103. Elaine M. Brody and Stanley J. Brody, "Aged: Services," in *Encyclopedia of Social Work*, vol. 1, pp. 33–34.

104. Ibid., p. 34.

105. Ibid., p. 40.

106. Ken Dychtwald with Joe Fowler, *Age Wave: The Challenges and Opportunities of an Aging America* (Los Angeles: J. P. Tarcher, 1989).

CHAPTER 8

Diversity in Family Lifestyles

M AJOR THEMES DISCUSSED IN THIS CHAPTER:

1. *Social class and family life.* Family patterns vary along class lines in the United States. Differences among middle-class, working-class, poverty-class, and affluent families are described.

2. *Families in ethnic and racial communities.* Since American society is composed of many racial and ethnic groups, variation in family life exists along racial and ethnic lines. Seven generalizations about how family ideals in racial- and ethnic-minority communities differ from the ideals of the middle class are presented. The family lifestyles of black-American, Native American, Hispanic, and Asian-American families are described in some detail.

3. *Family life outside marriage: Gay and lesbian couples.* As permanent relationships are increasing in the gay and lesbian community, roles, norms, values, and traditions for homosexual coupling are emerging in contemporary society.

4. *Implications for practice.* Americans seem to be striving for a consistent set of family lifestyle ideals. These include monogamy, greater equality between husbands and wives, more democratic parent-child interaction, and stronger ties to kin. Social service workers must allow for the ideals and aspirations of the individuals and families with whom they work. Assessment should focus on the ways in which the social environment and the psychological development of individuals foster or limit family well-being. Plans for intervention following from assessment may attempt to make both the individuals and the environment more supportive of family goals or to improve family functioning by attention to the members' attitudes, perceptions, behaviors, and abilities.

T HIS CHAPTER will look at diversity in the family lifestyles — the roles, norms, values, and traditions of family life — which are likely to be found in different communities in American society. In particular, we will examine differences in family lifestyles deriving from social class and race and ethnicity, as well as the family lifestyle being developed by gay and lesbian couples in long-term relationships. In considering these communities, we will show that, regardless of the diverse reality, most Americans seem to be striving for similar family lifestyle ideals: monogamy in long-term sexual relationships, greater equality in spousal roles, more democratic parent-child relations, strong ties with kin, and a nurturing and supportive interpersonal emotional climate. These are the ideals that guide us as we struggle to redefine the family as a social institution.

SOCIAL CLASS AND FAMILY LIFE

Many social scientists believe that the nature of family life significantly varies as a consequence of the family's socioeconomic status. In this view, family lifestyle is a function of the status and roles of the head of the household in the economy of the society. Thus occupation and employment status are highly related to the form and dynamics of family life.[1]

As we noted in Chapter 3, social classes can be defined in terms of social roles or positions in the work force, particularly the opportunities provided for a person to exercise self-direction in performing the work. Melvin Kohn maintains that such self-direction is unattainable to the extent that a worker is highly supervised, or the work is highly routinized and provides only limited ways to carry out the routines, or the work is simple and lacks challenge.[2] Higher-class status accompanies occupations that are challenging, varied, and unsupervised, and lower-class status accompanies those that are unchallenging, routinized, and highly supervised. Middle-class occupations are somewhere between these two extremes. Status is lowest in the poverty class, where just getting or keeping a job is the primary concern.

Much of the following discussion on class differences in family lifestyle is influenced by an article by Rayna Rapp.[3] Just as there are no rigid boundaries between social classes, there are no rigid differences in family forms related to social class. Rather, there are tendencies among middle-class, working-class, poverty-class, and upper-class individuals and communities which are reflected in certain tendencies in family life. These tendencies are described here.

MIDDLE-CLASS FAMILIES

Most studies of contemporary family life focus on the middle class on the assumption that these families not only are the most numerous, they also personify the ideal of the society as a whole. Rapp defines middle-class families as those headed by men (or women) who "own small amounts of productive resources and have control over their working conditions." [4] Middle-class family heads depend largely on wage labor to maintain the household, but they generally have occupations with a fair amount of prestige and autonomy — professional and managerial occupations in industry or government. In general, these families have a stable economic base which allows for some degree of luxury and discretionary spending.

Middle-class families aspire to the equal-partner marriage, in which husband and wife share responsibilities and make mutual decisions. As we have seen, however, equality in the family often is more illusion than reality.[5] In the traditional middle-class family, the career of the husband was all-important, but women were expected to be knowledgeable so they could entertain intelligently and instill the proper educational and social values in the children. In the contemporary middle-class family, women are likely to have careers of their own and to regard them as personally satisfying. As the old ideals and role expectations change, family tensions surface. When both partners work outside the home, conflict over whose career is to be considered most important and who is to perform the necessary household chores and child-care functions increases. Moreover, the **supermother**, the woman who exhausts herself trying to simultaneously satisfy the demands of career and home and family, is not uncommon. This has led some women to reevaluate the promise of the women's movement that they "could have it all." According to Betty Friedan, an early leader of the movement, the goal now is to learn how to live as equals without denying women's needs for fulfillment through love, nurture, and the home.[6]

By middle-class ideals, children are to be loved and nurtured unconditionally. Physical punishment is avoided, and every effort is made to let children develop and discover their full potential. Lineal and generational ties are very important in providing for the proper education of children, helping them establish careers or professional practices, or financing weddings and the formation of neolocal families. The accumulation of money and resources and the development of strategies for passing them on from one generation to the next is a central concern in middle-class families. In its socialization of children, the family attempts to assure that as adults they will have comfortable middle-class living standards and will not move downward into the working or poverty classes.

Friendship networks also serve a utilitarian or status-seeking function, and there is considerable concern that friends are the "right" kind of people as regards their education, work, residential neighborhoods, clothing, and club memberships. Friendships are a badge of status and a connection to be used in getting ahead and assuring proper marriages for children.

WORKING-CLASS FAMILIES

Working-class families may be getting closer to middle-class families in terms of ideals, but there are some important differences which undoubtedly emerge

The nuclear household is highly valued in all
ethnic groups: a middle-class Hispanic family
stands proudly in front of its suburban home.
Bob Daemmrich/The Image Works, Inc.

as a function of their economic position. The most distinctive feature of the stable working class is its dependency for survival on labor for wages. The household sends out its members to work and bring in an income, which provides food and shelter and allows for child rearing and the consumption of goods and services. How many members must be sent out to work depends on how much money each can bring in. It has been estimated that in the late 1970s, the average working-class family had the equivalent of 1.7 full-time wage earners.[7]

Young working-class couples generally marry for love, with the hope that love will last forever. Following the traditional family pattern, they accept the man's position as head of the family and the woman's as homemaker and child-care provider. The ideal is that the family will serve as a nest of love and nurture, but, as Lillian Rubin points out, the economic realities of maintaining the household often overwhelm the newlyweds (see the box, Facing Reality in the Working-Class Family, in Chapter 10).[8]

Until relatively recently, the financial problems of working-class families were eased by having many children who eventually could earns wages and contribute to the family's support. Labor laws now prevent children and adolescents from assuming such responsibilities, and parents are more likely to want their children in school than in the work force.[9] Working-class children, in fact, may be kept ignorant of their parents' economic burdens. This creates tension because peer pressure and advertising encourage children to "need" more things, and they feel deprived if their parents cannot or will not satisfy these needs.[10]

Working-class husbands and wives generally judge their marriages not so much in terms of personal fulfillment and happiness but in terms of their ability to fulfill their primary roles in maintaining the household (see Chapter 10). Ideally, a good husband works steadily, supports the family, and never harms anyone in it. A good wife is able to run the house without bothering the husband; she prepares good meals, keeps the house clean, and controls the children so the husband can relax at home and get ready for the next day's work. There is little room for compromise when both must get ready for the next day's work. Lillian Rubin points out that working-class women in the labor force do not "want to" work so much as feel they "have to" work to assure the solvency of the family.[11] They continue to do most of the housework in addition to their job work. Their housework also contributes to economic survival of the family, because it eliminates the need to pay for cooking, cleaning, and caring for children. When the wife has to perform two roles at the same time, family tensions invariably surface.

POVERTY-CLASS FAMILIES

Poverty-class families are statistically identified as having incomes below the poverty level, which is determined each year by the federal government on the basis of household money income and the Consumer Price Index. In 1986, the money income of 10.9 percent of all families and 13.6 percent of all persons in the U.S. population was officially below poverty level, which was $11,203 for a family of four. The poverty index does not take into account noncash benefits such as food stamps, Medicaid, and subsidized housing (see Chapter 10).[12]

The adults in poverty-class families are chronically unemployed, underemployed, dependent on welfare, or working for a subsistence wage. The family structure is altogether different from the one that prevails in the middle class. Both in the majority white community and the minority racial and ethnic communities, lower-class families are typified by high rates of divorce, births to unwed parents, and female-headed, single-parent families. Father figures are likely to be absent, and physical punishment is a common child-rearing technique. Family life is centered around networks of two or more households, usually those of relatives but sometimes those of friends. Carol Stack calls this arrangement a **domestic network**, "an extended cluster of kinsmen related chiefly through children but also through marriage and friendship, who align to provide domestic functions." In the black urban neighborhoods she has studied, these networks form around women because of their role in child care, but men play a positive role in them as fathers of the children and contributors to the resources of the network.[13]

Examples of poverty-class families often come from the study of family life in ethnic-minority communities, which will be considered in the following section. The major debate about poverty-class family life is whether the norms and values governing it are inferior to those for families in the middle and upper classes, or whether lower-class family arrangements represent a reasonable adaptation to the economic insecurities confronting poor people. This is an extension of the two explanations for the continued existence of poverty as the result of a culture of poverty or the effects of discrimination, which were examined in Chapter 6. Studies of lower-class black and Puerto Rican family life point to its positive aspects, such as willingness to take in children of relatives and build resource networks which spread out economic and interpersonal risks.[14] The love and nurturance provided children in such families often is as great as or greater than that provided in more affluent families. According to Stack, "The value placed on children, the love, attention, and affection children receive from women and men, and the web of social relationships spun from the birth of a child are all basic to the high birth rate among the poor."[15]

While networks of families living in poverty survive, it often is at great personal cost. The sharing of resources produces a leveling effect under which no one is expected to aspire to live better than the rest of the network. There is great pressure to keep everyone involved, and this makes marriage and stable family life, as well as upward mobility, difficult. Women in domestic networks find it impossible to simultaneously meet the expectations of their kin and the expectations of a spouse.[16] Moreover, a society in which upward mobility, competition, and individual effort are emphasized places great personal and interpersonal stress on members of the poverty class.

THE FAMILIES OF THE RICH

In the class of people to whom the term *rich* can be applied, income and wealth are derived from executive positions in large corporations, ownership of large businesses or professional practices, or sizable blocks of corporate stocks and other investments. This upper class includes the approximately 5 percent of families with annual incomes of $75,000 or more, who control about 16 percent of the income earned in the United States.[17]

The family lives of the very rich have not been studied often, and little real knowledge about them exists. From the evidence, Rapp suggests that while male dominance is unchallenged, women have a central role in the family and the society. These households usually include domestic help, which frees the wife to socialize the children, take part in civic affairs, and organize social gatherings. According to Rapp, because women in upper-class families represent the idea of family to the rest of society, they profoundly influence percep-

SAINTS AND ROUGHNECKS

Differences in the social class standing of families can have a profound effect on the life chances of the children. William Chambliss followed the careers of two groups of white boys in a small-town high school: "the Saints," from upper-middle class families, and "the Roughnecks," from lower-class families.

The Saints were popular, good pre-college students, active in school affairs. Using participant observation techniques, Chambliss found that these boys were frequently truant and involved in vandalism and petty theft. They drank heavily and drove at breakneck speed, endangering lives, both their own and others'. In the two years he observed them, none was arrested. They were clever in performing delinquent acts away from the sight of adults, or when they were caught, they acted contrite and respectful and were dismissed. In spite of their delinquency, police officers, merchants, and teachers saw them as the strength of America, "saints." To be sure, seven out of the eight members went on to college and subsequently held responsible positions in the community.

The Roughnecks were boys from "the other side of the tracks" who received average grades in schools and were constantly in trouble with the police, though their rate of delinquency was about equal to that of the Saints. Since they did not have cars or much money, they actually drank less than the Saints. They were most involved in petty theft and fights. If they were stopped by an authority, they reacted with hostility and disdain. Lack of a car also made it impossible to get away from the center of town

tions about the wife's role. This is an unfortunate image, since less wealthy women cannot have the same lifestyle as the rich.[18] Another family pattern is found in two-career families where the wife's income, added to the husband's, places the family in the upper-income class. In these families the availability of live-in household and child-care help greatly adds to the woman's ability to advance in her career.

The few studies that have been made of the children of the rich have focused on delinquency. It has been argued that these children are as delinquent as the children of the poor, but they are less likely to be caught or, if caught, more likely to be let off with a warning. The least delinquency has been found in stable middle-class or working-class families. Wealthy children have been involved in delinquency since the early days of capitalism and industrialization. These "rakes" or "young gallants," as they were called, are the prototype of the adolescent subgroups that later were named "Socialites, Elites, Shiddities, Colleges, Ivy Leaguers, Swingers, and Preppies."[19] The differences in the

to perform their delinquency, so their mischief was often done in full view of the authorities. In the period of observation each member was arrested at least once, and they were regarded by teachers, police, and merchants as delinquents, as "roughnecks." Two of the boys, who never finished high school, ended up in prison; another became a small-time gambler, and another drove a truck. Two boys received college athletic scholarships and became teachers, coaches, and family men.

According to Chambliss, the different treatment of the two equally delinquent gangs was due to their social class background, their visibility, and the biased perceptions of their activities by the authorities and the community. He concludes:

. . . visible, poor, nonmobile, outspoken, undiplomatic "tough" kids will be noticed, whether their actions are seriously delinquent or not. Other kids, who have established a reputation for being bright . . . , disciplined and involved in respectable activities, who are mobile and monied, will be invisible when they deviate from sanctioned activities. They'll sow their wild oats—perhaps even wider and thicker than their lower-class cohorts—but they won't be noticed.

The police and the community reacted to the Saints as though they were good, upstanding young men with bright futures and to the Roughnecks as though they were tough, young criminals headed for trouble. And by and large, the boys lived up to these expectations.

Source: William Chambliss, "The Saints and the Roughnecks," *Society*, vol. 11 (November-December 1973), p. 24–31.

delinquency of upper-middle-class or rich adolescents and poor adolescents and in the way they are treated by authorities have been documented by William Chambliss (see box, Saints and Roughnecks).

FAMILY LIFE IN RACIAL AND ETHNIC COMMUNITIES

In a multiethnic society such as that in the United States, variation in family life along racial and ethnic lines is to be expected. As Chapter 7 pointed out, family lifestyles have few universal features, and the diversity in them reflects historical and cultural relativity. In our consideration of racial and ethnic communities, we will maintain the relativist position that there is no one way by which families are or ought to be organized.

CHARACTERISTICS OF HOUSEHOLDS AND FAMILIES, 1970–1986: WHITES, BLACKS, AND HISPANICS

Data on family characteristics in various racial and ethnic communities are presented in terms of households or families. Using the Census Bureau definitions, a family is a group of persons related by birth, marriage, or adoption who reside together in a household. A household includes the related family members and everyone else who occupies a housing unit. A nonfamily household may be an individual living alone or a group of unrelated persons sharing the same housing unit.

Examination of the data for 1970, 1980, and 1986 provides a statistical portrait of trends in family lifestyles. Note, for instance, that the percentages of both families with a female householder and nonfamily households increased steadily for all three communities, whites, blacks, and Hispanics, but the smallest percentage growth in the 1980s was among blacks. Nevertheless, blacks continued to lead in the percentage of children under 18 living with the mother only or neither parent.

	1970	1980	1986
HOUSEHOLD TYPE (percent of total households):			
White households			
Family households	81.6%	73.8%	71.8%
Married couple	72.5	63.2	60.0
Female householder	7.2	8.6	9.3
Nonfamily households	18.4	26.2	28.2
Black households			
Family households	78.0	72.0	70.6
Married couple	53.3	40.0	37.6
Female householder	21.8	29.1	29.3
Nonfamily households	22.0	28.0	29.4

In the United States, differences in family life in various racial and ethnic communities are usually studied in terms of whites, blacks, and Hispanics. Data compiled by the U.S. Bureau of the Census most often are derived from these three groups (see box, Characteristics of Households and Families). Studies of family lifestyles in these groups and in others, such as Native Americans and Asian Americans, also have contributed to knowledge about the diversity of family life in American society.

Ethnic-minority families often have been studied with an eye toward uncovering presumably inherent **pathologies**, or abnormalities.[20] With the white, middle-class family taken as the norm, black families, especially, have been seen as "disorganized" because on the surface they do not resemble such mainstream families. Specifically, they appear to be matriarchal rather than

	1970	1980	1986
Hispanic households			
Family households	87.0	82.2	80.7
Married couple	70.1	61.9	56.8
Female householder	13.3	16.6	18.8
Nonfamily households	13.0	17.8	19.3
FAMILY SIZE (average number of members):			
White	3.52	3.23	3.15
Black	4.13	3.67	3.55
Hispanic	NA	3.90	3.87
FAMILIES WITH FOUR OR MORE CHILDREN (percent of total families)			
White	8.8%	3.6%	2.4%
Black	18.5	8.2	5.9
Hispanic	18.1	9.9	7.1
CHILDREN UNDER 18 YEARS OLD (percent of total children in community):			
Living with both parents			
White	89.5%	82.7%	79.9%
Black	58.5	42.2	40.6
Hispanic	77.7	75.4	66.5
Living with mother only			
White	7.8	13.5	15.7
Black	29.5	43.9	50.6
Hispanic	NA	19.6	27.7
Living with neither parent			
White	1.8	2.2	1.9
Black	9.7	11.9	6.3
Hispanic	NA	3.5	3.1

Source: U.S. Bureau of the Census, *Statistical Abstract of the United States 1988* (Washington, DC, 1987), Tables 58, 67, 69.

patriarchal; often, in fact, the fathers are absent. Native American families have been criticized for their matriarchal patterns and permissiveness in child rearing,[21] and Mexican-American families have been criticized for being too "familistic" and having patriarchal norms that are *too* strong.[22] These conditions have been labeled pathologies and taken as the basis for explaining away the deprived socioeconomic status of many ethnic minorities. Pathological family lifestyles, not discrimination or a lack of legitimate educational and occupational opportunities, are said to be responsible for the persistent poverty and unemployment experienced by such families.

In this section we take a **cultural relativist** position. Family lifestyle patterns develop for a multiplicity of reasons, and no family pattern is inherently better than another. They may develop because they are fervently desired, or because the social and economic conditions confronted in everyday life by members of the community force adaptations that are necessary, if not always desirable. Often both reasons operate simultaneously.

Taking a cultural relativist position does not mean presenting only the strengths of minority family life and disregarding the weaknesses, as some social scientists, reacting against the pathology viewpoint, have done.[23] While social service workers and policymakers must build on the strengths of minority groups, they cannot avoid examining the negative aspects of family life, in both minority and majority groups.[24] No one family pattern is superior, but some patterns, given the nature of the environment in which they operate, have more liabilities than others.

It is important for social service workers to get in touch with the aspirations of minority as well as majority communities. Therefore, in considering the family as a social institution in racial- and ethnic-minority communities, we start with some generalizations about the ideals that guide these diverse family lifestyles. Then these generalizations are illustrated with descriptions of the rich complexity of family lifestyle patterns found among Native Americans, American blacks, Hispanics, and Asian Americans.

GENERALIZATIONS ON FAMILY IDEALS AND NORMS

Generalizations summarize a body of knowledge and serve as an orientation to expected behaviors and attitudes. They have built-in limitations, however, and should not be taken to mean that every person or family in a group fits the description. A good generalization describes as many people in a group as possible, but, by definition, it allows for exceptions. To generalize, after all, is only to speak "in general."

In making the following generalizations, therefore, we start with the assumption that all minority-group families are not the same. Each group is a distinct, complex entity, and there is likely to be variation within groups as well as between groups. The generalizations in this section should serve to sensitize social service workers to probable differences. They are rules of thumb

Although extended kin rarely live under the same roof today, extended family ties are still important to this Asian family, as well as to other ethnic and racial groups. *Don Smetzer/Tony Stone Worldwide.*

which provide a starting point for assessing minority families, and they should be quickly discarded when they do not seem to fit.

1. Families in racial- and ethnic-minority communities in the United States aspire to the same ideals as those to which white, middle-class families aspire.

This might seem to be a surprising generalization, but the literature appears to support it. While most social scientists and social service workers use the terminology of cultural diversity, they also give considerable attention to cultural similarity. People in minority and majority groups alike espouse the ideals of heterosexuality, monogamy, two-parent nuclear family, relatively egalitarian roles between husband and wife, involvement in the rearing of children by both parents, and the maintenance of close kinship ties. In terms of the ambience of family life, most people, in both minority and majority communities, aspire to endow family life with the qualities of caring, acceptance, nurturing, warmth, cooperativeness, and openness. There are a few racial- and ethnic-community members who advocate truly alternative family structures; Paula Gunn Allen, for instance, argues for large matriarchal, matrilocal, extended-kin families among Native Americans.[25] But few minority-group members champion such family forms as cohabitation or single-parent families, and none would suggest that family life should be typified by such qualities as coldness, insensitivity, neglect, or abuse.

Jerold Heiss presents data that help support this generalization. He examined 1974 and 1979 national surveys and compared the attitudes of black and white women on a number of family issues. He found that while there were some differences in attitudes, most of them were trivial, and the differences in the history and experiences of blacks and whites had not produced major differences in their attitudes toward the family.[26] A number of studies of family life take the same position. Studies by Walter Allen and John McAdoo, for instance, demonstrate the similarities of black and white fathers.[27] The generalization is supported with respect to other groups as well. John Price notes that today most Native Americans and Alaskan Native adhere to family lifestyle patterns that are more or less in keeping with middle-class aspirations.[28]

2. When racial- and ethnic-minority families do not aspire to middle-class ideals, generational differences may be operating.

Differences between minority and majority families most often center around husband-wife and parent-child relations, as well as relations with kin. A major reason for variations in the family lifestyles of racial and ethnic minorities is that these patterns were established in different cultures or native homelands. Their family lifestyles in the United States are carryovers from another social context. As the different groups that make up the mosaic of contemporary American society became incorporated, they brought with them certain values and preferences about the way family life ought to be organized. In their own eyes their ways of organizing family life were correct and natural, but in the United States they were confronted with different values and realities. While many immigrants strove to retain their old ways, as each generation came to adulthood it began to adopt the family-lifestyle aspirations of mainstream Americans.

The painful changes that were made by southern and eastern European Catholics and Jews as they confronted life in the United States have been described by Michael Novak. Assimilation into the American mainstream for these immigrants meant exchanging the extended-kin family form for more nuclear family forms and discarding patterns of self-help. In the process they had to learn to accept loneliness and the disintegration of family ties; they had to learn that it was all right to put their own interests above those of others, including family members; and they had to learn to rely only on themselves and not to expect family help.[29]

Families whose historical origins are in African, Asian, European, or Latin American societies contain structural and functional elements associated with family life in those societies. These elements will be more visible if a particular family is newly arrived and less visible when the family has been in the United States for several generations. For recent immigrant groups like East Indians, Mexicans, and Haitians and new refugee groups like Cubans, Vietnamese, and Central Americans, the ideals of the home country are fresh in their minds. In most of these new groups there is likely to be greater control over family life by members of the older generation, greater emphasis on male dominance, and greater respect for parental authority than in middle-class American families. Joan Jensen reports, for instance, that concerns about male and parental authority are common among East Indian immigrants to the United States:

> The economic independence of some women concerned their husbands; working wives were not able to provide traditional care and services. . . . Parents were concerned about the erosion of traditional family authority, and the effect it would have on their children as they grew up. They worried about the lack of respect for the elderly.[30]

Similarly, Mary Bowen Wright reports that Vietnamese refugees rebelled against the family attitudes that were being taught their children in the refugee camps: "The program stressed assertiveness and independence . . . which clashed sharply with the tradition of respect for and submission to parental wishes." Vietnamese families often were large extended families dominated by a patriarch, and thus they were offended by the "pressure on family heads to split up their extended families into smaller units."[31]

3. When racial- and ethnic-minority families do not aspire to middle-class ideals, continued contact with a foreign homeland or social isolation from the dominant white majority may be operating.

Families that have been in the United States for many generations may continue to espouse ideals that are somewhat at variance with middle-class ideals. One reason that a culturally different pattern may continue to exist is that the

link with the native culture has not been entirely broken, and the pattern continues to be reinforced.[32] Family life in Mexican-American and Puerto Rican
communities is a case in point. Because of geographical proximity to the native
culture and the relative ease in going to and from the native land, these families can be expected to maintain their Latin American cultural traditions.
Many make numerous trips between their homeland and the United States
and maintain close ties to relatives there.

A second reason a culturally different pattern may continue to exist is that
the experiences of the minority group in the United States are so hostile that
it becomes socially and physically isolated from the dominant group. Under
these conditions the group must rely on its own inner strengths, resources, and
traditions in order to maintain dignity and cohesion. In black and Native
American families, family life has a history of existing in a context of hostility.[33] American Indians were forced to live on reservations, and blacks were
segregated from whites and their mobility was severely restricted. Systematic
efforts were made by the white majority group to eliminate family traditions.
In the case of blacks, marriage between slaves was illegal, and couples who considered themselves a family could be broken up at the whim of a slave owner.
In the case of Native Americans, Christian missionaries systematically undermined all forms of family life that did not correspond to the patriarchal, nuclear
family. Nevertheless, family life continued to be strong in both groups. There
is evidence that black family life persisted even under slavery,[34] and the west
African heritage has continued to influence the family life of American
blacks.[35] Similarly, matriarchal norms have persisted among Native American
families, in spite of all attempts to make them patriarchal. In at least one-fourth
of the federally recognized tribes, women function as council members and
tribal chairs, and many tribes have women as heads of state.[36]

   4. When racial- and ethnic-minority families do not conform to middle-class
      ideals, social class factors within the group may be operating.

The relevance of social class factors in explaining differences among racial
and ethnic groups is a subject of debate. It has been pointed out that comparisons between the white and black middle classes are hazardous because the
criteria used to measure white middle-class status are not accurate for the black
middle class.[37] Similarly, most of the literature on Mexican Americans and
other Hispanics has emphasized that cultural traditions are more relevant than
class to differences in individual and family behavior. Others, however, have
presented data indicating the relevance of social class.[38] The point is not that
class is more relevant than culture but rather that, within a culture, social class
differences operate to bring about diversity.

The reality of family life for any particular minority family may not conform
to middle-class ideals or even to the cultural ideals of the minority group. Thus
Robert Hill acknowledges that there are families within the black community
that deviate from its norms, even as he quite correctly denies that the black
community is by definition deviant.[39] These kinds of within-group differences

are better explained by socioeconomic factors than by cultural factors; that is, they do not reflect the values and traditions of a group so much as they reflect adaptations to the improved socioeconomic circumstances of many people in minority groups.

5. When the ideals of racial- and ethnic-minority families differ from middle-class ideals, a desire for greater involvement in extended-kin networks is likely to be evident.

Both minority- and majority-group families differ in their involvement with extended-kin networks. The traditional extended-kin family included several generations of related individuals living under one roof and headed by a matriarch or patriarch.[40] For the most part, such families do not exist in contemporary American society, except possibly among some Native American tribes.[41] More likely are **multigenerational families** or **modified extended families**, networks of independent households living in relative proximity which serve as a source of mutual assistance and maintain strong affiliations.[42] While the basis of the ties among household members is usually common blood **(consanguinity)**, it is also not unusual for **fictive relatives**, that is, close friends, to also achieve status as family members. The literature on minority-group families, much of which is not empirical, suggests that ethnic-minority families are more involved with extended-kin networks than majority families are.

This distinction should be made cautiously, however. Although the nuclear family has replaced the traditional extended-kin family in most industrialized nations, ties to extended kin remain strong.[43] Kinfolk serve many important functions, and a focus on intergenerational ties is the basis of much social work with white middle-class families.[44]

In any case, the literature on minority groups does emphasize kin ties. Certainly, for many Asian Americans, respect for elders and acquiescence to their authority are essential. Among Native Americans, Puerto Ricans, and Mexican Americans, **familism**, a byword meaning strong extended-kin attachments, is frequently used. Puerto Ricans and Mexicans also have strong ties to fictive relatives, giving them such titles as uncle, aunt, godparent (*padrino*, *madrina*), or co-parent (compadre, comadre). Because of their intense family involvement, it is often believed that in these groups family needs supersede individual needs, and the family takes precedence over the individual. Extended family relationships — those that go beyond the nuclear family — are also highly visible in the black community. Elmer and Joanne Martin describe the black family as a "multigenerational, interdependent kinship system which is welded together by a sense of obligation to relatives." A typical family network may include five or more "affiliated households" centered around a "base household" with an informally acknowledged "dominant family figure." The leader is often an elderly couple or female. The base and affiliated households may include blood relatives or relatives through marriage but also may include friends.[45]

For many racial and ethnic groups, the ideal of intense involvement with kin may not be evident in reality. While multigenerational families may be necessary to help minorities deal with racism, only mixed support has been found in studies which have attempted to document the existence of strong cooperative, intergenerational ties among minorities. There is little evidence that minorities are exceptionally committed to caring for elderly parents or demonstrating filial responsibility. In these respects, social class and generational differences may be as important as cultural differences.[46] Intense multigenerational involvement thus may be more of an ideal, something to be desired and striven for, than a reality.

6. When the ideals of racial- and ethnic-minority families differ from middle-class ideals, a greater adherence to paternalistic values is likely to be apparent.

This generalization also must be advanced cautiously. The debate in American society about more egalitarian relations between spouses in marriage applies to minority communities. In certain groups, in particular Asian Americans and Hispanics, paternalistic norms are clearly evident. In other groups, such as blacks and Native Americans, they are not.

Before their unwilling incorporation into American society, both blacks and Native Americans had strong matriarchal norms. According to certain anthropologists, some Indian tribes or nations were patriarchal and others were matriarchal, but even in the matriarchal tribes women held inferior positions to men. Paula Gunn Allen challenges these assertions, maintaining that the behaviors and thinking of American Indian tribes have been misinterpreted, and "traditional tribal lifestyles are more gynocratic [matriarchal, matrilineal, and matrilocal] than not, and they are never patriarchal."[47] In any case, most writers on Native Americans believe that patriarchal norms now have come into existence as the result of assimilation into the white majority and have been internalized by Indian tribal cultures.[48] It may be that because of the large number of Native American and Alaskan native peoples, such generalizations should not be made.

Debate on the role of the male in the black family is particularly heated. It has been argued that the black family is matriarchal, and men have only an auxiliary role in it. Increasingly, however, much more variation in black family life is becoming evident. While lower-class black men may have a secondary place in family life, middle-class black men assume roles that are not very different from those of white middle-class men. In general, there is no evidence that black culture values matriarchy higher than patriarchy. Moreover, when black men are absent from home, the reasons are likely to be related to the socioeconomic difficulties they encounter in American society. The argument is that the self-esteem of black men is constantly threatened by racism and economic exploitation, and efforts must be made to call attention to their needs, acknowledge their strengths, and increase their stature.[49] Some writers on the roles of black males clearly assume that they are and should be the rightful head of the family, while others support more egalitarian relationships.[50]

7. When the ideals of racial- and ethnic-minority families differ from middle-class ideals, a greater adherence to authoritarian values is likely to be apparent.

In keeping with the multigenerational ideals of many ethnic-minority families, parental obedience and respect for elders are important values. Authoritarian norms are likely to govern parent-child relationships, both between minor children and their parents and between adult children and their elderly parents.

Authoritarian does not necessarily mean that the power structure in minority families is cruel, overbearing, or arbitrary. Parental authority can be expressed in a number of ways: through physical punishment and coercion, social and monetary rewards, or *authoritativeness*, that is, expression of the parents' greater experience and knowledge. In family systems that adhere to authoritarian norms, the vertical hierarchy is clearly specified, and parents or elders are clearly in the role of decision maker. Family life reflects a centralized authority, not a group of peers in which everyone, regardless of age, has more-or-less equal influence.

In the traditional Mexican-American family, a major characteristic is "subordination of the younger to the older."[51] In the Japanese community, *oya-koko* prescribes the respect, awareness of obligation, and dependence that should be reflected in relationships between parents and children.[52] It is considered the cornerstone of morality in the family, requiring children to give their parents unquestioning obedience and loyalty and to be sensitive to their family duties. According to Man Keung Ho, filial piety and dominance and deference based on paternalism are cultural values among all Asian-American groups. Discussion and debate about decisions is precluded in Asian families: "The role of the parent is to define the law; the duty of the child is to listen and obey."[53]

The literature on blacks and Native Americans is less clear in respect to this generalization, and it may not apply. In relations between parents and minor children, Native Americans are likely to reflect the opposite of authoritarian norms, and permissive child rearing appears to be the ideal. However, as John Red Horse observes, the role of elders in family life and tribal interactions cannot be underestimated: "Elders are important and provide continuity of world view; they also lend wisdom to daily life and bring order to chaos. Elders are reminders of heritage and survival and strength."[54]

With respect to black families, the evidence is also not very clear. In some studies black parents were found to be less permissive than other types of parents.[55] Other studies indicated that while physical punishment of children is likely in black families, it is not likely to be harsh and probably is counterbalanced with a great deal of love. As a result, parent-child relations often are free of the anxiety often found in white middle-class families. After interviewing 160 black mothers and fathers, Karen Bartz and Elaine Levine concluded that black parents typically expect early autonomy in children, do not allow wasted time, are both highly supportive and controlling, value strictness, and encourage egalitarian family roles.[56]

AN OVERVIEW OF RACIAL- AND ETHNIC-MINORITY FAMILIES

To illustrate some of the seven generalizations about minority family norms and ideals, this section examines more closely the family lifestyles of Native Americans, American blacks, Hispanics, and Asian Americans.

Native Americans and Alaskan Natives

There is no single, definite "American Indian" culture. In colonial times there were hundreds of groups of indigenous peoples, ethnically and even racially distinct, living in the area that is now the United States. The cultural variation that existed among Native Americans and Alaskan Natives was greater than the variation among European groups; that is, the differences between such peoples as the Mohawk, Menominee, Navajo, and Klamath were probably greater than those between the Italians, Germans, Irish, and Polish. These variations were evident in language, in the economy, government, and religion, and in family life patterns and institutions. Price notes that "almost all of the world's major variants of marriage, incest prohibitions, postmarriage residence customs, and in-law relations were practiced by one native North American society or another."[57] In about 20 percent of the native groups, polygamy and homosexual coupling were also practiced.[58]

To demonstrate the diversity that existed among the various groups, Price compared the Eskimo, Hopi, and Kwakiutl tribes in the colonial era of the United States. Eskimos lived in bands in the Arctic region and built their economy around hunting and gathering. They permitted premarital sex; practiced monogamy, although wives were often given to male guests as a token of good manners; had neolocal postmarital residence (the married couple set up their own household); and acknowledged **bilateral descent** (traced through both sets of parents). There was a division of labor in the band; men hunted, women gathered, and both fished and built the houses. There was little display of emotion between husband and wife. Sometimes the relationship may have been close, affectionate, and satisfying, but at least from the point of view of outside observers, it appears to have been strained. Eskimo society was patriarchal; men treated their wives as inferiors and avoided deep interpersonal relations with them. The rights of parents over children were not questioned. Infanticide was common; the mother decided whether a newborn was strong and healthy enough to survive the inhospitable climate of the Arctic. Infants who were desired were indulged and nurtured with intense, continuous, warm maternal care.

The Hopi, who continue to live in their ancestral lands in what is now the state of Arizona, subsisted from communal agriculture. They permitted premarital sex but insisted on monogamy in marriage. Newly married couples moved to the home of the wife's mother, and descent was traced through the maternal line. However, Hopi men retained ritual, leadership, and disciplinary roles in their family of origin. It was the "social father," that is, the mother's brother, that disciplined the children. The biological father had a passive child-rearing role in his wife's household. The socialization of children was extremely permissive, with little explicit discipline and very gradual weaning and toilet training. The Hopi extended-kin and tribal system allowed for little privacy, and gossip and punishment through ridicule and religious ritual (the *Kiva*) was common. Men hunted and women cultivated; weaving was done by men and house building by both men and women.

The Kwakiutl, who inhabited the Northwest coastal area, were organized into chiefdoms and subsisted largely through fishing. They prohibited premarital sex but allowed for polygamy. The newly married couple moved to the husband's father's residence, and descent was traced through the paternal line. Men hunted and women gathered, but both were involved in fishing. Men did the house building, and women did the weaving.

For many native tribes, co-residence by same-sex partners was also acceptable. The term **berdache** was introduced by Europeans to describe the custom of reversal of the customary gender roles in native cultures. Indian tribes are likely to have their own terms for homosexually inclined people. The Lakota use *koskalaka* to describe a "woman who doesn't want to marry" and *winkte* to describe such a male.[59] In earlier centuries, it was not uncommon for a man or a woman to cross-dress, cross-work, or cross-speak. The man-woman or woman-man was often bisexual, but it is also likely that many were exclusively homosexual. The cross-sex berdache would also live in a sexual relationship with a same-sex partner, and homosexual relations may have existed among others. In any case, sex segregation was common in many tribes, with women and men living in separate structures.

The diverse forms of family life found among the various native groups were looked on with horror by the colonizing Europeans. As they gained superiority, Europeans set out to impose their own concept of "proper" family life on the native populations. As we showed in Chapter 4, they systematically set out to eliminate polygamy, homosexuality, and matrilineal customs and to support patriarchal norms. This was done not only through the activities of Christian missionaries but through legislation, including the reservations system and other attempts to alter the economic institutions that undergirded native cultures. Native groups were forced to give up their hunting and gathering and turn to agriculture as the major form of subsistence. More recently, they have turned to industrialization and tourism.

Recent Changes. Changes in the economy of the various tribes brought changes in their family life. Today most Native Americans and Alaskan Natives have family lifestyles that are more or less in keeping with the norms of

American society. Monogamous, patrilineal, nuclear families increasingly predominate.[60] Although kin networks are still strong and supportive, multi-family residences and corporate kinship groups such as lineages and clans have been abandoned. The elderly are still respected, but it is not uncommon for tribal elders to experience a loss of status and a sense of alienation. One Native American elder put it this way:

> We were put on the sidelines. Left on the bench. There was a time when this was not true. When age and experience was a vital and dynamic part of the Native culture. Traditionally, the elders were held in high regard. They were listened to, honored, and included in the ongoing life of the Indian community. There was no shame in having lived a good and full life. On the contrary, the older Indian was considered wise and knowledgeable. When problems arose, it was our answers, our advice and counsel, to which the people turned. We were the guides, the conscience, of the Indian nation. We were as much a part of tribal life as anyone else. We had our place, our home, among the family of Native people.[61]

The likelihood that an American Indian tribe has adapted its cultural and family life to conform to middle-class norms in the United States is related to a number of conditions. One is the historical and geographic isolation of the group from American culture. To the extent that the group continues to live on reservations apart from the white mainstream, the chances of retaining Indian ways are higher. The Hopi and the Eskimos have managed to escape most of the destruction and intrusion of European cultures, and in many ways their social patterns and strong tribal identity have prevailed. Yet changes are apparent. The Hopi, for instance, have never been Christianized, and while they have accepted English as the primary language, they retain their native tongue as a second language. They also continue to have strong matriarchal tendencies. But they have accepted free-market economic activities; they work for wages, attend non-Hopi schools, use automobiles and electrical appliances, shop at supermarkets, and wear Western dress.

It is believed that deep changes in family lifestyles will occur as more Native Americans move away from reservations and establish themselves in large cities. So far, knowledge of these changes is limited, however. It appears that when Indians move from the reservation to a city, relatives function to buffer the move.[62] It is also likely that urban enclaves of Native Americans form in a city to serve as a temporary reference group for new arrivals and help them with the problems of adjustment. Red Horse agrees that the urban environment has not profoundly influenced family and kin network patterns among Native Americans.[63] But high rates of intermarriage across different Indian groups or with non-Native Americans help dissipate these enclaves. Moreover, some studies suggest that Native Americans do not congregate in particular neighborhoods in cities but are integrated,[64] and there are differences among those who live in cities. One study found a wide range in degree of attachment to and involvement in American Indian ways, but in general tribal preferences were not strong.[65]

Further changes are likely as the American economic system increasingly predominates and class divisions are created within tribes. Studies on the Menominee of Wisconsin are important in this regard. George and Louise Spindler found five social segments in this tribe, of either acculturated or nonacculturated types. The nonacculturated, those who attempted to adhere to the traditional Menominee culture, include the "native oriented" and the Peotists, who believe that children are reincarnated elders and have supernatural power. The acculturated types include those undergoing transition from the traditional Indian to American culture and the lower-class and elite acculturated. The acculturated derive pride and identity from the native heritage but aspire to imitate the ways of the white American majority.[66]

American Blacks

In the forced introduction of American blacks into American society through slave trafficking, the slaves generally were not members of the African societies with which Europeans traded but rather were their captives. Thus, from the beginning, black slaves were cut off from their kinship networks and native cultures. This separation was reinforced on the journey to the United States, since slave masters tried to forestall rebellion by deliberately mixing captives of different societies. Once here, the slaves were subjected to restrictive laws which served to prevent the development of community and ethnicity (see Chapter 4). Slaves could not hire out their own time or find their own work. They were forbidden to vote, to be a witness in court against a white person, to become educated, or to legally marry and have families. Slave owners sometimes promoted marriage and family for their own purposes, but the practice had no legal backing.

The effects of slavery on black family life are hotly debated. Early in the twentieth century, E. Franklin Frazier argued that slaveholders often disrespected spouse and parent relationships in selling slaves.[67] As a result of this hostile environment, black two-parent family life never had a chance to take hold, and a strong matriarchal pattern emerged. His argument has been used to explain the higher incidence of single-parent families and unwed parents among lower-class blacks today.

Recent evidence has called this scenario into question. Herbert Gutman and his associates examined census schedules and other documents in the period 1750 to 1925 and found evidence that most slaves formed stable unions, living together until they died unless one of them was sold away. Most slave children thus grew up in two-parent families with strong ties to a larger kin group. Furthermore, a high percentage of black families living in Harlem as late as 1925, well after slaves were emancipated, had two parents.[68]

There are significant trends in the contemporary black family. Prior to World War II, age at first marriage was younger for blacks than for whites. Now this trend has been completely reversed. At the same time, the rate for out-of-wedlock childbearing has been increasing for white women, especially white teenagers. Nevertheless, it is still overwhelmingly more likely for black women than for white women to bear children out of wedlock. Among whites, 14.5 percent of all births were to unmarried women in 1985, compared to 60.1 percent of all births to unmarried women among blacks.[69] According to Andrew Cherlin, "having a first child and getting married appear to have become unrelated events for more and more black women during the postwar period." To be sure, he acknowledges that this is also true for whites, but the situation is far more pervasive for blacks.[70]

Focusing on such data as these has encouraged the stereotype of black family life as pathological. Theories of juvenile delinquency among lower-class blacks have emphasized a matriarchal family structure typified by neurotic, ambivalent relationships between mothers and their male offspring in families with absent fathers,[71] or they have blamed "dysfunctional" family life for continued poverty among blacks.[72] While family structure and dynamics may play some role in causing delinquency and maintaining poverty, family factors cannot be seen as the primary cause, nor can family factors be separated from the social context which produced them in the first place.[73]

Andrew Billingsley argues that black families must be understood in terms of their variation and complexity.[74] This perspective acknowledges that the black community is diverse and incorporates a number of family lifestyles. What might appear on the outside to be unusual or pathological may not be so on closer inspection. In the case of single-parent black families, for instance, the idea of a single parent suggests a lonely woman in social isolation struggling to rear her children, but this situation is not common in the black community. A single-parent family often includes a number of kin, such as a mother, aunt, or brother, in a number of households making up a domestic network. The network of supportive relatives is the family, rather than the single parent herself.

Diversity in Lifestyles.   Much of the diversity in family lifestyles in the black community is class-based. Black families in which the husband and wife have stable employment are probably not much different from working-class and middle-class white families. Poverty-class blacks are likely to have a very different family pattern, however. In attempting to describe the complexity of the black community, Ulf Hannerz presents an interesting classification of four lifestyles: mainstreamers, swingers, street families, and street-corner men. In a similar vein, Charles Willie has distinguished among the family lifestyles of conformists, innovators, and rebels.[75] In both of these typologies, social class is the underlying dimension. The following sketches of family lifestyle differences incorporate the ideas of Hannerz and Willie.

Affluent blacks are likely to be described as **mainstreamers**. They aspire to the ideal of the middle-class family and probably approximate it quite well in reality. Their values and beliefs, and their organization of family life, make them largely indistinguishable from other middle-class Americans. They have a Puritanical orientation which emphasizes work, success, and self-reliance. They have managed to overcome prejudice and discrimination and to achieve material success, but this often makes them sensitive to racism and the way it hinders the well-being of blacks. They generally are married, live in nuclear families, and maintain stable family relations. Their relatively high incomes largely are attributable to two-parent employment. They attach great value to home ownership, educational achievement, and family-oriented leisure activities. Because both parents work, however, there is likely to be little socializing. As blacks continue to achieve middle-class status, the mainstreamer perspective on family life can be expected to increase.

Swingers are often the children of mainstreamers. In many ways they are like "liberated" white, middle-class, young adults, in which peer-oriented social, athletic, economic, and political activities predominate. They generally are not family oriented but spend their leisure time exploring personal interests. Swingers are experimenting with the opportunities available to single people in contemporary society. This lifestyle is related more to young-adult status than to a permanent way of life. Eventually many swingers will marry, settle down, and take up lifestyles similar to those of mainstreamers.

Working-class black families are described as **innovators**. In these families, caught up in a struggle for survival, family cohesiveness is based less on understanding and tenderness than on the need to stave off adversity. Working-class couples are likely to have many children and to live near relatives who can give social support. They take great pride in their children and consider them successful when they can avoid the many opportunities in the neighborhood to get in trouble with the law. They have a strong sense of morality and are often deeply religious, even if they do not participate fully in church activities. The relationship between husband and wife is likely to be egalitarian, since cooperation is essential to survival. Nevertheless, male and female roles are specified clearly: husbands make financial and housing decisions and give advice to boys, while wives clean, cook, and give advice to girls. Their values emphasize upward mobility, and they are committed to rearing children as good citizens.

Poor black families are "forced to make a number of necessary, clever, and sometimes foolish arrangements," according to Willie.[76] The term **street families** most often is applied to the poor, single-parent, female-headed family. This family pattern is associated with blacks in the urban underclass, living in abject poverty. The single mother, lacking in education and employment opportunities, must struggle to maintain the family household. Street families are often viewed with contempt, not only by whites, who see in them all the pathology of black community life, but also by middle-class blacks, who object to what they perceive as instability and a lack of concern for sexual and family respectability. But, as we have noted, street families headed by single mothers often are attached to a network of households which provide some social support and economic security. By expanding the family in this way, economic and social resources can be shared. The flexibility of the network of street families, their willingness to include friends as well as relatives and to share and cooperate, is crucial to the survival of unemployed and underemployed blacks. Willie notes, however, that these families are likely to experience internal conflict. They move often, bringing a rapid succession of jobs, houses, and neighborhoods. Parents love their children but seldom understand them; the scapegoating of deviant children is common. The hold of the network is strong; men and women become sexually involved but are afraid to marry and entrust their futures solely to one another.

Street-corner men represent the other side of the street families. Where street families are usually headed by women, street-corner society is male-dominated, made up of lower-class men of all ages. Street-corner men have been the subject of a number of studies.[77] With limited educational and economic opportunities, they make few domestic attachments. Often they live among others like themselves, filling the ranks of the homeless. They may survive by making temporary attachments to street families, by working at occasional jobs, or by seizing illegal opportunities. There is a comaraderie among the men which offers economic and emotional support, but there is also animosity and violence. It is a difficult life, made up of monotonous routines.

Hispanics

The central role of family life in Hispanic communities has been described as familism. In the Mexican-American community, the term includes immediate family, extended kin (aunts, uncles, grandparents, cousins, and in-laws), and co-parents or god parents.[78] In Puerto Rican culture, although the nuclear family pattern is increasingly apparent, value is also attached to strong, intimate ties with kin and **companion parents**, that is, godparents, witnesses at a marriage, or close friends. As with blacks living in poverty, single-parent families and common-law marriages are frequent among impoverished Puerto Ricans, but ties to the households of relatives and companion parents remain strong.[79]

The traditional Hispanic culture emphasized a strict dichotomy between men and women in the family. Men were supposed to be macho, while women were supposed to be bound to the house, caring for children and husband, uninterested in sexual fulfillment yet submitting to the desires of their husbands out of respect for male "needs." Today this sexual division has been labeled **machismo** for men and **marianismo** (after the Blessed Virgin Mary) for women, and many inside the Hispanic community see it as a major source of strain in family life. In writing about Puerto Rican culture, Sonia Ghali draws a particularly negative image of the Puerto Rican male in the traditional marriage: "He advocates a double standard of sexual morality. The Puerto Rican husband may not be home often, preferring the company of his male friends or his mistress. The married woman, usually aware of her husband's extramarital affairs, is expected to suffer in silence."[80]

Yet there is considerable ambivalence toward these roles within the Hispanic community. Some see the male's role as a positive attribute. They point out that the contemporary American use of the term *macho* distorts the true meaning of the word. David Alvirez, Frank Bean, and Dorie Williams, for instance, caution against a narrow, overly sexual interpretation. While they do not deny that the macho tradition gave the male license to pursue sexual affairs, they argue that it also imposed important values such as "courage, honor, and re-spect for others, as well as the notion of providing fully for one's family and maintaining close ties with the extended-kin family". Male authority in the household was never absolute and was always expected to be used in a just and fair manner.[81]

Studies of class differences among Mexican Americans suggest that, com-pared to lower-class families, middle-class families are less patriarchal and relationships between spouses are more egalitarian. When middle-class Mexican-American women were asked what they expected from their hus-bands, they demonstrated a greater desire for expressive qualities (sensitivity to needs and affection), while lower-class Mexican-American women were more likely to want instrumental qualities (doing house repairs, mowing the lawn, etc.). While middle-class Mexican-American women are more likely than lower-class Mexican-American women to desire an egalitarian relation-ship with their husbands, in neither group was this preference cited by even half of the women.[82]

Asian Americans

In both the Chinese and Japanese communities, family life is strong. Accord-ing to Ishisaka and Takagi, the importance of the family in Chinese culture cannot be overemphasized, and the Japanese show great concern for family reputation and strive not to bring shame on the family line. In both groups, the effect of an individual's actions on the family governs behavior, and the per-sonal desires of the individual are expected to be subordinated to the needs of the family. The Japanese term *kenshin* expresses the renunciation of selfish desires in favor of common family interests. In both groups, also, the family is multigenerational and includes extended kin, although fictive relatives do not have an important role in Japanese and Chinese family life.[83]

Traditional Japanese and Chinese families were strongly hierarchal, with male authority clearly in control. In Chinese culture the ideal family is mul-tigenerational, marked by patrilineal descent and patrilocal residence. In Japa-nese culture maintenance of the reputation of the *ie*, the lineage of the father, is of most concern: "As the Emperor would expect loyalty from his subjects, and a prefectural baron from his feudal vassals, so too would a lineage patri-arch expect loyalty and obedience from his family . . . . The head of the fam-ily is accorded the respect due his position. In general, males are accorded prerogatives and status superior to those accorded women."[84]

The survival of the Japanese family and its traditions has been the subject of a recent study by Harry Kitano. He notes that with improvement in the so-cioeconomic status of Japanese Americans during the past few decades, the rate of outgroup marriages has increased greatly. For instance, in 1971 in Los Angeles county, 47 percent of those with Japanese surnames married in-dividuals with non-Japanese surnames; eight years later, the rate of outmarri-ages had risen to over 60 percent. Japanese-American females were more likely to marry out than Japanese-American males, and Japanese in general were more likely to marry into the dominant white community than any other group. Kitano suggests that the same phenomenon may be apparent in other Asian groups as well. During the 1970s, around 40 percent of Chinese and 30 percent of Koreans married outside the group. Since Chinese and Koreans include large numbers of first-generation immigrants, who are less likely to marry outside the group, the rate for these groups is surprisingly high.[85]

FAMILY LIFE OUTSIDE MARRIAGE: GAY AND LESBIAN COUPLES

As we noted in Chapter 7, lesbian and gay couples seldom are included in definitions of marriage or the family. Nevertheless, the number of homosexuals seeking to form lasting relationships apparently is growing, and as they live together they are fashioning family lifestyles with unique roles, norms, and values.

The ways gays and lesbians form lasting relationships, and the problems they experience in doing so, are affected by the discrimination they face in American society. As was done with Native Americans and blacks, legal and social obstacles are erected to obstruct the efforts of this group to achieve a family lifestyle. We have shown how the extended-kin, plural-marriage, matriarchal family pattern of Native Americans was considered savage and its eradication was attempted, and how slaveholders tried to destroy black family life by outlawing marriage and separating families. The implications of two lesbians or two gay men forming a long-term union are equally threatening to those who see in homosexuality a challenge to the nuclear family. Clerics and conservatives have been the most vocal critics of efforts in the late 1980s for passage of local ordinances to permit cohabiting couples, both heterosexual and homosexual, to register their relationships in much the same way as couples apply for marriage licenses. Such "domestic partners" then have the same legal standing as families in specific matters such as medical insurance coverage and residential zoning regulations. Legislation of this type is said to redefine the family by function rather than structure, and it is regarded as a threat to the traditional support of marriage and family life in American society.

HOMOSEXUAL COUPLES IN A HETEROGENEOUS WORLD

Homosexual couples with lifestyles analogous to those of heterosexual couples constitute a relatively new development in Western societies. In ancient Greece and Rome and in Victorian England, homosexuality apparently existed within a heterosexual context. Some married men (such as the tragic Oscar Wilde) lived bisexual lives, compartmentalizing their homosexual and heterosexual interests.[86] Today, studies show that quite a few lesbians and gays are or have been heterosexually married (see the next section).[87]

Many believe that gay and lesbian couples imitate heterosexual couples,

"Gay Liberation," a sculpture by George Segal, advocates human rights for gays and lesbians. As an indication that these rights have not been achieved, the sculpture has been repeatedly vandalized since it was placed in a park in Madison, Wisconsin, in 1987.

with one taking the role of the husband and the other the role of the wife. The historical evidence on this arrangement is sketchy, but it suggests that imitation of heterosexual roles was prevalent in the past. For instance, in the berdache custom, many American Indian tribes allowed for marriages between same-sex partners. Sometimes, as among the Zuni, this included a ceremony recognized by the whole community. The berdache always involved a man who became a woman or a woman who became a man, each fulfilling the achieved gender role according to the customs of the tribe.[88] While information on the nature of the relationship in homosexual couples in Western societies is very limited, it appears that even in the recent past it was quite common for these couples to imitate heterosexual role patterns. Two well-known homosexual couples who are said to have adopted the heterosexual role pattern were Gertrude Stein, who apparently played husband to Alice B. Toklas, and George Merrill, who apparently assumed the wife role for Edward Carpenter.[89]

CRAFTING A CONTEMPORARY LIFESTYLE

The gay and lesbian community in contemporary American society is necessarily creating its own ideals—roles, norms, and values—to govern long-term relationships as couples. Homosexual couples must define their roles with few models of same-sex intimacy to guide them. An article in *Practice Digest* notes that such couples are:

> raised by heterosexual parents, lacking marriage manuals and images of conjugal bliss on film or television, faced with a situation where gay couples who do develop successful relationships are seldom visible, unable to acquire the socially sanctioned same-sex dating experiences equivalent to that which non-gay men and women get with each other during adolescence, and lacking structured courtship rituals, . . . [90]

Like other minority groups, the gay and lesbian community is extremely diverse. Same-sex couples living together represent only one lifestyle for lesbians and gays (see box, Diversity in Homosexual Lifestyles). While the practice of coupling is growing, it has not yet been institutionalized in the community because the appropriate values to sustain long-lasting relationships have not been developed. According to Philip Blumstein and Pepper Schwartz in their study of American couples:

> There is a general fear in both gay and lesbian circles that relationships are unlikely to last. Long-lasting relationships are seen as quite special. They are unexpected and therefore newly formed couples are not treated as though they will remain together for fifty years. People are less likely to ask, "How's Jerry?" and more likely to say, "Are you still with your lover?."[91]

The ideals for which gays and lesbians are searching as they seek out relatively same-age, long-term partners are more egalitarian than imitating the role patterns of heterosexual partners would be. David McWhirter and An-

DIVERSITY IN HOMOSEXUAL LIFESTYLES

In their study titled *Homosexualities: A Study of Diversity among Men and Women*, Alan Bell and Martin Weinberg identify five types of homosexuals.

Closed couples are gays or lesbians in long-term relationships in which the partners are deeply involved and rely on each other for sexual and interpersonal satisfaction. They are the most well adjusted psychologically and the least likely to regret being homosexual. Closed-coupled males represented 13.8 of the study sample and closed-couple females constituted 38.4 percent.

Open couples are lesbians or gays who live with sexual partners in long-term relationships but find them unsatisfying. Individuals in open relationships tend to have other sexual affairs. They are as psychologically well adjusted as the average homosexual. Open couples represented 24.7 percent of the male sample and 24.1 percent of the female sample.

Functionals are homosexuals who come close to the idea of "swinging singles," organizing their lives around sexual activities. They are the least likely to regret being homosexual and are involved in the lesbian and gay community. Their good psychological profiles may be attributed to their personalities; they are energetic, self-reliant, cheerful, and optimistic. They do not score quite as high as closed couples in psychological adjustment. Functionals represented 21 percent of the male sample and 14.2 percent of the female sample.

Dysfunctionals are homosexuals who most resemble the negative stereotype of the gay or lesbian. They are the most unhappy homosexuals and tend to regret having this status. The are likely to have a fair amount of sex but feel inadequate about finding and keeping a partner; generally, they think of themselves as sexually unappealing. They often have had negative experiences associated with being homosexual, such as robbery, assault, extortion and job difficulties. Dysfunctionals represented 17.7 percent of the men and 7.6 percent of the women in the sample.

Asexuals are gay men and lesbians who have little social and sexual involvement with others. The men tend to be unhappy, and the women are likely to give up on finding professional help with sexual issues. Asexuals have the highest incidence of suicidal thought. They are the least likely to think of themselves as exclusively homosexual, and the men, especially, have few homosexual friends. Asexuals constituted 22.7 percent of the males and 15.6 percent of the females in the sample.

Source: Adapted from Alan P. Bell and Martin S. Weinberg, *Homosexualities: A Study of Diversity among Men and Women* (New York: Simon and Schuster, 1978), pp. 217–28.

drew Mattison surveyed 156 male couples and found that only among older couples, those who had been together for over 20 years, was the male-female, husband-wife pattern followed.[92] Lesbian families including children typically make nonsexist role assignments in which the mother and her partner, as well as the children, take a wider range of family roles than would be the case in the heterosexual family.[93] Alan Bell and Marvin Weinberg also found relatively little evidence for widespread imitation of heterosexual gender roles among gay and lesbian couples. For instance, both lesbians and gays, particularly those who are younger, have relatively larger repertoires of sexual techniques and interests.[94]

It is generally believed by heterosexuals that homosexual liaisons are temporary and promiscuous, and, in fact, gay men generally have experienced many sexual encounters in their lives. Among the homosexual males surveyed by Bell and Weinberg, almost half of the whites and one-third of the blacks said they had had at least 500 different sexual partners. They also found that lesbians are likely to have had multiple experiences, but in not nearly the numbers reported by gay men. About a quarter of the homosexual females they surveyed said they had had fewer than 5 liaisons, nearly one-third said they had had between 5 and 9, and an additional third said they had had between 10 and 50.[95]

Even long-term sexual relationships among gay men are not likely to emphasize sexual fidelity. McWhirter and Mattison conclude that

> the majority of couples in our study, and all of the couples together for longer than five years, were not continuously sexually exclusive with each other. Although many had long periods of sexual exclusivity, it was not the ongoing expectation for most. We found that gay men *expect* mutual emotional dependability with their partners and that relationship fidelity transcends concerns about sexuality and exclusivity."[96]

In contrast, the norm of sexual fidelity is expected in lesbian relationships. However, Blumstein and Schwartz note that because the lesbian community is based on tightly knit friendship groups, unlike the more open gay male community, it also tends to undermine sexual fidelity. The closeness of the friendship ties often slips over into love relationships which disrupt the friendship network.[97]

The evidence on number of partners and sexual fidelity suggests that homosexual men have generated norms which are significantly different from those of either heterosexual or lesbian couples. For some writers on the subject, multiple sexual partners and emotional dependability without sexual exclusiveness, is the meaning of liberation. They argue that heterosexual norms are hypocritical at best and unnecessarily repressive at worst, and so they do not use the term *promiscuity* in reference to the sexual behavior of gay men.[98] Other writers do not take a moral stance on the issue but explain it in terms of male socialization, both heterosexual and homosexual. Men in contemporary society are expected to be more sexually active, more independent, and less intimate than women. Given an all-male culture, it should be expected that exclusivity and faithfulness would not figure very prominently.[99] Still others see the norms as an indication of the oppressive circumstances confronted by gay men, an aberration that will disappear as gays achieve greater legitimacy and respectability within society.

One recent development which is likely to encourage greater reliance on monogamous, long-term relationships is the prevalence of AIDS (acquired immune deficiency syndrome) in the homosexual male community. AIDS is a viral disease which destroys the immune system and has always been fatal. It may be transmitted sexually; intravenously, through infected blood transfusions or infected hypodermic needles; or through significant contact with the bodily fluids of a diseased person. While cases among heterosexuals abound in Africa and are on the rise in Western societies, about 75 percent of the first cases in the United States were among homosexual men.[100] In the late 1980s, however, the numbers of women and intravenous drug users found to be infected with the virus that causes AIDS began to rise.[101]

Thus, while there are a number of unique qualities in homosexual relationships, in many ways gay and lesbian couples face the same social situations and problems as heterosexual couples do. As an article in the special issue of *Practice Digest* on working with gay and lesbian clients observes, the problems of couples in both kinds of sexual orientation include "different expectations due to having grown up in different cultural or socioeconomic contexts, or having come from different racial, religious or educational backgrounds." Like heterosexual couples, lesbian and gay couples "go to work, plan vacations, pay bills, and deal with illness, aging parents and the deaths of family and friends."[102]

Lesbians and Gay Men as Heterosexual Family Members

According to Alfred Kinsey and his colleagues, only a small percentage of men and women are exclusively homosexual throughout their lives.[103] Many women and men are bisexual or go through a period of relatively homosexual or heterosexual behavior. Indeed, lesbians and gay men often are heterosexual spouses and parents. A few studies on this topic are beginning to surface in the social work literature.

Gay men and lesbians who marry do so often before they become aware of their sexual orientation or before they can adequately accept themselves as gay or lesbian. Del Martin and Phyllis Lyon observe that lesbian mothers

> . . . are women who were unaware of their Lesbian tendencies until after they had married and had children. Or they are women who suppressed their Lesbian feelings, convinced, as most heterosexuals are, that these feelings merely represented a natural phase in their lives and would disappear after they experienced marriage and motherhood.[104]

Norman Wyers asked a nonrandom sample of 77 lesbian wives and gay husbands why they had married. Among the lesbian wives, the three primary reasons given were "always expected to" (38 percent), "love of spouse" (24 percent), and "pregnancy" (18 percent). Among the gay husbands, the primary reasons were "love of spouse" (34 percent), "always expected to" (28 percent), and hopes for "conversion to heterosexuality" (19 percent). Most of the lesbians and gay men responding to this survey had divorced or were separated from their heterosexual spouses. Among the lesbian wives, the most important reason given for the divorce was that they and their husbands were "always incompatible." Only secondarily did the women believe they had divorced because of their homosexual orientation. The gay husbands, on the other hand, overwhelmingly indicated that their homosexual orientation was the major reason for the divorce.[105]

When gay husbands and lesbian wives announce their sexual orientation, the heterosexual spouse is clearly affected. Sandra Auerback and Charles Moser did group work with 50 heterosexual wives of gay and bisexual men. The majority had been married for over ten years, and very few of the wives suspected their husbands' sexual orientation before they married. After learning of their husbands' homosexuality, the wives had to work through some difficult feelings, including anger, hurt, a sense of betrayal, homophobia, fears for their children, and fear of AIDS. The wives were in need of social support and tended to regard themselves as "superwomen" because of the extraordinary effort required to cope with their situation.[106]

Having children presents special difficulties for lesbian wives and gay husbands. In the Wyers survey, gay fathers said they feared that their sexual orientation might damage their children and were more tentative about their willingness to inform their children of it than lesbian mothers were. Gay fathers generally were less likely than lesbian mothers to have custody of their children after divorce and more likely to be dissatisfied with the custody arrangements. Many of the fathers who had informed their children of their sexual orientation believed it had had a negative impact on the relationship. Lesbian mothers were more comfortable about informing their children of their sexual orientation, and many of those who had done so believed it had enhanced their relationship.[107]

Nevertheless, lesbian mothers often live in fear that they will lose custody of their children. This fear has a realistic basis. The harshest discrimination a lesbian mother can encounter is losing custody of her children on the grounds that she is "unfit" to mother. Courts have removed custody from lesbian mothers, contending that they will molest their daughters or encourage their children to grow up homosexual. Yet studies do not demonstrate that lesbian mothers are unfit. In one study, a psychiatric team found no more emotional or gender disturbances among the children of lesbians than among heterosexual women. In another, it was found that motherhood, not the pursuit of self-indulgent sexuality, was the central organizing factor in the lives of lesbian mothers.[108]

This is not to suggest that children of lesbian mothers or gay fathers experience no difficulties as they grow and develop. When Karen Gail Lewis studied 21 children of eight mothers who were newly declared lesbians, she found that the children were proud of their mothers for the step they had taken.

Nevertheless, many of the children did not feel free to express their ambivalence about their mother's behavior, they worried about their own sexuality, and they indicated a lack of support from other family members, from peers, and from society in general.[109] Sensitive counseling, building social support among children of gays and lesbians, and promoting greater social acceptance should go a long way toward assuring that children of gays and lesbians mature and develop in positive ways.

IMPLICATIONS FOR PRACTICE

This chapter has explored diversity in family lifestyles according to social class and racial and ethnic communities in contemporary American society. There are differences between and within the various social classes, and between and among racial- and ethnic minority groups. In all of these, however, movement toward the same ideals is clearly evident. Family dynamics are working toward a redefinition of the family as a social institution. Contemporary family relations seem to involve a search for marriage, monogamy, more egalitarian gender-role expectations, more democratic parent-child relations, and close kinship ties in a nurturing and emotionally supportive environment. Similar aspirations are evident in the long-term commitments of lesbian and gay couples. In developing a family lifestyle outside of marriage, these couples are adopting egalitarian roles that do not emulate traditional heterosexual roles and are stressing monogamy (or loyalty in the case of gay men) and mutual respect.

Although Americans seem to be moving toward a consistent set of family-life ideals, communities differ in the extent to which they are promoting these ideals. Very close kin ties and paternalistic and authoritarian norms, for instance, are considered more desirable in some communities than in others. The reasons for these differences include such considerations as generation or length of time in the United States, social isolation from a foreign homeland or from the American mainstream, and economic necessity. Social service workers have to respect, understand, and support differences in family ideals, even as they work to help people achieve new ones.

The ability to achieve ideals also varies from family to family. It should not always be assumed that the behaviors exhibited by a family or couple represent their ideals. There is often a large gap between ideals and actual behaviors. In no community, even the white middle class, have the ideals discussed here been totally achieved. Social-environmental, biophysical, and psychological reasons can limit the ability of individuals to achieve the ideals to which they aspire.

To build strong helping relationships with families and couples, social service workers need to understand the connection between the ideals people hold and the services they require. Families and couples often seek service when their lifestyle does not conform to their ideals or those of their community. When this happens many come voluntarily into service — spouses and partners who cannot seem to resolve the inequalities in their relationships, for instance, or adult children whose ties to parents and siblings create deep stress. Involuntary services for families and couples whose behaviors stray too far from the ideals of their communities may be mandated by law, as in the case of families beset by violence toward elderly members, children, or spouses.

If social workers are to meet the needs of families and couples, they must begin by tuning in to their ideals and aspirations. Assessment should focus on clarifying the ideals and the ways in which the social environment as well as the psychological and biophysical development of family members foster or limit the attainment of ideals and aspirations. Plans for intervention, of course, follow from this assessment. Where the social environment limits the attainment of family ideals, ways must be found to make both the individuals and the social systems more supportive. When the failure to achieve ideals resides in the development of individual members, plans must be made to improve their functioning by attention to their attitudes, perceptions, behaviors, and abilities.

DISCUSSION QUESTIONS AND CLASS PROJECTS

1. Determine the social class background of each student. Have each person discuss the extent to which their own experiences fit with the research on family life in different social classes. Compare the experiences of people who were raised in the same social class situation. How similar were these experiences?

2. List and discuss the seven generalizations on similarities and differences between the ideals of white middle-class families and racial- and ethnic-minority families. Design a class project to test one or all of these generalizations. For instance, you could decide to talk to Hispanics or to Asian Americans about the family ideals and norms they see in their families.

3. Describe the family patterns found in each of the following communities, paying particular attention to the social class, generational, and other differences that are likely to be seen in any one group: Black Americans, Native Americans, Hispanics, or Asian Americans.

4. Identify a particular subgroup from one ethnic or racial community (Jamaican Americans, Haitian Americans, Navajos, Urban Indians, Cuban Americans, Dominican Americans, Korean Americans, or Vietnamese) and gather information from your library or from professionals about the family patterns that might be evident in them. Pay particular attention to the difference between family ideals and family realities.

5. Hispanic men are often believed to be *macho*. How do people in the United States use this term? How is this usage different from the usage among Hispanic people?

6. How did you think sexual relations between gay men and lesbians were organized before you read this chapter? Did any of their norms and ideals surprise you?

7. Define and identify the importance of the following terms:

mainstreamers
swingers
innovators
street families
street-corner men
familism
marianismo

companion parents	open couples
berdache	functionals
domestic network	dysfunctionals
closed couples	asexuals

NOTES

1. See Mark Poster, *A Critical Theory of the Family* (New York: Seabury Press, 1978), and Eli Zaretsky, *Capitalism, the Family and Personal Life* (New York: Harper Colophon, 1973).

2. Melvin L. Kohn, "The Effects of Social Class on Parental Values and Practices," in P. Voydanoff (editor), *Work and Family* (Palo Alto, CA: Mayfield, 1984).

3. Rayna Rapp, "Family and Class in Contemporary America: Notes toward an Understanding of Ideology," in B. Thorne (editor) with M. Yalom, *Rethinking the Family: Some Feminist Questions* (New York: Longmans, 1982), pp. 168–87.

4. Ibid., p. 180.

5. Ibid., pp. 180–81.

6. Betty Friedan, *The Second Stage* (New York: Summit Books, 1981), p. 30.

7. Rapp, "Family and Class in Contemporary America," p. 172.

8. Lillian Brewslow Rubin, *Worlds of Pain* (New York: Basic Books, Harper Colophon, 1976), pp. 69–92.

9. Joseph Kett, *Rites of Passage* (New York: Basic Books, Harper Colophon, 1977), pp. 168–71.

10. Yankelovich, Skelly, and White, *Raising Children in a Changing Society*, the General Mills American Family Report, 1976–77 (Minneapolis, MN, 1977).

11. Lillian B. Rubin, *Intimate Strangers: Men and Women Together* (New York: Harper Colophon, 1984).

12. U.S. Bureau of the Census, *Statistical Abstract of the United States 1988* (Washington, DC, 1987), Tables 713 and 718.

13. Carol B. Stack, "Sex Roles and Survival Strategies in an Urban Black Community," in H. R. Clark and C. Clark, *So-cial Interaction: Readings in Sociology* (New York: St. Martin's Press, 1983), p. 423. Based on Chapter 7 in Stack, *All Our Kin: Strategies for Survival in a Black Community* (New York: Harper and Row, 1974).

14. See, for example, Stack, *All Our Kin*, and Oscar Lewis, *La Vida* (New York: Random House, 1966).

15. Stack, "Sex Roles and Strategic Survival," p. 434.

16. Stack, *All Our Kin*, pp. 32–45, 105–07.

17. Robert D. Plotnick, "Income Distribution," *Encyclopedia of Social Work*, 18th ed., vol. 1 (Silver Spring, MD: National Association of Social Workers, 1987), pp. 882–83.

18. Rapp, "Family and Class in Contemporary America," pp. 182–83.

19. Herman Schwendinger and Julia Siegel Schwendinger, *Adolescent Subcultures and Delinquency* (New York: Praeger, 1985), pp. 3–58.

20. Jualynne Dodson, "Conceptualizations of Black Families," in H.P. McAdoo (editor), *Black Families* (Beverly Hills, CA: Sage, 1981), pp. 23–36.

21. See Howard M. Bahr, Bruce A. Chadwick, and Joseph H. Strauss, *American Ethnicity* (Lexington, MA: D. C. Heath, 1979), pp. 504–08.

22. Miguel Montiel, "The Social Science Myth of the Mexican American Family," *El Grito: A Journal of Contemporary Mexican American Thought*, vol. 3 (Summer 1970), pp. 56–63.

23. See Robert B. Hill, *The Strengths of Black Families* (New York: Emerson Hall, 1971); Robert Staples, "The Black American Family," in C. H. Mindel and R. W. Habenstein (editors), *Ethnic Families in*

America: Patterns and Variations, 2nd ed. (New York: Elsevier, 1981), pp. 215–44; and Robert Staples and Alfredo Mirande, "Racial and Cultural Variations among American Families: A Decennial Review of the Literature on Minority Families," *Journal of Marriage and the Family*, vol. 4 (November 1980), pp. 151–73.

24. William Julius Wilson, "Cycles of Deprivation and the Underclass Debate," *Social Service Review*, vol. 59 (December 1985), pp. 541–59.

25. Paula Gunn Allen, *The Sacred Hoop: Recovering the Feminine in American Indian Traditions* (Boston, MA: Beacon, 1986).

26. Jerold Heiss, "Women's Values Regarding Marriage and the Family," in McAdoo (editor), *Black Families*, p. 197.

27. Walter R. Allen, "Moms, Dads, and Boys: Race and Sex Differences in the Socialization of Male Children," and John L. McAdoo, "Involvement of Fathers in the Socialization of Black Children," both in L. Gary (editor), *Black Men* (Beverly Hills, CA: Sage, 1981), pp. 99–114 and 225–37.

28. John A. Price, "North American Indian Families," in Mindel and Habenstein (editors), *Ethnic Families in America*, p. 265.

29. Michael Novak, *The Rise of the Unmeltable Ethnics* (New York: Macmillan, 1973), pp. 103–36.

30. Joan M. Jensen, "East Indians," in S. Thernstrom (editor), *Harvard Encyclopedia of American Ethnic Groups* (Cambridge, MA: Belknap Press, 1980), pp. 299–300.

31. Mary Bowen Wright, "Indochinese," in *Harvard Encyclopedia of American Ethnic Groups*, p. 510.

32. Leon F. Williams and Carmen Diaz, "Family: Multigenerational," in *Encyclopedia of Social Work*, vol. 1, p. 532.

33. Leon Chestang, "Character Development in a Hostile Environment," in M. Bloom (editor), *Life Span Development*, 1st ed. (New York: Macmillan, 1980), pp. 40–50.

34. Herbert G. Gutman, *The Black Family in Slavery and Freedom: 1750–1925* (New York: Pantheon, 1976).

35. Niara Sudarkasa, "Interpreting the African Heritage in Afro American Family Organization, in McAdoo (editor), *Black Families*, pp. 37–53.

36. Allen, *Sacred Hoop*, pp. 1–7, 31.

37. Dodson, "Conceptualization of Black Families," pp. 23–36.

38. See Heiss, "Women's Values Regarding Marriage," pp. 186–98; Allen, "Moms, Dads, and Boys," pp. 99–114; and McAdoo, "Involvement of Fathers in Socialization," pp. 225–37.

39. Hill, *Strengths of Black Families*.

40. Christopher C. Harris, *The Family and Industrial Society* (London, England: George Allen and Unwin, 1983), pp. 97–100.

41. John G. Red Horse, "Family Structure and Value Orientation in American Indians," *Social Casework*, vol. 61 (October 1980), pp. 462–67.

42. Williams and Diaz, "Family: Multigenerational," pp. 530–32.

43. See Eugene Litwak, "Extended Kin Relations in an Industrial Democratic Society," and Marvin B. Sussman, "Relationships of Adult Children with Their Parents," both in E. Shanas and G. Streib (editors), *Social Structure and the Family* (Englewood Cliffs, NJ: Prentice-Hall, 1965), pp. 290–323 and 62–92.

44. Elizabeth A. Carter and Monica McGoldrick, *The Family Life Cycle: A Framework for Family Therapy* (New York: Gardner, 1980), pp. 3–20.

45. Elmer P. Martin and Joanne Mitchell Martin, *The Black Extended Family* (Chicago: University of Chicago Press, 1978), p. 1.

46. Williams and Diaz, "Family: Multigenerational," pp. 534–35.

47. Allen, *Sacred Hoop*, p. 2.

48. Price, "North American Indian Families."

49. Thomas J. Hopkins, "The Role of the Agency in Supporting Black Manhood," *Social Work*, vol. 18 (January 1973), pp. 53–58. Also see Gary (editor), *Black Men*.

50. See Allen, "Moms, Dads, and Boys," pp. 99–113, and McAdoo, "Involvement of Fathers in Socialization," pp. 225–37.

51. David Alvirez, Frank D. Bean, and Dorie Williams, "The Mexican American

Family," in Mindel and Habenstein (editors), *Ethnic Families in America*, pp. 269-92.

52. Hideki A. Ishisaka and Calvin Y. Takagi, "Social Work with Asian- and Pacific-Americans," in J. W. Green, *Cultural Awareness in the Human Services* (Englewood Cliffs, NJ: Prentice-Hall, 1982), p. 136.

53. Man Keung Ho, "Social Work with Asian Americans," *Social Casework*, vol. 57 (March 1976), p. 196.

54. Red Horse, "Family Structure and Value Orientation," p. 466.

55. Mary E. Durrett, Shirley L. O'Bryant, and James W. Pennebaker, "Child Rearing Reports of White, Black and Mexican American Families," *Developmental Psychology*, vol. 11 (June 1975), p. 871.

56. Karen W. Bartz and Elaine S. Levine, "Childbearing by Black Parents: A Description and Comparison to Anglo and Chicano Parents," *Journal of Marriage and the Family*, vol. 40 (November 1978), pp. 709-19.

57. Price, "North American Indian Families," p. 246.

58. Jonathan Katz, *Gay American History* (New York: Discus/Avon, 1978).

59. Gunn Allen, *Sacred Hoop*, pp. 258-59.

60. Price, "North American Indian Families," p. 265.

61. Quoted in *The Continuum of Life: Health Concerns of the Indian Elderly*, final report on the Second National Indian Conference on Aging, Billings, Montana, August 15-18, 1978 (Albuquerque, NM: National Indian Council on Aging, 1979), p. 176.

62. Charlotte Dickinson Moore with Dorothy L. Miller, "The Native American Family: The Urban Way," in *Families Today*, vol. 1, National Institute of Mental Health Science Monograph (Washington DC: U.S. Dept. of Health Education and Welfare, 1979), pp. 441-84.

63. Red Horse, "Family Structure and Value Orientation," p. 463.

64. Price, "North American Indian Families," p. 263.

65. Nancy Brown Miller, "Social Work Services to Urban Indians," in Green (editor), *Cultural Awareness in the Human Services*, pp. 157-83.

66. George Spindler and Louise Spindler, *Dreamers without Power: The Menomini Indians* (New York: Holt, Rinehart and Winston, 1971), pp. 2-6.

67. Edward Franklin Frazier, *The Negro Family in the United States* (Chicago: University of Chicago Press, 1939).

68. Gutman, *Black Family in Slavery and Freedom*, pp. 455-56.

69. U.S. Bureau of the Census, *Statistical Abstract 1988*, Table 86.

70. Andrew Cherlin, *Marriage, Divorce, Remarriage* (Cambridge, MA: Harvard University Press, 1981), pp. 95-97.

71. See, for instance, Walter B. Miller, "Lower-class Culture as a Generating Milieu of Gang Delinquency," *Journal of Social Issues*, vol. 14 (Summer 1958), pp. 5-19.

72. Daniel P. Moynihan, *Maximum Feasible Misunderstanding: Community Action in the War on Poverty* (New York: Free Press, 1969).

73. Ludwig L. Geismar and Katherine M. Wood, *Family and Delinquency: Resocializing the Young Offender* (New York: Human Sciences Press, 1986).

74. Andrew Billingsley, *Black Families in White America* (Englewood Cliffs, NJ: Prentice-Hall, 1968), pp. 3-4.

75. Ulf Hannerz, *Soulside: Inquiries into Ghetto Culture and Community* (New York: Columbia University Press, 1969; Charles Vert Willie, *A New Look at Black Families*, 2nd ed. (New York: General Hall, 1981).

76. Willie, *New Look at Black Families*, p. 55.

77. For a study by a social worker, see Douglas G. Glasgow, *The Black Underclass: Poverty, Unemployment and Entrapment of Ghetto Youth* (New York: Vintage, 1981). Also see Elliott Liebow, *Tally's Corner: A Study of Negro Streetcorner Men* (Boston: Little, Brown, 1967).

78. Jack Rothman, "Spoken but Not Heard: Communication Gaps between Minorities and Social Service Professionals," *UCLA Social Welfare*, vol. 1 (Spring 1986), pp. 13-15.

79. Sonia Badillo Ghali, "Understanding Puerto Rican Traditions," *Social Work*, vol. 21 (January 1982), pp. 98-102.

80. Ibid., p. 99.

81. Alvirez, Bean, and Williams, "Mexican American Family."

82. Ibid., pp. 184-87.

83. Ishisaka and Takagi, "Social Work with Asian- and Pacific-Americans," pp. 129, 135-38.

84. Ibid., p. 135.

85. Harry H. L. Kitano, "Will Your Daughter Marry One?" *UCLA Social Welfare*, vol. 1 (Spring 1986), pp. 5-6.

86. Jeffrey Weeks, *Sex, Politics, and Society: The Regulation of Sexuality since 1800* (New York: Longmans, 1981), pp. 97-121.

87. See Marny Hall, "Lesbian Families: Cultural and Clinical Issues," *Social Work*, vol. 23 (September 1978), pp. 380-87; also see Allen P. Bell and Martin S. Weinberg, *Homosexualities: A Study of Diversity among Men and Women* (New York: Simon and Schuster, 1978), pp. 106-11, 160-70.

88. Katz, *Gay American History*, pp. 423-29.

89. Sheila Rowbotham and Jeffrey Weeks, *Socialism and the New Life: The Personal and Sexual Politics of Edward Carpenter and Havelock Ellis* (London, England: Pluto Press, 1977). Also see Charles Shively, "Couples, Clones, and Capitalism," *Out* (Madison, WI), March 1986, p. 12.

90. "Counseling for Gay and Lesbian Couples," *Practice Digest*, vol. 7 (Summer 1984), p. 14.

91. Philip Blumstein and Pepper Schwartz, *American Couples* (New York: William Morrow, 1983), p. 322.

92. David McWhirter and Andrew M. Mattison, *The Male Couple: How Relationships Develop* (Englewood Cliffs, NJ: Prentice-Hall, 1984), p. 231.

93. D. G. Wolf, *Lesbian Community* (Berkeley: University of California Press, 1979).

94. Bell and Weinberg, *Homosexualities*, pp. 106-11.

95. Ibid., pp. 85, 93.

96. McWhirter and Mattison, *Male Couple*, p. 285; italics in original.

97. Blumstein and Schwartz, *American Couples*, pp. 322-23.

98. Spivey, "Couples, Clones and Capitalism."

99. Blumstein and Schwartz, *American Couples*, pp. 319-24.

100. Ray Berger, "Homosexuality: Gay Men," in *Encyclopedia of Social Work*, vol. 1, pp. 798-99.

101. "More Women's AIDS Cases," news item, *Chicago Tribune*, February 16, 1989, sect. 1, p. 3.

102. "Counseling for Gay and Lesbian Couples," p. 14.

103. Alfred C. Kinsey et al., *Sexual Behavior in the Human Female* (Philadelphia: W. B. Saunders, 1953), and Kinsey et al., *Sexual Behavior in the Human Male* (Philadelphia: W. B. Saunders, 1948).

104. Quoted in Sandra J. Potter and Trudy E. Darty, "Social Work and the Invisible Minority: An Exploration of Lesbianism," *Social Work*, vol. 26 (May 1981), p. 190.

105. Norman L. Wyers, "Homosexuality in the Family: Lesbian and Gay Spouses," *Social Work*, vol. 32 (March–April 1987), pp. 143-48.

106. Sandra Auerback and Charles Moser, "Groups for the Wives of Gay and Bisexual Men," *Social Work*, vol. 32 (July–August 1987), pp. 321-25.

107. Wyers, "Homosexuality in the Family," pp. 145-46.

108. See Potter and Darty, "Social Work and the Invisible Minority," p. 190.

109. Karen Gail Lewis, "Children of Lesbians: Their Point of View, *Social Work*, vol. 25 (May 1980), pp. 198-203.

CHAPTER 9

The Family as a Social Organization: Identifying Well-Being

M AJOR THEMES DISCUSSED IN THIS CHAPTER:

1. *Identifying family well-being: Healthy families and happy marriages.* The assessment of family life is both a primary task for social service professionals and a means of studying the family. Research has determined various characteristics of healthy families and happy marriages.

2. *Family functioning.* Study of the family as a social organization focuses on determining how families diverge from some optimum level of functioning and identifying directions for change. Understanding of how the family functions as a holon has been furthered by examination of how well a family can satisfy its needs, including survival needs in poor or minority families, as well as family boundaries and structural and interactional patterns within families.

3. *Family problems: domestic violence.* Although family life offers numerous pleasant and rewarding experiences, it also has a darker side. Violence, neglect, and abuse are problems in many families today. Three forms of violence are of special concern—violence against spouses, against children, and against elderly family members.

4. *Family problems: Marriage, divorce, and other stressful patterns.* Family lifestyles in contemporary society create a number of stresses. Growing numbers of individuals are likely to have children outside of marriage; to cohabit without marriage; to marry, separate, or divorce; to live for some period as sin-

gle parents; or to remarry after divorce or the death of a spouse. The stresses associated with all these behaviors are explored.

5. *Implications for practice.* This overview of the identification of strengths and problems in families has implications for primary prevention, early intervention, and crisis and long-term treatment of families.

T HE STUDY of the family as a social institution, the topic of Chapters 7 and 8, forms the basis for social service practice and policy on family life. In practice with families, however, another dimension of family life must be considered: the family as a social organization, which focuses on the functioning of actual families in their everyday lives. In this dimension the family is viewed from the systems perspective as a **holon**, simultaneously a whole and a part of a larger system. It is concerned with the interactions within families and between families and the social environment of which they are a part.

While most approaches to social service work with families claim in one way or another to be based on the systems perspective, many of them examine the family only as a whole with subsystems: the spouse subsystem, the parental subsystem, the sibling subsystem, the parent-child subsystem, the adult child-elderly subsystem. These approaches do not conceptualize the family as a part of a larger community and social system.[1] Chapters 9 and 10 take a **holistic** approach to study of the family as a social organization, seeking to identify and analyze **family well-being**, or the optimum level of **family functioning**: how well the family satisfies its needs, keeps its boundaries open and flexible, and maintains beneficial structural and interactional patterns. This chapter is concerned with identification of the strengths and problems of families and how they differ in terms of family functioning. Chapter 10 discusses five perspectives on family functioning with different points of view on analyzing family well-being and dealing with the problems experienced by families.

IDENTIFYING FAMILY WELL-BEING: HEALTHY FAMILIES AND HAPPY MARRIAGES

The assessment of family life not only is a primary task of social service professionals, it also is a means of studying what makes for well-being or ill-being in family functioning. Most social service work with families now takes the approach of **family therapy**, in which treatment is directed not to individuals with problems but to the family systems of which they are a part. Salvador Minuchin has defined the framework of **structural family treatment** as a body of theory and techniques in which the individual is placed in a social context. Changes in the structure of the family also change the positions of family members, and thus the individuals also change.[2]

When the family is the client — or the patient, in the therapeutic sense — the

Healthy families have no racial and ethnic
boundaries. Here a young Afro-American family
enjoys being together. *Mike Tappin*.

treatment goal is to achieve a state of health in the family. The characteristics of healthy families and happy marriages in contemporary American society have been variously identified by numerous researchers.

CHARACTERISTICS OF HEALTHY FAMILIES

Definitions of the healthy family usually are stated in terms of their characteristics. In *Traits of a Healthy Family*, Dolores Curran, for instance, presents a list of characteristics based on the opinions of professionals.[3] She consulted "the teachers, doctors, principals, pastoral ministers, directors of religious education, boy scout directors, YMCA leaders, Big Brothers, 4-H leaders, family counselors, and other persons of similar positions who work closely with lots of families" and concluded that the healthy family:

1. Communicates and listens.
2. Fosters table time and conversation.
3. Affirms and supports one another.
4. Teaches respect for others.
5. Develops a sense of trust.
6. Has a sense of play and humor.
7. Has a balance of interactions among members.
8. Shares leisure time.
9. Exhibits a sense of shared responsibility.
10. Teaches a sense of right and wrong.
11. Has a strong sense of family in which rituals and traditions abound.
12. Has a shared religious core.
13. Respects one another's privacy.
14. Values service to others.
15. Admits to and seeks help with problems.

Researchers also have taken two other approaches to determining the qualities of healthy families: direct study of families which think of themselves as healthy, and clinical observation of families which consider themselves in trouble (see box, The Healthy Family). In a review of these studies, Ted Bowman identifies the qualities of healthy families that were cited by three or more researchers:[4]

1. Direct and open communication patterns.
2. Appreciation and respect for one another.
3. Spiritual and religious commitment.
4. Adaptability and flexibility.
5. Clarity of family rules.

VARIATIONS IN HAPPY MARRIAGES

The characteristics considered typical of healthy families all have a quality of goodness about them and reflect the cultural ideals described in Chapter 8.

They give the impression that in these families conflict is at a minimum and always under control, and all family members always (or at least most of the time) behave in an exemplary manner.

This view of healthy relationships in the family may not be too realistic, however. John Cuber and Peggy Harroff challenge the rosy picture created by many researchers on family life. They chose to study "normal" couples, those "who had not received clinical help for whatever problems they may have had" or "who were apparently self-directed, not failures in any reasonable sense of the word." Starting from a larger sample, they interviewed 107 men and 104 women who had been married to the same partner for at least 12 years and who had never seriously considered divorce or separation. They concluded that there are at least five types of happy marriages, two of which might qualify as healthy families, but some of which in no way resemble them.[5]

The total marriage, which does have qualities similar to those described by other researchers, is very rare but does exist and can endure. Cuber and Harroff describe the **total marriage** as multifaceted, vital relationships in which there is practically no pretense between the partners, and almost all of the important focuses of life are shared. The various parts of the relationship reinforce one another, and there are few areas of tension. Differences of opinion may exist, but they are settled easily through yielding or compromising.

The vital marriage also comes close to the healthy family model. It is less multifaceted than the total marriage and somewhat more common. In the **vital marriage**, sharing between the partners and togetherness are genuine, and the relationship is the essence of life for each of them. There is an exciting mutuality in the ways the partners operate, but they do not lose their separate identities, and on occasion they can be rivals and competitive. When there is conflict it is usually over important issues, and it is handled without resorting to name-calling or accusation.

In contrast to these two types of happy marriages, which resemble the stereotypical happy family, are three other types: conflict-habituated, devitalized, and passive-congenial. In the **conflict-habituated marriage** there is considerable tension and conflict, although they are mostly controlled. At best the couple is discreet and mannerly in public, though the verbal barbs may start flying. At worst, they indulge in private quarreling, nagging, and "bringing up the past." The conflict-habituated couple seems to need conflict and depend on it to solidify the relationship. Indeed, to stop quarreling would probably end the relationship.

In the **devitalized marriage**, the love and romance that marked the early years of marriage have given way to a sense of duty and obligation. This kind of marriage is exceedingly common. Where the partners were once deeply in love, enjoyed sex, and spent a great deal of time together, they now more or less go their separate ways. Their time together is likely to be structured around activities involving the children, extended kin, or community responsibilities. There is typically very little sharing of important life events beyond acknowledgment of their mutual dependency on each other. There is a gracefulness between partners and even the sense that the marriage has meaning. They do share occasionally, and they have memories of a more vital past. They see themselves as being like most of their friends. Many believe that the marriage is no more and no less than what should be expected in the middle years of life.

The **passive-congenial marriage** usually does not have a loving or romantic past. From the beginning, the passive-congenial marriage has been a passive relationship with little expectation for anything else, so there is little sense that anything has been lost or that there was ever anything special about it. The

THE HEALTHY FAMILY

The characteristics of a strong or healthy family have been defined in different terms by various researchers. A review of the literature by Ted W. Bowman produced several lists of characteristics, including the following:

Frameworks of Family Strengths (Otto, 1975)

1. The ability to provide for the physical, emotional, and spiritual needs of a family.
2. The ability to "give and take" in the area of child-rearing practices and discipline.
3. The ability to communicate effectively.
4. The ability to provide support, security, and encouragement.
5. The ability to initiate and maintain growth-producing relationships and experiences within and without the family.
6. The capacity to maintain and create constructive and responsible community relationships in the neighborhood, town, school, and so on.
7. The ability to grow with and through children.
8. An ability for self-help, and the ability to accept help when appropriate.
9. An ability to perform family functions and roles flexibly.
10. Mutual respect for the individuality of family members.
11. The ability to use a crisis or a seemingly injurious experience as a means of growth.
12. A concern for family unity, loyalty, and intrafamily cooperation.

Four Key Factors (Satir, 1972)

1. Promotion of positive self-worth.
2. Open communication system.
3. Clarity as to family rules and expectations (motivaton emerging from self-initiative, not from sense of obligation).

couple feels comfortable and adequate, and there is little conflict. Some couples become passive-congenial by default, others by intention. The partners have found their real pleasures and interests outside the marriage, in their careers, children, or community activities. But the marriage fits their needs in a utilitarian sense. They are seen as family people. There is peace and quiet in the home. There may even be love and gratitude that the spouse is like she or he is. For people who require considerable independence and freedom, this kind of relationship can be fulfilling.

4. Link to wider society—commitment beyond the family.

Six Qualities of Strong Families (Stinnet, 1979)

1. Members express a great deal of appreciation for one another.
2. Family members make the effort to structure their lifestyles so that they have time to spend together.
3. Direct communication.
4. Portion of each other's happiness and well-being.
5. Commitment to a spiritual lifestyle.
6. An ability to cope with crisis.

Characteristics of a Self-Actualizing Family, a Family That Grows (Whitaker, 1980)

1. A family "with everybody in it"—a sense of the whole.
2. An ability to understand time and space—the members see their family moving.
3. Availability of all roles to all people.
4. Flexible family relationships.
5. Freedom to join and to separate.
6. Presence of an intrapsychic family—verbal history, mythologies, and stories.
7. An open system—available for contact with the networks around them.
8. A family where any member can be worked on.

Source: Adapted from Ted W. Bowman, "Promoting Family Wellness," in David R. Mace (editor), *Prevention in Family Services*, pp. 42–44, copyright 1983 by Sage Publications, Inc. Reprinted by permission of Sage Publications, Inc. Studies reviewed by Bowman include: Herbert A. Otto, *The Use of Family Strength Concepts and Methods in Family Life Education* (Beverly Hills, CA: Holistic Press, 1975); Virginia Satir, *Peoplemaking* (Palo Alto, CA: Science and Behavior Books, 1972); and Nick Stinnet, "Strong Families: A Portrait," in Mace (editor), *Prevention in Family Services*, pp. 27–38. Carl Whitaker's list is derived from a talk he gave at a workshop in Minneapolis on September 8, 1980.

FAMILY FUNCTIONING

The study of family functioning directs attention to various aspects of the family as a holon, a system made up of its parts and also interacting within the social environment. Family well-being can be determined by studying how well the family satisfies its needs. It also is related to the family's boundaries — the members and their roles, norms, values, and traditions, which distinguish the family from other families — and to its structural and interactional patterns.

NEEDS SATISFACTION

A major theme in the assessment of family well-being is evaluating the ability of families to satisfy their needs. Kenneth Terkelsen notes that the ultimate purpose of family life is to provide "the context that supports need attainment for all its individual members."[6] Following Abraham Maslow, he outlines two basic kinds of needs: survival needs and developmental needs. **Survival needs** are basic requirements for nourishment, shelter, and protection, while **developmental needs** have to do with psychological well-being, sensing that one belongs, experiencing self-esteem, and fulfilling one's developmental potential.

FAMILY NEEDS AND ENVIRONMENTAL RESOURCES

NEED	RESOURCE
Nutrition	Adequate, varied diet
	Clean air
	Pure, plentiful water
Shelter	Housing (space, light, warmth, privacy, communality, safety)
Protection	Safe neighborhoods
	Police, fire fighting, traffic control
Health	Clean environment
	Preventive, developmental, and rehabilitative health care
	Adequate, accessible medical system
Belongingness, intimacy, connectedness	Lovers, kin, friends
	Neighbors, social organizations, interest groups

Only when survival needs have been met does meeting dev
become possible (see Chapter 11).

Ann Hartman and Joan Laird also focus on family nee
tion to needs of both survival and developmental types ar
resources that must be available to families in order to sat.
box, Family Needs and Environmental Resources). The ecologica r
they take is an assessment of the social context of family life and how it u.
or does not support the family (see Chapter 10).[7] In their perspective, the extent
to which a particular family can meet its needs is dependent on the resources
available to it. Thus a family's needs for nutrition can only be met if an adequate, varied diet, clean air, and pure and plentiful water are available to it.
Likewise the family's need for shelter can only be met if the available, afford-
able housing provides living conditions which meet requirements for space,
light, warmth, privacy, communality, and safety.

Survival Needs in Poor and Minority Families

Family scholars have focused on developmental rather than survival needs. Indeed, most studies on the internal dynamics of family life fail to address how

NEED	RESOURCE
Communication, mobility	Telephone and postal systems, newspapers Public and private transportation
Education, enrichment	Good schools (for children and adults) Arts, recreation
Spiritual needs	Religious organizations Opportunities to share meaning and values Preservation of cultural, ethnic, racial, and other differences
Autonomy	Gratifying work in or out of home Community participation Opportunities for new experiences
Generativity	Opportunities to contribute to the future

Source: Adapted with permission of The Free Press, a Division of Macmillan, Inc. from
Family Centered Social Work Practice by Ann Hartman and Joan Laird. Copyright © 1983 by
The Free Press.

‚e need for basic survival impinges on interpersonal well-being. One reason is that most studies are based on white, middle-class families. Since it is likely that in these families basic survival needs are being met, researchers are inclined to gloss over the real survival needs of some families.

Researchers who have been sensitive to the issue of family survival are those who have focused on poor families, including many racial- and ethnic-minority families and single-parent families headed by women, including whites. In examining the life cycle of multiproblem poor families, Fernando Colon, for instance, suggests that family assessment must address their physical situation (level of food and clothing, condition of housing), employment situation (income, unemployment or under-employment), and social context (isolation, alienation from others).[8] Assessment of the well-being of such families must take into account the likelihood that the environmental resources necessary to meet their survival needs are at least partially unavailable. When economic insecurity pervades family life, there undoubtedly are deficiencies in the resources available to sustain the family.

It should not be assumed, however, that all families struggling for survival will suffer from some form of pathology. Families can be amazingly resilient, even under conditions of severe emotional stress. The strengths of families as well as their deficiencies must be acknowledged. According to Robert Hill, black families demonstrate a number of strengths which enable them to survive racial discrimination and economic insecurity. Although he does not doubt that some families collapse under such stress, he believes that most black families provide adequately for the physical, emotional, and spiritual needs of members; show concern for family unity, loyalty, and cooperation; develop healthy interpersonal relationships; help each other in healthy ways; and perform family roles flexibly. Examining the literature on black families leads him to assert that in most families there are strong kinship bonds, a strong work ethic, a strong need to achieve, a strong religious orientation, and very adaptive family roles.[9]

FAMILY BOUNDARIES

The family is a bounded system in interaction with its environment. Within the family boundary are its members and their roles, norms, values, traditions, and goals, plus other elements that distinguish one family from another and from the social environment. Researchers have looked at family boundaries in terms of their implications for good family functioning. In general, they have found that families whose boundaries are open and flexible are the most healthy.

Families with random, closed, and open types of family boundaries have been described in terms of their ability to meet survival and developmental needs by David Kantor and William Lehr.[10] The most unhealthy families are considered to be **random families**, which typically have boundaries that lack clarity or are constantly shifting and changing. There is no sense of family co-hesion, and each member seems to be doing his or her own thing. Closed families, in contrast, tend to be rigid, with well-defined roles. They are well organized and directed by planned goals and schedules. Family projects and concerns take precedence over individual desires; the family always comes first, and family stability is of great importance. Kantor and Lehr do not consider these families to be necessarily unhealthy. Because of their closed nature, however, they do not deal adequately with the normal crises that arise in family life.

The healthiest families are **open families**, which are well organized in the sense that there is a clear boundary; goals, roles, and membership are well defined and well understood. But there also is flexibility in these families. While the concerns of individual members are responded to, there is genuine concern for the family as a whole.

Structural Patterns and Family Well-Being

Family well-being has also been examined in terms of the operational or trans-actional patterns evident in families. Following the earlier work of Minuchin, research by Harry Aponte and John Van Deusen which originated in ther-apeutic work with the families of 12 poor Puerto Rican or black delinquents contributed to the development of structural family therapy.[11] This technique has been used in work with middle-class families as well as those with limited economic resources.

Aponte and Van Deusen argue that families living under poverty are "partic-ularly vulnerable to dysfunction."[12] They clearly state, however, that their work should not be taken to mean that poor Puerto Rican and black families are always dysfunctional. They focus on three elements of the family system: the boundaries among members, the power structure of the family, and the alignment that exists among members. Dysfunctions may arise from any of these.

In this perspective *boundary* refers not to relations between the family and its environment but to the **boundaries among family members**, defined in terms of rules about who may and may not participate in any family activity. In the healthy family, the boundary among members is neither too rigid nor too dif-fuse. The individuals are independent of one another yet united and focused on the needs of the family as a whole. Unhealthy families are described as either enmeshed or disengaged. In **enmeshed families**, the boundaries between some or all of the family members are undifferentiated, permeable, and fluid. The individuals lack a sense of independence and act as if they were physically and emotionally dependent on one another. In **disengaged families**, the members have little to do with one another, and the independence of each member is rigidly respected.

Family alignment refers to "the joining or opposition of one member to another,"[13] or the coalitions that form among members and the manner in which they compete or cooperate. Coalitions are not necessarily dysfunctional, and neither is a certain amount of competition among them, provided the coalitions are not rigid. As long as family members can move in and out of these coalitions easily, they can be quite useful for decision making. Coalitions are like family party politics; if members of a coalition always follow the party line and never cross it, dysfunction can result. This could take three forms: stable coalitions, triangulation, or detouring coalitions. **Stable coalitions** exist where two or more members have rigidly joined together against the others. **Triangulation** exists when individuals are caught in the middle between two coalitions and are forced to join one or the other. **Detouring coalitions** project their internal conflict onto others outside them.

All families require a **power structure**, a "force" which makes decisions possible. In the ideal, the power structure operates in a democratic way, with all members participating, up to the level of their developmental capacity, in family decisions, and all members capable of influencing one another. In underorganized families, the force is not distributed in an orderly fashion. It may be concentrated in one person who makes all the decisions, or it may be decentralized, with too many people exerting influence and no one person responsible for making the decisions. In both there is a lack of functional power in the way the family functions.

INTERACTIONAL PATTERNS AND FAMILY WELL-BEING

Family well-being is also related to the nature of the interactional patterns operating within the family. A guide for identifying interactional patterns which contribute to family well-being has been developed by Jerry M. Lewis. His work is based on an in-depth analysis of a sample of 12 white, middle-class, two-parent families with an adolescent child, in an urban, southern setting.[14] It is also based on his own clinical practice and his observations of personal friends and their families. Lewis believes that there is "no single thread" in healthy families, and a number of factors can combine to produce the result. These factors have to do with the marriage itself, power relations, closeness, communication, problem-solving abilities, the expression of feelings, dealing with loss, family values, and intimacy and autonomy. His work identifies the good marriage and the healthy family in terms of optimally functioning interactions.[15]

According to Lewis, in good marriages power is shared between husband and wife. Both parties are competent and have areas of special expertise. They like each other as friends, trust each other, and do not feel vulnerable in the relationship. They maintain their autonomy and are not fused as a couple. They define themselves as being "in love," though many years may have passed. Sexual intercourse might not be frequent, but the relationship is considered good by both partners.

Decision-making power is fully in the hands of the parents in healthy families. Power is expressed as a quality of easy leadership, with a sincere interest in the points of view of the children. These families are closely knit, and each member feels strongly connected. Because there is no effort to have everyone agree on everything, individuality is also evident. Healthy families have good communication patterns, Lewis says. They make things clear between one another, and there is little difficulty knowing what each member thinks or feels. They handle problems well: identify them early, do not deny them, do not try to blame or scapegoat a member for them, and solve them constructively.

These families express feelings freely—sad, angry, loving, hurt, fearful. There is a great sense of openness. The families are able to deal with loss openly. Lewis maintains that healthy families share a value premise which assumes that people are mostly good rather than evil. There is little authoritarianism in these families. They combine intimacy and individual autonomy easily. They also are very much involved with the world around them and are not isolated but are active participants.

In addition to defining healthy or optimally functioning families, Lewis describes the **faltering family**, which "just misses" being healthy. These are competent families, but considerable pain is evident. The primary difference between healthy and faltering families appears to be in the relationship in the married couple. In the faltering family the parents are somehow unable to meet each other's needs, but this does not reflect on how they raise the children. The children turn out healthy, and problems arising from the outside environment are handled pretty well. According to Lewis, "The failure of the couple to achieve the intimate level of communication is the central flaw in these families."[16]

Lewis suggests that there are three levels of faltering or troubled families. In **dominated families**, one parent takes control, and a level of closed relations results. When the other partner accepts the subordinated position, the family may get along fairly well. Some dominated families are marked by constant conflict and rebellion, however. In **conflicted families**, power is not shared or controlled by one of the partners. There is an open struggle between them to control one another, and no stable set of rules and roles is developed. Coalitions are common but often fleeting. Anger and other hostile feelings are expressed; nurturing, loving feelings are not. Blaming others is common. Family values are often intensely competitive. The severely disturbed families are **chaotic families.** The couple fails miserably in attempts to meet each other's needs and the needs of the children. No one has enough power to structure the family. Communication lacks clarity, and the flow of ideas is confusing and obscure. The family cannot solve problems at all, and individuality, independence, autonomy, and change are discouraged.[17]

Interactional Patterns in Black Families

Charles Willie paints a picture of black family life which he considers healthy but which nevertheless does not fit the interactional patterns that have been identified as characterizing healthy families. He notes, for instance, that regardless of socioeconomic level, black families have relatively little togetherness and are relatively isolated from the community. Affluent and middle-class blacks spend so much time working that little involvement in community affairs is possible. They are so concerned with staving off the effects of racism that all their energies are directed at making sure family members do not fail and fall behind. Similarly, at the working-class and poverty-class levels, blacks are so occupied with meeting survival needs that socializing, spending time together, communications, and the like require real effort. His point is not that these families are therefore unhealthy but that the sources of cohesiveness and strength lie elsewhere. Their strength derives from their ability to survive despite heavy odds against them. Family members coalesce around the need to stave off adversity.[18]

FAMILY PROBLEMS: DOMESTIC VIOLENCE

The identification of healthy families and happy marriages lends credence to the popular idea of family life as being inherently good. A darker side must be recognized, however. Domestic violence in all its forms — spouse abuse, abuse of the elderly, child abuse and neglect — is becoming increasingly evident.

Violence in the family usually is defined as physical injury or sexual abuse, but it also may include emotional abuse as well as neglect or abandonment. Barbara Star considers the term **domestic violence** to be synonymous with family violence, and she uses it to describe any form of violence in the family, including wife battering, elder abuse, and the physical and sexual abuse of children.[19]

Domestic violence is by no means new. In the traditional family, however, greater autonomy was exercised by men over women and by parents over children. It is even likely that there was more family violence in the past than there is today. As we pointed out in Chapter 7, infanticide and abandonment, as well as sex with children and child beating, were acceptable practices in earlier eras. Wife beating was also commonly accepted and supported by law. As changes have occurred in the norms and ideals governing family relationships, and patriarchal, authoritarian norms have begun to give way to more egalitarian, more democratic norms, more attention is being paid to domestic violence. Thus family violence appears to have been "discovered" in recent times.[20]

Social service workers have had a role in making society aware of domestic violence. Direct-service social workers in family and child welfare services not only have provided treatment in instances of domestic violence but have served to identify cases and to advocate for preventive programs and policies. The abuse of elders (parent battering), particularly, was identified through case findings by agency personnel in contact with the elderly.

Social workers must deal with the ugly side of family
life. *Mark Antman/The Image Works, Inc.*

SPOUSE ABUSE

The true incidence of domestic violence cannot be known, since many instances are not reported. Spouse abuse is no exception, but homicide statistics show that one-half of all murders among family members involve one spouse killing the other. It has been estimated that one-fourth of all couples have engaged in at least one violent episode during the life of their marriage. A true incidence rate may involve up to 60 percent of all couples.[21]

With the exception of homicide by spouses, in which men and women are equally victimized, women are believed to be more likely to suffer serious injury as victims of domestic violence. Federal Bureau of Investigation reports indicate that in 1986, 85 percent of the persons arrested in the crime category of offenses against family and children were males, and 62 percent of those arrested were in the age category of 25–44 years.[22] The view that women are the abused and men the abusers has been challenged recently, however. It is pointed out that surveys showing men with higher arrest rates are based on official law enforcement records, which are flawed methodologically and use samples which are not representative. Moreover, women are more likely to make victimization reports, and much of the information on spouse abuse derives from clinical populations, especially women receiving shelter services.[23]

In any case, spouse abuse appears to occur in the context of psychological abuse and exploitation. In the verbal abuse that often accompanies physical abuse, women may be made to feel worthless, incompetent, unlovable, insignificant, and less than human. Abuse rarely occurs just once. After the barrier to physical abuse has been broken, it often becomes an integral part of the husband-wife relationship.

Although spouse abuse is evident in all ethnic groups and in all social classes, there is evidence of higher incidences among lower-income and blue-collar couples and among blacks, Hispanics, and other ethnic minorities. Studies from services that offer shelter to abused women suggest that white women are more likely to seek help than ethnic-minority women.

Battered Women

Shelters for **battered women** are a service provided in most cities and regions of the United States. In spite of repeated battering, a significant number of these women remain with their spouses or partners. One reason is that many women still are economically dependent on the men who abuse them. One study of battered women found that the probability of wives returning to abusive husbands increased considerably if their husbands were their sole source of income.[24]

Battered women experience a good deal of psychological and emotional turmoil as well. Susan Turner describes separation from abusive husbands as a series of losses which initiates a mourning process. Since women are socialized to need relationships, they may feel inadequate and lonely when on their own.

Marriage represents an idealized relationship to which women bring very high expectations. When the marriage proves abusive, this relationship is lost. Marriage also represents an expansion of roles and a gain in status; a woman thus becomes a wife, often a mother, and a full adult in the community. Separating from an abusive husband, then, is a role loss, and it is often perceived as a sign of personal failure as well. The woman also may lose economic security, safety, social support, esteem, and fulfillment.[25]

These various losses must be mourned. At first the mourning may be expressed through denial — denying the battering, covering up bruises, or being ashamed to admit what has happened. Often when the abuse has been acknowledged, anger sets in, either openly or in the form of a high level of energy or self-punishment. Grief is likely to be present throughout the mourning period. It is often difficult to detect, however, and may take the form of feeling tired or other somatic, or physical, complaints.

The period during which an actual decision is made to stay with or leave the relationship is often typified by bargaining. Husbands may attempt to apologize and may feel dejected or promise to change. Wives may be willing to listen, given the losses they are experiencing. It is not uncommon for battered wives to maintain a good deal of loyalty toward their spouses and to find it difficult to contemplate leaving. They often find themselves torn between wanting to assure their own and their children's safety and wanting to shield and help the abuser.

ELDER ABUSE

Less is known about the incidence of elder abuse than that of any other form of domestic violence. Star reports that no nationwide study has been conducted, and no accurate statistics are available.[26] Knowledge about elder abuse largely comes from the victims themselves. The kinds of abuse they are most likely to report are psychological and financial abuse and physical neglect; direct physical abuse is less commonly reported. The elderly may be unwilling to report abuse because they are afraid of retaliation, they feel shame and do not want to admit that their children have abused them, or they fear being removed from the family and institutionalized.

The few studies that have been done suggest certain demographic and psychological characteristics in abuse of the elderly. Women are more likely to be victims than men, especially widows who live with the abuser. Many of the elderly abused seem to have physical and mental disabilities which make them dependent on family members to meet their needs. Especially vulnerable are the bedridden elderly.

There are contradictory findings with respect to those who are most likely to abuse the elderly. One study found that middle-aged women, related to the older person by blood or marriage and providing primary care, were more likely to be abusers. Another study found that middle-aged men of low socioeconomic status were the most likely abusers.[27]

Child Abuse and Neglect

There has been a dramatic rise in the attention shown to the maltreatment of children in the past 25 years.[28] In part the attention being paid to child abuse and neglect has been stimulated by the development of more accurate diagnostic techniques by the medical profession, such as designation of the term *battered child syndrome* to describe evidence of maltreatment. In part, too, it reflects changing expectations about the exercise of authority by parents and others in their relations with children. And in part it reflects the passage of legislation in most states which requires social workers, doctors, and others dealing with children to report bruises, burns, or broken bones, other visible signs of abuse or neglect, and behaviors that might indicate fear, shame, or confusion in children's dealings with adults. The rate of reports of child neglect and abuse by state child protective services to the National Study on Child Neglect and Abuse Reporting doubled between 1978 and 1985, going from 2.7 per 1,000 population to 5.4 per thousand (see box, Child Maltreatment Cases Reported).[29]

Abuse and neglect of children can be distinguished in a number of ways. **Child abuse** usually involves some kind of act perpetrated against a child,

CHILD MALTREATMENT CASES REPORTED, 1976–1985

The data on child maltreatment cases reported by state child protective services to the National Study on Child Neglect and Abuse Reporting provide an official portrait of the abused and the abuser. While the number of cases reported grew precipitously between 1976 and 1985, the characteristics of the children and the perpetrators involved varied little. The racial ratios must be viewed in the light of representation in the U.S. population. In 1985 blacks, for instance, represented 12 percent of the population but 21 percent of the children and 19 percent of the perpetrators in child abuse and neglect cases.

	1976	1980	1985
No. of children reported (1,000)	669	1,154	1,928
Characteristics of child			
Age (average years)	7.7	7.3	7.1
Sex (percent of total)			
Male	50.0%	49.8%	48.1%
Female	50.0	50.2	51.9
Race (percent of total)			
White	61.1	69.4	67.0*

while **child neglect** usually involves abandoning responsibility for the welfare of the child. These definitions usually include intention on the part of parents (see box, Intention in Child Abuse). Both abuse and neglect can have emotional as well as physical aspects. The criteria for identifying physical abuse are much clearer than for any other form of abuse or neglect, yet reports of maltreatment by neglect are more common. "Deprivation of necessities" accounted for 56 percent of all cases of child maltreatment reported in 1985, while minor physical injuries accounted for 15 percent and major physical injuries for just 2 percent.[30] Given the lack of clarity in the criteria for identifying the various kinds of abuse and neglect, social workers and others providing service must be cautious in assessing cases.

Interpreting the Data

The data on abuse and neglect are difficult to interpret. Estimates on prevalence derive from widely varied sources. Official data taken from child welfare services are likely to give very different information than unofficial data taken from direct surveys of children and families. It does appear, however, that the official data underestimate the true incidence of abuse and neglect in the popu-

	1976	1980	1985
Black	19.8	18.8	20.8*
Hispanic	11.1	9.7	9.6*
Characteristics of perpetrator			
Age (average years)	32.3	31.4	31.5
Sex (percent of total)			
Male	39.0%	41.2%	40.6%
Female	61.0	58.8	59.4
Race (percent of total)			
White	65.1	72.0	69.9*
Black	17.7	17.6	19.1*
Hispanic	9.5	8.3	9.3*
Family characteristics			
Single-parent, female-headed families (percent)	38.5%	39.3%	37.4%
Children in household (average number)	2.3	2.2	2.3

* 1984, latest data available.

Source: U.S. Bureau of the Census, *Statistical Abstract of the United States 1988* (Washington, DC, 1987), Table 277.

lation. A conservative estimate would be that between 10 to 20 out of each 1,000 children experience abuse or neglect at some time. There also appears to be a leveling off of reported incidents in the past few years.[31]

Knowledge of the demographic characteristics of victims of abuse and neglect derives in large part from official statistics. Thus it may reflect the extent to which people report incidents involving children and how they deal with such problems rather than the true characteristics of victims. In general, the likelihood that a child will experience neglect or abuse increases with age. Adolescent children have the highest incidence, followed by preadolescents, preschool children, and infants. If only the data on physical neglect are examined, however, the youngest children have the greatest likelihood of being victims. Boys and girls have an equal likelihood of experiencing abuse and ne-

INTENTION IN CHILD ABUSE

There is a fine line in Illinois law that separates a child murderer from an unintentional killer. Within a few months in 1986, two men were convicted of getting angry at the toddlers they were taking care of and beating the children to death. One man was convicted of murder and sentenced to 70 years in prison. The other was convicted of involuntary manslaughter and received the maximum possible sentence — 10 years' imprisonment.

In an article in the *Chicago Tribune* for March 31, 1986, Linnet Myers analyzed the difference in convictions and sentences:

It isn't the way the child dies: Bruises covered the legs, arms, buttocks, and abdomens of both toddlers, one 22 months old and one 24 months. Both also had severe internal injuries.

It isn't the motive: In both cases, the children were beaten because they had an accident while being toilet trained. They were "disciplined."

It isn't the evidence: Both men admitted they hit the children, but said they didn't mean to kill them.

The difference lies in a few lines of Illinois law. If the killer knew he was creating "a strong probability of great bodily harm" to the baby, he is a murderer. If he killed the baby "recklessly," he is not.

The law, according to the state's attorney, is "crystal clear — it all goes to the state of mind." Deciding a person's state of mind in cases where a child is killed as the result of "discipline" is extremely difficult, however. The crucial difference is the judge assigned to the case and the judge's particular interpretation of the law. Many judges find it hard to believe that anyone would deliberately murder a child.

Source: Linnet Myers, "Technicality Decides When Killing a Baby Isn't Murder," *Chicago Tribune*, March 31, 1986, sect. 1, p. 7.

glect. While all ethnic, racial, and socioeconomic groups are represented in the statistics, it appears that blacks and other lower socioeconomic groups are overrepresented.

The great majority of child abusers are parents, and they are likely to be natural or biological parents. Mothers are more likely to be implicated in cases of abuse and neglect than fathers. It has been suggested that child abusers were often abused themselves as children, but more recent data question this conclusion. Kinard reports that "careful examination of the empirical evidence reveals that only a small proportion of abusing parents experienced abuse in childhood. Thus, many abusing parents were not abused as children, and many parents who were abused as children do not abuse their own children."[32]

Child Sexual Abuse

Child sexual abuse, which is distinguished from physical and emotional abuse by the explicitly sexual nature of the act, is particularly troublesome. Criteria for identifying sexual abuse usually specify an age difference between the sexual partners of five or more years, use of force or coercion, and determination of developmentally appropriate behavior.[33] Especially with regard to the latter criterion, there may be ambiguity as to whether a particular act is abusive. While it is clear that coercive sexual intercourse between a father and a child is abusive, it may not be considered abusive for a father or mother to walk around the house naked.

As with other domestic violence, there are few reliable and valid statistics on child sexual abuse, and trends are difficult to discern. Official data are considered inaccurate measures of the true incidence in the total population, but studies of social populations, such as college students and people in psychotherapy, suggest an incidence so high it would be disbelieved. The methodologically soundest studies suggest that some 20 to 30 percent of all adults were sexually abused before their 18th birthdays. These studies also indicate that in the majority of cases, sexual abuse takes place within the context of family life and is perpetrated by men — fathers, stepfathers, grandfathers, brothers, and friends of the family.[34] Little is known of the ethnic, racial, and socioeconomic correlates of child sexual abuse.

Although all victims do not suffer severe or permanent harm, sexual abuse by family members and friends is extremely difficult for children to handle. John Conte notes that abused children can experience a wide range of negative effects, including "depression, guilt, learning difficulties, sexual acting out, running away, somatic complaints (such as headaches and stomachaches), hysterical seizures, phobias, nightmares, compulsive rituals, self-destructive behaviors, and suicide."[35] These effects can continue to plague the individual well into adulthood, taking such forms as a negative self-image, depression, and sexual problems.

FAMILY PROBLEMS:
MARRIAGE, DIVORCE, REMARRIAGE

Family dissolution, or the end of a marriage, has always been a possible outcome in family life. In the past, however, family dissolution was largely a result

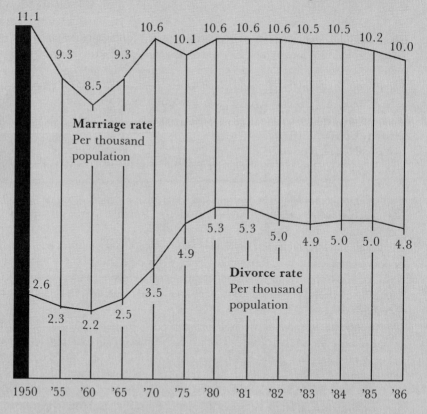

CHANGES IN MARRIAGE AND DIVORCE RATES, 1950–1986

The U.S. Bureau of the Census measures marital status in terms of marriage rates, the number of marriages per 1,000 population in a given period, and divorce rates, the number of divorces per 1,000 population. In the 1980s, both the marriage rate and the divorce rate began to decline.

Source: U.S. Bureau of the Census, *Statistical Abstract of the United States 1988* (Washington, DC, 1987), Table 81.

of the death of a parent or, in some cases, both parents. Today it is much more likely to be a result of divorce.

MARRIAGE AND DIVORCE RATES

In 1860 about 5 percent of all couples who married could be expected to divorce eventually. In the next 100 years, the divorce rate generally increased, but between 1960 and 1980 it more than doubled.[36] In 1981, when the number of divorces peaked at 1.21 million, there were twice as many marriages, 2.42 million. The **marriage rate**, 10.6 marriages per 1,000 population, was also double the **divorce rate**, 5.3 divorces per 1,000 population.[37] In terms of a ratio of divorces to marriages, there were about 500 divorces for every 1,000 marriages in 1981 (see box, Changes in Marriage and Divorce Rates).

The divorce rate began to decline after 1981, falling to 4.8 per 1,000 population in 1986. The marriage rate also declined, but slightly more, falling to 10.0 that year.[38] Still, demographers were predicting that about half of all marriages would end in divorce.

While divorce affects all socioeconomic and racial and ethnic groups, it correlates more highly with some sectors than with others. The likelihood of divorce is higher for blacks than for whites. There is evidence, however, that Mexican Americans have less marital instability than whites and that increases in divorces have been smaller among Mexican Americans than among whites.[39] The relationship between divorce and educational level, one indicator of social class, is quite complex (see box, Young Adults and Divorce). In general, the likelihood of divorce is lowest among college graduates, but while it is significantly higher for women whose education goes beyond a college degree, the same does not hold true for men.[40] A similar situation is found for another socioeconomic indicator, income. While for men each increase in income brings less likelihood of divorce, just the opposite is true for women. Divorce rates are highest among women earning high incomes and lowest among those earning little or no income.[41]

For some years it has been possible to state that over 90 percent of the adult population of the United States will be married at one time or another in their lifetimes. The marriage rate has fluctuated, however; for instance, the rate went from 10.3 in 1925 to 9.2 in 1930 and back up to 10.4 in 1935 and to 12.2 in 1945. It ranged between 9.9 and 10.9 in the period 1968–1982, and between 1983 and 1986 it fell by 0.5.

THE NEVER-MARRIED AND THE REMARRIED

The population of single, never-married people in the United States was higher at the turn of the twentieth century than it is now. In 1890, for instance, 27 percent of men and 15 percent of women between the ages of 30 and 34 had never married. This percentage dropped considerably in the 1950s and rose again in the 1970s, and in 1982 17 percent of all men and 12 percent of all women between the ages of 30 and 34 had never married.[42] In the entire population aged 18 and over in 1986, 25 percent of the males were single and 65 percent were married, while 18 percent of the females were single and 61 percent were married.[43] Among women, staying single is related to education and occupation; those

YOUNG ADULTS AND DIVORCE

About half of the first marriages of people aged 25 to 34 in 1980 may end in divorce, but the chances of divorce vary by education. Young adults who do not complete college have the greatest possibility of divorce; men with postgraduate educations have a much lower likelihood of divorce than women with the same level of education.

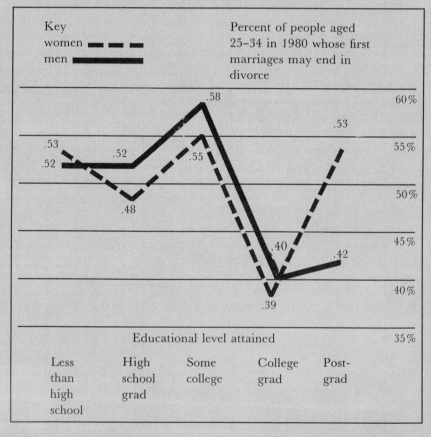

Source: Paul C. Glick, "How American Families Are Changing," *American Demographics*, vol. 6 (January 1984), p. 24.

with more education and career potential are less likely to marry. There are no comparable data on never married men.[44]

Remarriage is fairly common after divorce, but, according to census data, the percentage of people who remarry after a first divorce has steadily declined since 1971. Divorced men are more likely to remarry than divorced women. In 1971, 80 percent of all first-divorced men and 74 percent of all first-divorced women remarried, compared to 68 percent of divorced men and 64 percent of divorced women in 1985.[45] The likelihood that a woman will remarry is also related to education. All things being equal, divorced women with no college education remarry rather quickly, while those with a college education are far less likely to do so.[46]

Few people experience divorce twice, but their numbers are growing. Whites are more likely to have multiple divorces than blacks. Contrary to common assumptions, second marriages are more likely to end in divorce than first marriages. Paul Glick projects that 61 percent of men and 54 percent of women in their thirties in 1980 who marry a second time will experience a second divorce.[47]

INTERPRETING THE DATA

The data on marriage, divorce, and remarriage are difficult to interpret. Some see in them overwhelming evidence that family life is diminishing in importance in American society; that is, the data are said to demonstrate the ill-being of family life.[48] Others do not agree. Mary Jo Bane believes that divorce and remarriage rates merely show that the specific marital partner is being rejected, not marriage itself. She demonstrates that Americans continue to be committed to a stable family life and the nurturing of children.[49]

Most of the argument about the meaning of marriage and divorce rates is best understood as an assessment of the traditional two-parent, never-divorced family as a social institution. There is an implicit assumption that anything less than the traditional nuclear family is harmful for society. The single-parent families and even the stepfamilies that follow divorce thus may be judged to be deviant and therefore troubled. As we noted in Chapter 7, we view the family as a changing institution, and diversity in the structure and organization of family life as simply an indication of ongoing changes. A particular form of family life should not be seen as itself deviant. However, change predictably brings about stress and conflict.

STRESSFUL FAMILY PATTERNS

The stress associated with divorce affects not only the couple separating and their children but the family patterns which follow. The economic problems of single-parent families are heightened by psychological problems when they are formed as a result of divorce. Remarriage and the formation of blended or reconstituted families with the children of one or both partners have their own stressful circumstances. When marriage is avoided by the formation of single-parent families, especially when the head of the household is a teenaged girl, psychological stress is added to economic burdens. These families and the family lifestyles developed by cohabiting heterosexual and homosexual couples are subject to the particular stress of societal disapproval.

THE STRESS OF DIVORCE

Divorce undoubtedly produces stress, as the life-cycle perspective on study of the family demonstrates (see Chapter 10). It is not clear, however, that the stress is always intense or long-lasting. According to Doris Jacobson, most studies show that divorcing and divorced adults experience depression, loneliness, low work and school efficiency, trouble sleeping, somatic symptoms, feelings of incompetence, and even suicidal or homicidal feelings. Children involved in divorce commonly show increased acting out, antisocial or aggressive behavior, and feelings of anger, sadness, or guilt. Although these findings make intuitive sense, they should be evaluated cautiously. Many of these studies suffer from methodological weaknesses such as nonrandom samples and overreliance on white, middle-class subjects. They also tend to emphasize short-term effects. Considerable distress is reported among children, for instance, during the first two years after separation or divorce, but there is little knowledge of whether this leads to later psychological problems. Similarly, most studies of the effects of divorce on adults focus on the divorce period and its immediate aftermath.[50]

Moreover, all studies do not find evidence of negative emotional effects. Jacobson reports that the least distress has been found among divorced women who do not remarry. In addition, children from intact but conflict-ridden households have been found to have more psychological troubles than children from divorced or separated households in which there is less conflict (see box, Divorce or Stay Together). Social and psychological factors have been identified as mediating factors which determine the extent to which emotional problems will be experienced. Jacobson describes such factors as preexisting psychiatric disturbances, self-esteem attitudes, and willingness to accept nontraditional gender roles as being helpful in mediating the negative effects of divorce on adults. With respect to children, studies have found that the nature of parent-child interaction, economic stability, and the existence of social support networks can significantly reduce psychological disturbances.

Judith Wallerstein, whose California Children of Divorce Study was completed in 1980, has followed up with a study of how divorced men and women and their children have fared since the divorce. In *Second Chance*, she points to the importance of resolving feelings of anger and betrayal and reclaiming self-esteem in order to cope with the stress of divorce. To help the children of divorce, she suggests that it is vital for both of the parents to maintain their parenting roles by exercising visitation rights or following through on joint custody arrangements. A decade after divorce, the youngest children, girls especially, were doing the best; those who had been preadolescents and adolescents at the time of the divorce were having the most trouble. While the evidence bore out the finding that a good divorce is better than a bad marriage, in many postdivorce families the conflict continued. Many children went through a second divorce, and for only one out of seven children were both parents happily remarried. The economic condition of one out of four children dropped severely and stayed that way.[51]

Some differences in the adjustments children make to divorce relate to the ways they have been socialized. In a survey of children between the ages of 6 and 13, 49 percent agreed with the statement, "Parents should separate if they are not happy." Among children from families that did not stress marriage as a sacred institution, this percentage rose to 58 percent.[52]

THE STRESS OF SINGLE PARENTHOOD AFTER DIVORCE

Single-parent families formed by women after divorce are likely to experience not only economic problems but psychological disruption. These families often find themselves in poverty; in 1986, 34 percent of all persons in families with female householders and no spouse present (and 54 percent of the children in these families) were living below the poverty level.[53] As a group, their economic position has deteriorated since the passage, by 1970, of no-fault divorce laws in most states. Lenore J. Weitzman concludes that "the major economic result of the divorce law revolution is the systematic impoverishment of divorced women and their children." She found that, on average, divorced women and the children living with them suffer a 73 percent drop in their standard of living the first year after a divorce. In the same period, the standard of living of divorced men increases 42 percent.[54]

Mothers of young children are also expected to be able to support themselves and their families in short order. According to Weitzman, since no-fault divorce became the rule some 87 percent of young mothers have received no alimony. Very little child support is awarded—an average of $200 a month for two children—and when it is awarded it is difficult to collect from the father. Moreover, because a couple's property and assets are supposed to be divided equally, women and children often lose the family home when it is sold so the proceeds can be divided. The husband keeps the family's biggest assets—his education and training, his earning capacity, and his pension, health insurance, and other employment benefits.

Women and children experience numerous other consequences of divorce. When they must move from their former neighborhoods, important social networks and support may be lost. Many divorced women enter the full-time labor force for the first time, which may bring changes in their identity. The time mothers can spend with their children is shortened, and the mental health of both the mother and the children may suffer for various reasons. Single mothers report substantially higher rates of anxiety and depression than married women and men do, and service utilization statistics indicate that single-parent families with children headed by mothers consume a large share of community mental health services.[55]

FAMILIES OF UNWED MOTHERS

When single parenthood results from a child being born out of wedlock, other stressful consequences may occur, and they are heightened when the mother is a teenager. While the unmarried teen pregnancy rate is actually declining, the number of girls who are deciding to give birth and keep their babies is grow-

---

DIVORCE OR STAY TOGETHER:
TWO SIDES OF THE QUESTION

The following letters contributed by readers to Ann Landers's popular advice column eloquently express the dilemma for children caught in a conflict-ridden family situation. Though they are profoundly affected by the decision to divorce or stay together, they have no real voice in it. Together these letters state the case that while divorce is likely to be stressful, so is maintaining a bad marriage.

Dear Ann Landers:
   The worst thing that can happen to children is to have their parents get a divorce.
   It makes kids want to fall to the ground and die. When people ask why you changed schools or why your mom and dad aren't at the baseball game, it is agony to try to think of a sensible answer.
   Parents always say they would never do anything to hurt their children, but no physical abuse can be as bad as the pain of having parents split. Why can't they understand our feelings? We cry to our friends. We cry to our brothers and sisters. We cry to our pets. We even beg our parents to change their minds. They say we are too young to understand.
   We remember all the nights when we heard those terrible arguments. Why would married people say such awful things to each other? We try to block out the fighting but it's impossible. If they hate each other so much why did they get married? Is it possible to go from love to hate? It makes us afraid to get married.
   It's not fair for us to have to change schools and lose our friends. Don't they see what they do to our lives when they break up the family? It hurts something awful. I know because it's happening to my brothers and sisters and to me right now. No name, just—

"A Girl Age 12"

Dear Girl:
   I'm sad for you, but I hope the next letter will help you understand the other side of the story. Please share it with your brothers and sisters.

ing. Between 1960 and 1985, the rate of births to unmarried women aged 15–19 more than doubled, from 15.3 per 1,000 to 31.6 per 1,000. Rates of out-of-wedlock births among women aged 20–24 also increased, from 39.7 per 1,000 in 1960 to 46.8 per 1,000 in 1985, but they declined for women 25 years old and older. Births to unmarried women constituted 22 percent of all births in the United States in 1985, but they represented 15 percent of the births among whites and 60 percent of those among blacks.[56]

Teenage mothers are generally unprepared to be mothers and heads of households. The initial awareness of pregnancy brings about difficulties with parents, school authorities, and boyfriends. Many teenagers receive little

Dear Ann Landers:

Every now and then we see an unhappily married couple who stayed together "for the children." I have been wanting to write this letter for a long time. Today I am doing it.

My parents will celebrate their 50th wedding anniversary next year. None of their five children has ever acknowledged their parents' wedding anniversaries because it would have been so phony.

Our mother is a bitter and reclusive woman with a martyr complex. Our father is an unpleasant alcoholic with a mean mouth and a rotten temper. Every one of us kids was messed up because we never learned how to develop positive relationships until we reached our 30's. We have all experienced failed marriages and had other troubles in our lives.

Each of us is engaged in an ongoing struggle to erase the tapes of the destructive and awful behavior of our parents so we will not emulate them. It hasn't been easy. I am writing to tell all parents who are considering staying together for the children's sake to forget it. You will do them no favors.

T.O.

Dear T.O.:

Thanks for the powerful testimony. I am sure your letter was not an easy one to write. I appreciate the effort, as will many readers who are on the fence about this issue.

Every effort should be made to save the troubled marriage when children are involved. Counseling should be sought. But if the situation is down-right intolerable, it is an injustice to the children to stay together and feed on one another's neurosis and misery.

Source: Ann Landers, syndicated column, *The Oregonian*, August 12, 1986. Reprinted with permission of Ann Landers, Creators, and The Los Angeles Times Syndicates.

prenatal care, and their children often are born small, weak, or with birth defects. Because young mothers have trouble completing high school, they also have trouble providing for themselves and their children. Relatively few receive any support from the father, and dependence on public welfare often is necessary. There is a likelihood that additional children will be born out of wedlock. Child neglect and abuse are common, and the children of young mothers may suffer cognitive development deficits and eventually may become teenaged parents themselves.[57]

THE STRESS OF REMARRIAGE

Remarriage after divorce carries a high level of motivation to succeed, to avoid past failures in family lifestyles, and to assure the continued growth and development of family members. One obstacle to success lies in the social context of stepfamilies, which often are not accorded the same respect as other families. Legal problems are likely to arise as well. A stepparent does not always have the right to make medical decisions for a stepchild, and stepchildren do not automatically become heirs of the stepparent.[58]

Some of the stress in stepfamilies is likely to be of a psychological nature, as remarried individuals attempt to deal with the tasks involved in setting up another long-term emotional relationship. A. Goetting has described six tasks of remarriage, each of which carries a different kind of stress:[59]

1. Emotional remarriage, the process of establishing a new bond with a chosen partner.
2. Psychic remarriage, the process of changing one's identity from a single individual to a couple.
3. Community remarriage, the process of establishing relationships outside the marriage.
4. Parental remarriage, the process of establishing bonds with the children of a partner.
5. Economic remarriage, the process of becoming interdependent in terms of financial needs and responsibilities.
6. Legal remarriage, the process of settling financial and other responsibilities toward children and former partners.

Similarly, Patricia Papernow has described seven stages of stepfamily development, each of which poses a potential problem for remarried adults and their children. First, people planning to remarry are likely to entertain the **fantasy** that they will be rescuing their new partner or any children from the deficiencies of a previous marriage. These fantasies are likely to be played out in the second stage, **assimilation. Awareness** is the period in which the fantasy ends and the remarried couple comes to recognize the reality of their situation. **Mobilization** of energies and resources then takes place, the new family members attempt to pull together to solve common problems. **Action** is the process by which the family members begin to work together in an effective way. **Con-**

tact describes the growing sense of realistic intimacy likely to be experienced by family members working together effectively. Finally, **resolution** is the stage at which the reconstituted family feels and behaves as a solid unit.[60]

STRESSES IN COHABITATION

Heterosexual and homosexual cohabitation is susceptible to numerous stresses and difficulties. Since they fall outside the norms of marriage and family life, individuals in such arrangements are not likely to find support in the larger society. The relatively clear expectations that govern heterosexual marital relationships and child rearing are absent, and the couple must delineate its own expectations of how the relationship should work. Heterosexual and homosexual cohabitation, therefore, can be seen as "experimental forms of marriage."[61]

Cohabitation as a way of life is believed to be unstable, due in large part to society's lack of approval of these arrangements. For instance, the parents of a cohabiting person may not want to acknowledge their child's partner as a member of the family or may not know how to respond to the partner comfortably or naturally. This is a problem for heterosexual cohabitors, but it is greater for homosexual couples. The love that may exist for the couple often is insufficient to overcome the hostility and pressure toward conformity that derives from family, friends, and civic authorities. Moreover, even if a homosexual couple wishes to get married, mainstream and fundamentalist Judeo-Christian religions forbid it.[62]

For cohabitation to provide stable, family-like relations, it would have to become institutionalized or at least develop rules and regulations that are sanctioned by society.[63] While these have not developed, acceptance of premarital heterosexual coupling has become quite common, and in the gay and lesbian community, norms, roles, values, and traditions are being developed by couples in long-term relationships (see Chapter 8). Many social resources which can be used for support by homosexual couples have been established in churches, colleges and universities, professional associations, and local communities. Within the legal profession, for instance, a guide has been published giving information on all legal aspects of homosexual couples living together, including buying and selling property, relating to former spouses, child custody and visitation rights, estate planning, and living arrangements.[64]

IMPLICATIONS FOR PRACTICE

Study of the family as a social organization is a more concrete guide to assessment and intervention in family problems than study of the family as an institution is. Taken together, however, the two approaches demonstrate how critical social service workers can address public issues through their interactions with clients who have private troubles (see the box, The Family as Institution and Organization, in Chapter 7). When a married couple considering divorce or a legal separation seek help, for instance, the central issue for a critical social service worker is whether all marriages should be saved. Those who see in divorce the destruction of American family life would argue that saving marriages is a proper role for social workers. Those who believe that divorce is a rejection of the partner but not necessarily of marriage and parental responsibility would define the social worker's role differently. Divorce may be a necessary step in freeing the couple from a negative, dead-end relationship. Thus social workers must help to determine if divorce is truly necessary. If not, they might help revitalize the relationship to make it meet the needs of all the family's members. If divorce is considered necessary, they must try to deal with the stresses generated by the family dissolution.

Primary Prevention, Early Intervention, and Rehabilitation

Family practice and family treatment have become exceedingly popular in social work in recent decades, as well they should. As Anne Hartman has emphasized, the family has been the historical concern of social work and one of the concerns that distinguishes social workers from other helping professionals.[65] Two practice tasks are served by the assessment of family well-being: determining how families diverge from some optimum level of functioning (the identification of problems and strengths), and determining directions for change in order to improve functioning (intervention objectives). A number of other social work objectives, roles, and tasks also emerge from the consideration of family well-being. These are concerned with primary prevention, early intervention, and rehabilitation.

Primary prevention includes advocacy to assure that economic and other survival needs can be met. It also includes the development of policy and programs in support of greater educational opportunities, greater equality in the incomes of male and female workers, greater access to child care, and better enforcement of child support orders. Community and educational services can be promoted to call attention to family problems, including spouse, child, and elderly abuse. Providing information on the conditions that produce such problems and promoting skills that make it possible to overcome them should they arise can contribute to a decline in the number of such incidents.

Early intervention in families likely to experience difficulties also serves to prevent more serious problems. Social workers can set up and facilitate support or mutual-aid groups among people who have recently married or are cohabiting, have been divorced or remarried, or have been victims or perpetrators of family violence. **Support groups** help people understand that the difficulties they are experiencing are not unique but are often shared by others in similar circumstances. They can be educational, providing information on likely experiences and difficulties, and they can build skills, helping people develop the capacity to handle difficulties when they arise.[66]

Since social workers are most likely to work in the **rehabilitation** of families that are experiencing difficulties, they need to develop skills for crisis intervention and more long-term treatment. Crisis intervention often is needed to provide immediate help or support for families. At the time of a family dispute, divorce or separation, or a violent act, the task of the social worker is to listen and empathize, reinforce strengths, and assist clients in holding their lives together by assuring the satisfaction of their survival needs. More long-term family treatment can explore the whys and wherefores of family problems.

DISCUSSION QUESTIONS AND CLASS PROJECTS

1. Review the characteristics of healthy families presented in this chapter. Do these represent your idea of a healthy family? Would you delete any? Would you add any?

2. Define the following types of marriages: total marriage, vital marriage, conflict-habituated marriage, devitalized marriage, and passive-congenial marriage. Do you think all these types can be "normal" marriages? Do you agree that all can be "happy marriages"?

3. Describe the difference between survival and developmental family needs. Write three sets of themes or questions you might use in an interview to assess whether a family is meeting the survival needs of its members.

4. Family boundaries, both the boundary between families and their environments and the boundary between individual members in a family, have been studied for their implications for family well-being. Review the findings of researchers on both kinds of boundaries.

5. Internal family alignments and power structures have also been studied. What have researchers found about the relationship between these and family well-being?

6. Define and identify the significance of the following terms:
random families
closed families
triangulation
detouring coalitions
stable coalitions
faltering families
dominated families
conflicted families
chaotic families
disengaged families
enmeshed families

7. What is meant by domestic violence? What are the three major forms of domestic violence, and what is known of their incidence within families?

8. Those who work in shelters for battered women find that many women choose to remain with husbands who have abused them. Why would this be the case?

9. Define and distinguish among child abuse, child neglect, and child sexual abuse. How clear are definitions of sexual abuse?

10. Do you think that all marriages are worth saving? How would you distinguish between those that are and those that are not?

11. Without forcing any one to speak, inquire into the experiences of people in class who have gone through a divorce or separation, either as an adult or child. What stresses did they endure? What kinds of help did they ask for or receive? What kind of help would they have liked to have?

12. Goetting has described six tasks of remarriage. List and describe each.

13. Papernow has described seven stages of stepfamily development. List and describe each.

14. Again without forcing anyone to speak, inquire into the experience of people in class who have gone through remarriage either as an adult or child. What was the experience like? Do Goetting's tasks and Papernow's stages fit any of their experiences?

NOTES

1. Harriet Johnson, "Emerging Concerns in Family Therapy," *Social Work*, vol. 31 (July–August 1986), pp. 299–306.

2. Salvador Minuchin, *Families and Family Therapy* (Cambridge, MA: Harvard University Press, 1974).

3. Dolores Curran, *Traits of a Healthy Family* (Minneapolis, MN: Winston Press, 1983), p. 19.

4. Ted W. Bowman, "Promoting Family Wellness: Implications and Issues," in D. R. Mace (editor), *Prevention in Family Services: Approaches to Family Wellness* (Beverly Hills, CA: Sage, 1983), pp. 42–44.

5. John F. Cuber and Peggy B. Harroff, *Sex and the Significant Americans* (Baltimore, MD: Pelican Books, 1968).

6. Kenneth G. Terkelsen, "Toward a Theory of the Family Life Cycle," in E. A. Carter and M. McGoldrick, *The Family Life Cycle: A Framework for Family Therapy* (New York: Gardner, 1980), pp. 21–52.

7. Ann Hartman and Joan Laird, *Family-Centered Social Work Practice* (New York: Free Press, 1983), p. 165.

8. Fernando Colon, "The Family Life Cycle of the Multi-Problem Poor Family," in Carter and McGoldrick, *Family Life Cycle*, pp. 343–81.

9. Robert B. Hill, *The Strength of Black Families* (New York: Emerson Hall, 1971).

10. David Kantor and William Lehr, *Inside the Family* (San Francisco, CA: Jossey-Bass, 1975), pp. 119–42.

11. Harry J. Aponte and John M. Van Deusen, "Structural Family Therapy," in A. S. Gurman and D. P. Kniskern (editors), *Handbook of Family Therapy* (New York: Brunner Mazel, 1981), pp. 310–60; Aponte, "Underorganization in the Poor Family," in P. J. Guerin, Jr. (editor), *Family Therapy: Theory and Practice* (New York: Gardner, 1976), pp. 432–48. Also see Salvador Minuchin et al., *Families of the Slums: An Exploration of Their Structure and Treatment* (New York: Basic Books, 1967).

12. Aponte, "Underorganization in the Poor Family," p. 433.

13. Ibid.

14. Jerry M. Lewis, W. Robert Beavers, John T. Gossett, and Virginia A. Phillips, *No Single Thread: Psychological Health in Family Systems* (New York: Bruner Mazel, 1976).

15. Jerry M. Lewis, *How's Your Family: A Guide to Identifying Your Family's Strengths and Weaknesses* (New York: Bruner Mazel, 1979), pp. 85–96.

16. Ibid., pp. 111–20.

17. Ibid., pp. 121–31.

18. Charles Vert Willie, *A New Look at Black Families*, 2nd ed. (New York: General Hall, 1981).

19. Barbara Star, "Domestic Violence," in *Encyclopedia of Social Work*, 18th edition, vol. 1 (Silver Spring, MD: National Association of Social Workers, 1987), pp. 463–76. The discussion of domestic violence is based in large part on this article.

20. Stephen J. Pfohl, "The 'Discovery' of Child Abuse," *Social Problems*, vol. 24 (February 1977), pp. 310–23.

21. Star, "Domestic Violence."

22. U.S. Bureau of the Census, *Statistical Abstract of the United States 1988* (Washington, DC, 1987), Table 279.

23. R. L. McNeely and Gloria Robinson-Simpson, "The Truth about Domestic Violence: A Falsely Framed Issue," *Social Work*, vol. 32 (November–December 1987), pp. 485–90.

24. B. E. Aguirre, "Why Do They Return? Abused Wives in Shelters," *Social Work*, vol. 30 (July–August 1985), pp. 350–54.

25. Susan F. Turner, "Battered Women: Mourning the Death of a Relationship," *Social Work*, vol. 31 (September–October 1986), pp. 372–76.

26. Star, "Domestic Violence," pp. 468–69.

27. Ibid.

28. Much of this section is derived from E. Milling Kinard, "Child Abuse and Neglect," in *Encyclopedia of Social Work*, vol. 1, pp. 223–31.

29. U.S. Bureau of the Census, *Statistical Abstract 1988*, Table 276.

30. Ibid., Table 277.

31. Kinard, "Child Abuse and Neglect," pp. 224–25.

32. Ibid., p. 228.

33. Much of the discussion of child sexual abuse is derived from John R. Conte, "Child Sexual Abuse," in *Encyclopedia of Social Work*, vol. 1, pp. 255–60.

34. Ibid., pp. 225–56.

35. Ibid., p. 257.

36. James A. Weed, "Divorce: Americans' Style," *American Demographics*, vol. 4 (March 1982), pp. 13–17.

37. U.S. Bureau of the Census, *Statistical Abstract 1988*, Table 126.

38. Ibid., Table 81.

39. W. Parker Frisbie, Wolfgang Opitz, and William R. Kelly, "Marital Instability Trends among Mexican Americans as Compared to Blacks and Anglos: New Evidence," *Social Science Quarterly*, vol. 66 (September 1985), pp. 587–601.

40. Paul C. Glick, "How American Families Are Changing," *American Demographics*, vol. 6 (January 1984), p. 24.

41. Doris S. Jacobson, "Divorce and Separation," in *Encyclopedia of Social Work*, vol. 1, pp. 450–51.

42. Edward L. Kain, "Surprising Singles," *American Demographics*, vol. 6 (August 1984), pp. 16–19, 39.

43. U.S. Bureau of the Census, *Statistical Abstract 1988*, Table 48.

44. Kain, "Surprising Singles."

45. Reported in *USA Today*, Thursday, May 1, 1986, p. 1.

46. Glick, "How American Families Are Changing."

47. Ibid.

48. Victor R. Fuchs, *How We Live: An Economic Perspective on Americans from Birth to Death* (Cambridge, MA: Harvard University Press, 1983), pp. 220–26.

49. Mary Jo Bane, *Here to Stay: American Families in the 20th Century* (New York: Basic Books, 1976), p. 19.

50. Jacobson, "Divorce and Separation," pp. 451–57.

51. Judith S. Wallerstein and K. B. Kelly, *Surviving the Breakup: How Children and Parents Cope with Divorce* (New York: Basic Books, 1980); Wallerstein and Sandra Blakeslee, *Second Chances: Men, Women, and Children a Decade After Divorce* (New York: Ticknor and Fields, 1989).

52. Yankelovich, Skelly, and White, *Raising Children in a Changing Society*, General Mills American Family Report, 1976–77 (Minneapolis, MN, 1977), p. 128.

53. U.S. Bureau of the Census, *Statistical Abstract 1988*, Table 714.

54. Lenore J. Weitzman, *The Divorce Revolution* (New York: Free Press, 1985).

55. Jacobson, "Divorce and Separation."

56. U.S. Bureau of the Census, *Statistical Abstract 1988*, Table 87.

57. Kristin A. Moore and Martha R. Burt, *Private Crisis, Public Cost: Policy Perspectives on Teenage Childbearing* (Washington, DC: Urban Institute Press, 1982).

58. Esther Wald, "Family: Stepfamilies," in *Encyclopedia of Social Work*, vol. 1, pp. 558–59.

59. A. Goetting, "The Six Stations of Remarriage: Developmental Tasks of Remarriage and Divorce," in L. Cargan (editor), *Marriage and Family: Coping with Change*, (Belmont, CA: Wadsworth, 1985), pp. 323–33.

60. Patricia Papernow, "The Seven Stages of Step-Family Development," *Family Relations*, vol. 33 (July 1984), pp. 355–63.

61. Philip Blumstein and Pepper Schwartz, *American Couples: Money, Work, Sex* (New York: William Morrow, 1983), pp. 355–63.

62. Natalie J. Woodman, "Homosexuality: Lesbian Women," in *Encyclopedia of Social Work*, vol. 1, pp. 808–09.

63. Blumstein and Schwartz, *American Couples*, pp. 318–19.

64. Hayden Curry and Denis Clifford, *A Legal Guide for Lesbian and Gay Couples* (Reading, MA: Addison-Wesley, 1980).

65. Ann Hartman, "The Family: A Central Concept for Practice," *Social Work*, vol. 26 (January 1981), pp. 7–13.

66. See Alex Gitterman and Lawrence Shulman, *Mutual Aid Groups and the Life Cycle* (Itasca, IL: F. E. Peacock Publishers, 1986). Chapters are included on support groups for single parents, parents of sexually victimized children, men who batter their wives, and homeless women.

CHAPTER 10

The Family as a Social Organization: Analyzing Well-Being

M AJOR THEMES DISCUSSED IN THIS CHAPTER:

1. *Perspectives on family functioning.* Five perspectives for assessing the problems experienced by families are presented: the ecological model, the psychodynamic model, the developmental model, role theory, and conflict theory.

2. *The ecological perspective.* The ecological model locates family problems in the stresses caused by the interaction between the family and the groups, organizations, and institutions that make up its environment.

3. *The psychodynamic perspective.* The psychodynamic model locates the origins of family troubles in unconscious, neurotic needs and drives.

4. *The developmental perspective.* The developmental or family life-cycle approach locates the causes of family problems in the expected and predictable tasks family members must deal with as they enter into, maintain, and end family relationships.

5. *The role perspective.* Role theory focuses on the strain created by trying to meet the expectations of others, inside and outside the family, as well as expectations of the self.

6. *The conflict perspective.* Conflict theory emphasizes how contradictions and inequalities which are supported by contemporary Western societies set up tensions that are easily converted into conflict and coercion.

7. *Implications for practice.* When used together these perspectives can

contribute to the assessment phase of practice and the planning of interventions.

THIS CHAPTER considers how to understand the differences in the strengths and problems faced by various families. Why is it that, over time, some families continue to show strength, while others get mired in troubles? No one theory of family life is able to account completely for such differences in family well-being, but many theories offer insightful leads. Our interest is in theoretical perspectives which can be incorporated into a systems approach to study of the family as an organization.

PERSPECTIVES ON FAMILY FUNCTIONING

An understanding of the psychosocial functioning of family life, involving both psychological and social aspects, requires knowledge of both the external social context in which the family is situated and the internal dynamics which operate inside it. Since all systems exist in a state of dynamic change, family processes of interaction and development also must be examined.

In the following sections we will examine five perspectives which have been used in analyzing everyday family life. In the ecological perspective, family problems are located in the stresses created by the interactions between the family and the groups, organizations, and institutions that make up its environment, while in the psychodynamic perspective, the origins are located in the irrational, unconscious, and neurotic needs that govern intimate relationships. The developmental or family life-cycle perspective locates the causes of family problems in the expected and predictable tasks family members must deal with as they enter into, maintain, and end family relationships. Role theory focuses on the strain created by trying to meet the expectations of others as well as of the self, and conflict theory emphasizes how self-interest motivates family members to put self ahead of others. Each of these perspectives contributes to an understanding of the family as an organization.

THE ECOLOGICAL PERSPECTIVE

A major technique of family theorists in examining the relationships between the family and its social context has been the use of the **ecological model**. Essentially, this model attempts to locate families in terms of their interdependence with other social systems: schools, workplaces, churches, community organizations, welfare agencies, and the other organizations and individuals with which they interact daily and which exist both as sources of trouble and sources of strength. One approach taking this perspective views the family's environment in terms of exosystems and macrosystems and in relation to the economic stresses experienced by some families. Others use tools which have been developed specifically to study the social context of particular families. The most important of these are the eco-map and the genogram.

MACROSYSTEMS AND ECOSYSTEMS

As we noted in Chapter 1, transactions between a society and the individuals in it are likely to involve the micro environment of individual beliefs, attitudes, and behaviors as well as the macro environment of social institutions and processes. Thus, in the ecological approach to study of the family, private troubles are seen in relation to public issues in the domain of macrosystems. James Garbarino has developed a way of describing the social context of families which orders environmental systems in terms of their size and social distance from the individual.[1]

Garbarino's focal system is the individual, but his ideas also can be applied to the family. The family thus is seen as a **microsystem** surrounded by a mesosystem, exosystem, and macrosystem. The **mesosystem** includes those individuals, groups, and organizations with which the family must deal directly: other families, friends, church, schools, workplaces, and so on. The **exosystem** includes organizations with which the family may never have to deal directly but which nevertheless can influence its well-being. The exosystem might include local government and local voluntary associations like the Chamber of Commerce whose interests may or may not coincide with those of particular types of families. The **macrosystem** reflects the cultural context of family life: the values, traditions, and authority patterns inherent in social institutions.

The problems of American social institutions which affect the everyday well-being of families exist in the exosystem and macrosystem. The effects on families come through the operation of specific organizations and institutions and through institutionalized patterns such as classism, racism, and sexism which are present in the society but are not necessarily identified with specific organizations. In contemporary American society, one of the major sources of stress for families in the macrosystems and exosystems surrounding them is the institution of the national economy.

THE FAMILY AND ECONOMIC STRESS

Although adults marry or cohabit in the hope of building an intimate relationship supported by love and respect, they also create a household which has to be sheltered, fed, clothed, and entertained. Supporting the household, therefore, is a primary task of families, and difficulties in completing this task adversely affect the well-being of families. A 1986 survey of 2,555 Americans conducted by *Money* magazine found that the principal cause of family strife, according to respondents, was money.[2]

The capitalist or free-market economy operating in the United States has produced a high level of affluence, yet it continues to keep some families in poverty and to produce other problems which impact heavily on families. Problems of inequality, poverty, unemployment, economic cycles, and debt continue to affect certain sectors of American society.

Inequality

Except perhaps for the very rich, most families live in a perpetual state of economic risk. Even in the best of times, when the economy is not in recession and inflation and unemployment are low, goods and resources are inequitably distributed. The ideals of capitalism champion economic opportunity in the form of free competition. In theory, those who have the motivation to "go for it" will achieve; those who are not able to compete or fail in the competition fall behind. Capitalism recognizes neither equality of effort (it's not how well you play the game but whether you win or lose) nor equality of result. Two men with the same education and the same occupational skills may get paid differently simply because one sector of the economy can command more resources than another. Similarly, a woman with less education, less skill, and perhaps even making less of a contribution to the general welfare than another woman can command greater income and wealth simply because of the operation of the free market.

Income has been defined as the "flow of purchasing power during a fixed time period."[3] As officially measured in government statistics, money income includes wages, pensions, dividends, interest, and rents but excludes such significant sources of income as capital gains and fringe benefits. In 1986, the median money income of families, the point in a distribution of incomes at which 50 percent of the families had higher incomes and 50 percent had lower incomes, was $29,458. Approximately 21 percent of American families had incomes of less than $15,000, and another 21 percent earned $50,000 or more. The lowest fifth (20 percent) of families earned just 4.6 percent of all income earned, while the top fifth earned 43.7 percent.[4]

Inequality in income in the United States is not only great, it is growing. At the time of the Great Depression of the 1930s, social welfare services, social security, and income tax policies were designed in part to reduce extremes in inequality. Between 1929 and 1947 there was a small reduction, but social and economic policies since then have actually increased the inequalities in income distribution[5] (see box, Changing Shares of Money Income of Families, in Chapter 4).

Poverty

There are various definitions of poverty. The federal government classifies families and individuals as having incomes above or below a designated **poverty level**, using the poverty index originated by the Social Security Administration in 1964 and revised in 1969 and 1980. The **poverty index** is based solely on money income and does not include the noncash benefits such as food stamps, Medicaid, and public housing received by many low-income families. The basis for the index is the Department of Agriculture's 1961 economy food plan, but the income thresholds are updated every year to reflect changes in the Consumer Price Index. The different consumption requirements of families, according to their size and composition, are taken into account.[6]

The poverty index is an example of an absolute definition of poverty, in which poverty is regarded as a lack of the necessities of life. By this definition, when all families attain incomes at or higher than the specified level at which family needs presumably can be satisfied, poverty will have been eliminated. A relative definition of poverty would always reflect the bottom of the distribution of wealth or income in the population (such as the bottom fifth), regardless of what the various median incomes are. Poverty is defined in a relative sense by comparing the average income in a society with the income of the poorest people in it. Thus there would always be a portion of the population living in poverty, and greater inequality means greater poverty.[7]

The Persistence of Poverty.   In 1959, 22.4 percent of the population was officially living below the poverty level. The persistence of poverty despite an otherwise affluent society in the United States was brought to public attention in the early 1960s by Michael Harrington in *The Other America*. He describes an "invisible land" in which "tens of millions of Americans are, at this very moment, maimed in body and spirit, existing at levels beneath those necessary for human decency." The main "subcultures of poverty" are identified as the aged, minorities, agricultural workers, and "industrial rejects." Children, families with a female head, and people with little education were also at a disadvantage.[8]

The governmental response to this problem was a series of social welfare programs and policies which became known as the War on Poverty. As a result, absolute poverty declined between 1965 and 1978. According to the relative measure, however, no decline in poverty was noted during the early part of this period, and there was an increase in the later part.[9] Between 1978 and 1984, regardless of the measure, poverty in the United States increased. Officially, however, the proportion of the population living below the poverty threshold declined from 14.4 percent in 1984 to 13.6 percent in 1986.[10]

William O'Hare has identified a number of persistent myths about poverty which many people, including social service workers, continue to regard as facts. One myth is that more people are poor because they refuse to work. He points out that of the 7.3 million families living in poverty in 1984, in more than half at least one family member was working, and in over one-fifth two or more were working. Poor families headed by men are actually more common than poor families headed by women, since they include both married-couple and single-parent families. Similarly, there are more white families among the poor than black families, because whites are by far the majority in the population, and there are more rural and suburban poor families than poor inner-city families.[11]

The burden of poverty does fall disproportionately on minorities and women and children, however. In 1986, 14 percent of all persons were classified as poor, or with incomes below the poverty level. Yet 38 percent of the persons in families with female householders and 30 percent of blacks in families were poor, compared to 9 percent of whites in families. Among persons 65 years old and over, 12 percent had incomes below the poverty line in 1986.[12]

Unemployment and Underemployment

Official rates of joblessness are derived from monthly household surveys conducted by the Department of Labor. To be considered unemployed, a person must be 16 years or older, presently out of work, available for work, and have been looking for work during the preceding four weeks. Using this definition, the **unemployment rate**, or the proportion of the civilian labor force who were unemployed in 1986, was 7.0 percent. The rate for whites was 6.0 percent; for blacks, 14.5 percent, and for Hispanics, 10.6 percent. By age, the rate was highest, 18.3 percent, for males and females 16–19 years old, and the highest rate of all was 39.3 percent for blacks in this age category. The lowest rate, 2.8 percent, was for females 65 years and older, most of whom were not considered unemployed because they were not looking for work.[13]

Official rates are believed to underestimate actual unemployment. Among other shortcomings, they do not include **discouraged workers**, those who have been out of work a long time and have given up looking for employment. There were 1.8 million discouraged workers in December 1982, when unemployment rates reached their highest point since the Great Depression before starting to decline, according to the U.S. Department of Labor.[14] In 1986, about 4.5 million males and 3.7 million females were designated as long-term jobless, having been out of work 15 weeks or more.[15]

Underemployment is "a condition in which workers' jobs are incommensurate with their skills, training, expectations, and earning capacity, given the type or amount of work they are equipped to perform."[16] No data are available to measure underemployment adequately. Included are those who work part-time involuntarily, because no full-time work is available, and those who work full time in jobs that do not provide adequate income.

Effects of a Capitalist Economy on Families

A capitalist, free-market economy is subject to cyclical periods of recession and prosperity or inflation. In a recession or depression, jobs and incomes are lost, and families must tighten their belts. In a period of inflation, the price of basic necessities rises faster than incomes. Both make it difficult for families to meet their needs.

Economic booms and busts also play on the emotions of the family. Researchers found that in 1974–1975, in the midst of a severe recession, 37 percent of parents surveyed said that their standard of living was worse than in the year before, while only 14 percent said it was better. In 1976–1977, these proportions were almost reversed.[17] Economic conditions rarely remain stable for long. A National Broadcasting Company poll in 1987 found that 65 percent of the people interviewed said it was becoming more difficult for middle-class people to maintain their standard of living.[18]

Consumption and Debt.   The capitalist economy in contemporary American society also places great emphasis on the consumptive function of the family. Until the early twentieth century, the economy was concerned with production and supplying the basic needs of families for food, shelter, and clothing. Today, technological advances have created an economy capable of producing about as much as it wants to. Consuming everything it produces is another matter.

Lee Rainwater has documented the importance of the function of consumption for the perceived well-being of Americans. He notes that, in general, people assess their well-being not on the basis of how their own lives have improved but on the relative improvement in their lives compared to how much they perceive others' lives have improved. In the early 1970s, national surveys indicated that to "get along" families thought they needed about 106 percent of their take-home pay.[19] When the income earned does not seem to be enough to meet a family's "needs," it goes into debt. A recent series of articles in the *Wall Street Journal* estimated that "half of the 76 million baby-boomers consume products of a price and quality far beyond what might be expected for their means."[20]

In the consumer society that has evolved in the United States, people have been trained to desire more and more. The traditional values of thrift and delayed gratification have been abandoned, and new values based on conspicuous consumption and immediate gratification have been instilled. The advertising industry plays a crucial role in this regard, using numerous tactics to encourage consumption.[21] Advertising aims to make people believe that their happiness, indeed their self-esteem, is dependent on buying the "right" clothes, car, sunglasses, electric carving knives, and so on. It is increasingly being directed at young people, and children are encouraged to develop the "gimmees": give me this and give me that. Thus the need to consume has led to deficit spending in most American families. Savings are low and debt is high. Philip Slater calls the emphasis on consumption **wealth addiction**, comparing the need to consume and to accumulate to a powerful drug which gives a temporary high but eventually weakens and destroys.[22]

Economic Hardship and Stress.   The economic conditions generated by a consumer-oriented, high technology, capitalist economy produce a great deal of stress for families. The urge to consume, to immediately satisfy every perceived need or desire, affects affluent families as well as those who have to struggle to make ends meet. Job security has virtually disappeared as corporations have merged and been bought out, and a college education no longer guarantees a good job. The tensions created by household debt and the need to consume hit across the board.

Nevertheless, economic stress has the greatest impact on families with lower incomes. Survival needs are much more pressing than needs for self-

gratification, and other problems are magnified. Domestic violence, for instance, is found in families at all socioeconomic levels, but studies indicate that
they appear disproportionately in families of lower socioeconomic status.[23]
The economic problems confronted by poor and working-class families cannot
be exaggerated.

Lillian Rubin sensitively describes the development of a working-class family, from the time, as newlyweds, their dreams of marital bliss are invaded by
the need for economic survival (see box, Facing Reality in the Working-Class
Family). The economic hardships worsen with the birth of the first child, which
occurs early, often within the first year of marriage. Instead of added happiness, quarrels begin. The wife feels unappreciated; the husband feels nagged
at. They begin to live in fear that the unhappiness they saw in their parents'
lives, which they swore could never happen to them, is indeed about to surface.
They begin to realize that much of their parents' unhappiness was due to economic difficulties like the ones they are facing. This insight fails to help them,
however. They start to blame each other for their problems.[24]

Rubin describes how the romance of marriage fades by the middle years.
When working-class partners do not divorce, they come to redefine their notions of a good marriage. Romance, happiness, and personal fulfillment are no
longer important goals. Even though the husband might be a steady worker
and his income rises, financial security cannot be taken for granted. Unemployment is a constant threat, especially if the wife is not employed outside the
home and is completely dependent. "He's a steady worker, he doesn't drink;
he doesn't hit me" becomes the definition of a good husband. A good wife runs
the household competently, keeps the children under control, and sees that the
breadwinner's needs are met.

Social service workers often ignore the economic issues surrounding family
life. In a good deal of the literature on family functioning, the implicit assumption is that economic considerations are irrelevant, and only personal and interpersonal dynamics need to be taken into consideration. Thomas Keefe argues eloquently that empathy, a primary relational skill in social work practice,
must be based on a sound understanding of economic structures and
processes.[25] In order to truly comprehend the frustrations and anger experienced by many clients, the economic realities they confront must be appreciated and shared on an emotional level.

The Eco-Map: Studying the Social Context of the Family

The eco-map, developed by Ann Hartman, is a major tool for studying the social context of families. It is primarily offered as a way for practitioners to assess
and plan interventions for specific troubles clients bring when they seek service. The **eco-map** is a paper-and-pencil simulation; the worker and the clients
actually draw a map which shows the "major systems that are a part of the
family's life and the nature of the family's relationship with the various systems."[26] In the ecological perspective, the term *systems* refers to the particular

groups and associations, formal organizations, families, and individuals with which a particular family interacts.

To draw an eco-map, a circle is placed on a large, blank sheet of paper (see box, Setting Up an Eco-Map). This circle represents the particular family or focal system a practitioner wishes to describe. The composition of the family is indicated with small squares representing males and small circles representing females, and the symbols for the parents are placed in hierarchical position above those for the children. A number of other circles are then drawn in the area surrounding the family circle. These circles represent the other systems — the individuals, families, groups, associations, and organizations — with which the family ordinarily interacts.

In order to describe the nature of the relationship between family and environment, different kinds of lines are drawn connecting the family to each of the other systems. When discussion with the client indicates that the relationship between a system and the family is supportive, a solid line is drawn. A solid, thin line means that the system is an ordinary resource for the client, and a solid, thick line means there is a very strong positive relationship between the client and the system. By identifying these sources of ordinary and strong support, this ecological model avoids recognizing only the weaknesses in clients' surroundings.

When the relationship between a system and the family is tenuous or uncertain, a broken line is drawn on the eco-map. Tenuous relationships may be in-

FACING REALITY IN THE WORKING-CLASS FAMILY

Lillian Rubin describes the particular problems faced by young marrieds from working-class families as they try to establish a household and get started as a family. Like all young people, they approach marriage in dreamlike terms: a white dress, presents and congratulations from family and friends, romance and living happily ever after. Soon, however, reality strikes.

Both the male and the female in these families typically hold very traditional views about their gender roles. At the beginning of the marriage the young wife usually has a job, but she thinks of it as a temporary measure, to help the family get off to a good start. The young husband believes it is his duty to support his family, but earning a steady income proves to be surprisingly difficult. The adjustments they must make are very painful.

One young husband describes his feelings this way:

. . . Before I got married, I only had to do for myself; after, there was somebody else along all the time. I mean, before, there was my family but that was different.

terpreted in different ways; for instance, they may be regarded as having little to do with either the troubles presented by clients or the solutions for these troubles. When the relationship is conflicting or stressful, a slashed line is drawn. Stressful relationships concern conditions related to the troubles presented by clients. In a child-abuse case, for instance, the fact that the parents are unemployed, in debt, fighting with relatives, or unable to locate child-care services may be associated with the abuse. Resources will have to be found in the client or in the environment to overcome these sources of stress.

The analysis of family strengths and stresses can be furthered by the use of arrows on the eco-map to identify the direction of the flow of energy. An arrow pointing in the direction of another system means that family energy, in the form of resources, communication, or adaptation, is being directed toward that system. An arrow pointing to the family means that resources and energy are flowing from the other system to the family.

Use of an Eco-Map with a Hypothetical Family

The way an eco-map is used to study the social environment of a family can be illustrated with the case of the Garcias, a hypothetical family (see box, Eco-Map of the Garcias). Ricky Garcia, the oldest son, has been truant and is not doing well in his studies, as indicated by the arrows between the symbols for the Garcias and the school. His mother and the school social worker have a

They weren't there all the time; and even though I had to help out at home, they weren't absolutely depending on me.

Then, I suddenly found I had to worry about where we'd live and whether we had enough money, and all those things like that. Before, I could always get a job and make enough money to take care of me and give something to the house. Then, after we got married, I suddenly had all those responsibilities. Before, it didn't make a difference if I didn't feel like going to work sometimes. Then, all of a sudden, it made one hell of a difference because the rent might not get paid or, if it got paid, there might not be enough food money.

A young wife describes being overwhelmed by financial problems:

. . . I don't know how we survived that period. The first thing that hit us was all those financial problems. We were dirt poor. Here I'd gotten married with all those dreams and then I got stuck right away trying to manage on $1.50 an hour—and a lot of days he didn't work very many hours.

It felt like there was nothing to life but scrimping and saving; only there wasn't any saving, just scrimping.

Source: Lillian Breslow Rubin, *Worlds of Pain* (New York: Basic Books, 1976), pp. 70–71.

SETTING UP AN ECO-MAP

An eco-map is a tool for depicting the relationship between a focal system and its social enviroment. On an eco-map, a circle representing a family as the focal system is surrounded with other circles representing the individuals, groups, organizations, and institutions which make up its social environment.

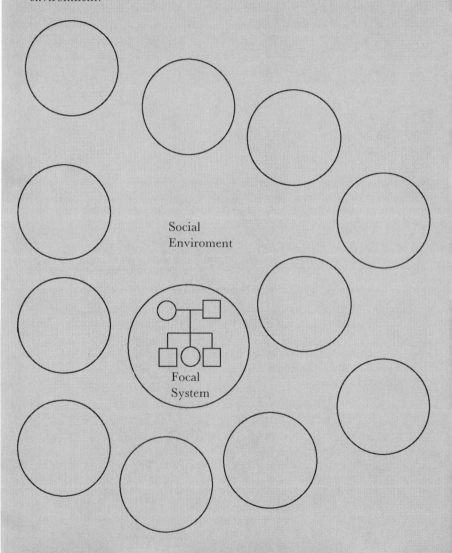

positive relationship, and Mrs. Garcia comes in to discuss the problems Ricky is having. Together with the social worker, she considers the various resources available to improve his progress in school. In developing the eco-map the social worker, with Mrs. Garcia's help, is able to identify some of the strengths and weaknesses within the family's social context:

> The Garcias are a fairly traditional family made up of husband and wife and three children. Their social context includes a number of organizations, such as the world of work (Mr. Garcia is employed and Mrs. Garcia, who is disabled, is at home); local government, especially mass transit and mental health services; and the school (the three children are all enrolled in the local elementary school).

> The family lives in a *barrio*, or Mexican-American neighborhood, which is adjacent to an Anglo neighborhood, and many of the residents in both areas have strong negative attitudes about the other ethnic group. The Garcias have few close friends, but they depend a great deal on relatives who live close by. Mr. Garcia's job is threatened and he has been forced to take a cut in pay. The family has many debts, so paying for a private tutor is out of the question.

> The use of mental health services is a possibility because there is good public transportation, but Mrs. Garcia does not want to use them; she doesn't want her child to be thought of as having mental problems. Besides, because of local politics, the mental health service is located in the Anglo neighborhood, and Mrs. Garcia believes that the service available there will not be suitable for Ricky.

> The Garcias are strongly tied to their extended-kin family, however. She has a niece and a nephew who are a few years older than Ricky and who have been excellent students. Mrs. Garcia decides to seek their help, and a plan is set up to ask them to tutor Ricky on a regular basis.

The technique of the eco-map is useful as a means for social service workers to identify the relationships among particular individuals and families and the individuals, groups, and organizations making up their environment. Its usefulness in developing a more general understanding of how societal and cultural factors impinge on family organization and functioning is limited, however.

THE GENOGRAM: STUDYING THE INDIVIDUAL IN THE FAMILY SYSTEM

A technique which can serve as an extension of the eco-map is the genogram, which was developed by a psychiatrist, Murray Bowen. The **genogram** provides a closer look at the relationships that exist within a family network by displaying family patterns across time and space and makes it possible to examine how these patterns affect members of the family. This technique is predicated on the assumption that "the family is the primary and, except in rare instances, the most powerful system to which a person ever belongs."[27] Maggie Scarf, who gives an engrossing example of use of a genogram, says, "A genogram is a road map laying out the important emotional attachments of each of the partners — attachments that lead backward in time, to the parents' and grand-

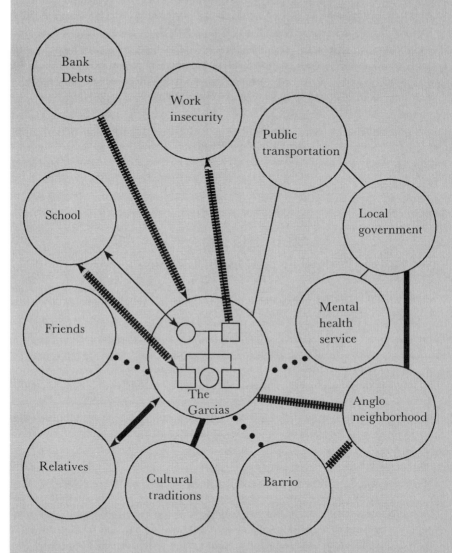

ECO-MAP OF THE GARCIAS, A HYPOTHETICAL FAMILY

Bank Debts

Work insecurity

Public transportation

School

Local government

Friends

Mental health service

The Garcias

Anglo neighborhood

Relatives

Cultural traditions

Barrio

Key:
Tenuous resource/relationship
Strong resource/relationship
Very-strong resource/relationship
Conflicted resource/relationship

parents' generations, and forward to the new one, the children (if any) of the present union."[28]

While the genogram is promoted as a family therapy technique, it does not use the family as the focal system. Instead it identifies an **index person**, the person with the problem or symptom, and uses the family as part of that person's present and past social context. Thus genograms promote understanding not so much of family problems as of individual problems. The genogram of a hypothetical family (see box) portrays the relations among a troubled husband, his wife, their children, and their wider family network.

Indicating Family Patterns on the Genogram

There is no one way to draw a genogram; the method described here was developed by Monica McGoldrick and Randy Gerson.[29] As in the eco-map, men are depicted by squares and women by circles. The older generation is depicted along the top of the chart, and later generations are shown below. Solid lines connect blood- and marriage- related generations (grandparents, parents, children, aunts, uncles, cousins), while dotted lines connect divorced or separated people. Deceased members are depicted by an X over the square or circle representing them.

Once the basic outline of the family network is drawn, three types of information are recorded: demographic information, functioning information, and critical family events. **Demographic information** includes ages, birth and death dates, locations, occupations, and educational levels. **Functioning information** includes more-or-less objective descriptions of the physical, emotional, and behavioral functioning of different family members. **Family events** includes important life changes such as shifts in relationships, losses, failures, gains, and successes.

After this information has been recorded, interpersonal relations are described with the use of various symbols connecting circles and squares. This involves a good deal of inference, as data are acquired from various family members and from direct observation. Six kinds of relationships can be identified: close, poor or conflictive, very close or fused, fused and conflictive, estranged or cut off, and distant relationships (see box, Symbols for Family Relationships Used in the Genogram).

Interpreting the Genogram

The genogram offers a number of lines of interpretation to assist in understanding the troubles presented by an individual family member. One area for exploration is the basic family structure. This concerns the composition of the household: single-parent, nuclear, extended-kin, or other family forms. The sibling constellation and birth order might also be considered. From these interpretations hypotheses can be stated about the working agreements or norms

GENOGRAM OF A HYPOTHETICAL FAMILY MEMBER

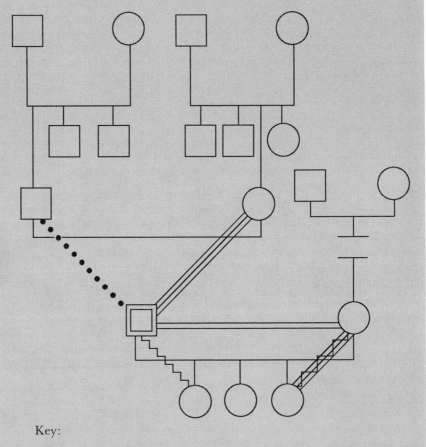

Key:

Focal person ▣ ◎

Male □

Female ○

Parents and children

that govern family functioning. Through testing these hypotheses, the relationship between family norms and the family's problems may be uncovered.

A second area for interpretation involves determining the family life cycle. Life-cycle issues will be discussed later in this chapter.

The third area of interpretation concerns family history and the repetition of patterns across generations. This makes it possible to determine if a particular problem is a recurring one in the family. By examining past problems, future problems can be predicted, and preventive intervention may be able to help the family avoid them.

A fourth area considers relational patterns and triangles. Interpersonal relationships between and among family members are examined to determine to what extent they are fused, conflicted, cut off, or distant. Diadic (two-person) functioning is common, but the genogram also can be used to examine triangles (three-person functioning). This may uncover coalitions of two against one, and the connection between one set of antagonisms and another set of loyalties may become clear.

The functional whole of a family is considered in interpretations of family balance and imbalance. In well-functioning families, there is believed to be a pull toward equilibrium in which family characteristics balance one another. Examining how the whole system functions may identify imbalances and show how they might be corrected.

Taken together, these various lines of interpretation make the genogram an

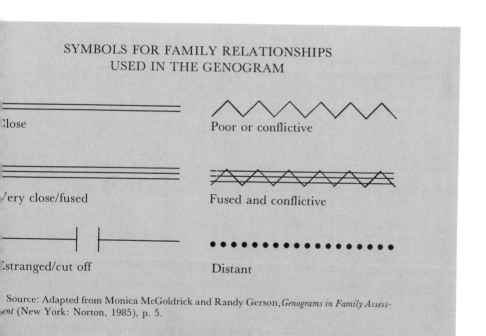

SYMBOLS FOR FAMILY RELATIONSHIPS
USED IN THE GENOGRAM

Close

Poor or conflictive

Very close/fused

Fused and conflictive

Estranged/cut off

Distant

Source: Adapted from Monica McGoldrick and Randy Gerson, *Genograms in Family Assessment* (New York: Norton, 1985), p. 5.

extremely useful tool in examining the social context of the family and the individuals in it. As Scarf says, "Genograms provide a systematic way of looking at each partner's own natural context—the family subculture in which he or she was reared—and discerning those repetitive themes, issues, myths, patterns of behavior, etc., which have been brought forward from the past and resurrected in the marriage of the present."[30]

THE PSYCHODYNAMIC PERSPECTIVE

Psychodynamic perspectives on the family rely heavily on the thinking of Sigmund Freud, which will be discussed further in Chapter 14. Freud believed that unconscious drives and needs, often connected with the gratification of sensual pleasure, guide human behavior. When parent-child relations go awry, the needs and drives may be converted into neuroses which interfere with interpersonal relations in later life.

The psychodynamic perspective has been examined by Herbert Strean. He maintains that individuals enter marriage with **inner scripts**, that is, a set of internalized needs. If their psychosexual developmental experiences in early life were gratifying, the chances are high that the marriage will prove successful, because the inner scripts are healthy. If these experiences were frustrating or were dealt with ambivalently or inconsistently, the marriage will be difficult, because the inner scripts are neurotic.[31]

In psychodynamic thinking, falling in love is an irrational process in the sense that unconscious needs and drives dominate conscious attitudes and beliefs. We may think we are getting married because we love someone, or find him or her attractive, warm, and sincere, but the reality is often quite different. We fall in love in an attempt to fulfill deeper inner needs.

Immature love, which is driven by unresolved, frustrating early-life experiences, takes many forms. Strean describes ten of these: clinging love, sadistic love, rescuing love, compulsive love, unrequited love, celibate love, critical love, revengeful love, love of the partner's parents, and homosexual love.[32] These forms of love often lie behind marital conflicts and represent the real source of many marital problems.

Clinging love lacks self-confidence. People who love by clinging never feel quite worthy of their partners and are always submissive to them, saying, in effect, "I will do anything for you; just love me in return." In **sadistic love**, a partner is chosen who can be derogated and demeaned as a way of compensating for and defending against one's own sense of weakness. **Rescuing love** is an attraction based on the need to be a savior for unhappy people. This is found more often among men who believe their love will change the lot of their partners and bring them happiness. **Compulsive love** is based on self-doubt. Initially, compulsive lovers must constantly prove themselves, incessantly declaring their love and involving themselves with others who will give them complete attention. As the relationship progresses, however, their real needs are not met, and they begin to resent their partners. Often they drive their partners off with displays of anger.

Unrequited love is the search for the perfect partner. The more unavailable and unattainable the partner appears, the more in love the other person feels. Unrequited love is usually based on feelings of guilt. An unattainable partner is chosen as a way of assuring that it will never really be necessary to prove oneself as a lover. **Celibate love** is another attempt to find the perfect partner, so perfect, indeed, that the partner is treated like a parent. Then an incest taboo is applied to the relationship; there can be only tender affection for the partner-parent, and no erotic feelings. Sometimes, indeed, it is not the search for a perfect partner that motivates love but the search for a perfect parent. Individuals who were deprived of loving parents in their childhood may unconsciously long for the **love of their partners' parents**, in the hope that they will come to be prized as sons or daughters. In **critical love**, externally one partner always seems to be annoyed with the other, while internally there is secret admiration. People who love critically search for partners who enjoy being punished for real or imagined transgressions. Critical lovers complain about all the things that are wrong with the partner as a way of warding off their own childish needs and impulses. **Revengeful love** is based on attempts to overcome feelings of having been scapegoated as a child. People who love in a revengeful way try to get even with their parents through their love relationships.

According to Strean, **homosexual love** is also a form of immature love. He writes: "Having experienced poor role models who failed to demonstrate that love between members of the opposite sex can be enjoyable and enriching, homosexual men and women are in an acute rage most of the time — even though much of their rage is unconscious."[33] In making this assertion, Strean goes against the view of homosexuals as a discriminated-against minority, the view we have taken. He also appears to go against the position of the American Psychiatric Association, which no longer lists homosexual behavior as a mental disorder.[34]

Often in marriage neurotic complementarity occurs; people having difficulties believe they are being victimized by their partners, and if they had another partner all would be well. They fail to realize that their own unconscious needs are at the base of the troubles they are experiencing. They also fail to realize that the conflict itself gratifies and protects them; they wouldn't want it any other way. The partners have unconsciously colluded, that is, entered into an agreement which requires them to complement each other's neurosis and thereby maintain a balance in the relationship:

> Married men and women who habitually complain about their spouses' sexual unresponsiveness are those who constantly disparage their spouses' attempts to respond sexually. Those husbands and wives who deride their spouses for their lack of cooperation are also those who frequently frustrate their partners' attempts to cooperate. And those marriage partners who chronically complain that their

spouses are poor parents for their children are frequently sabotaging their spouses' efforts to relate to their children.[35]

THE DEVELOPMENTAL OR LIFE-CYCLE PERSPECTIVE

Some researchers have taken a developmental approach in their attempts to understand the processes of family formation, maintenance, and dissolution. In their view, there is a **family life cycle** composed of a natural sequence of stages or periods, and many of the troubles families confront have to do with how transitions are made from one period to the next. The family is seen as "a basic unit of emotional development," and the focus is on psychological well-being as people proceed through the phases of family life.

The idea that the family should be understood as a unique system, with unique developmental propensities separate from the personalities of the members comprising it, has been around for a number of years.[36] Many theories of family development have been proposed, but no agreement exists on such basic issues as the number of developmental periods or the tasks associated with each of them. In this section, the ideas of Elizabeth Carter and Monica McGoldrick, which represent a synthesis of much of the literature, are highlighted.[37]

THE NORMAL TROUBLES OF FAMILY LIFE

The life-cycle approach makes an important contribution to the understanding of why families ordinarily have troubles. Family developmental theorists relate family troubles to **normative stress**, the normal and expected difficulties of living up to society's expectations. Carter and McGoldrick use the term *horizontal or normative stressors* to explain "the anxiety produced by the stresses of the family as it moves forward through time, coping with the changes and transitions of the family life cycle."[38]

Normative stress, however, is not the only recognized source of difficulties in family life in this approach. Two other sources are transgenerational stress and the stress of living in this place at this time. **Transgenerational stress** derives from the fact that the family is a three-generational unit which includes the entire kin network of a focal family. Since individuals are reared in their family of origin and then, as they mature, form their own family of procreation, their experiences in the first carry over to the second. According to Carter and McGoldrick, there is a "flow of anxiety" in family life which operates by passing on "family attitudes, taboos, expectations, labels and loaded issues" across generations. As children grow they are socialized into the culture and history of their family and thereby internalize them. When they marry, they bring this history with them into their relationships with their spouses and their children. The stress of **living in this place at this time** is a concept that is not very well developed by Carter and McGoldrick but nevertheless is important. As examples of this kind of stress they cite the public issues of stress created by women's liberation, the sexual revolution, and ecological pollution. The everyday stresses generated by changing social institutions and pre create troubles for families.

The primary contribution of the life-cycle model, however, is to tion to normative sources of stress. In this concept, Carter and N emphasize that family troubles (perceived stress and anxiety) are normal and to be expected. There is no such thing as a family without troubles. Moreover, just because a family has troubles it should not be assumed that the family is somehow abnormal. The troubles families confront are predictable, because they derive from specific developmental processes through which all family members pass. These processes are related to family life events, such as getting married or having a baby, but also the developmental stage the family member is in, such as young adulthood, middle adulthood, or old age.

Six Stages of the Family Life Cycle

The six life-cycle developmental stages identified by Carter and McGoldrick are:

1. The unattached young adult.
2. The joining of families through marriage.
3. The family with young children.
4. The family with adolescents.
5. The launching of children and moving on.
6. The family in later life.

These phases describe the family as a series of membership changes, changes in social roles and statuses, and changes in boundaries, as new members continually enter and old members continually leave.

Unattached young adults must deal with separating from the family of origin and achieving independence. In this process they must differentiate their own identity, learn how to form intimate adult relationships, and establish an occupational or work identity. When young adults marry, a new emotional process takes place in which the couple learns to commit themselves to a new family, their own family of procreation. Troubles may arise in the tasks of forming a healthy marital relationship, becoming committed to a spouse, and realigning relationships with extended families and friends to include the spouse.

Ginny didn't move beyond this stage

When a child is born to the couple, the task is to incorporate a new member in the family. The marital relationship has to be joined with a parental relationship. Husbands and wives become fathers and mothers; in-laws become aunts and uncles; parents become grandparents. There are normal difficulties in assuming the new set of roles, all of which require personal and interpersonal adjustments. Adolescence brings new kinds of stress to the family. Whereas family boundaries tend to close in as a way of assuring protection with young children, with adolescents the family boundary must open up to allow their search for independence. The couple has to start thinking of themselves less as mother and father and more as husband and wife; they must begin to rediscover themselves in their midlife crisis.

When adolescents become young adults and leave home, new troubles surface. The couple must confront each other and renegotiate their dyadic relation in an "empty nest." They must prepare to take on the role of grandparent, accept their own aging, and deal with the disability and death of their own parents. Major shifts in status take place as the family loses members and takes on new ones.

In later life, the couple must accept their age-related roles. Their physical decline is evident, the death of a partner is inevitable, and their adult children, likely with adolescents at home, must assume responsibility for their care, even as they begin to face their own mortality.

Derailed Families

Many families take the normal troubles of family life in stride. As families confront the tasks presented by the various life phases, however, it is quite possible for family troubles to become serious. All families cannot successfully meet the difficulties presented at all developmental phases. When they cannot, Carter and McGoldrick consider them **derailed families**, in need of being placed back on track. Derailments lead to conflict and occasionally to domestic violence. According to Carter and McGoldrick:

> Family life cycle passages are concerned with shifting membership over time, and the changing family status of family members in relation to each other. Dysfunctional families characteristically confuse shifts in status, exits, and functions. . . . Parents may pretend that their children are not growing up and leaving, or that their own parents are not dying when they are. . . . This occurs [when] the family pretends to have more power over the membership or status of family members than it actually has.[39]

DIVERSITY IN THE FAMILY LIFE CYCLE

While the family life-cycle perspective has made significant contributions to knowledge of family well-being, it is not without its limitations. There is a clear and often acknowledged emphasis on the traditional two-parent, white, middle-class family with a small number of children who are born within a few years of one another and progress through the life stages more or less at the same time. Other forms of family life are not adequately handled. Recent work has begun to apply the developmental model to nontraditional and alternative family forms. David McWhirter and Andrew Mattison, for instance, have applied the idea of developmental stages in family life to homosexual male couples. They identify seven stages in these relationships which can overlap, go forward or backward, and even go in circles: blending, the first year; nesting, the second and third years; maintaining, the fourth and fifth years; building, the sixth through tenth year; releasing, the 11th through 20th year; and renewing, beyond 20 years.[40]

Divorce, Single Parenthood, and Remarriage

Within the family life-cycle perspective, divorces are sometimes referred to as **dislocations**. Divorcing families often go through additional developmental phases with distinctive sources of stress before the separated partners and the children can get back on the normal developmental track. First, divorcing couples face the task of deciding to divorce. That is, they need to accept that they are unable to resolve the troubles they have confronted as a couple. Second, after the decision is made, they must take on the task of breaking up the family system. Divorce requires cooperation in decisions on custody, visitation, and financial settlements. Extended-family members must be faced and brought into the process. Ties to in-laws must be redefined. Third, the actual divorce brings a number of difficult tasks to be completed. The attachments to the former spouse do not automatically disappear, and mourning for the lost relationship and family is normal. New relationships between the divorced husband and wife must be worked out.

Other stressful family patterns described in Chapter 9 also are related to divorce. For both the custodial and noncustodial parents, there is the emotional task of maintaining personal contact and supporting healthy relationships with the children. There is also a need to rebuild the social network of the new single-parent family. When divorced parents remarry and form stepfamilies, the emotional tasks involve entering a new relationship, joining together in a new marriage, and reconstituting or blending two families. The partner or partners who have been divorced must recover from the loss of the first partner, master fears about entering a new relationship, and be patient as new roles, boundaries, and feelings are confronted. The new family must accept itself as a different, nontraditional family with boundaries that are much more permeable.

Poor and Racial- and Ethnic-Minority Families

Poor and minority families must adapt to the considerable stress that comes from living in this place at this time, in Carter and McGoldrick's terms. Both the time and the place typically are harsh, with substandard housing, poor-quality food and clothing, and deteriorating neighborhoods. They are likely to be underemployed if not unemployed, and often they are isolated and alienated from other types of individuals and families. As a result, their family life cycles often lack certain elements which usually are present. According to Fernando Colon, the multiproblem poor family has only three developmental phases: unattached young adults, family with children, and family in later life. Colon also says that the effects of a hostile social, economic, and physical context make for considerable underorganization in family life.[41]

Ethnic family life cycles differ. Study of the life cycles of the various ethnic groups making up American society has only begun, however. C. J. Falicov and B. M. Karrer did clinical practice with Mexican-American families in a large Midwestern city. They note that there is the same number of life-cycle phases as in Anglo families, but the speed with which they are negotiated differs. In the Mexican-American family, marriage is often at an earlier age; children become a part of the family earlier, go to school later, and complete or drop out of school earlier; and later-life family relations may be cut off earlier by death.[42]

Usefulness of the Family Life-Cycle Model

The life-cycle model directs attention to the normal and predictable troubles which both traditional and nontraditional families are likely to experience as they traverse their life course. By normalizing troubles, it helps to reduce victim blaming. When things go wrong in families, it is not necessarily the fault of family members.

Social service workers can apply this model to help derailed or dislocated families get back on track. Through family therapy techniques, they can help enable family members to fulfill the tasks associated with the family life-cycle phase they are in and to anticipate changes and make the transitions from one period to the next.

The family life-cycle model is more descriptive than explanatory, however. It teaches what kinds of troubles to expect, but it does not adequately explain why some families handle troubles effectively and others do not. Some reasons are hinted at: external here-and-now stresses, deficiencies in individual competence, neuroses derived from experiences in the family of origin. But the perspective does little to increase understanding of why such troubles as domestic violence or divorce occur.

ROLE THEORY AND THE FAMILY

Role theory in contemporary sociology and psychology has emerged from diverse sources. As used most frequently, it is heavily influenced by structural functional thinking (see Chapters 2 and 13). Those who have used the role perspective with regard to family life point out that basic units which make up the family as a system, as well as all other human systems, are social positions which are referred to as roles and statuses. **Status** refers to the position or "office" itself, but often it also implies some rank in a social hierarchy. **Role** refers to the more dynamic aspects of the position; it has more to do with what the people in various positions do or are expected to do. In family life, roles and statuses include husband, wife, lover, companion, mother, father, son, daughter, sister, brother, grandmother, grandfather, aunt, uncle, and the like. In the family, individuals only exist within the context of the roles and statuses they occupy; for instance, Mary as wife and stepmother, John as husband and

Families are multigenerational systems. How many
generations can you pick out in this photo? What
kinds of tasks are the people in each generation likely
to be dealing with? *Billy E. Barnes*.

father. Role theory maintains that the behaviors of family members cannot be understood outside the context of the roles they occupy.[43]

DYNAMICS OF ROLE RELATIONSHIPS

Roles can be defined in three ways: the prescribed role, from the point of view of others; the perceived role, from the point of view of the person in the role; and the enacted role, from the point of view of the actual behaviors performed by the person in the role (see box, Three Ways of Defining Role, in Chapter 2).[44] To understand the roles of members of a particular family, all three definitions have to be taken into account. Family therapists, for instance, have to inquire of all family members what they expect of others and of themselves and then observe what they actually do in their roles.

To illustrate the dynamics of role relationships, we will focus on the role of Martha, the mother in the hypothetical Jones family. This is a reconstituted or stepfamily of three blacks: Martha, her husband, John, and his son Tom by a previous marriage. The role of mother is defined in terms of the expectations of others, Martha's own expectations, and her actual behaviors.

Family Roles and the Expectations of Others

Martha receives expectations from her husband and her stepson as to how her role as stepmother is to be enacted. In the form of verbal and nonverbal messages, they instruct her as to how they expect her to function in the mother role. John tells her he would like her to play the role in the same way his mother did, and Tom wants her to play it just like his best friend's mother does. Members of the immediate family are not the only ones who communicate their expectations about how Martha is to perform the role of mother. Jerome, her widowed father; Susan, her sister; and Margaret, her mother-in-law, also have expectations, as do some of the groups and organizations with which she interacts. The school tells her what a mother who is supportive of a sound education should be like. The church she belongs to tells her what a religious mother should be like. The community of which she is a part also has expectations. Because she is a black woman, she receives expectations from the black community about how a good mother should be. Because she is an American black woman living today, she receives expectations from the larger society about how she should be an American mother in the latter part of the twentieth century.

Family Roles as Expectations of Self

When the role of mother is defined in terms of expectations of the person occupying the role, the emphasis is on how Martha—with her own socialization history, her own personality, her own developmental stage, and her own perceptions and values — makes up her mind about what she should be like in the role of mother. It involves sorting through many of the expectations she has been receiving from others, as well as being aware of her own needs and interests.

Family Roles as Actual Behaviors

The mother role may also be seen in terms of Martha's actual feelings, thoughts, and actions as a stepmother. Expectations emanating from self and others are just that: things that are expected. Sometimes we conform to the expectations of others, but we do not always do what others expect of us. Sometimes we do what we ourselves want, but just as often we put aside our own needs and interests. Sometimes the things we do are influenced by a complex decision-making process, sorting through the things others expect of us and the things we expect of ourselves and coming to a conclusion about what we are to do. Sometimes the things we do just seem to happen, a mystery to ourselves and others.

ROLE CONFLICT OR STRAIN

The special contribution of role theory to the study of family problems lies in the concept of role conflict or strain. Role theorists point out that many of the troubles individuals experience derive directly from problems which are inherent in social roles. They argue that understanding troubled families in terms of role conflict is more accurate than assuming that personal deficiencies or abnormalities are at the root of family troubles. The concept of **role conflict**, like the concept of normative stress, emphasizes the normality of conflict and change; conflict is expected to occur because it is inherent in the nature of family roles. In structural functionalist terms, role conflict and change contribute to the ultimate survival of the system.

Multiple Roles

The members of families take on not just one role but multiple roles. Some of these roles are defined exclusively as lying within the focal system. Thus Martha, in addition to being a stepmother, is also a wife and a lover in this nuclear family. Other roles are related to the groups to which people belong. Martha belongs to the extended family and so is also a daughter-in-law, a daughter, and a sister. She may take on the role of friend to a neighbor. Since Martha is employed she is also in the role of worker (a working stepmother), and since she is actively involved in her stepson's education, she has the role of PTA member. Martha may be functioning in a number of other roles which are not directly connected to but nevertheless influence her role as mother in the Jones family. She may be a member of a religious group, a political party, and a neighborhood association, for example.

Intrarole Conflict

The fact that many people have different ideas on how any family role should be enacted raises the possibility of **intrarole conflict**. If Martha's stepson, husband, father, sister, and mother-in-law, as well as first-grader Tom's teacher, all see eye to eye on how Martha is to be a mother, she is likely to avoid trouble in filling her role. When each of these individuals has different expectations of Martha in the role of mother, the disparity is likely to involve her in intrarole conflict (see box, An Example of Intrarole Conflict). If the teacher wants her to insist that her stepson keeps up with the class; if her father reminds her that she is not the boy's natural mother and should not assume the responsibility of making him learn; if her husband wants her to lay off because Tom is "only a kid"; if her mother-in-law tells her she should be strict with the boy, the same way she was strict with her sons — if all these people have different expectations for how Martha should be a stepmother, she will have trouble filling the role. If she goes to a therapist who tells her not to pay attention to others and to do what she thinks is right, the therapist is likely to add to Martha's troubles.

Interrole Conflict

The fact that individuals simultaneously function in a number of roles sets up the possibility of **interrole conflict**. There are at least two kinds of interrole conflict: that associated with playing different roles in different focal systems, and that associated with playing different roles within the same focal system. In the first kind, when all the different expectations emanating from others outside the focal system are in agreement with the expectations of those inside it, a person's social world exists in consensus, and all the person's roles are compatible. When the expectations from inside and outside the family differ, the social world exists in dissensus, and the person may be pulled and pushed and tormented by the competing expectations (see box, An Example of Interrole Conflict).

For instance, Martha the worker may have a boss who wants her in the office at 9:00 AM, or he will give her job to one of the unemployed people waiting to take it; Martha the mother has a stepson who wants her to stay home because he has a sore throat; Martha the wife has a husband who wants her to take the family car in for service because he will not be paid unless he works all day; and Martha the relative has a sister who is in a marital crisis and needs desperately to talk to Martha. When different expectations operate all at the same time, interrole conflict produces a good deal of trouble.

The second kind of interrole conflict occurs in situations within a single focal system. Many systems, such as the family, are complex, and individuals often

AN EXAMPLE OF INTRAROLE CONFLICT

Intrarole conflict occurs when the expectations of others compete so that a person in a family role cannot please all family members at the same time.

AN EXAMPLE OF INTERROLE CONFLICT

One kind of interrole conflict occurs when the expectations of others outside the family complete with the expectations of others inside the family.

find themselves playing more than one role in them. Martha the wife is also Martha the mother, and competing expectations from husband and stepson can put her in interrole conflict. When her stepson wants Martha to read him a story and at the same time her husband wants Martha to devote some attention to him alone, Martha is forced to make a decision that causes her stress.

Mixed Messages as Role Conflict

Individuals may communicate in such a way that two competing expectations are being promoted at the same time. Often one message exists at the verbal level but another message exists at the nonverbal level. Suppose Martha is trying to decide whether she should take a new job which offers her more money, prestige, and security. She feels that John's approval is essential, so she asks him what he thinks about her role as working mother and wife. John says: "Honey, it's up to you. Do what you want. I only want what's good for you." On the surface he appears very supportive, but Martha is uneasy; he just didn't say it right. He turned his head away from her, and there was something wrong about his tone. Somehow it sounded like: "If you only want to think of yourself, then do it, but if you really loved me you wouldn't." When people trying to fulfill a role hear such **mixed messages**, they may experience them as role conflict. They may become stymied and unable to make decisions; they experience trouble (see box, An Example of Mixed Messages as Role Conflict).

Personality-Role Conflict

Sometimes the roles individuals occupy are well suited to them, and they have the proper attitudes, knowledge, and skills to carry them out. Martha really likes being a homemaker, for instance; while it is a lot of work, she likes to keep house, to cook and sew and clean. She recognizes that having children is a lot of responsibility, but she genuinely wants lots of children. She was proud of her family name but willingly gave it up and took on her husbands'. She might like to have a career, but she is content to think of her work as a means to a supplemental income. Since Martha's whole being is caught up in the role of homemaker, she would not be overwhelmed by the conflicts that multiple roles and expectations might bring. If she were not really suited for or happy in that role, she would be likely to experience trouble in the form of **personality-role conflict** (see box, An Example of Personality-Role Conflict).

Role Overload

Even though individuals are suited to their roles and the expectations of others are not necessarily incompatible, they can experience conflict in the form of **role overload** if there do not seem to be enough hours in the day to complete all the tasks required of them. Martha may feel obliged to work eight hours a day, to cook and clean, to spend time with her aging mother-in-law and her energetic father, to be the ideal romantic partner for her husband, to help her stepson learn to read and her sister to deal with her problems. If she wants to do all these things equally much, she is likely to be troubled by having more things to do than she can handle.

FAMILY RESPONSES TO ROLE CONFLICT OR STRAIN

All the various forms of role conflict have in common a breakdown in the working agreements within and between systems in the family and its environment. Whether or not a family experiences role conflict or strain depends on whether or not there is consensus in expectations and they are clearly stated. In regard to role strain in the family, Wesley Burr et al. put forth the following propositions:[45]

AN EXAMPLE OF MIXED MESSAGES AS ROLE CONFLICT

Mixed messages occur when a family member says one thing but means another thing or says one thing one time and another thing another time.

1. The more individuals perceive consensus in the expectations about a role they occupy, the less their role strain.
2. The greater the perceived clarity of role expectations, the less the role strain.

The responses of family members to the various role conflict situations range along a continuum from conformity to nonconformity. A person in a role usually conforms to the expectations of others, as long as the expectations are clear and consensus exists among the various expectations. The structural functionalist and other consensus approaches to the analysis of social systems on which role theory is based assume that people in systems share values and function to maintain the system. Indeed, there is considerable evidence that conformity is the usual response to the expectations of others, but not necessar-

AN EXAMPLE OF PERSONALITY-ROLE CONFLICT

sonality-role conflict occurs when a person's character, self-image, or efs are in contradiction with the expectations of others.

Father   Son

ily because people want to conform. Sometimes people conform because they feel they have to.

Clarifying expectations may be necessary in order to achieve conformity. Role theory generally assumes that dissensus in expectations is not real but rather reflects poor communication. On the surface there is a communication breakdown, but underneath there is consensus. Thus when strain is evident, people in roles attempt to communicate better and clarify their expectations. Once clarification occurs, conformity with expectations follows.

Sometimes nonconformity results when people in roles attempt to make innovations in what is expected of them through feedback to other system participants or to other systems. If the innovation is accepted, the system is righted again and in balance; if it is not accepted, the process begins again. When consensus cannot be reached, the family system is likely to break apart (through divorce) or to be trapped in various forms of domestic violence.

CONFLICT THEORY AND THE FAMILY

Conflict theory refers to perspectives which hold in common the notion that utilitarian self-interest is at the core of human behavior. Unlike structural functionalists, who maintain that conflict and change are normal only when they contribute to maintenance of the system, conflict theorists believe that conflict and change are the normal and expected state in any system, and stability can only be achieved if it reflects equality among the elements of the system (see the box, A Comparison of Structural Functionalist and Conflict Theories, in Chapter 2).

When the theory is applied to the family, conflict is believed to develop because each member is expected to look out for his or her own best interests, even at the expense of other members. There is no assumption that the family is some kind of special system in which love and altruism predominate. To conflict theorists, conflict does not represent a breakdown in normal, stable relations; instead it indicates that systems are functioning in the expected way. Indeed, if stability and harmony were present, conflict theorists would get suspicious. They would suspect that some family members are forcing their wills on other family members.

Family conflict in contemporary Western, capitalist societies is studied in the context of **Marxian conflict theory**, which starts with the assumption that self-interest among family members is promoted under the influence of capitalism. As the search for rewards and profits became more acceptable in everyday life, it also became more acceptable within the family. The self-interest evident in the family has led some to argue that the family is so corrupt it should be abandoned and replaced. For instance, David Cooper denounces the family as a destructive social institution rife with emotional blackmail and terrorism.[46]

THE FAMILY AS AN OASIS IN CAPITALISM

Recently, conflict theorists have argued that the family represents on oasis in capitalism rather than an expression of its values. In this view, the family is a humane institution besieged by capitalism and in need of protection from it. Capitalism is said to have subverted the human values underlying social relations. As a result, the masses are exploited and have lost control over their creative processes. They are treated and treat themselves like commodities with a specific economic value, packaged like so many bottles of beer to be placed on sale, bought, and consumed. Family life is understood within a context of contradictions and competing values.

Philip Wexler, for instance, describes negotiations over contradictions in values as the **dialectic of intimate relations**. In advanced capitalist societies, he argues, there are at the same time tendencies toward social fragmentation and excessive individualism, rationalization and routinization, and alienation and exploitation. Competing tendencies exist simultaneously. People yearn for cooperation and communal attachments, for spontaneity and playfulness, for personal autonomy, control, and competence all at once. Family life is the struggle to resolve these competing values: urges to exploit and control versus urges to share and cooperate; urges to treat others as human beings versus urges to make them into objects to be used and consumed; urges to look out for the common good versus urges to look out for self. Wexler believes tradition favors humanist solutions; the family has been institutionalized to foster cooperation, personalism, and collectivism. As capitalist values have become inculcated into everyday life, however, there is less and less support for these values, and this creates continual stress.[47]

Similarly, Ralph LaRossa notes that there are no really acceptable alternatives to family life. From childhood, most people assume they will get married and have children. Thus when people come together to form intimate relations, there is an ambivalence born out of not knowing what else is possible which sets up tensions. Two people are likely to feel simultaneously pulled toward and away from the relationship. Feelings of attraction and repulsion, of being connected yet wanting to be separate, of unity and individuality exist side by side.[48]

INEQUALITIES IN THE FAMILY INSTITUTION

The way family life has been institutionalized also sets up tensions which must be dealt with. As we noted in Chapter 7, the status of women and children generally remains subordinate to that of men in society and in the family. Social norms traditionally have dictated the position of the husband as the head of the household and the authority of parents over children.

Marxian conflict theorists have argued that the source of gender and generational inequality can be traced to free-market economic institutions. In contrast, feminist conflict theorists have argued that the source of inequality lies more in gender conflict than in class conflict.[49] In many societies, although not all, men have been able to set up patriarchal norms which create advantage for them and disadvantage for women and children.

Regardless of their origins and legality, three major sources of potential conflict exist in the family: conflict over economic property rights, conflict over sexual possession, and conflict over intergenerational control.[50] Family and other intimate relations exist on the razor's edge. The issues surrounding these inequalities can erupt at any moment into conflict. These issues have to do with how much power various family members are to have, how the power is to be used, who is to participate in decisions and to what extent, what rewards members are entitled to, and what privileges and obligations go with the roles they occupy.

In conflict theory, the possibility for conflict is always present because self-interest is inherent in the statuses family members occupy. Most men and adults behave in ways that will protect their power and privilege over women and children; many women and children try to improve their statuses and reduce those held by men and adults, encouraged by women's and children's rights movements which have brought into question the authority of males and adults. The successful challenge to male dominance in adult relationships was discussed in Chapter 7. Efforts to make families less patriarchal and more egalitarian and democratic often have inspired family conflict.

Conflict theory thus sees life in the family as a negotiation in which members attempt to resolve the ambivalence, contradictions, and constraints generated by capitalist and patriarchal institutions. They manipulate whatever resources they have available as a way of holding on to or increasing wealth, power, status, prestige, and other economic and sexual benefits. They also attempt to affirm humanist values such as cooperation, the common good, personal respect, and autonomy.

CONFLICT BETWEEN HUSBANDS AND WIVES

Because Western societies have generally adopted sexist norms, men have traditionally held authority over women in the family. This authority is evident in both the economic and sexual spheres. While its extent has been reduced in recent years, male domination nevertheless persists; men and women still do not have equal status, either in the society or in the family. Thus, as women and men attempt to manage the ambivalence and contradictions generated by social institutions, there is a tendency for men to exploit women and a consequent tendency for women to assert their autonomy.

According to Marxian theory, the struggle between men and women in the family is intimately related to control over the economy. Traditionally, men attempted to exploit the labor of women by keeping them out of the work force and maintaining them in the home to do the work of keeping the house and nurturing the family without pay. In this view, women's economic dependence on men is the key to understanding their subordination in society.

Feminists do not necessarily dispute the economic competition between men and women. They argue, however, that the origins of female-male conflict lie in the exploitation of female sexuality for purposes of male sexual gratification. In taking a feminist position, Randall Collins makes three assumptions:[51]

1. Humans have the strongest sexual drives.
2. Males are, on average, bigger and stronger than females and thus will more often coerce and be aggressive against women.
3. Coercion on the part of males will likely be countered by aggression on the part of females.

From these assumptions, Collins concludes that husbands will claim the right to total sexual possession of wives but will not necessarily grant wives the right to sexual possession over them. In this view, women become the sexual property of men through marriage, and it is the control and use of this "sexual" property that forms the basis of conflict between them.

Male-female relations have historically involved an exchange between the economic and material rewards that men are able to offer and the sexual attractiveness and gratification that women are able to offer. To win his woman, the male attempts to become economically powerful. To win her man, the female attempts to appear attractive and as inaccessible as possible. The posture of women to men is usually defensive and involves a strong degree of sexual repressiveness. Woman cannot appear to like sex. The posture of men to women is aggressive and involves devaluing her capacities.

Yet women have power to influence men. Men do fear that women will supplant their authority. Traditional gender-role norms limit the ability of men to express emotions and therefore men fear the expressive powers of women. Women also serve to validate male sexuality. Men fear that women can make them impotent and thereby emasculate them. These fears give women leverage over men.

The nature of the economy does have a role in conflict between men and women. In an affluent market economy, such as the United States experienced in the 1970s, employment opportunities for women reduce their dependence on men, and they are freer to strike their own bargains. Under such conditions, a women's liberation movement could flourish, and divorce rates could be expected to rise as women exercise their options to go it alone. As long as women continue to experience occupational segregation and lower median incomes, however, they still cannot compete with men as equals.

Competition among men in the economy also tends to reinforce traditional gender roles. Many working-class and middle-class men experience alienation and exploitation in their jobs. They attempt to exercise power in the only place they have an opportunity to do so, their own homes.

Other forms of social relations also reinforce men's traditional gender roles. Joseph Pleck argues that these roles are maintained not only by the way women and men have responded to each other's self-interest, but also by the ways men respond to other men. The male-male bond reinforces the male's exploitation of the female. It is in the context of the competition among men which is set up by patriarchal norms that definitions of masculinity are formulated. Thus men define the acceptable forms of masculinity in relations with one another, as well as the unacceptable forms, such as homosexuality. The worst names men can call each other are "queer," "fag," or "sissy," but other forms of masculinity also are devalued. Traditionally, only aggressive, dominating, competitive, materially oriented men are valued.[52]

CONFLICT BETWEEN PARENTS AND CHILDREN

Through socialization, adults help children learn to become competent members of society. According to Collins, the traditional literature on socialization considers childhood almost entirely from the point of view of an idealized adult society. It accepts adults' rationalization of their exercise of authority by failing to acknowledge underlying tensions in parent-child relationships. Collins believes that socialization has been regarded as the process which "tames the little barbarians who enter the world as infants and makes it possible for them to associate in the civilized world [of adults]."[53]

In this respect, Collins and other Marxian-oriented scholars of the family believe that Freudian ideas about early-life socialization patterns are not far off the mark. Freud assumed an inherent conflict between individuals and society. He exposed the basic conflict in parent-child relations by maintaining that newborn children are polymorphous perverse, that is, driven by their need for pleasure, and so can only enter the civilized world of adults by taking on a superego. Freud made an important error, in the view of conflict theorists. He failed to realize that the Victorian family was not a universal type, existing everywhere and at all times in the same way. He took a nonhistorical approach to the family.

Collins's conflict approach sees socialization processes as a struggle for control over the emotional, behavioral, and cognitive life of the child. Children learn what parents believe are the acceptable ways of feeling, thinking, and behaving. That is, they learn their parents' personal solutions and difficulties with respect to the ambivalence and contradictions generated by society. This is an important point. Whereas the traditional literature on socialization makes it seem as though parents pass on clear and consistent norms and traditions, conflict theory emphasizes that parents pass on a maze of ambivalence and contradictions. Moreover, while children are subordinate to parents, they are not powerless: "The socialization of the child even in infancy, is not simply an imposition of the parent's culture . . . upon the child, but a negotiated product which can change as the resources available to the parties change."[54]

Resources and Strategies of Control

Parents' ability to use their authority to control children rests, according to Collins, in a time advantage; the parents are older and presumably wiser and smarter. They are also bigger and have more strength. And, perhaps of most consequence, children are attracted to parents and need to be loved and protected. Parents also control the material benefits a child may receive, and parental authority is to a large extent supported and reinforced by society. Children in contemporary society who are labeled *incorrigible*, or ungovernable, and who habitually disobey or run away from their parents may be declared delinquent.

Parents exercise their advantage primarily through either rewards or punishments such as shaming, love deprivation, or physical violence. The strategies they use are in part controlled by culturally based norms. For instance, the state has increasingly limited the violence and obvious coercion to which parents can subject their children. Society now supports the use of rewards rather than punishments and more subtle ways of manipulating the emotions, behaviors, and perceptions of children. The goal is for children to believe that their parents are not operating out of self-interest.

The ability of children to check the authority of parents depends on their age. Infants have few resources other than their ability to be cute and loving and their capacity for crying and making a nuisance of themselves. Young children are very vulnerable and likely to internalize the ambivalence and contradictions of the parents. The older children are, the more they are able to match brains and brawn with adults. Eventually they can shame parents, withdraw love, run away, or even use physical violence, or they can reward parents with love, affection, good grades, and the like. Children can use their own ambivalence and contradictions to influence parents. Even older children are likely to be economically dependent, however, and thus parents inevitably have the upper hand.

IMPLICATIONS FOR PRACTICE

Each of the five perspectives on family life examined in this chapter — the ecological, psychodynamic, and developmental models and role and conflict theories — makes a unique contribution to understanding the problems confronted by families. They are particularly helpful to social service workers in the first two steps of practice problem-solving, the assessment phase, in which the task is to identify and analyze family problems, and the intervention-planning phase, in which the task is to formulate a plan for resolving the problems.

The ecological model demonstrates that family problems are generated as a result of interaction with other individuals, groups, organizations, and social institutions. This model is useful because it supplies two excellent assessment instruments, the eco-map and the genogram. These tools make it possible to look closely at the relationship between a family and its social environment and to consider the changes that are needed in the environment.

The psychodynamic model looks inside the individuals making up the family to determine their unconscious needs and drives. It proposes that happiness in marriage is largely a function of early-life, family-based experiences. Women and men are attracted to each other based on unconscious needs, but those who bring unresolved, frustrating experiences into their marriages will love in immature ways and will develop ways of protecting against appropriate resolutions of their neuroses. Although most social workers will not be sufficiently trained to assess unconscious motives and drives, some basic understanding of them is necessary in analyzing problems.

The developmental or family life-cycle model shows how to look at the way family members and intimate partners are adapting to expected tasks and stresses as they enter, maintain, and end relationships. It sensitizes workers to the likely troubles people have as they decide to marry or become involved, have children or decide not to, see their children start school, and so on. Role theory focuses on the strain and conflict experienced as family members attempt to meet their own expectations and those of other family members and other people outside the family. Conflict theory emphasizes how contradictions and inequalities supported by the larger society set up tensions that are easily converted into conflict and coercion.

All of the perspectives contribute to good social work assessment, yet, taken independently, each has limitations. For instance, the ecological model is more a general guide than a perspective with substance. It does not provide a very good understanding of the internal dynamics of family life. The psychodynamic model fails to define the societal context of family life adequately and does not promote understanding of the conscious aspects of personality. Although the developmental, role, and conflict perspectives are all social-psychological, the strengths of one seem to be the weaknesses of others. Developmental models and role theory do not call sufficient attention to the harsh realities of industrial societies. Conflict theory pays insufficient attention to the human tendencies for cooperation and harmony.

It would be a mistake, therefore, for social service workers to favor one of these perspectives over the other. The insights provided by each model or theory must be taken into account in the assessment of family well-being.

DISCUSSION QUESTIONS AND CLASS PROJECTS

1. Define and identify the following: ecomap, genogram, microsystem, mesosystem, exosystem, macrosystem.

2. What kinds of economic stress are likely to be experienced by families today? Do you see any of these stresses operating in the families you are working with? Has your own family experienced any of these?

3. Separate into pairs and have one person take the role of social worker and the other the role of client. The social worker interviews the client in an attempt to complete an eco-map of the client. When the map is completed, reverse roles and begin over again. Come together as a class to clarify the use of the eco-map and the difficulties a social worker might have in doing one.

4. Describe the assessment areas a social worker can get into through the use of a genogram.

5. Separate into pairs and have one person take the role of social worker and the other the role of client. The social worker interviews the client to complete a genogram. When the genogram is completed, reverse roles and begin again. Come together as a class to clarify the use of the genogram and the difficulties a social worker might have in doing one.

6. Do you think that unconscious motives and drives operate in family troubles?

7. Describe what Strean means by immature love. What are the ways it can be exhibited? Do you agree that these ways are immature? Do you think you see immature love in your clients, in your friends, or in yourself?

8. Define and identify the following:
derailed families

dislocated families
transgenerational stress
normative stress
the stress of living in this place at this time

9. List and describe Carter and McGoldrick's stages of family development.

10. What are some of the tasks and stresses that should be expected when people go through divorce and remarriage?

11. Form groups of four or five students. Each person should describe his or her own family life (of origin, of procreation, of partnering) in terms of its stage of development. What do you see as the normal tasks and problems associated with that phase? Do you see that members of your own family are adapting to these?

12. List and define five major forms of family role conflict. Can you give concrete examples of each? Can you give specific examples by describing situations experienced by your clients, by your friends, or by yourself?

13. What are the ways by which role conflict can be resolved? In thinking about the examples you have given of role conflict, how were they, or how are they likely to be, resolved?

14. What is meant by conflict theory? How does it sensitize us to conflict between husbands and wives, and conflict between parents and children? Do you ever find yourself dealing with the potential conflict created by status inequalities in the family?

15. Name and define the five perspectives on family functioning discussed in this chapter.

NOTES

1. James Garbarino, *Children and Families in the Social Environment* (New York: Aldine, 1982), pp. 21-16.

2. Peter A. Brown, "Money Called Top Cause of Family Strife," *Capital Times*, Madison, Wisconsin, October 22, 1986, p. 1.

3. Robert D. Plotnick, "Income Distribution," in *Encyclopedia of Social Work*, 18th ed., vol. 1 (Silver Spring, MD: National Association of Social Workers, 1987), p. 881.

4. U.S. Bureau of the Census, *Statistical Abstract of the United States 1988* (Washington, DC, 1987), Tables 699, 701.

5. Plotnick, "Income Distribution," p. 883.

6. U.S. Bureau of the Census, *Statistical Abstract 1988*, p. 405.

7. James William Coleman and Donald R. Cressey, *Social Problems* (New York: Harper and Row, 1984), pp. 162-63.

8. Michael Harrington, *The Other America: Poverty in the United States* (Baltimore, MD: Penguin Books, 1973), pp. 1, 195-202. Also see Harrington, *Decade of Decision* (New York: Simon and Schuster, 1980), and *The New American Poverty* (New York: Holt, Rinehart and Winston, 1984).

9. Sheldon Danziger, "Poverty," in *Encyclopedia of Social Work*, vol. 2, p. 195.

10. U.S. Bureau of the Census, *Statistical Abstract 1988*, Table 714.

11. William O'Hare, "The Eight Myths of Poverty," *American Demographics*, vol. 8 (May 1986), pp. 22-25.

12. U.S. Bureau of the Census, *Statistical Abstract 1988*, Tables 714, 716.

13. Ibid., Table 632.

14. News item, *Chicago Tribune*, January 8, 1983, sect. 1, p. 1.

15. U.S. Bureau of the Census, *Statistical Abstract 1988*, Table 633.

16. Katherine Briar, "Unemployment and Underemployment," in *Encyclopedia of Social Work*, vol. 2, p. 779.

17. Yankelovich, Skelly, and White, *Raising Children in a Changing Society*, the General Mills American Family Report, 1976-77 (Minneapolis, MN, 1977), p. 58.

18. NBC News poll, *Wall Street Journal*, March 11, 1987, sect. 2, p. 1.

19. Lee Rainwater, *What Money Buys: Inequality and the Social Meaning of Income* (New York: Basic Books, 1974), p. 53.

20. John Koten, "The Shattered Middle Class: Upheaval in Middle-Class Market Forces Changes in Selling Strategies," *Wall Street Journal*, March 13, 1987, p. 21. For a more systematic sociological analysis of the same theme, see Richard Parker, *The Myth of the Middle Class* (New York: Harper Colophon, 1972).

21. Stuart Ewen, *Captains of Consciousness: Advertising and the Social Roots of the Consumer Culture* (New York: McGraw-Hill, 1976).

22. Philip Slater, *Wealth Addiction* (New York: Dutton, 1980).

23. E. Milling Kinard, "Child Abuse and Neglect," and Barbara Star, "Domestic Violence," both in *Encyclopedia of Social Work*, vol. 1, pp. 226, 468-69.

24. Lillian B. Rubin, *Worlds of Pain* (New York: Basic Books, 1976), pp. 70-71.

25. Thomas Keefe has written extensively on the theme of empathic understanding of the economic stresses on family life. See "The Economic Context of Empathy," *Social Work*, vol. 23 (November 1978), pp. 460-66 and "The Stresses of Unemployment," *Social Work*, vol. 29 (May-June 1984), pp. 264-69.

26. Ann Hartman, "Diagrammatic Assessment of Family Relationships," *Social Casework*, vol. 59 (October 1978), pp. 465-76.

27. Monica McGoldrick and Randy Gerson, *Genograms in Family Assessment* (New York: Norton, 1985), p. 5.

28. Maggie Scarf, *Intimate Partners: Patterns in Love and Marriage* (New York: Random House, 1987), p. 8. The story of "the Bretts," illustrated with the development of their family genogram, is told in Part I, pp. 27-100.

29. McGoldrick and Gerson, *Genograms in Family Assessment*.

30. Scarf, *Intimate Partners*, p. 40.

31. Herbert S. Strean, *Resolving Marital*

Conflicts: A Psychodynamic Perspective (New York: John Wiley and Sons, 1985).

32. Ibid., pp. 10–22.

33. Ibid., pp. 19–20.

34. American Psychiatric Association, *Diagnostic and Statistical Manual of Mental Disorders*, 3rd ed. rev. (Washington, DC, 1987).

35. Strean, *Resolving Marital Conflicts*, p. 43.

36. Evelyn Duvall was one of the first sociologists to describe the family as a unit or system. See her *Marriage and Family Development*, 5th ed. (Philadelphia: J. P. Lippincott, 1971), p. 145.

37. Elizabeth A. Carter and Monica McGoldrick, "The Family Life Cycle and Family Therapy: An Overview," in E. Carter and M. McGoldrick (editors), *The Family Life Cycle: A Framework for Family Therapy* (New York: Gardner, 1980), pp. 3–20.

38. Ibid., p. 10.

39. Ibid., p. 12.

40. David McWhirter and Andrew M. Mattison, *The Male Couple: How Relationships Develop* (Englewood Cliffs, NJ: Prentice-Hall, 1984), pp. 14–18.

41. Fernando Colon, "The Family Life Cycle of the Multiproblem Poor Family," in Carter and McGoldrick, *Family Life Cycle*, pp. 343–81.

42. C. J. Falicov and B. M. Karrer, "Cultural Variations in the Family Life Cycle: The Mexican American Family," in Carter and McGoldrick, *Family Life Cycle*, pp. 383–425.

43. Wesley R. Burr, Geoffrey K. Leigh,

Randall D. Day and John Constantine, "Symbolic Interaction and the Family," in W. R. Burr, R. Hill, F. I. Nye, and I. L. Reiss (editors), *Contemporary Theories about the Family*, vol. 2 (New York: Free Press, 1979), pp. 78–84.

44. Morton Deutsch and Robert M. Krauss, *Theories in Social Psychology* (New York: Basic Books, 1965), pp. 175–77.

45. Burr, Leigh, Day, and Constantine, "Symbolic Interaction and the Family," pp. 78–84.

46. David Cooper, *Death of the Family* (New York: Vintage Books, 1970).

47. Philip Wexler, *Critical Social Psychology* (Boston, MA: Routledge and Kegan Paul, 1983), pp. 141–56.

48. Ralph LaRossa, *Conflict and Power in Marriage: Expecting the First Child* (Beverly Hills, CA: Sage Publications, 1977), pp. 105–14. The reader may also wish to read pp. 103–51.

49. Randall Collins, *Sociology of Marriage and the Family: Gender, Love and Prosperity* (Chicago: Nelson-Hall, 1985), p. 26.

50. Ibid., p. 39.

51. Randall Collins, *Conflict Sociology* (New York: Academic Press, 1975), pp. 221–28.

52. Joseph H. Pleck, "Men's Power with Women, Other Men, and Society: A Men's Movement Analysis," in R. A. Lewis (editor), *Men in Difficult Times* (Englewood Cliffs, NJ: Prentice-Hall, 1981), pp. 234–44.

53. Collins, *Conflict Sociology*, pp. 259–60.

54. Ibid., p. 260.

PART IV

The Individual as a System

CHAPTER 11

Psychological Well-Being

M AJOR THEMES DISCUSSED IN THIS CHAPTER:

1. Domains of *psychological well-being*. The psychological well-being of the individual includes emotional, cognitive, and behavioral functioning. Psychological well-being has been studied in terms of abnormal functioning, or mental disorders, and in terms of normal functioning, or normality.

2. *The study of abnormality: Mental disorders.* The *Diagnostic and Statistical Manual* of the American Psychiatric Association is used widely in mental health settings. Its strengths and limitations for studying well-being are discussed.

3. *The study of normality.* The study of normality is in its infancy. Normality can be defined as average, health, utopia, or transaction.

4. *Toward an integrated approach to normality.* Normality is the outcome of transactions between individuals and between individuals and their social environment. It is a social construction of reality which changes according to cultural, historical, interpersonal, and personal processes. Transactions can lead to abnormality or to normality as average, health, or utopia.

5. *Normality and the disabled.* As a result of interpersonal transactions, the social reality of people with disabilities is changing from abnormal to normal. The physically disabled are distinguished from the developmentally disabled.

6. *Implications for practice.* In order to accomplish the task of assessing the psychological well-being of clients, social service workers must have knowledge of what constitutes normality. Part IV takes the utopian approach to the study of psychological well-being, focusing on the full human potential.

I N THE systems perspective, individuals are seen as systems comprised of biophysical and psychological domains (see Chapter 2). They are bounded by their skin and other phenotypical attributes, which gives them a distinct and recognizable appearance. They also are bounded by such psychological attributes as character, personality, and sense of self. They are socially bounded as well, set off from others by their names, which identify them as individuals, and their positions, which identify the roles and statuses they occupy within a family, a group, a community, or a society.

This chapter serves as an introduction to Part IV and the extremely complex issue of psychological well-being. In the primary social service task of assessing the psychological well-being of clients, thorough knowledge is required of the affective, cognitive, and behavioral subsystems in the psychological domain of the individual. These subsystems, which also are referred to as domains in their own right, are intimately interrelated and cannot be understood without consideration of all three. In order to be able to promote psychological well-being in clients, the concept of normality also must be studied and understood.

DOMAINS OF PSYCHOLOGICAL WELL-BEING

Psychological well-being may be defined in terms of a number of domains of functioning, primarily the affective or emotional, the cognitive, and the behavioral. **Emotional well-being** is related to the emotional structures and processes in the inner life of individuals, their motivations, needs, drives, feelings, attitudes, and interests as they are played out in specific situations or as they are internalized into character and personality. Emotional processes may also include interpersonal attitudes, perceptions, skills, and behavioral intentions toward others. **Cognitive well-being** is concerned with intellectual functioning and the processes involved in obtaining knowledge and becoming aware of the self and the environment. Cognition refers to such things as perception, memory, thinking, imagination, judgment, reasoning, language, and intelligence. **Behavioral well-being** can be narrowly defined in terms of the things people do or can do, their activities and abilities for action. Behavioral well-being also encompasses interpersonal skills and processes.

While each of these psychological domains can be conceptualized independently of the others, the differences among them are easily blurred. For instance, morality may be understood as cognitive (thinking morally), emotional (feeling guilt, remorse, or shame), and behavioral (acting morally). For social service workers, the trouble of individual clients can cut across all the domains of well-being. A mother receiving public assistance may have emotional difficulties, for instance, but she may also be unable to perform certain tasks and have a limited intellectual capacity. The domains of well-being are also highly interdependent, each influencing the other and collectively making up the psychological functioning of the individual as a whole. How we feel is influenced by how we think and how we behave.

The most usual distinction made in connection with any domain of individual functioning has to do with the relative normalcy of the individual. Thus clients may be seen as basically normal and therefore not in need of service, or they may be seen as falling short, or at least in danger of falling short and therefore in need of service. The criteria by which such determinations can be made are found in the two major approaches to the study of psychological well-being. One is through the study of abnormal functioning, that is, **abnormality**, or mental disorders, and the other is through the study of normal functioning, that is, **normality**.

THE STUDY OF ABNORMALITY: MENTAL DISORDERS

A widely used tool for assessing normality in individuals is the *Diagnostic and Statistical Manual of Mental Disorders* developed by the American Psychiatric Association. This manual is based on an international system for the categorization of diseases which was developed by the World Health Organization. Early editions were not very successful, but the third edition, informally known as the *DSM-III*, has achieved widespread use in the United States. A revised edition, the *DSM-III-R*, was published in 1987.[1]

The *DSM* describes mental disorders and other symptoms which may not be disorders but for which psychiatric treatment may be sought. A number of major diagnostic categories of disorders are identified in the *DSM-III-R* (see box, Major Diagnostic Categories). For each disorder the manual lists the essential features, prevalence, the likely age of onset, the sex ratio, the familial pattern, predisposing factors, the likely course of the disorder, and any physical impairments or other complications that may be associated with it. Individuals who are not normal, according to the manual, are characterized by behavioral and psychosocial functioning which conforms to one or the other of the identified disorders. Thus, the *DSM* offers relatively specific criteria for determining psychosocial ill-being.

The *DSM* allows for a fairly complex assessment of individual functioning. Through the development of a **multiaxial system**, it encourages the assessment of not just the disorder for which treatment is sought, or the **presenting disorder**, but also other aspects of psychosocial functioning. Diagnosticians make five diagnoses, one for each of the following axes:

1. Axis I, an assessment of the mental disorder or condition that is the focus of treatment.
2. Axis II, an assessment of any personality disorders or specific developmental disorders that may exist along with the mental disorder.
3. Axis III, an assessment of any physical disorders and conditions that may be present.

4. Axis IV, an assessment of the severity of the psychosocial stressors being experienced.
5. Axis V, a global assessment of the highest level of adaptive functioning at the present and during the previous year.

By requiring diagnosticians to pay attention to other circumstances than the clinical disorder alone, the multiaxial system supplies a more holistic picture

MAJOR DIAGNOSTIC CATEGORIES

The *Diagnostic and Statistical Manual of Mental Disorders* published by the American Psychiatric Association provides a vast and highly detailed categorical system for use in the diagnosis and study of abnormal behavior. The 14 major categories in the third revised edition and examples of the disorders in these categories are as follows:

1. Disorders usually first evident in infancy, childhood, or adolescence — mental retardation, eating disorders, autism, attention-deficit disorders.
2. Organic mental disorders — dementia, substance-induced disorders, delirium.
3. Psychoactive substance-use disorders — substance abuse and dependence.
4. Schizophrenic disorders — schizophrenia.
5. Delusional (paranoid) disorders — paranoia.
6. Mood disorders — bipolar disorder (mixed, manic, or depressed); major depression
7. Anxiety disorders — phobias, anxiety states, post-traumatic stress disorder.
8. Somatoform disorders — psychogenic pain disorder, hypochondriasis.
9. Dissociative disorders — psychogenic amnesia, multiple personality.
10. Psychosexual disorders — gender identity disorders, fetishism, transvestism, inhibited sexual desire.
11. Factitious disorders — artificially produced disorders with psychological or physical symptoms.
12. Sleep disorders.
13. Impulse-control disorders — pathological gambling, kleptomania.
14. Adjustment disorders.

Source: American Psychiatric Association, *Diagnostic and Statistical Manual of Mental Disorders*, 3rd ed., rev. (Washington, DC, 1980).

of people seeking treatment. And, because it is a medical manual, the *DSM* promotes the ideal that the organic basis of a problem in living must be ruled out before psychological and social causes can be considered.

EVALUATION OF THE DSM-III

The *Diagnostic and Statistical Manual* is valuable because it contributes to better communication among mental health professionals, leads to comprehensive assessments and effective treatment, and is useful as an educational tool.[2] The strength of the manual is that it lists relatively clear, concise, and standardized categories of the abnormal behavior, something that few other approaches to the study of individual behavior, not even a systems approach, are capable of doing.

Social service workers do not all accept the manual, however. It has been criticized as a tool for negative labeling, for instance. Francis Turner believes that social workers should take an anticlassification position: They cannot altogether avoid the use of labels, but they should avoid their misuse and negative consequences for clients. Diagnostic categories like those in the *DSM* make clients appear one-dimensional, stereotype them, encourage self-fulfilling prophesies, emphasize problems rather than strengths, and may not always be based on adequate theoretical or empirical support.[3] Florence Lieberman charges that many of the childhood disorders listed in the *DSM-III* are not based on extensive research and are not appropriately treated by psychiatry. She suggests that it is culturally insensitive, excludes psychodynamic formulations, neglects humanistic approaches, and fosters a "cookbook" approach to assessment.[4]

Herb Kutchins and Stuart Kirk note that many social workers who do not endorse the manual and its medical focus nevertheless use it because *DSM* diagnoses are required for reimbursement by insurance programs. They suggest, in fact, that social workers who use the manual may be led to adopt unethical practices and run the risk of being the target of malpractice suits; they are likely to fail to follow the diagnostic procedures and to assign arbitrary diagnostic codes. As a result, Kutchins and Kirk believe that social workers will eventually be driven out of the mental health field. The conclude that the *DSM* is good neither for clients (especially children) nor for social work.[5]

One major reason for the success of the *DSM-III* is its reputed reliability. Earlier editions of the manual were marred by imprecision in the use of the categories. If five psychiatrists applied the manual to the same client, each was likely to arrive at a completely different diagnosis. In the *DSM-III*, tests were reported which indicated that this lack of reliability was no longer likely to occur. The American Psychiatric Association claimed that if the manual were used properly, quite acceptable levels of reliability would result.

In a recent review of the literature, however, Kutchins and Kirk assert that most of the studies on which the claim of reliability rests are highly suspect.

They contend that although the *DSM-III* may indeed produce highly reliable diagnoses, there is no good evidence that this, in fact, is the case.[6] Obviously the question of the reliability of the *DSM-III* is the subject of considerable controversy which is not likely to be resolved for some time. In the *DSM-III-R*, the newest edition, however, no chapter on the reliability of diagnoses is included, so it can be assumed that the American Psychiatric Association believes reliability is a dead issue, and no further proof is necessary. In the light of the Kutchins and Kirk review, this is indeed an unfortunate conclusion.

The *Diagnostic and Statistical Manual* may or may not be a useful tool to social workers. In any case, we will not use it here as the basis for teaching about normality. In addition to the criticisms noted, the manual is insufficient preparation for social workers on the subject of psychosocial well-being. It is a manual of disorders with no particular point of view on well-being or on human behavior. The manual lists the conventional wisdom, derived from the experiences of psychiatrists and to a lesser degree from more objective research, on what is problematic in human behavior, or abnormality. It has no coherent view of what might be right in human behavior, or normality.

THE STUDY OF NORMALITY

Knowledge of normality is still in its infancy, and no simple definitions can be stated. In studying normality, the complexity of the concept must be appreciated, and as much as possible an understanding of what it means to be psychologically normal must be developed. A good deal of caution must be exercised by social service workers in applying ideas about normality to their clients.

At least four different definitions of normality have been advanced, each with very different implications about well-being. Daniel Offer and Melvin Sabshin have described these as normality as average, normality as health, normality as utopia, and normality as transaction or transactional systems.[7]

NORMALITY AS AVERAGE

The concept of normality often is stated in terms of a statistical principle. On a bell-shaped or **normal curve**, normality is depicted as the center of the bulge at the top of the curve or some range around that center. The center can be described as the **mean**, an average score or standing; as the **median**, the point where 50 percent of the scores fall above and 50 percent fall below; or as the **mode**, the most common score or standing. The range around the center is often described in terms of scores around or **standard deviations** from the mean. For instance, normal intelligence is usually defined as an IQ score somewhere between 100 and 130. Individuals who score somewhat below 100 are said to have low, although normal, intelligence, and those who score below 70 are considered to be "retarded." Individuals who score somewhat above 130 are seen as "precocious" and those who score above 160 as "geniuses." Individuals at both extremes are suspect, since they are not like most everybody else but are either too dull-witted or too intelligent and therefore not normal.

The idea of **normality as average** pervades much of the research literature on individual well-being. Middle-class people feel normal because they are neither too rich nor too poor. People feel emotionally stable when they are neither seriously depressed nor seriously hyper or manic. Those who vote for moderate political candidates feel socially normal in that they are not extremists of the reactionary right or the radical left. People who are of average height and weight are normal — not too tall, not too short, not too fat, not too skinny. People with names like Steve and Brad and Cindi and Lori are normal because they do not stand out like people with names such as Rosario and Rafael, or Eiko and Kenji.

Pros and Cons

Normality defined as an average is a useful concept in making assessments of individual functioning. Humans, being social animals, can take comfort in the knowledge that they are "just like everybody else." Averages can also serve as relatively objective standards which help people evaluate how they are growing and maturing. Normality as average is the basis of much research on human behavior and development. Developmental psychologists in particular have used it to plot expected markers in biological maturation and psychological development. In child development, it is important to know when children are likely to cut their first teeth, walk, talk, control their bladders, and so on (see box, Normal as Average). In adult development, it is important to know the likelihood of physical and intellectual deterioration.

But there are many times when normality as average is not a helpful concept. It has a conformist connotation, and sometimes an intolerant one. Whatever is not average, not normal, is considered bad or deviant. Thus girls who do not like to play with dolls, or boys who are left-handed, or teenagers who like classical music, or unmarried single adults, or grandmothers who are interested in sex are made to feel out of step, presumably not like everybody else. Many people feel good about being just like everybody else, though some like to think of themselves as different, usually a little better than everybody else. Normality as average is the basis for social norms under which diversity is scorned and neutrality or conformity is championed.

NORMALITY AS HEALTH

The term *normality* often is used in a medical or psychiatric context to signify a positive level of individual functioning which usually is described not as some optimum level but as the absence of pathology or illness. Offer and Sabshin call it a "*reasonable* rather than an *optimal* state of functioning."[8] The *Diagnostic and Statistical Manual* is an application of the idea of **normality as health**, or the absence of pathology. The concept of normality as health is often used as the basis of studies of social indicators of personal satisfaction and happiness, as well as epidemiological studies of mental health.[9] **Epidemiological studies** examine the incidence and distribution of a disease, illness, or personal or social problem in a population. Often, patterns are studied by examining official records. Perhaps the most famous and earliest epidemiological study using this technique was the work of Emile Durkheim on suicide in Europe in the nineteenth century.[10] In the twentieth century, epidemiological techniques were used to trace the relationship between place of residence in a city and the distribution of first admissions to mental hospitals.[11]

More recently, sophisticated survey techniques have been introduced to examine the incidence of mental illness among the noninstitutionalized population. Beginning in 1979, the National Institute of Mental Health (NIMH) began funding a five-year program to provide information on the prevalence of specific mental disorders in the population and estimates of the number of people in need of mental health services. It was estimated that some 15 percent of the American population had some mental disorder, as defined in the *Diagnostic and Statistical Manual*, and in the other 85 percent there was an "absence of a diagnosable disorder." Estimates of the number of mentally healthy people "at risk" of some mental disorder indicated that a significant proportion — some 30 to 50 million people — would "experience a stressful life event that immobilizes their capacity to cope."[12] Results of the NIMH Epidemiologic Catchment Area Program, a survey conducted over several years in the early 1980s, were released in full in 1988. More than 18,000 adults were interviewed in households in New Haven, CT, Baltimore, St. Louis, Los Angeles, and Durham, NC. Answers to detailed, carefully constructed questions indicated that in a given six-month period, approximately one out of five Americans (more than 19 percent) was suffering from some type of major mental health problem. Of those with diagnosable mental problems, only 17 percent said they had seen a mental-health professional.[13]

Pros and Cons

Normality as health is the most common approach to normalcy used by social service practitioners. It acknowledges the debilitating potential of stressful life events and the relatively high proportion of the population that does not have psychiatric symptoms. The pragmatic approach provides a basis for using reasonable and specific criteria in making diagnoses, and research such as the NIMH-sponsored programs has fostered improved mental health services.

There are some difficulties with the concept, however. When measuring physical health, some adequate level of functioning is relatively easy to describe. Health is the absence of a fever or a virus or some other incapacitation. In relation to mental health, however, adequate functioning is much more difficult to describe, since it involves any number of biological, psychological, and social considerations.

Some psychological disturbances such as schizophrenia may indeed be biological in origin and therefore lend themselves to notions of health and illness. Other disturbances seem far more social or psychological in their origins, and it is only the meanings attached to the behaviors that cause some to be designated as health and others as illness. Thus some social scientists have pointed out that the language of health and illness ought to be replaced by the idea of **problems in living.**[14] In this view, health and illness are labels applied by

NORMAL AS AVERAGE: PHYSICAL CHANGES AND MOTOR DEVELOPMENT THROUGH CHILDHOOD

Age	Physical Changes	Motor Developments
1st Year (birth to 12 months)	Weight and height: The average child weighs about 7 pounds at birth and is about 20 inches in length. By the end of the first year, an average child weighs between 21 and 24 pounds and is about 29 inches in height. Feeding: From 5 to 8 times a day to 3 regular meals plus snacks; teeth begin to erupt. Sleeping: From 20 hours a day to about 12 hours, plus naps. Sensory: From learning to use oral and visual modes of exploration to greater differentiation and control of these modes. It takes about a year to develop normal vision. Mortality: Males have higher mortality rates than females during the first year. Lower-class black infants have about twice the mortaily rate of white infants.	Development of control over various portions of the body; turning head, lifting head, turning body, purposive grasping, apposition of thumb and forefingers, sitting up, crawling, climbing up low furniture, cruising (walking with support). Black children are a little larger than whites, and they tend to mature somewhat sooner.
2nd Year (12 to 24 months)	Feeding: Able to grasp objects (finger-thumb apposition), to feed self. Sleeping: About 13 hours at night, 1 long daytime nap. Sensory: More hand-eye coordination, as in drawing on paper.	High level of activity: walks, creeps upstairs and down; jumps, both feet; seats self in chair; turns pages, several at a time; runs; other gross motor skills in play. Basic control of body is complete: bladder control—dry during day; capable of bowel control. Feeds self.
3rd Year (25 to 36 months)	Sleeping: About 12 hours at night, some short naps.	Continued high-level activity; jumps; is able to ride a tricycle. Helps to dress him/herself.

more powerful people to less powerful people when they cause more discomfort than the powerful are willing to endure.

Normality as health also is related to the idea of **psychological survival.** The literature on social work often focuses on developing clients' skills at **coping** and **adaptation**, to help them survive difficult situations, endure stress, and deal with the problems of contemporary life. Indeed, many people regard themselves as doing good if they are just surviving. An ability to survive the

Age	Physical Changes	Motor Developments
4th Year (37 to 48 months)	No significant differences in height and weight between the sexes.	Dresses him- or herself. Increasing large muscle control and some small muscle control. Eye-hand coordination developing. Brushes teeth.
5th Year (49 to 60 months)	Muscles growing more rapidly than rest of body. Appetite is usually good.	Mature motor control, with increasing developments in small muscle movements.
6th Year (61 to 72 months)	Eruption of first permanent teeth. General growth continues. Appetite good. Sensory: About one fifth of all children have some visual problems; another 3 percent have hearing impairments.	Very active physically, but still clumsy; apt to have accidents. Works hard in sports but tires easily.
7th to 11th Year	Beginnings of physical differences of the sexes: Onset of prepubescence (accelerating growth) in girls (about 10 years) with boys starting later (around 12). Wide variations in developments within and between the sexes. Ages 9-12 often the healthiest because lymphoid masses (which fight infection) have reached their maximum (about twice adult amount), vigorous activities, eating, etc.	More integrated and coordinated motor activity. High expenditure of energy and experimentation with new skills. Shows poise. However, half a million children between 6 and 11 years have accidents on bikes, swings, and skateboards, requiring emergency room visits.

Source: Reprinted with permission of Macmillan Publishing Company from *Life Span Development* by Martin Bloom. Copyright © 1985 by Martin Bloom.

hardships of life is undeniably important, but the emphasis on survival also implies that people cannot be and should not be expected to be in control of social circumstances and their own lives. The emphasis on coping and adapting also can be taken to mean that social reality must always be accepted, and societal conditions and situations can never be changed.[15] Perhaps the best example of this kind of thinking has been done by William Glasser. He asserts that normality is best thought of as responsible behavior, and this requires an acceptance of reality and a willingness to meet personal needs within the constraints of that reality. According to Glasser:

> . . . our basic job as therapists is to become involved with the patient and then get him to face reality. When confronted with reality . . . he is forced again and again to decide whether or not he wishes to take the responsible path. Reality may be painful, it may be harsh, it may be dangerous, but it changes slowly. All any man can hope to do is to struggle within it in a responsible way by doing right and enjoying the pleasure or suffering the pain that may follow.[16]

The concept of adaptation, which derives from the European psychoanalytic literature, became a central concept in the United States when ego psychology was imported by psychoanalysts escaping Nazi Germany. It has nevertheless been characterized as a very American concept: "In the United States, ego psychologists made their goal of psychotherapy a reflection of the culturally encouraged virtue of fitting in — getting the patient to adapt to the environment.[17] Thus normality, defined as adequate functioning or absence of disorder, may not always be an acceptable criterion for judging psychological well-being.

In many ways the concept of normality as health is not too different from the concept of normality as average. By focusing on the absence of illness rather than some optimal level of functioning, researchers are obviously using some notion of average. The World Health Organization and other commissions attempting to define health have been opposed to definitions that promote reasonable and adequate functioning. These groups would prefer to define health in more positive terms, as the enhancement of health or as "a state of complete physical, mental and social well-being."[18]

NORMALITY AS UTOPIA

The idea of **normality as utopia** is an attempt to state a maximum level of human functioning. It goes beyond averages and adequate functioning to envision realization of the full psychological potential of human beings. Thus it may be seen as unworkable, of interest to dreamers but not to researchers, clinicians, and other serious students of human development and behavior.[19] In many ways the difference between normality as health and normality as utopia is one of degree. Those with utopian visions of normality call for the development of more than the ability to cope and adapt to social reality. They espouse development of the ability to create new and more positive realities.

Much of the literature on human behavior fits this definition of normality. For instance, social service practice theory has begun to emphasize the notion of individual competence, which derives from the work of Robert W. White and other egopsychologists.[20] Competence sets a higher standard for assessing coping and adaptation because the individual is expected to go beyond survival toward mastery of social reality. **Competence** is defined in both objective and subjective ways. Objectively, it is the capacity, based on cumulative experiences, to interact effectively with the environment. Subjectively, it is the perception that one has accumulated the strengths and abilities required to control one's destiny.

Another concept that fits a utopian vision of normalcy is that of **empowerment**: The individual must confront social situations which are oppressive or which distort psychological well-being and gain power or control over them. Elaine Pinderhughes defines **power** as the "capacity to influence the forces which affect one's life space for one's own benefit." She believes that the ultimate goal of social workers ought to be helping clients exert power in a way that enables them to obtain the resources to meet their needs. Social work treatment should give people "the ability and capacity to cope constructively with the forces that undermine and hinder coping, the achievement of some reasonable control over their destiny."[21]

Some humanist psychologists go further than notions of empowerment. Abraham Maslow introduced a theory of human behavior in which self-actualization is the highest need motivating human behavior.[22] First there are basic human needs that enable survival, such as the needs for food, clothing, shelter, and safety. Maslow refers to these as **physiological needs** and **safety needs.** Unless these basic human needs are satisfied, the individual will strive for nothing more; all attention will be focused on organic survival. Once these survival needs are satisfied, the individual can strive to fill the **need for belongingness and love.** Behavior is motivated by the need for friendship and the intimacy and love of family members and lovers. As these needs are met, **esteem needs** can be addressed. These needs are expressed in terms of self-esteem, "the desire for strength, for achievement, for adequacy, for mastery and competence, for confidence in the face of the world, and for independence and freedom," and in terms of the esteem of others, "the desire for reputation and prestige . . . , status, dominance, recognition, attention, importance, or appreciation."[23] Finally, individuals who have achieved self-esteem can turn their attention to the **need for self-actualization**, or self-fulfillment, "the desire to become more and more what one is, to become everything that one is capable of becoming."[24] Thus realizing one's potential is the ultimate human need.

The important point, according to Maslow, is that only when the more basic survival needs have been met will individuals begin to sense and be able to satisfy the higher-level needs for esteem and self-actualization. Needs exist in a hierarchy, often pictured in the form of a pyramid with survival needs at the base and self-actualization needs, the ultimate goal of normal human beings, at the pinnacle (see box, Maslow's Hierarchy of Needs). As William Glasser and Leonard Zunin put it:

> Maslow believed most individuals have a capacity for creativeness, spontaneity, caring for others, curiosity, continual growth, the ability to love and be loved, and all other characteristics found in self-actualized people. A person who is behaving badly is reacting to the deprivation of his basic needs. If his behavior improves, he begins to develop his true potential and move toward greater health and normalcy as a human.[25]

Radical theorists go even further, introducing the notions of **freedom** and **liberation**. Eric Fromm, for instance, wrote about the oppressiveness of free-market, industrial societies, arguing that they are dehumanizing and inculcate

MASLOW'S HIERARCHY OF NEEDS

In Abraham Maslow's needs theory, behavior is motivated by needs or values which are related to one another in order of their strength and priority, in a manner which is both heirarchical and developmental. Gratification of a lower-level need opens the individual's consciousness to the next higher-level need. Thus self-actualization, the level at which the individual's highest potential can be realized, cannot be addressed until physiological, safety, belongingness and love, and esteem needs have been satisfied in turn.

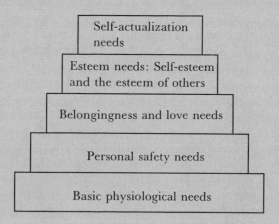

Source: Abraham H. Maslow, *Motivation and Personality* (New York: Harper and Row, 1954), and "Synergy in the Society and in the Individual, "*Journal of Individual Psychology,* vol. 20 (1968), pp. 153-64.

authoritarian needs, destructiveness, and conformity. In such societies individuals are unable to liberate themselves; they have a fear of freedom from which they cannot escape. Rather than defining normality in terms of ability to fulfill social roles in a society, Fromm sees normalcy "as the optimum of growth and happiness of the individual."[26] In his view, individuals should aspire to ultimate liberation from the demands of oppressive social circumstances.

Pros and Cons

The concept of normality as utopia has all kinds of problems. Pragmatists will note that the visions are dreamlike. Researchers will note that the visions are vague and difficult to make sufficiently concrete for study; they are not easily stated in ways that enable them to be measured. Sociologists will note that there is no consensus among the visions, and that they represent the interests of particular theorists and particular ideologies. They may even be labeled as *theoreticomorphism*, or the tendency of researchers to idealize the goals of human behavior in terms of their own theories.[27]

Yet this vision of normality as utopia is noble. It suits critical social service practice because it rejects the status quo of reality and encourages striving for the best possible world and the best possible place in it for humans. Although the concept is vague and means too many things to too many people, this can be seen as a strength, not a shortcoming. Utopian visions represent the human spirit in its highest form of creativity.

Normality as Transactional Systems

All of the definitions of normality mentioned so far stress particular characteristics or traits of individuals; the average individual, the adapting individual, the competent, empowered, or liberated individual. **Normality as transaction** starts with the premise that humans are social systems embedded in social contexts. Normality therefore is not a characteristic of an individual but a characteristic of the *interaction* between individuals and their environments.

The transactional point of view combines some of the notions of the other definitions yet arrives at a unique understanding of human well-being. As with normality as health, it recognizes that there is an intrinsic limit to individual well-being. Humans are a social animal and cannot exist without other people. Other people have their needs as well, and therefore people's needs often are in conflict. A built-in tension exists in all human interaction, a tension between the quest for one's own well-being and the quest for the collective well-being. Normality as transaction is not an egocentric, or personal, vision of well-being. It stresses that personal normality requires a collective search for the common good.

Normality as transaction is unique in its separation from egocentric visions of normality, but it also suggests that environments must be normal. In this respect it is much like the utopian visions. It suggests that it is not always necessary to conform to other systems making up a social environment, and these systems have certain responsibilities for meeting the needs of individuals who must deal with them. Besides making demands on people, environments ought to supply opportunities for well-being, for justice, for autonomy and self-control, and for equitable outcomes.

The conflict among the needs and interests of individuals and their environments is real and can be seen daily in social work practice. A father comes in and wants the social worker to make his son, Bruiser, obey, that is, to do what the father thinks is important. The social worker talks with Bruiser and finds that he has some legitimate gripes about his father and would like to enlist her support in getting his father to be a "better man." Or the police bring in Ophelia and expect the worker to stop her from a life of prostitution; that is, to conform to the accepted image of a woman. After talking with Ophelia, the worker realizes that women with little education and very limited legitimate economic opportunities do not think they are in need of change. Or John and Mary seek help because they cannot deal with the pressure they are getting from their parents; they want support for their decision to live together without a marriage license.

As these examples suggest, there are differences between conformity to others and the conformity of others. In numerous cases, social service workers earnestly believe that people should conform, for their own well-being and that of the society. None would justify murder as a way of liberation from the anti-murder norms of society. Most would insist that employers and landlords conform to laws and regulations prohibiting discrimination against women and minorities. There are also many cases where social service workers earnestly believe that society should conform to individuals' expectations about rights and opportunities. Most believe that it ought to be possible for women to share the occupational status and pay men can achieve. Most also would not insist on respect for traditional expectations about the role of husband and wife; they would not expect all women to stay home, mind the children, and care for their working husbands.

When conflicts in the needs and interests of individuals exist, mediation in the form of negotiation and compromise is often required. In this process the concern is for the **goodness of fit**, or the fit between the person and the environment. The role of the social service worker is to negotiate the boundary, that is, the line between individuals and the expectations of others.

TOWARD AN INTEGRATED APPROACH TO NORMALITY

Normality as average, as health, and as utopia are three independent yet not completely distinct **types of normality**. They all can have their uses in the assessment of psychological well-being, and often they are combined in an **eclectic approach**. The notion of normality as transaction refers not so much to a type of normality as to a **source of normality**. Individuals become or achieve normality as a function of transactions that take place between them and their social environments. Transactions between individuals and environments, therefore, generate all three types of normality. As a result of transactions with others, an individual may turn out to be normal; or, like most others, surviving without any serious disorders; or near perfect (see box, Normality: Source, Domains, and Types).

THE TRANSACTIONAL CONTEXT OF PSYCHOLOGICAL NORMALITY

Normality is a social construction of reality. What is average, what is healthy adaptation, and what is utopian are all defined by individuals in their interaction with other individuals in the context of groups, families, communities, and organizations. David Karp and William Yoels point out that

> the sense or intelligibility of interactions depends on the meanings individuals attribute to their environments. The perceived meanings of behaviors are always liable to revision as individuals piece together information about themselves and others and the arenas in which they interact. The social world cannot be seen as independent of people's definitions of it.[28]

Thus, according to Karp and Yoels, "The existence of shared meaning structures or a common definition of social reality must be assumed, but everyone does not construct an identical version of reality."[29]

A focus on the transactions between individuals and other individuals in the context of groups, families, communities, and organizations demonstrates that many aspects of normality are quite variable, differing according to cultural traditions and historical periods, interpersonal expectations, and indeed particular persons. Psychological normality, whether defined as average, health, or utopia, is a social construction of reality which changes from culture to culture, from one historical moment to the next, from one specific interpersonal situation to another, and from one person's thoughts and beliefs to another's.

NORMALITY: SOURCE, DOMAINS, AND TYPES

Source of Normality	Domains of Normality	Types of Normality		
		As Average	As Health	As Utopia
Transactions with others	Cognitive	Like most others	Without disorder	Near perfect
	Emotional			
	Behavioral			

As such, there are no behaviors, emotions, or beliefs, in and of themselves, that are inherently normal or, for that matter, abnormal.

The Influence of Culture

Standards of normal, expectable behavior vary from society to society and, within a particular society, from community to community. Examples of such social norms or standards are the age at which toddlers are expected to walk and talk, the age at which young people are expected to engage in sexual intercourse and become financially independent, and the age at which adults are expected to retire from work. Other expectations govern such areas as personal self-fulfillment and autonomy, normal male and female behavior, and the care and treatment of the elderly and infirm. Even such seemingly abnormal behavior as having hallucinations and talking to spirits is not always defined as abnormal in a particular culture.

The Influence of History

Standards for evaluating normalcy change over time within a culture. In each public debate over each social problem, new definitions of normalcy are developed. Before marijuana and other drug laws came into existence, it was not considered abnormal to be addicted.[30] The recent attention to the issue of child abuse has generated new definitions about the normal way for adults to respond to the children under their care.[31] Laws, traditions, norms, and mores change from generation to generation, in a continual although not necessarily progressive process of separating the normal from the abnormal.

Interpersonal Influence

Face-to-face experiences such as family relationships, friendships, and work group interactions also contribute to the definition of standards of normal behavior. Couples establish goals and expectations for themselves, for their partners, and for their relationships. These expectations reflect not only cultural and historical influences, but the very personal solutions of the individuals involved. Thus it is not unusual for one couple to reject traditional gender-role stereotyping while another accepts it fervently, not as something imposed from the outside but as their own free choice. Studies of the expectations of families with children demonstrate this clearly. Parents vary widely in their tolerance of children's behaviors. Some have very narrow definitions of the characteristics of a good child, while others have extremely tolerant definitions.[32] In the study of infant behavior it is not unusual to find a tendency to **adultomorphism**, or imputing adult attributes and experiences to the behaviors of children. This is done in both negative terms, imputing evil intentions, and in positive terms, idealizing the infant as representing a lost adult innocence.

The Person

Each individual in the course of life develops her or his own sense of what it means to be normal. By sorting through their experiences with others and listening to their own needs and attitudes, individuals define their own goals. These may include desirable levels of economic success, interpersonal success, and personal satisfaction and competence. Individuals develop their own values and attitudes about what they expect of themselves and others. Their definition of the situation, including their role in it, is a crucial element in their psychological well-being.

NORMALITY AND THE DISABLED

The normality of the disabled seems to be a contradiction in terms. A physically, cognitively, or emotionally disabled person, by definition, would appear to be deficient in health and to vary from statistical averages. Yet because of interpersonal transactions currently taking place in groups, families, communities, and organizations, a new social construction of reality is taking form which is reshaping American culture. In contemporary society, the belief that normality must be redefined to include people with disabilities is gaining strength.

The term *disability* is itself a social construction of reality; just what is and is not a disability is an issue that is being openly debated in contemporary society. Two overlapping types of the disabled have been identified. **Physically disabled** people have any kind of physical impairment brought about in any way.[34] Medical definitions consider as physically disabled those who have experienced "chronic disease leading to various courses of treament" and those who suffer from postpolio complications, cerebral palsy, epilepsy, and so on.[35] Thus the physically disabled can include people who have suffered from accidents and are not able to complete certain physical functions connected with work and everyday living, or people who have experienced an illness or a birth-related defect which has left them chronically impaired. **Developmentally disabled** people have severe and chronic disabilities which are attributable to mental as well as physical impairments, which are manifested before the person attains 22 years of age, and which are likely to continue indefinitely.[36] Developmental disabilities may include severe, moderate, and mild forms, but usually only the more serious handicaps require intervention. Nevertheless, developmental and physical disabilities both can limit individuals' abilities in the areas of self-care, receptive and expressive language, learning, mobility, self-direction, capacity for independent living, and economic self-sufficiency.

In the recent past, people with disabilities were essentially cut off from society. Labels such as *invalid* or *crippled* were applied as a way of indicating their status as abnormal. In definitions today, the more likely argument is that people with disabilities make up minority or disadvantaged groups which experience systematic prejudice and discrimination:

In the psychosocial model, disability is related to society. It is not taken for granted that medical illness, economic definition, or functional limitation by themselves say what is significant about disability. Rather, what is significant can be revealed only by the ecological framework in which the disabled person exists, by the interactions through which society engages a disability, by the attitudes that others hold, and by the architecture, means of transportation, and social organization constructed by the able-bodied.[37]

As a consequence of changing social definitions, people with disabilities now are being **mainstreamed**, or included with people of normal capabilities in the mainstream of society. Instead of being segregated in a protective environment, they are being viewed as capable of performing within the range of normalcy in classrooms, workplaces, and living arrangements.[38]

IMPLICATIONS FOR PRACTICE

When individuals seek assistance from social service workers, they most often are concerned with personal difficulties which involve social and psychological functioning. Voluntary clients usually express their own concerns: They feel bad about themselves, they have done things they regret, they are unhappy with a social relationship, they want to improve their economic situation, and so on. With involuntary clients, the concern is usually expressed by others and may be denied by clients whose behaviors and attitudes have been judged by others to be inappropriate. In some instances social service workers reach out to clients who may not be demonstrating serious personal difficulties. This type of service, in the form of both primary prevention and early intervention, is usually predicated on the assumption that the prospective clients are **at risk** of experiencing personal difficulties.

Regardless of how clients and social service workers come together, a principal task of the worker is to make an assessment of the psychological well-being of the client in three interrelated domains: affective or emotional, cognitive, and behavioral. The responsibilities associated with that task require serious attention to the study of normality.

One approach to this study is through the medical model articulated in the *Diagnostic and Statistical Manual of Mental Diseases* published by the American Psychiatric Association. The medical model is not used in this book. While the diagnostic categories in the manual have proven useful to some social service workers, there is evidence that they lack reliability. More important is the manual's failure to provide a theoretical basis through which human behavior can be understood or a positive vision of what constitutes psychological well-being. It presents lists of ill-being without guidance as to what constitutes well-being.

There are no easy answers to the question of what constitutes well-being, however. A fruitful way to approach the subject is through the concept of normality. Three distinct but overlapping ways of defining normality are to view it as average, as health, or as utopia. Normality, furthermore, is an outcome,

Physically disabled people have many unrecognized abilities. How many abled people could play basketball in a wheelchair? *Charles Gatewood/Stock, Boston.*

a result of transactions among people in a particular culture and at a particular moment in time. An example of historically based cultural, interpersonal, and personal change is the status of people with disabilities in contemporary society. Disabled people, who used to be thought of as abnormal, are increasingly being mainstreamed into society and included in the idea of normal.

In assessing the well-being of individual clients, social service workers need to examine the transactions taking place between individuals and their social environments. They must ask, "In what ways do these transactions lead to emotional, cognitive, and behavioral normalcy in clients?" As they think about normality itself, they must sort out and integrate the meanings of the term and use the meaning most appropriate to their situation. Normality as average forces workers to think about how their clients compare and should compare with other people. Normality as health forces workers to think about how their clients are able to cope, adapt, and survive and maintain themselves free of debilitating conditions. Normality as utopia forces workers to think about the full potential for growth and development in their clients.

In the remaining chapters of Part IV, a utopian approach will be taken to the study of psychological well-being. Although no one view of normality is inherently better than another, the utopian vision seems to be the best for purposes of critical analysis. Focusing on the full human potential takes into consideration the **pragmatic**, what is probable and possible, as well as the **ideological**, what is the maximum to be expected. In social service practice, the pragmatic is likely to win out, since the task is to help clients when they need it and in the best way possible. By highlighting a utopian view, however, the torch can be lit for progress through individual change and, utimately, social reform.

DISCUSSION QUESTIONS AND CLASS PROJECTS

1. Describe three domains of psychological well-being. In your work with clients, is one type more salient than others?

2. Identify the following:
Diagnostic and Statistical Manual
physically disabled
developmentally disabled
normal as average
normal as health
normal as utopia
normal as transaction

3. Describe the multiaxial system around which diagnoses are performed using the Diagnostic and Statistical Manual.

4. What do social workers regard as the contributions and limitations of the Diagnostic and Statistical Manual?

5. Identify professional social workers in your area who are working in a mental health setting. Interview them about their experiences in using the DSM. Ask them what they think are the uses and limitations of the DSM.

6. Describe the four meanings of normality described in this chapter. Give examples of each.

7. What do you see as the strengths and weaknesses of each meaning of normality?

8. Distinguish between a type of normality and a source of normality.

9. From a transactional point of view, what are four considerations that need to be taken into account in assessing the psychological well-being of a person?

10. Can you explain the box, Normality: Source, Domains, and Types? How might it be useful in helping you think about assessing the psychological well-being of a person?

11. Are you acquainted with any disabled individuals? Do you think they see themselves as normal or as abnormal? Do you think they would rather be separated from others or mainstreamed?

12. Are you familiar with any programs for the disabled in your community? If not, identify programs for the physically or developmentally disabled and see if you can arrange to talk to someone who understands the program intimately. Determine what their policies are with respect to their clients. Do they try to shelter their clients or mainstream them?

NOTES

1. American Psychiatric Association, *Diagnostic and Statistical Manual of Mental Disorders*, 3rd ed. (Washington, DC, 1980), and 3rd ed., rev. (Washington, DC, 1987).

2. See Janet B. W. Williams, "Diagnostic and Statistical Manual," in *Encyclopedia of Social Work*, 18th ed., vol. 1 (Silver Spring, MD: National Association of Social Workers, 1987), pp. 389–93.

3. Francis J. Turner, "Mental Disorders in Social Work Practice," in F. J. Turner (editor), *Adult Psychopathology: A Social Work Perspective* (New York: Free Press, 1984), pp. 1–5.

4. Florence Lieberman, "Mental Health and Illness in Children," in *Encyclopedia of Social Work*, vol. 2, p. 114.

5. Herb Kutchins and Stuart A. Kirk, "DSM-III and Social Work Malpractice," *Social Work*, vol. 32 (May–June 1987), pp. 205–11.

6. Herb Kutchins and Stuart A. Kirk, "The Reliability of DSM-III: A Critical Review," *Social Work Research and Abstracts*, vol. 22, (Winter 1986), pp. 3–13.

7. Daniel Offer and Melvin Sabshin (editors), *Normality and the Life Cycle: A Critical Integration* (New York: Basic Books, 1984), pp. xii–xiii.

8. Ibid, p. xii; italics in original.

9. See Gerald L. Klerman and Myrna M. Weissman, "An Epidemiologic View of Mental Illness, Mental Health, and Normality," in Offer and Sabshin (editors), *Normality and the Life Cycle*, p. 341.

10. Emile Durkheim, *Suicide* (New York: Free Press, 1951).

11. R. E. L. Faris and H. W. Durham, *Mental Disorders in Urban Areas: An Ecological Study of Schizophrenia and Other Psychoses* (Chicago: University of Chicago Press, 1967).

12. Klerman and Weissman, "Epidemiologic View of Mental Illness," pp. 328, 331, 333.

13. *Chicago Tribune Magazine*, February 25, 1989, pp. 27–29.

14. Thomas Szasz, *The Myth of Mental Illness* (New York: Harper and Row, 1961).

15. Christopher Lasch, *The Minimal Self: Psychic Survival in Troubled Times* (New York: W. W. Norton, 1984).

16. William Glasser, *Reality Therapy* (New York: Harper and Row, 1965), p. 41.

17. Daniel Offer and Melvin Sabshin, "Patterns of Normal Development," in Offer and Sabshin (editors), *Normality and the Life Cycle*, p. 412.

18. Daniel Offer and Melvin Sabshin, "Implications and New Directions," in Offer and Sabshin (editors), *Normality and the Life Cycle*, p. 428.

19. This idea is expressed in Bennett L. Leventhal and Kenneth Dawson, "Middle Childhood: Normality as Integration and Interaction," in Offer and Sabshin (editors) *Normality and the Life Cycle*, p. 31.

20. Anthony N. Maluccio, *Promoting Competence in Clients: A New/Old Approach to Social Work Practice* (New York: Free Press, 1981). Some of the writings of Robert W. White are "Motivation Reconsidered: The Concept of Competence," *Psychological Review*, vol. 66 (September 1959), pp. 297-333, and "Competence and the Psychosexual Stages of Development," in M. Jones (editor), *Nebraska Symposium on Motivation* (Lincoln: University of Nebraska Press, 1960), pp. 97-141.

21. Elaine B. Pinderhughes, "Empowerment for Our Clients and for Ourselves," *Social Casework*, vol. 64 (June 1983), pp. 331-38.

22. Abraham H. Maslow, *Motivation and Personality* (New York: Harper and Row, 1954), pp. 80-92.

23. Ibid., p. 90.

24. Ibid., p. 92.

25. William Glasser and Leonard M. Zunin, "Reality Therapy," in R. J. Corsini (editor), *Current Psychotherapies*, 2nd ed. (Itasca, IL: F. E. Peacock Publishers, 1979), p. 305.

26. Eric Fromm, *Escape from Freedom* (New York: Avon Books, 1965), p. 159.

27. See Robert N. Emde and James F. Scorce, "Infancy: Perspectives on Normality," in Offer and Sabshin (editors), *Normality and the Life Cycle*, p. 4.

28. David A. Karp and William C. Yoels, *Sociology and Everyday Life* (Itasca, IL: F. E. Peacock Publishers, 1986), p. 37.

29. Ibid., p. 38.

30. See Howard S. Becker, *The Outsiders* (New York: Free Press, 1963), pp. 135-46.

31. Stephen J. Pfohl, "The Discovery of Child Abuse," *Social Problems*, vol. 24 (February 1977), pp. 310-23.

32. For a discussion of a specific study see Bennett L. Leventhal and Kenneth Dawson, "Middle Childhood: Normality as Integration and Interaction," in Offer and Sabshin (editors), *Normality and the Life Cycle*, p. 32.

33. Emde and Scorce, "Infancy," p. 4.

34. William Roth, "Disabilities: Physical," in *Encyclopedia of Social Work*, vol. 1, pp. 434-48.

35. Ibid., p. 434.

36. Lynn McDonald-Wickler, "Disabilities: Developmental," in *Encyclopedia of Social Work*, vol. 1, pp. 422-34.

37. Roth, "Disabilities: Physical," p. 434.

38. Emde and Scorce, "Infancy," p. 21.

CHAPTER 12

Interpersonal Well-Being: Behavioral and Marxian Theories

MAJOR THEMES DISCUSSED IN THIS CHAPTER:

1. *Behavioral theories: Social exchange and learning.* Our investigation of a critical utopian transactional approach to the study of individual psychological well-being begins with consideration of behavioral theories of human social interaction. Both social exchange and learning theories are based in classical economic theory and view the individual as self-interested, rational, and motivated by utilitarian and hedonistic values.

2. *Learning theories.* Learning theories describe the processes by which behavior is learned, maintained, and unlearned. Three approaches have influenced social work practice: classical conditioning, operant conditioning, and social learning theory. Although learning theories can be described as transactional, they offer no utopian vision of normal human behavior.

3. *Social exchange theory: Equity.* Social exchange theory uses an image of economic exchanges in the marketplace to study human social interaction. Individuals are self-interested and attempt to maximize their rewards and minimize their costs in interaction with others. When people judge that there is an inequity between the rewards they are achieving and the costs they are incurring, they are likely to feel angry and aggrieved. These feelings lead them to seek what they perceive to be equity and fairness in transactions with others. Implications for practice deriving from exchange theory are discussed.

4. *Marxian theory: Exploitation and alienation.* Marx believed that humans

are not by nature egocentric and self-interested but had become so as a result of the development of capitalism as a social institution. Capitalism encourages people to exploit one another and produces alienation, and exploitation and alienation require efforts at resolution. Marxian theorists believe these effects can only be overcome by struggling against the forces that promote them and by substituting the value of equality. Implications for practice deriving from Marxian theory, including social service workers' own feelings of alienation and attempts to resolve them, are discussed.

ALL OF THE perspectives on normality examined in Chapter 11 have their strengths and weaknesses, and none can be used without consideration of the others. Two of these perspectives are especially appropriate to the objectives of this book, however. A critical perspective on social service practice requires a *utopian vision,* the formulation of goals and objectives which lead to social and human progress. And a systems approach requires a *transactional vision,* in which the source of normality is seen as the relationship between person and environment (see the box, Person in Environment, in Chapter 2).

In this chapter and the next we will apply a **utopian transactional approach** to the study of individual, psychological well-being. Four social psychological frameworks which focus on the interaction between individuals and their environments will be described. These are the behavioral, Marxian, structural functional, and symbolic interaction theories. The other two chapters of Part IV deal with ego psychology and the complementary theory of cognitive development, which also offer a utopian vision. Their particular vision is that as people age they can continually develop their psychological capacities (see box, Theoretical Frameworks and Utopian Visions of Well-Being).

All these five perspectives are transactional because they look at person in environment, but the first four make the environment more explicit than ego psychology does. In ego psychology, the environment is a subjective reality, a perception in the minds of people. In the others, the subjective experience of the environment is important but only as it follows from concrete experiences with other people. Thus the environment is also conceptualized as an objective condition which must be understood in its own terms. For this reason, behavioral, Marxian, structural functional, and symbolic interaction theories tend to be concerned with interpersonal well-being, the well-being of individuals as they interact with others as members of specific groups. This makes these approaches not only useful when the client is an individual but when the client is a small group such as a family or a larger group such as an organization or a community. Ego psychology, in contrast, tends to be concerned with intrapsychic or intrapersonal well-being and thus is useful largely when the client is an individual.

The four social interactional frameworks discussed in Chapters 12 and 13 are useful in understanding all the transactional processes which were described in Chapter 2: recruitment, socialization, interaction, innovation, and social control. The focus here, however, will be on the interactional, that is, on the continual, overarching process through which individuals influence one another and social systems are shaped and reshaped. Thus, in looking at interaction we are in effect looking at all of the transactional processes.

The four social interactional frameworks are also important for social service assessment and intervention planning, because they can help workers understand problems that occur in the transactions between clients and their social environments. Each provides a unique utopian vision about how normal social transactions ought to take place in groups, families, organizations, and communities. Behavioral theory incorporates both learning theory and social exchange theory. The first utopian vision is presented in the discussion of social exchange, which sees the problems that arise when the rewards emanating from relationships are inequitable and calls for a search for equity and fairness. Marxian theory points to the problems of exploitation and alienation and calls for building relationships free of them. Structural functionalism sees the prob-

THEORETICAL FRAMEWORKS AND UTOPIAN VISIONS OF WELL-BEING

The theoretical frameworks concerned with the study of individual, psychological well-being include four social-interactional theories and ego psychology. Each has a particular utopian vision of how human progress is to be achieved.

THEORIES	UTOPIAN VISIONS
Behavioral theory Social exchange	Equity and distributive justice
Marxian theory	Equality and the absence of alienation and exploitation
Stuctural functionalism Anomie	Consensus and shared values
Symbolic interactionism Labeling	Mutual self-respect and the absence of labeling
Ego psychology	Development across the life course

lems that arise when people do not conform to social norms and calls for equal opportunity in the pursuit of socially desirable goals. Symbolic interactionism locates perfection in relationships that generate self-esteem for all members.

BEHAVIORAL THEORIES: SOCIAL EXCHANGE AND LEARNING

The origins of the concept of **social exchange** lie in early economic theory.[1] The elements of contemporary theories of social exchange can be found in the work of Jeremy Bentham, Adam Smith, and other classical political economists. The basic proposition is very simple: "an individual will act in a certain way if the consequences of doing so are pleasurable and refrain from doing so if the consequences are painful."[2] Behind this simple proposition, however, lie some not so simple and even debatable assumptions about human nature. The proposition assumes that humans are self-interested, rational creatures operating primarily from utilitarian and hedonistic, or pleasure-seeking, motives. As will be pointed out, some social psychologists do not accept these assumptions.

Social exchange theory is not the only one in contemporary psychology that shares these underlying assumptions of human nature. Learning theory, including social learning theory, also views the individual as self-interested and rational and motivated by utilitarian and hedonistic values. Not surprisingly, learning theory also has its roots in classical economic theory. Because both social exchange and learning theories emphasize the actual behaviors of people rather than their attitudes and perceptions, they are often referred to as **behavioral theories**. John B. Watson, an American psychologist, is usually credited with being the founder of behaviorism. He proposed that the legitimate subject matter of psychology is behavior, not mind or consciousness.[3]

LEARNING THEORIES AND PRINCIPLES OF LEARNING

Learning theories, which are predicated on the idea that most human behavior is learned as a function of transactions between individuals and their social environments, devotes a good deal of attention to deciphering the principles under which learning takes places. These theories have contributed three important concepts: classical conditioning, operant conditioning, and social learning. Classical, or respondent, and operant conditioning are the two major transactional processes by which people learn, either through responses to external or environmental stimuli or through responses which operate on the environment. Social-learning theory attempts to explain individual behavior, including personality characteristics, on the basis of classical and operant conditioning but also on the basis of cognitive processes.

CLASSICAL CONDITIONING

Classical conditioning derives from the work of Ivan Pavlov, a Russian phys-iologist who worked out its basic principles.[4] The idea of respondent or **classi-cal conditioning** is that when a neutral stimulus is repeatedly paired with an-other stimulus which normally elicits a particular response, the neutral stimulus itself will begin to elicit a similar response and thereby become learned or conditioned. In Pavlov's famous experiments, a hungry dog was shown meat and began to salivate. The meat acted as an **unconditioned stimulus** because it naturally produced salivation, an **unconditioned re-sponse**. Then a bell was rung shortly before the meat was shown to the dog. Normally the sound of the bell would not produce salivation, but because it had been paired with the sight of food, the bell alone became sufficient to gener-ate salivation in the dog. The bell became the **conditioned stimulus**, and sali-vation became the **conditioned response** (see box, The Classical Conditioning Process).

The ideas involved in classical conditioning have led to the development of two important therapeutic techniques, systematic desensitization and aversion therapy. **Systematic desensitization** is often used to treat phobias (fears) and anxiety, which are believed to develop through classical conditioning. A neu-tral experience (getting on a plane, having sexual intercourse, washing one's hands) becomes associated with an experience that previously had produced fear or anxiety (having knowledge that a plane had crashed, believing that it will not be possible to arouse a partner or pregnancy could result, being ac-cused of sloppiness or dirtiness). The treatment technique then is to desensitize or **countercondition** the person through the use of relaxation, so that fear and anxiety are no longer associated with the experience.[5]

Aversion therapy is used to eliminate a conditioned but unwanted or un-desirable behavior. It has been used to treat addiction to substances such as alcohol and cigarettes, as well as sexual addictions such as homosexual and transvestite (cross-dressing) behavior. Since the undesirable behavior is be-lieved to have come about through association with some positive stimulus, the treatment involves associating the behavior with a negative stimulus. The usual technique is to pair the behavior with electric shock, nausea-inducing chemicals, or aversive symbols. Despite some claims of success, aversion ther-apy is not used a great deal today.[6]

OPERANT CONDITIONING

Operant conditioning derives from the work of Watson and B. F. Skinner, an American psychologist who differentiated between learning through classical conditioning and learning through instrumental or operant conditioning.[7] In **operant conditioning** a neutral response is operated upon by a **reinforcing stimulus** to produce a particular response. For instance, if a pigeon receives

THE CLASSICAL CONDITIONING PROCESS

Ivan Pavlov was director of the physiological laboratory at the Institute of Experimental Medicine in St. Petersburg, Russia, until his death in 1936. While working on the digestive system, he devised an experimental apparatus which made it possible to measure the amount of saliva secreted by dogs when food was placed in their mouths. His observation that dogs in the apparatus began to salivate at the sight of the attendant bringing the food, or even at the sound of his footsteps, led to his statement of the principle of classical conditioning, an important phenomenon in explaining how the organism learns and adapts to its environment. The classical conditioning experiment included the following steps in the conditioning process:

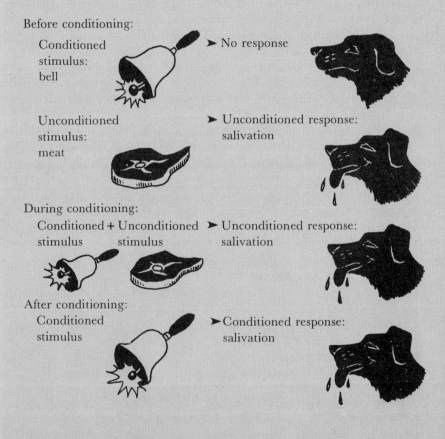

Before conditioning:

Conditioned
stimulus:
bell

➤ No response

Unconditioned
stimulus:
meat

➤ Unconditioned response:
salivation

During conditioning:

Conditioned + Unconditioned
stimulus   stimulus

➤ Unconditioned response:
salivation

After conditioning:

Conditioned
stimulus

➤ Conditioned response:
salivation

Source: Adapted from Dan G. Perkins, "Classical Conditioning: Pavlov," in G.M. Gadza, R. J. Corsini, and contributors, *Theories of Learning* (Itasca, IL: F. E. Peacock Publishers, 1980), pp. 35-36.

a food pellet (the reinforcing stimulus) each time it touches a lever (the desired response), in due time the pigeon begins to act as if it knows that by touching the lever it can obtain food. The pigeon has learned that the lever response produces a reward.

Shaping occurs when the subject is reinforced for approximating the desired response. Since it might take months for the pigeon to touch the lever in the first place, the behavior is shaped or encouraged by rewarding **successive approximations**, behavior that comes closer and closer to the desired result. The food pellet is released further each time the pigeon gets closer to the lever, but only when the pigeon actually touches the lever does it get the food.

Positive and Negative Reinforcement

Behaviors are increased or learned to the extent that they are reinforced, either positively or negatively. In general, the more a behavior is reinforced, the more it will be repeated. To increase a behavior through **positive reinforcement**, a favorable event or outcome is applied to the behavior, such as giving a reward each time the behavior is exhibited. To increase a behavior through **negative reinforcement**, an undesirable event or outcome is removed, such as taking away a punishment when the behavior is discontinued.

Determining exactly what is reinforcing can be a problem. Certain events are almost always reinforcing, such as giving food or water to a hungry or thirsty person. Other events do not work as readily as reinforcers. Practitioners attempting to use reinforcement techniques may be asked to conduct an empirical test, either observing clients to determine what normally reinforces their behavior or interviewing them about their likes and dislikes.[8]

At some point a positive or negative reinforcer is likely to stop being useful in eliciting a behavior. **Satiation** is said to occur when "so much of a reinforcer is provided that it no longer increases behavior that follows it." If the goal is to increase a response, therefore, a positive reinforcer should be chosen which will not be tired of easily. If the goal is to decrease a response, one strategy is to offer so much of a positive reinforcer that it fails to be effective.

Punishment and Extinction

Unlearning occurs in a number of ways. In **punishment**, an aversive stimulus is made contingent on a behavioral response; the stimulus will be administered if the undesirable behavior persists. Certain conditions must be met if punishment is to eliminate a behavior, however. First, since the initial reaction to punishment is likely to be escape or avoidance, the reinforcing environment must be made escape-proof. Second, punishment is only effective when it occurs at the same time as the undesirable response; a punishment that is not associated with the response will not be of any use. Third, punishment must be severe enough. It is often impossible to meet all these conditions in everyday life. If a father punishes a child for smoking, for instance, it is unlikely that the child will actually stop smoking. More likely, the child will attempt to escape further detection by smoking behind the father's back and without his knowledge.

A form of punishment which is often used in work with children is "time-out," whereby undesirable behavior is punished by making the child spend a short time alone. During the time-out interval, the child is not receiving any reinforcements and also is not able to commit the undesirable behavior.[10]

Because the conditions under which punishment is likely to be effective often cannot be met, extinction is preferred by many learning theorists as the way to eliminate unwanted behaviors. In **extinction**, reinforcement of a behavior is discontinued; a previously rewarded response is no longer rewarded. If the pigeon has been rewarded with a food pellet for pressing the lever, it no longer receives a pellet when it presses the lever. If the child has been rewarded with parental affection and attention when it has a tantrum, the affection and attention are withdrawn when a tantrum starts. Extinction is not automatic and, depending on how the rewards were administered in the first place, it may be difficult. Parents using extinction techniques to eliminate undesirable behaviors in their children must be extremely patient and must be sure not to administer rewards that have reinforced such behaviors.

Social-Learning Theory

In explaining the development of personality characteristics and social behavior, **social-learning theory** gives particular attention to processes of imitation and vicarious acquisition. In human learning, particularly, such laborious processes as shaping do not seem to capture the way learning takes place. When we learn to drive a car, for instance, we are not shaped or rewarded each time we approach a car, sit in it, touch the steering wheel, put a key in the ignition, and so on. Humans have a capacity for **vicarious acquisition**; from their observation of others who take the role of **models**, they can blueprint complex series of behaviors, think about the models and their behaviors, and make choices about **imitation** as a way of acquiring those behaviors. Thus we learn to drive pretty much by observing how others drive and imitating what they do. Similarly, children can learn prosocial or antisocial behavior by observing and imitating parents, peers, and even television shows.

Classical and operant conditioning theories of learning have been described as "empty-headed" approaches to human behavior because they make no room for psychological processes. They assume no psychological mediating functions, no cognitions, motivations, attitudes, identity, or personality beyond some basic hedonistic and utilitarian need to seek rewards. The learning in classical conditioning assumes a completely passive subject. In operant conditions it assumes that rewards and punishments supplied by the environment in and of themselves produce behavior. In this sense they are transactional only in the most minimal sense.

Social-learning theory is different. Since its origins, it has allowed for cognitive processes and thereby established that learning takes place regardless of rewarding or punishing consequences.[11] Albert Bandura, a leading proponent of social learning, conducted interesting laboratory experiments to determine whether awareness of the reinforcement of a model affects imitation of the model's actions by others. In one study, three groups of children saw a model misbehaving. One group saw the model being punished for his actions; the second group saw the model being ignored; and the third group saw him being rewarded for his actions. Later the imitative behaviors of the children who had observed the model were recorded. The group that had seen the model rewarded exhibited the most imitative behaviors, while the group that saw him punished exhibited the least. Then, without any further training, the children were told that they would be rewarded if they could demonstrate the behavior of the model. All of them, regardless of the group they were in, were equally able to imitate the behavior.[12] As this experiment demonstrated, learning involves cognitive processes and should be distinguished from behavioral responses alone, which are more likely to be controlled by incentives.

Cognitive Processes in Behavioral Responses

In social-learning theory, behavioral responses are recognized as a function of the processes of attention, retention, production, and motivation, in addition to rewarding and nonrewarding consequences.[13] The cognitive process of **attention** is the starting point; learning cannot take place unless the observer is aware of the models and the events being modeled. Not only the personal and social attributes of the models but the unique characteristics of the events being modeled affect the level of attention given by the observer. More attention is paid when the events are distinct, novel, salient, and somewhat complex. Characteristics of the observer such as the capacity to be aroused, personal needs, and perceptual readiness also influence the level of attention.

Social learning also requires the cognitive process of **retention**, the ability to store information observed and remember it when necessary. This process includes organization and such symbolic processes as **rehearsal**, that is, going over the event and the things learned from it in the mind.

Behavioral production processes are the third dimension in social learning. **Production** refers to the process of converting the retained information, cognitively stored and rehearsed, into action. The observer must have the ability to pull together all the components of the behavior and the physical capacity to actually recreate the behavior. The observer also must have the ability to judge the correctness of recreated behavior and learn from mistakes, through self-evaluation or feedback from others.

Social learning ties in with operant conditioning in the fourth dimension, **motivational processes**. This kind of learning does not require reinforcement; people can store much more information than they ever convert into behavior. But reinforcement, either from within or without, supplies the motivation for the actual performance of a behavior. External incentives to behave include tangible rewards such as money and social rewards such as approval and praise. Internal self-incentives include the tangible rewards individuals give themselves and the positive self-evaluation they feel in doing something they want to do.

The role the individual has in regulating her or his own behavior has recently been recognized as a component of social learning. As Bandura notes, "People do not behave just to suit the preferences of others. Much of their behavior is motivated and regulated through internal standards and self-evaluative reactions to their own actions."[14] The capacities to observe the self, to judge the self, and to react to the self allow for self-regulation.

Social service practitioners need to examine these four cognitive processes in order to assess why a client fails to behave in a particular way when supposedly the client has learned that behavioral response. The behavior may not have been attended to adequately, retained adequately, carried out adequately, or motivated by reinforcement from others or the client's self-evaluation.

SOCIAL EXCHANGE THEORY: EQUITY

Social exchange theory is a behavioral approach which shares the assumptions about individuals' utilitarian and hedonistic motives with all three learning theories discussed in the preceding section. Like social learning, it incorporates a more elaborate understanding of cognitive and motivational processes than classical and operant conditioning do. In all social exchange approaches, the connection with learning principles is clearly evident. Nevertheless, **social exchange theory** differs significantly from learning theories in that it focuses specifically on interactions between individuals and their social environment. Most often, a "person" is in interaction with an "other," and the person and the other form a dyad, that is, they are two individuals who may in turn be interacting within the context of groups, families, communities, or organizations. The concept of social exchange has also been applied to study the interactions between organizational elements in a society, or relationships between organizations, between units of an organization, or between communities. Thus social exchange theory is more in keeping with a systems (transactional) approach than learning theories are, because it looks at the interaction between one system or element of a system — group, community, family, or individual — and another. Furthermore, social exchange differs from learning theories in that it offers a clearly utopian vision about what exchanges should be like. It says that unless exchanges are fair, social interaction will falter. Learning theories are content to describe the processes by which behaviors are learned, maintained, or unlearned, without taking a step into critical theory. They offer no utopian vision to social service workers.

Social exchange theory has been the basis of considerable research on individual and group behavior, but it has not had the impact on social service practice that learning theories have had, and this is unfortunate. Nevertheless, it has been systematically applied to study of the family, the relationship between some clients and the social services they receive, and the interaction be-tween social worker and client.[15] It is a theory, therefore, that has considerable potential in social service practice.

THE MARKETPLACE ANALOGY AND THE SYSTEMS APPROACH

Social exchange theory uses an analogy of the economic marketplace in inves-tigating human social interaction. The basic idea is that individuals approach social interaction with the expectation of maximizing their own rewards while minimizing their own losses. All interactions, therefore, involve self-interested, profit-and-loss calculations, as each individual attempts to gain as much as possible at minimum cost. Thus as people exchange rewards, they try to profit from one another. Upon entering a social interaction, each person cal-culates her or his possible interpersonal **profits**, or **payoff**, for the interaction by subtracting the expected **costs** from the likely **rewards** (see box, The Calcu-lation of Interpersonal Profit in Interactions).[16] Something like the following process is believed to take place in the mind of each participant: If I do such and such, I am likely to give up such and such (costs) but I am also likely to obtain such and such (rewards) in return. If I tell you I care about you, I am likely to feel embarrassed but I am also likely to learn that you care about me. Thus, since your friendship is important to me, the embarrassment I will suffer in making my feelings known is well worth it.

Social exchange is a systems approach because the actual outcomes or payoffs individuals obtain are a result of the bartering and negotiating that take

THE CALCULATION OF INTERPERSONAL PROFIT IN INTERACTIONS

In social exchange transactions, each individual calculates the possible costs to be paid and profits to be gained by entering the transaction. The calculation can be expressed as follows:

Interpersonal profit = Rewards to be obtained − Costs to be incurred

The rewards in such transactions can be intrinsic or extrinsic to the situ-ation; unilateral or reciprocal, involving just one participant or both; and entering directly into the interaction or deferred. The costs can be direct costs, with an immediate payoff; investment costs, with a long-term re-turn; or opportunity costs, the cost of giving up other alternatives when one is chosen.

Source: Peter M. Blau, *Excahnge and Power in Everyday Life* (New York: John Wiley, 1964).

place in the transactions between individuals and others in the social environment. The person and the other have behavioral control over one another, which can be differentiated from fate control or autonomous control. In **fate control**, the other is totally in control of the outcomes the person receives. Put another way, the person is completely dependent on the other. **Autonomous control** is the opposite of fate control; in this situation, the person is totally in control of his or her own outcomes; the other has no way of influencing the profit. Fate control and autonomous control represent extreme cases of power in interpersonal relations. For this reason, they are unusual in social interaction; it is rare for others to be able to completely determine our destiny or for us to be able to do so.

Behavior control, the more usual form of control, is what makes social exchange a systems theory. **Behavior control** refers to interpersonal situations in which each partner is able to alter the behavior of the other. The other may influence the person's outcomes in important ways, but they are also influenced by how the person responds as an individual.[17] The profits of the person and the other actually are interdependent. In other words, in most situations when you and I interact, what I do to try to maximize my rewards is as important as what you do to try to minimize my rewards and maximize your own.

INTIMATE RELATIONS AND EXCHANGE RELATIONSHIPS

There are limits to how far we can take the image of marketplace relationships into the interpersonal realm. When we think of people interacting for monetary benefit — buying and selling, owning and working, giving services for fees — it seems to make good sense. But the image is less obvious in other realms of human social interaction such as intimate relations. Many theorists maintain that deep personal relationships such as love, family life, and friendship cannot be fruitfully understood as market exchanges. Marxists and other humanists believe that family relationships, for instance, are inherently nurturing, supportive, and free of utilitarian value, though a powerful free-market economy continually threatens to force on family life the values of a capitalist market philosophy. When intimate relations do take on the characteristics of market exchanges, it is because the market philosophy has successfully invaded them (see Chapter 10).

Nevertheless, exchange theorists who have studied friendship and love in contemporary society have concluded that intimate relations make sense in terms of social exchange. To be sure, love and friendship exchanges do not work in exactly the same way as business and market exchanges. For instance, friendship may be rewarding in itself, since having a friend gives pleasure and security. Friends are not always bargaining over the need for rewards and do not expect to be paid back immediately when they give rewards. But eventually friends have to reward one another, or the friendship is likely to deteriorate and the friends will go their separate ways.

Love and family relationships operate on similar principles as friendships do, but it is much more difficult to separate the individual from the family.[18] Peter Blau and Zick Rubin, who have studied heterosexual attraction in terms of social exchange processes, have concluded that attractiveness is often measured in supply-and-demand terms. Individuals seem to be attracted to others depending on how available they are, how attractive they are to other people, how difficult they are to conquer, and the like. In courtship, the participants manipulate their scarcity value as a way of increasing their reward value. Potential love partners are less likely to invest heavily in the beginning so they do not lose too much if the relationship does not work out. People who have many opportunities for partners are less likely to make a commitment to any one partner.[19]

Even after a commitment is made in intimate relations, self-interest is apparent. Exchange theorists conclude that "selfless devotion generally rests on an interest in maintaining the other's love."[20] Ivan Nye and his associates applied social exchange theory to family life and concluded that behavioral choices made by family members follow a specific, rank-order pattern:[21]

1. Family members choose those alternatives from which they expect the most profit.
2. Costs being equal, they choose alternatives from which they anticipate the greatest rewards.
3. Rewards being equal, they choose alternatives from which they anticipate the fewest costs.
4. Immediate outcomes being equal, they choose alternatives that promise better long-term outcomes.
5. Long-term outcomes being perceived as equal, they choose alternatives providing better immediate outcomes.

THE CALCULATION OF REWARDS IN EXCHANGE TRANSACTIONS

People in social interaction exchange rewards, but rewards can mean many things to many people. Money, the most obvious reward, is often used to influence people. Gifts and prizes can be rewarding in the same way. Opportunities may also be exchanged; I will give you the opportunity to play if you give me the opportunity to rest. More usually, however, exchange transactions involve social rewards such as approval, liking or loving, or bestowing esteem, respect, or prestige. A wide range of rewards can be bartered and negotiated in interpersonal encounters.

In the marketplace, the value of rewards is more-or-less standardized. Since a monetary system is used, the value of a dollar, a pound, a peso, or a yen is standardized not only with a society but in different societies. Items are usually priced: a toaster costs $30, a worker is paid $5 an hour; a house is valued at $110,000. In human social interaction no standardized monetary system, pay scale, or price schedule exists. In such an interpersonal marketplace, how do people determine how much reward they are getting or are willing to accept or to give? Social exchange theorists explain the procedure in terms of a number of social psychological structures and processes.

George C. Homans has identified some of the processes and principles underlying the attribution of value to rewards and the effect on exchange transactions. Most of these have a commonsense meaning; the value proposition, for instance, states that "the more valuable to a person is the result of his action, the more likely he is to perform the action." In the process of supply and demand, rewards that are scarcer have more psychological value than rewards that are plentiful. To the extent that individuals have been deprived of a reward in the past, they are likely to value the reward more in the present. Conversely, the more often in the recent past individuals have received a particular reward, the less value any further unit of that reward becomes for them. This is Homans's principle of deprivation-satiation, which is built around the notion of supply and demand.[22]

Social comparison processes provide a richer understanding of cognitive and motivational processes. **Social comparison** means that people evaluate rewards and punishments on the basis of the kinds of experiences they have had. Two such processes have been described by John Thibaut and Harold Kelley. At the **comparison level**, present rewards and costs are evaluated in terms of past experiences. Thus a person accustomed to receiving substantial rewards in the past is not likely to be pleased when lower rewards are offered. At the **comparison level for alternatives**, expected outcomes in one exchange relationship are compared with opportunities to receive potentially better rewards in another exchange relationship. That is, to the extent that people have limited means for obtaining rewards, they become dependent on the relationship and willing to accept the reward, even though it might not be as great as wished.[23]

A social structure used in evaluating rewards is the individual's **reference groups**, the groups and individuals whose beliefs, attitudes, and behaviors the individual respects and is influenced by. Reference groups often supply the norms that regulate behaviors and serve as a source of comparison in evaluating individual well-being.[24] To the extent that an individual's reference groups consider a particular reward valuable, or others in these groups are accepting the same kind of reward, it is likely that the individual will find the reward valuable and will accept it.

COOPERATION, RECIPROCITY, AND FAIRNESS IN SOCIAL EXCHANGE

The marketplace image — the quest for profits — always puts the person and the other in contention. Each person (or each system) is in pursuit of his or her best interest, as measured by profit outcomes. In contending with one another, each attempts to maximize her or his power and profit over the other's power and profit. A number of strategies, both negative and positive, can be used toward these ends.[25] A negative strategy is oneupmanship, calling attention to one's indifference to the relationship and the existence of other alternatives. Another

Comparable worth is a public issue. Although women
now earn $.66 for every dollar earned by men, the
American economy is still unwilling to give equal pay
for equal work. *Reprinted with special permission of King
Features Syndicate, Inc.*

is putting down the other person by suggesting that what is being offered has minimal value. The person also can attempt to thwart the other's attempts to achieve a desired reward by raising the costs involved. On the positive side, the person can improve her or his ability to be rewarding or can create a need in the other for the rewards being offered.

With all this competition it might seem that conflict is the only possible outcome. Yet because of the behavioral control people have over one another, social exchange theorists predict that the outcome in social relationships is more likely to be cooperation than conflict. In this view, negotiation and bartering in interpersonal relations lead to stabilizing, relatively harmonious **norms of cooperation**. Cooperation is likely to be generated by **norms of reciprocity**; we treat others as they have treated us. And the **principle of distributive justice** operates to create norms of fairness, under which the participants in an interaction receive according to what they have given. As Homans describes this principle, "a man in an exchange relation with another will expect that the rewards of each man be proportional to his costs — the greater the reward, the greater the costs — and the new rewards, or profits, of each man be proportional to his investment — the greater the investments, the greater the profit."[26]

Social exchange theorists suggest at least two reasons why the norms of cooperation and fairness come to dominate in exchange transactions. First, since approval by others is an important human need, cooperation is likely to flow automatically: If I scratch your back, you will probably scratch mine. Second, when real conflicts of interest occur, the competing parties are likely to build formal rules (norms, laws, and institutions) to regulate the conflict and assure the well-being of all. Reciprocity and justice are the likely foundations for such rules.[27]

This does not mean that the society or, for that matter, interpersonal relations will be typified by stability and cooperation or that all people in the society will benefit equally from the exchanges being made. According to Blau, the more stable and cooperative some exchange relationships are, the more likely are other relationships involving the same parties to become unstable and unbalanced.[28] Moreover, nineteenth-century economic exchange theorists argued that the good society does not offer equal rewards to everybody but only gives them to the majority, in order to secure the greatest good for the greatest number. That a minority would not do well in such an exchange was not seen as a problem. Thus the classical economists, like many in contemporary society, were not concerned with helping those who come away from social exchange transactions without profits or rewards. A utopian transactional approach to the study of individual well-being derives from a different tradition, one that attempts to secure justice and fairness for all.

Equity Theory

Distributive justice has been defined in terms of the concept of **equity**, or perceived fairness in social exchange. Equity is said to exist when the benefits received by each person are perceived to be in balance with the contributions each makes (see box, Equity in Social Relationships).

In equity, social exchange theory provides a key concept for understanding the transactional problems that can emerge between individuals and their environments. When human relations are strong and stable, norms of reciprocity are likely to be operating, and each person in a transaction is likely to believe that the rewards they are receiving are just and fair. When the norms of reciprocity are not working, inequity will be perceived, and the partners in the exchange are likely to feel angry and aggrieved. According to Homans's aggressive-approval propositions:

> . . . (a) When a person's action does not receive the reward he expected, or receives punishment he did not expect, he will be angry; he becomes more likely to perform aggressive behavior, and the results of such behavior become more valuable to him. (b) When a person's action receives the reward he expected, especially greater reward than expected, or does not receive punishment he expected,

EQUITY IN SOCIAL RELATIONSHIPS

The extent to which equity is achieved in social transactions depends on the person's and the other's investment or contributions, what each puts into a transaction, as well as the person's and the other's profits or outcomes in terms of rewards and costs. Fairness is said to characterize the exchange when the outcomes of each participant match his or her investment in the following manner:

$$\frac{\text{Person's rewards} - \text{person's costs}}{\text{Person's investment}} = \frac{\text{Other's rewards} - \text{other's costs}}{\text{Other's investment}}$$

OR

$$\frac{\text{Person's outcomes}}{\text{Person's inputs}} = \frac{\text{Other's outcomes}}{\text{Other's inputs}}$$

The important measure in this equation is not whether the inputs or outcomes for the person and the other are equal, but whether the *ratios* between these factors match. In an equitable transaction, the outcomes for each participant are related to that individual's inputs, and the outcomes of all participants, their rewards minus their costs, are approximately in balance. Thus those who put more into a transaction equitably receive more from it, and equity is a relative judgment.

Source: Gerald Leventhal, "Fairness in Social Relationships," in J. Thibaut, J. T. Spence, and R. Carson (editors), *Contemporary Topics in Social Psychology* (Morristown, NJ: General Learning Press, 1976).

he will be pleased; he becomes more likely to perform approving behavior, and the results of such behavior become more valuable to him.[29]

In the theory of equity proposed by J. Stacey Adams, a sense of fairness enters into all calculations about rewards and costs in social transactions. Distributive justice, or equity, exists when both parties in an exchange come away believing that each is getting profits out of the relationship which are consonant with what they have put into the relationship.[30] When people perceive inequity in their social relationships, Adams suggests a number of changes they might make:[31]

1. They can alter their inputs of investments. If they think they are doing too much, they might reduce their efforts. If they are doing too little, they might increase them.

2. They might alter their outcomes. If they think what they are getting out of the relationship is too little, they might reevaluate their outcomes in a more favorable light.

3. As a way of reevaluating inputs or outcomes, they might alter their reference groups and individuals. Instead of comparing themselves with people who seem to be getting so much more out of relationships, they might compare themselves to people who are getting less.

4. They might cognitively distort their inputs or outcomes. People can come to misperceive the reality, seeing things not as they are but distorted, so they sense either more or less equity than actually exists.

5. They might abandon the relationship. When people do not get what they want out of a relationship, the option exists to separate and free themselves from it.

6. They might attempt to get the other person to change. The other person could be asked to increase his or her inputs or to decrease his or her expectations for reward.

All the strategies Adams proposes are designed to convert an inequitable exchange or outcome into an equitable one.

IMPLICATIONS OF SOCIAL EXCHANGE FOR SOCIAL SERVICE PRACTICE

Social exchange theory sees perfection in human social interaction, whether the interaction is in dyads, small groups, families, organizations, or communities, as involving norms of reciprocity and the principle of distributive justice. If we accept the assumption that humans are by nature self-interested, then perfection can be no more than fairness and justice, that is, equity.

Equity should not be confused with equality. Equality means that the outcomes people receive in social interaction are more or less the same. Equity allows for a good deal of inequality as a result of social transactions in which each participant's outcomes are in keeping with her or his inputs. This inequality is justified to the extent that the participants accept it as fair and just, in view of the rewards each receives minus the costs each incurs in the transaction.

Social service workers must deal with many situations in which relationships are perceived as inequitable. Working in organizations, including social service agencies, for instance, they often encounter situations in which some individuals are accused of not pulling their weight and detracting from the effectiveness and productivity of the whole. In working with small groups, social workers often hear complaints that some are contributing more to a discussion or task than others are. In working with married couples, the problem often is that one partner believes she or he is putting more into the relationship than the other one is.

In such situations, social workers can use social exchange theory to assess interpersonal relationships in terms of the degree of equity in them. In the assessment process, they can explore the ways that individual members calculate their rewards — the value they hold for the relationship or for the group, their past experiences in similar relationships, the alternatives available to them, the experiences of others whose opinions they value. If inequity is indeed found in the interaction, they can lay out the possible solutions to resolve it. In doing so, however, they will find that equity theory is not able to predict how particular individuals are likely to deal with inequity. A number of solutions are possible: distorting perceptions, reducing the amount of energy put into the relationship, trying to change the other person, leaving the relationship, even learning to accept and put up with the inequity. Nor does equity theory propose that any one solution is inherently better than another; all of them are of equal value.

In some respects this may not be of great concern. The role of a social worker who accepts the ethic of client self-determination may simply be to help clients identify inequities, offer alternative solutions, and help them achieve the solution they wish. On the other hand, many social workers believe that inequity should be resolved in favor of the aggrieved party. This value judgment is implicit in the work of Nancy Weinberg with the response of physically disabled people to perceived violations of their rights. In this research she examined autobiographies and interviewed a nonrandom sample of the orthopedically disabled. She discovered that people disabled this way believe the able-bodied violate their rights in four common ways: continual staring, intrusive questioning, unsolicited assistance, and public humiliation.[32]

In Weinberg's study, all of these acts provoked feelings of inequity in the disabled (dissatisfaction, anger, hostility, and so forth), in response to which they developed certain strategies of coping (see Chapter 14). Most of them, however, used "passive or accommodating" strategies which left them still feeling the injustice. The usual way of coping with continual staring was to ignore it; the usual way of handling intrusive questions was to respond politely, hoping to terminate the interaction; the usual way of dealing with unsolicited help was to let it pass without comment; and the usual way of responding to humiliation was through emotional displays. More assertive and even aggressive strategies were used by some, but with less frequency.

In most cases, therefore, the experienced inequity was left unresolved, unlike the outcome in the strategies proposed by Adams. Weinberg recommends the use of group intervention techniques to allow the disabled to describe their encounters with social inequity and practice ways of resolving it which would force others to respect their rights. She suggests that often people do not resolve inequity so much as they endure it, learn to put up with it, or learn not to let it bother them. When people cope with inequity in this way, the situations continue to be inequitable.

Weinberg is dismayed that the disabled generally resolve inequity in ways that leave the situation essentially unchanged. She maintains that the disabled should *require* the able-bodied to treat them with greater fairness and justice. In taking this position, however, Weinberg goes beyond exchange theory. More discussion and research obviously are needed if the role of the social worker with respect to inequity is to be understood.

MARXIAN THEORY: EXPLOITATION AND ALIENATION

Karl Marx developed his theory of social behavior in large part as a response to the ideas underlying social exchange theory. Marx was an economist schooled in the classical exchange tradition, but he criticized that tradition, dismissed it, and went on to build his own framework for understanding human behavior.

Marxian theory can be understood on a number of levels. It is most usually thought of as an attempt to understand situations at the macro or societal level involving conflict between communities of people in different economic positions and social classes. Nevertheless, Marx's theory includes a number of social psychological principles, and, as an extremely holistic theory of human behavior, it is suited to the study of individual well-being in both small and large groups.[33] As we shall see, it is particularly useful in helping social workers understand the large formal organizations or bureaucracies in which they and their clients often work.

Marxian theory promotes a particular utopian vision about well-being in which social interaction is ideally free of exploitation and alienation. Marx's own work, however, deals largely with the opposite of this ideal, the ways in which social relationships under capitalism are organized to produce exploitation and alienation.

MARX'S THEORY OF SOCIAL BEHAVIOR

Marx's ideas about human nature are more in keeping with those of contemporary **humanist psychology** than those of social exchange theory. Humanists stress the individual's worth and capacity for self-actualization through reason. Marx saw humans as an inherently social species; humans need one another not just to satisfy their self-interest, because they can profit from one another, but for the nurturing, camaraderie, and stimulation interaction provides. For Marx, the distinguishing feature of human beings is their capacity for creative, purposive activity in the company of others. Together, humans can create things and master their environment. They can take a piece of wood and whittle it into a beautiful figurine, see grass and realize its potential for wheat and bread, hear words and convert them into poetry.[34]

Marx's position on human nature nevertheless maintains some elements of the social exchange philosophy. In particular, Marx accepts the assumption that humans are rational creatures concerned with their self-interest. For Marx, however, this is a collective self-interest, the interest of others along with oneself, not egocentric, individualistic self-interest seeking to maximize personal profits and minimize personal costs.

People interacting with other people create society and its institutions. The products of their social creativity do not always turn out to be beneficial, however; sometimes humans create ideas and things that actually do them harm. For instance, Marx believed that gods are the creations of humans and often do them harm. He argues that gods did not make people in their image and likeness, as religious doctrine holds, but rather that gods were made in the image and likeness of people. Marx also believed that a product created by human creativity often is treated as if it had a life independent of its creators. Thus when gods incarnated through religious interpreters tell people what they should and should not do, people have lost control over the gods they have created.

Marx refers to the process by which social creations come to have an independent life and exert control over their creators as **reification**, or giving material properties to an abstract idea. It was his belief that the economic systems created through social processes had been reified and so were seen as human nature, and they often exerted a destructive force in social relationships. Nineteenth-century capitalism had dehumanized people and was socially destructive. While capitalism was based on exchange principles, they worked in very different ways than the classical economic theorists believed they did.

In contemporary society, the belief that "looking out for No. 1" is normal, self-evident, and does not need any particular explanation is widely accepted. Individual self-interest, even in love and friendship, is regarded as human nature. To Marx, these ideas were not human nature but evidence of the ways in which capitalism had debased the human spirit. He argues that such a marketplace, or exchange, mentality developed because as humans created capitalism, they internalized its values. These values eventually pervaded all interpersonal relations, not just those related to work and business. Thus utilitarian social exchange is not natural but is a corruption of the true creative and social nature of humans. Contemporary Marxists argue that social exchange theories are doing little more than helping to further reify and thus perpetuate the values of capitalism.[35]

CAPITALISM AS A SOCIAL RELATIONSHIP

Marx defined capitalism as a particular form of social relationship. What made capitalism unique to Marx was not its industrial technology but the way it organized interpersonal relations in the workplace. In his view, capitalism consists of the relationships among the owners and managers and the workers in businesses and industries which form the basis for social class position (see Chapter 3). The economic and social relationships of feudalism, which preceded capitalism, were different; property consisted of land owned by a lord and worked by serfs or peasants who were tied to the land by birth. With capitalism came two new classes, owners and managers on the one hand and free workers on the other. The change from serfs to free workers was a great advance which should not be discounted. The free workers, no longer tied to the land and completely beholden to a lord, could find their own employment and had the potential to better their position.

Nevertheless, Marx believed that the things that were wrong with capitalism as a social relationship were so wrong that constructive criticism aimed at improving it was not possible. Instead he proposed ruthless criticism, which could only destroy the capitalistic system.[36] Today, the difference between liberals and radicals on the political left is akin to the difference between constructive criticism and ruthless criticism. The two things Marx saw as most wrong with capitalism had to do with social relations in the workplace: They are exploitative, and they produce alienation.

Ruthless Criticism 1: Capitalism Exploits Workers

While capitalism was an advance over feudalism, Marx detected some basic contradictions or flaws in the system. One basic flaw is that it generates and depends on social inequality. Marx starts with the assumption that workers and owners contribute equally to the work process. The owner gets the money to build a canal, buys the tools, and hires the labor; these are important inputs. But the worker actually builds the canal with sweat and muscle, and this too is an important input. Marx reasons that since the owner and the worker put in equal efforts and resources, the worker's benefits — income and wealth and prestige and power — ought to equal those of the owner. If the benefits are not equal, the relationship between the owner and the worker is one of **exploitation**, in which the owner benefits at the expense of the worker. Owners get far more out of such a relationship than they put in it, while workers get much less out of it than they put in it.

This sounds like equity theory. In some ways there are differences between the concepts of inequity and exploitation, and in other ways there are not. Inequity and exploitation both are complaints that a situation is unfair and unjust. But equity theory accepts the possibility of inequality, while Marxian theory aspires to achieve equal outcomes.

Unlike most other social scientists, Marx had no illusions about being neutral in his approach. He deliberately tried to see the world from the point of view of working-class people in the nineteenth century, a time of great social and labor unrest. Conservatives at that time, more or less like conservatives today, argued that workers have no right to demand fair treatment. Since, presumably, equity existed and distributive justice and the norm of reciprocity prevailed, workers had no rational basis for complaint. If they calculated their inputs and outputs and weighed them against those of the owners and managers, they would understand that they were getting what they were worth. Marx says that the trouble with this position is that the calculation was being rigged against the workers. It was built on a **norm of negative reciprocity**, which allows some people to get more out of a situation or relationship than others, regardless of how much they put into it.[37]

While owners were trying to convince workers they had nothing to complain about, they were trying to influence the government to create laws which would lend credence to the idea that those who take the risks of starting and maintaining a business should receive greater rewards and privileges than those who only do the work. Indeed, they were quite successful. Most workers today have accepted the owners' point of view and have come to believe that owners ought to profit more than workers do. Marx argues that since workers contribute as much as owners, they should be equal in every respect; there should be no difference whatever in the rewards, privileges, and prestige gained by workers and owners. If workers are not treated as equals, they are experiencing not mere inequity, but exploitation (see box, Comparable Worth).

Ruthless Criticism 2: Capitalism Alienates Workers

Marx also argues that the social relationship between workers and owners is alienating. By **alienation** Marx means that under capitalism, free workers lose their human quality and are dehumanized. The concept of alienation refers both to the social situation in which people find themselves (an alienating situation) and to the perceptions of individuals in those situations (a feeling of being less than human). Alienation is therefore a social as well as psychological phenomenon.[38]

Marx describes four types of alienation. The first and most important is **alienation from production**. There is a contradiction in the change from serfs to free workers; they became free to find jobs and work at what they chose, but once having accepted a job they had to do as the owner or manager wished. Thus through capitalism, workers become separated from the means of production. They cannot use their human powers for creativity, because in taking jobs they give up their right to self-determination. Owners and managers tell workers what to do, when to do it, and how to do it. Workers are not supposed to reason why but simply to do as they are told.

Free workers are also alienated in that the things they produce or the services they give are not theirs and have no necessary relation to them as individuals. This is what Marx called **alienation from the product**. It is one thing to decide to build a house for one's own pleasure and another to build a house for the pleasure of somebody else. Moreover, many of the things Americans produce and the services they perform seem to be devoid of real value. This is the ultimate criticism of consumerism. As we noted in Chapter 10 in regard to the family, urged on by advertising, Americans buy endless amounts of consumer goods, trying to satisfy their "needs." They earn their living making products and providing services that do not necessarily contribute to any objective social good.

A third form of alienation Marx called **alienation from others**. Capitalism is based on free competition not only among businesses but among workers. At its best, it offers equal opportunities to all free workers, that is, equal opportunities to compete for unequal rewards. In a world of competition, the inherent social nature of humans is debased. People treat one another not as in-

COMPARABLE WORTH: INEQUITY MEETS EXPLOITATION

The issue of comparable worth in contemporary American society is relevant to both the idea of inequity as defined in social exchange theory and the ideas of exploitation and inequality as defined in Marxian theory. The concepts indeed converge and become blurred, especially in eras like the present in which definitions of fairness are being challenged.

Comparable worth has been considered to be a women's issue. On average, women do not earn as much as men even when they have the same qualifications and abilities (see Chapter 7). The pay gap is largely the result of occupational segregation under which women are limited to jobs and positions which do not pay as well as those traditionally held by men. Under Title VII of the Civil Rights Act of 1964, equal employment opportunities were to be provided to women, but they have been able to make only small inroads into the male-dominated, better-paid occupations. Comparable worth, or pay equity, is a more direct approach to occupational equality for women. The idea is that women should be paid the same as men for jobs that are not precisely equal but are comparable in skill, effort, responsibility, and social and economic value. In practice the goal is being achieved by raising pay scales for the jobs traditionally held by women in business and government.

Thus, despite arguments that supply and demand in the free-labor market ought to be allowed to dictate how much a particular job is worth, women are beginning to make their point that being paid according to their skills, qualifications, and contributions is fair and not being paid on that basis is exploitative and inequitable. Comparable worth goes beyond the well-being of women, however. The same point also applies to many minorities and working-class people. Moreover, even to a casual observer, it is obvious that the principles by which the free-market economy operates

dividuals with common human needs, equally worthy of dignity and respect, but as competitors.

The fourth kind of alienation is **alienation from the self**. Capitalism not only debases social relationships, deemphasizing love and nurturing while emphasizing competition and self-interest, it debases human nature, the essence of the individual, as well. Alienation from the self results from marketplace values which lead people to think of themselves less as humans and more as things or objects to be bought and sold (see box, Alienation from Self: Executive Packaging). Thus we become no different from a product, a machine, a cog in a wheel, a paper pusher. We wear the right clothes, say the right things,

have nothing to do with equal pay for equal work. A rock star without a high school education will make more than a senator, or a congressperson, or even a Supreme Court justice. A medical doctor with seven years of advanced education will make far more than a university professor with a similar seven years of advanced education. People with degrees in social work are unlikely to command the same salaries as people with degrees in business. The idle daughter of a multi-millionaire will acquire, simply through the accident of her birth, far more wealth than the hard-working daughter of an equally hard-working truck driver.

While the U.S. Civil Rights Commission has supported the need for equity, defined as "fair pay," "equal pay for equal work," and "equal reward for equal preparation," it stops short of advocating equality of outcome, the idea that everyone should have the same rewards. Comparable worth is a principle that is not compatible with capitalism because it challenges the norm of negative reciprocity, by which some people derive more profit in a relationship than others do. Conservatives believe that comparable worth is a move in the direction of socialism. They maintain that employees should continue to calculate their inputs and outputs based on a norm of negative reciprocity. Furthermore, salaries and wage rates should be set according to free-market principles of supply and demand. Thus a person who chooses to become a social worker rather than a business administrator or a medical doctor has no right to maintain that the salary paid a social worker is unfair.

Those who argue for the principle of comparable worth maintain that the work of women, minorities, and working-class people is often inequitably rewarded. While they do not advocate equality of outcomes, they do propose that comparable skills, effort, responsibility, and contributions should be rewarded comparably.

live in the right places, go to the right schools. We package and sell ourselves in ways we hope will increase our worth to employers and others who matter to us.

MARX'S SOLUTION FOR EXPLOITATION AND ALIENATION

Marx's critical analysis of capitalism led him to espouse an idea that he hoped would resolve the problems of exploitation and alienation. He called this idea scientific socialism to distinguish it from the other forms of socialism that were being discussed in the nineteenth century. By using the term *scientific* he meant that his solution for exploitation and alienation had been arrived at by means of scientific investigation and analysis. **Scientific socialism** is the idea that control over the economy was to be wrested from the hands of owners and placed in the hands of workers, who would then begin to set up social relationships based on equality of input and output. In the beginning phases workers would set up a socialism based on equal rights to goods and resources; norms of equal reciprocity were to prevail and people were to receive in proportion to what they contribute. In the latter phases — indeed, in a distant future — the norms of reciprocity would no longer be needed, and a communism based on "from each according to his ability, to each according to his needs" would become the prevailing norm.

The process of change would not be easy, Marx recognized, but he argued

---

ALIENATION FROM SELF: EXECUTIVE PACKAGING

The perceived need for American business executives to present themselves not as they naturally are but in the way they are expected to look is an example of how capitalism has encouraged alienation from self. The emergence of an industry of personal image consultants to help executives package themselves in the proper image for success was described in a 1985 article in *Time* magazine:

> Underneath that overweight, stuttering, bumbling, scuffed-shoe exterior there may be someone with intelligence, wit, competence and true competitive ability. But who knows unless the exterior reveals the interior? And so an industry has come along dedicated to making men and women look good on the job so they can perhaps rise to top management posts in their companies.
>
> The operative word of this business is image, and the practitioners call themselves image consultants. First seen a decade ago, they are now multiplying like reflections off a ballroom mirror . . .
>
> The stylemakers offer to shape, polish and crease almost all aspects of a person to achieve success in the corridors of corporate power . . .
>
> At fees that can hit $225 an hour, the specialists try to create a complete

that all major changes that had taken place in society had come about through conflict. Capitalists could not be expected to give up their power and control freely, since they themselves had wrested control through violence in the French Revolution and the American War of Independence. To Marx, the history of the world was a history of conflict, and alienation and exploitation had to be met head on.

His followers have since tempered Marx's support of conflict, even to the point of violence. After Marx's death, Friedrich Engels, his collaborator and friend, suggested that armed rebellion might no longer be necessary. Working-class people had made significant gains such as the right to vote without owning property, and fair-labor practices such as workers' compensation, a minimum wage, and the 40-hour week were being mandated by law.[39] Non-Marxist leaders such as Mahatma Gandhi and Martin Luther King also demonstrated that organized, nonviolent confrontation was able to bring about change.[40]

ALIENATION IN CONTEMPORARY SOCIETY

Can it be said that Marx's criticisms of social relationships under capitalism, written in the nineteenth century, still hold in the late twentieth century? He largely described the situation of factory workers in a production-oriented society. Capitalism has changed; we are now in **advanced capitalism**, described

image—from corporate hairstyle to speech—for the ambitious man or woman who is still a few tantalizing rungs from the top. Self-styled "wardrobe engineers" advise men to discard cheap ties and reject anything in polyester. Women executives are cautioned to button up at the collar and resist the current custom of walking into the office in running shoes.

Honing one's social small-talk skills is also urged. For those with no interests outside their jobs, *Image Impact for Men*, a new book, has succinct advice: "Develop some." Readers are advised that a person's face must be carefully controlled; let positive feelings show, but reveal negative ones selectively. The complete executive commands a "repertoire of effective facial expressions," writes James G. Gray, a consultant in Washington. . . .

The advisers offer "personal public relations" guidance on looking and acting like an expert in a particular field. Clients are even taught how to stand for success. John T. Molloy, one of the most successful image-makers, says that the "power stance" is with arms hanging down, feet apart, almost in a military fashion.

Source: Excerpted from John S. DeMott, "Looking Good: Consultants Polish Images," *Time*, April 8, 1985, p. 56. Copyright 1985 Time Inc. Reprinted by permission.

variously as the postindustrial state or the information society.[41] Especially in the United States, production-oriented industries have declined as service-oriented industries have proliferated. Consumption of goods, not production of goods, is now the driving force of the American economy.

Some who might accept the outlines of Marxian theory nevertheless believe that the contemporary world is so different from Marx's world that his analyses of class relations must be altered a great deal. They argue that Marxian conflict theory (conflict between worker and owner) must be completely reinterpreted in the twentieth century.[42] Others believe that although there have been many positive changes since Marx's criticisms, such as child labor laws, unemployment compensation, more white-collar and middle-class occupations, fringe benefits, social security, food stamps, and Aid for Families with Dependent Children, the basic flaws of capitalism are still evident. Capitalism is still based on exploitative norms of negative reciprocity. Capitalism still alienates people from production, from the products they produce, from others, and from themselves.

The theme of alienation is very powerful and has drawn the attention of many contemporary thinkers, Marxians and non-Marxians alike.[43] The terms that Marx invented to describe alienation are generally not used, and the concept of alienation has been broadened to include situations outside the workplace. Nevertheless, the ideas generated by Marx continue to have an influence on the thinking of social scientists.

Melvin Seaman has described how Marx's ideas on alienation have been adapted to fit contemporary life.[44] The idea of alienation from production has been redefined as **powerlessness**, people's sense that their behavior cannot determine their outcomes, that somehow they are not in control of their destiny. Barbara Solomon has defined powerlessness as the inability to manage emotions, skills, knowledge, or material resources so that effective performance of valued social roles provides personal gratification.[45]

Alienation from the product is seen in the contemporary concept of **meaninglessness**, people's feelings that they cannot make sense of the situations in which they are involved. Things don't add up; everything is routine and repetitious, without challenge. People work or study because they have to, not because they want to. Powerlessness and meaninglessness contribute to the alienation suffered by some social service workers (see box, Burnout as Alienation among Social Service Workers).

Social isolation is the term likely to be used today to describe alienation from others. People feel that they are apart from society, out of step with the rest of the world. There is a sense that the things others are interested in are not the things they are interested in. Social isolation includes the feeling that others have left them out and they cannot get back in.

The term **self-estrangement** is used today instead of alienation from the self. People have a sense of some ideal human condition they would like to achieve, but they do not believe they measure up to it. People experience themselves

The struggle against economic exploitation is still going on in affluent America. *UPI/Bettmann Newsphotos.*

as aliens. They have no real sense of what makes them tick, only a sense that they are not what they would like to be.

The Alienating Effects of Unequal Status

The work of Karl Marx is particularly helpful in understanding interpersonal relationships connected with work; powerless and meaningless relations with superiors, competitive relationships with peers, and self-debasing behaviors. But all social relationships do not occur within the context of formal organizations and bureaucracies. Many other social relationships in an advanced capitalist society resemble the alienating relationship between workers and management described by Marx. Social relationships in the economic sphere are reflected in social relationships in all other spheres of a society.

W. Peter Archibald has developed a Marxian-oriented theory describing the alienating effects of class, status, and power divisions on interactions between people of unequal status in everyday life.[46] As we have noted, social classes are defined in terms of roles or positions in the economy, such as blue-collar worker, white-collar worker, manager, and owner (see the box, Social Stratification and Social Classes, in Chapter 3). Status refers to prestige, and power refers to the ability of one person or system to influence the decisions of another.

Differences in status and power are seen in any number of relationships out-

BURNOUT AS ALIENATION AMONG SOCIAL SERVICE WORKERS

A private trouble social service workers themselves may encounter is burnout, or physical and emotional exhaustion and defeat. Its symptons are evident in feelings of being stressed out, tedium, a sense of not accomplishing anything, absenteeism, worker turnover, and actual physical ailments. The symptoms have been especially documented among child welfare workers, but workers in other fields of practice also are subject to burnout. Could burnout be alienation? A number of social work writers certainly think so.

Social workers are not supposed to experience alienation. They are one of the newer middle-class occupations which developed in the twentieth century and which have been defined as professions. According to S. K. Khinducka, "Professional status offers an individual resources, immunities, privileges and autonomy." Thus, as professionals, social workers are supposed to be in control of their work activities. Working with clients, direct-service social workers are supposed to make independent assess-

side of formal organizations and bureaucracies. In many ways the status and power of women and men in the family and in society in general are traditionally unequal. The status and power of people of color and white people have also been historically unequal. The relationship between adults and minors is another area in which status and power inequality is evident.

Archibald asserts that all interpersonal encounters, whether they take place in small groups, families, organizations, or in the community, are threatening to the participants. People simply are not at ease in interpersonal relations, especially if the participants are unequal in class, status, and power. When they meet in face-to-face encounters, they may respond to the threat and discomfort of participating in such interaction by making four different adaptations. Archibald defines these adaptations in terms of the following generalizations.[47]

The **detachment generalization** is that individuals of different class, status, and power adapt by trying to avoid one another. Different neighborhoods are developed by the rich and the poor, by whites and by blacks, Hispanics, or other groups they regard as unequal in status. Children are separated from adults, though they are always supervised by adults. Young people congregate in singles bars, groups, and apartment buildings designed to cater to their interests. Men's clubs are incorporated to exclude women, and women form groups to exclude men.

The **means-end generalization** is that when individuals of different class, status, or power do interact, the interaction tends to be very narrow and role-

ments of client needs and tailor services to meet those needs. This may be an impossibility, however. Often what a social worker can do with and for a client is rigidly defined by social welfare policy, or the worker is subordinate to a policy planner or administrator who operates through bureaucratic rules and procedures.

It has been suggested that social work may best be thought of an as occupation, not as a profession. Michael Fabricant has articulated the increasing "industrialization" of social work, a process whereby social workers are being stripped of their autonomy and increasingly made subject to administrators. When the rewards of the work also are inadequate in terms of pay and working conditions, burnout is not unusual.

Sources: Howard Karger, "Burnout as Alienation," *Social Service Review*, vol. 55 (June 1981), pp. 270–83; S. K. Khinducka, "Social Work and the Human Services," in *Encyclopedia of Social Work*, vol. 2 (Silver Spring, MD: National Association of Social Workers, 1987), p. 682; Irwin Epstein and Kayla Conrad, "The Empirical Limits of Social Work Professionalization," in R. Sarri and Y. Hasenfeld (editors), *The Management of Human Services* (New York: Columbia University Press, 1978), pp. 163–83; Michael Fabricant, "The Industrialization of Social Work," *Social Work*, vol. 30 (September-October 1985), pp. 389–401.

specific. People try to relate to one another within the context of the formal, impersonal roles they occupy and the expectations for these roles. In turn they avoid getting to know each other in a more personal way. If you are a student and I am a professor, we will keep within the bounds of that relationship even if we should meet at a party or in a restaurant. In short, people tend to "use" one another according to their roles.

The **control-purposiveness generalization** is that individuals of high class, status, or power tend to initiate activity, make attempts to influence others, and actually do influence others more than individuals in lower-status positions do.

The **feelings generalization** is that hostility underlies much of the interaction between unequals, so that occasionally rebellion surfaces. Although there may be evident rapport, unequals always tend to dislike one another.

CONTEMPORARY VIEWS ON RESOLVING EXPLOITATION AND ALIENATION

Marx believed that exploitation and alienation could only be overcome by systematically doing away with the status hierarchies that had produced them. But all these hierarchies were not to be abandoned. According to Engels, authority relationships are destructive only to the extent that they are exploitative and alienating.[48] Thus the socialist ideal was to eliminate oppressive hierarchies and replace them with social relationships based on equality of input and output.

This is another respect in which Marxian theory differs from exchange theory. In social exchange, inequity can be resolved in any number of ways. Marx assumed that exploitation and alienation could only be resolved by forcing more powerful people to amend their ways. Workers, therefore, should be dedicated to confronting owners and managers. But history has shown that workers, or any other individuals in situations of social domination, do not always confront their superiors. Resolution of the conflict in any number of ways, as predicted in equity theory, is more likely. Marxian thinkers today themselves are apt to recognize a variety of individual solutions to the problems of exploitation and alienation.

Resolutions in Everyday Life

Peter Leonard recognizes the gap between Marxian theory and practice which resulted from the prediction that subordinate workers would rise up against their superiors. Leonard sets out to shed light on Marx's failure to develop an integrated understanding of the individual in society, or person in environment.[49]

Individual personality is constructed through experiences in the economy, the family, and the state, or government. Since each of these institutional sectors is full of contradictions, these experiences present conflict to the individual. The contradictions in work organizations have already been discussed; in the search to fulfill their human social and creative nature, people encounter alienating and exploitative social relationships. In the family, the values of sharing, caring, and cooperation must accommodate the need for socialization into the realities of the societal hierarchies of gender, age, class, ethnicity, and sexual orientation. In the state, the goal of cultural pluralism, with a shared identity and national cooperation, is contradicted by the realities of competing points of view. Through the development of laws and the establishment of traditions, the state functions to mediate conflict among the competing sectors of society, each of which is trying to impose its point of view about cultural identity and cooperation. In a capitalist society, the state often favors the dominant interests in its definitions of normality and deviance and the hierarchies of the society. The dominant interests also are favored in the establishment and enforcement of social welfare services.

Such conflictful experiences determine how personalities are formed and individuals locate themselves within the various hierarchies. As a general **sense of superordinancy and subordinancy** is inculcated into the personality, individuals come to feel superior or subordinate in their relations with others. Leonard argues that subordinated people—working-class members, people in stigmatized racial and ethnic groups, women, gays and lesbians, the very young and the very old, the disabled—adopt modes of avoidance, resistance, or dissent as ways of dealing with the contradictions of social institutions which are internalized in their general sense of self. In Leonard's terms, contradictory consciousness, unconscious resistance, the development of individual capacities, and participation in collective action are the principal ways in which subordinates respond to the demands of the dominant interests.[50]

Contradictory Consciousness. Dominant interests often are successful in inculcating in subordinated individuals values and beliefs that support their own point of view. When they are successful, the subordinated will experience the contradictions in social institutions and relationships as a private trouble, some indication of personal failure or deficiency. They may continue to submit to the dominant order, albeit often with reservations, but they may also engage in acts of deviance. They may steal, commit industrial sabotage, or engage in other unlawful behavior as an attempt to undermine the authority of dominant interests. Yet by being deviant they do not attempt to change their circumstance and thereby, as with conformist submission, work against their own interests.

Unconscious Resistance. As contradictions are experienced by subordinate people, they may make unconscious attempts to repress drives and needs which they perceive as unacceptable to the dominant interests. Women repress their urges to achieve and excel; gays and lesbians repress their urge to fulfill their desires and try desperately to go straight; the disabled repress their anger and try to accept with humility the stigma attached to their status; racial and ethnic minorities repress their urge to speak out and try to ingratiate themselves. In their milder forms, such repression may produce anxiety and neurosis. In their more severe forms, full-blown mental illnesses may develop.

Development of Individual Capacities.   Subordinated individuals may deal with contradictions by cultivating skills and interests that somehow take them out of the conflict or make them feel an exception to the rule. They may read literary works, engage in hobbies, or take up spectator sports and activities. They may attempt to locate themselves within the contradictions in a way that reduces the strain. They may strive for more education or a different occupation, or they may try their hand at becoming entrepreneurs in the hope that this new niche will help them avoid contradictory feelings.

In these three adaptations, subordinated individuals attempt to conform as best they can to the demands of the dominant interests. They may deviate, go insane, or locate a protective niche, but in each case they never confront the contradiction head on or try to resolve it, as they do in the fourth adaptation, collective action.

Participation in Collective Action.   Subordinated individuals may come together in an attempt to deal directly with the contradictions they experience through their participation in the economy, in the family, and in the nation as a whole. Although collective action generates new contradictions, between hope and despair and between optimism and depression, the advantages to the individual far outweigh the disadvantages. Collective action provides the opportunity to develop the capacities necessary for effective struggle in developing an altered sense of the self, one that is freer of the contradictions in social institutions and in their own personality.

Resolutions in Social Service Organizations

Noting the powerlessness social service workers often experience as they attempt to help their clients, Wendy Sherman and Stanley Wenocur propose six ways of resolving their feelings of alienation. Four of these can be considered forms of conformity. **Capitulation** involves identifying with agency administrators and incorporating values and behaviors that maintain the alienation of clients from the service. **Niche-finding** is an attempt to sidestep the conflict between client needs and administrative needs by searching out a special position that will give the worker an independent base of power. **Withdrawal** essentially refers to leaving the job. The worker hopes to avoid the conflict by wrongly assuming that it is just a problem in a certain agency or service and will not be a problem in the next one. **Martyrdom** refers to adaptations in which workers come to identify with the alienation of their clients; they see themselves as alienated but cannot bring themselves to do anything about it. They become victims incorporating a sense of powerlessness, a sense that there is no solution at all.[51]

The fifth adaptation can be considered deviant or nonconformist. In **noncapitulation**, workers reject the alienation and exploitation of agency directors and attempt to challenge or undermine the agency. According to Sherman and Wenocur, this is not a good solution to agency conflict because workers who forcefully challenge the system may be isolated and "identified as mavericks or house radicals. At best they are discounted as unrealistic, immature, unable to cope. More frequently, noncapitulators will be harassed, 'counseled out,' or simply fired, if they do not first resign."[52]

The sixth adaptation is in keeping with how contemporary Marxists generally view positive solutions to exploitation and alienation. **Functional non-capitulation** occurs when workers organize together in mutual support and attempt to negotiate with agency administrators about the conditions of their work with clients. This is a form of compromise, but it is a productive adaptation in which workers consciously and actively decide whether to capitulate or to hold firm. They maintain a stance of always being willing to negotiate: "Thus, these workers maintain a range of responses from refusal to acceptance, with a large middle ground wherein to seek workable compromises. They also develop realistic expectations for changing the organization and establish boundaries of acceptability regarding the demands placed on them."[53]

Conclusions about Resolutions

The ideas of Leonard and those of Sherman and Wenocur are quite similar and suggest certain generalizations about the ways in which exploited and alienated people are likely to deal with their situations. Three basic adjustments are:

1. Conformity or functional capitulation, which involves all strategies by individuals and groups that in effect work to maintain existing exploitative and alienating relationships.
2. Deviance or noncapitulation, which involves rebellious acts by individuals and groups which undermine and subvert but which do not engage the system directly in change.
3. Collective action or functional noncapitulation, which involves individual and collective attempts to engage the system in a process of compromise and negotiation.

Marxian theory holds that only the third option, functional noncapitulation or collective action, can resolve alienation and exploitation. Some Marxists have used the term *false consciousness* to refer to solutions such as conformity and deviance which further the power of the dominant interests to exploit and alienate.[54] False consciousness is probably not a very useful term because it suggests that there is only one truth, and that truth is self-evident. There are many reasons why people may choose to conform or to deviate in the face of alienation and exploitation. Not the least is that they often come to perceive that their situation is not so bad or at least that it could be far worse. When they look around them and calculate their ability to command higher rewards, reflect on their past experiences, examine their alternatives, or compare their situation to those of others, they may very well conclude that their situation is not so bad after all. The Marxian position that there is only one effective solution is challenged by evidence that in practice, people do not always choose to directly confront alienation and exploitation.

IMPLICATIONS OF MARXIAN THEORY FOR SOCIAL SERVICE PRACTICE

In social service practice, Marxian theory is concerned with helping workers put functional noncapitulation into practice. More often than not, social workers influenced by Marx turn their attention to large-scale social movements and social change. Or, when an organization is the client system, they articulate the need for workers to unite to produce better and more humane working conditions for themselves and, in turn, better opportunitites to serve the interests of their clients.[55] But Marxian theory also can be fruitfully used in social work with individuals. It directs workers to assess the degree to which individuals are in exploitative and alienating relationships, be they in friendship networks, small groups, families, or organizations. It suggests that intervention plans should offer clients the clear opportunity to confront such situations, and, when clients agree to such confrontations, that workers should assist in facilitating these opportunities.

Leonard emphasizes that services to individuals should combine reflection, or consciousness of alienation and exploitation, with action, or actually doing things to alter social circumstances.[56] However, Marxist-influenced practitioners appear to be developing approaches that give emphasis to one or the other of these functions. **Action-oriented practice** puts considerable emphasis on achieving concrete changes through such interventions as community organization, community development, and social action. Clients of action-oriented services may have experiences which enable them to develop a new and better sense of self, but no deliberate attempt is made to assure this. **Consciousness-oriented practice** places its emphasis on altering the personality and inculcating better ways of responding to exploitation and alienation. Interventions may focus on rap groups, support groups, consciousness-raising groups, and possibly individual psychotherapy. Involvement in direct social action is hoped for, but it is not the principal focus of the intervention.

CHAPTER SUMMARY

In this chapter two theories that focus on the interaction between individuals and their social environment have been presented. Social exchange theory starts with the assumption that humans are by nature self-interested creatures. Marxian theory begins with the assumption that humans are special, inherently social and drawn to others and inherently creative. Because of these varying assumptions, their visions of utopia in social relationships differ markedly.

Social exchange theorists see ultimate perfection in fairness and justice; social inequalities may exist, but only insofar as they are based on norms of reciprocity and the principle of distributive justice. Fairness and justice can be achieved in a number of ways which do not necessarily alter any objective ideas about what would be fair and just but which nevertheless can satisfy the participants in the interaction. Marxian theorists use ultimate perfection in equality of outcome; exploitation and alienation must be overcome if social relationships are to fulfill their promise. Although people may deal with exploitative and alienating situations in any number of ways, only one way — direct attempts to do away with inequality — is regarded as effective.

DISCUSSION QUESTIONS AND CLASS PROJECTS

1. Distinguish between classical conditioning, operant conditioning, and social-learning theories. Indicate how each has been used in social service practice.

2. Describe the four cognitive processes that produce behavioral responses, according to social-learning theory.

3. Identify and describe the following:
aversion therapy
systematic desensitization
positive reinforcement
negative reinforcement
successive approximations
shaping
satiation
punishment
extinction
models

4. Distinguish between the methods of successive approximation and vicarious acquisition. Which do you think is the more normal form of learning among humans?

5. Do you believe that social exchange processes are a good way to describe the interaction between two people who are in love? Between parents and children?

6. Describe the principles and processes by which rewards are calculated according to social exchange theory.

7. Distinguish among fate control, behavioral control, and autonomous control.

8. Identify and define the following:
comparison level
comparison level for alternatives
the principle of distributive justice
norms of reciprocity
norms of negative reciprocity
comparable worth
scientific socialism
reification

9. When people experience inequity in social relationships, what is likely to happen?

10. Do you think people should be paid according to the principle of comparable worth or according to market principles?

11. Give some examples of inequity in social relationships from your clients' experiences or your own life. How were they resolved? Do you think the resolution was a good one?

12. What is the vision of human nature that underlies Marxian theory?

13. Describe Marx's two critiques of nineteenth-century capitalism. Do you think they still apply in the twentieth century?

14. What are the four kinds of alienation described by Marx? How have these been redefined in the twentieth century? Can you think of examples when you have experienced alienation?

15. Have you ever explored the situations your clients find themselves in in terms of alienation and exploitation? Think of a series of interview questions or issues that would enable you to assess alienation and exploitation in their lives.

16. According to Archibald, what kinds of interaction are you likely to see between people of unequal status? Can you recognize any of your own behaviors in these terms? For instance, does it describe your behavior with respect to professors?

17. According to Sherman and Wenocur, what are the ways that social workers are likely to handle exploitation and alienation on the job? Can you see your own behavior or the behavior of people you have worked with in these terms?

18. When social workers feel burned out, do you think they are experiencing alienation? Identify a representative group of so-

cial service workers in both the public and private sectors and interview them about how their practice is organized and how it may lead to burnout and alienation.

19. Identify and describe the importance of the following terms:

unconscious resistance
contradictory consciousness
development of individual capacities
participation in collective action
capitulation
niche-finding
withdrawal
martyrdom
noncapitulation
functional noncapitulation
the detachment generalization
the means-end generalization
the control-purposiveness
  generalization
the feelings generalization

NOTES

1. See W. Peter Archibald, *Social Psychology as Political Economy* (Toronto, Canada: McGraw-Hill, 1978), pp. 16–31.

2. Ibid., p. 17.

3. John B. Watson, *Behaviorism* (New York: W. W. Norton, 1925).

4. Ivan P. Pavlov, *Conditioned Reflexes* (London, England: Clarendon Press, 1927).

5. See G. Terence Wilson and K. Daniel O'Leary, *Principles of Behavior Therapy* (Englewood Cliffs, NJ: Prentice-Hall, 1980), pp. 152–64.

6. Ibid., pp. 176–82.

7. B. F. Skinner, *The Behavior of Organisms: An Experimental Analysis* (New York: Appleton-Century-Crofts, 1938).

8. Wilson and O'Leary, *Principles of Behavior Therapy*, pp. 98–101.

9. Eileen Gambrill, *Casework: A Competency-Based Approach* (Englewood Cliffs, NJ: Prentice-Hall, 1983), pp. 210, 291.

10. Robert M. Liebert, Rita Wicks-Nelson, and Robert V. Kail, *Developmental Psychology*, 4th ed. (Englewood Cliffs, NJ: Prentice-Hall, 1986), p. 298.

11. See Ted L. Rosenthal and Barry J. Zimmerman, *Social Learning and Cognition* (New York: Academic Press, 1978), pp. 71–74.

12. Albert Bandura, "Influence of a Model's Reinforcement Contingencies on the Acquisition of Imitative Responses," *Journal of Personality and Social Psychology*, vol. 1 (June 1965), pp. 589–95.

13. Albert Bandura, *Social Learning Theory* (Englewood Cliffs, NJ: Prentice-Hall, 1977), pp. 22–29. Also see Albert Bandura, "Model of Causality in Social Learning Theory," in S. Sukemune (editor), *Advances in Social Learning Theory* (Tokyo: Kaneko Shobo, 1983).

14. Bandura, "Model of Causality," p. 92.

15. F. Ivan Nye et al., "Choice, Exchange and the Family," in W. R. Burr et al. (editors), *Contemporary Theories of the Family* (New York: Free Press, 1979), pp. 1–41; Robert Pruger, "Social Policy: Unilateral Transfer or Reciprocal Exchange," *Journal of Social Policy*, vol. 2 (October 1973), pp. 289–302; John S. Wodarski, "Clinical Practice and the Social Learning Paradigm," *Social Work*, vol. 28 (March–April 1983), pp. 154–60.

16. Peter M. Blau, *Exchange and Power in Social Life* (New York: John Wiley, 1964).

17. See Marvin E. Shaw and Philip R. Costanzo, *Theories of Social Psychology*, 2nd ed. (New York: McGraw-Hill, 1982), pp. 96–97.

18. See Nye et al., "Choice, Exchange and the Family," pp. 9–10.

19. See Blau, *Exchange and Power in Social Life*; and Zick Rubin, *Liking and Loving: An Invitation to Social Psychology* (New York: John Wiley, 1973).

20. Archibald, *Social Psychology as Political Economy*, p. 27.

21. Nye et al., "Choice, Exchange and the Family," p. 6.

22. George C. Homans, *Social Behavior: Its Elementary Forms*, 2nd ed. (New York: Harcourt, Brace, Jovanovich, 1974).

23. John W. Thibaut and Harold H. Kelley, *The Social Psychology of Groups* (New York: John Wiley, 1959), pp. 21–24, 80–99, and 100–03.

24. See H. H. Kelley, "Two Functions of Reference Groups," in G. E. Swanson, T. M. Newcomb, and E. L. Hartley (editors), *Readings in Social Psychology*, rev. ed. (New York: Holt, Rinehart and Winston, 1952), pp. 41–44.

25. See Shaw and Costanzo, *Theories of Social Psychology*, p. 100.

26. Homans, *Social Behavior: Its Elementary Forms*, 1st ed. (New York: Harcourt, Brace, Jovanovich, 1961), p. 75.

27. See Archibald, *Social Psychology as Political Economy*, p. 19.

28. Blau, *Exchange and Power in Social Life*.

29. Homans, *Social Behavior*, 2nd ed., p. 37.

30. For a discussion of equity theory, see J. Stacey Adams, "Toward an Understanding of Inequity," *Journal of Abnormal and Social Psychology*, vol. 67 (1963), pp. 422–36; J. Stacey Adams and Sara Freedman, "Equity Theory Revisited," in L. Berkowitz (editor), *Advances in Experimental Social Psychology*, vol. 9 (New York: Academic Press, 1976), pp. 43–90; Elaine E. Walster, Ellen Berscheid, and G. William Walster, "New Direction in Equity Research," *Journal of Personality and Social Psychology*, vol. 25 (February 1973), pp. 151–76; and G. William Walster and Ellen Berscheid, *Equity: Theory and Research* (Boston, MA: Allyn and Bacon, 1978).

31. J. Stacey Adams, "Inequity in Social Exchange," in L. Berkowitz (editor), *Advances in Experimental Social Psychology*, vol. 2 (1965), pp. 283–95.

32. Nancy Weinberg, "Social Equity and the Physically Disabled," *Social Work*, vol. 28 (September–October 1983), pp. 365–69.

33. George Ritzer, *Toward an Integrated Sociological Paradigm* (Boston, MA: Allyn and Bacon, 1981), pp. 31–69.

34. For relatively easy reading of Karl Marx's writing on human nature see "The German Ideology, Part I" in E. C. Tucker (editor), *The Marx-Engels Reader* (New York: W. W. Norton, 1972), pp. 113–19.

35. See Archibald, *Social Psychology as Political Economy*, pp. 24–31.

36. Karl Marx, "For a Ruthless Criticism of Everything Existing," in Tucker (editor), *Marx-Engels Reader*, pp. 7–10.

37. This concept comes from the anthropologist Marshall D. Sahlins. See Archibald, *Social Psychology as Political Economy*, pp. 106–14.

38. Karl Marx, "Alienated Labor," translated by Eric and Mary Redman Josephson, in E. and M. Josephson (editors), *Man Alone* (New York: Dell/Laurel, 1962), pp. 93–105.

39. Friedrich Engels, "The Tactics of Social Democracy," in Tucker (editor), *Marx-Engels Reader*, pp. 406–23.

40. See Richard B. Gregg, *The Power of Nonviolence*, 2nd rev. ed. (New York: Shocken Books, 1966).

41. See John Naisbitt, *Megatrends* (New York: Warner Books, 1982).

42. Ralf Dahrendorf, *Class and Class Conflict in Industrial Society* (Palo Alto, CA: Stanford University Press, 1959), pp. 36–72.

43. Melvin Seeman, "Alienation Motif in Contemporary Theorizing: The Hidden Continuity of the Classic Themes," *Social Psychology Quarterly*, vol. 46 (September 1983), pp. 171–84.

44. Melvin Seeman, "On the Meaning of Alienation," *American Sociological Review*, vol. 24 (December 1959), pp. 784–90.

45. Barbara Bryant Solomon, *Black Empowerment: Social Work in Oppressed Communities* (New York: Columbia University Press, 1976), p. 16.

46. W. Peter Archibald, "Face-to-Face: The Alienating Effects of Class, Status and Power Division," *American Sociological Review*, vol. 41 (October 1976), pp. 819–37.

47. Ibid., pp. 820–21.

48. Friedrich Engels, "On Authority," in Tucker (editor), *Marx-Engels Reader*, pp. 662–65.

49. Peter Leonard, *Personality and Ideology: Towards a Materialist Understanding of the Individual* (London, England: Macmillan, 1984), pp. 5–7.

50. Ibid., pp. 103–15.

51. Wendy Ruth Sherman and Stanley Wenocur, "Empowering Public Welfare Workers through Mutual Support," *Social Work*, vol. 28 (September–October 1983), pp. 375–79.

52. Ibid., p. 367.

53. Ibid., p. 377.

54. Guenter Lawy, *False Consciousness: An Essay on Mystification* (New Brunswick, NJ: Transaction Books, 1987).

55. See, for instance, Robert Knicker-meyer, "A Marxist Approach to Social Work," *Social Work*, vol. 17 (July 1972), pp. 58–65; and Paul Adams and Gary Free-man, "On the Political Character of Social Service Work," *Catalyst*, no. 7, vol. 2 (1980), pp. 71–82.

56. Leonard, *Personality and Ideology*.

CHAPTER 13

Interpersonal Well-Being: Structural Functional and Symbolic Interaction Theories

M AJOR THEMES DISCUSSED IN THIS CHAPTER:

1. *Structural functionalism and anomie.* Structural functionalism proposes that social relationships are normal when agreement exists about values, goals, roles, and tasks and when opportunities for complying with these agreements are made available to all participants. The concept of anomie represents breakdowns in the social system when these opportunities are not present. In social service practice, workers must take into account the social situation in addition to the perceptions of the client in assessing anomie.

2. *Stress as a form of anomie.* In stress theory, which is rooted in physiology rather than sociology, there are echoes of anomie. Stress is seen as a private trouble resulting from unexpected changes in life events to which the individual must adapt. In social service practice, stress management programs have been developed to help clients cope with the effects of stress.

3. *Symbolic interactionism.* This perspective focuses on the social processes through which individuals attach meaning to the objects, events, and situations that make up their world. It has been particularly concerned with the ways in which meaning is attached to the self, that is, the ways people come to understand themselves as an object in social situations. Its utopian vision

is that social relationships are normal when each party in a transaction is able to come out of it with a positive sense of self.

4. *Symbolic interaction and labeling*. The labeling perspective is a major contribution to understanding the development of negative self-images and low self-esteem. Labeling has been applied to the study of achieved labels, negative messages about the self that result from people's actions which annoy others, and ascribed labels, negative messages about the self that result from the groups and communities people belong to or into which they are born. In social service practice, the potential for stigmatizing clients in the assessment process is very real. Workers must avoid the application of negative labels and strive to sustain positive self-images in clients.

T̲HIS CHAPTER continues the examination of psychological well-being by looking at the contributions to the utopian transactional approach of two additional schools of thought: structural functionalism and symbolic interactionism. Both of these theories shed light on the relationship between individuals and their social environments, and both present utopian visions which are useful in guiding social service practice. In structural functionalism, social relationships are regarded as normal when agreement exists as to values, goals, roles, and tasks and when opportunities for complying with these agreements are made available to all participants. In symbolic interactionism, social relationships are considered normal when mutual self-respect prevails.

STRUCTURAL FUNCTIONALISM AND ANOMIE

The origins of structural functionalism, like those of the social exchange and Marxian theories discussed in Chapter 12, are in the nineteenth century, and the theory emerged as a response to both classical economic exchange theory and Marxian theory.[1] Structural functional perspectives dominate the contemporary social sciences, including social work. Indeed, as we pointed out in Chapter 2, most approaches to the study of social systems in the social services have applied the assumptions and concepts of structural functionalism.[2] When social workers refer to systems theory, they usually mean functionalism.

THE UTOPIAN VISION

Emile Durkheim, a French sociologist in the late nineteenth and early twentieth centuries, made significant contributions to structural functional thinking. He saw society as a whole, held together by a collective conscience, a normative or moral order, and a social contract. Today the same concepts are likely to be referred to as cultural norms and values. Norms and values, Durkheim believed, are absolutely essential to social life because they set up the goals for which people should strive and inform people of what is expected of them in achieving those goals. In other words, norms and values establish the working agreements governing social transactions, without which transactions could not occur and social life would disintegrate.

The division of labor in a society is such that the unit or parts are integrated into a whole. Each unit or part serves a purpose, and each contributes to the maintenance of the whole. In these ideas lies the meaning of **structural functionalism**. Each unit of a system, or *structure*, serves a positive purpose, or *function*, for the whole. In the ideal form of human social interaction, therefore, there would be a consensus in values and expectations, and everyone would contribute to this consensus by acting to assure the survival and continued development of the system. This is a utopian vision of perfect harmony which is rarely found in reality. Technological and social changes from outside the system are often believed to cause dysfunction or breakdown in the system. The chances for achieving harmony are enhanced by limiting conflict, clarifying expectations, generating consensus, and encouraging conformity.

Anomie Theory: Breakdowns in the Social System

Durkheim coined the term **anomie** to describe breakdowns that threaten the viability of a system. Anomie has two meanings. First, anomie means **normlessness**, a condition in which the **social contract**, or the norms and values governing social interaction, seem to have broken down and disintegrated. Under such conditions of **normative breakdown**, people no longer know what is expected of themselves or others. Second, anomie refers to a condition in which the complex, multiple norms and values which regulate social interaction somehow contradict one another. Under conditions of **contradictory norms**, people are pulled in different directions at the same time. Regardless of the form anomie takes, they become confused and disoriented and are forced to adapt.

When Durkheim looked at the nineteenth century, he did not see the norms of fair reciprocal exchange that the classical economists saw, nor did he see the exploitation and alienation that Marx saw. Instead he saw anomie in the breakdown of the old feudal order and the rise of the new industrial order, a condition of normlessness in which people were transacting with each other in hesitant, awkward, and confused ways. And he saw the terrible social problems that were arising from this condition.

Anomie and Suicide in the Nineteenth Century

Among the problems of normlessness Durkheim saw, he focused on high rates of suicide.[3] His examination of official records in a number of European countries showed that suicide rates increased during times of social disruption, both when things were getting worse and when they were getting better. It was social change, or a breakdown in the normal order, that was disorienting.

Durkheim's study of recorded suicides led him to some interesting and unexpected observations about the relationship between the society and individual behavior. For instance, living in poverty and squalor did not appear to drive people to suicide. In poor countries the rates of suicide were actually lower than in more wealthy countries. Similarly, in Protestant countries, where individuality and individual responsibility were championed, suicide rates were higher than where moral principles were laid down and enforced by the Catholic Church. In any of these countries, however, change produced higher rates of suicide. When economic conditions were stable, suicide rates declined. When they deteriorated and people lost wealth and incomes, suicide rates increased. They also increased when economic conditions improved and people began to gain wealth and increase their status and income. Any kind of change, not the condition people normally find themselves in, could create private troubles. Thus poverty and authoritarian regimes could produce a comfortable social order, and industrialization and norms supporting individual rights could produce a dysfunctional social order.

Anomie and Deviance in the 1950s

In the twentieth century, when Robert Merton considered the idea of anomie, he emphasized contradictions among norms rather than normlessness.[4] Merton, like Durkheim, was trying to understand social deviance, why people break the norms of society and act to threaten its survival. He believed, too, that society is held together by a moral order which includes a morality about goals and the ways of achieving them.

Merton's social world was American society in the 1950s. While television and the media promote an image of the fifties as "happy days" in which life was more orderly than it is today, Merton saw it very differently. When he looked at the fifties he saw anomie, or contradictions in the social order.

On the one hand, Merton observed, Americans were tied together by a common value: the goal of economic success and material well-being. Merton saw nothing wrong with this goal; this was, after all, the meaning of the American dream and the reason for the emergence of the United States as a strong and wealthy nation. Furthermore, the vast majority of Americans shared in this dream. On this issue there were no cultural or class differences. Almost everyone dreamed of a house in the suburbs, a car or two, nice clothes, good food, and everything that goes with material success.

On the other hand, there were many social problems in the United States. The goal of economic success was contradicted by the fact that everybody did not have the same opportunities to achieve it. The route to economic success was not always clear and not always available. Equal opportunities did not exist, and many Americans who earnestly wanted to participate in the American dream found that the means for doing so were blocked. Thus for large numbers of people, especially for the poor and the working class, a situation of anomie existed.

Although some poor people achieve the American dream, the lack of economic opportunities in inner city ghettoes often leads to theft, drug and alcohol dependency, and gang fighting. *Mike Tappin.*

Out of the contradictions between the goals of success and the lack of means of success, Merton believed, deviance was taking such forms as crime and delinquency, mental illness, drug and alcohol abuse, depression and disillusionment, social violence, and the like. People were being forced to adapt to these contradictions, and they did not always do so in functional or positive ways.

Adaptations to Anomie.   Merton described five ways individuals adapt to anomie, ways which are still evident today (see box, Merton's Anomie and Adaptations).[5] He argued that even in the face of contradictions, most people respond with **conformity**, trying to achieve the American dream and exhausting every possible legitimate opportunity to do so. If at first they don't succeed they try, try again. Some, however, turn to deviant adaptations. One of these Merton called **innovation**, which refers to achieving success through illegitimate means such as cheating, stealing, embezzling, committing fraud, selling drugs, or prostitution. Through such means people might achieve the American dream, but not in acceptable ways.

Some people adapt by giving up on the goal of economic success altogether. They become satisfied with what they have and do not feel compelled to pursue the material goals of other Americans. They do not upset the system or cause trouble but continue to perform their expected tasks, though with no real purpose. Merton referred to this kind of deviant adaptation as **ritualism**, in which people just go through the motions of getting ahead. On the surface they ap-

MERTON'S ANOMIE AND ADAPTATIONS

According to Robert Merton, anomie is the result of contradictions between success goals and opportunities for success. People experiencing anomie are said to adapt in one of five ways:

Conformity	Continual pursuit of success goals using available legitimate opportunities
Innovation	Continual pursuit of success goals using available illegitimate opportunities
Ritualism	Giving up on success goals but continuing to go through the motions of using legitimate opportunities
Retreatism	Giving up on success goals and dropping out of legitimate opportunities
Rebellion	Giving up on success goals and legitimate opportunities. Setting up alternative goals and opportunities.

Source: Robert K. Merton, *Social Theory and Social Structure*, enlarged ed. (New York: Free Press, 1951), pp. 193–211.

pear to be conforming, but they do just what is expected of them, no more and no less.

People making the **retreatism** adaptation give up not only on the goal of economic success but also on any legitimate attempt to pursue that goal. They do not even go through the motions. Merton identified retreatist adaptations in those who abuse drugs, including alcohol. He also saw mental illness as a retreat from reality into hallucination and fantasy. **Rebellion** goes a step further. Not only do people give up on success goals and on legitimate attempts to achieve them, they substitute new goals and devise new ways of achieving them. Merton and others have seen violent youth gangs as the major example of rebellion. These gangs reject economic success in favor of toughness and excitement, and they reject the work ethic in favor of an ethic of violence. In the 1960s, the rebellious adaptation also was found among "hippie dropouts" who left school and competition in the marketplace and went in search of the simple life, sometimes living in egalitarian communes.

Anomie and Anomia

The concept of anomie was used by Durkheim and Merton only to describe an objective, environmental situation in which people find themselves. Both of them studiously avoided using the term to refer to any subjective or inner states of individuals. Anomie, as described by Durkheim and Merton, is not a feeling or a perception. Thus, even in his ideas about adaptation, Merton insists that he is not describing personality traits or types of people. He deliberately does not use the terms *conformist, innovator, ritualist, retreatist,* or *rebel.* He offers types of adaptations that anybody might choose, depending on the circumstances.

Other theorists have coined the terms *anomia* (or *anomy*) to refer to the most subjective aspects of anomie. **Anomia** has to do with feelings of normlessness and the conscious experience of contradictions. According to Robert MacIver, "Anomy signifies the *state of mind* of one who has been pulled up by his moral roots, who has no longer any standards but only disconnected urges, who has no longer any sense of continuity, of form, of obligation."[6]

To Merton, anomia is not an irrelevant concept, but it cannot be substituted for anomie. People experiencing anomie do not have to realize that the situation is anomic to adapt in the various ways he suggests. For instance, thieves will not say they are "innovating" because they are experiencing a contradiction between their desire for success and the legal opportunities available to them. Those who promote the concept of anomia, however, believe that anomie must be experienced on some level by the individual if it is to provoke the need for adaptation.[7]

Direct-service social workers can use Merton's idea of anomie to examine the fit between person and environment, but they will find themselves working as much in the environment as in the person. Just asking clients about their perceptions of the opportunities available to them and their feelings about any lack

of opportunities is not enough. Social workers must learn about the community, the way it is organized and the opportunities that are actually available
to clients. They have to examine anomie as well as anomia.

COMPARING MERTON, MARX, AND SOCIAL EXCHANGE

Merton, Marx, and social exchange theorists all are concerned with a similar
dimension, the achievement of rewards. While for Merton and Marx the principle emphasis is on material rewards, both theories are easily altered to include a broader range of social rewards, as in social exchange. The points of
departure in these three theories are quite different, however. In exchange theory, human nature is assumed to be self-interested, so a system like capitalism
is inevitable, a natural law, and an ultimate good. In Marxian theory, humans
are rational creatures concerned with collective self-interest who nevertheless
produce a system like capitalism and reify it; capitalism is humankind gone
wrong. Merton does not see human nature as necessarily self-interested or
question the effects of capitalism. He does not look much deeper than the
general goal of material success, nor does he argue for or against inequitable
outcomes, or take a stand on competitiveness, exploitation, and alienation.

Merton does take a stand on how people should respond in situations where
opportunities may not be available: They should conform, or keep trying
against all odds. Social exchange theory maintains that people should respond
to inequity in any way that will reestablish a sense of equity. The Marxian
stand on how exploitation and alienation should be handled is at odds with
Merton as well as with social exchange. While Marxians do not espouse
deviance—such acts as stealing, cheating, dropping out, martyrdom, or
repressing needs—they do not champion conformity, either. Marx in fact
champions rebellion, the substitution of new goals and new means for established goals and means. In Marxian theory, as we noted in Chapter 12, rebellious behavior in the form of social action and functional noncapitulation is the
proper response to problems in the organization of society.

Obviously Marx and Merton (and Durkheim) held very different views
about the normality of capitalism as a social context. For Marx, capitalism itself was an aberration. For Merton it was basically good and only needed some
tinkering. For Durkheim the particular system, and the goals and values guiding it, did not matter. The only social context of value was the stability that
comes with clear and concrete social expectations.

The ideas of Merton and Durkheim demonstrate why functionalist analysis
ultimately leans in the direction of conservatism. The argument is that everyone wants to and should conform, and only breakdowns or contradictions in
norms will prevent conformity. If only people knew what was expected of
them, or if they only had the opportunities to fulfill those expectations, they
would gladly do what is expected. People who do not do what is expected—
even when the expectations are not clear or are contradictory—are deviants,
potential threats to the survival of the system.

Nevertheless, the structural functionalist theory of anomie has had an important, positive impact on society. In pointing to the contradictions between the goal of economic success and the limited opportunities for achieving it that existed in American society, Merton introduced ideas which were incorporated in the social welfare policies of the Great Society and the War on Poverty of the 1970s.[8] Anomie theory forced Americans to put their free-market house in order. Applying the theory of anomie, efforts were made to mobilize the poor and racial and ethnic minorities and to seek changes in the economic system to provide them with new and greater opportunities. Since capitalism offers the opportunity to compete with others for economic success, equality of opportunity was adopted as social policy. But the goal was not equality of outcome or even equity of outcome. Anomie theory led to liberal and progressive changes, but it never aspired to bring about radical change.

ANOMIE AND JUVENILE DELINQUENCY

One of the principal applications of anomie theory has been in the study of deviancy, especially juvenile crime or delinquency. In Merton's words, "It is only when a system of cultural values extols, virtually above all else, certain *common* success-goals for the population at large while the social structure rigorously restricts or completely closes access to approved modes of reaching these goals *for a considerable part of the same population*, that deviant behavior ensues on a large scale."[9]

Merton's deviant adaptations helped demonstrate why poor people and minorities disproportionately turn to illegitimate opportunities, rebel, abuse drugs, or develop mental disorders. The study of the relationship of anomie to delinquency has been constructively criticized, however, by other social scientists working within the functionalist tradition. Noting that Merton examined the relationship between the organization of society as a whole and the private troubles of individuals, they point out that the community, peer group relations, and the family operate as intervening variables which must be taken into consideration. Everyone in an anomic society does not turn to deviance; depending on community and family patterns, they may conform or make different adaptations.

Legitimate and Illegitimate Opportunities

In Merton's terms, anomie describes the state of a society as a whole, and the adaptations represent the normal or deviant response of individuals to it. Between the contradictions in society and the individual adaptations, however, are different social contexts which influence these adaptations.

Richard Cloward and Lloyd Ohlin have concluded, along with Merton, that various types of delinquent subcultures have developed as a response to the contradictions between the society's goals of economic success and the availability of opportunities to achieve it.[10] They direct attention to the influence of neighborhood life on the adaptations made by young people to the condition of anomie in a society, noting that neighborhoods provide both legitimate and illegitimate opportunities to youngsters. In the neighborhood young people learn from friends and acquaintances what opportunities are available and how to use them. Because legitimate opportunities are limited in lower-class neighborhoods, illegitimate opportunities fill the gap. The form of these **illegitimate opportunities** varies, depending on the delinquent subculture in the neighborhood. In the **criminal subculture**, material success is gained by theft, extortion, and fraud, and connections are made to organized crime. These neighborhoods thus produce innovative responses to anomie. In other neighborhoods, the **retreatist subculture** provides opportunities for drug and alcohol use and abuse. The **conflict subculture** in still other neighborhoods presents opportunities to substitute aggressive, violent goals for economic goals. These neighborhoods produce a rebellious response.[11]

Merton also directed attention to the role of the family in promoting adaptations to anomie. As we noted in Part II, family life is varied, representing class and ethnic differences. Through socialization, children learn from parents and others the goals and values of the class and ethnic groups to which they belong, not necessarily those of the larger society. Citing studies which indicate that many lower-class and black parents hold very high ambitions for their children, Merton points out that frustration (anomie) may be particularly acute in these families, which are the least able to model for their children the proper ways of achieving legitimate goals. The children internalize the value of economic success and are deeply frustrated when they fail to accomplish it.[12]

Other Contradictions for Adolescents

An important study of how the concept of anomie relates to juvenile delinquency was undertaken by David Greenberg.[13] He begins with a constructive criticism of Merton, noting that all forms of delinquent behavior cannot be understood by examining contradictions between success goals and opportunities for achieving them. Other kinds of contradictions also have to be examined.

Using arrest rates in the 1970s, Greenberg notes that arrests for crime and delinquency were overwhelmingly highest for young males. Few children were arrested below the age of 12, arrest rates rose sharply between ages 12 and 17 and then started to decline slowly, and relatively few people over the age of 35 or 40 were arrested. These data have not changed considerably since the time of his study. In 1986, males represented 83 percent of all arrests; 5 percent of all arrestees were under 15 years old and 17 percent were under 18. Most arrests were in the age categories of 18–14 (32 percent) and 25–44 years old (43 percent). Only 5 percent of those arrested were 45–54 years old, 2 percent were 55–64, and 0.9 percent were 65 and over.[14]

Greenberg then sets out to determine what there is about being young and male that provokes participation in crime and delinquency. He looks at the way age is structured in society, at the goals of youth as a culture and the opportunities available to youth to achieve those goals. In addition to economic contradictions, he notes contradictions created by the schools and by the peer culture.

Economic contradictions are indeed at work. Teenagers are as much a part of the consumer society as everyone else. They want material rewards, and they go after them. Many teenagers can satisfy this goal legitimately by taking part-time jobs, which are abundantly available in service-oriented occupations in many neighborhoods (see box, Part-Time Work and Adolescent Development). Yet many adolescents, legally defined as children, are economically dependent. Having the desire for consumer goods but lacking the resources to achieve them, they innovate by stealing. Class differences do not operate, because the economic resources to participate in youth activities increase with higher social class, and upper-class youths experience anomie as much as lower-class youths do (see the box, Saints and Roughnecks, in Chapter 8). As evidence of the strength of this urge, arrests for theft (auto theft, burglary, and robbery) easily constitute the greatest percentage of arrests in the United States for both young and old, males and females. According to Greenberg, "Adolescent theft then occurs as a response to the disjunction between the desire to participate in social activities with peers and the absence of legitimate sources of funds needed to finance this participation."[15]

While contradictions between economic goals and economic opportunities lead to utilitarian responses such as shoplifting and theft to acquire material things, some delinquent acts do not appear to be utilitarian. Greenberg argues that other kinds of contradictions cause youths to participate in nonutilitarian acts such as vandalism, arson, and thefts in which objects are abandoned or destroyed.

Because youth cultures value autonomy and freedom, frustrations build up in connection with the schools. Schools put youths in a dependent position, symbolizing the limits to self-expression for adolescents who are required to attend school, have little autonomy over what they do there, and if they do not perform well academically, may be publicly humiliated. Greenberg believes that denial of autonomy and public degradation are the features of schooling that cause nonutilitarian delinquency. When going to school is experienced as a frustration, it is not surprising that the greatest amount of vandalism and destruction involves school property.

There are also contradictions in the special sexual status of adolescents, who are at the age of socialization into gender roles. In spite of changes in the roles of males and females in society, the peer culture of adolescence still strongly favors traditional male and female behaviors. For boys, the traditional role requires toughness, strength, self-sufficiency, bravery, daring, and other stereotypically masculine behaviors. Those who do not have opportunities to demonstrate such supposedly masculine virtues experience a good deal of anxiety and concern and are likely to turn to fighting and other forms of violence to prove their masculinity. Greenberg notes that "men who experience such anxiety because they are prevented from fulfilling conventional male role expectations may attempt to alleviate their anxiety by exaggerating those traditionally male traits that can be expressed. Attempts to dominate women (including rape) and patterns of interpersonal violence can be seen in these terms."[16]

STRESS AS A FORM OF ANOMIE

The social work literature has given a prominent place to the study of stress. Stress is seen as a cause of private troubles, and social service interventions known as stress management have been devised to overcome it.[17]

Stress theory and anomie theory are two distinct perspectives which should not be confused. Anomie theory is rooted in sociology, structural functionalism in particular, and has been used to explain deviance and other social behaviors which are not considered normal. Stress theory is rooted in physiology and the

PART-TIME WORK AND ADOLESCENT DEVELOPMENT

The availability of employment opportunities for young people has become a social and political issue in American society. Proposed legislation to raise the minimum wage was promptly vetoed in June 1989, partly because it did not include adequate provisions for a lower training wage; the administration's position was that long-term lower entry-level wages would mean more jobs for young people and minorities. Substantial numbers of young people had joined the labor force for part-time and temporary work in the 1960s and 1970s, as a result of social policies designed to open up more employment opportunities for them. The growth of service industries, particularly in urban and suburban neighborhoods, also vastly increased the opportunities for teenagers to earn wages while still attending school.

Some social scientists have questioned whether the availability of work opportunities has made a positive contribution to adolescent development. When Ellen Greenberger and Laurence Steinberg surveyed a sample of 530 youths from largely middle-class backgrounds, 82 percent white, 10 percent Hispanic, and 8 percent black or Asian (chiefly the latter), they found some disconcerting results. When teenagers work, academic grades are likely to decline, money earned is rarely saved but is spent on consumer goods, and students internalize many negative values associated with the competitiveness of the economic order. Greenberger and Steinberg conclude that "excessive commitment to a job may pose an impediment to development, by causing adolescents to spend too much time and energy in a role that is too constraining and involves tasks that are too simple, not very challenging, and irrelevant to their future to promote development." The problem may be not that adolescents, at least those in the middle class, lack economic resources but that they have too many and have become overly involved in trying to gain immediate material rewards.

study of the endocrine system. It is useful in understanding physical health and illness and relies heavily on psychology. Nevertheless, stress theory does echo a number of the ideas underlying anomie theory, and stress may be interpreted as a form of anomie.

THE GENERAL ADAPTATION SYNDROME

Hans Selye introduced the term **general adaptation syndrome** in 1936 as "a nonspecific response of the body to readjust itself following any demand made

For lower-class adolescents, however, another recent study espoused meaningful work activities for pay as a way of opening opportunities. Terry Williams and William Kornblum developed a program based on the completion of difficult writing assignments. They were concerned with deterring adolescents in a neighborhood abandoned by industry, leaving a scarcity of jobs, from turning to crime or prostitution in order to achieve material well-being. They trained 86 disadvantaged youths between the ages of 14 and 20 to participate in the world of work by having them write assignments on such topics as "life histories of themselves and their peers, interviews with their peers and parents, descriptions of their experience in other employment situations, field notes about events in their neighborhoods, and evaluations of their experience in the demonstration." The results indicate that success is possible, given close supervision, support, and demanding assignments. Nevertheless, the researchers refer to the lack of legitimate opportunities, the problem Merton highlighted in the 1950s, as "social dynamite." Lower-class teens continue to turn to illegitimate opportunities when legitimate opportunities are not available.

While on the surface these two studies point in different directions, in many ways they are not at odds. Both indicate that work experiences for youth should assure positive personal and interpersonal development. They also affirm that work will be of developmental value only if it is challenging, meaningful, well supervised, and leads to increased opportunities in the future. Work simply for conspicuous consumption has no value.

Sources: *Youth: Transition to Adulthood*, report of the Panel on Youth of the President's Science Advisory Committee (Chicago: University of Chicago Press, 1974); Ellen Greenberger and Laurence Steinberg, *When Teen-Agers Work: The Psychological and Social Costs of Adolescent Employment* (New York: Basic Books, 1986), quote on p. 7; and Terry Williams and William Kornblum, *Growing up Poor* (Lexington, MA: Lexington Books, 1985).

upon it." This produces stress, which itself is defined as "the physiological changes in the body that prepare it for fight or flight."[18] These changes are elicited by the direct influence on body tissues of neural impulses from the hypothalamus in the brain and by the secondary influence on these tissues of the release of epinephrine or adrenaline.

The general adaptation syndrome involves three stages. In the first stage, **alarm**, the whole organism is involved in a generalized activation and mobilization of defensive responses. In the second stage, **resistance**, the responses are more localized, specialized, and effectively contained. The third stage, **exhaustion**, occurs when the reponses are strained beyond their capacity and the defenses collapse; eventually the organism dies.[19]

The defensive responses or changes in the body that occur with stress include increased blood glucose, blood glycerol, and fatty acids, more rapid heart rate, higher blood pressure, faster breathing rate, dilated air passages, and greater blood flow to skeletal muscle. Stress arises as a function of both physical and emotional arousal. When it arises from vigorous exercise and physical activity, the body seems to adjust and respond in positive ways. When it arises from emotional trauma, the diastolic pressure increases as the body tenses and additional strain is put on the heart. Continuous emotionally induced stress can lead to the coronary damage that often results in heart attacks.[20] Seyle identifies a long list of "distress signals" which can indicate responses to stress, including general irritability and excitability, pounding of the heart, dryness of the throat and mouth, impulsive behavior, inability to concentrate, accident proneness, floating anxiety, stuttering, insomnia, excessive sweating, and loss of or excessive appetite.[21] Stress can also lead to sadness and depression, listlessness, and other negative psychological conditions. Stress theory is an attempt to understand the debilitating physical and psychological effects of emotional arousal on the behavior of individuals.

STRESSORS IN THE ENVIRONMENT

The origin of stress in individuals is found in changes in the physical or social environment. Some events act as **stressors**, situations that provoke the physiological response or stress. Stress theory and anomie theory come together in the way stressors are understood. Like anomie theory, stress theory starts with the assumption that change of any sort creates problems for people. In his pioneering studies, Selye discovered that if rats were injected with a variety of foreign substances, the same physiological response was always produced: The intrusion of any foreign matter produced stress.[22]

In the study of human stress and adaptations to it, the events or stressors are believed to be social rather than biological intrusions. The most common way of measuring stress in humans is with the Schedule of Recent Experiences (SRE) or one of its variations. This instrument is based on the observation that there is a relation between life changes and physical and psychological problems.[23] People filling out the SRE are asked to rate the extent to which they had experienced stress as a result of the situations listed (see box, Life Events Provoking Stress).

Responses to the SRE indicate that any event representing some change in the situation in which people find themselves can induce stress. When the normal routine breaks down, emotional arousal is followed by physiological arousal, and people are forced to adjust. As Durkheim found with suicide, these changes can be of a positive or negative nature. Although most of the

LIFE EVENTS PROVOKING STRESS, BY RANK

The extent to which various life events provoke stress has been measured with the Schedule of Recent Experiences. Rankings on this scale are based on the number of times a particular event is cited by a group of respondents as having been a recent stressful experience for them. A loss in family relationships was by far the most frequently checked event on the list of stressful experiences in the 1960s:

RANK	LIFE EVENT
1	Death of spouse
2	Divorce
3	Marital separation
4	Jail term
5	Death of close family member
6	Personal injury or illness
7	Marriage
8	Fired at work
9	Marital reconciliation
10	Retirement
11	Change in health of family member
12	Pregnancy
13	Sex difficulties
14	Gain of new family members
15	Business adjustment
16	Change in financial state
17	Death of a close friend
18	Change to different line of work
19	Change in number of arguments with spouse
20	Mortgage over $10,000

Source: T. H. Holmes and R. H. Rahe, "The Social Readjustment Rating Scale," *Journal of Psychosomatic Research*, vol. 11, no. 2 (1967), Journal no. 227, p. 214. Reprinted with permission of Pergamon Press.

stressors are negative changes (death, divorce, marital separation), there are also positive changes (marriage, marital reconciliation, pregnancy, and the addition of new family members). Some of the life events included in the scale simply highlight periods of change (change in financial state, change in number of arguments with spouse, change to a different line of work).

The Relation of Stress to Unexpected Change in Life Events

The concept of stress has been used to study difficulties encountered in aging throughout the life cycle, which can be seen as a series of life events related to biological, psychological, and social factors. Some of these events are normative in the sense that they are expected. We expect to go to school, be popular with our peers, choose and enter a career, leave home, get married, have children, become economically successful, grow old gracefully with our loved ones, see our children become even happier than we have been, become grandparents, and die peacefully when we are old. These are the **normative expectations** of life. Often normative expectations are related to chronological age, that is, they are **normative age-graded influences** on development. We are expected to go to school at age 6, graduate from high school at age 18, get married for the first time around age 25, die at age 75 or 80. Other normative expectations have more to do with the historical era in which individuals live and the age cohort (people born more or less at the same time) they belong to. Thus the expectations for people born during the Great Depression of the 1930s were very different from the expectations of people born in the baby boom years of the 1950s or the social-movement years of the late 1960s and early 1970s. These influences on development are referred to as **normative history-graded influences**.[24]

Sometimes life events do not occur when they are expected or in quite the way they are expected to occur. This is especially the case as people age. We expect to be economically successful, so being poor or unemployed is jarring. We expect to marry and live happily ever after, so if we quarrel, are divorced, or become widowed, our expectations are shattered. These **nonnormative influences** on development are not easily discernible because they are not what people have prepared themselves to expect.

Normative life events, according to some researchers, do not cause stress; it is nonnormative events that are stressors. According to Bernice Neugarten,

> . . . it can be argued that the normal and expectable life events are not themselves life crises. Leaving the parent's home, marriage, parenthood, occupational achievement, one's own children leaving home, the climacteric, grandparenthood, retirement — these are the normal turning points, the punctuation marks along the life line. They call forth changes in self-concept and identity, but whether or not they produce crises depends on their timing. For instance, for the majority of middle-aged women the departure of children is not a crisis. It is, instead, when children do *not* leave home on time that a crisis is created for both parent and child.[25]

Neugarten says that even death is normal and expectable; it is a tragic event only when it occurs at too young an age.

THE PSYCHOLOGICAL RESPONSE TO STRESS

Where Durkheim and Merton examined only those social situations that provoke anomie, stress theorists, like those who emphasize anomia, have been more concerned with the psychological response to stress. Stress theory gives a great deal of attention to **perceived stress**, that is, individuals' reactions to stressors. They argue that no stressor in and of itself automatically provokes stress. What is important is how the individual perceives the change. Thus what may be stressful for one person may not be stressful for another, and some people are affected more or less than others by the same level of stress. In short, people's definition of the situation is what counts; stress only exists if they think it does.

People also respond or adapt to stress in different ways. The primary adaptive mechanism is believed to be cognitive; people respond by appraising the situation they are in. Two relatively complex subprocesses in the appraisal process have been described by R. S. Lazarus and his associates.[26] **Primary appraisal** has to do with determining the relevance for personal well-being of a life experience. It involves evaluating the "threat value" of a life change. Upon evaluation, a person decides whether the situation is irrelevant, benign, or stressful. A person who appraises an event as stressful must make further appraisals. The threat may be seen to have already caused significant harm or loss or as being likely to do so. Or the threat may be appraised as a challenge, a situation with potential for personal growth and development. **Secondary appraisal** has to do with evaluating what can be accomplished. People take into account the options available to them, the likelihood that a particular option will have the desired results, and their ability to use the available option effectively.

STRESS THEORY AND MANAGEMENT IN SOCIAL SERVICE PRACTICE

Since stress theory has been developed largely by clinically oriented scientists, it can be directed more explicitly to direct-service social workers than anomie theory can. Emotionally induced stress often leads to physical or psychological difficulties. When people appraise their situations and are unable to find within themselves the personal resources necessary to cope, they are likely to turn to professional helpers. The role of the helper or social worker is to convert the negative experience of stress into an experience that promotes positive growth. The worker therefore leads clients through a reappraisal process, helping them see the challenge and positive potential of the experience. Then the worker aids clients to determine their options, evaluate them, and use them effectively.

Stress management programs usually have four components. The first is decreasing the physiological arousal of stress by teaching relaxation techniques. The second component usually is coping with maladaptive thinking by supplying information about stress and stress reactions. In this step clients are encouraged to see stress as a challenge which offers the potential for personal development. They are taught adaptive self-statements to use in preparing for, confronting, and dealing with stressors. In the third component, training in problem-solving strategies, clients learn to identify problem situations, reflect on them, generate solutions, and implement them. The fourth component is mobilizing personal resources by such means as linking clients to social support networks.[27]

Stress theory and stress management make very useful, concrete contributions to social service practice. They fall short only in providing a critical understanding of human behavior. Stress theory carries no social message and no utopian vision. Since stressors are seen as largely neutral but unfortunate facts of life, there is no analysis of how society generates private troubles. There is no relation of stress to inequity, exploitation, alienation, or a lack of opportunities. There is no appreciation of sexism, racism, or ageism. Stressors only become a problem if people perceive them to be a problem. Likewise, stress management usually has no social-change component. It may include **assertiveness training**, whereby people are helped to speak up and be more forceful in terms of their perceived rights, but this rarely is translated into any larger political or social movement.

Thus, while stress theory and stress management help people to conform and adjust, they rarely contribute to critical commentaries about society. Stress management depoliticizes human struggles. For stress theory to be really useful in a critical theory for social service practice, more systematic analysis on the societal roots of stress would have to be undertaken.

IMPLICATIONS OF STRUCTURAL FUNCTIONALISM FOR PRACTICE

Structural functionalism is a major theoretical perspective which has been highly influential in social service work. It has contributed the important concept of anomie, which in turn is reflected in ideas on stress and individual development across the life cycle.

Structural functionalism has a clear utopian vision of how interpersonal and other social relationships ideally should function. Harmony and stability, derived from common, shared values and expectations, should prevail. Everyone should be assured equal opportunity to achieve the socially acknowledged goals to which they aspire. What these values are is of much less consequence than agreement about them and opportunities to achieve them. When harmony is broken, that is, when social change occurs or when contradictions in norms and expectations exist, then anomie, stress, and developmental crises may surface. These strains or stressors force individuals to adjust their behaviors, positively or negatively. A positive adaptation, from the viewpoint of functionalism, is usually one that reinforces the existing values while assuring improved opportunities to achieve them. A negative adaptation is one that produces deviance, physical illness, or psychological disturbance.

The role of the social service worker is to assess the degree to which clients are in situations of anomie or stress. Following stress theory, the worker must inquire into the social changes or stressors operating on clients and into the cognitive processes by which clients define and attempt to deal with them. Following anomie theory, the worker must identify the social norms operating in the society and in the communities in which clients actually live. It is also necessary to assess the opportunities, both legitimate and illegitimate, which are available to clients. In part this can be done by asking clients to describe their opportunities as they perceive them, but a more complete interpretation of anomie requires the worker to go out into the community and study its norms and opportunities directly. Furthermore, the worker must identify the conditions in the family, in friendship or peer groups, and in other community organizations which impinge upon the situation and make it likely that certain kinds of adaptations will be favored over others.

When it is determined that anomie or stress is affecting a client, the worker can plan strategies for altering either the situation or the ways the client is responding to it. Anomie theory leads workers to reinforce attachment to prevailing social norms and increase the available legitimate opportunities by developing and maintaining community resources and linking people to them. Stress theory leads workers to help people acknowledge and manage stress so they can continue to function and develop despite present and future stress.

SYMBOLIC INTERACTIONISM

Symbolic interactionism is a perspective on human behavior which has its origins in the United States in the early twentieth century. In important ways it too represents a criticism of classical economic theory, particularly its behaviorist and utilitarian characteristics. David Karp and William Yoels define **symbolic interactionism** as "a theoretical perspective in sociology which focuses attention on the processes through which persons interpret and give meanings to the objects, events, and situations that make up their social worlds." **Social worlds** represent the "totality of the various social locations individuals occupy in a society."[28] Thus members of different social classes, racial and ethnic groups, religions, sexual orientations, and so on inhabit different social worlds.

George Herbert Mead, a major figure in symbolic interactionism, argues that habits developed through social reinforcement processes, as in classical and operant conditioning (see Chapter 12), are only one small and often inconsequential aspect of human behavior. Taking issue with the "empty headedness" of such ideas on conditioning, he argues that the mind is an essential consideration in the understanding of human behavior.[29]

Mind and Self in the Context of Society

Mind is a function of certain unique features of humans as a biological species which allows for three specific abilities. First, humans have the ability to create **symbols**. That is, through language and other cognitive processes, they can name and designate objects, feelings, and behaviors in their environment and within themselves. Second, humans have the ability to think and to rehearse alternative lines of action. Thinking is a covert or hidden action which goes on inside the head; it is a private conversation we have with ourselves about what is going on, what we feel, and what we want to do. Mead refers to this as **imaginative rehearsal**. Third, humans have the ability to make decisions about their feelings and behaviors and to **give meaning** to their social worlds. In this respect, mind makes active participation in everyday events possible. Humans influence these events by the way they interpret them, express feelings and attitudes about them, and actually behave in them. No other species can do this in the sophisticated and efficient way that humans can.[30]

While mind is inherent in the biological nature of man, it does not exist outside the context of society. Mind not only produces human society, it is influenced and shaped by that society. How humans symbolize, develop and use language, and communicate with one another are all developed through social interaction. Thus humans are involved with one another not as mechanical and utilitarian social rewarders and punishers but as participants in a symbolic interaction. Through such interaction, society, the social system composed of norms, values, social institutions, and institutionalized social arrangements (see Chapter 2), is continually shaped and reshaped.

Self is one of the products created from the relation of mind to society. Karp and Yoels define **self** as "the view of oneself derived from the ability to evaluate one's behaviors from the point of view of others, ultimately from the point of view of the standards of society as a whole."[31] The self is one of those symbols, one of those imaginative rehearsals, one of those meaningful lines of action people decide to take.

Different aspects of self have been identified. **Identity** establishes who and what we are in social terms: "I am a man, an Hispanic, a social worker."[32] **Self-image** refers to the sense of self as unique and how we attempt to present ourselves in everyday interaction with others: "I am a secure, confident woman." Sometimes self-image exists in contrast to the **ideal self**, the person we wish we were or want to be: "I wish I were more sophisticated and worldly wise."[33] Sometimes this ideal exists in contrast to the **possible self**, which is what we could be if we tried: "I could be less shy and awkward."[34] The self-image, the ideal self, and the possible self are representations of the essence of humans as individuals, statements about how they see themselves most of the time, if not always. More transitory representations of the self are referred to as **self-precepts**; when we fail at a particular task we may think of ourselves as incompetent, though we do not normally think of ourselves that way. Another aspect of self is **self-esteem**, which refers to how we evaluate ourselves favorably or unfavorably as a result of a particular event: "What a mess I am," or "What a nice person I am."

Since self is only possible because of the symbolic capacities of humans, it is attached to mind. Self is also attached to society, because it is only through interaction with others that the person gives meaning to and makes sense of who she or he is. Mind, self, and society are all processes. Unlike many other perspectives, symbolic interactionism does not consider stable or unstable social structures. In this perspective everything exists in a state of flux, always emerging but never quite arriving. Mind, self, and society are in continual development.

The Development of the Self

Perhaps no other process is more central to symbolic interaction than the development of the self. Mead proposes that the self has two components, the I and the me. The **I** is subjective, concerned with how we see ourselves, while the **me** is objective, concerned with how others see us. The I also is more spontaneous, creative, and unpredictable, while the me is more conventional, conforming, and rule-abiding.[35] Mead emphasized the objective nature of the self, the me, and noted that it occurs at an earlier phase of development than the I. Thus we see ourselves as others see us before we come to some understanding of our own image of ourselves. Charles Horton Cooley, another early symbolic interactionist, emphasized the development of the more personal, subjective I.[36] The important point is that the development and emergence of the self comes about not only as others respond to us but also as we respond to ourselves.

The basic process in the development of the self involves the objective me and the ability to take the role of the other. Role-taking must be distinguished from role-playing. **Role-taking** is analogous to seeing the world, including the self, from the point of view of others. In particular, it is "the process whereby an individual imaginatively constructs the attitudes of the other, and thus anticipates the behavior of the other."[37] **Role-playing** refers to the behaviors associated with and undertaken in a particular social position. Thus the self emerges out of the ability to step into the role of others and see oneself through their eyes. The ability to symbolize makes it possible to read the minds of others with whom interactions take place.

There are three phases in the development of the self: imitation and symbolizing, play, and games. The self develops across the life cycle as humans physically mature and decline. At birth, individuals are not able to take the role of others, to play, or to see themselves as unique. Infants imitate others, but these **imitative behaviors** have no meaning for them. Soon, however, the gestures and behaviors of the child acquire meaning and purpose. Even before children can talk, they can understand the attitudes of others through language.[38]

A sense of self, then, emerges as cognitive abilities mature. Role-playing follows role-taking, the ability to take the role of the other. In **play**, children become able to look at themselves from the point of view of others and to practice the roles they are learning in interaction. A girl raised in a traditional family may play at being a mother or a beauty queen. A boy raised in a traditional family may play at being a father or a football player. The girl treats a doll as her parents have been treating her, cuddling, feeding, and dressing it in pretty clothes, or she dresses up in her mother's hats and shoes. The boy carries around a briefcase and wears a necktie in imitation of his father or hurtles around in imitation of the football stars he sees on television. Children at play not only take the roles of others but also role-play, becoming an object to themselves and externalizing their behaviors so they can be understood and evaluated.

Children's play is unorganized, however; in play they learn to take the roles of particular others but not the social roles through which society is organized. The final phase in the early development of the self is the ability to participate in **games**, which have organized rules and involve many players at once. Thus games enable children to understand where they fit in relation to other players. Mead used the example of a baseball game. A child who becomes the catcher in baseball must understand this position and how it relates to the position of the pitcher, the basemen, the outfielders, and even the coaches.

Generalized Others, Reference Groups, and Significant Others

All social interaction is not equally influential in the development of the self. Mead developed the concept of the **generalized other** to describe the "organized community or social group which gives to the individual his unity of self."[39] Karp and Yoels define the generalized other as "all of those persons whose behaviors and expectations are considered by individuals in formulating their own behavior." [40] This idea has also been expressed by symbolic interactionists in terms of the reference group or the reference other.[41] The **reference group**, introduced in Chapter 12, is very much like the generalized other. It has to do with those groups or individuals with which people identify and which are therefore capable of influencing them. Such **referents** are used in two ways: in a normative way, to provide standards, norms, attitudes, and values that individuals come to identify as their own, and in a comparative way, to allow individuals to evaluate themselves and their positions.[42]

Reference groups and others need not be actual persons or groups; it is not necessary to have contact with them or to belong to them as members. Referents *may* be actual people we know, parents, friends, religious leaders, or others we have come to know and respect, or they may be people we do not actually know but only know of or aspire to be like or to be connected with. For instance, a lower-class male whose parents never went to college may aspire to become a college-educated professional. In the process, his referent stops being his membership group (his family) and becomes the professional group to which he aspires. Referents may also be imaginary or symbolic. They may simply exist as ideas in our heads; we may want to be sophisticated or quiet and unassuming, traditional or radical, feminine or masculine, and so on.[43]

Reference groups and others are not always positive referents. **Negative reference groups** are those we do not want to imitate and whose influence we want to avoid. Such negative referents can be important as a source of behavior and self-image. Knowing that you do not want to be a narrow-minded conservative, for instance, can shape your behavior as much as knowing that you want to be an open-minded liberal.

The concept of **significant others** is also associated with the development of the self. Significant others are usually considered to be actual people with whom individuals interact and who have influence over them.[44] Most often they are members of the primary groups in which intimate, person-to-person interactions take place at the interactional level (see Chapter 2). Thus significant others usually are members of the individual's family, friendship groups, or communities based on common identity. But significant others may also be involved in secondary groups in which meaningful interaction takes place on a more restricted, less personal basis on the sociocultural level. Thus a teacher may serve as a significant other for a student or a boss can do so for a worker.

Social Interaction

The self first emerges in childhood, but it is subject to continual change and reshaping throughout life as a function of interactions with others. **Interaction** can be defined as "the reciprocally influenced behavior of two or more people," [45] or, as noted in Chapter 2, as a continual, overarching process through which individuals influence one another and social systems are shaped. As one of the basic social processes identified by George McCall and J. L. Simmons, interaction operates along with recruitment, socialization, innovation, and control to maintain or change social systems.[46]

Situations and Social Positions

Social interaction always takes place in situations. **Situations** can be defined objectively as the actual circumstances under which individuals come together, or they can be defined subjectively in terms of the meaning of the circumstances for the individuals who are interacting. At the objective level, a situation could involve, for instance, encounters in the family, among friends, at school, or at work, and these encounters could be further identified as a family dinner, an accidental meeting in an elevator, a student study group, or an evaluation of work performance.

People understand themselves and others only through the social positions they occupy in the situation. **Social position** is defined in role theory in terms of the related concepts of status and role (see Chapters 2 and 10). Status is equivalent to the position itself—member of the family, stranger, lover or spouse, student or teacher, boss or worker, social worker or client. Role refers to the dynamic aspects of the position, the actions of mothers, strangers, lovers and spouses, students and teachers, bosses and workers, and social workers and clients. Social interaction functions so that people are recruited and socialized into positions where they may maintain or change the behaviors and attitudes expected of people in their position.

Definition of the Situation

Symbolic interactionists are especially interested in the subjective **definition of the situation**, the stage of examination and deliberation which precedes action. To define a situation is to give it and the role of the individual in it the meaning necessary for interaction to occur. McCall and Simmons outline the process in the following terms:[47]

1. As humans, we are thinkers, planners, schemers.
2. Things take on meaning in relation to our plans.
3. We act toward things in terms of their meaning for our plan of action.
4. Therefore, we must identify every "thing" we encounter and discover its meaning.
5. For social plans of action [things that are done with others], the meanings of "things" must be consensual; that is, there must be agreement among the participants about those meanings.

The definition of the situation gives the concept of role a special interpretation in symbolic interactionism. As we have noted, people's roles are defined in terms of both the expectations others have of them and the expectations they have of themselves. Thus while there are certain cultural and interpersonal expectations about the way a mother, a student, or a social worker should behave, how individuals interpret these roles is of paramount importance. Mary's definition of mother is likely to be quite different from Maria's definition of mother. Your definition of student may be quite different from the definition of student the person next to you in class would give. Symbolic interactionists emphasize the subjective aspects of role.

Negotiated Lines of Action: Behaviors and Self-Definitions

Because there are often differences between the expectations others have of us (the objective situation) and the expectations we have of ourselves (the subjective situation), all social interaction involves negotiation and bargaining about how the behaviors associated with roles are to be enacted. A certain amount of agreement has to be reached in the situation in order for the interaction to go smoothly. This is what McCall and Simmons refer to as the **negotiation of lines of action**.[48]

Behaviors and other role-related tasks are not the only things negotiated in social interaction. Individuals also negotiate their own identities within the situation, that is, how they present themselves. Specifically, they negotiate how much of their own selves they can bring to the situation. Two working agreements must be reached, one with the self and one with the others in the situation. For instance, the negotiation could involve how much of the real Mary and how much of the expected Mary a mother can bring into an encounter with her 15-year-old daughter, Margaret. Mary may be a quite liberal, open-minded person, but she feels she should be more conservative in talking about sex with her daughter. Margaret may want her mother to open up and tell her about her own experiences as a teenager, but Mary may choose to hide or reinterpret some of the facts of her past in accordance with how she believes teenaged girls ought to behave. Similarly, a social worker may need to negotiate how much of her real self and how much of her expected self as a worker she should bring into an encounter with a client in an unwanted pregnancy. The real self may feel very strongly that abortion is wrong or even a sin but nevertheless feel constrained by the ethics of the social work profession to allow the client self-determination. Even though the client wants the worker to advise her honestly and openly about all the alternatives available, the worker may feel the urge to promote the alternative that agrees with her personal views.

McCall and Simmons divide negotiation into four moments or processes: imputation of the role of other, improvisation of a role for self, presentation of self, and altercasting. **Imputation of the role of other** involves the moment of role-taking. We try to step into the roles of others in order to understand where they are coming from. We are interested in their qualities as people, but more important we need to understand the roles that are being played and interpreted, that is, the identity they are trying to project. We are interested in the others' plans and schemes so we will know what is giving their role-playing direction, coherence, and meaning. We may not be correct in our understanding of others, but we at least attempt to figure them out. Having reflected on how others are playing their roles, **improvisation of a role for self** is the moment when we come to decisions about how we will play our role. How we play the role, then, is influenced both by our assessment of others and by our own decisions.

Presentation of self is the moment when we express ourselves through our behaviors. The term reflects what has been called a **dramaturgical** approach to human behavior, which is that "individuals present themselves in a manner analogous to a stage actor's presentation of a role to an audience."[49] Erving Goffman, the leading proponent of this view, describes the presentation of self as a process in which the individual "makes an implicit or explicit claim to be a person of a particular kind, [and] automatically exerts a moral demand upon the others, obliging them to value and treat [the individual] in the manner that persons of this kind have a right to expect."[50] **Altercasting** is the moment when we project back to others who we think they should be and what we think they should do. We pass on to them our expectations for them.

THE EFFECTS OF SOCIAL INTERACTION ON THE SELF

The outcomes of all social interactions affect individuals. In the process of negotiating lines of actions and identities they come to either maintain or change the meanings they have previously attached to themselves. Some situations do not affect individuals deeply; what they do in them or how they present themselves in them can be disregarded as being basically irrelevant to the real self. Self-precepts may develop in which they think negatively about themselves, but these pass with time. The term **ingratiation** has often been used to describe those positive presentations of self that are more-or-less momentary, utilitarian, and little involved with the real self.[51] Ingratiation techniques are extremely important in situations of threat or in relationships with superiors. When someone has power over others, they will often try to control it by being agreeable and compliant. They do not necessarily want to act that way but they do anyway, because they sense, often quite rightly, that their survival depends on it.

Other situations affect individuals more deeply. What happens in them somehow gets right to the core of the self-image, so that the real self becomes embedded in and indistinguishable from the situation. When the situations that affect individuals deeply are rewarding and enable them to think positively about themselves, considerable self-esteem can be built. However, when deeply affecting situations are not satisfying and make individuals unhappy about themselves, the result may be a devalued self, a spoiled identity, or a stigma. Such situations involve what symbolic interactionists call labeling.

SYMBOLIC INTERACTIONISM AND LABELING

One perspective within the symbolic interaction tradition is eminently suitable to a critical social service practice because it sheds light on a common problem: Why do so many clients lack self-esteem and suffer from a negative self-image? In the **labeling** perspective the answer is that their self-image reflects how others have responded to them. Negative self-images reflect negative social situations.

The labeling perspective emerged out of the attempt to understand social deviance and abnormal behavior. It made its initial contribution in the areas of delinquency and mental helath and has since been used more broadly to study the negative self-images of individuals who are not necessarily deviant. For instance, Barry Adam has used the perspective to explain feelings of self-hate among Jews, blacks, and homosexuals, and Edwin Schur has used it in examining the process by which women are devalued in contemporary society.[52]

The concept of **labeling** has brought a critical vision to practice. If social service professionals can prevent clients from internalizing negative labels, they will have gone a long way toward helping those who have done things or who belong to groups which somehow offend others.

Labeling in Everyday Life

According to the labeling perspective, no status, attribute, or act is in and of itself inherently negative. Negative evaluations derive from the social process of trying to reach consensus or working agreements about how society and the social interactions within it ought to be organized.

This social process takes place on three levels. At the level of **collective decision making** (that is, the society), working agreements in the form of laws, social policies, traditions, and norms which confer rights and obligations, duties and privileges, are reached. As a result, certain statuses, attributes, and acts come to be valued and others become devalued. At the level of **organizational decision making**, bureaucracies, voluntary associations, schools, clubs, families, and the like reach working agreements about the expectations of members. As a result, certain kinds of participation come to be valued and other kinds become devalued. At the **interpersonal level**, people generate labels that distinguish favorable or acceptable partners from unfavorable or unacceptable partners as they devise their own definitions of friendship, love, and other interpersonal relationships.

Labeling is a natural process. It is also unavoidable; social life is impossible unless humans can define things and give them meaning—bad or negative things as well as good or positive things. Negative labeling thus is an unfortunate consequence of symbolic interaction which can be extremely destructive to the self. There are two ways by which individuals come to have negative labels: They can do things that offend others and thus acquire achieved labels, or they can have the misfortune of being born into a social status that is negatively valued in the society and thus acquire ascribed labels.

Achieved Labels: Blemishes to Individual Character

Most of the work on achieved labels has focused on the applications of such labels as *deviant, delinquent, mentally ill,* or *misfit.* These are stigmatizing labels; Goffman refers to them as **blemishes of individual character** and says they result in a **spoiled identity**.[53] The assumption is that no act is deviant or a sign of mental illness in and of itself. Acts only acquire these meanings through collective or organizational decision making or through interpersonal processes. For such a label to be achieved, the individual must do something which offends others and, moreover, must be caught; that is, the act must come to public attention.

Perhaps the greatest influence of labeling theory has been in the areas of delinquency and mental health. Labeling theory was the basis of programs for diversion and the deinstitutionalization movement which have called for treatment and supervision in the local community rather than in institutions whenever possible. It has also sensitized workers to the need to avoid further psychological damage to delinquent or disturbed clients by being cautious in their use of stigmatizing terminology.

Labeling theorists distinguish primary deviance from secondary deviance.[54] **Primary deviance** refers to commission of an act which might be considered deviant if it is noticed and censured. Nearly everyone performs acts of primary deviance like breaking rules or committing victimless crimes such as gambling and prostitution. Deviance remains primary as long as those who commit such acts define them as incidental to their real self-identity. Labeling theory is not concerned with primary deviance, since commission of an act which does not entail a negative response from society is not assumed to have any consequence for the identity of a person. An individual may be doing things that are not expected of those who are law-abiding or normal, but since no one who would be disturbed by such acts is aware of them, the deviant individual as well as the others continue to think of the individual as a good, normal citizen. **Secondary deviance**, which refers to commission of an act even though it has identified the individual as deviant, is another matter. Once an individual is caught committing an act considered by society to be deviant, a situation is set up where the individual's personal identity can be transformed from law-abiding or normal to deviant or abnormal.

Labeling and Delinquency

Labeling theorists have had much to say about the effects on adolescents of being named delinquent. The term came into use with the development of the juvenile court, a major social invention in the United States. The Illinois legislation under which the first juvenile court was established in Chicago in 1899 officially designated children who break laws as delinquent rather than criminal. It set the age below which a person could not be treated as a criminal and made provisions for governing and evaluating the behavior of delinquents in hearings rather than trials. The work of the court was placed under chancery (or equity) jurisdiction, so delinquent children became wards of the state. All states now have juvenile court laws, most of which apply to persons under age 18.

The objective of juvenile court proceedings is not to establish the guilt or innocence of a person accused of an offense, as in the criminal court, but rather to ensure the well-being of the child. Children's right to nurturance and rehabilitation are differentiated from adults' right to due process of the law and punishment if convicted.[55] The juvenile court legislation also established the special category of **status offenses**, under which certain behaviors are violations if committed by a minor but not if committed by an adult. In earlier times status offenses included a very wide and vague range of behaviors, including such things as immoral or indecent conduct, growing up in idleness, patronizing a public poolroom, wandering about railroad yards, or using vile or vulgar language.[56] Today status offenses are limited to such misbehavior as not obeying parents (unmanageable behavior), not living at home (runaways), not attending school (truants), staying out late at night (curfew violations), or purchasing cigarettes, liquor, or the like.

The homeless are a stigmatized group who endure
"blemishes to individual character." *Mark Antman/The
Image Works, Inc.*

The juvenile justice system was, in many ways still is, considered very progressive. Nevertheless, in the 1960s it came under attack from labeling theorists who charged that instead of nurturing and rehabilitating children, the system was labeling them, that is, turning them into **career deviants** with spoiled identities. These critics agreed that the juvenile justice system had been institutionalized as collective decision making based on a philosophy of delinquency and specified offenses. It was being operated as organizational decision making about how rehabilitation was to be accomplished. And at the interpersonal level, court counselors, probation officers, and others within the system were fulfilling their tasks by labeling offenders. According to their argument, the self-images of potentially well-adjusted, normal adolescents were being systematically destroyed.

Labeling theorists have proposed that the juvenile justice system should use **radical nonintervention** and try to affect those brought before it as little as possible.[57] In various states, diversion programs have been set up to avoid court hearings and incarceration in correctional institutions, and attempts have been made to decriminalize status offenses or at least reduce their number. Deinstitutionalization, especially for status offenders, has been used as a way to avoid locking up youths who commit less serious offenses with more hardened offenders. Court decisions and legislation have revised juvenile court proceedings, requiring them to adopt criminal-trial procedures to determine innocence or guilt beyond a reasonable doubt and to observe many of the due-process protections accorded adults, including notice in writing of specific charges, the right to be represented by counsel, and the right to avoid self-incrimination. The goal of all these procedures is to help juveniles accused of delinquent acts avoid internalizing the negative label of delinquent or deviant.

Opposition to the Labeling Argument.   Labeling theorists provoked considerable controversy when they attacked the juvenile justice system. Opposition from court counselors, many of whom are social workers, soon arose. A major concern of labeling theory critics is whether the response to troubled adolescents of others, especially people in authority, in fact leads them to take on spoiled identities as career deviants.

Milton Mankoff, one of the first to argue that this is not the case, points out that delinquency is an achieved status, not a status ascribed by birth. The fact that an offense was committed cannot be avoided, and labeling can take place even though the offender is not caught or processed by an authority. Thus an identity as a career delinquent could develop through interaction with peers, whether or not the adolescent is ever brought into custody.[58] Support for this argument comes from Howard Becker, who helped define the labeling perspective. According to Becker, the development of career deviants is facilitated by their involvement in delinquent subcultures.[59] Walter Gove also emphasizes this point, noting that "a pattern of deviant behavior and low self-esteem occurs long before official labeling. Furthermore, it clearly appears that it is the informal reactions of others, or unofficial acts, that is the major deterrent to deviant behavior."[60] In addition, all youths who pass through the justice system do not end up with spoiled identities. Many ex-offenders are in fact rehabilitated and go on to lead healthy and productive lives.

Whether a young person involved in delinquency incorporates a negative self-image therefore depends on numerous factors. The operation of the juvenile justice system, or, for that matter, any other social service that proposes to treat people who deviate from social norms, is only one contributing factor. The self is not the result of a single experience but develops across the life cycle through interaction with innumerable other individuals. There are endless possibilities for acquiring new identities and for changing old ones.

Labeling and Mental Illness

Labeling theory has also been used in the study of the causes and maintenance of mental illness. Thomas Szasz argues that the **medical model**, in which mental illness is regarded as a diagnosable disease and normality is regarded as health (see Chapter 11), is inappropriate for understanding the emotional troubles and disturbances individuals experience. Although a thermometer and other objective instruments can be used to give a fairly accurate measure of physical health, there are no such instruments available for determining mental health. Mental illness, Szasz and others believe, is a myth. The behaviors designated as pathogenic are no more than labels applied to people who have given other people trouble. The application of the label, through laws, hospitals and clinics, and contact with psychiatrists and other helping professionals, is a political act through which individuals are forced to take on spoiled identities as mentally ill people. Labeling theorists propose that a more appropriate term in reference to emotional troubles is *problems in living*, rather than mental illnesses.[61]

Erving Goffman, a leading symbolic interactionist, documents the ways in which the medical model has been applied in institutions to stigmatize patients, thus contributing to the maintenance of the problem. He describes the mental hospital as an example of a **total institution**, "a place of residence and work where a large number of like-situated individuals, cut off from the wider society for an appreciable period of time, together lead an enclosed, formally administered round of life."[62] Residents are completely engulfed in total institutions, and all aspects of life are conducted in the same place, with little privacy; eating, dressing, sleeping, bathing, and so on, are all done in the company of others. Daily life consists of enforced activities, tightly scheduled and controlled. Officially these activities are supposed to follow a rational plan to realize the official aim of the organization, that is, to cure the patients. Goffman argues that in practice mental hospitals are demeaning, and many patients experience **mortification of the self** which causes them to accept a spoiled identity. The community mental health programs initiated in the 1960s as part of the deinstitutionalization movement were a response to public reaction against the cruel and demeaning conditions of mental hospitals and the stigma and deprivation that ordinarily results for individuals committed to them.

Murray Edelman believes that labeling common, everyday activities as though they are medical interventions is a political act whereby superior and subordinate roles are identified. He regards popular use of the term *therapy* as the ultimate metaphor for the medical model. Mental health professionals redefine common, everyday activities in therapeutic terms, so sitting down and talking about problems becomes psychotherapy; asking clients to read books becomes bibliotherapy; having a dance becomes dance therapy; teaching marketable skills becomes occupational therapy, and so on. Professional language, or jargon, thus is used as a tool of communication to create status differences and remind clients of their inferior position.[63]

In fact, labeling is more likely to occur when people with symptoms of mental illness use mental health services than when they do not. According to Bruce Link, labeling is not just a function of direct, face-to-face interaction with professionals. Stereotypes about the mentally ill are inculcated into individual beliefs through socialization. As a result, people who use mental health services expect to be devalued and discriminated against and act accordingly—a self-fulfilling prophecy. Link presents data to show that people who do not use mental health services, even though they have symptoms that would seem to require it, do not suffer a loss in self-esteem because of their symptoms. He concludes that to the extent that people believe they can handle their own problems, they are less likely to think of themselves as mentally ill.[64]

Challenges to Labeling.   The conclusions of labeling theory in respect to the mental health system have been attacked in the same way as its conclusions in respect to juvenile delinquency, using similar arguments. One argument which specifically challenges labeling theory as applied to mental illness, however, utilized research which establishes that some problems in living are indeed illnesses.

For years schizophrenia, for instance, has been described as a kind of mental illness, and there has been a fair amount of consensus that is is caused by internal psychological conflicts created by neurotic parents who send mixed messages to their children. Recently the search for psychological and social causes has all but come to a standstill, however. Neuropsychiatric studies using advanced biomedical techniques have convincingly defined schizophrenia as an illness, and researchers at the National Institute of Mental Health classify it as a group of brain diseases. According to Edward Taylor, "It is known that individuals with the illness may undergo both structural and functional neurological changes. How the abnormalities occur remains largely a mystery." Viral infections, genetic makeup, and chemical or hormonal dysfunctions have been suggested as causes, and in the future the illness may be described as a group of neurobehavioral diseases.[65]

ASCRIBED LABELS: TRIBAL STIGMAS

Labels are not always acquired as a result of actions which offend others. Some people are born with negative labels. Goffman refers to this kind of negative labeling as **tribal stigmas** which engulf individuals because they happen to be born into a particular race, ethnic group, or religion. Through collective decision making, societies create status hierarchies that bestow advantages, prestige, and privilege on certain groups, while creating disadvantages for other groups.

Self-Esteem among Minority Groups

Stigmatized people have been said to internalize the negative labels others ascribe to them. The research data, however, do not always support such sweeping statements.

The self-esteem that minorities such as blacks, Jews, and homosexuals develop has been looked at very closely, for instance. Barry Adam contends that these minorities frequently develop low levels of self-esteem. Because they constantly have to cope with domination by others, these groups internalize the hateful, hostile messages they receive and come to think of themselves as inferior. Adam suggests that minority-group members may try to cope with a hostile environment by trying to escape from their identity, withdrawing socially and psychologically, performing "guilt expiation" rituals, accepting "magical ideologies" that promise to release them from bondage, or experiencing self-hate.[66] Goffman's study of interaction between normal and stigmatized people certainly supports these ideas. According to Goffman, "The stigmatized individual tends to hold the same beliefs about identity that [normals] do; this is a pivotal fact."[67]

Many years before either Adam or Goffman, Gordon Allport had identified **traits due to victimization** in minority-group members. In his studies, minority members reacted to living under constant victimization by trying to deny their membership in the despised group, withdrawing from social relations and becoming passive, or acting clownish and silly, and they would actually hate themselves.[68] After World War II, survivors of the Holocaust noted that some Jews had "identified with the aggressor" to obtain medical and other attention.[69] Observing that sexism has given women the status of a minority group, Gloria Donadello notes that "women take on the behaviors and attitudes of minority-group individuals: self-contempt, helplessness, hopelessness, a sense of inferiority and incompetence, to name some of the most common."[70]

Leon Chestang, a social worker, has suggested that the effects of racism in producing a hostile environment can have negative consequences for personality development. He hypothesizes that many blacks have a sense of injustice, inconsistency, and impotence. Like others experiencing a hostile environment, blacks may be left with a depreciated character.[72] Even as children, many blacks develop low self-esteem (see box, Black Dolls and Black Children's Self-Esteem).

It should not be surprising that people who live continuously with oppression begin to believe the things they hear about themselves. Yet Adam's conclusions on low self-esteem among blacks[72] created quite a stir. A number of studies had

BLACK DOLLS AND BLACK CHILDREN'S SELF-ESTEEM

Dolls representing whites and blacks were used in an early study by Kenneth and Mamie Clark to investigate the consciousness of self and racial identity of black children. In 1939, they asked black children 3 to 7 years old to choose whether they wanted to play with a black or white doll, which one they considered "nice," which one "looks bad," and which one was a "nice color." Generally, the black children preferred the white doll and rejected the black one. Over two-thirds (67 percent) wanted to play with the white doll, over half (59 percent) said the white doll was nice and the black doll looked bad, and 60 percent said the white doll was a nice color.

These findings, later substantiated in numerous studies using various test methods and settings, have been interpreted to mean that black children lack group pride and suffer from low self-esteem. On the basis of these findings K. J. Morland, for instance, generalizes that "in a multiracial society in which there is a dominant and subordinate race, young children of the subordinate race tend to prefer and identify with members of the dominant race, while children of the dominant race tend to prefer and identify with members of their own race."

In 1969, when Joseph Hraba and Geoffrey Grant duplicated the doll study in an integrated elementary school setting, they found that black children who had had opportunities to associate with white children preferred and identified with the black doll. In this study, 72 percent of the black children chose to play with the black doll, compared to 32 percent in the Clarks' study. Hraba and Grant interpreted this as evidence that the black children had internalized the message that "black is beautiful."

Almost 20 years later, however, at the 1987 meeting of the American Psychological Association, Darlene Powell-Hopson and Sharon McNichol reported on their independent replications of the Clark study in the United States and Trinidad. These two new studies of black children showed that they are still very likely to prefer to play with the white doll. The researchers concluded that blacks' feelings of inferiority have not disappeared, in spite of the civil rights efforts initiated in the 1960s and 1970s.

Sources: Kenneth B. Clark and Mamie P. Clark, "The Development of Consciousness of Self and the Emergence of Racial Identification in Negro Preschool Children," *Journal of Social Psychology*, vol. 10 (1939), pp. 591–99; K. J. Morland, "Racial Awareness among American and Hong Kong Chinese Children," *American Journal of Sociology*, vol. 75 (November 1969), p. 360; Joseph Hraba and Geoffrey Grant, "Black Is Beautiful: A Reexamination of Racial Preference and Identification," *Journal of Personality and Social Psychology*, vol. 16 (November 1970), pp. 398–402. APA meeting reported by Daniel Goleman, "Feeling of Inferiority Reportedly Common in Black Children," *The New York Times*, August 31, 1987, pp. 1, 13.

indicated that self-esteem, at least in blacks, is not related to societal factors.[73] Thus, while racism might exist in a society, it did not have any bearing on the self-esteem of blacks. Roberta Simmons and her associates, for instance, consistently reported no difference in the self-esteem of blacks and whites.[74] When the *Journal of Social Psychology* asked her to reply to Adam, she acknowledged that earlier studies did find low self-esteem among blacks, but this had changed, for any number of reasons. The change could simply be a function of the way self-esteem is measured; later studies were comparatively more scientific and objective. Moreover, historical processes can produce changes in self-esteem. In the 1950s, before the civil rights movement, a sense of inferiority could take hold, but several decades of "Black is beautiful" had helped blacks take on a more positive self-image. Simmons also argues that an individual's self-concept may be determined more by family and community than by the larger society. Blacks may be receiving negative messages from whites, but they are receiving positive messages from the people who really count — their friends and families.

While Adam and Simmons disagree on whether minority people always internalize low self-esteem, they agree on how dominated people ought to respond to their dominators. Both emphasize the importance of minority-group members challenging the authority of their persecutors. Adam proposes that minority members should participate in the **arts of contraversion**, that is, develop alternative, more positive definitions of themselves by building support and information networks, develop positive literary and artistic traditions, and encourage other members to subvert the authority and power of those in positions of domination and demand their rights.[75]

RESPONDING TO LABELS

The evidence is clear that societal labels developed and used by those in dominant positions, including social service professionals, do have the potential for creating spoiled identities. Whether negative labels become internalized into the self-image of people depends on a number of factors, however. One is history; to the extent that social movements exist which counter oppressive forces and enable stigmatized people to feel proud about themselves, negative labels are not likely to be internalized. Another major factor is the role of friends and family; to the extent that they offer a buffer against the assault of people in dominant positions, negative labels are not likely to be internalized.

SOCIAL SERVICE WORK AND LABELING

From the perspective of labeling theory, the potential ability of social service workers to stigmatize clients is very real. With respect to clients who have offended others, a worker may inadvertently become one of the "others" who help transform them from normal to deviant. With respect to clients who carry tribal stigmas because of the discrimination suffered by the groups into which they are born, the worker may unknowingly be one of the "others" who continue to reinforce the stigma. In both instances, social workers must be careful lest they contribute to the development of poor self-images and low self-esteem in their clients.

The assessment process in direct-service social work is inherently a labeling process, since identifying the problems of clients entails calling attention to their deficits. Moreover, labeling is a normal process; it is not possible to give meaning to the social world without creating divisions between normal and abnormal, deviant and nondeviant, good and bad. Social service workers therefore cannot avoid labeling, but they can attempt to make assessments in ways that minimize the possibility of leaving clients emotionally scarred. While it is important for social workers to be descriptive of the presenting problem and to locate the specific situational context in which particular deficiencies occur, they can also redefine labels in a way that reflects the troubles clients are experiencing more positively. For instance, they can redefine *handicapped* as *differently abled*; a *frigid* woman as *preorgasmic*; or *disordered* as *experiencing problems in living*. They can refer to a person with AIDS instead of to a victim of AIDS. Use of such more positive terms reduces the negative impact of applying a label.

Social service professionals generally should avoid using **essentialist labels**, descriptions which locate the cause of all problems in the character and personality of the client. Examples of essentialist labels include *neurotic, paranoid, delinquent, criminal, retarded*, and the like. They should avoid engulfing clients in a one-dimensional identity as a deviant, rather than a multidimensional identity which recognizes strengths as well as deficiencies. A client may have committed a crime or suffered an emotional collapse, but the client also may be intelligent, have good values, be motivated to self-improvement, or may be thoughtful and considerate of others. Social service professionals also have an important role in helping people who have been negatively labeled respond assertively to the labels applied to them by others.

IMPLICATIONS OF SYMBOLIC INTERACTIONISM FOR PRACTICE

The symbolic interactionist tradition starts with the premise that the cognitive abilities possessed by humans make them special. Only humans have the full capacity for communication which makes it possible to invent and manipulate symbols. Through this ability human society develops on the communal level and individuals develop a sense of self. The self, like society, is best thought of as a process, always emerging and coming into being. It never just is.

In the continual process of developing a self, the images individuals have of who and what they are become extremely important. To the extent that these images are negative, a spoiled sense of self can evolve. Symbolic interactionists maintain that such spoiled identities ought to be avoided. In their utopian vision of ideal social relations, mutual respect and understanding would constantly produce positive self-images. The message of symbolic interactionism to social service workers is clear: Help clients deal effectively with those who negatively label them, and avoid as much as possible applying to clients labels that stigmatize.

DISCUSSION QUESTIONS AND CLASS PROJECTS

1. Identify and distinguish the ways in which Merton and Durkheim approached the study of anomie.

2. According to Merton, what are the ways in which anomie can be adapted to?

3. Greenberg applied anomie to juvenile delinquency in the 1970s. What contradictions did he see? Do you think these are still important sources of anomie today?

4. Keeping in mind the issue of confidentiality, discuss the situation of a client you are working with. Do you think anomie applies? How do you see it affecting your client? What adaptation to anomie would you say your client is making?

5. Have you ever experienced anomie in your life? If so, describe the situation. What adaptation to anomie did you make?

6. Compare Merton's adaptations to anomie with Marx's adaptation to exploitation and alienation. What do you make of the differences in terms of working with clients?

7. What have studies found with regard to adolescents who are given the opportunity to work? Do you think adolescents should be given the opportunity to work? Will any kind of work do, or should work be organized in a special way?

8. Identify and describe:
normlessness
contradictory norms
anomie
anomia
ritualism
rebellion
retreatism
conformity
illegitimate opportunities
normative expectations
normative age-graded influences
normative history-graded influences
nonnormative influences

9. What is stress? What causes it? What can be done about it?

10. Identify and describe:
general adaptation syndrome
primary appraisal
secondary appraisal
stress management
stressors
perceived stress

11. Identify and describe the importance of the following concepts from the symbolic interactionist perspective.
mind
self-image
ascribed labels
achieved labels
primary deviance
secondary deviance
imaginative rehearsal
spoiled identity
significant others
reference groups
role-taking
role-playing
self-precepts
the me

12. Describe the process that leads to the development of the self in childhood.

13. What is meant by a negotiated line of action? What four processes are involved in negotiation? Do you think the assessment process in social work practice can be seen as an example of negotiating lines of action?

14. What is meant by the labeling per-

spective? What contribution does it make to understanding normal human behavior?

15. Do you think that members of minority groups are likely to experience low self-esteem and internalize a spoiled identity?

16. Social critics have accused social workers and other helping professionals of spoiling the identities of delinquent and disturbed clients. To what extent do you think this is a valid criticism?

17. Identify some friends of yours who have received social service for personal problems. Talk to them about their experiences with the services. Inquire as to whether they experienced a threat to their self-image as a result of the service. Inquire what they think helpers ought to do to avoid labeling people.

18. Select a representative sample of so-

cial workers working in mental health and juvenile delinquency. Interview them to determine their attitudes toward labeling. Ask them such things as what they think a label is, whether they believe labeling goes on in their service, whether they believe labeling can or should be avoided, and in what ways they try to minimize labeling.

19. What specific ways are recommended for social workers to avoid or minimize the potential for labeling? Can you think of other recommendations?

20. Identify and describe the following:
tribal stigma
blemishes of individual character
arts of contraversion
essentialist labels
traits due to victimization
total institutions
mortification of the self

NOTES

1. See W. Peter Archibald, *Social Psychology as Political Economy* (Toronto, Canada: McGraw-Hill, 1978), pp. 50–57.

2. See Ralph E. Anderson and Irl Carter, *Human Behavior in the Social Environment*, 3rd ed. (New York: Aldine, 1984).

3. Emile Durkheim, *Suicide* (New York: Free Press, 1951), pp. 241–76.

4. Robert K. Merton, *Social Theory and Social Structure*, enlarged ed. (New York: Free Press, 1968), pp. 185–248.

5. Ibid., pp. 193–211.

6. Robert M. MacIver, *The Ramparts We Guard* (New York: Macmillan, 1950), pp. 84–85.

7. Merton, *Social Theory and Social Structure*, pp. 215–20.

8. See Lamar Empey, *American Delinquency: Its Meaning and Construction*, rev. ed. (Homewood, IL: Dorsey Press, 1982), pp. 240–45.

9. Merton, *Social Theory and Social Structure*, rev. ed. (1957), p. 146; italics in original.

10. See Richard A. Cloward, "Illegiti-

mate Means, Anomie, and Deviant Behavior," *American Sociological Review*, vol. 24 (April 1959), pp. 164–76, and Richard A. Cloward and Lloyd E. Ohlin, *Delinquency and Opportunity: A Theory of Delinquent Gangs* (New York: Free Press, 1960).

11. Cloward and Ohlin, *Delinquency and Opportunity*, pp. 111–24.

12. Merton, *Social Theory and Social Structure*, enlarged ed. (1968), pp. 212–13.

13. David F. Greenberg, "Delinquency and the Age Structure of Society," in D. F. Greenberg (editor), *Crime and Capitalism* (Palo Alto, CA: Mayfield, 1981).

14. U.S. Bureau of the Census, *Statistical Abstract of the United States 1988* (Washington, DC, 1987), Table 279.

15. Greenberg, "Delinquency and Age Structure," p. 123.

16. Ibid., p. 131.

17. Richard Tolman and Sheldon D. Rose, "Coping with Stress: A Multimodal Approach," *Social Work*, vol. 30 (March–April 1985), pp. 151–52.

18. Cited in Kent M. Van De Graaff and

Stuart Ira Fox, *Concepts of Human Anatomy and Physiology* (Dubuque, IA: William C. Brown Publishers, 1986), p. 600. See Hans Selye, *The Stress of Life* (New York: McGraw-Hill, 1956) and *Stress without Distress* (Philadelphia: J. B. Lippincott, 1974).

19. See Franklin C. Shontz, "Constitutional Theories of Personality," in R. J. Corsini (editor), *Current Personality Theories* (Itasca, IL: F. E. Peacock Publishers, 1977), p. 309.

20. American Medical Association, *Guide to Heart Care*, rev. and updated ed. (New York: Random House, 1984), pp. 65-66.

21. Hans Selye, "Stress," in *Health 83/84, Annual Editions*, (Guilford, CT: Dushkin, 1983), p. 55.

22. See DeGraaff and Fox, *Concepts of Human Anatomy and Physiology*, p. 600.

23. See James H. Johnson, *Life Events as Stressors in Childhood and Adolescence* (Beverly Hills, CA: Sage, 1986) pp. 23-26.

24. Paul B. Baltes, "Life-Span Developmental Psychology: Some Converging Observations on History and Theory," in P. B. Baltes and O. G. Brim, Jr. (editors), *Life Span Development and Behavior*, vol. 2 (New York: Academic Press, 1979).

25. Bernice L. Neugarten, "Time, Age, and the Life Cycle," in M. Bloom (editor), *Life Span Development*, 2nd ed. (New York: Macmillan, 1985), p. 361, italics in original.

26. See Johnson, *Life Events as Stressors*, pp. 20-22.

27. Ibid., pp. 132-36.

28. David A. Karp and William C. Yoels, *Sociology and Everyday Life* (Itasca, IL: F. E. Peacock Publishers, 1986), p. 31.

29. George Herbert Mead, *Mind, Self and Society*, edited by Charles Morris (Chicago: University of Chicago Press, 1934).

30. See Robert H. Lauer and Warren H. Handel, *Social Psychology: The Theory and Application of Symbolic Interactionism*, 2nd ed. (Englewood Cliffs, NJ: Prentice-Hall, 1983), p. 6.

31. Karp and Yoels, *Sociology and Everyday Life*, p. 56.

32. See Ronald Fernandez, *The I, The Me, and You: An Introduction to Social Psychology* (New York: Praeger, 1977), p. 39.

33. See Lauer and Handel, *Social Psychology*, p. 256.

34. See Hazel Markus and Paula Nurius, "Possible Selves," *American Psychologist*, vol. 41 (September 1986), pp. 954-69.

35. Karp and Yoels, *Sociology and Everyday Life*, pp. 48-50, 57.

36. Charles Horton Cooley, *Human Nature and the Social Order* (New York: Scribner, 1902).

37. See Lauer and Handel, *Social Psychology*, p. 104.

38. See Norman K. Denzin, "The Genius of Self in Early Childhood," *Sociological Quarterly*, vol. 13 (Summer 1972), pp. 291-314.

39. See Lauer and Handel, *Social Psychology*, p. 115.

40. Karp and Yoels, *Sociology and Everyday Life*, pp. 48, 57.

41. Raymond L. Schmitt, *The Reference Other Orientation* (Carbondale: Southern Illinois University Press, 1972).

42. Harold H. Kelley, "Two Functions of Reference Groups," in G. E. Swanson, T. M. Newcomb, and E. L. Hartley (editors), *Readings in Social Psychology* (New York: Henry Holt, 1952), pp. 410-14.

43. See Lauer and Handel, *Social Psychology*, pp. 117-18.

44. See Fernandez, *The I, The Me and You*, pp. 42-45, 271-73.

45. See Lauer and Handel, *Social Psychology*, p. 87.

46. George J. McCall and J. L. Simmons, *Social Psychology: A Sociological Approach* (New York: Free Press, 1982), pp. 75-183.

47. McCall and Simmons, *Social Psychology*, pp. 25-26.

48. Ibid., pp. 39-40.

49. Karp and Yoels, *Sociology and Everyday Life*, p. 87.

50. Erving Goffman, *The Presentation of Self in Everyday Life* (New York: Doubleday/Anchor, 1959), p. 13.

51. Edward E. Jones, *Ingratiation* (New York: Appleton, Century, Crofts, 1964).

52. Barry D. Adam, *The Survival of Domination* (New York: Elsevier, 1978); Edwin M. Schur, *Labeling Women Deviant* (New York: Random House, 1984).

53. Erving Goffman, *Stigma: Notes on the*

Management of Spoiled Identity (Englewood Cliffs, NJ: Prentice-Hall, 1963), p. 4.

54. See Edwin Lemert, *Social Pathology* (New York: McGraw-Hill, 1951; also see Karp and Yoels, *Sociology and Everyday Life*.

55. Empey, *American Delinquency*, pp. 63–64.

56. Gene Kasebaum, *Delinquency and Social Policy* (Englewood Cliffs, NJ: Prentice-Hall, 1974), pp. 11–12.

57. Edwin M. Schur, *Radical Non-Intervention* (Englewood Cliffs, NJ: Prentice-Hall, 1973); see Empey, *American Delinquency*, pp. 481–89.

58. Milton Mankoff, "Societal Reaction and Career Deviance: A Critical Analysis," *The Sociological Quarterly*, vol. 12 (Spring 1971), pp. 204–18.

59. Howard Becker, *The Outsiders* (New York: Free Press, 1963).

60. Walter R. Gove (editor), *The Labelling of Deviance*, 2nd ed. (Beverly Hills, CA: Sage, 1980), p. 407.

61. Thomas S. Szasz, "The Myth of Mental Illness," in T. S. Szasz, *Ideology and Insanity: Essays on the Psychiatric Dehumanization of Man* (Garden City, NY: Doubleday/Anchor, 1970). Also see Thomas Scheff, *Being Mentally Ill: A Sociological Theory*, 2nd ed. (Chicago: Aldine, 1984).

62. Erving Goffman, *Asylums: Essays on the Social Situation of Mental Patients and Other Inmates* (Garden City, NY: Doubleday/Anchor, 1961), p. xiii.

63. Murray Edelman, *Political Language: Words that Succeed and Policies that Fail* (New York: Academic Press, 1977), pp. 57–75.

64. Bruce G. Link, "Understanding Labeling Effects in the Area of Mental Disorders: An Assessment of the Effects of Expectations of Rejection," *American Sociological Review*, vol. 2 (February 1987), pp. 96–112.

65. Edward H. Taylor, "The Biological Basis of Schizophrenia," *Social Work*, vol. 32 (March–April 1987), p. 115.

66. Adam, *Survival of Domination*.

67. Goffman, *Stigma*, p. 7.

68. Gordon Allport, *The Nature of Prejudice* (Garden City, NY: Doubleday/Anchor, 1958), pp. 142–62.

69. Bruno Bettelheim, "The Dynamism of Anti-Semitism in Gentile and Jew," *Journal of Abnormal and Social Psychology*, vol. 42 (1947), pp. 153–68.

70. Gloria Donadello, "Women and Mental Health," in E. Norman and A. Mancuso (editors), *Women's Issues and Social Work Practice* (Itasca, IL: F. E. Peacock Publishers, 1980), p. 206.

71. Leon Chestang, "Character Development in a Hostile Environment," in M. Bloom (editor), *Life Span Development*, 1st ed. (New York: Macmillan, 1980), pp. 40–51.

72. Barry D. Adam, "Inferiorization and Self-Esteem," *Social Psychology Quarterly*, vol. 41 (March 1978), pp. 47–53.

73. Ruth C. Wylie, *The Self-Concept*, rev. ed. (Lincoln: University of Nebraska Press, 1979), pp. 138–61.

74. Roberta G. Simmons, "Blacks and High Self-Esteem: A Puzzle," *Social Psychology Quarterly*, vol. 41 (March 1978), pp. 54–57.

75. Adam, *Survival of Domination*, pp. 115–18.

CHAPTER 14

Intrapersonal Well-Being: Ego Psychology and Cognitive Development Theories

M AJOR THEMES DISCUSSED IN THIS CHAPTER:

1. *The study of ego psychology and psychosocial development.* Ego psychology is one of the most important theories of human behavior for social service workers. Its particular utopian vision is psychosocial development, or continuous psychological progress throughout the life span.

2. *The Freudian base of ego psychology.* The origins of ego psychology in Freudian theory are evident in the concern with individuals' inner space. Freud's recognized contributions are balanced by debates concerning his views on the importance of early-childhood experiences, development in women, sex-role identification, and homosexual behavior.

3. *Ego psychology.* Ego psychology focuses on both conscious and unconscious functioning of the "executive arm of the personality." Areas of study include the ego in conflict and defense mechanisms, the ego in harmony and the operation of autonomous functions such as coping, and object relations.

4. *Cognitive development.* The work of Piaget and Kohlberg on cognitive

development, particularly the study of moral judgment, complements the study of autonomous functions in ego psychology. Kohlberg's view of female morality is a topic of debate, and different ideas on the roots of moral behavior have been proposed.

5. *Implications for practice.* The points of view presented in this chapter provide different slants on the utopian ideal of human development. In Freudian theory, the basis of ego psychology, it includes internalizing the norms and traditions of society, identification with same-sex parents, and genital sexual gratification. In ego psychology, human development includes ego strength and competence, and self psychology adds the ideal of a cohesive nuclear self. In cognitive development, an ability for abstract reasoning is the utopian ideal. Direct-service social work assessment requires identifying the strengths and deficiencies of clients with respect to all these perspectives.

THE PERSPECTIVES discussed in Chapters 12 and 13 focus on interpersonal well-being. Each of these perspectives — behavioral (learning and social exchange), Marxian, structural functional, and symbolic interaction — frames the problem of psychological well-being in terms of specific transactions occurring between individuals and others. Each concludes that certain kinds of relationships, described in such terms as inequitable, exploitative, alienating, anomic, and labeling, produce ill-being not only within a person but also between people.

Ego psychology and the cognitive theories of Jean Piaget and Lawrence Kohlberg, the perspectives to be presented in this chapter, frame the issue of psychological well-being differently. **Cognitive development theory** is concerned with the way people attend, learn, think, and reason as they grow older. **Ego psychology** is concerned with the affective or emotional dimension of behavior and development. Both, however, share a common utopian vision: Humans have the capacity to continually develop, psychologically and cognitively.

Both are also concerned with intrapsychic or **intrapersonal well-being**, that is, with what is going on inside the heads of people. The concept of inner space is central to ego psychology. **Inner space** has been defined as the "mental representation of experience, the process involved in reviewing and interpreting experience, and the capacity to plan for new experiences."[1] Ego psychology and cognitive theory do take note of the environment, but generally only the subjective environment, that is, the perceptions individuals have of the external world and their motivations in relation to others. The objective reality is less important, because, as ego psychologists assume, people live within what Heinz Hartman calls an **average expectable environment**, an external world which provides essential support for the development of human potential.[2] Thus important environmental transactions largely take place in the heads of individuals, as physical, cognitive, and emotional processes interpenetrate and generate behavior. For this reason, ego psychology and cognitive development are theories of intrapersonal or intrapsychic well-being.

Throughout much of the history of social work, theories of intrapersonal functioning have been exceedingly important. However, some social service professionals believe that the advent of the various system and ecological approaches, the intrapersonal dimension of human functioning has been neglected.[3] The emphasis on person in situation or person in environment, they contend, has produced an imbalance in favor of interpersonal and other social-context considerations. While it is doubtful that this is the case, the point is well taken. Social workers in direct service, particularly, cannot ignore the inner life of their clients. Ego psychology and the complementary cognitive development theory have been championed as the appropriate psychological theories of intrapersonal functioning to provide balance for the more socially oriented general systems and ecological theories.[4] They provide the conceptual base of many direct-service social work practice models, including the psychoanalytic, psychosocial, problem-solving, and crisis intervention models.[5]

THE STUDY OF EGO PSYCHOLOGY AND PSYCHOSOCIAL DEVELOPMENT

The origins of ego psychology are in Freudian theory, but as it has emerged over the past quarter of a century, it has begun to incorporate many diverse perspectives. While it is no longer strictly Freudian, it nevertheless remains a perspective concerned with normal intrapsychic functioning. Thus ego psychology is a composite of related theoretical ideas about human behavior which are based in Freudian theory.

According to Eda Goldstein, who has examined the application of ego psychology to social work practice, this theory gives primary attention to "the executive arm of the personality — the ego — and its relationship to other aspects of the personality and to the external environment."[6] She lists seven propositions which characterize ego psychology:[7]

1. Ego psychology assumes that people are born with a capacity to function adaptively.
2. The ego is the part of the personality that allows for successful adaptation to the environment.
3. Ego development takes place as a function of meeting needs, identifying with others, learning, mastering tasks, and effectively coping and solving problems.
4. The ego is only one part of the personality and must be understood in relation to the id and superego.
5. The ego mediates between the individual and the environment but also mediates conflict that arises among the various components of the personality.

6. The social environment shapes the personality and provides the conditions that facilitate or hinder coping.

7. Private troubles are a function of deficits in coping capacity and the fit among needs, capacities, and environmental conditions and resources.

Ego psychology is replete with utopian visions of human behavior. One is the vision of **psychosocial development**: Individuals should show continuous psychological progress throughout their lives. Even as they mature and decline physically, their inner life should continue to evolve in a positive direction. At every stage in life people should improve their ability to meet the challenges posed by the biological and social changes taking place around them.

The study of human development involves examination of the physical, cognitive, emotional, and social changes in individuals as they go from conception to death. The concept of psychosocial development carries the connotation of progress. When theorists refer to cognitive, emotional, and social development, they often mean the process whereby humans continually improve their psychological and social functioning. Development thus carries the connotations of unidirectionality and irreversibility; a person goes in one direction from less developed to more developed, and, once there, cannot go back.[8]

DEVELOPMENT AND CHANGE

The concept of development should be distinguished from growth, differentiation, maturation, and change. **Change** refers to alterations from one condition to another and carries no connotation of progress. As Henry Maier notes, "Change implies a transition from one state to another, while development focuses upon the dynamic, one-directional elements of change."[9] Change can be physical or biologcial as well as psychological and social. Change may be for better or worse; no direction or irreversibility is implied.

Growth, differentiation, and maturation all describe progressive physical change. **Growth** refers to physical changes by way of cell or tissue enlargement. In the simplest terms, the body and its organs get bigger. **Differentiation** refers to structural changes through which the interrelations among cells, tissues, and organs or their parts become more specialized and complex. **Maturation** sometimes means a combination of growth and differentiation, but the term also connotes the ability to procreate; a physically mature person is capable of reproducing life. The opposite of growth, differentiation, and maturation is **decline**. As humans mature, their physical capacities stabilize and then begin to decline toward inevitable death.

Psychosocial development, or progressive psychosocial change, is not a fact of life. Studies show that individuals continually change; they do not automatically progress cognitively, emotionally, and socially as they age. There are large intra-individual and inter-individual differences in human behavior, and change is often multidirectional and reversible. A particular individual may show different rates of change at different periods in his or her life; sometimes changing quickly, sometimes slowly; sometimes not changing and sometimes declining. The changes may appear to be in a progressive direction or regressive. Similarly, two people of the same chronological age may show very different patterns of change; one may show continuous progress and the other may not. Change across the life cycle, therefore, is believed to take place in multidirectional and reversible ways (see box, Behavioral Change Across a 50-Year Life Span).[10]

By their attention to the goal of continuous psychosocial development, ego psychologists help social service workers understand the internal struggles individuals encounter and the tasks they must accomplish in order to develop in a progressive direction. Their message to direct-service social workers, in particular, is: Help clients to continually improve their psychosocial functioning.

THE FREUDIAN BASE OF EGO PSYCHOLOGY

Ego psychology has its origins in the work of Sigmund Freud, who must be ranked among the most influential thinkers of all time. Freud was one of the first to approach the study of individual behavior using the scientific method. He observed his patients, devised techniques such as free association and dream analysis to study their personalities, wrote up case studies, and generated hypotheses about human behavior. As a man of science, he lifted thinking about emotional problems out of the realm of religious mysticism. Before Freud introduced the medical model in which emotional problems are regarded as mental illnesses, people with such problems were believed to be controlled by spirits or demons. Freud also established the importance of unconscious, often erotic needs to an understanding of individual behavior. While these ideas probably do not appear startling now, they were quite revolutionary during Freud's time. Furthermore, Freud's theory of human behavior has become so much a part of the cultural heritage that even scholars who deny his importance and criticize many particulars of his theories use and therefore promote his ideas. Terms such as *the unconscious, ego defenses, superego,* and *neurosis* which are common in everyday usage were popularized in his work.

Freud was a voluminous writer whose thinking changed over time. Furthermore, analysts trained by Freud and his followers continue to make changes in his theory. Freudian theory, therefore, should not be thought of as some final, finished product. The following description must be regarded as a gross oversimplification. It is useful only as a basic introduction to Freud's ideas.[11]

A Theory of Psychosexual Development

Freud was concerned with emotional development, that is, with the development of individuals' drives, needs, motivations, and feelings. To Freud, a **drive** is "a genetically determined, psychic constituent which, when operative, produces a state of psychic excitation or . . . tension."[12] He posited that

BEHAVIORAL CHANGE ACROSS A 50-YEAR LIFE SPAN

Changes may occur in many directions over the life span, both within a person and between people. The figure shows how the behavior of five hypothetical people (A–E) might change at 20-year intervals, as they grow from 10 years old to 50 years old.

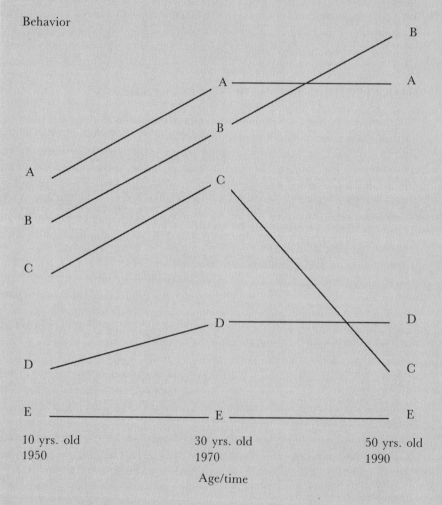

Behavior

Source: Adapted from M. M. Lerner and D. F. Hultsch, *Human Development: A Life-Span Perspective* (New York: McGraw-Hill, 1983), p. 9. Reproduced with permission.

along with survival needs (hunger and thirst), there are two basic instincts, the drive for erotic or sexual gratification (**eros**) and the drive for aggression or destruction (**thanatos**). Most of his work on individual behavior, however, was built around the drive for sexual gratification, and thus his work is referred to as a theory of psychosexual development. Freud believed that the need for erotic gratification — a primary, unlearned, instinctual, drive — is present at birth and driven by an energy which he called **libido**. Although sexual gratification is a fundamental driving force, Freud defined it rather broadly. He saw sexual gratification as deriving from all pleasurable sensual sensations, not simply genital orgasm and ejaculation. Since from birth all humans exhibit a concern for pleasurable sensations, children as well as adults were seen as sexual.

Personality Structure and Dynamics

The central concern in human development for Freud was the personality, structured around three parts: the id, the ego, and the superego. He regarded the personality as a dynamic system, each part in transaction with the others and the whole in transaction with both the somatic or physical apparatus and the external environment.

Freud believed that there is a basic conflict between individuals and society. Instinct drives people to seek their own pleasure, unconcerned about the needs of others. In this respect, Freudian theory can be seen as a conflict theory of human behavior (see Chapter 2). Instinct operates unconsciously in that part of the personality known as the **id**. Especially through family life, society imposes a set of rules to control children's unbridled pleasure-seeking. Early-childhood socialization and development, therefore, represent the struggle between the needs of individual children and the demands of society, as expressed by their parents. Healthy development requires the building of a **superego**, a conscience which offers ideals to strive for at the same time it acts to prohibit undesirable behavior and attitudes. As the internalization of parental standards and moral values, the superego makes it possible to fulfill personal needs while coping with the demands of society. The **ego** is that part of the personality which mediates between libidinal or erotic energies and superego constraints. In his early work, Freud emphasized the place of the id in child development. Only in his later work was the emphasis placed on the ego.

Early-life experiences are considered central to personality development. For Freud, individual personality — the continual dynamic transactions among the id, ego, and superego — is generally set by the time a person is 5 or 6 years old. It may develop a bit further during puberty, but essentially the adult personality, for better or worse, is a stable playing-out of childhood patterns.

While Freud did not work directly with children, his theory is about early-childhood development. For instance, in the case of Little Hans, a 5-year-old boy with a phobia for horses, Freud obtained all his information and carried out the treatment through the parents.[13] Nevertheless, Freud maintained that most of the psychological difficulties adults experience result from unresolved conflicts in their childhood. Struggles to meet libidinal needs in childhood could leave an adult fixated in a particular developmental period and therefore neurotic, with a distorted perception of reality. Then only psychoanalysis, a long-term, in-depth therapy developed by Freud which aims to uncover and replay childhood memories and fantasies, could alter the adult personality. The effects of early-life experiences on personality development have been questioned by later Freudians, however (see box, How Important Are Early-Life Experiences?).[14]

FREUD'S DEVELOPMENTAL STAGES

Freud describes five psychosexual stages of development: oral, anal, genital, latency, and puberty. Adulthood is not seen as a period in which development

HOW IMPORTANT ARE EARLY-LIFE EXPERIENCES?

Most contemporary scholars agree that early-life experiences are important to personality development, but they do not regard them as quite as
important as Freud believed them to be. Indeed, contemporary Freudians
such as Erik Erikson and Daniel Levinson (see Chapter 15) have shown
that the human personality can develop and change throughout the entire
life cycle. And life-span theorists, some of whom are more wedded to ego
psychology than others, have demonstrated that while there is considerable consistency of cognitive and emotional development across the life cycle, there also are considerable change and variability.

Research has shown that individuals' early-life conditions do not necessarily predict subsequent developmental levels. Reviewing studies on infants who suffered through premature and physically debilitating births,
for instance, Arnold Sameroff concludes that their subsequent physical,
cognitive, and emotional development will not necessarily be limited.
Similarly, Jerome Kagan presents evidence that extreme cultural differences in the ways adults care for children do not necessarily alter the level
of development that can be expected of the children in later life.

Kagan compares the treatment of American children with that of infants
in rural Guatemala, who spend their first year confined to a small, dark
hut. They are poorly nourished, are not played with, and rarely are even
spoken to. Only when they are about 4 or 5 years old does their social
world open so they begin to play with other children and participate in the
work of their parents. American parents treat their infants very differently.

takes place. In the **oral phase**, the libido and therefore the search for pleasure is centered in the area of the mouth, in the **anal phase** it moves to the area of the anus, and in the **genital phase** it is centered in the genital area. In each of these phases the child is using the parent, largely the mother, to fulfill his or her needs. Unbridled, infants would remain at their mothers' breasts, biting and hurting them as their teeth emerge. Left to their own devices, children would wallow in the pleasure of their bowel movements, playing with their feces. Given free reign, they would strive to masturbate and would use their mothers, or anyone else, for genital pleasure. Children, Freud believed, are **polymorphous perverse**; that is, they exhibit sexual tendencies even before they can identify the genitals as the principal sexual organs or coitus as the principal sexual activity. During these stages of development, parents struggle to keep children from total immersion in their perversity and teach them to control their sucking, their bowels, and their genital responses.

They believe that unless children are stimulated socially, intellectually, and emotionally, developmental retardation will result. Kagan found that while the cognitive development of Guatemalan children did appear retarded at early ages, by adolescence there was relatively little difference between them and American adolescents on tests of memory and reasoning.

Longitudinal studies which have traced individuals across their life course have found that although some personality variables remain more or less stable, others show a good deal of variation. For instance, many children, both male and female, show such personality traits as dependence, passivity, and aggression in infancy and childhood. Nevertheless, apparently through sex-role learning, boys are far more likely to lose the stereotypical feminine traits and retain the stereotypical masculine traits, while girls tend to retain the stereotypical feminine traits and shed the masculine ones. In another study of working-class and middle-class adults who had grown up in intact homes in Ohio, Kagan and H. A. Moss found little relation between such psychological qualities as fearfulness, irritability, or activity during the first three years of life and any aspect of behavior in adulthood.

Sources: Arnold J. Sameroff, "Early Influences on Development: Fact or Fancy?" in M. Bloom (editor), *Life Span Development*, 1st ed. (New York: Macmillan, 1980), pp. 105–19; Jerome Kagan, "The Baby's Elastic Mind," *Human Nature Magazine*, vol. 1 (January 1978), pp. 66–73; Jerome Kagan and H. A. Moss, *Birth to Maturity* (New York: John Wiley, 1962). Studies on traits are discussed in Richard M. Lerner and David F. Hultsch, *Human Development: A Life Span Perspective* (New York: McGraw-Hill, 1983), p. 517.

The Oedipal Conflict

The conflict between the instinctual needs of children and the social demands of parents is particularly evident during the genital phase. Freud postulated that all children pass through an Oedipal period. In the Greek legend, Oedipus, an abandoned child, grows up, becomes king, and unknowingly marries his mother. When he discovers his sin against the gods, he is so overcome by guilt that he blinds himself with a pin taken from his mother's garment and wanders off. He is finally hounded to his death.[15] Freud saw in this myth a symbol of normal, human development gone awry. All children, in search of genital satisfaction, attempt to use their parents as their first sexual objects. Since this is socially objectionable and taboo, this behavior must be warded off and checked. If the child actually achieved its sexual wish, as Oedipus did, the enormous guilt produced would destroy it. The drive is so intense that it can only be prevented by scaring, even threatening, the child.

Freud describes the psychological result of the male child's attachment to his mother and consequent jealousy of and hostility toward his father as the **Oedipus complex**. The boy experiences **castration anxiety** out of fear that his rival, a bigger and more powerful father, will cut off his penis, thus making it impossible for him to achieve pleasure. As a result, he represses his desires for his mother and over the following development stages, transfers his desires to more appropriate women. The female child, according to Freud, goes through a similar experience in the genital period which culminates in the **Electra complex**, named after a daughter in Greek legend who conspires with her brother to murder their mother. The female child believes she has already been castrated, since she has a clitoris but no penis. Out of unconscious envy, she is attracted to her father and turns away from her mother, whom she regards as a rival. The girl must also repress her attraction to the opposite-sex parent and transfer her sexual desires to more appropriate men. Freud's ideas on female development and **penis envy** have been attacked by twentieth-century feminists and others, as we will show.

As a direct result of the Oedipal struggle, which includes the Oedipus complex in males and the Electra complex in girls, the superego, or morality, develops. Freud postulates that girls and boys learn to accept authority and to prefer heterosexual genital satisfaction by identifying with their same-sex parent. This identification comes about out of **fear of loss of love**, a basic motive to ensure a positive relationship. For male children, it also comes through **identification with the aggressor**; that is, to ward off the fear of castration, boys internalize the values and behaviors of the father, and in the process they learn to repress genital activity during childhood. Freud maintains that because females do not experience castration anxiety, their superego does not develop as fully as the male superego.

The Latency and Puberty Phases

Once the genital conflict is resolved, children enter the **latency phase**, a period in which erotic urges apparently are dormant. Then, in the puberty phase, they begin the physical transformation into adulthood (see Chapter 15). With sexual maturation, the Oedipal tensions resurface; they now must be dealt with positively and put to rest. Children in puberty must once again channel their sexual interests away from the parent and toward the outside community of appropriate opposite-sex friends. Thus for Freud, human development, the ultimate outcome for a normal person, means internalizing the norms and traditions of society, identifying with the same-sex parent, and fulfilling sexual gratification through genital/genital contact with a member of the opposite sex.

FREUD ON FEMALE DEVELOPMENT

Freudian theory has been criticized for its apparent sexist bias. Although the great majority of Freud's patients were women, he never was able to put together a coherent theory of female development. One critic speculates that Freud's theory may derive more from self-analysis than from analysis of his female clients.[16] In any case, Freud devoted relatively little attention to women, concentrating most of his scientific energy on the development of the male personality.

This is true not only of Freud but of Freudians in general. Mary Schwartz notes that Erik Erikson, a Freudian who will be discussed in Chapter 15, commits a serious sin of omission. As a result of such bias, students of personality learn almost nothing about the female and receive a subtle message that female development is unimportant.[17] In fact, the sexism in Freudian theory may go beyond a sin of omission to a sin of commission. The few things that are said about women suggest a negative understanding of female development.

Freud suggests that girls resolve the Electra complex in a peculiarly feminine way which he does not seem to have thought out very clearly. The dilemma of the genital period is similar for boys and girls; both are attached to and desire genital pleasure from the opposite-sex parent, and both are forced to give up this urge. Boys must come to identify with their fathers and channel their affection to other women, and girls must come to identify with their mothers and channel their affection to men other than their fathers. According to Freud, the male personality develops out of fear of castration, and, because the female does not have this fear and has no penis, her moral development is weaker and she feels incomplete and envies the male his penis. This envy causes girls to reject their mothers and love their fathers as a means of acquiring at least the control of a penis. Freud says it is also penis envy which underlies the woman's desire to have a child; in childbirth, if only for the moment, she has a penis.

Penis Envy and Women's Position in Society

Not surprisingly, many feminist psychologists have rejected the idea of penis envy and see in such an assertion the essence of sexism.[18] They argue that women are not inferior beings; they are proud of their genital organs and do not feel at all castrated or wish to become men. But some feminists have supported Freud's position. Juliet Mitchell, for instance, argues that the notion of penis envy has been misunderstood, and to some extent Freud's ideas make sense. Thus penis envy may exist in the unconscious, as Freud suggests, even though it certainly does not exist in the consciousness of women. At the level of consciousness it is experienced only as a wish to love and possess men and bear children. To those who do not believe that an unconscious exists, the question of penis envy is irrelevant, since there is no conscious penis envy. Mitchell says that the only reason the wish for a penis exists even in the unconscious is because of the sexism and patriarchal norms in the society. Thus penis envy is an unconscious feeling in women because they have been coerced into a devalued social position.[19]

Mitchell's interpretation suggests that Freud may have been correct in his observations of the unconscious drives of the affluent women he treated around the turn of the twentieth century. However, her analysis also suggests that with women's suffrage and the present women's movement, the status of women in Western society has risen. Thus it is less likely that early-childhood genital urges in females will enter the unconscious as envy of the male. In contemporary society, especially in families where nonsexist behaviors and attitudes are valued, female children are more likely to develop unconscious feelings of wholeness, equality, and independence.

In a recent work, Erikson seems to agree with Mitchell. Although he also generally focused on male development, his work is viewed somewhat more positively by feminists than Freud's is. He acknowledges that during the infantile genital stage of development, boys and girls alike have feelings of both intrusion and inclusion, that is, a **bisexual propensity**. The inability of girls to intrude (meet their masculine needs) and of boys to include (meet their feminine needs) can create difficulties for both. In a patriarchal, exploitative society, girls may develop envy and become excessively dependent. Boys in such societies can fear castration and become excessively aggressive. Erikson believes, however, that neither outcome necessarily occurs "under enlightened conditions."[20]

THE COMPLEX PROCESS OF SEX-ROLE DEVELOPMENT

According to Freudian theory, girls and boys learn to be women and men as a result of emotional conflicts. Early-life experiences continually narrow the range of satisfactions that are permitted the child and that the child permits itself. These experiences reach their culmination in the genital or Oedipal period. The boy who desires his mother is threatened by the father, fears cas-

Gender role patterns are changing. As more girls
learn that women can have valued careers and
participate equally in society, the likelihood of
unconsciously envying men decreases. *Elizabeth Crews.*

tration, and as a result comes to identify with the father and men in general. The girl who desires her mother feels she has already been castrated and identifies with her mother's sexuality as a way of symbolically obtaining a penis. The Freudian model of sex-role learning suggests that a set of convoluted emotional responses and counterresponses results in identification with the same-sex parent and the internalization of heterosexual mores.

The Biology of Sex

A major difficulty in unraveling the processes by which men and women take on a sexual identity is that sex or gender itself is not easily identified. (Sexual development is described more fully in Chapter 15.) Katherine and Kermit Hoyenga point out that there are at least eight different aspects of gender, not necessarily related to one another. Some aspects are **genotypical**, that is, internal to the organism and not visible to the naked eye. These include chromosomal, gonadal, hormonal, and organal gender. Other gender categories are **phenotypical**, that is, external to the organism and therefore visible. These include genital gender, the gender of rearing, gender identity, and gender role (see box, Eight Definitions of Gender).[21]

The most basic way of defining gender is genotypical, in terms of differences in **chromosomal gender**. Each cell consists of 46 chromosomes, or 23 pairs with one set from the mother and the other from the father. One pair is responsible for sex determination. When sperm meets ovum during conception, females normally inherit an XX pair of chromosomes and males normally inherit an XY pair (see Chapter 15). If this does not occur, the embryo is often aborted. Other pairings of chromosomes are possible, however. In Turner's syndrome only one chromosome, an X, is present in the fetus. A person with this syndrome will look female but will almost always be infertile. In Klinefelter's syndrome, a person is born with a Y chromosome coupled with two or more X chromosomes. The person is male, yet the multiple X chromosomes often overwhelm the Y chromosome, and complete masculinization does not take place. The person has a male chromosome but often has a small penis, low levels of testosterone (the male hormone), breast enlargement, and little body hair. Other persons are born with one X chromosome and two Y chromosomes. There is some speculation that such double-Y chromosome men are particularly aggressive, but the data are not clear; many such men appear to live normal lives.

Other genotypical definitions are gonadal and hormonal gender and the gender of the internal accessory organs. **Gonadal gender** refers to testes in males and ovaries in females. Gonads produce hormones, which enter the brain and affect behavior. Although males and females share all hormones, **hormonal gender** is determined in males by the testes, which mostly produce androgens (as testosterone), and in females by the ovaries, which mostly produce estrogen and progesterone. **Organal gender** refers to the internal accessory organs. In males, these include prostate glands, ejaculatory ducts, the vas deferens, and seminal vesicles. In women, they consist of the uterus and the fallopian tubes.

Some XX fetuses (females) emit high amounts of androgen (male hormones), while some XY fetuses (males) appear to be insensitive to androgen. When this occurs the XX fetus can become masculinized and the XY fetus becomes feminized in the external organs. Thus while the internal apparatus may be of one gender, the external appearance may be of another. Sometimes these processes can reverse themselves. For instance, it was discovered that enzyme deficiencies were occurring to males born in rural villages in the Dominican Republic. Upon birth, the boys looked like females and were dressed and treated accordingly. At puberty, however, they began to produce testosterone, their testes descended, their penis emerged, their voices deepened, and their muscles developed in conformity with the male body.[22]

Among the phenotypical definitions, **genital gender**, the physical external appearance of the genitals at birth, most often determines how a child will be raised (the **gender of rearing**). **Gender identity**, or self-identification as male or female, and **gender role**, the taking on and preference for culturally ap-

EIGHT DEFINITIONS OF GENDER

Sex-role or gender-role development is a complicated process involving eight different ways of differentiating males from females. Theories of sex-role development must examine the relationship between the genotypical (internal and not visible) and phenotypical (external and visible) aspects of gender.

Types of Definition	Males	Females
Genotypical		
Chromosomal gender	XY	XX
Gonadal gender	Testes	Ovaries
Hormonal gender	Mostly androgens	Mostly estrogens
Organal gender	Prostate glands, ejaculatory ducts, vas deferens, and seminal vesicles	Uterus and fallopian tubes
Phenotypical		
Genital gender	Penis and scrotal sacs	Clitoris, labia, and vagina
Gender of rearing	"It's a boy"	"It's a girl"
Gender identity	_X_ Male ___ Female	___ Male _X_ Female
Gender role	Masculine behavior	Feminine behavior

Source: Adapted from Katherine B. Hoyenga and Kermit Hoyenga, *The Question of Sex Differences* (Boston: Little, Brown, 1979), p. 5.

propriate male and female behaviors, are the concern of Freudian and other sex-role theorists.

Theories of gender-role or sex-role development must examine the relationship between genotypical and phenotypical gender. Studies of individuals whose genotypes differ from their phenotypes are especially important, although very few such studies exist. In general, these studies demonstrate that biology and socialization are equally important. For instance, the enzyme-deficient boys in the Dominican Republic who were reared as girls took on all the expected demeanor of girls, suggesting the importance of socialization. Nevertheless, all but two of them easily assumed male identities once their genotypic gender became apparent, suggesting the importance of biology. Most theories of sex-role identity are limited to explaining the relationships among the gender of external genitals, gender role, and gender identity.

Gender-Role Identification

Barbara and Philip Newman, who work within the ego psychology tradition, have formulated a theory of gender identity and gender role which relies on Freudian ideas but incorporates work outside the Freudian tradition. They describe four processes in the development of sex-role identification: understanding, sex-role standards, identification with same-sex parents, and sex-role preference.[23]

Understanding gender is largely a cognitive process which requires the child to become knowledgeable about his or her physical appearance (gender of external genitals). Four elements make up understanding. First, children come to correctly use the gender label others are applying to them. They reply "I'm a boy" or "I'm a girl" when asked, "Are you a boy or a girl?" Second, they come to understand that gender is stable and lasts a lifetime; boys become men and girls become women. Third, they come to understand that gender is constant, which means that a child is a girl or boy regardless of clothing, hairstyle, toys, and the like. Fourth, they come to understand the genital basis of gender and learn that sexual identity has to do with the appearance of the genitals.

The second process concerns **sex-role standards**, the cultural expectations about appropriate behavior for boys and girls, men and women. Although these expectations are often unclear or undergoing change, they are the bases on which parents socialize children. As should be evident from Freud, mothers and fathers have much to do with the sexual identity of their children. They reward and punish the behavior of their children in accordance with their own understanding of cultural expectations. There is evidence that by the time children are 5 years old they have internalized their parents' expectations and are applying them to themselves and to other children. During the early school years children seem to have clearly fixed sex-role stereotypes, and they are especially strict with regard to proper sex-role behavior.

The third process is **identification with the same-sex parent**. Following Freud, the Newmans refer to fear of loss of love and identification with the aggressor as two primary motivations for sex-role identification, but they take into account at least two others. One is the need for status and power, an idea which derives from social-learning theory (see Chapter 12). When children are confronted with two models, one of whom controls rewards and the other of whom receives them, they will imitate the behavior of the person who controls, that is, the more powerful person. Rewards, of course, affect the actual behaviors of children. Thus, while they are likely to imitate the parent, they must be rewarded for performing the imitation.[24] The other motive is perceived similarity. Children behave like their same-sex parents in order to increase the similarity they perceive exists between them. The three major ways in which children realize their similarity to their same-sex parents are by observing physical and psychological similarities themselves, adopting their parents' behaviors, and being told by others that they are similar to their parents.[25] But the Newmans accept the idea that children are bisexual by nature and see no strong evidence to indicate that boys inherently identify with their fathers and girls with their mothers. They suggest that it is the warmth and dominance of the parent rather than the actual sex-role behaviors of the parents that promote identification.

The fourth process is **sex-role preference**. Children who understand the genital origins of their sex, who are taught culturally approved sex-role standards, and who identify with their same-sex parents come to prefer a culturally approved gender identity and gender role for themselves. Sex-role preference depends on three factors. The more the child's innate competencies approximate sex-role standards, the more will that child prefer being a member of his or her sex. Similarly, the more the child likes the parent of the same sex, the more will that child prefer being a member of that sex. Cultural values about the status of the child's own sex also influence preference. The Newmans say that where the society gives more status to the male, males are more likely to prefer being male and females "are likely to experience some ambivalence toward, if not rejection of, their sex groups."[26] This, of course, echoes Mitchell's and Erikson's ideas on female development. Freudian theory suggests that women raised in a sexist society are likely to develop gender ambivalence, possible rejection of other women, and an unconscious envy of men.

Freud on Homosexual Behavior

In Freudian theory, a homosexual identity and preference develop because certain things go wrong in early-childhood development. Homosexuality is believed to come about as a result of traumas in pre-Oedipal and Oedipal periods, and thus it represents neurosis. Erikson includes the capacity for heterosexual, procreative sex in his definition of a normal adult. For the Newmans, it is clear that a homosexual identification and preference will come about only if children do not understand sex, cultural standards are not taken into account, motivations break down, or the person's competencies do not fit the expected mold.

In 1973, The American Psychiatric Association voted not to include homosexuality as a mental illness or disorder in their *Diagnostic and Statistical Manual*. The revised third edition of the *DSM* does include an entry for "persistent and marked distress about one's sexual orientation" in the category of "sexual disorders not otherwise specified." This "ego-dystonic homosexuality" pertains, however, only to those who are disturbed by their homosexual behavior and wish to alter it.[27] There are those, both in and outside of the psychiatric community, who propose that homosexuality ought to be reintroduced as psychopathology. They often cite the work of Freudians to defend their point of view, in which homosexuality is seen as an illness.[28]

Freud himself was inconsistent on the issue of homosexuality. Mitchell argues forcefully that the justification for considering homosexuality a disorder is not to be found in Freud, since he always recognized the bisexual nature of human behavior. She quotes a letter from Freud to a distraught mother in which his opinion on homosexuality was quite enlightened:

> . . . Homosexuality is assuredly no advantage, but it is nothing to be ashamed of, no vice, no degradation; it cannot be classified as an illness; we consider it to be a variation of the sexual function. . . . Many highly respectable individuals of ancient and modern times have been homosexuals, several of the greatest men among them. . . . It is a great injustice to persecute homosexuality as a crime — and a cruelty too. . . .
>
> By asking me if I can help you, you mean, I suppose, if I can abolish homosexuality and make normal heterosexuality take its place. . . .
>
> What [psycho] analysis can do for your son runs in a different line. If he is unhappy, neurotic, torn by conflicts, inhibited in his social life, analysis may bring him harmony, peace of mind, full efficiency whether he remains homosexual or gets changed. . . . [29]

Knowledge of sexual development — behaviors, identifications, and preferences — is only in its infancy. No one theory seems to adequately handle the complexity of biological, social, and psychological factors that are likely to be operating. In the same way theories of female development have become increasingly sensitive to the psychological consequences of being raised in a sexist society, sensitivity is required with respect to homosexual development.

FREUD'S CONTRIBUTIONS TO THE STUDY OF HUMAN BEHAVIOR

Although Freud's theories have been debated and are being extended in directions he may not have even considered, it is clear that he made significant contributions to the study of human behavior. No direct-service social worker seriously interested in assessing and intervening in the troubles of clients can overlook the work of Freud and his followers.

Freud's contributions include the following ideas:[30]

1. Psychological processes determine all human behavior; this is the idea of psychic determination.

2. There is a personality composed of conflicting elements which must be understood as a psychodynamic system.

3. Unconscious mental activity is a primary motivating force in human behavior.

4. Two primary drives are eros, the drive for sensual pleasure, and thanatos, the drive for aggression.

5. The drive for sensual pleasure can be fruitfully studied as a function of psychosexual stages of development.

6. The method of treatment for emotionally disturbed adults is long-term, in-depth psychoanalysis in which childhood memories are examined.

The discussion presented here suggests that Freud also made a contribution to defining the nature of human development. For Freud, development means internalizing the norms and traditions of society, identifying with the same-sex parent, and achieving sexual gratification through genital/genital contact. In psychoanalysis and other methods of helping people whose psychosexual development is in question, this definition is used as an objective for intervention.

As Freud developed his theory, he began to recognize the role of conscious mental activity in determining human behavior. However, his work on this factor remained incipient, and most of it has been done by Freudians who call themselves ego psychologists.

EGO PSYCHOLOGY

While Freud stated in his early work that the ego is not present at birth, he came to believe that the ego exerts an influence over the personality from the beginning of life. The term *ego* was coined by Freud, but the major work on the concept was done by Anna Freud, his daughter, and by Heinz Hartman and others.[31]

Psychoanalytic study of the ego has been done in two areas. One, which focuses on the ego in conflict with the id, is more firmly anchored in the Freudian tradition in which the problem of development is seen as an inherent conflict between the individual and society. The other area, which focuses on the conflict-free zone of the ego, emphasizes the individual's conscious adaptive and coping responses. In some respects the two areas represent two sides of a coin, as in the conflict and consensus (or structural functional) theories of social interaction (see box, Conflict or Consensus, in Chapter 2).

THE EGO IN CONFLICT: EGO-DEFENSE MECHANISMS

The ego is that part of the personality which mediates between the individual and the environment as well as between the id and the superego. Since libidinal needs are so strong and surface in ways that may threaten individuals, the personality must find a way to fulfill libidinal demands and at the same time control them so that they are not overwhelming. One way the individual does this

ing **ego-defense mechanisms,** "specific intrapsychic processes,
uconsciously, which are employed to seek relief from anxiety."[32]
unconscious strategies, ego-defense mechanisms are used by everyone,
at is, they are part of the normal functioning of the individual. They may
be either adaptive or maladaptive. The maladaptive use of defenses prevents
personality development whereas the adaptive use promotes it. The particular
defense used is not itself adaptive or maladaptive behavior. Rather, in adaptive
use, the defense must simultaneously protect and enable optimal functioning;
it is temporary and flexible, and the conflict that provokes the defense is eventually resolved. In maladaptive use, the defense is rigid, and, while it might
protect for a while, it does not enable optimal functioning.

A number of ego-defense mechanisms have been identified.[33] **Regression** is
unconsciously returning to a type of thought, feeling, or behavior associated
with an earlier stage of development to avoid present anxieties and fears.
Adults who start to behave as if they were children are regressing. **Repression**
involves unconsciously keeping unwanted thoughts, feelings, and behaviors
out of awareness. Individuals who do not allow themselves to think about certain things are using repression. In **denial**, the individual unconsciously
negates or refuses to accept as real something that is in fact real, such as refus-
ing to acknowledge that a loved one has died. **Rationalization** is the unconscious use of convincing reasons to justify unacceptable thoughts, feelings, and
behaviors. Students may be rationalizing when they convince themselves that
a low grade was due to a tricky exam or the instructor's lack of clarity about
expectations, instead of admitting that they were not prepared.

Other ego defenses include **projection**, unconsciously attributing unacceptable thoughts and feelings to others. Instead of admitting to a particular
thought, a person may attribute it to others. **Displacement** is unconsciously
shifting unacceptable feelings about one person or situation onto another. A
woman, for instance, may get angry at her husband instead of getting angry
at her boss. **Sublimation** is unconsciously converting a socially objectionable
thought, feeling, or behavior into a socially acceptable one. A man, for instance, may channel his aggression to football or boxing as a way of positively
expressing hostility, instead of battering his wife. Sublimation is believed to be
the most mature, most effective way to deal with anxiety or fear.

Almost any thought, feeling, or behavior may be considered a defense as
long as it functions unconsciously and is an attempt to ward off anxiety. For
this reason, the labeling of behaviors as ego-defense mechanisms must be done
cautiously.

THE EGO IN HARMONY: AUTONOMOUS FUNCTIONS

Hartman was the first to study the conflict-free aspects of the ego, that is, those
functions that are not tied to instinctual drives but are **autonomous functions**.
These are the tools individuals use to deal directly and adaptively with their
environment, such as intelligence, perception, motility (inner feelings of ac-

tion), speech, thinking, language, and memory. Hartman accepted the function of ego defenses in the personality, but he believed that the study of the ego could be enhanced by looking at its nondefensive, adaptive functions. His work demonstrates the capacity of the ego for neutralizing conflict and fostering adaptations. Thus it forms the basis of much contemporary psychotherapy.[34]

A number of ego functions have been identified in the autonomous sphere.[35] **Reality testing** refers to the ability to perceive the difference between inner, subjective states, such as wishes, fantasies, hopes, and desires, and objective conditions outside the person, or what is actually taking place. Reality testing emphasizes the need to perceive the world accurately and to understand cause-and-effect relations. The ego also functions to enable the development of a sense of **reality of the world** and **reality of the self** as separate entities at the feeling level rather than the perceptual level. A person may be able to test (that is, perceive) reality accurately but still not be able to sense, feel, or experience the difference between inner and outer reality. **Judgment** involves the ability to sort out different possible responses to objective reality, weigh their consequences, and determine the most appropriate response.

The ego also serves to regulate and control drives, emotions, and impulses. It provides for thought processes which are organized, logical, and oriented to objective reality, but it allows a certain amount of regression; when people are confronted by a reality that appears to overwhelm them, they can let go of their organized, goal-directed thinking, relax, and perhaps come up with more creative adaptations. Other autonomous functions, such as attention, concentration, memory, learning, and perception, are facilitated by the ego, even under circumstances of stress or conflict.

Coping Mechanisms

While ego-defense mechanisms function unconsciously in attempts to ward off anxiety, coping is a broader concept which includes both conscious and unconscious adaptive strategies. The extent to which a behavior is under conscious control and is adaptive is what differentiates a coping mechanism from a defense mechanism. **Coping** is the mechanism used by the ego to consciously deal with actual situations, actively testing reality, making judgments, and regulating and controlling impulses. For instance, repression, an ego defense, involves keeping unwanted feelings out of awareness; suppression, a coping mechanism, involves consciously deciding to control those feelings.

Robert W. White has identified three components of coping: the ability to gain and process new information, the ability to control one's emotional state, and the ability to move freely within one's environment.[36] There can be an endless variety of coping strategies, most of which are created by individuals in accordance with their own personalities and needs. For instance, when confronted with a difficult interpersonal relation with a loved one, different people will cope by going to a therapist, talking to friends, consulting self-help books on intimate relations, ignoring the difficulty, or confronting the loved one with their feelings. Each strategy can be understood as a way to gain information, control emotions, and continue to function socially.

Competence

When ego psychologists turned their attention to autonomous ego processes, the existence of an inborn motive for mastery over the environment became apparent.[37] **Competence** has to do with a person's capacity to interact in an effective way with the environment. It is the ability to adapt beyond merely surviving, muddling through, or coping. Carel Germain identifies competence as a drive to interact effectively with the environment which leads to learning, interests, skills, and a sense of identity and esteem.[38]

White's work has been particularly influential in promoting the concept of competence. He starts with the assumption that inherent biological energies in the ego, or **effectance**, motivate people to strive for competence. Then he describes the actual skills individuals should learn in the course of their development in order to interact effectively with their environment: self-confidence, trusting one's own judgment, and the ability to make decisions. According to White, mastery of these skills produces a **sense of competence**, the subjective feeling or perception of acting in a competent manner, and a **feeling of efficacy**, the experience of satisfaction and positive self-esteem as a result of having done something active and being in control over one's life.[39]

Anthony Maluccio uses the concept of competence in a different way. He argues that competence is not a set of personal attributes but a product of the transactions between individuals and their environment, that is, the relationship between the person's needs, qualities, and coping patterns and the properties of the impinging environment.[40] In this transactional view, the attributes of a person are only one component of competence. The nature of the macro, mezzo, and micro environments and the way they support competence are of equal consequence to individual development (see box, Levels of Systems within Individuals, in Chapter 2).

Ego Strength

The concept of ego strength summarizes what many ego psychologists mean by development. **Ego strength** implies "a composite picture of the internal psychological equipment or capacities that an individual brings to his interaction with others and with the social environment." [41] Its opposite is **ego weakness**, which signifies the deficiencies a person brings to social relationships.

People who have ego strength use their defenses adequately, cope well, perceive reality correctly, and have a good sense of themselves and others. They make good judgments, regulate their drives, and think in logical, goal-oriented ways but can let go of logic when necessary. They continue to attend, concentrate, and learn even under stress, and they maintain mature interpersonal relations. In sum, people with ego strength have the qualities that allow for competence in interaction with the social environment. Ego weakness is evident in individuals with deficiencies in internal functioning, so that the ego is unable to perceive, experience, and deal adequately with the demands imposed by reality.[42]

The Study of Object Relations

As ego psychology continued to emerge, more attention was given to the social environment, especially the family. A major school of thought which has resulted is concerned with **object relations**, the study of the attitudes people hold toward other people and how these attitudes influence human social behavior.[43] Object relations, also referred to as interpersonal relations, may refer to the individual's sense of self and sense of other people or to the capacity for mature interpersonal relations.

Within the Freudian tradition, subjective reality, including fantasy and the imagery evoked by it, often is considered more important than actual events or objective reality. Early in his career, Freud believed that actual traumatic events experienced during infancy accounted for the neurotic symptoms exhibited by his adult patients. For instance, many of his female clients spoke of memories of incestuous events with their fathers. Later Freud came to believe that in fact these traumatic, seductive events never occurred and existed only in the fantasy of his clients. The reason Freud changed his mind has been debated. Jeffrey Masson argues that it was more for personal than for scientific reasons; Freud was unwilling to challenge the medical community or to unmask the behaviors of close associates.[44] Alvin Rosenfeld argues that Freud reversed himself because clinical observations and new insights had raised doubts as to the validity of the accounts of seduction by his patients.[45] In any case, analytically oriented practitioners still give most of their attention to the fantasies of the individual.[46]

The intense emotions of early childhood lead individuals to incorporate into their personalities images of the important people in their lives which they later project onto others. Thus perception is always selective. Individuals form attitudes about others based on a complex combination of what the other persons objectively are and what they are expected to be.

Transference and Countertransference

One example of this projection can be seen in analytically oriented therapeutic encounters in which clients transfer their fantasies about their parents onto the therapist. In turn, therapists who are not careful may countertransfer these fantasies onto clients. **Transference** has been defined as the unconscious projection onto the therapist of the client's attitudes toward a powerful figure in early childhood. **Countertransference** refers to the reactions of the therapist to being treated as a father or a mother. It is a reaction to the patient's neurotic displacements.[47]

While the study of transference and countertransference is, strictly speaking, limited to the therapeutic encounter, analogies with interpersonal behavior in everyday life are readily apparent. As individuals interact and build relationships with others, they are constantly evoking fantasies and images of the people in their past. Such remarks as "He's attracted to her because she reminds him of his mother" or "She married him because he's a father figure" are common. Some of the images are very pleasant, and what may be called a positive transference takes place: Individuals attribute to others good things and are drawn to them. Some of the images are very unpleasant and a negative transference takes place: Individuals can see no good in others and spurn them. Most images are highly ambivalent, mixed images reflecting love and hate simultaneously: Individuals are drawn to others just as they are wary of them. Object relations, then, is the study of how internalized childhood patterns, often based in fantasy rather then real-life events, penetrate the psyche and shape interactions with others.

Self Psychology

Self psychology, influenced heavily by the works of Heinz Kohut and Margaret S. Mahler, is a prominent area in the study of object relations.[48] It proposes the existence of a set of motives which differ from Freud's instinctual, antisocial, libidinal, aggressive drives. In **self psychology**, drives are much more social in nature.

Newborn infants are believed to have an innate ability to inform others of their needs; they are eager learners, mentally active, and able to observe the world in a structured way. If the response infants evoke from those who care for them is empathic, the primary care-giver becomes a **self-object**. Through such self-objects, which constitute the empathic environment into which the child is born, the child begins to internalize a **nuclear self**, a central, enduring, and organized sector of the personality. If the child cannot evoke an empathic response, or if the care-giver is emotionally dull, unavailable, or otherwise unable to respond to the child, the child will not develop a cohesive, vigorous, and harmonious nuclear self. Then development is unlikely, and the child's personality could become weak and fragmented.

The self is **bipolar**, that is, it comes into being through two streams of experience, "that of being mirrored, admired, and guided; and that of being permitted to merge with the power and wisdom of an idealized self-object." [49] In this respect, self psychology and symbolic interactionism (see Chapter 13) posit similar processes in the development of the self. While being comforted, held, fed, and changed, the newborn merges or becomes one with the primary care-giver, who becomes a self-object for the infant. The process of internalizing the empathic responses of others in a nuclear self is defined as **transmutation**, to indicate that the individual does not simply incorporate the self of others but is transformed into something unique. Thus the mirroring, guiding, and confirming functions of self-objects become **self-functions** for the infant, such as the capacity to regulate self-esteem, to monitor stress, and to define and pursue realistic goals. The complementary processes of separation and individuation are involved in transmutation. In **separation**, infants move away from the merged state they have achieved with their primary care-givers, and in **individuation** they develop and assert their own unique characteristics.[50]

In keeping with contemporary views of development, self psychology recognizes the individual's potential for development throughout the entire life cycle. As people go from one age status to the next, the self-objects that influence the nuclear self widen. Some self-objects are given up and others are added, and the role of self-object goes from parents and other care-givers to peers, teachers, fellow workers, partners, and lovers. Self-objects are not necessarily actual people, however; they may also be preferences or vocational, professional, religious, civic, and cultural ideals that take on values. For development to occur, the nuclear self must be reevaluated and restructured at each stage.

COGNITIVE DEVELOPMENT

Ego psychology has its origins in clinical practice, but other traditions in psychology have developed along with it. The cognitive theory of Jean Piaget and the theory of moral development of Lawrence Kohlberg, for instance, describe the development of such capacities as learning, memory, attention, and reasoning and thereby enhance understanding of the autonomous ego functions.

PIAGET'S STAGES OF COGNITIVE DEVELOPMENT

Piaget is by no means a Freudian, or even an ego psychologist. Both Piaget and Freud were interested in inner-life experiences, and both offered theories of human development, but Freud's concern was with emotional development in individuals, while Piaget's was with cognitive development. It is precisely because of this concern that Piaget is often read by ego psychologists. He too believes in human developmental progress, but on an intellectual rather than an emotional level.

Piaget was a Swiss naturalist and biologist whose interest in childhood development was aroused when he became a father. The early development of his theory of cognitive development was based on observations of normal children (his own children, as a matter of fact) and simple experimentation with their learning processes.

The Process of Adaptation

For Piaget, development is the synthesis of biological maturation and environmental experiences which takes place through the process of **adaptation**. In this process, individuals seek to establish an equilibrium between their selves and their environment through the logical coding and ordering of intellectual experiences and the behaviors associated with them. Piaget's theory of cognitive development takes into account three levels of thought, or orders of cognition. The lowest is the level of **schema**, sensory and motor patterns which make meaningful, repeatable behaviors possible. **Structures** are related to the organization of thinking; they are subprocesses which link thought and action and are generally associated with more complex cognitive processes. In **operations**, schema and structures may be reversed, transformed, or otherwise manipulated by cognitive processes. Operations are complex patterns which approximate some kind of logical model.

Schema, structures, and operations are the products of adaptation, particularly through the subprocesses of assimilation and accommodation. **Assimilation** refers to individuals' attempts to adapt the environment to themselves. Experiences are processed and accepted only to the extent that they fit into the existing cognitive equilibrium. Thus to make sense of new ideas or experiences, individuals try to fit them into old ideas or experiences. For instance, children can learn to jump rope by comparing the skill to others they already have, such as jumping up and down, jumping over a rock, or hopping over a line. **Accommodation** refers to the opposite procedure, accepting new experiences, regardless of how different they may be from what is known. The unique aspects of jumping rope are attended to, and no comparisons are made with other forms of jumping. Jumping rope thus is different from jumping over a rock or hopping over a line.

When individuals encounter new experiences, they simultaneously assimilate and accommodate them. They fit them into their thinking patterns even as they alter those patterns. Assimilation and accommodation represent a push-and-pull pattern which emphasizes the dynamic nature of cognitive development.

Four Stages of Cognitive Development

The three levels of thought produced by assimilation and accommodation in Piaget's theory of cognitive development ordinarily are learned from birth to adolescence in four stages, each with a number of substages. The four major stages are sensorimotor, preoperational, concrete operational, and formal operational thought.[51]

The Sensorimotor Stage. The stage of sensorimotor intelligence, generally from birth to 18 or 24 months of age, is the period in which children are socially the most dependent and physically the most limited. For infants, reality has no beginning or end. They and their environment are one and the same, and their experience is limited to what can be seen, touched, heard, or smelled. Objects are real when they are present and cease to exist as soon as they disappear. At this stage children perceive and act but do not have internal representations of the environment. They must work within these confines to create and control their social world in order to meet their needs. Reflexive behaviors such as sucking slowly take on meaning, become repeatable, and thus form schema in the cognitive repertoire, and by the end of this stage children can endow objects in the environment with **object permanence**. Once they have internalized basic sensorimotor schema and are capable of imagery, they begin to replace the sensorimotor approach to problem solving with elements of conscious thinking.

The Preoperational Stage.   The stage of **preoperational intelligence**, usually between the ages of 2 to 7, allows for a transition between the egocentric, sensorimotor adaptations of infancy and the more socialized structures of later childhood. During this stage children begin to derive concepts from experiences. Learning occurs through first-hand sensorimotor activities. Thinking is very concrete; reality is exactly what is perceived, no more and no less, and there is little ability to consider alternatives. Intuitive thinking and deliberate behaviors emerge, enhanced by the development of language and the ability to play and pretend.

Rolf Muus identifies three factors which limit preoperational thinking. Children are still dependent on direct sensorimotor experiences, they are unable to consider multiple dimensions simultaneously and so must focus on one aspect of an object, neglecting other aspects, and they cannot rearrange or reorganize information in their minds.[52] They also are unable to comprehend the **principle of conservation**. For adults, a quart container holds a specific quantity of liquid which remains the same regardless of how the contents may be distributed or redistributed. If a quart of milk is divided into four glasses, adults can recognize that it is still a quart. Nothing has changed except that the milk has been redistributed. At the preoperational stage children do not recognize this principle. If they are shown a quart of milk and then it is divided into four glasses, they will say that this makes more milk, since what was just one container of milk now is four. If the four glasses are poured back into the quart bottle, they will say there is less milk.

The Concrete Operational Stage.   The principle of conservation becomes evident at this stage, in which **concrete operational intelligence** emerges around age 8 and continues into puberty. Children begin to be able to perform logical and mathematical operations, but they cannot deal with abstract matters, only with concrete or real objects. For instance, they have a sense of what a particular number is and how it can be presented in different ways: $2 + 3 = 5$, but so does $7 - 2$.

Concrete operational thinking enables children to solve problems of **classification**. They can divide fruits into apples, oranges, and peaches, for instance, or distinguish animals from humans and divide animals into four-legged animals like dogs and horses and flying animals like birds and ducks. Classification skills are enhanced by the ability to understand the logic of relations. Children at the concrete operational stage can order things by their relative size from small to large. They can also begin to think abstractly about what certain things have or do not have in common.

The Formal Operational Stage.   The fourth and highest stage of cognitive development is **formal operational intelligence**, which does not emerge until adolescence or later. At this point reasoning becomes less a matter of trial and error and more a process of thinking through a problem. Abstract reasoning, in the form of propositional thinking (i.e., if this, then that) and combinatorial analysis (i.e., all things being equal) is possible, and the person is able to state and test hypotheses. With formal operational thinking, it is possible to solve problems by varying one factor while holding all other factors constant and systematically excluding explanations until the correct one can be abstracted.

An example of the use of formal operational intelligence is in the pendulum task, for which participants are given a series of weights, strings of varying lengths, and a rod from which to suspend the weights. They are asked to state the principle which determines how fast a weight can go back and forth within a given period. They are likely to start by proposing that the principle involves either the length of string or the size of the weight, or some combination of the two. They might decide to see what happens if they alter the length of string while holding the weight constant or change the weight while holding the length of the string constant. In any case, they will conclude that it is the length of the string, not the weight, that determines the speed at which a pendulum swings.

While formal operational thinking is believed to appear around adolescence, it is not unusual for college freshmen or even seniors to lack it. Studies have shown that a significant proportion of the population may never attain the ability to think in formal operational terms. Piaget believes that all normal people can reach this level,[53] but he acknowledges that cognitive aptitude becomes differentiated in adolescence and adulthood. Thus while some people have cognitive skills in logic, mathematics, or physics, others have them in literature, linguistics, or art.

KOHLBERG'S STAGES OF MORAL DEVELOPMENT

In his work on problem solving, Piaget prescribes a shift in moral judgment from **heteronomous morality**, based on fixed, unchangeable rules, to **autonomous morality**, based on cooperative agreements. Lawrence Kohlberg has adapted and expanded on these ideas and incorporated them in an influential theory on the development of moral judgments in cognitive thinking. Kohlberg has tested his theory by presenting verbal or written accounts of problem situations or dilemmas and asking children or adults to state the "right" solution in each instance. The answers given indicate the stage of moral development that has been achieved by the test participant.

The problems Kohlberg presents are built around such issues as:[54]

1. Should a doctor practice "mercy killing" to end the life of a fatally ill woman who requests death because she is in great pain?
2. Is it better to save the life of one important person or many unimportant people?

Kohlberg's descriptions of the situations built around such issues pose moral dilemmas. The mercy killing issue, for instance, is presented as a problem facing Heinz, whose wife is near death from cancer and who cannot afford a new drug which might save her. The druggist who has discovered the drug paid $200 for the radium he uses in it, but he charges $2,000 for a small dose. Heinz can only raise $1,000. The druggist will not lower his price or let Heinz pay later, so Heinz steals the drug. Respondents then must decide whether Heinz rightly took the drug and why they think so. Kohlberg asks them to consider such questions as whether the husband is motivated by love of wife or regard for humanity and whether the pharmacist has a right to property he has created.[55]

Kohlberg is not interested in the actual solution to a problem, that is, the specific attitudes or beliefs expressed, but in the way the child or adult reasons and thinks through the solution. It is inconsequential whether or not the individual believes in mercy killing or that it is or is not better to save one important person. The reason behind the individual's attitude is the only pertinent point. The morality of individuals is related to their decision-making abilities and their ego capacities rather than their moral habits or feelings. Kohlberg identifies five ego capacities which he believes are related to moral behavior:[56]

1. General intelligence.
2. The ability to anticipate future events and to choose a greater future reward over a lesser immediate one.
3. The capacity to maintain stable, focused attention.
4. The capacity to control unsocialized fantasies.
5. Satisfaction with the self and others.

Six Stages of Moral Development

In his early work, Kohlberg postulated three basic stages of moral development: preconventional, conventional, and postconventional thinking. These generally correspond to Piaget's preoperational, concrete, and formal organizational stages of cognitive development (see box, Stages of Development: Piaget and Kohlberg). Later Kohlberg redefined these three stages, dividing each into two substages to reflect a more social perspective in which moral development is seen as moving from self-centeredness to awareness of the rights and needs of others.[57] Thus Kohlberg proposes an order of progression in moral development which includes three levels and six stages.

Moral thinking is not present in Piaget's sensorimotor stage of development. Kohlberg, like Freud, believes the earliest stage begins around 4 years of age with **preconventional moral development**, which is limited to thoughts about punishment first and then reward. In stage 1, the "egocentric stage," moral judgments are based on fear of punishment and unquestioning deference to authority or superior power. In stage 2, the "concrete individualistic stage," the physical consequences of action, regardless of its human meaning or values, determine for the child whether the behavior is right or wrong. Thus, with respect to mercy killing, a 4-year-old is likely to say it is wrong because "you can go to jail." Somewhat later the child begins to understand the role of rewards in motivating behavior. Some behaviors are considered good because they bring satisfaction in the form of rewards. This is often coupled with basic ideas about reciprocity: "If I am good to you, you will be good to me." Then the child is likely to believe that a doctor in a mercy-killing situation should behave in a way that will produce a reward.

Conventional moral development begins around age 10, when children be-

STAGES OF DEVELOPMENT: PIAGET AND KOHLBERG

The taxonomies of developmental skills presented by Jean Piaget and Lawrence Kohlberg can be considered congruently because development is said to occur at certain ages or with the mastery of certain skills. Neither theory proposes that development will begin or end at these points, however. In fact, formal operational intelligence and postconventional morality may never be achieved by many individuals.

PIAGET'S STAGES OF COGNITIVE DEVELOPMENT	KOHLBERG'S STAGES OF MORAL DEVELOPMENT
Stage 1: Sensorimotor Intelligence Birth to age 18 or 24 months	No moral development
Stage 2: Preoperational Intelligence Ages 2 to 7	Level 1 (Stages 1 and 2): Preconventional Morality Begins about age 4 Moral judgments utilize preoperational intelligence skills
Stage 3: Concrete Operational Intelligence Ages 8 to puberty (about 11)	Level 2 (Stages 3 and 4): Conventional Morality Begins about age 10 Moral judgments utilize concrete operational skills
Stage 4: Formal Operational Intelligence May begin in adolescence	Level 3 (Stages 5 and 6): Postconventional Morality May begin in adolescence Moral judgments utilize formal operational skills

come aware of social expectations and norms and are motivated to conform to them. Stage 3 is characterized by "mutual interpersonal expectations." According to Ralph Anderson and Irl Carter, "The child now takes the role of the other, and can see the situation (and self) from the other's perspective."[58] This level of development has a "good boy-nice girl" orientation. Children follow rules; they want to be considered nice and to receive praise and avoid blame. They seem to be motivated by their ideas of majority or "normal," "natural" behavior, and, for the first time, the intentions of their behavior become important. Thus 10-year-olds believe a doctor should strive to do what is right, should be nice, should mean well, and should try not to hurt anyone. In stage 4, characterized by "the societal point of view," the child recognizes the need to obey laws, perform duties, and respect authority. There is a sense that society could not exist if the existing authority is not upheld. Thus doctors should follow the rules of their profession and obey the law; the only way for them to earn respect is to satisfy their professional obligations.

For most of the population, moral development never gets beyond stages 3 and 4; it is estimated that only about 5 percent ever get as far as stage 6. The postconventional level is the most controversial of Kohlberg's taxonomy. While the first four stages clearly emerged from his research, other theorists maintain that stages 5 and 6 are based more on philosophical ideas than on scientific investigation. Nevertheless, they do follow logically from the first four stages.[59]

In **postconventional moral development**, stages 5 and 6 are characterized by a "prior to society perspective," incorporating the ideas of the social contract and individual rights. These stages do not begin before adolescence and, if they are achieved, it will not be before young adulthood. In stage 5, the dominant idea is the social contract. Personal moral values are recognized as relevant, but the need to show concern for the welfare of others is also appreciated. A legalistic point of view emerges. Values are debated using acceptable procedures in order to reach a consensus which will meet the needs of the majority of the people. But laws are not considered to be intrinsically good, and if they no longer serve the common good, they can be changed. Kohlberg believes that the official morality of the American government reflects this level of thinking. Stage 6 is marked by "orientation toward the decisions of conscience and toward self-chosen ethical principles appealing to logical comprehensiveness, universality and consistency."[60] Concrete moral rules such as the Ten Commandments are likely to be rejected in favor of more universal ethical principles such as the Golden Rule or the categorical imperative. These principles reflect a sense of justice, equal rights, and respect for the dignity of all human beings.

Kohlberg's research is ongoing. On the basis of cross-cultural studies and research on social class factors, he argues that the stages of moral development can be found across all cultures and all classes and thus should be considered universal, unlearned developmental processes. He notes, however, that children in the United States are more likely to reach the higher levels of moral development than children in less developed countries such as Mexico, Turkey, and Taiwan. He also says middle-class children are likely to develop moral think-judgment principles faster and further than those in the lower classes. Religious background is not significant, however; Catholics, Protestants, Jews, Buddhists, Moslems, and aetheists go through similar stages of moral development.[61]

WOMEN'S MORAL DEVELOPMENT

Carol Gilligan argues that much of the literature on human development, both emotional and cognitive, is sexist; that is, it considers humans as men and largely ignores female development. Gilligan, who worked with Kohlberg at Harvard, believes that moral thinking in women progresses differently than it does in men. She proposes that men and women reason in very different ways, and even when they may agree or reach the same conclusion about a moral dilemma, the inductive rules they use to reach that conclusion are quite different.

According to Gilligan, developmental theorists see the goal of development as the achievement of personal autonomy. In Kohlberg's stage 6, for instance, the highest level of thinking is evident in the man who is able to determine his

DIFFERENT VOICES IN CHILD WELFARE

Ann Hartman and Diane Vinokur-Kaplan have examined the differences in the "world views" of male and female child welfare teachers and workers to determine whether their judgments and decisions in practice are affected by gender; that is, whether they hear different voices, as Carol Gilligan suggests. They asked 684 men and 1,315 women working or teaching in child welfare to rate the importance of various content areas in education for child welfare practice. The greatest difference between the replies of women and men was found on the item called psychological and social processes of separation and loss, which women rated much higher than men did. A second area, including items concerned with preservation of the family and the prevention of placement of dependent children, such as working with families toward reunification, treating troubled families, and preventive outreach to families, was considered important by both genders but was significantly ranked higher by women. The researchers state that these findings bear out Gilligan's view that women value connection while men value separation, and women have a greater investment in the maintenance of attachment while men's investment is in personal autonomy and achievement.

The four items that men ranked higher than women did were decision making in child placement, working with involuntary clients, family

own ethical principles and apply them as he sees fit. Women, Gilligan says, define themselves in terms of relationships with others rather than personal autonomy, and therefore "male and female voices typically speak of the importance of different truths, the former of the role of separation as it defines and empowers the self, the latter of the ongoing process of attachment that creates and sustains the human community."[62] As a result, women's responses to Kohlberg's moral problems are at a lower level of development than the appropriate responses specified for men at the various stages, or they do not fit at any stage.

For Gilligan, the central issue in women's development is how to reconcile responsible, caring relationships with the personal autonomy and individual achievement that are more valued as the goal of human development. The moral judgment of women differs from men's because "sensitivity to the needs of others and the assumption of responsibility for taking care [of others] lead women to listen to the voices of others and to include in their judgment points of view other than their own."[63] This difference has been found to extend to the opinions and attitudes of women and men in child welfare teaching and practice (see box, Different Voices in Child Welfare).

breakdown, and working with troubled adolescents. These findings suggested that male child welfare workers tend to use separation developmentally, and "their concern may well be to help teens and children going into placement to make use of these experiences for growth and individuation."

A major difference that emerged from this study was that "women seem to be more concerned about separation and loss, connectedness, and the maintenance of the family." Whether this difference is translated into the decisions on child placement made by female and male workers was suggested as a topic for further study. In particular, three questions that might be addressed are suggested by Hartman and Vinokur-Kaplan:

1. Are programs headed by females likely to put less emphasis on placement and more on preventive services?
2. Are male direct-service workers more likely than female workers to place a child outside the family or to place an adolescent in a group setting?
3. When administrators and staff members are of different sexes, do gender issues escalate strain and conflict between supervisors and workers in child welfare services?

Source: Ann Hartman and Diane Vinokur-Kaplan, "Women and Men Working in Child Welfare: Different Voices," *Child Welfare*, vol. 64 (May-June 1985), pp. 307–14.

While Gilligan's critique challenges the destructive force of sexism, the results of her studies may not stand up to empirical scrutiny. As we noted in Chapter 2, other research has demonstrated that innate, psychological male-female differences prove to be nonexistent or exaggerated when examined closely. Recent reviews of the literature have found little or no evidence for gender differences in moral development.[64] Lawrence Walker, for instance, found that while some studies indicate higher moral development in adult males, these studies did not control adequately for education and occupation, and "contrary to the prevailing stereotype, very few sex differences in moral development have been found."[65]

The Roots of Moral Behavior

Freud, Piaget, and Kohlberg all suggest that moral thinking and feeling are not evident in infancy. Research on empathy, however, suggests that the ability to empathize and take the perspective of others makes children receptive to moral teaching. The Newmans define empathy as "the vicarious experience of an emotional state that is being expressed by another person."[66] By watching facial expressions and gestures and listening to the sounds of others, infants can discern others' feelings. Studies have found that when one infant in a hospital nursery cries, so do the others, and three-year-olds can recognize emotions such as happy and unhappy, as well as afraid, sad, and angry.[67] These early empathic abilities appear to be the foundation on which moral development rests.

Kohlberg stresses that moral development has to do with an evolving ability to think through ethical problems and dilemmas. For Freud, moral development has to do with the acquisition of a superego as a result of successfully resolving the Oedipal conflict in the genital stage of development. Thus Kohlberg is concerned with thinking morally and Freud with feeling moral. But what of behaving morally? Learning theory and research on parental discipline and moral decision making are useful in integrating Kohlberg's and Freud's ideas into a more complete understanding of how moral development takes place.

Social learning theory (see Chapter 12) presents evidence that children learn prosocial and antisocial behaviors by observing others. To the extent that the prosocial behavior of others is rewarded, children are likely to imitate it, and to the extent that the antisocial behavior of others is punished, they are likely to inhibit that behavior. Moral behavior also is influenced by social situations and the expectations, values, and objectives of the people involved in them.[68] For instance, people who place a high value on academic achievement may feel pressured to cheat on exams when they fear they will not do well, but it may never occur to them to cheat their friends in money matters. Similarly, if people believe antisocial behavior will not be caught or punished, they are more likely to engage in it.

Parental discipline techniques are also important in instilling moral values and encouraging moral behavior. The Newmans conclude that the discipline techniques that instill moral behavior are those that help children control their own behavior, understand the meaning of it for others, and increase their capacity for empathy. They propose a technique for disciplining children which includes four elements:[69]

1. Discipline should interrupt or inhibit the undesirable behavior.
2. Discipline should demonstrate a more acceptable form of behavior; knowing what to do is as important as knowing what not to do.
3. Discipline should include an explanation, at a level the child can understand, of why an action is right or wrong.
4. Discipline should stimulate the child's empathy for the victim of the misdeed; a boy, for instance, should be encouraged to put himself in the place of his victim and see how the victim feels.

A synthesis of all the theories on psychosocial development discussed in this chapter, within a perspective which takes into account the behavioral, affective, and cognitive dimensions of morality, has been proposed by James Rest. His proposal seeks answers to the question, "What do we have to suppose went on in the head of a person who acts morally in a situation?" All phases of moral decision making require the cognitive ability to understand and judge as well as the emotional ability to feel and emphathize. Thus a person confronted with a situation which calls for moral judgment must first gather information on the situation and the others in it and interpret the situation in terms of how a proposed action would affect the welfare of others. Then the person must formulate a moral course of action, identifying the competing ideals which might be realized in response to the situation. The next step is to select one ideal from among those possible and decide whether to try to achieve it. Finally, in executing and implementing the intended action, the person must call on ego strength and coping skills in order to overcome any obstacles to the moral behavior.[70]

Thus Rest's ideas on moral behavior are very much in keeping with the thrust of ego psychology. The emphasis is on coping mechanisms which utilize what ego psychologists would call reality testing, a sense of reality of the world and of the self, and judgment.

IMPLICATIONS FOR PRACTICE

Ego psychology has a utopian vision about normal human behavior which embraces the possibility of continuous progress across the life cycle, that is, human development. Its special merit for social service workers is that it offers descriptions of a normally developed person at various stages and identifies the factors that promote or hinder development.

As a perspective, ego psychology owes a great deal to Freud. The value of Freud's theory to social service workers is that it sensitizes them to clients' unconscious needs and motives, provides a theoretical framework for the study of personality structure and dynamics, and promotes an understanding of psychosexual development. Contemporary Freudians continue to alter his theory and make their own contributions. Freud's emphasis on early-life development, his rather tentative explanation of female development, and his ideas about homosexuality are in continuous revision. Freudians today focus less on the id and the unconscious and more on the ego, ego defenses, ego functions, and object relations. Many of them have incorporated these ideas from the study of cognitive processes and development as well as social-learning theory.

Points of View on Human Development

The points of view described in this chapter provide different ways of thinking about human development. For Freud, development is achieved with the acquisition of a superego as a result of successfully dealing with the Oedipal conflict. Human development has to do with internalizing the values of the society, identifying with the same-sex parent, and achieving sexual gratification through heterosexual, genital relations.

For ego psychologists, development has to do with the adequate use of defenses and the ability to cope with and master the environment. The concept of ego strength is central. Individuals who have ego strength can use their defenses, perceive reality accurately, have a good sense of themselves and others, and make good moral judgments. They can regulate their drives; think in logical, goal-oriented ways yet let go of logic when necessary; continue to attend, concentrate, and learn even under stress; and maintain mature inter-personal relations. They have the qualities that allow for competence in inter-action with the environment. In contrast, ego weakness is evident when deficiencies in internal functioning limit the ego's ability to perceive, experience, and deal with the demands imposed by reality.

One aspect of ego psychology is self psychology, in which the ideal of development is regarded as the achievement of a cohesive nuclear self, that is, a central, enduring, organized sector of the personality which emerges through interaction with others. Development is achieved when people can see themselves and others as separate, three-dimensional individuals. It is aborted for those who seem fragmented, unseparated from others, and unable to achieve individual well-being.

In cognitive development theory, development is the progressive ability to use abstract reasoning. The ultimate stage of cognitive development is reached when individuals become capable of formal logic, or combinatorial and propositional thinking. In terms of morality, ultimate development requires the individual to become less centered on the self and more aware of the rights and needs of others.

APPLICATION IN ASSESSMENT AND INTERVENTION

For a direct-service social worker, the first decision is whether an ego-oriented assessment should be made of a particular client. Goldstein warns that such assessments are not appropriate in some forms of practice, as in determining client's needs for entitlement to services such as financial maintenance and homemaker assistance.[71] Ego strength should not be equated with personal worth or goodness, and ego weaknesses should not be used as a reason to disqualify clients from receiving services. However, when the service being provided has to do with personal and interpersonal problems in living, then the various perspectives on psychosocial development can be useful.

Psychosocial development is especially pertinent in the assessment phase of practice. The various points of view about this development can be useful in examining the extent to which a client's problems are related to deficiencies in fulfilling drives, in developing ego strength and a nuclear self, or in thinking and reasoning. Yet these perspectives are not just problem-focused; they also provide help in identifying the internal strengths and capacities of clients which can be mobilized in helping them. An assessment must take note of the development that the client has achieved. Then, three forms of intervention can be used. The worker can try to nurture, maintain, enhance, or modify the client's inner capacities; mobilize, improve, or change environmental conditions that impinge on those capacities; or improve the fit between inner capacities and external circumstances.

In using developmental principles, the biological age of the person must be taken into account. Development takes place across the life span, and at different ages it has different meanings and consequences. In the next chapter we will consider the work of ego psychologists with respect to development throughout the life cycle.

DISCUSSION QUESTIONS AND CLASS PROJECTS

1. List the seven propositions associated with ego psychology. To what extent would you say that they are in keeping with the systems approach described in Chapter 2?

2. Distinguish among the following concepts: growth, differentiation, maturation, development, and change.

3. Why is development better thought of as a value rather than an inevitable fact of life?

4. Identify at least five contributions made by Freud to the study of human behavior.

5. Distinguish among the id, ego, and superego. To what extent do you believe

that there are instinctual drives and motives that operate unconsciously in people? As a social worker, how would you know that unconscious drives are operating?

6. What does Freudian theory mean by penis envy? Do you think it is an apt concept to capture the unconscious feelings of women in a sexist society? To what extent do you think that women are ambivalent toward their sexual identity? To what extent are men not ambivalent toward their sexual identity?

7. In what ways can it be said that Freud was indecisive on the question of the normalcy of homosexuality?

8. Describe the Newmans' theory of sex-role identification. In what ways might it be useful in assessing sex-role problems of women and children? In what ways does it help you understand homosexual behavior? Do you see any limitations in their perspective?

9. What is meant by ego defenses? How are these different from coping mechanisms?

10. Describe at least three ego defenses. Can you give examples from your own experience with clients or friends in which defenses were being used? Do you think that it is a sign of poor development when people use ego defenses?

11. What is meant by an autonomous ego function? List and describe at least three such functions.

12. What three components are believed to comprise coping?

13. What is meant by ego strength and ego weakness? Why are these important concepts for social workers?

14. Describe the following concepts from the study of object relations and self psychology:
object relations
self-object
nuclear self
separation
transference
countertransference
transmutation
individuation

15. Describe the following concepts from cognitive development theory:
adaptation
schema
structures
operations
assimilation
accommodation

16. Describe Piaget's four stages of cognitive development.

17. Describe Kohlberg's six stages of moral development.

18. How is Kohlberg's approach to moral development different from Freud's? What other approaches ought to be considered for a more complete understanding of moral behavior and development?

19. Choose one of the two examples of Kohlberg-type questions used in the study of moral development and have everyone in the class fill out as complete a response to the question as possible. There is no need to put your name on the response. Remember that Kohlberg is not interested in the yes or no aspect of the question but in the logic and reasoning used in the response. Collect the responses and pass them out again, being sure to mix them up as much as possible so no one gets his or her own reply. Attempt to determine the stage of development represented in the reply. Discuss the difficulties encountered in determining someone's stage of development. How might you revise the procedure to assure that someone's stage is made clearer? Do you think you would ever use such a procedure in working with children, adolescents, or adults?

20. For a variation on Question 19, have everyone indicate their sex on the response to determine if there are systematic gender-related differences in the responses. Does there appear to be a "male voice" and a "female voice"?

21. For another variation, interview acquaintances or strangers outside the class and ask for their responses to the question. Tell them only that you are studying moral development in class and assure them that their names will not be used. Both sexes and a number of age categories should be included in the sample.

22. Name the four related points of view on human development identified in the section on implications for practice. Describe the slant on the utopian vision of development promoted by each.

NOTES

1. Barbara M. Newman and Philip R. Newman, *Development through Life: A Psychosocial Approach*, 4th ed. (Chicago: Dorsey Press, 1987), p. 616.

2. Heinz Hartman, *Ego Psychology and the Problem of Adaptation* (New York: International Universities Press, 1939); also see Erik H. Erikson, *The Life Cycle Completed: A Review* (New York: W. W. Norton, 1982), p. 28.

3. See Judith Marks Mishne, "The Missing System in Social Work's Application of Systems Theory," *Social Casework*, vol. 63 (November 1982), pp. 547–53.

4. Carel Germain, "General Systems Theory and Ego Psychology: An Ecological Perspective," *Social Service Review*, vol. 52 (December 1978), pp. 535–49.

5. Eda G. Goldstein, *Ego Psychology and Social Work Practice* (New York: Free Press, 1984), pp. 37–38.

6. Ibid., p. xiv.

7. Ibid., pp. xv–xvi.

8. Paul B. Baltes, "Life-Span Developmental Psychology: Some Converging Observations on History and Theory," in P. B. Baltes and O. G. Brim, Jr. (editors), *Life-Span Development and Behavior*, vol. 2 (New York: Academic Press, 1979), p. 262.

9. Henry W. Maier, *Three Theories of Child Development* (New York: Harper and Row, 1969), pp. 4–5.

10. Baltes, "Life-Span Developmental Psychology," p. 263.

11. The account of Freudian theory is drawn from a wide range of Freud's work and the work of several of his followers. For a good introduction to Freud, see Charles Brenner, *An Elementary Textbook of Psychoanalysis* (New York: Doubleday/Anchor, 1957); Harry Guntrip, *Psychoanalytic Theory, Therapy, and the Self* (New York: Basic Books, 1973); Eunice F. Allen "Psychoanalytic Theory" in F. J. Turner (editor), *Social Work Treatment: Interlocking Theoretical Approaches,* 2nd ed. (New York: Free Press, 1979); and Katherine M. Wood, "The Contributions of Psychoanalysis and Ego Psychology to Social Casework," in H. Strean (editor), *Social Casework: Theories*

in Action (Metuchen, NJ: Scarecrow Press, 1971).

12. See Brenner, *Elementary Textbook of Psychoanalysis*, p. 18.

13. Eric Fromm, *The Crisis of Psychoanalysis: Essays on Freud, Marx, and Social Psychology* (New York: Holt, Rinehart and Winston, 1970), pp. 69–78.

14. See Ann M. Clarke and A. D. B. Clarke, *Early Experience: Myth and Evidence* (London: Open Books, 1976); Jerome Kagan, Richard B. Kearsley, and Philip R. Zelazo, *Infancy: Its Place in Human Development* (Cambridge, Mass.: Harvard University Press, 1978); and Hans Thomas, "The Concept of Development and Life-Span Developmental Psychology," in P. B. Baltes and O. G. Brim, Jr. (editors), *Life-Span Development and Behavior*, vol. 1 (New York: Academic Press, 1979), pp. 282–312.

15. Robert Graves, *The Greek Myths*, vol. 2 (New York: George Braziller, 1959), pp. 9–15.

16. Roger Brown, *Social Psychology* (New York: Free Press, 1965), pp. 374–81.

17. Mary C. Schwartz, "Sexism in the Social Work Curriculum," *Journal of Education for Social Work*, vol. 9 (Fall 1973), p. 66.

18. See, for instance, the discussion of Freud by Marie Richmond-Abbott, in *Masculine and Feminine: Sex Roles over the Life Cycle* (New York: Random House, 1983), pp. 26–27.

19. Juliet Mitchell, *Psychoanalysis and Feminism* (New York: Vintage, 1975), pp. 5–15, 95–104.

20. Erikson, *Life Cycle Completed*, pp. 38–39.

21. Katherine B. Hoyenga and Kermit Hoyenga, *The Question of Sex Differences* (Boston, MA: Little, Brown, 1979), p. 5.

22. See Richmond-Abbott, *Masculine and Feminine*, pp. 48–52.

23. Newman and Newman, *Development through Life*, pp. 236–45.

24. Walter Mishel, "A Social-Learning View of Sex Differences in Behavior," in E. Maccoby and C. Jacklin (editors), *The*

Psychology of Sex Differences (Stanford, CA: Stanford University Press, 1974), pp. 56–81.

25. Paul B. Mussen, J. J. Conger, and Jerome Kagan, *Child Development and Personality* (New York: Harper and Row, 1974).

26. Newman and Newman, *Development through Life*, p. 243.

27. American Psychiatric Association, *Diagnostic and Statistical Manual*, 3rd ed., rev. (Washington, DC, 1987), pp. 296, 560.

28. For a strong statement on homosexuality as a pathology, see Robert Endleman, *Psyche and Society: Exploration in Psychoanalytic Sociology* (New York: Columbia University Press, 1981), pp. 235–330.

29. Mitchell, *Psychoanalysis and Feminism*, p. 11.

30. Morton Deutsch and Robert M. Krauss, *Theories in Social Psychology* (New York: Basic Books, 1965), pp. 126–30.

31. See Heinz Hartman, *Ego Psychology and the Problem of Adaptation* (New York: International Universities Press, 1939), and Anna Freud, *The Ego and the Mechanisms of Defense* (New York: International Universities Press, 1936).

32. This definition is from the Psychiatric Glossary in Norman A. Polansky, *Integrated Ego Psychology* (New York: Aldine, 1982), p. 47.

33. Goldstein, *Ego Psychology and Social Work Practice*, pp. 70–77. This source is used for the descriptions of ego defenses and autonomous functions.

34. Hartman, *Ego Psychology*. Also see Germain, "General Systems Theory and Ego Psychology," p. 541.

35. Goldstein, *Ego Psychology and Social Work Practice*, pp. 43–64.

36. Robert W. White, "Strategies of Adaptation: An Attempt at Systematic Description," in G. V. Coelho, D. A. Hamburg, and J. E. Adams (editors), *Coping and Adaptation* (New York: Basic Books, 1974).

37. Goldstein, *Ego Psychology and Social Work Practice*, pp. 60–61.

38. Germain, "General Systems Theory and Ego Psychology," p. 545.

39. Robert W. White, "Competence and the Psychosexual Stages of Development," in M. R. Jones, editor, *Nebraska Symposium on Motivation* (Lincoln: University of Nebraska Press, 1960), pp. 97–124.

40. Anthony N. Maluccio, "Competence-Oriented Social Work Practice: An Ecological Approach," in A. N. Maluccio (editor), *Promoting Competence in Clients* (New York: Free Press, 1981), pp. 6–9.

41. Goldstein, *Ego Psychology and Social Work Practice*, p. 62.

42. Ibid.

43. Polansky, *Integrated Ego Psychology*, p. 17.

44. Jeffrey M. Masson, *The Assault on Truth: Freud's Suppression of the Seduction Theory* (New York: Farrar, Straus, and Giroux, 1984).

45. Alvin Rosenfeld, "Freud, Psychodynamics, and Incest," *Child Welfare*, vol. 66 (November/December 1987), pp. 488.

46. Polansky, *Integrated Ego Psychology*, pp. 189–91.

47. Ibid.

48. The description of self psychology is largely derived from Miriam Elson, *Self Psychology in Clinical Social Work* (New York: W. W. Norton, 1986). See especially pp. 8–22.

49. Ibid., p. 4.

50. Goldstein, *Ego Psychology and Social Work Practice*, pp. 106–07.

51. See Henry W. Maier, *Three Theories of Child Development* (New York: Harper and Row, 1969), pp. 81–157.

52. Rolf E. Muus, "Jean Piaget's Cognitive Theory of Adolescence," in R. E. Muus (editor), *Theories of Adolescence,* 4th ed. (New York: Random House, 1982), pp. 176–208.

53. Jean Piaget, "Intellectual Evolution from Adolescence to Adulthood," in R. E. Muus (editor), *Adolescent Behavior and Society: A Book of Readings,* 3rd ed. (New York: Random House, 1980), pp. 70–78.

54. Lawrence Kohlberg, "The Child as a Moral Philosopher," *Psychology Today*, vol. 1 (September 1968), p. 28.

55. Lawrence Kohlberg, "The Development of Children's Orientations toward a Moral Order: II. Social Experience, Social Conduct, and the Development of Moral Thought," *Vita Humana* (1963), pp. 18–19.

56. Lawrence Kohlberg, "Development of Moral Character and Moral Ideology," in M. Hoffman and L. Hoffman (editors), *Review of Child Development Research* (New York: Russell Sage Foundation, 1964), pp. 389–91. Also see John W. Lorton and Eveleen L. Lorton, *Human Development through the Lifespan* (Monterey, CA: Brooks/Cole, 1984), p. 248.

57. Kohlberg, "Child as Moral Philosopher," pp. 25–30, and Lawrence Kohlberg, "Revisions in the Theory and Practice of Moral Development," in W. Damon (editor), *Moral Development: New Directions for Child Development, No. 2* (San Francisco: Jossey-Bass, 1978), pp. 83–87.

58. Ralph E. Anderson and Irl Carter, *Human Behavior in the Social Environment: A Social Systems Approach,* 3rd ed. (New York: Aldine, 1984), p. 175.

59. Ibid., pp. 174–76.

60. Kohlberg, "Child as Moral Philosopher," p. 26.

61. Ibid., p. 30.

62. Carol Gilligan, *In a Different Voice: Psychological Theory and Women's Development* (Cambridge, MA: Harvard University Press, 1982), p. 156.

63. Carol Gilligan, "Why Should a Woman Be More Like a Man?", *Psychology Today*, vol. 16 (June 1982), p. 68.

64. Lawrence J. Walker, "Sex Differences in the Development of Moral Reasoning: A Critical Review," *Child Development,* vol. 55 (June 1984), pp. 677–91; John C. Gibbs, Kevin D. Arnold, and Jennifer Buckhardt, "Sex Differences in the Expression of Moral Judgment," *Child Development*, vol. 55 (August 1984), pp. 1040–43.

65. Walker, "Sex Differences in Development of Moral Reasoning," p. 688.

66. Newman and Newman, *Development through Life*, p. 250.

67. Ibid., pp. 251–52.

68. Walter Mischel, "Toward a Cognitive Social Learning Reconceptualization of Personality," *Psychological Review,* vol. 80 (July 1973), pp. 252–83.

69. Newman and Newman, *Development through Life*, p. 253.

70. James Rest, "The Major Components of Morality," in W. M. Kurtines and J. L. Gewirtz (editors), *Morality, Moral Behavior, and Moral Development* (New York: John Wiley, 1984), pp. 24–38.

71. Goldstein, *Ego Psychology and Social Work Practice,* p. 127.

CHAPTER 15

Ego Psychology and Development across the Life Course

$\mathbf{M}$AJOR THEMES DISCUSSED IN THIS CHAPTER:

1. *Stages of development.* Most ego psychologists believe that the life course consists of a series of stages, from birth to death. Biological, social, and psychological clocks are taken into consideration in determining a person's developmental stage.

2. *Prenatal development and birth.* For human development to take place, a child must be conceived and born. The period before birth sets the stage for development across the life course.

3. *Developmental tasks across the life course.* The life course can be regarded as a series of age-related tasks. Completion of these tasks in sequence makes development possible. Havighurst's concept of developmental tasks to be accomplished or learned at various stages of the life cycle has been influential in life-course psychology.

4. *Erikson's psychosocial crises.* Erikson maintains that human development occurs as a function of various inner crises or struggles. He identifies eight age-related stages of development, each marked by a particular psychosocial crisis. If the crisis is resolved, the individual acquires a basic strength; if it is not, the result is a core pathology.

5. *Developmental crises in maturity.* Erikson, like Freud and Piaget, pays most attention to the inner development of the individual from infancy through adolescence. Other theorists maintain that significant development occurs in adulthood. Levinson is particularly concerned with the crisis experienced at

mid-life, and Peck suggests ways in which people can resolve crises and continue to develop in old age.

      6. *The necessity of crises in the life course.* Must there be crises for development to take place? The literature on crises during adolescence and mid-life suggests that the answer is yes.

      7. *Implications for practice.* Social service workers can use developmental theory to determine the stage of life a person is in, identify developmental difficulties, search out their causes, and mobilize personal and social resources to overcome them.

F OR SOME ego psychologists, the utopian vision of individual progress or development covers the entire life course, from birth to death. They regard development not as a group of traits in the character of individuals but as a process which continually emerges as individuals live out their lives. In this view, development is best understood as the outcome of transactional processes; that is, the effects of complex, continual interactions among biological, social, and psychological factors.

STAGES OF DEVELOPMENT

Most psychologists segment the life course into sequential stages associated with the processes of physical growth and decline. At each stage, a unique set of tasks and crises determines the possibilities for development.[1] As a result, development is expressed in different traits and characteristics at each stage of life.

      There is no agreement as to the number of stages in the life course. Sigmund Freud's five stages of psychosexual development and Jean Piaget's four stages of cognitive development, discussed in Chapter 14, are examples. Erik Erikson, whose work is discussed in this chapter, describes eight stages of psychosocial development, but most contemporary writers add three or four more. Barbara and Philip Newman, for instance, include a prenatal period and divide adolescence and old age into two stages each, for a total of eleven stages of development.[2]

      Although a person's chronological age is associated with her or his stage of development, there is no established one-to-one relationship between age and stage. Stages of development are as much cultural invention as biological fact. Social historians point out, for instance, that childhood and adolescence were not recognized as periods of development prior to industrialization.[3] Adolescence, long believed to be a natural outgrowth of the pronounced biological changes that occur at puberty, is now believed to be a more arbitrary cultural phenomenon. Young people are classified as adolescents from preteens through college enrollment, and the term *adolescence* is no longer used as equivalent to puberty.[4] There is also no agreement on the definition of adulthood, its span, or its subdivisions.[5] Aging itself has little to do with proposed stages of development.[6] A longitudinal study of two samples of men, for instance, found adult life stages to be more-or-less independent of chronological age.[7]

Differences in response to the life cycle make it impossible to categorize individuals' stages of development solely on the basis of their age. The age at which children sit up, walk, talk, and control their bowels varies, as does the age at which puberty sets in cr young people gain independence. Adults today are flexible about when and if they will marry, have children, or begin a career. The diversity is particularly evident in women. One 21-year-old, for instance, may decide to concentrate on beginning a career and put off marriage and a family: at age 35, she may be ready to bear and rear a child. Another woman may marry at 21 and begin rearing children and then, at 35, return to school for a degree or start a new career. Because of such diversity, these two women of the same age cannot be considered in the same stage of development.

BIOLOGICAL, SOCIAL, AND PSYCHOLOGICAL CLOCKS

An individual's stage of development in the life cycle is best thought of as a function of the independent, internal clocks ticking away. A **biological clock** measures chronological age as each person advances in years. Since the state of physical development is important to human behavior, chronological age must always be taken into account in trying to understand the tasks and crises individuals are facing. But chronological age alone is an insufficient basis for identifying cognitive and emotional development.

A **social clock** operates in terms of the roles and statuses an individual occupies across the life course, which are closely related to the tasks and crises confronting the individual.[8] The social clock measures stages of development as a series of structured social roles which individuals move in and out of and which are more-or-less connected with chronological age.[9] Martin Kohli suggests that in industrial societies, four **age strata** are derived from roles in the economy. Infants play; that is, they have no tasks with respect to the economy. Children and adolescents are given tasks in school to prepare them for participation in economic activities. Adults have the principal roles in economic and household production and services, and older people generally have been retired or released from these roles.[10] Age strata can also be defined in terms of sexual rights and obligations. Children are preparing for participation in procreative roles and are not expected to engage in sexual activity; adults are expected to take on procreative roles within the family but also have the right to seek sexual fulfillment. The cultural norm that older people have no interest in sex and so make up a third age stratum in this respect is increasingly being rejected.

A **psychological clock** measures how individuals feel about themselves, what their abilities are, what they perceive their expectations to be, and how they behave. Some people feel old when they are 35 years of age, while others feel young at 70. Some adolescents are quite mature, independent, and able to form intimate relations, and some adults are not.

PRENATAL DEVELOPMENT AND BIRTH

Human development across the life span begins with conception and the prenatal period. Although ego-psychological theories usually do not include prenatal growth as a period of development with specific tasks and crises, it is clear that the period before birth is extremely important in setting the stage for development of the **fetus** (the organism from the third through ninth month) and the birth of the infant.

THE PARENTS' INFLUENCE

The physical well-being of the unborn child is inseparable from the physical, social, and psychological well-being of the adults responsible for bringing it into the world. If these adults are living at a subsistence level, with poor nutrition, barely able to feed and shelter themselves, the conception and prenatal and postnatal development of the child will surely be affected. There is clear evidence that the socioeconomic position of parents has a great deal to do with problems in prenatal and postnatal development.[11]

The age, nutrition, and physical condition of the mother have a direct influence on the prenatal development of the fetus. The optimal ages for women to conceive and bear children are between 18 and 35. Infants carried by women younger or older than these ages have a higher risk of birth defects, premature birth, and infant mortality,[12] though advances in prenatal care and diagnosis of potential difficulties have made it safer for women to begin their families later if they choose. Since the mother is the only source of nutrition for the fetus, her diet is a vital concern. A number of correlational studies have indicated a relationship between deficiencies in maternal diet and stillbirths, prematurity, low birth weight, and growth retardation and poor mental functioning in the infant.[13] The mother's physical health or condition also is a concern; for instance, **rubella**, or German measles, is very harmful to the fetus if the mother contracts the disease in the first three months of pregnancy. The internal characteristics of the mother and the fetus occasionally are incompatible; different **Rh factors** in red blood cells, for instance, can result in anemia or even miscarriage and early death.

There has been increasing evidence that the destructive habits of mothers can adversely affect the fetus. Excessive alcohol consumption can lead to **fetal alcohol syndrome**, an irreversible condition characterized by prenatal and postnatal growth deficiency, abnormally small heads, joint defects, and abnormalities in heart development and facial characteristics. Expectant mothers who smoke cigarettes have been found to have more unsuccessful pregnancies and premature babies than those who do not. Even the excessive consumption of caffeine in coffee and other beverages is being discouraged. In the environment, toxins and other health hazards such as radiation and pollution can lead to miscarriages, sterility, or birth defects.[14]

In their review of the effects of drugs on pregnancy, John and Eveleen Lorton conclude that prenatal and postnatal development are negatively affected when expectant mothers regularly use addictive drugs.[15] A mother addicted to heroin, morphine, or methadone often gives birth to an infant who is addicted at birth and displays drug withdrawal symptoms. An increasing number of babies are being born with birth defects to mothers who used cocaine during pregnancy. The drug is absorbed through the mother's placenta, cutting off the flow of oxygen to the baby and causing permanent brain damage. Other likely consequences are retarded growth, seizures, abnormalities of the genital and urinary organs, and incomplete intestines. The babies are irritable, upset by the slightest stimulus, and unable to focus on sights or sounds. They often withdraw into a deep protective sleep. Mothers infected with the AIDS virus through contaminated hypodermic needles or unprotected sexual practices give birth to infants who already have the disease and whose brief lives are full of suffering.

The mother's emotional state also can be a profound influence on prenatal development. Pregnancy is a time of stress for almost every woman.[16] It reshapes the body and can cause physical discomfort, irritability, or nausea. The women is projected into new roles and statuses in preparation for motherhood. An expectant mother's peers and parents and the father-to-be all are likely to treat her differently and expect different things of her than they did before she became pregnant. Such changes require considerable adaptation.

The stresses of pregnancy are particularly harmful if the expectant mother has little understanding of the process of conception, how the fetus grows, and the needs of newborns. If these stresses are not handled well or they are worsened by a lack of social support or conflict with parents, peers, or the father, the development of the fetus or the newborn child may be threatened. Women suffering from postpartum (after-birth) depression may even subject their infants to neglect or abuse.

There are significant differences between the birth weight and health of infants born out of wedlock and those born to married couples. Even in the latter case, an infant who is unplanned for or unwanted is at a disadvantage.[17] A review of the literature found evidence that a few upsetting experiences during pregnancy are not likely to harm the fetus, but prolonged emotional distress is. Tense and anxious mothers are more likely to have colicky babies. Women with a positive attitude toward pregnancy and motherhood will spend more time in face-to-face contact with their newborn children and interact more with them during their infancy.[18]

Fathers are becoming more involved in the pregnancy and the birth process. Both are enhanced if the father is present, supportive, interested in learning, and capable of sharing the mother's feelings about the coming child. Fathers who participate actively in the delivery and care of the infant are likely to become engrossed with the child. They are more visually and tactilely aware of the infant and its distinctive characteristics and may well perceive it as perfect.[19]

GENETIC INHERITANCE

Internal and external physical characteristics are inherited through the parental genes, carried in the chromosomes of the female ovum and the male sperm, which unite in an act of conception. A **gene** may be defined as a chromosomal unit of inheritance; specifically, a segment of a DNA (deoxyribonucleic acid) molecule which contains a complex chemical code providing all the biochemical information needed to enable cells to make the many kinds of molecules that determine physical characteristics.[20]

One of the important bits of information carried in the chromosome is information on sex (see the section on the biology of sex in Chapter 14). The 46 chromosomes in each cell are made up of 23 pairs with one chromosome from the sperm and one from the ovum. Of these 23 pairs, 22 are similar; the 23rd, which distinguishes sex, is different. In females, the 23rd chromosome is an XX pair, while in males it is an XY pair. The sex of the child is highly influenced by the chromosomal information carried in the sperm of the father. If the sperm that fertilizes the ovum carries a Y chromosome, the child will likely be a male. If the sperm carries an X chromosome, the child will likely be a female.

Genetic inheritance is not a simple addition of the traits of the father and the traits of the mother. The sum total of what individuals inherit is called their **genotype**. What they look like on the outside, their physical appearance, is called their **phenotype**. Some genes are dominant while others are recessive. When a dominant gene meets a recessive gene, the **dominant gene** is incorporated in the phenotype, while the **recessive gene** remains in the genotype, where it may affect the development of an individual in a future generation. The meeting of the dominant and recessive genes is the process through which many characteristics are passed on from parents to children, including hair color, eye color, and blood type. The children, therefore, may look like one parent or the other, like a combination of the two, or different from either one.

Much of the human inheritance is affected by many genes operating simultaneously, a process referred to as **polygenic inheritance**. Almost all complex human characteristics, such as intelligence, behavioral and emotional patterns, and physical abilities, are acquired through this process. Nevertheless, very few human characteristics are purely genetic in origin. For instance, Americans are much taller than they would be if height were determined simply on the basis of genetic inheritance. Due to the effects of environmental factors such as changes in nutrition and health care, between 1860 and 1960 American adults became, on average, six inches taller than their forefathers. These effects are less visible today, which seems to imply that height has reached a plateau or possibly even its outer human limit.[21]

The individual's cognitive, emotional, and behavioral development also is affected by environmental conditions as well as genetic inheritance. Temperament, for instance, apparently is influenced by genetic endowments. In an often-cited series of studies, Alexander Thomas, Stella Chess, and Herbert Birch found nine basic personality dimensions in which children were likely to vary at birth.[22] On the basis of interviews with parents who were asked to describe the characteristics of their children, babies were found to differ in level of activity, rhythm, willingness to approach new things, adaptability, intensity of reactions, responsiveness, moods, distractibility, and attention span. Based on these dimensions, the researchers could categorize many of the children they studied into three basic personality types. The **easy child** is biologically regular and rhythmical, eats and sleeps more or less on schedule, accepts new food and new people with relative ease, and is not easily frustrated. Forty percent of the children studied were of this type. The **slow-to-warm-up child** (15 percent of those studied) tends to withdraw quietly but shows interest in new things when not forced and given time to adapt. The **difficult child** (10 percent of those studied) is negative, withdraws noisily, and is very slow to adapt. Approximately 35 percent of the children studied were not easily classified into these three categories.[23]

The temperaments evident at birth do not always survive infancy. Thomas and Chess found that while a number of characteristics identified were maintained, others changed as children grew older, and by adolescence many of them evidenced different personality traits than they had at birth.[24] Infants' temperaments affect their early interaction with parents and other adults. Rather than being passive creatures unable to influence their environments, even very young infants are quite active and can trigger emotions in their care-givers. The physical appearance of a child, for instance, can elicit positive or negative reactions from adults. The emotional treatment of babies born prematurely often suffers because of their unattractive appearance; indeed, there is evidence of a link between prematurity and the probability of child abuse.[25] The actions of an infant also can affect the giving or withdrawing of care. Crying behavior takes on a cyclical rhythm which becomes predictable to the care-giver, who responds with the necessary attention.[26] Excessive crying, however, can lead to the withdrawal of attention or even to punishment. In a study of 54 mothers, it was found that the attachment of mother to child builds during the first months after birth, but it decreases when a child will not stop crying.[27]

THE EMBRYONIC AND FETAL PERIODS

Human development begins at the moment of conception when a single male sperm joins with a single female ovum or egg cell to form a **zygote**. Usually this occurs through normal heterosexual intercourse, but a substantial number of couples are infertile, and conception does not take place. The two major reasons for infertility are low sperm count in the male and failure to ovulate in the female. The use of artificial insemination, fertility drugs, microsurgery to unblock the fallopian tubes, and, more recently, test-tube methods of impreg nation have increased the likelihood for infertile couples to conceive and have children.

If impregnation does take place, 24 hours later the single-celled zygote di vides into two, which soon become four, eight, sixteen, and so on. Within a week the **embryo**, or the developing human organism, contains more than 100 external and internal cells implanted in the uterus of the mother. Through the external cells of the embryo, nourishment is passed from the placenta; thus the embryo has an independent blood supply and also makes use of the mother's. The internal cells of the embryo are attached to the placenta through the umbil ical cord, which contains veins and arteries to carry nutrients in and waste products out.

The embryo grows rapidly and in an orderly fashion in the **embryonic period**, which lasts about seven weeks. Crucial structural development occurs with the appearance of an **ectoderm**, which becomes the skin; an **endoderm**, which becomes the digestive system and lungs; and a **mesoderm**, which be comes the musculature, skeleton, and other circulatory, excretionary, and reproductive organs. Often even before the woman knows she is pregnant, the embryo develops rudimental hands, arms, and fingers, and legs, feet, and toes, and a heartbeat can be distinguished. Miscarriages and spontaneous abortions are most likely to occur in the embryonic stage.

The third through ninth month (birth) of prenatal growth is referred to as the **fetal period**. The embryo is now a fetus, and the organs, limbs, and mus cles and other systems developed in the embryonic period become functional. Sex differentiation occurs around the third month of pregnancy. By the fifth month the fetus has sleeping and waking periods and mothers can feel it mov ing about. By the end of the sixth month the fetus is considered viable; that is, capable of surviving outside the womb if it is given special attention and placed in an incubator. During the ninth month growth begins to slow and the fetus stops changing position, turns head down, and moves into the woman's pelvic cavity in preparation for birth.

BIRTH

In a normal or **vaginal birth**, the muscles of the uterus begin to alternately contract and relax, and the cervix dilates or widens a centimeter or two. Labor begins as the contractions become more regular and closer together. By the end of the first stage of labor the cervix is wide enough to allow the baby's head to move from the uterus to the vaginal opening. This is a very difficult transition; for a successful normal birth, the woman must control her breathing and relax ation. In the second stage of labor the baby's head and body move through the vagina; the baby is delivered. In the third stage of labor, contractions of the uterus expel the placenta.

If a vaginal birth would threaten the life of the mother or baby or the labor process becomes too difficult, a surgical incision may be made in the wall of

domen and uterus for removal of the baby. Surgical methods
:an section have been improved to the point that the operation
: as a vaginal delivery. It is often recommended when the
iical characteristics or conditions which might complicate
1ay be used for the delivery of breech babies, who exit the
_ icet first; babies lying in a transverse presentation, crossway in the
womb; twins and other multiple births; large babies carried by small women;
and babies who show distress during the last weeks of pregnancy. Use of the
procedure has become so widespread that health-care providers and insurers
have begun to question its routine application in nonemergency situations.

THE NEWBORN BABY

Newborns usually breathe and cry as soon as they are born. To avoid overlook-
ing complications which can appear or develop at birth, an assessment instrument has been developed by Virginia Apgar for use in checking the physical
well-being of the newborn. The **Apgar scale** rates infants on heart rate, effort
in breathing, muscle tone, color, and reflex irritability.[28] If significant difficulties are detected, pediatricians are called in. The Apgar scale helps save many
new lives each year.

Birth complications include premature birth, low birth weight, and difficulties in breathing and respiratory distress. If labor has had to be induced, for-
ceps may have been used in the delivery, and medications and drugs may have
been administered to the mother. Most children overcome birth complications
and develop normally, provided there has been no brain damage, the socioeconomic status of the family is adequate, and the parents have positive attitudes
about the trouble.[29]

More severe birth disabilities can be detrimental to the child's cognitive and
emotional development. These include blindness, deafness, mental retardation, orthopedic handicaps, and neurological impairments, many of which are
organic in origin. When such a gross disability is evident at birth, the development of attachment between the parents and the child may be affected. Parents
generally are more helpful in furthering the development of a child whose disability develops after such an attachment has already been formed.[30]

DEVELOPMENTAL TASKS ACROSS THE LIFE COURSE

Robert J. Havighurst, an educational psychologist, has proposed a theory of
development based on the concept of **developmental tasks.** He believes that
development is achieved as the person, while physically growing and then
declining, learns and successfully completes a series of specific age-related
tasks. For Havighurst, life is learning: "The human individual learns his way
through life."[31] Thus his ideas are somewhat separated from the Freudian tradition, which emphasizes inherent, instinctual drives. According to
Havighurst, lower animals rely on instinctual processes, but humans rely on

learning. Nature offers wide possibilities for development, and which skills will be mastered depends on individual learning through socialization.

Havighurst describes a developmental task as "a task which arises at or about a certain period in the life of the individual, successful achievement of which leads to his happiness and to success with later tasks, while failure leads to unhappiness in the individual, disapproval by the society, and difficulty with later tasks."[32] In an ego-psychological theory of development, Barbara and Philip Newman define the term as an outcome of particular stages in the life cycle: "Developmental tasks consist of a set of skills and competencies that contribute to increased mastery over the environment." These tasks may represent a gain in motor skills, intellectual skills, social skills, or emotional skills.[33] The concept of task perhaps is best thought of as an assigned or expected behavioral, emotional, or cognitive chore to be performed or learned by a person.

According to Havighurst, developmental tasks have three interrelated sources. They may originate in the biophysical domain and express maturational urges and needs or in the cultural or social domain and reflect expectations about age roles and statuses, such as daughter, student, or civic leader. The third source is in the psychological domain, which emerges from the interaction between the biophysical and cultural domains. These tasks reflect values and aspirations internalized by the individual. Havighurst believes that by the age of 3 or 4, "the individual's self is effective in the defining and accomplishing of his developmental tasks."[34]

Because these tasks derive from biological needs, from society, and from the self, there is always the potential for conflict. In this respect the idea of developmental tasks is similar to the notion of roles (see Chapters 2 and 10). Role expectations derive from the individual and from society. When expectations for roles and tasks are unclear, mixed, or in other ways poorly communicated, conflict is likely to occur. Successful development, therefore, depends not only on the abilities of the individual to master the tasks but also on the support that is available in the society.

HAVIGHURST'S CLASSIFICATION OF TASKS

Havighurst differentiates between unique and recurrent developmental tasks. **Unique tasks** are associated with a particular age or stage of development. For these tasks, there is a **teachable moment** when a person is ready to learn them; toilet training is an example. **Recurring tasks** are never completely or finally learned. A good example is learning to be a man or a woman, roles which cannot be mastered at one moment in the life cycle but require continual attention. For instance, Havighurst describes the recurring sex-role task in these terms:

> In begins in earnest for most people about the time they start to school, and in its first phase it is pretty well mastered by the age of nine or ten. But the coming of puberty changes the nature of the task and it has to be carried on into a new phase, that of learning to get along with age-mates of the opposite sex. Soon another phase of the task develops — that of learning to get along with age-mates of both

sexes in a socially mature way, where one cooperates with others not because of friendship alone, but because of some impersonal purpose. And even then the task is not completed. The old person often faces it in a new guise when he has to learn to accept the fact of his age and to associate happily with the "elders" of the society.[36]

HAVIGHURST'S DEVELOPMENTAL TASKS ACROSS THE LIFE COURSE

In his classification of developmental tasks confronting the individual negotiating the life course, Robert J. Havighurst identifies six categories of tasks and the specific tasks of each type to be learned in infancy, middle childhood, adolescence, middle adulthood, and later maturity.

I.   Tasks Related to Growth and Maturation
    A. Infancy
        1. Walking
        2. Taking solid foods
        3. Controlling body wastes
        4. Achieving physiological stability
    B. Middle childhood
        1. Learning physical skills necessary for games
        2. Building wholesome attitudes toward self as a growing organism
    C. Adolescence
        1. Accepting one's physique and effectively using the body
    D. Middle adulthood
        1. Accepting the physiological changes of middle age
    E. Later maturity
        2. Adjusting to decreasing physical strength and health

II. Tasks Related to Sexuality and Sex Roles
    A. Infancy
        1. Learning sex differences and sexual modesty
    B. Middle childhood
        1. Learning appropriate masculine or feminine roles
    C. Adolescence
        1. Achieving a socially approved masculine or feminine role

III. Tasks Related to Family Life
    A. Infancy
        1. Learning to relate to parents, siblings, and others

Havighurst's unique and recurring tasks can be classified in six general categories. They include tasks associated with physical growth and maturation, sexuality and sex roles, family life, friendships, cognitive development, and moral and civic responsibility (see box, Havighurst's Developmental Tasks across the Life Course). Development occurs as individuals meet these unique

B. Adolescence
   1. Achieving independence from parents and other adults
   2. Preparing for marriage and family life
C. Early adulthood
   1. Selecting a mate
   2. Learning to live with a marriage partner
   3. Starting a family
   4. Rearing children
   5. Managing a home
D. Middle adulthood
   1. Assisting teenagers to become responsible and happy adults
   2. Relating oneself to one's spouse as a person
   3. Adjusting to aging parents
E. Later maturity
   1. Adjusting to death of a spouse

IV. Tasks Related to Social Friendships
   A. Middle childhood
      1. Learning to get along with age-mates
      2. Achieving personal independence
   B. Adolescence
      1. Achieving mature relations with age-mates of both sexes
      2. Achieving emotional independence from parents and others
   C. Early adulthood
      1. Finding a congenial small group
      2. Developing adult leisure-time activities
   D. Later maturity
      1. Establishing an explicit affiliation with one's age group

V. Tasks Related to Cognitive Development
   A. Infancy
      1. Forming simple concepts of social and physical reality

Continued on p. 500.

and recurring biological, cognitive, psychological, and social expectations and learn the appropriate tasks. Biological tasks occur as a direct result of physical maturation and decline. Cognitive tasks indicate Havighurst's interest in cognitive development theory, and sexual and sex-role tasks show the influence of Freud and ego psychology (see Chapter 14). Other tasks, which are social in nature, seem to represent Havighurst's own thinking about human development. In short, Havighurst provides a perspective which makes it possible to think about human development in a very broad way.

    B. Middle childhood
        1. Developing fundamental skills in reading, writing, and calculating
        2. Developing intellectual skills and concepts for civic competence

VI. Tasks Related to Moral and Civic Responsibility
    A. Infancy
        1. Learning to distinguish right from wrong and developing a conscience
    B. Middle childhood
        1. Developing concepts necessary for everyday living
        2. Developing a conscience, morality, and a scale of values
        3. Developing attitudes toward social groups and institutions
    C. Adolescence
        1. Achieving assurance of economic independence
        2. Selecting and preparing for an occupation
        3. Desiring and achieving socially responsible behavior
        4. Acquiring a set of values to guide behavior
    D. Young adulthood
        1. Getting started in an occupation
        2. Taking on civic responsibility
    E. Middle adulthood
        1. Achieving adult civic and social responsibility
        2. Establishing and maintaining an economic standard of living
    F. Later maturity
        1. Adjusting to retirement and reduced income
        2. Meeting social and civic obligations
        3. Establishing satisfactory physical living arrangements

Source: Adapted from R. J. Havighurst, *Developmental Tasks and Education* (New York: David McKay, 1952).

Rather than attempting to uncover universal laws of human development, Havighurst maintains that each society has distinctive developmental tasks. He explains that the tasks he has identified are to be interpreted only within the context of white, middle-class, American society in the middle of the twentieth century.

Most social scientists have incorporated the notion of developmental tasks into their ideas on the life course, and there have been few systematic attempts to improve on the work of Havighurst. Thus while his ideas about developmental tasks have been very influential, the specific tasks he has identified have not been systematically utilized or tested. They do have an ad hoc validity which makes them useful in social service practice, but they cannot be applied unthinkingly to individuals outside the mainstream of American society, such as the poor and racial and ethnic minorities. More research is needed on the concept of developmental tasks and specific unique and recurrent tasks throughout the life course.

ERIKSON'S PSYCHOSOCIAL CRISES

Other developmental theorists maintain that development occurs not simply as a function of completing specific age-related tasks, as Havighurst proposes, but as a function of various inner crises or struggles. The most influential theory built around this idea is Erik Erikson's conceptualization of the psychosocial crises confronting each person throughout the life course.

By identifying the psychological processes that occur as individuals live out their lives, Erikson has been of enormous significance to social service practice. His work is considered a theory of psychosocial development; it is deeply indebted to Freudian ideas but goes beyond them. Erikson maintains all the contours of the Freudian model, including the emphasis on biology, unconscious instinctual needs, the id, ego, and superego, and the centrality of sexuality. In addition, he recognizes the conflict inherent in transactions between the person and the society and acknowledges the roles of ego processes, social needs, and social expectations in human development. Erikson also breaks with Freud in his view of development as occurring across the entire life course. For Freud and Piaget, human development is largely completed by the end of adolescence. The early childhood years also are the most important in Erikson's formulation, but it takes into account the stages in which physically and sexually mature adults rework the crises of their earlier years and confront new crises as they age.

EIGHT STAGES OF PSYCHOSOCIAL DEVELOPMENT

Erickson postulates the existence of "eight stages of man," each of which occurs within a **radius of significant relationships** and in a particular social context or environment. In the first three stages, infancy, early childhood, and the play age, the child's social relationships are confined to the family and the role of son or daughter. The school-age and adolescence stages accompany puberty, when sexually maturing girls and boys are still very much involved in the family of origin but also are interacting in the world of the school, the neighborhood, and their peers. In the next two stages, young adulthood and adulthood, the person may take up the roles of spouse, parent, worker, and citizen. The last period, old age, involves the years of retirement when the roles of worker and householder have been released and the individual must confront the inevitability of death (see box, Erikson's Stages of Psychosocial Development).

Erikson's developmental stages are defined in terms of the **psychosocial crises** that typify each stage. In this term *crisis* does not mean some kind of extreme and traumatic experience but a set of **critical tasks** which require coping or adaptation. Each crisis poses a struggle from which a **basic strength** can emerge. Together, these strengths or ego qualities represent the ultimate possible development. If the crisis is not overcome, an ego weakness or **core pathology** can develop.

In ego psychology, resolution of the psychosocial crisis comes from the ego strengths built up from past experiences. These strengths involve the proper use of defense mechanisms as well as the conscious use of coping skills, the drive toward competence, and all the other autonomous ego functions. Resolu-

ERIKSON'S STAGES OF PSYCHOSOCIAL DEVELOPMENT

Erik Erikson's theory of psychosocial development covers the life course from infancy to old age. In each stage a particular psychosocial crisis must be resolved within a radius of significant relationships with others. Successful resolution endows the personality with a basic strength; the result of unsuccessful resolution is a core pathology.

Stage	Psychosocial Crisis	Radius of Significant Relationships	Basic Strength	Core Pathology
Infancy	Trust vs. mistrust	Maternal person	Hope	Withdrawal
Early childhood	Autonomy vs. shame, doubt	Parental persons	Will	Compulsion
Play age	Initiative vs. guilt	Basic family	Purpose	Inhibition
School age	Industry vs. inferiority	Neighborhood, school	Competence	Inertia

tion is also helped along by society or, more particularly, others in the radius of significant relationships. Erikson's focus on the individual's inner life does not provide a systematic understanding of the ways in which society can provoke or exacerbate crises or can support and help people through them. Borrowing the concept of average expectable environment from Heinz Hartman (see Chapter 14), he makes the assumption that all societies provide the support necessary for human development. Although this is a useful concept, it should be clear from the discussion in Chapters 12 and 13 and the attention we have given to the study of class status, racism, and sexism that everyone does not receive equal support in American society. Alienation, anomie, inequity, and attacks on self-esteem continue to plague some people of working-class and lower-class status, women, racial and ethnic minorities, the disabled, and homosexuals.

Erikson's stages are epigenetic in nature; that is, each follows from the other in a sequential order. According to the **epigenetic principle**, "proper developmental progress requires the meeting and surmounting of the distinctive critical tasks of each developmental phase at the proper time in the proper sequence."[36] Although the stages follow one after the other, the crisis of each stage is believed to exist in an embryonic form before that stage begins. Moreover, all the crises are believed to be systematically related to all the others, so

Stage	Psychosocial Crisis	Radius of Significant Relationships	Basic Strength	Core Pathology
Adolescence	Identity vs. confusion	Peers, outgroups, models of leadership	Fidelity	Repudiation
Young adulthood	Intimacy vs. isolation	Partners in friendship, sex, competition, cooperation	Love	Exclusivity
Adulthood	Generativity vs. stagnation	Divided labor and shared household	Care	Rejectivity
Old age	Integrity vs. despair	Mankind, my kind	Wisdom	Disdain

Source: Adapted from THE LIFE CYLE COMPLETED, A Review, by Erik H. Erikson, pp. 32–33, by permission of W. W. Norton & Company, Inc. Copyright © 1982 by Rikan Enterprises Ltd.

that as people work through any one crisis, they simultaneously work through past crises and lay the groundwork for the resolution of future crises. Thus Erikson believes individuals have endless possibilities to rework their inner experiences and reach maximum development. The idea that it is always possible to get people back on course, confronting new, past, and future crises in their development, is Erikson's major contribution to social service practice.

EARLY-LIFE STAGES OF DEVELOPMENT

Infancy and early childhood is a period of profound physiological growth and differentiation. Growth is extraordinarily rapid in the first two years after birth and continues through puberty. Children take on the tasks of walking, talking, controlling bodily wastes, and achieving physiological stability. Cognitive development proceeds from sensorimotor to preoperational abilities (see the discussion of Piaget's stages in Chapter 14). Children learn how to form simple concepts of social and psychological reality, including the first sense of self.

Erikson identifies three stages of psychosocial development during these early years of significant growth: infancy, early childhood, and the play age.[37] Each takes place within a radius of significant relationships. For infants this relation is with what Erikson refers to as the **maternal person**, that is, the person who assumes the mother role in caring for the child. In early childhood the significant relations open up to include other parental persons, and in the play age the entire family becomes the significant social context for development. It is up to these persons to supply the direct support necessary for development of the child.

During early life, crises centered around trust, autonomy, and initiative are experienced. If they are resolved adequately, hope, will, and purpose emerge as basic strengths to be used in confronting the crises of subsequent developmental periods. If they are not, withdrawal, compulsion, and inhibition emerge as pathologies.

Physical Growth and Development

At birth, American infants on average weigh about 7.5 pounds and are about 20 inches long. By the end of the second year they have grown a great deal. Most girls have achieved 52.8 percent of their final adult height and most boys have achieved 49.5 percent of theirs by the time they are 2 years of age.[38]

Many infants lose weight immediately after birth but soon begin to take it on rapidly; some double their birth weight in the first four months. Most of the initial weight gain is in the form of fat, which provides insulation and calories for nourishment. After about nine months, the weight gained goes more to bone and muscle. Once children start walking the proportion of body fat decreases, and by the time they are ready for school they have lost most of their "baby fat."

A big moment in childhood development. The school-age child will have to prove his/her competence and avoid a sense of inferiority. *Gale Zucker/Stock, Boston.*

The heads of newborn infants comprise about one-fourth of their total length, and with age this proportion decreases. By age 2 the brain weighs about 75 percent of what the adult brain does. The primary motor and sensory areas of the cortex, which control the senses and simple motor skills, increase most rapidly during the first months. Areas that coordinate more complex skills begin growth later.

Infants can lift their heads before they can sit up, and they sit up before they can stand. They first learn to move by pulling themselves along with their arms and usually progress to crawling on their hands and knees. At about a year they begin to walk tentatively. By age 2 most children can walk forwards and backwards, run, and climb stairs. There is continued maturation in motor abilities through the preschool years. Three-year olds pay less attention to what their feet are doing; four-year-olds can run fast or slowly, and five-year-olds can skip, balance on one foot, and move to the cadence of music.

Newborns can wave their arms when they see dangling objects, but they cannot aim well enough to grab them. By six months they can reach, grab, and hold on to a dangling object but have difficulty letting go. Then they develop the ability to pick up small objects and become more dexterous in manipulating the fingers. At birth there is involuntary release of waste products, but by four months more-or-less predictable intervals between feeding and bowel movements have been established.

Until recently it was believed that infants are born blind. Now it is known that they have blurred vision but can focus reasonably well on objects between 7 and 10 inches away. They often prefer to focus on faces, perhaps out of a social instinct but more likely because faces have interesting patterns. Babies seem to be curious about colorful, moving objects. Depth perception develops in the first months of life. Hearing also is well developed early in life. Sudden noises easily startle newborns and make them cry; rhythmic sounds such as lullabies are soothing and help put them to sleep. At one month many infants are able to distinguish their mothers' voice, and by the seventh month they can locate other sounds.

Family Life

Infants are extremely vulnerable and unable to perform the most basic tasks of life. They are usually sheltered in the protective environment of the family, where the mother's early importance soon is matched by that of the father, siblings, and other relatives. Although infants are dependent, they can enter into interactions with care-givers and can influence them.[39] Thus socialization is not a process whereby parents simply introduce completely malleable children to the tasks expected of them.

Since family roles and relations are central in the early years, infants and young children assume a number of family tasks. They learn to relate to parents, siblings, and other relatives as a son, daughter, brother, sister, niece, nephew, or cousin. They learn sex differences and sexual modesty. They also learn about society and social institutions indirectly, through the adults and older children caring for them. Their social class and political, social, ethnic, and racial status are completely ascribed, an accident of their birth. Their parents' advantages and disadvantages become their own. The struggles of disadvantaged parents against poverty, unemployment, low wages, prejudice, and discrimination, as well as the struggles of advantaged parents to sustain the privileges associated with their social class, race, and ethnicity, permeate the relationship between parent and child. The struggles of fathers and mothers to resolve issues related to sex-role status also affect their relations with their young children. Children are not so much socialized into society as they are socialized into the conflicts and changes taking place in it and their families' points of view or ambivalence in those conflicts.

Psychosocial Crises in Early Life

Erikson describes the psychosocial crisis of infancy as basic **trust vs. mistrust**. Infants are born relatively helpless and must learn to depend on, that is, to trust, adults. Since the mother usually is most responsible for the welfare of the infant, infants must trust that their mothers will not abandon them and will be there to nourish them and satisfy their needs. In gaining this basic trust, infants incorporate a larger sense of trust in the world and the adults who control it. The gaining of trust is an interactive process; it involves the things that mothers do and the things that infants do. Infants must learn not only to trust mother but also to trust their own ability to control their urges to bite and swallow and not injure mother. Mothers must learn to trust the child and to encourage trust from the child. Erikson notes that "babies control and bring up their families as much as they are controlled by them; in fact, we may say that the family brings up a baby by being brought up by him." [40]

The quality of the mother-child relationship is more important than the quantity of nourishment or love given. If the relationship goes well, **hope**, "an enduring belief that one can attain one's deep and essential wishes," [41] will be incorporated into the child's personality. If the relationship falters, a basic mistrust may be incorporated which will make it difficult for the person to form attachments throughout life. **Withdrawal** occurs; the person becomes "socially and emotionally detached." [42] Later stages of development may provide opportunities to rework the mother-child relationship and establish trust and hope, but failure to do so leaves a residue of mistrust and withdrawal.

In early childhood the psychosocial crisis is **autonomy vs. shame and doubt**. As the child's musculature matures and libidinal impulses center around the anus, new social needs and expectations are experienced. Parents motivate their children to control their bowels in particular and to control themselves in general, starting with arm and leg movements. Thus children begin to experiment with "holding on and letting go." If during this period they can learn to control themselves, they establish a **sense of autonomy** and develop the ego strength of a **will**, "a determination to exercise free choice and self-control." [43] If self-control is thwarted by the interaction of child and parents, a sense of shame and doubt comes to pervade the personality. **Shame** is the sense of being completely exposed, so everyone can see failures. It is demonstrated in self-consciousness and often exhibited by children as hiding their faces or sinking to the ground. **Doubt** is the sense of having a hidden side which others may expose. A sense of paranoia about being threatened or found out is experienced. Shame and doubt can lead to **compulsion**, "repetitive behaviors motivated by impulse or restrictions against the expression of impulse." [44] Compulsive people are excessively disciplined, orderly, neat, and organized and are easily shaken when their routines are interrupted.

Initiative vs. guilt is the psychosocial crisis of the play age. As children grow physically stronger and get greater control of themselves, their behavior becomes more deliberate, taking on the quality of undertaking, planning, and attacking which Erikson calls **initiative**. Since libidinal impulses are now focused in the genital area, the initiative is in part directed at genital pleasure with parents, usually the mother. But it need not be thought of only in terms of sexual development. Psychosocially this is a period in which more general ambitions and interests appear in the child's interactions with the entire family.

The play age is a particularly important phase in the life course because it marks the emergence of "the slow process of becoming a parent, a carrier of tradition." [45] In developing a superego, a sense of what is right and wrong about their needs and desires, children accept adult authority and lay the foundation for taking the role of adult themselves.

Mutual regulation of the behaviors of the child, parents, and siblings is essential. In this way children gain a sense that their plans and behaviors are good and proper and their initiative is being channeled correctly. They develop the ego strength of **purpose**, "the courage to imagine and pursue valued goals." [46] Without mutual regulation, children may experience deep guilt about their interests and goals. Then **inhibition** sets in, "a psychological restraint that prevents freedom of thought, expression and activity." [47]

SCHOOL AGE AND ADOLESCENCE

Erikson defines the stages of development in later childhood as school age and adolescence. These stages are marked by psychosocial crises involving the acquisition of industry and identity, within the context of continued physical growth and the significant biological changes of puberty. These crises are reasoned through the cognitive capacities for concrete operational thought and, in later adolescence, formal operational reasoning. The struggle to resolve them takes place in a wider radius of significant relationships which include not only the family but the school, the neighborhood, peer groups, and individuals representing models of leadership in the society. The ego strengths that can emerge from a successful resolution of these crises are competence and fidelity; the pathologies that can emerge from a poor resolution are inertia and repudiation.

Physical Growth and Maturation

School-age children do not grow at the same startling rate as preschool children but do continue to grow. They learn the physical skills necessary for complex physical maneuvers such as those needed in games and begin to acquire a positive sense of themselves as physical beings. With the arrival of the teen years and puberty, adolescents begin to accept their changing physiques and learn to deal with sex-role expectations. Cognitively, school-age children learn fundamental skills in reading, writing, and calculating and learn to follow rules. In adolescence they begin to acquire the intellectual skills necessary for eventual civic competence.

The most important biological experience during these years is **puberty**, "the time when the sexual organs become capable of reproduction and the influence of sex hormones first becomes prominent." [48] It is sometimes divided into two periods; **pubescence** describes the years just prior to puberty itself. Although males and females both undergo changes during puberty, the substance of the changes and the rate of change vary somewhat. Girls tend to develop earlier than boys and often are physically mature by age 16. [49] Boys begin pubescence later, and maturation proceeds at a slower pace and over a longer period.

Sexual Development in Girls.   Pubescence in females, which begins at approximately ages 8–11, is marked by distinct physical changes. The breasts enlarge, the nipples project, the body contours round out, the pelvic area broadens, and fatty pads develop around the hips. The vaginal lining thickens and pubic and auxiliary hair appears. About two years after the first signs of pubescence, **menarche**, or menstruation, the monthly discharge of blood and other material from the uterus through the vagina, begins. **Ovulation**, the release of a mature egg, begins about a year after the first menstrual period. With these developments, the girl is able to procreate; she has entered puberty.

There is great variation in the age at which females begin to menstruate and ovulate. For approximately half of all American girls, the age of ovulation is between 12.5 and 14.5 years. Nutrition, the physical environment, and physiological factors such as body weight all influence the onset of menstruation and ovulation.

During puberty the sex glands or **gonads** begin to produce and emit hormones which influence sexual desire and may also influence mental health. In females the gonads are the **ovaries**, which produce **estrogen**. This hormone controls body structure, is important in the development and functioning of the genital organs, and influences the menstrual cycle as well as the development of secondary sexual characteristics. The ovaries also produce **progesterone**, which is of primary importance in preparing the lining of the uterus for implantation of fertilized eggs and maintaining pregnancy. Progesterone also enlarges the breasts of pregnant females and inhibits premature uterine contractions as birth approaches.

Sexual Development in Boys.   Pubescence in males is also marked by physical changes. A "fat period" usually begins around age II. At the same time erections of the penis begin to occur, and as the penis and scrotum enlarge, erections are more frequent. **Ejaculation**, the expulsion of semen from the urethra, is usually possible by this time. The secretion of sperm follows, although mature sperm may not be present yet. Spontaneous nocturnal emissions of sperm, or "wet dreams," are common. Secondary sex characteristics such as the growth of pubic and auxiliary facial and body hair, changes in muscular and skeletal structures, and changes in the male voice, which drops about an octave, appear as puberty progresses.

The male gonads (**testes**) produce and emit **testosterone**. This hormone is responsible for the development and preservation of masculine secondary characteristics. Testosterone used to be considered responsible for the greater height of males, but this belief was discarded when it was learned that estrogen also controls height.[50] Each sex possesses hormones associated with the opposite sex, and excessive amounts can have implications for sexual functioning and secondary sexual characteristics.

Schools and Peer-Group Relations

School-age children learn to get along with age-mates and acquire a sense of personal independence. In later childhood they try to achieve mature social relationships with friends of both sexes. Adolescents are particularly involved in achieving emotional independence from parents and, as they approach the end of childhood, relationships with peers. Adolescence ends when young adults prepare to leave their family of origin and set up their own independent households.

Schools and peers are particularly influential during later childhood. This does not mean, however, that family relationships become less important. Although relationships with teachers and with peer group members account for much time and attention, older children generally remain very attached to and influenced by their families of origin.[51]

Education is the social institution which, along with the family, most directly affects children during these years. In an extension of the parent role, teachers assist children to develop the basic intellectual, moral, and behavioral tools necessary for entry into the adult world. Before public schools were common, the education of children was often through apprenticeships, a kind of on-the-job training in direct contact with experts in a particular task or craft. In the early schools, academies, and universities, students of very different ages often were taught together.[52] Education today is age-graded and much more formal, especially in the elementary, middle, and high school years.

As in the family, today's schools have both manifest and latent functions. At the manifest level, the purpose of schools is to prepare children for successful participation in society.[53] Students are introduced to concepts, theories, and relationships to enable them to organize their everyday experiences. They are taught and evaluated on knowledge in a range of disciplines, including arithmetic, language, art, music, science, and social science, and become acquainted with methods of investigating and solving problems. Contacts with teachers and exposure to the various disciplines help children discover their interests and channel their commitment to personal and career goals and standards.

At the latent level, the school's functions are similar to the family's, the socialization of children into the inequities associated with classism, racism, and sexism in the society. Christopher Jencks maintains that problems in education cannot be resolved without dealing with such social inequities.[54] It is often through the school that children first receive messages about what they can and cannot expect to accomplish as adults. Sex-role stereotypes, by which girls' interests are channeled to motherhood and traditional women's careers such as secretary or social worker[55] and boys' interests are directed to such careers as businessman, doctor, or lawyer, are no longer the rule, but they persist in some school districts. Because of the diverse ways in which schools are financed, teachers are motivated, and parents participate in the work of the school, children from lower-class and ethnic-minority groups are less likely to have educational experiences which will develop their interests and talents and encourage them to succeed. They therefore perceive the curriculum and the school experience as irrelevant and often have high dropout rates.

Peer-group relations become particularly influential as children reach puberty and the teen years. While friends are important during the early school years, becoming a member of a definable group now is essential, and pressure to become part of a particular group is felt from the family, the school, and friends.[56] As friendship cliques develop, children become associated with groups going by such names as "the leading crowd, populars, socialites, preppies, rah-rahs, jocks, eggheads, nerds, ginks, eraserheads, dirtballs, potheads, greasers, and hoods." Similar labels may be found in all schools, regardless of neighborhood.[57]

In conjunction with anomie and other sources of stress, some peer groups exert pressure on adolescents to become involved in delinquency. Although delinquent behavior is supported by cliques at all levels of society, working-class greasers and hoods are most likely to be caught and taken into custody by the police (see the box, Saints and Roughnecks, in Chapter 8). Peer-group relations also can cause adolescents who are not doing well in school to drop out.[58] Nevertheless, peer groups generally have positive functions. Through relations with their peers, adolescents learn the value of collective action, the increased influence of an individual which comes from participation with others. Peer groups support feelings of self-worth and offer protection from loneliness. When troubles exist between parents and children, peers can give comfort and nurture.[59]

Psychosocial Crises in Later Childhood and Adolescence

Erikson describes the psychosocial crisis faced by school-age children as **industry vs. inferiority**. Going off to school produces a new set of needs and demands. The egocentricity of earlier stages is abandoned as children begin to learn about their society and find they can win approval and recognition by their industry in producing things. Parents, friends, and especially the school focus on the ability to complete intellectual and physical tasks.

School-age children who learn to produce, that is, are successful academically, gain assurance that they are capable and can expect to participate effectively in society. They acquire the basic strength of **competence**, which in this sense means "the free exercise of skill and intelligence in the completion of tasks."[60] Competent children feel at one with the school and the society. They gain the sense that they can learn and do what is expected of them. Children whose school experiences are not productive may develop a sense of inferiority. They experience **inertia**, "a paralysis of action and thought that prevents productive work."[61] In other words, they doubt their abilities and become afraid of the tasks that are presented to them. They prefer to complete nothing rather than risk failure.

In adolescence, the crisis is **identity vs. identity confusion**. Puberty is a time of turmoil in which adolescents seem to feel the need to question all their earlier adaptations to the demands of parents and teachers. Adulthood lies just ahead, and needs become centered on locating the self within the society. Adolescents often are caught up in the issue of "what they appear to be in the eyes of others as compared with what they feel they are."[62]

In their search for identity, adolescents must make many decisions: who their real friends are and what kind of adult they want to be; what their sexual identities are and how to relate sexually to others; what their interests are and how to prepare for their chosen occupations. They may develop a political allegiance, question adult authority, and challenge traditional ideology. Adolescents who can manage the search for identity develop a clear sense of who they are and acquire the strength of **fidelity**, "the ability to freely pledge and sustain loyalties to others."[63] Thus they become able to commit themselves to friends and leaders whose values and way of life have meaning for them. When the crisis of adolescence is unresolved, adolescents suffer identity confusion which can follow them throughout life. This may be expressed in **repudiation**, the "rejection of roles and values that are viewed as alien to oneself."[64] Those who are not able to give fidelity to any one person tend to reject all loyalties. They approach life with indifference and sarcasm; nothing seems to have meaning for them.

YOUNG ADULTS AND ADULTHOOD

Erikson proposes two adult stages of development, young adulthood and adulthood. The first provokes a crisis of **intimacy**, which has to do with the ability for deep interpersonal relations. The second provokes a crisis of **generativity**, which has to do with the ability to contribute creatively and productively to society. If the personal and social resources available to adults enable them to resolve the crises over intimacy and generativity, development occurs, and love and care emerge as basic ego strengths. If not, the pathologies of exclusivity and rejectivity mark the personality.

Physical and Biological Changes

In early adulthood most individuals are at the peak of their biological and physiological capacities. Physical strength is at the maximum, and the ability to procreate has been achieved. Cognitive development is likely to be at the level of formal organizations, which allows for abstract reasoning in the solution of problems.

A period of physical stability can be expected until the mid-adult years, when the body becomes more susceptible to disease and decline. The rate of heart conditions per 1,000 persons in 1985 was 40.1 among those 18–44 years old but 129.0 among those 45–64 years old. The rate of hypertension increased from 64.1 for the 18–44 age group to 258.9 for the 45–64 age group, and the rate of diabetes increased from 9.1 to 51.9 in the same groups.[65] Skin and muscle start to lose elasticity and strength. The ability to see, hear, taste, smell, and even feel pain begins to diminish. Motor skills and reaction time decrease, and there is a loss of energy.

Cardiovascular diseases and cancer are the leading causes of death among older adults. In 1985, the death rate from heart disease went from 8.2 per 100,000 persons aged 25–34 years old to 38.0 among those aged 35–44 and 152.9 among those 55–64 years old. Deaths from cancer went from 45.7 per 100,000 at ages 25–34, to 169.1 at ages 35–44, and to 450.5 at ages 55–64.[66]

Although sexual pleasure can be enjoyed throughout the adult years, reproductive abilities decline in the **climacteric** period, and for women, they end. In men, the hormonal changes in testosterone and other androgens which limit reproduction take place gradually, over a long period. In women, the decrease in production of estrogen, referred to as the **menopause**, is more abrupt and takes place in their late 40s and early 50s. The climacteric may produce other physical symptoms such as impotence and difficulties in becoming aroused, and it may be accompanied by such psychological states as depression, a loss in self-esteem, and diminished interest in sexual relations. These physical and psychological troubles are related to the social context of aging, including sexism, and are not an inherent part of the aging process.[67]

Social Relationships

In the adult years the crises of intimacy and generativity are played out within a wide radius of significant relationships with acquaintances, friends and associates, and lovers. Most young adults aspire to form deep, enduring sexual and emotional commitments to other persons, and these intimate relationships are central to their individual well-being.[68] Most young adults devote considerable time to dating and selecting a partner, and most eventually marry and have or adopt children. They get involved in the tasks of learning to live with another person, rearing children, and managing a household. Quite a few eventually divorce and may remarry. They help their adolescent children become independent and leave home, and, as they age, they take on some of the tasks of caring for their own parents (see the section on the family life cycle in Chapter 10).

At the same time, most adults are striving for occupational success, a basic way in which creative capacities are unleashed. While this goal formerly occupied men more than women, most women now pursue it at some time during their adult years. Adults also join political, religious, and other voluntary associations in line with their personal views or to serve the interests of families, friends, and communities.

As adults interact within their radius of significant relationships, they experience the conflicts and contradictions in the society. There is, for instance, a greater tendency for conflict and competition in intimate relations in a society that is organized around inequitable sex roles. As Jessie Bernard points out, "her" marriage can be quite different from "his" marriage when the two partners come to have different understandings of their relationship. Noting that women are much less satisfied with marriage than men are, she proposes a "shock theory of marriage" which applies to women. The legal, social, and personal changes when women become "just housewives" produce a shock that threatens their independence and self-esteem and contributes to marital dissatisfaction.[69]

The various class, ethnic, racial, and sexual statuses that adults occupy also influence their ability to solve the crises of adulthood. The vulnerabilities imposed by unemployment, economic insecurity, limited opportunities, prejudice, and discrimination lead to the perception that society is hostile to the development of some individuals. Those in lower-status groups are more likely to experience alienation, anomie, and inequity in their dealings with society. That many in these groups do manage to develop satisfactorily is testimony to their own strengths and to the support they receive from family, friends, and others, including social workers, who join them in their developmental struggle.

Psychosocial Crises in the Adult Years

Young adulthood is marked by the psychosocial crisis of **intimacy vs. isolation.** A new set of needs and demands emerge as older adolescents complete their educations and become ready to enter the adult world. Young adults are ready for intimacy; that is, they have the capacity to commit themselves to concrete affiliations and partnerships and to abide by such commitments, even though doing so may require significant sacrifices and compromises. In large part, the intimacy is of a sexual nature, becoming legitimate through marriage, but it can also be thought of in terms of meaningful relationships with friends, teachers, family members, and fellow workers. In committing themselves to another, young adults give up a part of themselves. Thus the fear is ego loss; if they cannot achieve intimacy, they may develop a deep sense of isolation and self-absorption.

It is in early adulthood that sexual gratification is finally fulfilled. To Erikson, the "utopia" of sexuality means:[70]

1. mutuality of orgasm
2. with a loved partner
3. of the other sex
4. with whom one is able and willing to share a mutual trust
5. with whom one is able and willing to regulate the cycles of
   a. work
   b. procreation
   c. recreation
6. so as to secure to the offspring, too, all the stages of a satisfactory development.

Many other theorists, however, would not limit normal adulthood to heterosexual, procreative functions, as we noted in Chapter 7. Mutuality of orgasm and procreation are not always seen as values or indications of competent development by contemporary sexologists, and homosexual relations are no longer considered an indication of unhealthy development or mental disorder.

If the young adult does develop the ability to be intimate with others, love emerges as a strength. From a psychosocial point of view, **love** is defined as "the capacity for mutuality that transcends childhood dependency."[71] In other words, adult love is different from the love of parent for child. It involves the ability to take care of as well as to be taken care of, being able to depend on the other but also being dependable. Adults who become intimate must be able to meet each other's needs and accept each other's weaknesses. If a sense of isolation develops instead, the pathology of **exclusivity**, or a "shutting out of others,"[72] takes over the personality. Adults may become excessively possessive and jealous and try to control the love object, or they may become unable to include and therefore to commit themselves to others. They then are likely to spend the rest of their lives without experiencing love for others.

Generativity vs. stagnation is the psychosocial crisis of adulthood. Adults assume roles such as parent by which they become responsible for establishing and guiding the next generation. **Generativity**, or contributing to the continuance of the society, includes the drive to create objects, services, and ideas of any nature, but Erikson emphasizes its procreative aspects. He believes having children is essential to human development, although he acknowledges that "there are individuals who, through misfortune or because of special and genuine gifts in other directions, do not apply this drive to their own offspring. And indeed, the concept of generativity is meant to include such more popular synonyms as *productivity* and *creativity*, which, however, cannot replace it."[73]

Merely having children is not sufficient to establish generativity. The parent role must be taken seriously. Parents must be emotionally developed if they are to guide the younger generation. The crisis of adulthood is thus over productive and creative capacities emanating from physical, intellectual, and emotional maturation. The struggle is against **stagnation**, that is, not being able to accomplish anything. Stagnation occurs when adults do nothing or are thwarted in the use of their mature abilities. A sense of stagnation is often evident in people who are having difficulties in their roles as parent or worker. Resolving this adult crisis produces the strength of **care**, "the commitment to be concerned for what has been generated,"[74] in order to assure the next generation's life and strength. Decisions made in life are weighed against the interests of others, and attachment becomes complete, as much a commitment to their needs and interests as one's own. When the crisis overwhelms a person, the pathology of **rejectivity**, "the unwillingness to include certain others or groups of others in one's generative concern,"[75] marks the personality. These adults reject the feeling of caring about others and about society.

OLD AGE

Erikson describes old age as the last stage of development. Faced with inevitable physical decline and possible social isolation, individuals think through their lives introspectively, calling on their personal resources as they search for wisdom. The psychosocial crisis involves the conflict between ego integrity, leading to wisdom, and despair, leading to disdain.

Old age has traditionally been defined as beginning at 65 years of age, the time when employed people have been expected to retire and give up their role of worker. This definition no longer holds, since many workers retire much earlier and others continue to work well into their 70s. Physically and socially, too, the period of "old age" is being extended as life expectancy lengthens (see Chapter 7). The Census Bureau now reports some data in the categories of 65-74 years old, 75-84 years old, and 85 and older, rather than just 65 and over.

In any case, the period Erikson describes as old age or later adulthood is a distinct stage of the life course. The family's children are grown, often married and with children of their own, and may live far away. Spouses and friends can be expected to die, leaving an older person widowed, alone, and suffering bereavement. Physical and mental deterioration may require prolonged periods of physical dependence, and, for some, institutionalization in nursing homes. For these reasons, old age is sometimes described as a time of role loss or a period of disengagement, in which the elderly turn inward and are motivated to withdraw from society.[76]

Such pessimistic views of old age are not in keeping with the emphasis in ego psychology on development. While it is acknowledged that old age is a time

Older people have to adjust to their changing physical abilities, but happiness need not escape them. *Jim Wright/Nawrocki Stock Photo, Inc.*

of role exit, all phases of life can be thought of in terms of role entrances and exits which bring changes in associations, mood, and self-concept.[77] Cross-national studies of retired people have failed to demonstrate universal patterns of disengagement, even within similar environments.[78] The amount of activity or involvement with the environment varies considerably among older people. Different theories of aging see old age not as a period of loss but as a period of role transition or a time when older people are motivated to maintain a high degree of active involvement and strong relationships with others.[79] Thus while old age is for some a period of physical decline and deterioration, it need not be devoid of psychological development.

Life Expectancy and Physical Decline

Major changes in death rates have been observed over the past 100 years. The most likely period of death used to be infancy, and thereafter the likelihood of death was fairly constant across the life course. Comparatively few people now die before reaching old age in the United States. Life expectancy at birth, the average length of life for an individual, has increased steadily since 1920, when it was 54 years. Males born in 1986 could expect to live 71 years, and females born that year could expect to live seven years longer.[80]

Old age is without doubt a period of physical and intellectual decline and eventual deterioration. This does not mean that older people cannot be healthy and cannot function physically, sexually, and cognitively. As in all life stages, there are wide individual differences.

Studies of cognitive functioning among older people have found that while fluid intelligence declines with age, crystallized intelligence remains stable and may even increase, at least up to the eighth decade of life. **Crystallized intelligence** is the ability to use appropriately knowledge that has been accumulated through past experience. It has to do with verbal comprehension, including vocabulary, the evaluation of experiences, and the association of words and phrases (for instance, the ability to connect authors and titles). **Fluid intelligence** is akin to having a head on one's shoulders. It has to do with general reasoning skills, including the abilities to organize information, develop and test hypotheses, and approach new problems logically and systematically.[81]

Sexual enjoyment generally also declines with age. Most older people are slower to arouse, and the opportunities for sexual intercourse may not be present. According to William Masters and Virginia Johnson, however, this decline results from social and psychological considerations rather than from aging.[82] With respect to physical capacities, attention to exercise and good nutrition is allowing many older people to remain amazingly hearty, productive, and active. Nevertheless, few people older than 65 are entirely free of disabilities.[83] The decline in vision, hearing, taste, and other senses that begins to be noticed in late adulthood becomes very evident in old age. For instance, by age 70 almost two-thirds of the tastebuds and many of the sense receptors in the nose have died.[84] The rate of blindness and severe hearing loss goes up appreciably. Shrinking muscles, calcification of ligaments, and decreases in flexibility become obvious.

As the immune system produces fewer antibodies, the older person is left with less protection against disease and microorganisms, and acute and chronic illnesses are more likely.[85] About 80 percent of older people have at least one chronic condition, and multiple conditions are common.[86] Many of these, like rheumatism and arthritis, are not so debilitating that the person cannot function. In about 15 percent of the cases major limitations in functioning occur, and long-term care, in or out of the home, becomes necessary.[87]

The elderly are also vulnerable to organic mental disorders. These may involve temporary or permanent brain damage and cause impaired memory, poor judgment, intellectual decline, and disorientation. Chronic brain syndrome or **senile dementia** occurs in about 15 to 30 percent of the population 85 years old and over.[88] The principal form of nonreversible dementia in the middle-aged and elderly now is identified as **Alzheimer's disease**, a progressive deterioration in brain cells. This life-shortening illness can strike adults of all ages and produce such effects as memory loss, confusion, speech impairment, and personality changes. Recognition of the disease is helping to destroy the perception of a connection between senility and old age.

The Psychosocial Crisis in Old Age

Ego integrity vs. despair is the psychosocial crisis in old age, as individuals come to grips with the meaning of their lives and their place in the social world and the spiritual order. Ego integrity means coming to accept "one's one and only life cycle as something that had to be and that, by necessity, permitted of no other substitutions."[89] The person comes to love and respect not the self so much as all of humanity. Those who are not able to accept their life may fear death, be disgusted with self and humanity, and experience remorse and despair. While old age is marked by physical decline and deterioration, it nevertheless presents additional possibilities for development. If the crisis of old age is resolved, the strength of **wisdom**, "the detached yet active concern with life itself in the face of death"[90] pervades the personality. Wisdom requires a vision of humankind, that is, an idea of how all the past, present, and future generations fit together. If despair takes over, old age can generate the pathology of **disdain**, "a feeling of scorn for the weakness and frailty of oneself and others."[91] In this case, the older person becomes bitter.

DEVELOPMENTAL CRISES IN MATURITY

Erikson was among the first developmental theorists to call attention to periods of potential development beyond adolescence. Nevertheless, five of his eight stages are in the first 16 or 17 years of life, and only three are in the remaining

60 or more years in the average life course. Daniel Levinson and Robert Peck have developed ego-psychological theories which focus on additional periods of adult development.

LEVINSON AND THE SEASONS OF LIFE

The developmental theory proposed by Levinson and his colleagues is based on empirical research using biographical interviews with 40 North American men between the ages of 35 and 45. This sample was considered to represent diverse backgrounds and circumstances. One-fourth of the men were hourly workers in industry; one-fourth were top- and middle-management executives; one-fourth were university biologists, and one-fourth were novelists. Only 5 percent were black, and all had been heterosexually married at least once.[92]

Levinson did not include women in this study, but he suggests that his ideas are applicable to women as well as men (see box, Life Patterns for Women and

LIFE PATTERNS FOR WOMEN AND MEN

Research for the life-cycle study reported in *The Seasons of a Man's Life*, by Daniel J. Levinson and his colleagues, was limited to men because the differences between the genders were considered to be so great that separate analysis was needed. They concluded that women and men go through the same adult developmental periods, but they do so in partially different ways which reflect their biological inheritance and social circumstances.

While there have been no major studies on age-related sequences in female development which are comparable to that done by Levinson et al., Gail Sheehy built on their work in her best-seller *Passages: Predictable Crises of Adult Life*. Rather than concentrating on a single gender, she set out to compare the "developmental rhythms" of men and women. In her opinion, "The fundamental steps of expansion that will open a person, over time, to the full flowering of his or her individuality are the same for both genders. But men and women are rarely in the same place struggling with the same question at the same age" (p. 22).

To substantiate her ideas, Sheehy collected 115 life stories of Americans in the "pacesetter group"—healthy, motivated members of the middle class, from 18 to 55 years old. The men were students, professionals, or businessmen; the women were top achievers or in traditional nurturing roles. Sheehy found quite different "life patterns" for men and women, determined by the choices they made in their twenties.

Men). Moreover, while the study considered a relatively homogeneous sample of only 40 North American males in the middle of the twentieth century, the periods and transitions described are considered to be universal. Levinson maintains that life structures evolve through an orderly sequence during the adult years, and "the essential character of the sequence is the same for all the men in our study and for the other men whose biographies we examined."[93]

Levinson's thesis is that there are seasons in a man's life, "a series of periods or stages within the life cycle." His seasons, or eras, are based on chronological age, more-or-less unaffected by social or cultural considerations. The seasons he is interested in are early and middle adulthood, that is, the chronological years between ages 17 and 65. (There are two other eras, childhood and adolescence, 0–22 years, and late adulthood, 60 years and older.) Within each era he articulates **stable periods** of development lasting about six to eight years. These periods overlap and are joined by **transitional periods** of up to five years in which men evaluate their position in life and explore new options. In the transitional periods individuals acquire their **life structure**, the set of inter-

Sheehy classified the men as the *transients*, unwilling or unable to make firm commitments; the *locked in*, or committed; and the *wunderkind*, who create risks and play to win. Less common patterns were *never-married men; paranurturers*, such as clergymen or husbands who nurture their wives; and *latency boys*, who avoid the process of adolescence and remain bound to their mothers. A seventh category, the *integrators*, was created to describe those few men who try to balance their ambitions with a commitment to their families, consciously working to be ethical and of benefit to society while they ensure their own economic success.

She identifies fewer life patterns for the women, who "must improvise a timetable around the needs of others" (p. 157). Traditionally the most common have been the *caregivers*, who have no desire to go beyond the domestic role when they marry in their twenties. *Either-or* women feel required to choose between love and children or work and accomplishment. This category includes both nurturers who defer achievement and achievers who defer nurturing. *Integrators* try to do it all, integrating marriage, career, and children. There are also *never-married women*, and *transients*, who wander sexually, occupationally, and geographically in their twenties and most of their lives.

Source: Gail Sheehy, *Passages: Predictable Crises of Adult Life* (New York: Bantam Books, 1977).

nal values, ideals, and aspirations which are played out through participation in the external world of family and occupation.[94]

Transitional periods are extremely important because they are the times when established life structures are discarded or revised and new life structures are created. To Levinson, a developmental transition marks the termination of a time in a person's life. In these periods, the tasks are to accept the losses of the end of a period, review and evaluate the past, decide what to keep of the past and what to reject, and consider the possibilities for the future.

> One is suspended between past and future, and struggling to overcome the gap that separates them. Much from the past must be given up—separated from, cut out of one's life, rejected in anger, renounced in sadness or grief. And there is much that can be used as a basis for the future. Changes must be attempted in both self and world.[95]

The changes in the transitional periods leading to mature adult life are described by Judith Viorst this way:

> Breaking away from the pre-adult world—the Early Adult Transition—between ages seventeen and twenty-two. Making, during our twenties, our first commitments to a job, a life-style, a marriage. Revising our selections in our late twenties and early thirties—the Age Thirty Transition—to add what is missing, to modify and exclude. Settling down and investing ourselves, during most of our thirties, in work, friends, family, community, whatever. And reaching, at about forty, those bridging years which take us from early to middle adulthood. Levinson calls this time the Mid-Life Transition. For most of us it's a crisis—a mid-life crisis.[96]

The Mid-Life Crisis

Although the Levinson study could be used as a basis for delineating the periods and transitions throughout the life course, the major aim was to study men as they resolve the crisis of the mid-life transition, from about age 40 to 45. Levinson proposes that men form their **dream**, their vision of what adulthood will hold for them in occupational and familial terms, in the early adult transition, ages 17–22. In developing the dream and learning how to reach it, they benefit from a **mentor relationship** with another man, generally someone eight to ten years older, with experience and seniority in the world they wish to enter. The mentor is a transitory figure, someone extremely important only at that moment in the young man's life. The dream is played out in the stable **novice period** by choosing an occupation and starting a career. The other key relationship for the man in this period is with a woman he loves; this dream is played out by marrying and having a family. The special quality of the loved woman in the man's life at this stage is her connection to his dream, her ability to make him feel capable of achieving it.

Before settling down in early adulthood, the novice undergoes another transition between about ages 28 and 32 during which he works on the flaws and limitations of his dream. He is concerned about advancement, social rank, income, power, fame, creativity, and quality of family life and attacks the dream of life in earnest. He tries to become his own man and to establish his niche in life, to feel self-assured and confident. Sometimes he succeeds and sometimes he does not. By age 40, however, the settled man's quest for advancement, his early adult life structure, no longer is sufficient, and he enters the mid-life transition.

The dream is different for women, though Levinson found in a study of 45 women in their middle years that women go through the same sequence of periods at the same ages as men do, and even the most traditional women wrestle with a crisis in mid-life.[97] For men, the dream that motivates young adulthood is essentially centered on occupations; while they also have family dreams most believe they are taking care of their families through the economic support they provide. Women have more difficulty forming their dream of adulthood, since they are conflicted between yearnings for a career and yearnings for a family, and the two roles do not mesh as they do for men. Men are the heroes of their own dreams; women participate both in their own heroic dreams and the dreams of their husbands. As a result, many women with careers do not have long-term career goals, and some traditional women consciously marry men who will create a dream in which they can have a significant part. Moreover, few women have either of the relationships which men can rely on in their twenties, the mentor to help them get established in a career or a loving helpmate to provide domestic support.

For the increasingly smaller proportion of women who only participate in their husbands' dreams and devote themselves to family concerns, the mid-life crisis can take the form of the **empty-nest syndrome**, a feeling of loss when the youngest child leaves home. Most women today nurture their own occupational goals, however. Mid-life represents the time when, having fulfilled their child-care obligations, they can resume their careers or prepare for and take on new ones. Thus at the same time the husband may be resolving his mid-life crisis by reconsidering his career and making firmer attachments to his family, the wife may be devoting less attention to family and more to career. Psychologists call this problem being out of phase, or the **career trajectory problem**.[98]

During the mid-life crisis, both women and men must find themselves again by participating in a new search for identity. They become confused about what their actual desires, values, talents, and aspirations really are, and in clarifying them they seek to define and understand themselves. The mid-life crisis involves struggles at integration, or unifying opposing tendencies, in four polarities, each a statement about the nature of human development. The **young/old polarity** poses the questions, "What does it mean to no longer be young?" and "What does it mean to be old?" The **destruction/creation polarity** presents the problem of attempting to find a balance between aggressive needs and expressive, creative needs. The **masculine/feminine polarity** confronts individuals anew with their masculine and feminine sides and suggests the need to incorporate them in gender-role behavior. And in the **attach-**

ment/separation polarity, the task is to reconcile the masculine desire for autonomy and independence with the feminine desire for affiliation, affection, and approval.[99]

By age 45, these struggles must be resolved if adult development is to take place. The search for meaning in life requires building a new life structure and putting it into practice. Life goes on.

PECK ON DEVELOPMENT IN OLD AGE

Robert Peck, a student of Havighurst who came to know Erikson, developed a stage theory of old age. He postulates three crises in old age rather than only one. Two of these, **ego differentiation vs. work-role preoccupation** and **body transcendence vs. body preoccupation**, represent innovations over Erikson. The third, **ego transcendence vs. ego preoccupation**, is essentially a restatement of Erikson's ego integrity vs. despair. Although Peck, like so many developmental theorists, focuses on men, his ideas have been used as a framework for understanding older women as well.[100]

Peck acknowledges that old age is a time of role loss, the time when people retire from paid work, become widowed, lose friends, and no longer have direct responsibility for children. But he also acknowledges that it is a time of transition, in which these losses must be compensated for psychologically and new positive and useful definitions of the self must be acquired. He defines **ego differentiation** as the capacity to pursue and enjoy activities and to value oneself as a person, without relation to the roles of adulthood.

Old age is also a time of physical decline. To remain emotionally healthy, older people must be able to overcome their physical concerns and preoccupation with the deterioration of their bodies. **Body transcendence** is the capacity to feel whole, worthwhile, and happy because of one's social and mental powers and activities, regardless of physical health. It also involves the ability to be satisfied with one's body and to continue to have sexual interests.

As the inevitability of death becomes unavoidable, individuals tend to become preoccupied with their private, self-centered desires. **Ego transcendence** is the capacity to engage others in a direct, active, and emotionally gratifying manner. It involves the ability to remain concerned about others and find satisfaction in fulfilling the needs of others.

To partially test his theory, Peck studied personal adaptability and flexibility in a sample of men living in the Midwest during the 1950s who ranged in age from 45 to 65. He was interested in whether there is a decline in adaptive capacities as old age approaches; that is, whether older people are preoccupied with their work roles, bodies, and egos. On the basis of cultural stereotypes, he hypothesized that a decline in adaptability would be evident, and older people thus would be vulnerable to emotional turmoil. He concluded that this is not the case, however. Aging did not appear to produce any decline in emotional flexibility or ability to adapt. His data did show a positive correlation with social class; the higher the class, the greater the emotional stability and effectiveness.[101]

THE ROLE OF CRISES IN DEVELOPMENT

In the perspectives of Erikson, Levinson, and Peck, successful struggle against inner crises is necessary if development is to occur. Other studies have raised questions that human development occurs as a result of crisis or that crises are a sign of normal development. This section examines more closely the roles of conflict and crises in development in adolescence and adulthood.

THE ADOLESCENT CRISIS DEBATE

The teen years have traditionally been seen as particularly beset by conflict. G. Stanley Hall, the first psychologist to study this stage of development, defined adolescence in the United States at the turn of the twentieth century as a period of *Sturm und Drang*, storm and stress.[102] Others have followed suit. Anna Freud, for instance, characterized normal (or average) adolescence as a period in which

> aggressive impulses are intensified to the point of complete unruliness, hunger becomes voracity and the naughtiness of the latency period turns into the criminal behavior of adolescence. . . . Habits of cleanliness . . . give place to pleasure in dirt and disorder, and instead of modesty and sympathy we find exhibitionistic tendencies, brutality and cruelty to animals.[103]

As recently as 1983, Carl Tischler stated that "crisis, stormy emotions, and psychic instability are characteristic of adolescence."[104]

Crises and the Normal Adolescent

In a ten-year longitudinal study of "normal" adolescents, those who have not been adjudicated as delinquent or institutionalized for mental disorders, Daniel Offer found that a significant proportion do not experience turmoil. Only 21 percent of those he studied were classified as exhibiting severe turmoil, or **tumultuous growth**. They were troubled by self-doubt and escalating conflict with their parents, had debilitating inhibitions, and often responded inconsistently in social and academic environments. In contrast, **continuous growth** was demonstrated by 23 percent of the adolescents. They were purposeful and self-assured, accepting social norms and feeling comfortable in them. When they experienced trouble, they coped, using adaptive ego defenses. Another 35 percent demonstrated **surgent growth**. These adolescents were not as confident, and their self-esteem wavered. Some were afraid of their emerging sexual feelings and were awkward in relationships with members of the opposite sex. All in all, however, they coped with troubles and did not suffer from severe breakdown. The remaining 21 percent of the adolescents studied could not be classified in any category.[105]

Offer believes that his findings demonstrate that crises and conflict are not normal to adolescence, or, by extension, to any period in the life course. Using Offer's findings, David Oldham suggests that the stereotype of storm and stress should be discarded. Thus, rather than seeing adolescent conflict as normal, social service workers should take any such conflict seriously, as an indication of possible pathology.[106]

Offer's findings are suspect, however. Most of the adolescents studied experienced at least some turmoil, and 21 percent experienced tumultous growth. It might be assumed that some of the 21 percent who could not be classified did experience either surgent or tumultuous growth. He did not include abnormal adolescents in his study, all of whom could be said to have experienced tumultuous growth. He studied only white, middle-class youth, and even with this group there were differences in economic status; lower-middle-class boys were significantly more likely to evidence tumultuous growth than upper-middle class boys.

It is not surprising that one clinician who refers to the work of Offer and recognizes that all adolescents are not disturbed nevertheless concludes:

> It seems safe to assert that all adolescents are probably shaken by emotional storms and troublesome floods of impulse; for many, these experiences are transient and readily mastered, whereas for a minority, the same issues lead to far more serious reactions. . . . Anna Freud's observation about the normalcy of adolescent turmoil is probably as accurate a statement as one can make.[107]

Thus Offer's study can be used to support the view that turmoil is normal in adolescents, the same view he attempts to disprove.

James Marcia on Identity and Role Confusion

Using empirical methods, James Marcia identified four **identity statuses** representing the ways youths adapt during the years of adolescence. Following Erikson, he proposes that all youths must experience and resolve crises before they can establish a true identity. Abnormality consists in not experiencing the crisis, or in experiencing it and not being able to find a solution. His point of view, also supported by empirical studies, conflicts directly with the view of Offer.[108]

Marcia describes two kinds of identity status among normal youths. One is a **moratorium**, a state of crisis marked by active searching for the identity that will give form and coherence to their being. The second is **identity-achieved**, for those who experience the crisis and resolve it successfully. They truly understand who and what they are. He also describes two kinds of status among abnormal youths. The **identity-confused** youth has not yet experienced an identity crisis or made any commitment to a vocation or to a set of beliefs about the self and the social world. The **identity-foreclosed** youth has not yet experienced an identity crisis but nevertheless appears to have made a commitment to a particular identity.

From Marcia's point of view, it is necessary to distinguish between youths in turmoil because they are actively dealing with their identity and youths who have not allowed themselves to experience conflict. Both may need help.

IS THERE A CRISIS IN MID-LIFE?

Levinson argues that a mid-life crisis is normal, particularly in men, from about age 40 to age 45. He believes this crisis is a function of age per se and not of the social roles and situations that people find themselves in. He recognizes that some men do not experience a mid-life crisis, and some experience only a very minor crisis. For a great majority of men, however, Levinson says, "this is a period of great struggle within the self and with the external world."[109]

The idea of an age-40 crisis is suspect to many researchers, but it is the mid-life part rather than the crisis part that is suspect. A review of the literature on men and women in the middle-adult years indicates that while crisis is often evident, it is not singularly noticeable between the ages of 40 and 45. One study concluded that there is no universal mid-life crisis; while some do experience crisis at age 40, others thrive at the same age.[110]

George Vaillant analyzed the results of the Grant Study of Adult Development, which traced the long-range psychological health of 268 men who were Harvard students in the classes of 1942 and 1944. He found that these men worked hard at their careers between the ages of 25 and 35, and by age 30 their potential for excellence had been "lost to conformity." The years from 35 to 49 were much more tumultuous, marked by depression and doubts, but the men who faced up to the reappraisal of mid-life looked back at that period as the happiest in their lives.[111]

Most people, a little like Marcia's identity-diffused youth, seem to bury their heads in an attempt to deny and avoid crises. Conflict in adulthood thus appears to be very common, but it is not necessarily associated with any particular chronological age.

RECONSIDERING CRISES ACROSS THE LIFE COURSE

The evidence is not conclusive, but a fair amount of crisis apparently is endemic to the life course. Although some individuals appear to experience no conflict and others experience severe conflict, most seem to experience at least some crises. The crises, both in amount and intensity, are undoubtedly a function of biological changes, cognitive capacities, psychological needs, motives, and abilities, as well as environmental considerations such as the degree to which inequity, alienation, anomie, and labeling are present in the society.

Some caution is in order in making this generalization. There is a difference between the experience of conflict and the inability to resolve conflict. Experiencing conflict throughout life seems to be normal. Not being able to experience it or not being able to resolve it when it is experienced may be a sign of abnormal development. Developing people do not avoid conflict in their transactions with others. They do experience conflict, but they are able to deal with it effectively. The developed person passes through life, meeting one crisis after another successfully.

IMPLICATIONS FOR PRACTICE

This chapter has examined perspectives on stages of development across the life course. Our discussion of life stages suggests, however, that people cannot be pigeonholed into stages based solely on their chronological age. The social roles and positions they occupy as well as their psychological states and processes must be taken into account. Once that is done, the notion of stages can be very helpful in understanding the dynamics of individual development. Such an understanding is crucial to effective social service practice.

Although the time before birth is usually not thought of as a developmental period with tasks and crises, it clearly sets the stage for development across the life course. Knowledge of the prenatal period can be used in working with adults who are having children, not only as it affects the mother and father but as it affects the development of the child.

The notion of developmental tasks is popular in the ego-psychological literature. Havighurst, who introduced the concept, proposes that at each stage in life, individuals are met with a set of unique and recurring tasks derived from biophysical maturation, societal expectations, and psychological or personal needs. He identifies physical, cognitive, sexual, family, social friendship, and moral or civic tasks. Development is achieved when the various tasks are accomplished and learning takes place.

Three principal ego-psychological perspectives, each with its own vision of development, are those of Erikson, who considers development throughout the life course; Levinson, who concentrates on males at mid-life; and Peck, who describes the continuing development of old age. Erikson sees development as a series of ego strengths which emerge out of the successful resolution of crises. The developed person incorporates into the personality the successive strengths of hope, will, purpose, competence, fidelity, love, care, and wisdom. His work is particularly useful in social service practice because he identifies the pathologies that can form if development does not occur. In succession, these are withdrawal, compulsion, inhibition, inertia, repudiation, exclusivity, rejectivity, and disdain.

Levinson looks more closely at development in adulthood, postulating that development can occur as a result of a mid-life crisis. For him, development is not a series of personality qualities or strengths but mastery over four polarities. Developed adults understand that they are neither young nor old. They are able to put together and become comfortable with their masculine and feminine urges, their urges for creation and destruction, and their urges to be attached yet separate from others.

Building directly from Erikson, Peck proposes three stages of development in old age. The developmental tasks for older people include learning to think of themselves as differentiated individuals with many dimensions and aspects, not limited to the work roles they are giving up. They must learn to transcend their bodies and their selves and avoid getting caught up in their physical decline and inevitable death. They must continue to see the value of life and their own value as part of humankind.

DEALING WITH DEVELOPMENTAL DIFFICULTIES

These approaches all highlight the likelihood of crises throughout the life course. Empirical evidence does indeed show that crises and conflict are common, and it is unlikely that human development can take place without some minimal level of struggle among biophysical needs, social expectations, and personal proclivities. This means that social service workers should not see any and every indication of trouble as a sign of pathology. The troubles people experience exist on a continuum from mild to severe. Some people will pass through particular periods in life with very little trouble; others will experience a great deal. When a crisis is severe, and especially when a person seems unable to cope and adapt to it, the possibility of developmental breakdown should be anticipated.

Direct-service social workers can use ideas about development in thinking about the behavior of their individual clients. Assessment involves taking note of clients' ages, their social roles, and their psychological strengths and deficiencies. The social worker then considers what crises and tasks people in that particular bio-psycho-social configuration are likely to be dealing with. By empathic attention to clients, social workers can determine if crises or difficulties in completing tasks are causing the troubles presented.

If it is determined that an individual is experiencing developmental difficulties, the social worker must analyze the reasons for the difficulties. Ego psychology suggests that the reason will lie in the ego weaknesses of the person, in the lack of social support for development in the environment, or in some combination of ego weakness and an inhospitable environment. The social worker must determine the factors related to these difficulties and find ways to mobilize the personal strengths and social resources available to the individual. Psychotherapy, possibly even referral to psychoanalysis or psychiatry, may be warranted, but this is not the only appropriate form of intervention with respect to developmental crises and tasks. Sometimes counseling and advice are sufficient. Skills training, especially with respect to tasks, may also be useful. Referral to other services or even helping to develop services where none are present also can constitute a form of intervention.

DISCUSSION QUESTIONS AND CLASS PROJECTS

1. Describe three considerations that have to be taken into account in determining a person's stage in life.

2. In the period of conception through birth, the physical well-being of the unborn child is inseparable from the physical, psychological, and social well-being of the parents. Why is this the case?

3. How is the sex of the child determined by the father?

4. Identify the following terms:
zygote
embryo
fetus
gene
genotype
phenotype
rubella
fetal alcohol syndrome
cesarean section
Apgar scale
placenta
polygenic inheritance
puberty
menarche
menopause
gonads
progesterone
climacteric
crystallized intelligence
fluid intelligence
testosterone
estrogen
Alzheimer's disease

5. Children show distinct temperaments at birth. Describe three types of temperaments often seen at birth. Will these temperaments remain the same as the child grows into adulthood?

6. Identify students in the class who have given birth to or fathered a child (and wish to talk about it). Have them describe their experiences, using the chapter section on the prenatal period as a stimulus. They can either illustrate some of the issues discussed or introduce other issues.

7. Distinguish between Havighurst's unique and recurrent tasks. Can you give examples of each?

8. According to Havighurst, what are the sources of developmental tasks?

9. Describe the life course in terms of the physical growth or decline that can be expected in early childhood, later childhood, adulthood, and old age.

10. Describe the social relationships that are likely to influence development as people pass through early childhood, later childhood, adulthood, and old age.

11. List and describe Erikson's eight developmental crises. Do you believe they apply to women as well as to men? Do you believe they apply to all racial and ethnic groups in the United States?

12. What is meant by the epigenetic principle? Why is it important for social work?

13. Identify the following concepts; also identify the scientist who originated them.
basic strengths
core pathologies
season
period
tumultuous growth
surgent growth
continuous growth
identity confused
radius of significant relationships
average expectable environment
mentor relationship
transition
moratorium
identity-achieved
identity-foreclosed

14. According to Levinson, mid-life transitions for men and women are likely to produce inner crisis or conflict. What does he see as the origins of the crisis, and what are the polarities around which the crisis takes shape?

15. Robert Peck describes three crises of old-age. What are they? What is the likelihood that older people will not be able to deal with the crises of old age?

16. Compare Offer's view on adolescent development with Marcia's. Do you believe that human development occurs through the experience of a certain

amount of turmoil? Does that mean social workers should not take crises in clients seriously?

17. In groups of no more than six students, discuss the following: Do you believe you are in a particular stage of life? What stage is it? What do you see as the developmental tasks you are dealing with in the present? Do they resemble the tasks identified by Havighurst for someone of your general age category? What do you see as the developmental crises you are dealing with? Do they resemble the crisis Erikson discusses for someone in your general age category?

18. How might you use the terms *development, tasks, crises, radius of significant relationships, basic strengths*, and *core pathologies* in an interview with a client? Would you use these terms or try to find a jargon-free way of expressing them? Can you think of different ways of saying the same things? For instance, how could you ask clients what their stage of development is or what tasks and crises they are dealing with? How would you inquire into their basic strengths and possible pathologies?

19. The following role play can be done in front of the class or more privately as a three-person discussion group. One person plays the role of the social worker and the other the role of a client. The third person (or the class) plays the role of observer.

The social worker should engage the client to determine the developmental tasks and crises the client is dealing with. In conducting the interview, the social worker should try to use everyday, jargon-free language.

After the interview the observer(s) should comment on the interview, calling attention to the things the social worker did well as well as the things she or he did not do so well.

NOTES

1. All psychologists do not posit stages of life, and some critics argue that the emphasis on stages creates many more differences among people than actually exist. See Carel B. Germain's recent review of developmental perspectives, "Human Development in Contemporary Environments," *Social Service Review*, vol. 61 (December 1987), pp. 565–80. Also see Victoria Fries Rader, "The Social Construction of Ages and the Ideology of Stages," *Journal of Sociology and Social Welfare*, vol. 7 (September 1979), pp. 643–56.

2. Barbara M. Newman and Philip R. Newman, *Development through Life: A Psychosocial Approach*, 4th ed. (Chicago: Dorsey Press, 1987).

3. For social histories of childhood and adolescence, see, for instance, Phillipe Aries, *Centuries of Childhood: A Social History of Family Life*, translated by Robert Baldwick (New York: Vintage Books, 1962), and Joseph Kett, *Rites of Passage: Adolescence in America 1790 to the Present* (New York: Basic Books/Harper Colophon, 1977). Also see William Kessen, "The Child and Other Cultural Inventions," in F. Kessel and A. W. Sieger (editors), *Houston Symposium #4: The Child and Other Cultural Inventions* (New York: Frederick A. Praeger, 1983), pp. 26–39.

4. Daniel Offer and Melvin Sabshin, "Adolescence: Empirical Perspectives," in D. Offer and M. Sabshin (editors), *Normality and the Life Cycle: A Critical Integration* (New York: Basic Books, 1984), p. 77.

5. Robert L. Arnstein, "Young Adulthood: Stages of Maturity," in Offer and Sabshin (editors), *Normality and the Life Cycle*, p. 108.

6. K. Warner Schaie, "Psychological Changes from Midlife to Early Old Age:

Implications for the Maintenance of Mental Health," in C. H. Meyer (editor), *Social Work with the Aging* (Silver Spring, MD: National Association of Social Workers, 1986), pp. 44–63.

7. George E. Vaillant and Eva Milofsky, "Natural History of Male Psychological Health: IX. Empirical Evidence for Erikson's Model of the Life Cycle, *American Journal of Psychiatry*, vol. 137, No. 11 (November 1980), pp. 1348–59.

8. Bernice Neugarten coined the term *social clock* to mean subjective or "socially defined" time. We are using it in a somewhat different way; her use is more akin to what we call the psychological clock. She emphasizes personal expectations about when and how life events are to be experienced. See Bernice L. Neugarten, "Time, Age, and the Life Cycle," in M. Bloom (editor), *Life Span Development*, 2nd ed. (New York: Macmillan, 1985), pp. 360–69.

9. Linda K. George, *Role Transitions in Later Life* (Monterey, CA: Brooks/Cole, 1980), pp. 1–12.

10. These ideas are derived from Martin Kohli, "The World We Forgot: A Historical Review of the Life Course," in V. W. Marshall (editor), *Later Life: The Social Psychology of Aging* (Beverly Hills, CA: Sage, 1986), p. 272, and Fries Rader, "Social Construction of Ages."

11. Arnold J. Sameroff, "Early Influences on Development: Fact or Fancy?", in M. Bloom (editor), *Life Span Development*, 1st ed. (New York: Macmillan, 1980), pp. 107.

12. M. D. Jensen, R. C. Benson, and I. M. Bobak, *Maternity Care: The Nurse and the Family*, 2nd ed. (St. Louis, MO: Mosby, 1981).

13. Hilda Knobloch and Benjamin Pasamanick, *Gessell and Amatruda's Developmental Diagnosis* (New York: Harper and Row, 1974).

14. See Newman and Newman, *Development through Life*, pp. 137–38.

15. John W. Lorton and Eveleen L. Lorton, *Human Development through the Life Span* (Monterey, CA: Brooks/Cole, 1984), pp. 65–69.

16. Elaine R. Grimm, "Psychological and Social Factors in Pregnancy, Delivery and Outcome," in S. A. Richardson and A. F. Guttmacher (editors), *Childbearing: Its Social and Psychological Aspects* (Baltimore, MD: Williams and Wilkins, 1967), pp. 1–52.

17. Kathleen Stassen Berger, *The Developing Person* (New York: Worth, 1980), pp. 118–31.

18. Lorton and Lorton, *Human Development through the Life Span*, pp. 69–70.

19. Martin Greenberg and Normal Morris, "Engrossment: The Newborn's Impact upon the Father," *American Journal of Orthopsychiatry*, vol. 44 (July 1974), pp. 520–31.

20. Stassen Berger, *Developing Person*, p. 76.

21. Ibid., p. 86.

22. Alexander Thomas, Stella Chess, and Herbert G. Birch, *Temperament and Behavior Disorders in Children* (New York: New York University Press, 1963); Stella Chess, "Temperament in the Normal Infant," in J. Hellmuth (editor), *The Exceptional Infant*, vol. 1 (Seattle, WA: Special Child Publications, 1967); Alexander Thomas and Stella Chess, *Temperament and Development* (New York: Brunner/Mazel, 1977).

23. Thomas and Chess, *Temperament and Development*, pp. 21–23.

24. Ibid.

25. Michael E. Lamb (editor), *Social and Personality Development* (New York: Holt, Rinehart, and Winston, 1978).

26. Peter H. Wolff, *The Cause, Controls, and Organization of Behavior in the Neonate* (New York: International University Press, 1966).

27. Kenneth S. Robson and Howard A. Moss, "Patterns and Determinants of Maternal Attachment," *Journal of Pediatrics*, vol. 77 (December 1970), pp. 976–85.

28. Virginia Apgar, "Proposal for a New Method of Evaluating the Newborn Infant," *Anesthesia and Analgesia*, vol. 32 (1953), pp. 260–67.

29. See Sameroff, "Early Influences on Development"; Bruce Balow, Rosalyn Rubin, and Martha J. Rosen, "Perinatal Events as Precursors of Reading Disabilities," *Reading Research Quarterly*, vol. 11 (1975–1976), pp. 36–71; and Michael J. Chandler and Arnold Sameroff, "Repro-

ductive Risk and the Continuum of Caretaking Casualty," in F. D. Horowitz and F. Degen (editors), *Review of Child Development Research*, vol. 4 (Chicago: University of Chicago Press, 1975), pp. 187–244.

30. Harriet Johnson, "Human Development: Biological Perspective," in *Encyclopedia of Social Work*, 18th ed., vol. 1 (Silver Spring, MD: National Association of Social Workers, 1987), pp. 839–40.

31. Robert J. Havighurst, *Developmental Tasks and Education* (New York: David McKay, 1952), p. 1.

32. Ibid.

33. Newman and Newman, *Development through Life*, p. 32.

34. Havighurst, *Developmental Tasks and Education*, p. 4.

35. Ibid., p. 31.

36. Theodore Lidz, *The Person* (New York: Basic Books, 1968), p. 79.

37. Erik Erikson, *The Life Cycle Completed: A Review* (New York: W. W. Norton, 1982), p. 31. Also see Erikson, *Childhood and Society*, 2nd ed. (New York: W. W. Norton, 1963).

38. Richard M. Lerner and David F. Hultsch, *Human Development: A Life Span Perspective* (New York: McGraw-Hill, 1983), p. 144.

39. Richard Q. Bell and Lawrence V. Harper, *Child Effects on Adults* (New York: John Wiley and Sons, 1977), pp. 53–84, 158–71.

40. Erikson, *Childhood and Society*, p. 69.

41. Newman and Newman, *Development through Life*, p. 45.

42. Ibid., p. 46.

43. Ibid., p. 45.

44. Ibid., p. 46.

45. Erikson, *Childhood and Society*, p. 225.

46. Newman and Newman, *Development through Life*, p. 45.

47. Ibid., p. 46.

48. This section is largely derived from James Leslie McCary, *Human Sexuality: A Brief Edition.* (New York: D. Van Nostrand, 1973).

49. Offer and Sabshin, "Adolescence," p. 84.

50. Ibid.

51. See Fumiyo T. Hunter and James Youniss, "Changes in Functions of Three Relations during Adolescence," *Developmental Psychology*, vol. 18 (November 1982), pp. 806–11, and Martin Gold and Denise S. Yanof, "Mothers, Daughters, and Girlfriends," *Journal of Personality and Social Psychology*, vol. 49 (September 1985), pp. 654–59.

52. See Aries, *Centuries of Childhood*; also see Kett, *Rites of Passage*.

53. Manifest functions are stressed in their discussion of the importance of education in the lives of school-age children by Newman and Newman, *Development through Life*, pp. 306–08.

54. Christopher Jencks et al., *Inequality: A Reassessment of the Effect of Family and School in America* (New York: Harper and Row, 1972). For other critiques of school life, see Ralph W. Larkin, *Suburban Youth in Cultural Crisis* (New York: Oxford University Press, 1979), and Miriam Wasserman (editor), *Demystifying School: Writings and Experiences* (New York: Frederick A. Praeger, 1974).

55. See Betty Levy, "The School's Role in the Sex-Role Stereotyping of Girls: A Feminist Review of the Literature," and Phyllis Taube MacEwan, "Girls Don't Play with Cars, Linda," in Wasserman (editor), *Demystifying School*, pp. 111–14, 327–29.

56. Newman and Newman, *Development through Life*, p. 352.

57. Herman Schwendinger and Julia Siegel Schwendinger, *Adolescent Subcultures and Delinquency* (New York: Frederick A. Praeger, 1985), pp. 3–58.

58. Newman and Newman, *Development through Life*, p. 359.

59. Ibid., p. 357.

60. Ibid., p. 45.

61. Ibid., p. 46.

62. Erikson, *Childhood and Society*, p. 261.

63. Newman and Newman, *Development through Life*, p. 45.

64. Ibid., p. 46.

65. U.S. Bureau of the Census, *Statistical Abstract of the United States 1988* (Washington, DC, 1987), Table 172.

66. Ibid., Table 118.

67. Cleo S. Berkun, "In Behalf of Women over 40: Understanding the Im-

portance of the Menopause," *Social Work*, vol. 31 (September-October 1986), pp. 378–84.

68. Joseph Veroff, Elizabeth Douvan, and Richard A. Kulka, *The Inner American: Life, Work, and Mental Health from 1957 to 1967* (New York: Basic Books, 1981).

69. See Jessie Bernard, "The Paradox of the Happy Marriage," in Vivian Gornick and Barbara Moran, *Woman in Sexist Society* (New York: Signet Books, 1971), and *The Future of Marriage* (New York: Bantam Books, 1972).

70. Erikson, *Childhood and Society*, p. 266.

71. Newman and Newman, *Development through Life*, p. 45.

72. Ibid., p. 46.

73. Erikson, *Childhood and Society*, p. 267.

74. Newman and Newman, *Development through Life*, p. 45.

75. Ibid., p. 46.

76. See Neugarten, "Time, Age, and the Life Cycle," p. 366, and Elaine Cummings and William E. Henry, *Growing Old: The Process of Disengagement* (New York: Basic Books, 1961).

77. Zena Smith Blau, *Old Age in a Changing Society* (New York: New Viewpoints, 1973), pp. 243–44.

78. Vern L. Bengston, "Comparative Perspectives on the Microsociology of Aging: Methodological Problems and Theoretical Issues," in V. W. Marshall (editor), *Later Life: The Social Psychology of Aging* (Beverly Hills, CA: Sage, 1986), pp. 304–36.

79. George, *Role Transitions in Later Life*; Bengston, "Comparative Perspectives on Microsociology of Aging," pp. 312–13.

80. U.S. Bureau of the Census, *Statistical Abstract 1988*, Table 106.

81. John L. Horn, "The Rise and Fall of Human Abilities," *Journal of Research and Development in Education*, vol. 12 (Winter 1979), pp. 59–78.

82. William H. Masters and Virginia E. Johnson, *Human Sexual Response* (Boston, MA: Little Brown, 1966).

83. From a lecture by Vivian Wood, University of Wisconsin School of Social Work, May 1987.

84. Newman and Newman, *Development through Life*, p. 573.

85. Asenath La Rue and Lissy F. Javick, "Old Age and Behavioral Changes," in B. Wolman (editor), *Handbook of Developmental Psychology* (Englewood Cliffs, NJ: Prentice-Hall, 1982), pp. 791–806.

86. Newman and Newman, *Development through Life*, p. 573.

87. Riva Specht and Grace J. Craig, *Human Development: A Social Work Perspective*, 2nd ed. (Englewood Cliffs, NJ: Prentice-Hall, 1987), p. 241.

88. Ibid., p. 243.

89. Erikson, *Childhood and Society*, p. 232.

90. Newman and Newman, *Development through Life*, p. 45.

91. Ibid., p. 46.

92. Daniel J. Levinson with C. N. Darrow, E. B. Klein, M. H. Levinson, and B. McGee, *The Seasons of a Man's Life* (New York: Alfred A. Knopf, 1978).

93. Ibid., p. 49.

94. Vimala Pillari, *Human Behavior in the Social Environment* (Pacific Grove, CA: Brooks/Cole, 1988), p. 275.

95. Levinson, *Seasons of a Man's Life*, p. 51.

96. Judith Viorst, *Necessary Losses: The Loves, Illusions, Dependencies and Impossible Expectations That All of Us Have to Give Up in Order to Grow* (New York: Simon and Schuster, 1986), p. 266.

97. Preliminary results of this study were described in a news item by Patricia Leigh Brown, "Studying Seasons of a Woman's Life," *The New York Times*, September 14, 1987, p. 23.

98. Viorst, *Necessary Losses*, pp. 277–78.

99. Levinson et al, *Seasons of a Man's Life*.

100. Robert F. Peck and Howard Berkowitz, "Personality and Adjustment in Middle Age," in Bernice L. Neugarten (editor), *Personality in Middle and Late Life* (New York: Atherton Press, 1964), pp. 15–43. In her lecture to my human development class at the University of Wisconsin School of Social Work in May 1987,

Vivian Wood used Peck's theory as a framework for discussing old age and women.

101. Peck and Berkowitz, "Personality and Adjustment in Middle Age," p. 42.

102. See John and Virginia Demos, "Adolescence in Historical Perspective," *Journal of Marriage and the Family*, vol. 31 (November 1969), pp. 635-36.

103. Cited in Erikson, *Childhood and Society*, pp. 306-07.

104. Carl Tischler, "Detection and Prevention of Suicidal Behavior in Adolescents," in L. E. Arnold (editor), *Preventing Adolescent Alienation* (Lexington, MA: Lexington Books, 1983), p. 98.

105. Daniel Offer, "Adolescent Development: A Normative Perspective," in S. I. Greenspan and G. H. Pollock (editors), *The Course of Life, Vol. II: Latency, Adolescence, and Youth*, U.S. Department of Health and Human Services, Publication No. (ADM) 80-999 (Washington, DC: 1980), pp. 357-72.

106. David G. Oldham, "Adolescence Turmoil: A Myth Revisited," *Journal of Continuing Education in Psychiatry*, vol. 39 (March 1978), pp. 23-32.

107. Joseph D. Noshphitz, "Disturbances in Early Adolescent Development," in Greenspan and Pollock (editors), *Course of Life, Vol. II*, pp. 316-17.

108. James E. Marcia, "Identity in Adolescence," in J. Adelson (editor), *Handbook of Adolescent Psychology* (New York: John Wiley and Sons, 1980), pp. 159-87.

109. Levinson, *Seasons in a Man's Life*, p. 60.

110. Anne Rosenfeld and Elizabeth Stark, "The Prime of Our Lives," *Psychology Today*, vol. 21 (May 1987), pp. 62-72.

111. George E. Vaillant and Charles C. McArthur, "Natural History of Male Psychological Health: I. The Adult Life Cycle from 18-50," *Seminars in Psychiatry*, vol. 4 (November 1972), pp. 415-27.

PART V

Epilogue

CHAPTER 16

Toward a Reform-Oriented Theory for Practice

T HIS BOOK has covered a considerable amount of background information and numerous facts, issues, and theories. To bring it to a conclusion, we will review its intentions and summarize its main points. This should be of help in synthesizing the content and evaluating how well the book has accomplished its purposes.

The overall objective of *Human Behavior in the Social Environment* is to contribute to the development of a reform-oriented theory for social service practice. Such a theory offers a set of explanations about human behavior and the social environment which can guide social work assessment and intervention on the one hand and social policy and programs on the other. The book does not present a fully developed theory, however. Theory development in social work, as in the social and behavioral sciences, is not yet at a point where one particular point of view clearly answers all the questions that need to be addressed. Furthermore, many theories are capable of contributing to practice, so it is foolish to discard some prematurely in favor of others. Reform-oriented social service workers need to be familiar with a range of theories and to be able to draw out the implications for practice in each of them.

This book thus lays the *groundwork* for a reform-oriented theory for practice. In doing so, it draws on two frames of reference from the social sciences, a critical perspective and a systems approach. A critical perspective is dedicated to the evaluation of society and its social institutions. It is not a theory of human behavior so much as a theory of caring, a set of values, ideals, and assumptions about the nature of human behavior and society. A critical perspective presents social service workers with the need to evaluate the world they live in, to participate in the debates about social problems and issues, and to be prepared to offer alternatives or "passionate prescriptions" in the hope of creating a better society.

The critical perspective is not without detractors. Well-intentioned scientists and philosophers doubt the ability of social work and the other helping professions to produce progressive change. They point out that these professionals often do as much harm as good in developing policy, administering programs, and delivering services. Students therefore must critically evaluate the critical perspective and develop their own ideas about society, social progress, and the role professional helpers can take in them.

To provide an orienting framework capable of producing a reform-oriented theory for social work practice, we have combined the critical perspective with the systems approach. A system is defined as a "dynamic order of parts and processes standing in mutual interaction." All systems are holons, a whole and a part of the whole at the same time. Social service workers are interested in human systems, that is, those that are individual human beings or are composed of individuals, including families, communities, groups, organizations, and society. Workers are called upon to identify and analyze the strengths and problems of human systems and to design intervention strategies to help improve their functioning.

The notion of a system is implicit in any number of social and psychological theories. Accordingly, a systems approach to the study of human behavior in the social environment is best seen as a loose cluster of the theories and hypotheses about the behavior and functioning of human systems which are presented in various disciplines. In adopting the systems approach, we make two general substantive assumptions about human systems:

1. The state or condition of a system, at any point in time, is a function of the interaction between it and the environment in which it operates.
2. A system is never static; change or conflict are always evident.

The dual principles of critical analysis and the systems approach provide the basis for the chapters on communities, families, and individuals as systems which make up the principal parts of this book.

COMMUNITIES IN SOCIETY

Social service workers have good reason to study community life. They work directly with or on behalf of communities in such capacities as community organizer, community developer, program administrator, and policymaker. Community also is an important social context in assessment and intervention with individuals and families. In assessing the private troubles of individuals and families, workers must acknowledge that community-based roles (e.g., rural dweller, Asian American, blue-collar worker, lesbian, or Catholic) can put people at risk, and in intervening in private troubles, they must seek out community support and resources.

Communities are relatively large social systems which are nevertheless distinguished by the personal or affective nature of the ties that hold their members together. Like all social systems, communities are collections of individuals, each with his or her own biophysical and psychological makeup. But communities are more than the sum of the individuals comprising them. They are bounded social systems organized into units (families, groups, associations, organizations, institutions, and institutionalized arrangements), in which individuals hold different roles and statuses. The units are held together by working agreements in the form of expectations, norms, and traditions which may be experienced as a common value or as a coercive intrusion. Communities exist within a larger social context made up of the society, its institutions and institutionalized arrangements, other communities, and other organizations. The larger social context can constitute both a source of stress and a source of support or strength. For these reasons, communities are dynamic systems, always responding to internal and external pressures and therefore always subject to change and conflict.

Three overlapping kinds of communities are commonly identified: communities based on common residence (locational), on common identity (identificational), and on common interests. In the chapters on communities in society, identificational communities are emphasized. American society is made up of many such communities, based on such characteristics as social class, religious denomination, racial and ethnic identity, and sexual orientation.

THE CRITICAL THEMES: MAJORITY-MINORITY RELATIONS

Perhaps the major public issue with respect to community life in the United States is the relation between majority and minority, especially in racial and ethnic communities. The designations *majority* and *minority* are not based on numbers but reflect differences in power, prestige, and status. In the United States, new ethnic and racial groups have continually been incorporated into the society. In the past, most groups experienced minority status upon entering the country. Many of these groups, particularly immigrants from Europe, have managed to overcome this status and enter into the mainstream of American life. Others, especially people of color with origins in non-European nations, continue to live as minority groups. As a result, they have become mired in such social and economic problems as poverty, low wages, unemployment and underemployment, and low levels of educational achievement and attainment.

Reform-oriented social workers can design policies, set up programs, and provide services to enable ethnic and racial minorities to improve their status. Moreover, they can work to prevent new arrivals from being placed in the status of minorities.

The Systems Approach to the Issues

The low social and economic status of people of color in the United States today is best seen as a function of the interaction between them and the white European majority, an interaction which can be characterized as a situation of domination through coercion. Europeans conquered Native Americans and enslaved Afro-Americans. To some extent they also colonized Puerto Ricans and Mexican Americans. They subjected Japanese and Chinese Americans to exclusionary immigration regulations and legalized forms of discrimination. Prejudice, discrimination, racism, and ethnocentrism continue to reinforce this status. Although legalized discrimination has been prohibited, racism is still evident in neighborhood residential patterns, friendship networks, and choice of marital partners. There also are biological and cultural factors which can work against people of color as they attempt to achieve the American dream. Some researchers claim that genetic differences in IQ and differences in cultural values and group cohesiveness have helped keep some people of color in a minority status. More study of biological and cultural issues is necessary before a definitive answer can be given.

FAMILY LIFE

Family life is at the heart of social work practice. It provides the social context for understanding the private troubles of individuals; indeed, direct-service workers can hardly avoid working with families. Increasingly, family therapy and other forms of family practice are becoming the dominant mode for providing services. Social policy and program development are often aimed at strengthening family life and overcoming its limitations.

A satisfactory definition of what is meant by the family is almost impossible. The family is both a social institution, existing as a set of working agreements or norms emanating from the society, and a social organization, a specific group of individuals interacting in terms of their roles and statuses. Moreover, as anthropologists and social historians agree, family life has existed under so many different working agreements that applying the term *family* to all of them would conflict with present cultural ideals of what a family ought to be.

The so-called traditional family consists of an assertive husband who is the breadwinner and socioeconomic task leader, and a passive wife who is the homemaker and socioemotional leader. They live monogamously with their children, independently of their kin, in a private residence. This is hardly a universal definition of the family, however. At best it expresses an ideal to which many aspire, for better or worse. In reality, it is not a very common household arrangement, and important parts of the ideal are continually being rejected.

The traditional image of the family is changing, in any case. This is particularly evident in the tendency for couples to divorce and in changing relationships between spouses, between parents and children, and between adults and their parents. Traditional gender-role relationships and traditionally authoritarian parent-child relationships are being rejected in favor of more egalitarian, more democratic relationships. Moreover, households are taking a number of different forms. Along with only-once-married, two-parent families are many reconstituted or stepfamilies. Increasingly common are single-parent families formed prior to marriage or after divorce and usually (but not always) headed by women. Cohabitating heterosexual and homosexual couples, single-person households, and households formed of friends not in a sexual relationship are also more numerous.

The structure of family life and the values of family members differ as a function of social class position, ethnic and racial heritage, and sexual orientation. Among new immigrants (especially those from Third World nations) and in the lower and working classes, traditional gender-role relationships, authoritarian parent-child patterns, and greater power and control by the elderly are likely to be very visible. Nevertheless, most Americans appear to be searching for certain common goals: monogamy in sexual relationships, egalitarian relations among adult partners, democratic relations between parents and children, and close ties with kin, especially older parents and grandparents. In addition, the common goals embrace such values as the need for open communication and for emotional support and nurturance.

THE CRITICAL THEMES: CHANGING ROLES AND EXPECTATIONS

Family life has become a public issue in American society. There is wide acceptance of the idea that family life is breaking down, and only a return to traditional values and norms will restore it to its rightful place in society.

A reform-oriented theory of social work practice addresses debates about the definition of the family, gender-role expectations, and parent-child relations, within both the family of procreation and the family of origin. It expresses the belief that the family is not breaking down: rather, family life has always been diverse and is constantly changing. There never was one perfect tradition of family life. As people have interacted with other people, they have sought out family forms that can meet their own needs and those of the society.

The traditional family has had its share of problems. Most women today would not want to go back to the "good old days" when the husband ruled the roost and there was a double standard of sexuality. Most children would not want to return to the days when parents laid down the law and controlled the personal, marital, and occupational choices of their children. Afro-Americans and Native Americans would not want to return to the days when their family life was dismissed as being pathological and disorganized. Gays and lesbians would not want to return to the days when they were forced to live in the closet.

Reform-oriented social service workers who regard the family as a changing institution can facilitate the development of family lifestyles which are not sexist, racist, or ageist and therefore promote individual well-being. They can continue to champion the egalitarian and democratic goals for which Americans seem to be searching and which are implicit in most contemporary forms of family practice. They also can continue to work toward greater social tolerance and acceptance of alternative family lifestyles, so people who choose them need not feel deviant, pathological, or ostracized from community life.

THE SYSTEMS APPROACH TO THE ISSUES

As family life changes, a number of negative consequences are becoming evident. Most people expect to find their major life satisfaction in family relations, but recurring conflict, including child, spouse, and elder abuse, can produce stress, psychological problems, separation, or divorce. A systems approach helps social workers understand the reasons for these private troubles and facilitates the planning of interventions to improve family well-being.

Changing family life patterns and the family troubles that go along with them can best be understood as a function of the interaction between families and their social environments. Families are relatively small social systems in which members occupy such roles and statuses as spouse, partner, parent, and child. These positions are held together by working agreements which can be experienced as coercive or valued. Families also function within the context of a social environment consisting of the society at large, its institutions and institutionalized social arrangements, and other individuals, families, groups, communities, and organizations. The social environment may be a source of stress or a source of support.

Although no one theory satisfactorily captures all the dynamics of family life, a number of theoretical perspectives which shed light on important dimensions collectively constitute a systems approach. The ecological perspective is most useful in demonstrating the interaction between families and their social environment. It helps social workers identify the sources of strain and support deriving from the social environment. The family life-cycle or developmental perspective proposes that families pass through certain stages as they are formed, complete their procreative and socialization functions, and dissolve with divorce, separation, or death of members. The fulfillment of the normal tasks associated with these stages results in development, while inability to fulfill them results in dysfunction. Psychodynamic, Freudian theory proposes that the conflicts of family life derive from the unconscious, often pathological needs of family members. Role theory focuses on the communication of expectations among family members or between family members and the groups and organizations of which they are a part. It therefore helps social workers identify and analyze sources of strain both within families and between families and their social environments. Conflict theory emphasizes the coercive dynamics among family members that are created by economic exploitation, sexism, and ageism in the larger society.

THE INDIVIDUAL AS A SYSTEM

As the basic human system, the individual is the level of systems around which most social services are organized and with which most social service workers practice. The individual's system is comprised of biophysical and psychological domains including cognitive, emotional, and behavioral needs, capacities, and abilities. Individuals are bounded physically by their skin and outward appearance and psychologically by such dimensions as character, personality, and self. They are also socially bounded by the roles and statuses they occupy within families, groups, organizations, communities, and society.

Social service workers and other helping professionals are primarily concerned with the psychological well-being, or normality, of individuals. This involves two dimensions: intrapersonal well-being, associated with the inner relationships among the psychological and biophysical domains, and interpersonal well-being, associated with the external relationships between individuals and the various other individuals, groups, and organizations that make up their social environment. Standards for assessing normality are still in their infancy. This book rejects the medical-model approach of the American Psychiatric Association's *Diagnostic and Statistical Manual* in favor of one grounded in a systems understanding of well-being. In this approach normality is defined as the outcome of transactions between individuals and their social environments, which are influenced by cultural, historical, interpersonal, and personal processes.

THE CRITICAL THEMES: ACHIEVING PSYCHOLOGICAL WELL-BEING

Psychological well-being is a public issue which underlies many social problems. Sexism, racism, ageism, and poverty, as well as crime, deviance, and mental illness, are believed to result in or to be caused by psychological disturbances. The fact that these problems are widespread in American society is an indication of the numbers of individuals who are struggling to achieve the personal happiness and fulfillment associated with psychological well-being.

Normality, or well-being, has been defined in terms of three outcomes. Individuals can be average, that is, like most everybody else. They can be healthy, capable of adapting and coping with the exigencies of reality without noticeable mental disorders. And they can be better than average, beyond healthy; they can reach utopian perfection.

In a reform-oriented theory for social work practice, the ultimate goal is such perfection. Getting individuals to be like everybody else and helping them to survive despite a possibly coercive reality are worthy objectives, but they cannot be the primary goals of reform-oriented social workers. Utopian perfection probably does not exist, especially in the short run. But unless social service workers strive for it in the long run, their practice decisions may inadvertently impede both personal and social progress.

Many of the major theories of individual behavior offer utopian visions which can guide social service workers in assessing the troubles of clients and planning interventions to resolve them. Four of these theories are concerned with the achievement of interpersonal well-being through the interactions between individuals and their social environments. Social exchange theory offers the vision of achieving interpersonal well-being when the rewards obtained in social relationships are equal to the costs of participation. Marxian theory envisions the achievement of interpersonal well-being as being dependent on social relationships which are free of alienation and exploitation. In structural functional theory, the vision is for people to share values and make available appropriate opportunities for achieving them. In symbolic interactionism, it involves social relationships that are devoid of labeling and based in mutual self-respect.

A fifth theoretical orientation, ego psychology, offers a vision for individuals to achieve intrapersonal well-being by acquiring ego strength in the process of psychological development across the life course. Depending on the biological age of the individual, development occurs when such attributes as trust, autonomy, initiative, industriousness, a clear identity, intimacy, generativity, and integrity are incorporated into the personality.

THE SYSTEMS APPROACH TO THE ISSUES

Achieving normality, whether or not it is utopian, is a function of the transactions between people and their social environments. The major theories of interpersonal and intrapsychic well-being all share this point of view. They all use an implicit, if not always explicit, systems approach which recognizes that individuals constantly change as a function of interacting biophysical, psychological, and social processes.

The major theories all make contributions to the understanding of human nature, physical growth, and age-related behavioral, cognitive, and emotional capacities. The explanations of human behavior offered by these theories often are distinctly different, however. Symbolic interactionism proposes that humans are special animals capable of creating such symbols as language and thought to give meaning to others and themselves. Ego psychology and other development-oriented theories identify important emotional and cognitive processes, tasks, and crises and consider how they are influenced by biophysical changes, either age-related or as a function of health, fitness, or disease. Whereas social exchange and Marxian theories hold that adult behavior is governed by rational perceptions and motivations, so that individuals know what they want and need, other theorists, especially Freudians and the more psychologically oriented Marxians, say that behavior is governed by unconscious motives or childhood traumas which make it difficult for individuals to know their wants and needs. Another difference is in the amount of conflict between individuals and their social environments. Structural functionalism and symbolic interactionism emphasize the social nature of humans and see little inherent conflict, while Freudian psychology and social exchange theory maintain that competition and conflict among individuals are part of human nature. Marxian theory posits no inherent conflict but recognizes that social institutions, especially the nature of the economy, can foment constant conflict. Ego psychology recognizes both instinctual needs which are in conflict with society and conflict-free aspects of the human personality.

All of the major theories of interpersonal and intrapsychic well-being take into account the social environment in which people live. The environment is usually thought of as an objective phenomenon—the other individuals, groups, and organizations which influence individuals' behavior and development. But the environment can also be seen as a subjective phenomenon, that is, as a perception, a meaning, or a definition of the situation which guides behavior and development. The subjective environment is emphasized in ego psychology, and the objective environment is emphasized in structural functional and anomie theories. In the symbolic interaction, social exchange, and Marxian theories, relatively equal treatment is given to both types of environment.

The major theories also all shed light on the ways in which the social environment facilitates or hinders normal behavior and development. Ego psychology suggests that others in the environment create troubles for individuals through the countertransference of unconscious needs, unresolved crises, ego defensiveness, and conscious coping and adaptation. When individuals interact with others who have weak ego strength and have not developed appropriately, they are likely to demonstrate the same attributes. In social exchange theory, the key to understanding the ways others influence individual behavior and development is in the operation of norms of reciprocity or fair exchange. Those who get according to what they give are satisfied, and those who do not may experience psychological ill-being. Marxian theory posits that normal human behavior and development can only take place when the social institutions are such that they do not promote norms of negative reciprocity or expose individuals to powerlessness, meaninglessness, social isolation, or estrangement from the self. In anomie theory, normal behavior and development are said to be facilitated when people share working agreements—expectations and goals—and make available to one another the means for achieving them. Deviance occurs when either the working agreements are unclear or the means available for achieving them are unavailable. In symbolic interactionism, well-being is said to be obstructed by environments that do not allow individuals to develop a positive sense of self. People who receive messages that they are negatively valued are likely to behave and develop negatively.

Thus, although all these theories make contributions to a systems approach, they do not always agree on the key concepts or the dimensions of biophysical, psychological, and social processes which ought to be considered by social service workers as they assess and intervene in the problems of individuals. This can be troublesome for the social work student who would like a clear, unambiguous, and straightforward theory for a reform-oriented practice. Unfortunately, the state of social work knowledge makes this impossible, now or in the near future. Yet such students should not despair. In doing their jobs they can help develop theory by systematically applying these and the other perspectives learned in their studies. They may find certain theories to be useful or not useful in resolving the public issues in the society and ameliorating the private troubles of individuals, families, and communities. As reform-oriented social workers they have the duty of passing on their experiences and points of view. By this means, they can help maintain the position of social service work as a major force for social progress.

Subject Index

abnormality, 346
accommodation
    in cognitive development theory, 472
    in ethnic group relations, 98
acquired immune deficiency syndrome,
        257–258
action-oriented practice, 402
adaptation, 353, 471
adjustment disorder, 347
adolescence, 415–418, 490, 512, 525–526
adultomorphism, 360
advanced capitalism, 393–394
affective subsystem, 25
affirmative action, 93
Afro-Americans, 117–120
age strata, 490
AIDS, 257, 258, 492
Alaskan Natives, 113–117
    family, 244–247
alienation, 389–401
    as burnout, 396–397
    from others, 390–391
    from product, 389
    from production, 389
    from self, 391–392
    in contemporary society, 393–398
    resolutions of, 392–393, 398–402
        in everyday life, 398–400
        in social services, 400–401
altercasting, 431
Alzheimer's disease, 519
American blacks
    community, 73–76
    family, 247–250, 273–274, 277–278

innovators, 249
    mainstreamers, 248
    swingers, 249
American dream, 410–412
American Indians
    community, 113–117
    family, 244–247
American Psychiatric Association, 317
analytic descriptive, 6
anomia, 413–414
anomie, 407, 409–419
anomy, 413
anxiety disorders, 347
apartheid, 80, 157
Apgar scale, 496
arts of contraversion, 441
Asian Americans, 124
    Chinese, 124–125
    East Indians, 135–136
    family life, 251–252
    Filipinos, 124
    Indochinese, 138–139
    Japanese, 125–126
Asian Pacific Triangle, 134
assertiveness training, 424
assessment
    and developmental difficulties,
        529–530
    and ego psychology, 483
    and exchange theory, 385
    and Marxian theory, 402
    of family life, 266
    principles, 47–48

assimilation
    in cognitive development theory, 472
    in ethnic group relations, 98-99, 114,
        174-176
at risk, 362
attachment/separation polarity, 523-524
attention, 375
authoritarian norms, 243
autonomous control, 378
autonomous functions, 466-469
    judgment, 467
    reality of the self, 467
    reality of the world, 467
    reality testing, 467
autonomous morality, 474
autonomy
    sense of, 507
    vs. shame and doubt, 507
average expectable environment, 448
aversion therapy, 371
avoidance, 373

barrio, 311
basic strength, 502
battered child syndrome, 282
battered women, 280-281
behavioral
    production, 375
    subsystem, 25
    theories, 367, 370-386
    well-being, 345
behavior control, 378
berdache, 245
    koskalaka, 245
    winkte, 245
biculturation, 142, 172-173
    bicultural socialization, 142-144
bigots, 150
bilateral descent, 244
biological clock, 490
biology
    and gender roles, 212-214
    of sex, 460-462
biophysical domain, 22-24
bipolar self, 470
birth, 495-496
    cesarean section, 496
    vaginal birth, 495
bisexual propensity, 458
blacks, 117-120, 247-250
blaming the victim, 9-11
blemishes of individual character, 433
body transcendence, 524

breeding populations, 75
burnout, 396-397

career trajectory problem, 523
capitalism
    and family life, 333
    Marx's criticisms of, 387-392
capitulation, 400
castration anxiety, 456
celibate love, 317
cesarean section, 496
change, 450
child abusers, 283-285
child abuse/neglect, 282-285
child sexual abuse, 285
childhood, 504-508
childhood socialization, 346
children in society, 209
Chinese
    Chinese Exclusion Acts, 105, 125
clarifying expectations, 331-332
class conflict, 64
class consciousness, 66
classical conditioning, 371-372
classification, 473
climacteric, 513
clinging love, 316
clinical disorder, 347
closed systems, 30
cognitive development, 447, 448, 471-481
    concrete operational stage, 473
    formal operational stage, 473-474
    Kohlberg's stages of moral develop-
        ment, 474-478
    levels of thought, 472
    Piaget's stages of, 471-474
    preoperational stage, 473
    processes of adaptation, 471-472
    roots of moral development, 480-481
    sensorimotor stage, 472-473
    women's moral development, 478-480
cognitive processes, 375
cognitive subsystem, 24
cognitive well-being, 345
cohabitation, 203, 204, 295
cohabiting couples, 203
collective decision making, 433
colonialism, 101
    colonial analogy, 101
    colonized groups, 101
community, 56-91
    defined, 56-61
    ethnic, 76-80, 97

gay and lesbian, 69–73
identificational, 58, 60–61
interest, 60
in society, 539–40
locational, 58
racial, 73–76
religious denominations as, 68–69
social classes as, 61
companion parents, 250
comparable worth, 381, 390–391
comparison level for alternatives, 380
competence, 355, 468, 512
sense of, 468
competition, 98
compulsion, 508
compulsive love, 316
concrete operational intelligence, 473
conditioned response, 371
conditioned stimulus, 371
conflict, 382
functions of, 40
husbands and wives, 334–335
parents and children, 336–337
conflict subculture, 416
conflict theory, 39, 100
and family, 300, 331–337
Marxian theory, 332–334, 386
conformity, 331–332, 412
consciousness-oriented practice, 402
conservative humanism, 7
continuous growth, 525
contradictory consciousness, 399
control-purposiveness, 398
conventional moral development,
476–477
cooperation, 382
coping, 353
mechanisms, 467–468
core pathology, 502
corrective feedback, 173
costs, 377
countercondition, 371
countertransference, 469
criminal subculture, 416
crisis, in development, 525–528
adolescent crisis debate, 525–527
crisis across the life course, 527–528
crisis in mid-life, 527
critical love, 317
critical perspective, 5–9
theory, 14–15
crystallized intelligence, 518
cultural pluralism, 142, 170, 174–175

cultural relativist, 236
culture, 61, 165–173, 360
and gender roles, 212–214
and socioeconomic well-being, 174–176
influence on poverty, 165–167
cycle of race relations, 98

decision making
organizational, 433
decline, 450
defense mechanisms, 465–466
definition of the situation, 430–431
deinstitutionalization, 433, 436
delusional disorder, 347
denial, 466
depreciated character, 439
deprivation and satiation, 380
derailed families, 320
destruction/creation polarity, 523
detachment generalization, 397
detouring coalitions, 276
development
and change, 450–451
and growth, 504–506
in old age, 524–525
of individual capacities, 400
of the self, 427–429
role of crisis in, 525–528
developmental
crises in maturity, 488, 519–525
disorders, 361
perspective of family, 300, 318–322
processes, 27
developmental tasks, 496
Havighurst's classification of, 497–501
deviance, 410–413, 434–437
career deviance, 436
primary, 434
secondary, 434
deviant group, 70
Diagnostic and Statistical Manual (DSM),
346–349
dialectic of intimate relations, 333
differentiation, 450
difficult child, 494
disabled, 344
and equity theory, 385–386
developmentally, 344, 361
physically, 344, 361
discouraged worker, 305
discrimination, 149, 207
principle of nondiscrimination, 151–155
disengaged families, 275

dislocated families, 321
disorders first evident
    in infancy, childhood, and
        adolescence, 347
displacement, 466
dissociative disorders, 347
distributive justice, 382
divorce, 265, 286–289
    divorce rates, 286–287
    stress of, 290–291
domestic networks, 231
domestic violence, 265, 278–285
dominant gene, 493
doubt, 508
dramaturgical, 431
drive, 451
dual perspective, 170–173
dyad, 32

early intervention, 296
East Indians, 134–136
easy child, 494
ecological perspective, 19, 300, 301–316
eco-map, 307–312
economic stress, 302–307
effectance, 468
ego, 453
    autonomous functions, 466–469
        competence, 468
        coping mechanisms, 467–468
        ego strength, 468
        ego weakness, 468
        judgment, 467
        reality of the self, 467
        reality of the world, 467
        reality testing, 467
    defense mechanisms, 465–466
        denial, 466
        displacement, 466
        projection, 466
        rationalization, 466
        regression, 466
        repression, 466
        sublimation, 466
ego differentiation, 524
ego integrity vs. despair, 519
ego psychology, 354, 368, 447, 448,
        465–471
    and psychosocial development, 447,
        449–451
    contributions to study of human be-
        havior, 464–465
    ego-defense mechanisms, 465–466

developmental stages, 454–457
Freudian base of, 447, 451–465
Oedipal conflict, 456
personality structure and dynamics,
        453–454
sex-role development, 458–464
theory of psychosexual development,
        451–453
ego transcendence, 524
ejaculation, 510
elderly
    abuse of, 281
    in the family, 210–211, 219–220
Electra complex, 456
embryo, 495
embryonic period, 494–495
empowerment, 355
emotional well-being, 345
empty-nest syndrome, 523
enmeshed families, 275
environment
    objective, 51
    physical, 31
    social, 31, 50–51
    subjective, 50
epidemiological studies, 351
epigenetic principle, 503
equifinality, 29
equity
    and practice, 384–386
    theory, 382–384
eros, 453
estrogen, 509
ethclass, 67
ethnic groups, 76, 93
ethnicity, 76–80
ethnocentrism, 98, 148–149
    defined, 148
evaluative critical, 6
exclusivity, 515
exosystems, 302
expectations, 35
    of others, 324
    of self, 324–325
exploitation, 207, 388
expulsion, 175
extended kin family, 189, 241
extermination, 175
extinction, 374

factitious disorders, 347
false consciousness, 401
faltering families, 277

families
American Indian, 244–247
Asian American, 251–252
Black, 247–250, 277–278
chaotic, 277
closed, 275
conflicted, 277
ethnic/racial, 226, 234–252
dominated, 277
healthy, 265, 266–271
Hispanic, 250–251
middle class, 227–228
multigenerational, 219–220, 241
of the rich, 232–234
one parent, 201
open, 275
polyandrous, 190
polygamous, 189–190
poverty class, 230–231
step families, 202–203
two parent, 200–201
working class, 198–199, 228–230
familism, 241
family
alignment, 275–276
and exchange theory, 376
aristocratic, 195
as institution, 182, 184–191
as organization, 184
balance, 315
boundaries, 274–275
bourgeois, 196
definitions of, 187–188
emotional climate, 195–199
equal partner marriage, 183
extended kin, 189
ideals, 236–244
imbalance, 315
interactional patterns, 276–278
life cycle, 300, 318–322
monogamous families, 189
nuclear, 189, 190
of origin, 188
of procreation, 188
peasant, 195–196
plural marriage, 189
power structure, 276
racism and, 192
random families, 274
serial monogamy, 199
sexism and, 192–193
structural patterns, 275–276, 333–334
traditional nuclear, 183

working class, 198–199
family functioning, 265, 272–278
family functions, 182, 191–199
affection, 194
consumption, 194
latent functions, 192–193
manifest functions, 191, 193–195
procreation, 188, 191
production, 193
socialization, 191
family life, 541–543
and development, 506–507
changing roles and expectations,
205–220, 542–543
gay and lesbian, 226, 252–259
recent trends, 185–187
systems approach to, 543
unrelated individuals, 187
family life cycle, 300, 318–322
diversity in, 320
divorced families, 321
homosexual couples, 320
poor families, 321
racial minority families, 321
remarried families, 321
family politics, 206
family well-being, 266
fate control, 378
fear of loss of love, 456
feedback, 29–30
feeling generalization, 398
feminism, 84–85
fetal alcohol syndrome, 491
fetal period, 494–495
fictive relatives, 241
fidelity, 512
fit between person and environment,
358
fluid intelligence, 518
focal condition, 49
formal operational intelligence, 474
freedom, 119–120, 356
functional noncapitulation, 401

games, 428
gay men
as heterosexual parents, 257–259
community, 69–73
gay couples, 203–205, 226, 252–259
gemeinshaft, 57
gender
chromosomal, 460
definitions of, 461

gender (*Continued*)
  genital, 461
  gonadal, 460
  hormonal, 460
  identity, 461
  organal, 460
  role, 211–217, 461
gender-role identification, 462–463
  identification with same-sex parent,
    462
  sex-role preference, 463
  sex-role standards, 462
  understanding gender, 462
gene, 493
general adaptation syndrome, 419–420
general system model, 19
generalized other, 428
generativity, 513
  vs. stagnation, 515
genetic inheritance, 493–494
genogram, 311–315
genotype, 74, 460, 493
Gentlemen's Agreement, 125
gonads, 509, 510
goodness of fit, 358
group cohesiveness, 169
groups
  primary, 32
  secondary, 32
growth, 28, 458, 504–506

Haitians, 140–142
Hart-Cellar Act, 134
heteronomous morality, 474
Hispanics, 95
  Chicanos, 120–122
  family life, 250–251
  Mexican Americans, 120–122, 139–140
  Puerto Ricans, 122–124
history
  influence of, 360
holon, 31, 266
holistic approach to families, 266
homeostasis, 29–30
homophobia, 71
homosexual behavior, 463
homosexual couples, 203–205, 226,
    252–259
  diversity in, 255
  stages of, 320
homosexual love, 317
hope, 507
household, 187

human nature, 20–22
  in Marxian theory, 386–387
  male and female differences, 21
  theory of, 21–22
  vs. animal nature, 20
  vs. cultural determinants, 20
human progress, 8–9
humanism, 386–387
humanist psychology, 386–387

I (the), 427
identification with the aggressor, 456
identity, 426
  vs. identity confusion, 512
identity-achieved, 526
identity-confused, 526
identity-foreclosed, 526–527
imaginative rehearsal, 426
imitation, 374, 427
immature love, 316–317
immigrant analogy, 101
immigrants, 101, 103–113, 131, 134–136
  European, 106–113
immigration policies, 92, 103–106, 134,
    139
improvisation of role for self, 431
impulse control disorder, 347
imputation of role of other, 431
index person, 313
individual
  as a system, 22–31, 343, 544–547
  change and development, 27–28
individuation, 471
Indochinese, 138–139
industry vs. inferiority, 512
inequality
  and family well-being, 303
inertia, 512
information society, 393–394
ingratiation, 432
inhibition, 508
initiative vs. guilt, 508
inner scripts, 316
inner space, 448
innovation, 44, 412
institutional discrimination, 158
institutional racism, 39, 146, 156–162
institutional sexism, 39, 207
institutionalized social arrangements,
    38–39
intelligence
  and race, 163
  IQ controversy, 163–165

interaction, 32, 44, 429
intergroup conflict, 127
interpersonal influence, 360
interpersonal level, 433
intimacy, 512-513, 514-515
intimate relations, 378-379
intrapersonal well-being, 448

Jim Crow laws, 119
juvenile delinquency, 415-417

kin relations, 219-220

labels, 432-442
    achieved, 433-438
    ascribed, 438-441
    essentialist, 442
    responding to labels, 441
labeling, 441-442
law of segregation, 74
learning theories, 370-376
lesbians
    as heterosexual parents, 257-259
    community, 69-73
    couples, 203-205, 226, 252-259
levels of systems, 25-26
liberation, 356
libido, 453
life chances, 65
life course
    developmental tasks across the, 488,
        496-501
    prenatal development and birth, 488,
        491-496
    stages of development, 488, 489-491
life cycle, 422, 424, 427
life events, 319, 421-423
life structure, 521-522
love
    and exchange theory, 378-379
    psychosocial definition, 515
loving the partner's parents, 317

machismo, 250
macro environment, 11
macrosystems, 302
mainstreamed, 362
majority group, 85, 86
    defined, 81
marianismo, 250
marriage, 188, 265-299, 286-289
    conflict habituated, 269
    devitalized, 269
    passive-congenial, 270

total marriage, 269
vital marriage, 269
martyrdom, 400
Marxian theory, 367, 386-402
    compared to anomie, 414
    compared to social exchange, 414
masculine/feminine polarity, 523
maternal person, 504
matrilocal families, 219
maturation, 450
me (the), 427
meaninglessness, 394
meanings, 426
means-end generalization, 397-398
means of production, 389
median score, 349
mediators, 172
medical model, 437
menarche, 509
menopause, 513
men's issues
    delinquency, 417
    men's movement, 215-216
mental disorders, 344, 346-349
    adjustment disorders, 347
    anxiety disorders, 347
    delusional disorders, 347
    disorders evident in infancy,
        childhood, or adolescence, 347
    dissociative disorders, 347
    factitious disorders, 347
    impulse control disorders, 347
    organic mental disorders, 347
    psychosexual disorders, 347
    schizophrenic disorders, 347
    sleep disorders, 347
    somatoform disorders, 347
    substance-use disorders, 347
mental health, 344-364
    and labeling, 437-438
mentor relationship, 522
mesosystems, 302
micro environment, 11
microsystems, 302
middlemen minorities, 97
mid-life crisis, 522-524
mind, 426-427
minority group, 80-86
    behavioral minorities, 82-83
    cognitive minorities, 82
    defined, 80
    ethnic minorities, 81-82
    minority individuals, 81-82

minority group (*Continued*)
  physical minorities, 82
  responses to subordination, 85–86, 103
  self-esteem, 439–441
  women as a minority group, 83–85
minority-majority relations, 98–101, 540
mixed messages, 329
modal score, 349
models, 172, 374
modified kin families, 219
mood disorders, 347
moral behavior
  roots of, 480–481
moral development
  conventional stage, 476–477
  Kohlberg's stages of, 474–478
  postconventional stage, 477–478
  preconventional stage, 475–476
  women's, 478–480
moratorium, 526
mortification of self, 437
motivational processes, 375
multiaxial system of *DSM*, 346
multicentered approach, 11

National Institute of Mental Health, 351
Native Americans, 113–117
  family, 244–247
natural helping networks, 32
Naturalization Act of 1790, 104
needs
  developmental, 272
  for esteem, 355–356
  for self-actualization, 355–356
  human needs, 126–127
  need for belonging and love, 355–356
  of black families, 273–274
  of families, 272
  physiological needs, 355–356
  safety needs, 355–356
  survival, 272, 273–274
needs satisfaction, 272–274
negotiated lines of action, 430–431
negotiation of roles, 45
neolocal families, 219
neurotic complementary, 317
new arrivals, 131–144
newborn baby, 496
niche finding, 400
NIMH, 351
noncapitulation, 400–401
non-normative influences, 422

normality, 344, 346, 349–364
  as average, 349–350
  as health, 350–354
  as transaction, 357–358
  as utopia, 354–357
  psychological, 359–361
normative age-graded influences, 422
normative expectations, 422
normative history-graded influences, 422
normlessness, 409
norms
  breakdown of, 409
  contradictory, 409
  of negative reciprocity, 389
  of reciprocity, 382
  social, 35
northern and western european immigrants, 106–107
novice period, 522
nuclear self, 470
nurturance
  right to, 434

object permanence, 473
object relations, 469–471
  self psychology, 470–471
  transference and countertransference, 469–470
Oedipus complex, 456
open systems, 30
operant conditioning, 371–374
operation bootstrap, 123
operations, 472
opportunities
  illegitimate, 415–416
  legitimate, 415–416
organic mental disorder, 347
ovulation, 509

paranoid disorders, 347
parent-child relations, 336–337
  history of, 217–219
participation in collective action, 400
passionate prescription, 6
patriarchy, 206
patrilocal families, 219
payoff, 377
penis envy, 456, 457
  and women's position in society, 458
people of color, 113
person in environment, 41–47
personality
  disorders, 346

role conflict, 329
Marxian approach, 398-399
phenotype, 74, 460, 493
placid description, 6
play, 428
polygenic inheritance, 493
polymorphous perverse, 455
postconventional moral development,
    477-478
postindustrial state, 394
power, 98, 355
powerlessness, 394
poverty
    and family well-being, 303-305
    index, 303
    level, 303
preconventional moral development,
    475-476
prejudice, 149-151
prenatal development and birth, 488,
    491-496
    birth, 495-496
    embryonic and fetal periods, 494-495
    genetic inheritance, 493-494
    newborn baby, 496
    parents' influence, 491-493
preoperational intelligence, 473
prescribed role, 42
presentation of self, 431
presenting disorder, 346
prestige rankings, 62
primary appraisal, 423
primary prevention, 296
principle of conservation, 473
private troubles, 11-12
problem analysis, 47
problem-solving process, 47-48
problems in living, 352, 437
production, 375
professional ethics, 36-37
progesterone, 509
projection, 466
psychodynamic theory
    and families, 300, 316-317
psychological
    clock, 490-491
    domain, 24
    processes, 27
    survival, 353
    well-being, 344, 345-346
psychosocial crises, 501-519
    defined, 502
    in adult years, 514-516

in early life, 507-508
in later childhood and adolescence,
    512
in old age, 519
psychosocial development, 450
    Erikson's stages of, 488, 501-519
puberty, 509
public issues, 12
punishment, 373

race, 73
    contemporary ideas on, 75-76
    racial classification, 73-76
race relations, 92, 98-103
    cycle of, 98
racial distance, 152
racism, 148-149, 149-162
    formal, 158
    in family, 192
    informal, 158-162
    institutional, 156-162
    intentional, 158-162
    symbolic, 148
radical nonintervention, 436
radius of significant relationships, 501
rational humanism, 386-387
rationalism, 8
rationalization, 466
reality testing, 467
rebellion, 413
recessive gene, 493
reciprocity, 380-384
recruitment, 43-44
reference groups, 380, 428
    negative, 429
refugees, 136
    displaced persons, 131, 136-139
regression, 466
rehearsal, 375
reification, 387
reinforcement
    negative, 373
    positive, 373
reinforcing stimulus, 371
rejectivity, 516
religion
    and community life, 68-69
    and social attitudes, 68-69
remarriage, 286-289, 294
    rates of, 287-289
    stages in, 294-295
    stress of, 294-295
repression, 466

repudiation, 512
rescuing love, 316
resource identification, 48
retention, 375
retreatism, 413
retreatist subculture, 416
revengeful love, 317
revolution, 175
rewards, 377
    calculation of, 377, 379-380
Rh factors, 491
ritualism, 412
role
    as actual behaviors, 325
    enacted, 42
    expected, 42
    outcomes, 42
    perceived, 42, 324
    playing, 427
    repudiation of, 512
    sex-role development, 458-464
    strain, 330-332
    taking, 427
role conflict, 325-332
    and personality, 329, 331
    interrole, 326, 328
    intrarole, 326-327
    mixed messages, 329-330
    role overload, 329-330
roles, 18, 41-45
    in family, 182, 205-220, 211-217, 300
    multiple roles, 325
role theory, 322-332
rubella, 491

sadistic love, 316
satiation, 373
schema, 472
schizophrenia, 347, 438
schools
    and delinquency, 417
    and development, 510-511
scientific socialism, 392
seasons of life, 520-524
secession, 176
secondary appraisal, 423
self, 427-432
    development of, 427-429
    ideal, 426
    image, 426
    possible, 426
    precepts, 426

self-esteem, 426-427
    of minority groups, 439-441
self-estrangement, 394-396
self-functions, 470-471
self-object, 470
self psychology, 470
    bipolar self, 470
    individuation, 471
    nuclear self, 470
    self-functions, 470-471
    self-object, 470
    separation, 471
    transmutation, 470
senile dementia, 519
separation, 471
sexism
    and family, 192-193, 333-336
    and Freudian theory, 457
    institutionalized, 207
sex-role development, 458-464
    biology of sex, 460-462
    gender-role identification, 462-463
    homosexual behavior, 463-464
sex roles
    in family, 207
sexual abuse
    child, 285
sexual development
    development in boys, 509-510
    development in girls, 509
sexual disorders, 347
sexual exploitation, 207
shame, 508
shaping, 373
significant others, 429
singlehood, 205
    temporary, 206
    voluntary, 206
single people, 205-206
situations, 429
sleep disorders, 347
slow-to-warm-up child, 494
social change, 4-5
social classes, 61-68
    and families, 226, 227-234
    class conflict, 64
    class consciousness, 66
    class position, 64-66
    ethclass, 67
    Marxian definition of, 62-64
social clock, 490
social comparison, 380
social contract, 409

social control, 44-45
social distance, 135, 152
social exchange
    and the family, 376
    theory, 367, 370, 376-386
social indicators, 93-94
    objective measures, 94
    subjective measures, 94
social institutions, 35-38, 156
    family as, 182-221
social interaction, 429-432
social isolation, 394
social learning theory, 367, 374-376 6
social norms, 35
social positions, 429-430
social relationships, 513-514
social worlds, 425
socialization, 44
    of children, 191-193
sociocultural level, 32-39
socioeconomic achievement
    of racial and ethnic communities,
        93-97
socioemotional leader, 211-212
somataform disorders, 347
spoiled identity, 433
spouse abuse, 280
stable coalitions, 276
stages of development
    in families, 319-320
    in homosexual couples, 320
stagnation, 516
status, 42
    achieved, 78
    ascribed, 78
    face-to-face encounters, 397
    in family, 322
    unequal, 396-398
status offenses, 434
steady state
    in individuals, 29
stepfamilies, 202-203, 321
stereotypes, 152
stigma, 438-441
stratification, 61-64
    racial and ethnic, 67-68
    socioeconomic, 61
street-corner men, 250
street families, 249-250
strength of weak ties, 162
stress
    as a form of anomie, 407
    economic stress, 302-307

management, 423-424
normative stress, 318
of living, 318
perceived, 423
psychological response to, 423
theory, 418-424
transgenerational, 318
stressors, 420
structural functional theory, 39, 407,
    408-409, 424-425
structured family therapy, 266
structures, 472
sublimation, 466
subordinancy, 399
substance use disorder, 347
successive approximation
    method of, 373
suicide, 409
superego, 453
superordinancy, 399
supply and demand, 378-380
support groups, 296
support systems, 172
surgent growth, 525
symbolic interactionism, 407-408,
    425-443
symbols, 426
system
    approach, 18, 19, 377-378, 541
    boundaries, 30-31
    client, 48
    communities as, 57-58
    dynamics, 26-31
    focal, 48, 49
    human, 18, 20-22
    individual as a, 18, 20, 22-31
    social, 18, 20, 31-41
    target, 48
systematic desensitization, 371

tabula rasa, 20
task leader, 211
tasks, 497-501
    recurrent, 497
    unique, 497
taxonomies, 73
teachable moment, 497
testosterone, 510
thanatos, 453
theoreticomorphism, 357
theory for practice, 3
theory of caring, 5
theory of practice, 3

third world people, 113
total institutions, 437
traits due to victimization, 439
transaction-centered approach, 11
transactional
    processes, 43-45, 357-358, 367-368,
        376
transference, 469
translators, 172
transmutation, 470
Treaty of Guadalupe Hidalgo, 121
Treaty of Paris (1898), 122
triad, 32
triangulation, 276
tribal stigma, 438-441
trust vs. mistrust, 507
tumultuous growth, 525

unconditioned response, 371
unconditioned stimulus, 371
unconscious resistance, 399
underclass, 66, 168
underemployment, 305
underorganization
    in family, 321
undocumented aliens, 131, 139-142
unemployment, 305
    rate, 305
unequal status, 396-398
unintended consequences of change, 7-8
unrequited love, 317
unwed mothers, 291-293

utopian transactional approach, 368-370
utopian vision, 408-409

vaginal birth, 495
values, 5, 167-169
vicarious acquisition, 374

War on Poverty, 304, 415
wealth addiction, 306
will, 507
wisdom, 519
withdrawal, 507
women's issues
    and family, 206-209
    comparable worth, 381, 390-391
    discrimination, 206-209
    Electra complex, 456
    feminization of sex, 216-217
    human nature, 21
    husband/wife conflict, 334-335
    moral development, 478-480
    penis envy, 456-458
    supermother, 228
    women's movement, 206-209
    women as a minority, 83-85
working class families, 198-199, 228-230
World Health Organization, 346, 354

young/old polarity, 523

zygote, 494

Author Index

Adams, J., 384
Aponte, H., 275
Archibald, W., 370, 379, 382, 387, 396
Aries, P., 218
Bandura, A., 375, 376
Bane, M. J., 289
Becker, E., 6
Bell, A., 204, 205
Berger, P., 7
Bernard, J., 58
Billingsley, A., 248
Blauner, R., 101, 113, 121
Carter, E., 241, 318, 320
Cherlin, A., 186, 202–203, 205, 248
Chestang, L., 172, 439
Cloward, R., 66, 415–416
Cobb, J., 67–68
Coser, L., 40–41
Cowger, C., 11
Dahrendorf, R., 39
Danziger, S., 96, 97
de Anda, D., 142, 172
De Hoyos, A., 32
De Hoyos, G., 19, 32
Delgado, M., 172
DeMause, L., 209, 217
Devore, W., 67
Erikson, E., 448, 458, 504, 507, 512,
    515–516, 519, 525
Freud, A., 465
Gambrill, E., 373
Garbarino, J., 302
Germain, C., 449, 468
Gerson, R., 311, 313
Gerth, H., 36, 156

Gilligan, C., 22, 479
Goffman, E., 431, 433, 437
Goldstein, E., 449, 466, 467, 468–469,
    483
Gordon, M., 21
Green, J., 78, 79
Gutman, H., 240, 247
Hartman, A., 188, 273, 296, 307
Hartman, H., 448, 465, 466–467
Hearn, G., 19, 29, 31
Hill, R., 274
Humm-Delgado, D., 172
Kagle, J., 11
Kett, J., 230
Knowles, L., 157–158
Kohlberg, L., 474–478
Laird, J., 188, 273
Lasch, C., 194
Lehninger, R., 39
Leonard, P., 398, 402
Levinson, D., 520, 522, 527
Lewis, O., 165–167
Lum, D., 113
Maluccio, A., 355
Marcia, J., 526
Marx, K., 386–387, 388
Maslow, A., 126, 355, 356
Mead, G. H., 425
Merton, R., 150, 410, 413, 415, 416
McGoldrick, M., 241, 311, 313, 318, 320
Mills, C., 11, 36, 156
Minuchin, S., 31, 266
Newman, W., 70, 74, 81–83, 100–101, 113,
    149, 174
Norton, D., 170

Novak, M., 67, 107
Offer, D., 349, 350, 354
Ohlin, C., 415-416
Park, R., 98
Parsons, T., 194
Piaget, J., 474
Piven, F., 66
Poster, M., 189, 190, 195-196, 227
Prewitt, K., 157-158
Rapp, R., 227, 230, 232-233
Rubin, L., 230, 307
Ryan, W., 9, 10
Sabshin, M., 349, 350, 354
Schlesigner, E., 67
Schuman, H., 151, 153-154

Schur, E., 70
Selye, H., 420
Sennett, R., 67-68
Sherman, W., 400
Skinner, B. F., 371
Solomon, B., 394
Sowell, T., 103, 106-112, 118-119, 167-169
Stack, C., 231
Szasz, T., 352
von Bertanlanffy, L., 20, 29
Weber, M., 61
Weinberg, M., 204, 205
Willie, C., 162, 248, 249
Wilson, W. J., 66, 149, 159-162, 236
Zaretsky, E., 194-195

ABOUT THE AUTHOR

John. F. Longres is a professor of social work at the University of Wisconsin, Madison. He received a BA in psychology from New York University, an MSW from the University of California, Los Angeles, and a PhD in social work and social psychology from the University of Michigan.

His practice experience includes direct service work in public welfare, child and adolescent mental health, adoption services, and hospital social work. In addition, he has served on the board of directors for child welfare, juvenile, and drug and alcohol services. In 1983–84, he was chairperson of the Tri-County Youth Services Consortium in Portland, Oregon. Presently he is a member of the board of the Centro Hispano in Madison.

Professor Longres has published in leading professional journals in the area of minority issues, professional issues, and children and youth. He contributed articles to the 17th and 18th editions of the *Encyclopedia of Social Work* and in addition served as an editor of the latter. He is a co-author of the recently released *The Status of Children in Wisconsin*. His current research is in the area of service utilization patterns of racial and ethnic minorities.

His extensive teaching experience includes visits to Spain through the United States Short Term Assignment of Experts program and England as a visiting fellow at the University of Warwick. He was also a visiting professor at the University of Puerto Rico and a Fulbright lecturer at the Catholic University of Guayaquil, Ecuador.

In addition to extensive publications and teaching experience, Professor Longres has been active nationally in social work professional associations. He has served on the editorial board of *Social Work*, the journal of the National Association of Social Workers, and as a consulting editor for the *Journal of Social Work Education*. Presently, he is on the editorial boards of two new journals, *The Journal of Multicultural Social Work* and *The Journal of Progressive Social Work*.

THE BOOK'S MANUFACTURE

Human Behavior in the Social Environment
was typeset by Stanton Publication Services, Inc.,
Minneapolis, Minnesota.
The typefaces are Baskerville for text
and Zapf Chancery Bold for display.
Printing and binding were done by
Arcata Graphics, Kingsport, Tennessee.
Cover design and internal design by John B. Goetz,
Design & Production Services, Co., Chicago.